THE
·CHINESE·

The Chinese: Adapting the Past, Facing the Future is a joint project of Contemporary Learning Systems of East Lansing, Inc. and the Center for Chinese Studies at the University of Michigan.

Contemporary Learning Systems, Inc.

George A. Colburn, Director of Operations
David Kennard, Television Programming Consultant
Jane L. Scheiber, Director of Education Programs
John Ball, Projects Administrator
Emily Ball, Research Associate

Center for Chinese Studies

Michel Oksenberg, Director
Martin K. Whyte, Director of Publications
Walter Michener, Editor

This book was conceived as part of *The Chinese* telecourse project, created around the public television series "The Heart of the Dragon." Produced by ASH Films of London, which had negotiated hitherto unheard-of access rights for its film crews inside of China, "The Heart of the Dragon" won the 1985 International Emmy Award for Best Documentary following its premiere on Channel 4 in Great Britain. The telecourse was originally developed in 1985–86 by National Video Communications, Inc., an associate company of CLS, and South Carolina Educational Television, presenter of the series on public television. Funding for development and production of telecourse materials was provided by General Electric Company, underwriter of the PBS series.

THE
·CHINESE·

ADAPTING THE PAST
FACING THE FUTURE

Edited by

♦ Robert F. Dernberger ♦ Kenneth J. DeWoskin ♦
♦ Steven M. Goldstein ♦ Rhoads Murphey ♦
♦ Martin K. Whyte ♦

Center for Chinese Studies ♦ University of Michigan

Published by Center for Chinese Studies
The University of Michigan, Ann Arbor, Michigan 48109-1290

First edition published in 1986
as *The Chinese: Adapting the Past, Building the Future*

Second Edition 1991
Second printing 1992
Third printing 1993
Fourth printing 1996

Printed and made in the United States of America

∞ The paper used in this publication conforms with the
American National Standard for Information Sciences—
Permanence of Paper for Publications and Documents
in Libraries and Archives ANSI/NISO/Z39.48—1992.

Library of Congress Cataloging-in-Publication Data

The Chinese : adapting the past, facing the future /
edited by Robert F. Dernberger ... [et al.] — 2nd ed.
p.   cm.
Includes bibliographical references and index.
ISBN 0-89264-100-2 (alk. paper)
1. China.
I. Dernberger, Robert F.
II. University of Michigan. Center for Chinese Studies.
DS706   1991
951—dc20   91-19453
CIP

Contents

Part 3:   Society
Edited by Martin K. Whyte

Part 4: The Economy
Edited by Robert F. Dernberger

Agriculture

Industry

Part 6: The Future
Edited by Steven M. Goldstein

China's Prospects

Editors' Note

The Chinese is a book that leads two lives, one as a stand-alone text in college classrooms, the other as part of a telecourse package created by Contemporary Learning Systems of East Lansing, Inc. The telecourse is linked to the Emmy Award–winning public television series "The Heart of the Dragon" and includes a Study Guide for students.

In preparing this revision of *The Chinese* we have been mindful of its dual roles, and publication of the second edition has been coordinated with updating of the video segments by CLS and the preparation of a revised edition of the accompanying Study Guide, designed to be equally useful to both classroom and telecourse students. Inquiries about the telecourse should be directed to CLS at P.O. Box 6220, East Lansing, MI, 48826.

This edition of *The Chinese* also incorporates other changes: students interested in further reading in the original sources can easily identify them in a new section at the back of the book; teachers who prefer a chronological approach to the material will find a table grouping the readings by period; and a much-requested index has been included to help students and professors alike.

In the introductory essays and in the headnotes that precede each chapter, we have used the *pinyin* romanization system, providing Wade-Giles equivalents at the first mention of names and terms. Readings from sources using the Wade-Giles system have not been altered. In their original form, a number of the readings contain footnotes or other references which do not appear in this volume.

Preface to the Second Edition

Much has happened in China since 1986, when the Center for Chinese Studies at the University of Michigan published the first edition of *The Chinese: Adapting the Past, Facing the Future*. In the political realm, massive demonstrations shook Beijing and many other cities in the spring of 1989, followed by a harsh and violent crackdown that left thousands of civilians and soldiers dead and wounded. The hopes and tragedy of Beijing Spring, 1989, have left an indelible mark on China, and the legacy of those events will long shape Chinese history. The suppression altered, at least temporarily, both the perception of and behavior toward China of several foreign governments, especially the United States. In the five years since 1986, too, the Chinese economy has continued to grow rapidly, while planners in Beijing have seen their control over the economy continue to decline. In the social realm, the events of 1989 have not halted the rapid transition of the country from a largely agricultural, peasant society to an industrial, urban one. And culturally and ideologically, Hong Kong, Taiwan, and overseas Chinese are exerting increasing influence upon the mainland Chinese, especially in the coastal and southern regions.

The changes in China since 1986 have altered the balance between state and society and between the formal system of official control and the informal means of getting things done. In many respects, there has been a resurgence of tradition. In other respects, new problems have begun to appear on the national agenda, such as environmental deterioration and an increasing proportion of the population that is elderly and requires special care. In the light of these developments since the first edition, when the editors gathered to consider publication of a second edition, they came to two conclusions. First, its original rationale had become even more persuasive. This volume is designed to introduce the

XV

Chinese people, their history, and the challenges they face—political, social, economic, and cultural—in their search for a Chinese pattern of modernity. The editors believe that understanding of contemporary China must be rooted in an appreciation of Chinese tradition. The Communist revolution did not represent a sharp break with the past, and current approaches to solving China's problems grow out of previous ways of dealing with these issues. As the Chinese state's grip over the population possibly weakens, deeply embedded cultural and social traditions that have been suppressed under Communist rule may become even more important.

Second, the editors concluded that the new edition had to take into account recent events. And that necessitated substantial alterations to the original edition, especially in the sections devoted to politics and the future. The editors have revised, and some cases rewritten, the book's six introductory essays and have taken the opportunity to discard dated or superseded readings and to add new material throughout the volume. Altogether there are seventeen new readings. As before, the readings have been organized thematically rather than chronologically. Each section captures the powerful themes of both continuity and change as China has evolved politically, socially, economically, and culturally. But the readings can also be regrouped chronologically. I, for instance, organize my course on modern China chronologically: high Qing; late imperial China; the Republican era; the Mao era; and the Deng era. I attempt to convey a comprehensive understanding of China for each era. *The Chinese* can be very effectively adapted to such an approach, for it has excellent readings on the politics, economy, society, and culture of each period. For example, chapters 1, 2, and 3 by Fairbank and Kracke, chapters 11 and 12 on political traditions, chapters 19 and 20 on high Qing legal practices, chapter 26 on customary family law, chapter 31 on urban social controls, and chapter 42 on the marketing system, provide a powerful set of interrelated readings on the traditional system. This edition contains a complete grouping of chapters by historical period at the back of the book. I have found that approaching the readings in this way is quite effective, for it enables the student to see how the various facets of China were interconnected. At the end of the course, however, when I review the major themes, I encourage students to reread the material in the order in which it is presented in *The Chinese*. At that point, the themes of continuity and change emerge with special clarity, and I know of no other book that offers the breadth of this volume. In this sense, *The Chinese* is rooted in the best tradition of area studies. The individual articles draw upon the cutting-edge concepts of each author's discipline, but in aggregate they yield a wholistic view of China and illuminate how China's past shapes its present and future.

Michel Oksenberg

Part 1

History and Geography

Edited by Rhoads Murphey

Introduction

Rhoads Murphey

China is a very past-conscious society. If one is to understand China, and to understand also its future, one must know something of its past, and something of the way most Chinese see that past. It has been called the Great Tradition, and that may be the best brief statement of the Chinese sense of their own history. They are the heirs of greatness, and they see themselves that way. Pride in sharing a continuous tradition whose civilization and empire led the world for two thousand years is a basic part of being Chinese, and a part also of their hopes for the future. While other civilizations and empires rose and fell, imperial China and its culture remained more or less continuously intact from the third century B.C. until our own century.

Many would argue that the Communist state has in most respects continued the imperial tradition and that most of traditional Chinese culture remains vigorous, blended now with only some new elements. As China moves toward full contact with the outside world after its self-imposed isolation from 1949 to the 1970s, it is again taking pride in the past, which the revolution rejected during its radical phase. Maoist visionaries saw the past as an obstacle that must be swept aside to make way for a new China and the fundamental changes which they regarded as necessary. Today's leaders see the past as a source of strength and inspiration. China must strive to rejoin the world once more as a model or leader, the role it played for so long.

3

The Beginnings of Chinese Civilization: The Shang and the Zhou (Chou)

The origins of Chinese civilization are older than any surviving civilization in the West, and go back to about 2000 B.C. By that time on the north China plain there were the beginnings of walled towns with bronze metallurgy, writing, and the agricultural surpluses which made such developments possible. By about 1750 B.C. the first authenticated Chinese dynasty had emerged, the Shang, whose domains covered most of the Yellow River plain, where they built successive capitals on an increasingly large scale. Royal tombs have yielded magnificent bronze vessels, weapons, and decorated chariots complete with the skeletons of the horses which drew them and the grooms and retainers of the royal household. The Shang directly controlled only the central area around what is now the great bend of the Yellow River, but they had feudal-style dependencies on all frontiers of their kingdom. Those to the south, especially in the central Yangzi (Yangtse) valley, may have been as advanced as the Shang in agriculture, metallurgy, and city building and were probably more highly developed commercially. Already the predominant southern crop was rice, while the drier and colder north depended mainly on millet, which was slowly displaced by wheat as it entered China from western Asia after about 1500 B.C. Some of the kingdoms in the Yangzi valley were probably independent of Shang connections except in trade, as were those in southernmost China, but all had evolved bronze tools and weapons, an already recognizably Chinese system of writing, and a productive agricultural system. Each region was, however, still culturally and even ethnically distinct, with separate languages, writing systems, and group identities.

Shang rule was overthrown in 1122 B.C. by an internal revolt joined by the Zhou (Chou) kingdom, one of the Shang's dependencies which guarded the western frontier, with its capital near modern Xi'an (Sian). The Zhou had acquired most of Shang technology and culture, including writing. They gave their own account of the oppression of the Shang as justification for their conquest, and first voiced what was to become a standard Chinese line: "The iniquity of Shang is full; Heaven commands me to destroy it." In other words, the Shang had lost the Mandate (approval) of Heaven by its misgovernment, and it was the duty of responsible people to overthrow it. The Zhou extended the Shang system of feudatories whereby surrounding groups were linked to the

Zhou king as vassals to a sovereign. The parallel with medieval European feudalism a thousand years later is not exact in details, but the basic system was the same. For some centuries it worked reasonably well, dominated by an hereditary land-owning aristocracy. Bronze technology, writing systems, agriculture, city-building, and trade continued to develop. Probably soon after 1000 B.C. writing was increasingly done in longer texts with brush and ink on silk or bamboo strips rather than the earlier inscriptions on bone or bronze. The central body of the Chinese classics was first written down in this period: the *Book of Changes (Yijing [I-ching]*, a cryptic handbook for diviners), the *Book of Songs,* the *Book of Rituals,* and collections of historical documents.

But other changes were at work to disrupt and then to destroy the feudal structure. Iron was becoming cheaper and more plentiful as technology improved; iron-tipped plows came into use in China over a thousand years before the West. Irrigation was spreading, as was cultivated land. Spurred by rising farm output, the population grew more rapidly, but still there were surpluses, the basis for increasing trade. New productivity also freed workers from farm labor, to serve as artisans, soldiers, officials, scholars, and merchants. More and more towns began to dot the plain and the richer lands to the south in the Yangzi valley. Trade and cities grew rapidly, roads were built, and the bureaucratic apparatus of the state began to appear. Large armies became possible as soldiers could be spared from farming for at least part of the year and could be fed on surpluses. Most of the Zhou dependencies were becoming separate states, culturally and linguistically distinct from one another and divided also by chronic warfare. Serfdom and the power of the landed aristocracy seemed less and less suited to the changing conditions, as in the later periods of European feudalism. There was new opportunity for able commoners, at the expense of the hereditary nobles. The old rules and values were increasingly questioned.

For many, the change was welcome, but for some the passing of the old order and the disruptions of chronic warfare meant chaos and moral confusion. Confucius, who lived from about 551 to about 479 B.C. during what the Chinese call the "Period of the Warring States," was the most famous of these. His prescriptions were an effort to reestablish order, following the rules and values of what he saw as an earlier "golden age." Born to an aristocratic family which had seen better days, he combined teaching with periodic service as adviser to various feudal lords. Although he seems to have thought of himself as not very successful, he was the founder of the most successful moral and ethical system in human history, measured by the number of people in East Asia who followed his precepts for twenty-five hundred years and who are still profoundly affected by them. Confucianism urges benevolence in human affairs and in government, but with an essentially conservative stress on order, which is to be preserved by the morally upright behavior of those in authority, who should serve as models for others. These ideas, described by John K. Fairbank in chapter 1 (and in chapters 11 and 12 of Part 2), have helped to restrict selfish behavior by individuals, and oppressive action by the state, ever since. They were first institutionalized under the great Han empire (202 B.C.–A.D. 220), but before there could be an empire China had to be unified.

The First Empires: The Qin (Ch'in) and the Han

Unification was the work of the short-lived Qin (Ch'in) dynasty, which imposed its own rule in 221 B.C., after defeating all of the other warring states—like the Qin, breakaways from former Zhou hegemony. Our name "China" probably comes from "Qin," appropriately so since one can now for the first time speak of China as a single state and culture. The Emperor Qin Shihuangdi (Ch'in Shih Huang Ti) forcibly unified writing systems, weights and measures, currency, and even axle lengths throughout his newly conquered empire, which now also included the Canton area in the south and adjacent northern Vietnam. He began a network of imperial roads and canals, built a magnificent palace at his capital outside modern Xi'an, and completed the construction and unification of the Great Wall to mark the northern limits of the empire—all with forced labor. A million men are said to have died in building the wall, which was thus a monument to his tyranny as well as his ambition. It was a totalitarian state which followed the new school of Legalism—strict adherence to written laws—rather than the more humane model of Confucius. Merchants and scholars were regarded as parasites and trouble-makers. The emperor buried several hundred scholars alive for questioning his policies, and ordered all books burned which could promote "undesirable thoughts." These excesses earned him a very bad press from subsequent scholars, who after all are the people who write history. But his methods, harsh though they were, built an empire out of chaos and established the base of the Chinese state for all later periods, including the present. It is not surprising that his model of strong state control and the importance of hard work, frugality, and discipline, on a peasant-based state that distrusted merchants and intellectuals, was extolled during the Cultural Revolution from 1966 to 1976.

Many of the Qin reforms were in fact essential for the building of an empire. Among them was the abolition of the former hereditary feudal relationships and land tenure, and of the system of primogeniture whereby the eldest son inherited all of his father's property and status. Land became privately owned and could be freely bought and sold. Status was no longer inherited but won by achievement. A new uniform law code was applied to all people without discrimination, ending many centuries of aristocratic privilege. By Qin times most people were ready to break with their feudal past, and many saw the Qin as building a new and better society. Its excesses were soon rejected, and subsequent dynasties were more "human-hearted," as Confucius put it, in part because they were run largely by Confucian scholars who rejected Legalism. But most of the elements of state control forged by the Qin were necessarily retained in the service of empire; Chinese were ever after to cling to the idea of imperial unity, willing to pay the price it exacted, if not to the tyrannical extent of the Qin. A massive rebellion destroyed Qin power by 206 B.C., and in 202 a new dynasty emerged, the Han.

The Chinese still call themselves "people of Han." Under the new dynasty China took the territorial, political, and social shape it was to retain until the present century. The nearly four centuries of Han rule also saw an impressive and varied flowering of what was now a single Chinese culture in art, literature, music, philosophy, and administration. Agriculture became still more productive as technology continued to improve, and its surpluses paid the heavy costs of empire and supported the new sheen of culture. Han armies reconquered much of the south even beyond the Qin borders, and extended Chinese control and colonies for the first time into southern Manchuria and adjacent northern Korea. A little later most of Xinjiang (Sinkiang) was added to the empire, to guard the Silk Road westward, along which a string of watchtowers was built and garrisoned. Expeditions into central Asia west of Xinjiang, beyond its mountain borders, revealed to the Chinese no state or culture in the world that could rival China. The only possible rival, Rome, lay just beyond China's knowledge on the other side of the great desert of central Asia, although the Chinese had heard travellers' tales of such an empire far to the west to which most of their silk exports went, via a long chain of central Asian middlemen beyond Xinjiang. Paper was invented in Han China and was in common use by the first century B.C., especially for the proliferating documents of imperial administration. The Han capital, Chang'an (Ch'ang An, "Long Peace"), was in the Xi'an area, by now the traditional power base, placed there also to guard the northwestern frontier against nomadic raids. But Chang'an was remote from the empire's new center of gravity in the east and south, and in A.D. 25 the capital was moved eastward to Luoyang. There it remained until the dynasty fell, troubled with intrigue and corruption in its old age, in A.D. 220.

Division and Reunification

For the next nearly four centuries China was again divided into rival kingdoms. In most of the north these were in fact "barbarian" states founded by originally nomadic invaders from the steppe borderlands, while the south was split among a number of Chinese regimes, to which many Chinese fled from the north. Most of Han culture survived, and little of it was forgotten by educated people, but these centuries were seen as a time of troubles, and the loss of imperial unity and grandeur were keenly felt. Buddhism had spread from India during the Han, but became a mass religion only in the troubled centuries after the dynasty's fall as people turned to otherworldly promises of salvation in the face of a real world which many found unsatisfactory. Art and literature continued to flourish, perhaps also as forms of solace, but it was the imperial idea that still appealed to national pride. Nearly all Chinese wanted to see the Han model of greatness restored, but the country had first to be reunified and the imperial machine rebuilt. This was primarily the work of the brief Sui dynasty, which in 589 again welded contending states together by conquest, using many of the same methods as the Qin to the same end. Sui tyranny, too, provoked revolt, and in 618 was succeeded by a new dynasty, the Tang.

The High Culture of the Tang and Song (Sung)

Under Tang rule China achieved new prosperity, cultural greatness, and imperial power. Most of the Han-ruled territories were reclaimed by conquest, and Chinese settlement expanded farther into the south. By late Tang most of the revenue and the population—as well as tea, which became the basic Chinese drink—came from that more productive, flourishing region, including the Yangzi valley. Imperial tradition and defense of the still troublesome northwestern frontiers, however, kept the capital in the north at Chang'an; with about two million inhabitants, that cosmopolitan capital was the largest city in the world. The imperial civil service was reestablished in the Confucian pattern; and, with the encouragement of the early Tang emperors, learning and the arts blossomed. The Tang is still seen as the greatest period of Chinese poetry, especially the work of Li Bo (Li Po, 701–762) and Du Fu (Tu Fu, 712–770). By the early eighth century the art of printing had developed, first from carved wooden blocks, and by late Tang from movable type, more than six hundred years before its spread to Europe. Porcelain, too, had appeared by Tang times, and objects of exquisite beauty, never matched elsewhere, were made from it.

Renewed contact with more distant lands westward revealed, as in Han times, no other civilization that could rival the Celestial Empire. The Son of Heaven, as the Emperor was called, was seen as the lord of "all under heaven," meaning the four corners of the known world, within which China was clearly the zenith of sophistication and power. Like all dynasties, the Tang lost vigor eventually and was weakened by corruption. By 907 it dissolved into civil war, but after a confused period a young general proclaimed a new dynasty in 960 which was to last another three centuries: the Song.

The Song is in many ways the most unusual dynasty in Chinese history. Later generations of Chinese historians have criticized it because it failed to stem the tide of barbarian invasion and was ultimately overwhelmed by the hated Mongols. But, as Kracke points out in chapter 2, the Song also saw unprecedented changes which anticipated the modern Western world by many centuries; these included rapid commercial and urban growth and the beginnings of new technology which was later to lead to industrialization in the West. The Song capital at Kaifeng, near the great bend of the Yellow River, became a huge commercial center as well, with a population well over a million, linked to the productive Yangzi valley by the Grand Canal. In addition to trade, there was a boom in iron and steel production. By the eleventh century Song China probably produced more iron, steel, and metal goods than the whole of Europe until the mid-eighteenth century, and also preceded Europe by seven centuries in smelting and heating with coal. The Song rebuilt the civil service as the core of imperial administration, manned by scholar officials recruited through the imperial examination system, who had no power base of their own but did have a long tradition of public service in the Confucian mode. The further spread of mass printing promoted literacy and education and opened new opportunities to enter the elite group of scholar-gentry from whom officials were recruited, or to prosper in trade. Paper promissory notes and letters of credit were followed by mass government issue of paper money, to serve the growth of commerce. Government officials distributed printed pamphlets and promoted improved farming techniques: irrigation, fertilization, ingenious new metal tools and proto-machines, and new improved crop strains. Painting had a glorious development often patronized by rich urban merchants. It was in many ways a golden age of good government, prosperity, and creativity.

These developments were only briefly interrupted when the north was overrun by the Jurchen, ancestors of the Manchus from the northern steppe border, who sacked Kaifeng in 1127 after a long siege. The Song moved south, fixed their new capital at Hangzhou (Hangchow) in the Yangzi delta, and now could concentrate on China's richest and most populous half. Cut off from normal trade routes through the northwest, Song merchants turned to the sea routes to Southeast Asia. Chinese colonies grew in many Southeast Asian trade centers, and ports on China's southeast coast boomed. There were striking advances in the size and design of ocean-going ships, far larger than any place elsewhere until modern times. The earlier Chinese invention of the compass was a vital navigational aid; Song ships also pioneered the use of multiple masts, separate watertight compartments, and the stern-post rudder, predating modern ships by many centuries. Europeans much later reached China using all these Song innovations, plus Chinese-invented gunpowder, and recorded their profits on Chinese-invented paper. With the stimulus of new trade, Hangzhou's population probably reached a million and a half. Marco Polo, who saw it only later under Mongol rule when its greatness had declined, marvelled even then at its size and wealth; he and his several Western contemporaries who visited China during the brief Mongol period agreed that it was by far the largest and richest city in the world. New tools and simple machines, including pumps for irrigation, were also increasing farm output; early versions of textile machinery were appearing as well as water-powered mills. In these terms, China in the thirteenth century looked in some ways like eighteenth-century Europe. But all of China succumbed in 1279 to the Mongol conquest, which included most of Eurasia.

The Century of the Mongols

The Mongol conquerors took the dynastic title of Yuan for their rule of China, and ran the country largely through Chinese administrators and technicians. Nor could they have triumphed without the help of Chinese siege engineers and military technicians. The heavily fortified Chinese cities were both defended and attacked with explosive weapons. Gunpowder had been invented earlier in China, for fireworks, but this was the first certain use to propel projectiles. The Mongols also used many foreigners, whom they felt they could better trust, in their administration of China, including the Venetian Marco Polo, who served as a minor Yuan official from 1275 to 1292. His famous journal, widely read in Europe, was dismissed by many because it speaks in such extravagant terms about the wealth and splendor he encountered even in a China so recently devastated by a brutal conquest. But when his confessor urged him on his death bed to take back all those lies, Marco is said to have replied, "I have not told the half of what I saw."

The Last Empires: The Ming and the Qing (Ch'ing)

When the Ming dynasty (1368–1644) restored Chinese control after a century of Mongol rule, it strove understandably to resume the traditional imperial pattern and became in time conservative and inward-centered. Despite Ming traditionalism, many of the developments begun under the Song continued, especially the rising commercialization of the economy, the growth of overseas trade, and the consequent spurt in urbanization. An increasingly prominent merchant culture patronized the arts and promoted the growth of popular literature, including the world's first detective stories and a number of widely read novels and adventure tales. All of these trends continued under the Qing (Manchu) dynasty, China's last, which ended in 1911. Early Ming was notable for a brief series of impressive naval expeditions, a continuation of Song overseas probings, which sent fleets of large ships westward in the early fifteenth century to India and east Africa, perhaps even around the Cape of Good Hope, in search of trade and of tribute to the

Chinese throne from a long list of states and kingdoms along the sea route. But the expeditions were very expensive and were soon abandoned as China turned to its traditional concerns with the northern frontiers and its own internal problems.

By the time the first Portuguese traders and Jesuit missionaries arrived only a century later, soon after 1500, the Ming fleets were gone and China showed little interest in these "sea barbarians," who seemed to them crude and bizarre. The Jesuits, who made a few converts in court circles, were finally expelled when the Chinese took offense at the Pope's presuming to tell Chinese Christians what to believe. Europe was still in most respects less developed or impressive than China. Ming and early Qing rulers haughtily rejected Western requests for wider trade or for diplomatic representation at Beijing (Peking), the Ming and Qing capital. The magnificent city of Beijing was laid out and built largely by the Ming, on the ruins of the Mongol capital; it was enlarged and embellished by the Qing as a symbolic affirmation of imperial greatness and of China as the center of the world. There, as the documents in the History section reveal, Lord Macartney, George III's envoy, was kept waiting in 1793, only to be dismissed with a letter rejecting the British requests.

China's high culture and long tradition of good government by Confucian scholars greatly impressed European observers from Marco Polo to Macartney; the latter, despite his rebuff, wrote admiringly of the prosperity and sophistication of the empire. For another several decades Westerners were also unable to challenge China militarily, and their merchants continued to be confined to Canton under close government supervision. The Qing emperors Kang Xi (K'ang Hsi, 1661–1722) and Qian Long (Ch'ien Lung, 1735–99) were highly able, and under their leadership China was again probably the world's greatest power. Their military campaigns reconquered Xinjiang and Tibet and added Mongolia and their Manchurian homeland to the empire. Direct Chinese control and settlement incorporated the south, and large new acreage was brought under the plow. Merchants, trade, and cities continued the rapid growth begun under Song and Ming, although domestic commerce remained far more important than foreign trade. As an indication of new prosperity, the population doubled or tripled between 1700 and 1850, but the standard of living probably continued to rise until the late eighteenth century, when population growth began to outrun further increases in production. Even as late as the 1840s most European observers saw average economic welfare in China as still ahead of the European average, and the country as orderly and well administered, a tribute to Confucian principles. Painting and literature continued to flourish, under merchant as well as imperial patronage, and there was a notable growth in popular literature for the increasing audience of literate city dwellers. Qian Long took a special interest in the arts and in the encouragement of learning, and also directed the further embellishment of the imperial city at Beijing, as befitted his role as the monarch of "all under heaven."

But all was not well by the time of his death in 1799. The dynasty was growing old, troubled with corruption and palace intrigue, while the state was no longer able to stimulate new production to match a still growing population. The poorest areas suffered first, and there was local banditry and periodic rebellion, put down with increasing difficulty. The root problem was the lack of the new technology needed to produce the kind of agricultural and industrial growth which was taking place in the West. China had begun to fall behind in science and technology during the Ming, while Europe saw the Renaissance, Copernicus, Newton, Descartes, the scientific revolution of the eighteenth century, and the beginnings of the industrial revolution. China rested with increasing complacency on its past glories and its current successes, shortsightedly dismissing the Westerners as crude barbarians with nothing to offer from which China could benefit—witness the documents reprinted in the History section. In 1839 disputes over opium, the chief commodity brought to China by the Westerners, spilled over into war. The British navy demolished the antiquated Chinese fleets in short order, with the help of one of the early iron-clad, steam-driven vessels whose guns were also far superior in range and accuracy. British marines and their equally superior weapons easily defeated the far more numerous Chinese troops. The technological gap had become disastrous.

The treaty that ended the war in 1842 began what the Chinese called "the century of humiliation." As explained in more detail in Part 4, foreigners could live and trade in China wherever they liked, under the protection of their own law rather than Chinese law. Tariffs were kept low so that foreign goods could invade the domestic market. Missionaries preached the gospel all over the country and called the Chinese ignorant heathens. The largest and fastest growing cities were the so-called treaty ports, where foreigners had special privileges, ran the local administration, dominated trade and banking, and excluded Chinese from their parks and clubs. China was repeatedly humbled in successive small-scale wars which again demonstrated Western technical superiority, and brought still more concessions from the weakening Qing government.

A great rebellion by the Taipings from 1850 to 1864 was finally suppressed after devastating much of central China, but the Qing were unable to stem the economic and political decline which underlay the rebellion and were powerless to resist the foreign pressures which turned the country into a semi-colony. This humiliation was especially bitter for a people so proud of their traditional glories and their leadership of the world until so recently. Despite repeated object lessons, most Chinese found it hard to acknowledge that they could and should learn from these latest barbarians, or that they should discard or modify any elements of their ancient culture. Meanwhile, China's economic decline became precipitous as population outstripped production and the increasingly ineffective Qing government proved more and more unequal to the crisis situation.

In the 1860s, British and French forces burned the summer palace in Beijing to enforce China's recognition of the foreign "rights" granted in successive treaties. Following this second major humiliation, imperial power was slowly concentrated in the hands of the arch-conservative Empress Dowager, who plotted her way to the top and prevented or undercut the reform efforts of a few farsighted officials. She saw the problem as foreign intrusion rather than Chinese weakness. A few arsenals and the beginnings of a modern fleet were built, but the Empress, and many Chinese intellectuals and officials, urged a full-scale return to traditional ways—"Back to the Han"—as the best answer to China's problems. After China was humbled again when Japan easily defeated its new fleet and annexed Korea, China's protectorate, the Empress and her courtiers supported the mob efforts of the Boxers to kill all foreigners or drive them into the sea. An allied expeditionary force put down the Boxers in 1900 and imposed heavy indemnities on the Chinese government. The Empress died in 1908 of old age, and the dynasty soon after, in 1911, of similar causes, rather than because of the strength of the poorly organized revolutionary effort which overthrew it.

The Republic

Chinese nationalism, as opposed to simple cultural pride, had still to come of age, as Mary Wright points out in chapter 5. Attempts at a national republican government after 1911 were subverted by the military "strong man" Yuan Shikai (Yuan Shih-k'ai). When he died in 1916, after trying to declare himself emperor, China broke up into rival warlord regimes. But even in a divided and powerless China modern nationalism was growing, stimulated by foreign arrogance and Chinese despair over their country's humiliation. When the Japanese demanded the former German concession areas and other special rights and the victorious Allies at Versailles agreed to this vivisection in 1919, there were mass spontaneous demonstrations. Known as the May Fourth Movement, these demonstrations marked the real beginning of Chinese nationalism. The Chinese Communist Party was founded in 1921, and for a time worked with Sun Yat-sen's Guomindang, or Nationalist Party, to build a strong national government. With the warlords largely suppressed and most of China under a new republican government at Nanjing in 1927, president Chiang Kai-shek, Sun's political heir, turned on his Communist allies and nearly eliminated them. A few, including Mao Zedong (Mao Tse-tung), survived to retreat into the southeastern mountains, and then, in the Long March of 1934, to reach a new base in the remote northwest centered on Yenan. For ten years Chiang's Guomindang governed most of China and began some belated modernization until 1937, when the Japanese, who had already annexed Manchuria in 1931, invaded northern and eastern China.

The People's Republic

The Guomindang had become increasingly conservative, even reactionary, while the Communists preached the need for radical change to cure China's poverty and backwardness, and to enable it to expel imperialists and regain international equality. The eight years of anti-Japanese war left the Guomindang exhausted, its subjects thoroughly demoralized and impoverished by uncontrolled inflation. The Communists' guerrilla strategy against the Japanese won them widespread support, and at the war's end in 1945 they were incomparably stronger than they had ever been. More and more Chinese were coming to feel that the traditional system, which Chiang tried to revive, had been proven inadequate to cope with China's modern problems and that radical change was indeed necessary. A truce between the two rivals after the war soon broke down, and a series of victories, in which large numbers of Guomindang troops and their officers deserted to the other side, brought the Communists to full power in 1949.

The majority of Chinese welcomed the Communist victory, and echoed Mao's phrase, "China has stood up!" They had been a hundred years in the wilderness. Now China was to be made strong and great again. Long neglected problems of peasant poverty, inequality, elitism, the oppression of women, and corrupt or ineffective government were at last to be attacked, by a united people using mass action. The old scholar-gentry and their elitist life-style and manipulation of power were to be swept away, and China ruled by and for the peasants and workers, the vast majority of the Chinese people, who had been largely ignored or exploited by the handful of the elite, especially during the most recent century when the traditional imperial model had so disastrously stumbled and failed.

As the revolution progressed from reconstruction to the Great Leap Forward and the commune system in 1958, and then to the even more disruptive radicalism of the Cultural Revolution from 1966 to 1976, much of its early promise and the enthusiasm it evoked began to be clouded. Millions died of starvation, the result of ill-conceived policies of the Great Leap. Further millions were persecuted, driven to suicide, or killed in the madness of the Cultural Revolution. Education in those years, especially above primary levels, virtually ceased except for "political study." China will go on paying a high price for what most of its people now refer to as "the lost years"—most of the time from 1957 to 1978. "Self Reliance" was the theme of those years also, good for national morale but bad for the economic and technological development which China so urgently needed and which suffered while China cut herself off from most of the rest of the world. Perhaps there was need to purge China of the negative aspects of the past, but the revolution was increasingly seen as failing the traditional, and indeed universal, test of good government: concern for and positive impact on the welfare and improvement of the nation. Much constructive work was done; the revolution was far from being all bad. But when Mao died in 1976, most Chinese were ready for less ideology, less politics, and more rational planning and development. These, too, had all along been revolutionary goals. Now it was time to pursue them.

The changes after 1976 also included a reemerging pride in China's imperial past, a qualified return to respect for traditional Confucian values (although they survived even the radical years as the revolutionary imperative to "serve the people"), the pairing of power with responsibility, and more sober and realistic solutions to make up for the "lost years." China must rejoin the world, with pride. Slogans are no substitute for hard practical work. China has a long way to go, but it is determined to catch up, and perhaps in time to show the way. Its great past is now seen as a source of strength and of confidence. Being Chinese has always been a special privilege and distinction. Now over a billion people are bent on making good that claim in the world of the twenty-first century.

Unfortunately, from about the mid-1980s on, the economic system has been in growing trouble, as inflation, growing out of control, has caused great hardship. There has also been much resentment of the rampant corruption among Party officials and of the new rich, who profited from the relaxation of earlier controls on private enterprise. The aging Party leadership and the deadweight of the world's largest bureaucracy have been, in their rigidity and obstructionism, important factors contributing to China's sluggishness in improving the lot of many of its citizens, at a time when some have enjoyed new prosperity. As a direct result of the new openness to the outside world after 1978, there have also been growing pressures for freer expression. Fuelled by all these developments, protests and demonstrations, mainly by students, provoked in the end the bloody Beijing Massacre in June of 1989, repeated in other cities, and a return to a policy of hardline political controls. These actions earned widespread international condemnation and have critically slowed the exchanges and the flow of foreign technology China so urgently needs. Meanwhile, the economic situation has remained largely out of control, and bitterness against the government continues to smoulder. Thus, in its drive for "modernization" and full membership in the world community, China approaches the end of the century with mounting problems.

Unity out of Diversity

The centuries-old sense of pride in being Chinese is all the more remarkable when one considers the vastness of the Chinese state and the variety of its regions and its peoples. Since the time of Qin Shihuangdi, the first imperial unifier, the Chinese state has been a triumph of unity out of diversity, an imperial imprint on a highly varied landscape and its varied inhabitants. As we have seen, political unity was reasserted after every period of division, from the fall of the Han to the twentieth century. The empire first took shape on the north China plain, and then progressively incorporated the very different area of the south, originally occupied by separate cultures and independent states. Successive dynasties conquered and occupied Xinjiang, Inner Mongolia, Tibet, and Manchuria and added them to the empire.

All of these areas supported different peoples, most of them unrelated to the people of the north China plain and some of them traditional enemies, such as the nomadic groups of the steppe borderlands. The conquest of the south took place not only at the expense of Chinese-style states and cultures, as in the Yangzi valley and the Canton area, but also at the expense of a great variety of non-Chinese groups, who were subjugated and gradually displaced. Their descendants still live in the mountains of the south and still cling to their traditional cultures and languages today. Most of the people of the south, however, have been absorbed into, or came to form a part of, the greater Chinese whole, the people called *Han.* The Han people are distinguished from both the small but highly varied non-Han groups of the south and the somewhat more numerous non-Han people of the outer areas: Tibetans, Uighurs (in Xinjiang), Mongols, Kazaks, and Manchus. Except for Tibet, Han Chinese have become the dominant inhabitants of all these border areas, as they have in the south.

The present Chinese state, inherited from the empire, is inhabited by a population that is about 94 percent Han, but there remains a sharp distinction between what is called China Proper on the one hand, the eighteen provinces south of the Great Wall and east of Tibet and Xinjiang, and on the other hand the outer areas, which constitute half of the area of the state. Tibet and the adjacent related area of Qinghai (Tsinghai), all part of the "roof of the world," are almost the size of western Europe; Xinjiang is only slightly smaller, and Inner Mongolia plus Manchuria about the same size as Tibet. China is in fact the world's second largest country, exceeded only by the Soviet Union, but half of it is desert, arid steppe, mountains, or high alpine wasteland, all of which are very thinly settled. Relations between the Han inhabitants of China Proper and the non-Han groups of the south have traditionally been bad: a conquering majority coexists with oppressed minorities driven from their land and denied access to the mainstream of Chinese culture unless they were willing and able to adopt Han language and life-style. Tibetans, Uighurs, Kazaks, and Mongols in the outer areas have also tried to retain their own cultures and identities and have fought against or resented Chinese control. They came under Chinese domination as part of imperial expansion, but for much of Chinese history their military abilities as mounted nomads, plus the remoteness, mountains, and marginality of their homelands enabled them to keep their independence, and even to harry or occasionally conquer parts of China proper. From the founding of the Han dynasty until the fall of the Qing in 1911, all or large parts of China Proper were in fact ruled nearly half the time, though in Chinese style, by groups that were originally "barbarians" from the northern steppes. The Great Wall, designed to keep them out, was thus often breached or infiltrated, but it still serves as a line of demarcation between the traditional Han Chinese areas of settled agriculture and the realms beyond it, where until recently Hans did not venture except for military purposes.

The Problem of Minorities

The line of the Great Wall still follows approximately the climatic limits of agriculture under traditional conditions. Areas north of it are too dry for permanent farming except with irrigation, and also too cold until the recent development of crop strains suited to the climate. Chinese civilization traditionally depended on, and was coexistent with, agriculture. Han settlement therefore spread in time into all of the areas where farming was rewarding, leaving the steep slopes of the mountainous south and the dry, cold, or alpine regions of the outer areas to the variety of non-Han groups who still occupy them. Modern technology, especially irrigation, has made it possible to extend agriculture out into the steppe and into northern Manchuria. At the same time, railways and industrialization have encouraged large Han Chinese settlement in those areas and strengthened their importance to the state as sources of oil, iron ore, coal, metals, timber, and other basic raw materials. Han Chinese farmers, technicians, and industrial workers now outnumber Mongols ten to one in Inner Mongolia, constitute 95 percent of the inhabitants of Manchuria, about half of those in Xinjiang, and are a large group even in Tibet, although there they are primarily officials of the Chinese state. Technological change has also destroyed the former military balance and loaded it overwhelmingly in favor of the Han Chinese.

Unfortunately for the minorities, they are all together only about six percent of the national total, and they are divided among literally hundreds of very different groups who could not possibly, and would not choose to, make common cause. The largest groups, Uighurs, Mongols, and Tibetans, are not only totally different from one another but number only a few million each, a handful out of 1.2 billion. It will take much time before Han and non-Han can live together happily as simply fellow Chinese.

The present government's solution to this ancient problem is to recognize the validity of the minorities, and to promote the fiction that the Chinese nation is now a formally equal partnership between Han and non-Han "nationalities." Non-Hans are encouraged to preserve their traditional cultures, short of attitudes or activities which suggest real autonomy or separatism. Most non-Han groups are now associated with designated areas where their cultures are recognized and which carry their name. The smaller ones, mainly in the culturally complex mountainous parts of the south, are called "Autonomous Areas"; the larger ones are "Autonomous Regions," such as the Xinjiang-Uighur, Tibetan, and Inner Mongolian Autonomous Regions. But the ruling hand of the central Chinese state is strong in all of them, through officials who assert political control and national priorities. The one-child-per-family policy of population control (see Part 3) is not applied to these minorities, and they are given a few other concessions. But if they want to get ahead in modern China, they must adopt Han culture and language. China's policy toward its minorities is like Soviet policy toward the non-Russian groups in the U.S.S.R., which are given somewhat greater local autonomy but can move into the modern world only by following the Russian path. The difference is that Russians are in fact a minority in the U.S.S.R. and must therefore acknowledge the importance of other nationalities in their multi-national state. China is only by courtesy a multi-national state, and while the courtesy may be symbolically important to non-Han peoples who feel, with reason, that they have been treated for over two thousand years as enemies and oppressed victims, their small numbers and hopelessly fragmented situation leave them with no substantial role or power. A more appropriate analogy is with the American Indians in the United States, for three centuries the targets of extermination efforts by the whites, and only recently offered a place in American society—on predominantly white terms.

Manchuria, which the Chinese now call simply "the Northeast," is rather different from the other outer areas since it is so overwhelmingly Han in population. The Manchus are almost gone, outnumbered even in their original homeland by Mongols and other non-Han groups who shared it with them even before the Han dynasty occupation of the Liao River valley in southern Manchuria. The Qing dynasty tried to protect their ancestral lands from Chinese settlement, but after about 1890 such efforts were ineffective against a rising tide of immigration from north China. Manchuria was relatively empty, and especially its southern half in the Liao valley was physically similar to the north China plain, where overpopulation generated more and more peasant distress as China slid into chaos and economic decline. Between 1900 and 1940 about a million Chinese a year migrated to Manchuria. Japanese control after 1904 encouraged rather than dampened this flow, since the Japanese greatly expanded the railway system and built a commercial agriculture, a rapidly growing industrial plant, and booming cities and ports, all of which needed and rewarded huge amounts of Chinese labor. In 1945, with the end of the Pacific war, Manchuria was returned to China and became the backbone of the industrialization drive after 1949. In the last years of the Qing, Inner Mongolia also drew large numbers of Chinese settlers, increasingly supported by new irrigation and linked to the economy by rail lines. Major iron ore deposits were found there after 1949, and Chinese settlement was further augmented by technicians and workers. Outer Mongolia, never firmly under Chinese control, became the independent Mongolian Peoples' Republic in 1921, and has remained a Soviet satellite.

The Geographic Regions

China proper, within the Great Wall, still includes the bulk of the agricultural land, the vast majority of the Chinese people, and the roots and body of Chinese civilization. It centers primarily on three great river systems, the Yellow (Huang) for north China, the Yangzi for central China, and the Xi (Hsi, West) River for south China. Each rises in the mountainous west and flows across the breadth of the country, so that their usefulness is enhanced. The north China plain, where the empire was born, is almost entirely the flood plain of the Huang, deposited by the river over recent millennia and hence highly fertile, but plagued by recurrent drought, and until recently by periodic floods. The efforts at flood prevention by a series of dams and control works carried out since the 1950s have much reduced this problem, and new irrigation, from reservoirs and from deeper wells with pumps, has lessened the ravages of drought. But as de Crespigny points out in chapter 8, the north remains agriculturally marginal, and in general a poorer area than the better watered south. Rainfall lessens and becomes even more variable westward, farther from the monsoonal source of moisture, the sea. The northwestern provinces of Shanxi (Shensi) and Gansu (Kansu), bordering Xinjiang, approach desert conditions. Islam spread first into this area, from central Asia and Xinjiang, and it is still the home of some 60 million Chinese Muslims, recognized as yet another "nationality," although they are ethnically Han. Most of them are the descendants of Chinese converts, others of many centuries of intermarriage by original Muslim immigrants.

The Yangzi basin, with its many tributaries, covers about half of China Proper and contains over half of its population. The main stream is navigable for deep draft shipping as far as Wuhan, 630 miles from the sea, but local boats can use some 20,000 miles of waterways in the basin. Above Wuhan the Yangzi has cut a spectacular series of gorges, punctuated by rapids. A big new dam near Yizhang (Ichang), designed also for power generation, has raised the water level in the gorges, moderated the river's flow, and greatly improved navigation. There has long been talk of a much bigger dam near the mouth of the gorges, which would generate enormous amounts of power and open the upper Yangzi to ocean shipping; it would be extremely expensive, but it may well be built eventually as China's economic development proceeds and as the need for energy rises. Below Wuhan the river widens as it winds across the nearly level plain of east China and becomes a broad estuary a hundred miles from the sea. The land on both sides is watery, too, crisscrossed by an intricate network of deltaic streams and artificial canals linked together over many centuries of dense human occupancy which since ancient times has combined productive agriculture on this fertile alluvial soil with water-borne commerce. The Yangzi delta has always been China's premier area of urbanization, now dominated by Shanghai but containing also the old capitals of Nanjing, Suzhou (Soochow), and Hangzhou at the edge of the delta, plus many intermediate commercial centers, all interconnected by cheap water transport and supported by the intensively cultivated area of the lower Yangzi valley. In addition to irrigation from surface streams and wells, farming benefits from more adequate and reliable rainfall than in the north (as the maps in John Fairbank's brief account show), and the growing season is also far longer.

The mountains which cover most of west China include Sichuan (Szechuan), but in much of its "red basin," as it is called from the color of its soils, relief is gentle enough to permit intensive cultivation. The warm moist climate contributes to high yields, and hence to a large cluster of dense population, which shows up clearly on Fairbank's population map. In Sichuan, too, the Yangzi and its several tributaries have long supported an active commerce, a further basis for dense settlement.

In the south, steeper slopes occupy most of the landscape, leaving only small pockets of more level land until the West River, the major drainage system, emerges from the mountains about 300 miles from the sea and flows through a slowly widening flood plain, entering the delta just above Canton (now called Guangzhou). The Tropic of Cancer lies just north of the city, so that the delta is free of frost and supports three crops per year. More than ample rainfall and high temperatures combine with fertile alluvial soil to produce the highest yields in China, and the densest single cluster of population. As in the Yangzi delta and Sichuan, this has also long been a highly commercialized area, dependent on deltaic waterways which focus on Canton. From Canton and other ports on the southeast coasts, such as Amoy, Shatou (Swatow), and Fuzhou (Foochow), Chinese traders centuries ago built overseas trade networks throughout Southeast Asia. Although Shanghai has outdistanced them in size and trade flows, Chinese stereotypes still cast the Cantonese and Fujianese (Fukienese) as the preeminent merchants and entrepreneurs. The overpopulated coastal southeast was the source of almost all of the Chinese who settled abroad, first in Southeast Asia and then world-wide, including the United States. Cantonese and Fujianese have their own culture, a variation of Han Chinese culture, reflecting their different circumstances, relatively later inclusion in the empire, and longstanding overseas connections. Their languages, too, are different, not just dialects of Chinese, although during the two thousand years of close involvement with the empire they have incorporated many words from standard Chinese.

Resources for Development

China's biggest resource problem is the inadequate amount of good agricultural land to support its immense—and still growing—population. Roughly half of the country is desert, arid steppe, mountains, or alpine wasteland, and even within China Proper only about 30 percent of the land is cultivated, the rest being either too dry or too steep. The hard fact is that China has one of the smallest per-capita amounts of cultivated land in the world, less than one-sixth of that of the United States.

Irrigation projects since 1949 have already greatly extended the acreage under cultivation, in some cases beyond what is either economically or ecologically rational. Yields from existing farmland have risen considerably in the past forty years with new irrigation, increased application of fertilizer, and the use of higher-yielding strains produced by the so-called Green Revolution, and they will continue to do so, especially as the drought-plagued north is better irrigated. Yet the agricultural resource base for feeding China's population and supplying non-food crops to industry remains, as a whole, precariously limited. While total output has risen, though somewhat irregularly, it has kept only a little ahead of population growth, and the margin of surplus remains small and still threatened by the periodic weather shifts to which China is subject.

Another serious problem in the age of the chainsaw is continuing deforestation to feed the huge market for timber. Deforestation has already greatly worsened flooding problems, as well as producing massive erosion, which China can ill afford.

China does enjoy certain natural advantages, however. It is munificently supplied with coal. While the greatest output is in the north and northeast, coal is mined in every province and in Xinjiang, and is the country's major mineral resource. Ample cheap coal gives a strong boost to Chinese industrialization, though heavy use creates pollution problems that are already severe, especially in the industrialized cities. There are also major reserves of iron ore, many of them discovered since 1949, and equally important pools of petroleum, also discovered and exploited mainly since 1949, although, like coal, these resources are concentrated in the north and northeast. Export surpluses of tungsten, tin, and antinomy exist, mainly in the southwest, and there appear to be sufficient deposits of bauxite (aluminum ore), as well as a number of other minerals used in smaller quantities. Hydroelectric potential, especially on the Yangzi and its tributaries, is immense but expensive to develop, although some major projects have been completed. While shortages may arise as industrialization continues on the huge scale required for a market of over one billion people, in general China's industrialization and drive for "modernization" need not be retarded by a lack of natural resources.

Language and Culture

Language is of course a basically important aspect of culture, and a useful key to cultural differences. There are many regional variants within standard Chinese, but it is misleading to speak of "Mandarin Chinese" as if it were somehow a dialect instead of the common language of a billion people. Except for separate languages such as Cantonese or Fujianese (the latter spoken also in Taiwan, as Taiwanese, since most of its people came since the seventeenth century from Fujian), these regional variants are for the most part mutually intelligible. The range of dialectical or regional differences is probably very little more than that in the United States. Think, for example, of the considerable gulf between Black English, Chicano English, or Maine backwoods versus Louisiana bayou speech, between which mutual intelligibility may break down, as it does between some dialects in China. But linguistic commonality in China is rapidly widening with the spread of education, radio, and television, all of which use standard Chinese. Even in Canton that is the national language, and one now hears it spoken in shops or in the street, if not at home. The written language has, of course, always been uniform, and indeed was shared with Koreans, Vietnamese, and Japanese. The standard spoken language of China evolved from the speech of officials, who had to communicate with people in all parts of the empire, and with each other and the capital. The preferred model thus became the speech of Chang'an, then of Kaifeng (the Song capital), and finally, since the fourteenth century, of Beijing; the so-called "Beijing dialect," while distinctive, is just one of many forms of a genuinely national language spoken and understood by just about everyone, especially since 1949.

The nine "macroregions" defined and described in the selection by Skinner in chapter 9 also developed their own regional variants of spoken Chinese, and a wide spectrum of other distinctive regional characteristics. As he points out, most of them exhibited tendencies to break away from central control when the center was weak, as it was toward the close of each dynasty. Even China Proper is a huge area, with great regional differences in both physical and human terms. It was a triumph of statecraft to hold it together as a political unit at the best of times, although that job has been made immeasurably easier in the age of railways, telecommunications, and the vast apparatus of the modern state. But it is only natural to find centrifugal as well as centripetal forces operating in a continual interplay between regional and national pressures. Sichuanese, Cantonese, and other regional cultures see themselves as very different from one another, often as rivals within the national whole, and, when circumstances have permitted, as independent entities. This has been especially true of the regions remote from the capital: the Canton delta and the southeast coast, Sichuan, the Yunkuei (Yun-Kwei) region of the southwest, and (in recent centuries) the northwest. All have seen major rebellions against the central authority or bids for independence. The Canton delta was the major original base of the modern revolution, from its beginnings in the 1890s as a movement against the Qing dynasty to the qualified victory of the Guomindang in 1927. Food, house styles, aspects of dress, social systems, and other cultural characteristics are distinct in each of these regions. But there is a strong shared consciousness of Chineseness among all of them, thanks in part to their common heritage of the Great Tradition of Chinese civilization and empire, in which they jointly take pride. Separate regional identities are merged as members of a greater Chinese whole.

This unity has always been made easier by the commonality of the written language, its role as the carrier of the Great Tradition which belongs to all Chinese, and as the medium of empire. Empire was won and held only at heavy cost in blood, treasure, and energy, but from the time of the Han dynasty it has seemed right to most Chinese that their country should be one. Such a conviction was fed not only by the glory of the empire and the unity of literate culture, but, as we have seen, by China's image of the rest of the world. Lesser cultures and states around them acknowledged and even paid tribute to the Son of Heaven, the Emperor of China, as the supreme lord of "all under Heaven." That was good for national ego, but also seemed an appropriate reflection of the gap between "barbarians" and Chinese. Nature had been munificent in giving China Proper the world's largest portion of productive agricultural land; with the care lavished on it, it supported a quarter or more of the world's people, at a generally high level of well-being. Beyond every frontier the natural environment sharply deteriorated: too cold, too dry, too mountainous, too hot or jungly. Only in China was there a golden mean, with everything in appropriate balance. The Chinese called their country the middle kingdom, in part to reflect this conception, but also to imply their apparently heaven-ordained role to serve as a model of unity, greatness, and culture for less well endowed peoples elsewhere. Those at the top of the hierarchy have a responsibility to lead the way.

Such an attitude is clearly expressed in the selection of historical documents included in Part 1: "Our Celestial Dynasty rules over and supervises the myriad states. . . ." Within China, given the high level of its civilization, resting on so nourishing a geographical foundation whose favor and importance were openly acknowledged, it is understandable that the home base acquired a womb-like quality. This further sharpened the distinction in the Chinese mind between themselves, their culture and their territory on the one hand, and, on the other, the cultural and geographical "wilderness" of barbarian lands and peoples beyond their borders and beyond major mountain barriers behind which China matured in relative isolation. Self-sufficiency in time bred also self-satisfaction, and rigidifying attitudes toward the rest of the world, to China's heavy modern cost. But the special qualities seen as adhering to Chineseness, and as deriving at least in part from China's geographic good fortune, were linked with the consciousness of China as both a political and a cultural unit. Regional tensions remain, and policy will continue to swing between strengthening central control and responding to pressures for greater regional initiative or responsibility. But the great regional variety of which China is composed is bound more tightly than ever in the past within the larger frame of a unitary state, and in the service of a new national effort.

History

1

The Old Order

John K. Fairbank

John Fairbank is the dean of American historians of China. Now retired from Harvard but still very active, he has produced a long list of scholarly books and articles, but for all his learning he retains an enviable knack for summarizing huge and often complex matters in a brief, authoritative, yet lively fashion. The fourth edition his The United States and China *is widely acknowledged as the best single guide to Chinese history and civilization up to the late 1970s. The following selections provide a neat account of the traditional imperial system by which China was governed from the third century* B.C. *to the republican revolution of 1911. They focus appropriately on the role of Confucian ideology, the bureaucracy which embodied those values, and the nature of the resulting balance between individual and group or collective interest—themes which still relate closely to China today.*

Confucian Principles

The principles of Confucian government, which still lie somewhere below the surface of Chinese politics, were worked out before the time of Christ. Modifications made in later centuries, though extensive, have not been fundamental until recently. The past is still just around the corner.

First of all, from the beginning of Chinese history down to the third century B.C. there was a marked stratification into officials and nobility on the one hand, and the common people on the other.... This social distinction between the ancient ruling class and the common people gave rise to a particular type of aristocratic tradition which was preserved and transmitted through Confucianism. The former aristocrat became the scholar official, and Confucianism his ideology.

This Confucian aristocracy of merit or talent came closer to the original Greek idea of aristocracy, "government by the best," than did the subsequent European hereditary aristocracies of birth. In the era of warring states, when the empire was not yet unified and philosophers flourished, Chinese thinkers of all major schools turned against the principle of hereditary privilege, invoked by the rulers of the many family-states, and stressed the natural equality of men at birth: men are by nature good and have an innate moral sense.... This means that man is perfectible. He can be led in the right path through education, especially through his own effort at self-cultivation, within himself, but also through the emulation of models outside himself. In his own effort to do the right thing, he can be influenced by the example of the sages and superior men who have succeeded in putting right conduct ahead of all other considerations. This ancient Chinese stress on the moral educability of man has persisted down to the present. It still inspires the government to do the moral educating.

Government by Moral Prestige. The Confucian ideology did not, of course, begin with Confucius (551–479? B.C.). The interesting concept of the Mandate of Heaven, for example, went back to the early Chou period (ca. 1027–770 B.C.). According to the classic *Book of History,* the wickedness of the last ruler of the Shang, who was a tyrant, caused Heaven to give a mandate to the Chou to destroy him and supplant his dynasty, inasmuch as the Shang people themselves had failed to overthrow the tyrant. As later amplified, this ancient idea became the famous "right of rebellion," the last resort of the populace against tyrannical government. It emphasized the good conduct or virtue of the ruler as the ethical sanction for preserving his rule. Bad conduct on his part destroyed the sanction. Heaven withdrew its Mandate, and the people were justified in deposing the dynasty, if they could. Consequently any successful rebellion was justified, and a new rule sanctioned, by the very fact of its success. "Heaven decides as the people decide." The Chinese literati have censured bad government and rebels have risen against it in terms of this theory. It has also reinforced the belief that the ruler should be advised by learned men in order to ensure his right conduct.

Confucius and his fellow philosophers achieved their position by being teachers who advised rulers as to their conduct, in an age when feudal princes were competing for hegemony. Confucius was an aristocrat and maintained at his home a school for the elucidation and transmission of the moral principles of conduct and princely rule. Here he taught the upper class how to behave. He emphasized court etiquette, state ceremonies, and proper conduct toward one's ancestors and in the famous five degrees of relationships. One of the central principles of this code was expressed in the idea of "proper behavior according to status" *(li)*. The Confucian gentleman ("the superior man," "the princely man") was guided by *li,* the precepts of which were written in the classics.

It is important to note that this code which came to guide the conduct of the scholar-official did not originally apply to the common people, whose conduct was to be regulated by rewards and punishments rather than moral principles.

This complex system of abstruse rules which the Confucians became experts at applying stemmed from the relationship of Chinese man to nature.... This relation had early been expressed in a primitive animism in which the spirits of land, wind, and water were thought to play an active part in human affairs. The idea is still prevalent in the practice of Chinese geomancy or *feng-shui* (lit., "wind and water"), which sees to it that buildings in China are properly placed in their natural surroundings. Temples, for example, commonly face south with protecting hills behind them and a water course nearby. In its more rationalized form this idea of the close relation between human and natural phenomena led to the conception that human conduct is reflected in acts of nature. To put it another way, man is so much a part of the natural order that improper conduct on his part will throw the whole of nature out of joint. Therefore man's conduct must be made to harmonize with the unseen forces of nature, lest calamity ensue.

This was the rationale of the Confucian emphasis on right conduct on the part of the ruler, for the ruler was thought to intervene between mankind and the forces of nature. As the Son of Heaven he stood between Heaven above and the people below. He maintained the universal harmony of man and nature by doing the right thing at the right time. It was, therefore, logical to assume that when natural calamity came, it was the ruler's fault. He might acknowledge this by issuing a penitential edict.... It was also for this reason that the Confucian scholar became so important. Only he, by his knowledge of the rules of right conduct, could properly advise the ruler in his cosmic role.

The main point of this theory of "government by goodness," by which Confucianism achieved an emphasis so different from anything in the West, was the idea of virtue which was attached to right conduct. To conduct oneself according to the rules of propriety or *li* in itself gave one a moral status or prestige. This moral prestige in turn gave one influence over the people. "The people are like grass, the ruler like the wind"; as the wind blew, so the grass was inclined. Right conduct gave the ruler power.

On this basis the Confucian scholars established themselves as an essential part of the government, specially competent to maintain its moral nature and so retain the Mandate of Heaven. Where the Legalist philosophers of the Ch'in unification of 221 B.C. had had ruthlessly efficient methods of government but little moral justification for them, the Confucianists offered an ideological basis. They finally eclipsed the many other ancient schools of philosophy. As interpreters of the *li,* they became technical experts, whose explanations of natural portents and calamities and of the implications of the rulers' actions could be denied or rejected only on the basis of the classical doctrines of which they were themselves the masters. This gave them a strategic position from which to influence government policy. In return they provided the regime with a rational and ethical sanction for the exercise of its authority, at a time when most rulers of empires relied mainly upon religious sanctions. This was a great political invention.

Early Achievements in Bureaucratic Administration. Theory, moreover, was matched by practice in the techniques of government. The bureaucratic ruling class came into its own after the decentralized and family-based feudalism of ancient China gave way to an imperial government. The unification of 221 B.C., in which one of the warring states (Ch'in) finally swallowed the others, required violent dictatorial methods and a philosophy of absolutism (that of the so-called Legalist philosophers). But after the short-lived Ch'in dynasty was succeeded by the Han in 206 B.C., a less tyrannical system of administration evolved. The emperors came to rely upon a new class of administrators who superintended the great public works—dikes and ditches, walls, palaces and granaries—and who drafted peasant labor and collected the land tax. These administrators supplanted the hereditary nobility of feudal times and became the backbone of the imperial regime. They incorporated many of the Legalist methods in a new amalgam, imperial Confucianism.

In the two centuries before Christ the early Han rulers firmly established certain principles. First, the political authority in the state was centralized in the one man at the top who ruled as emperor. Second, the emperor's authority in the conduct of the administration was exercised on his behalf by his chief ministers, who stood at the top of a graded bureaucracy and who were responsible to him for the success or failure of their administration. Third, this bureaucracy was centralized in the vast palace at the capital where the emperor exercised the power of appointment to office. His chief task became the selection of civil servants, with an eye to the maintenance of his power and his dynasty. For this reason the appointment of relatives, particularly from the maternal side, became an early practice. (Maternal relatives were the one group of persons completely dependent upon the ruler's favor as well as tied to him by family bonds, in contrast to paternal relatives who might compete for the succession.) Fourth, the early Han rulers developed the institution of inspection which later became the censorate, whereby an official in the provinces was checked upon by another official of lower rank, who was sent independently and was not responsible for the acts of his superior.

In this and in many other ways the central problem of the imperial administration became that of selecting and controlling the bureaucrats. It was here that Confucianism gained strength from certain Legalist methods, and ancient China . . . led the world in developing basic principles of bureaucratic government: namely the impersonal use of specifically delegated powers in fixed areas of jurisdiction by appointed and salaried officials who regularly reported their acts during limited terms of office. For more than 2000 years this system of territorial bureaucracy has been epitomized in the walled administrative city of the *hsien* or county.

To find the talent for officialdom the Han emperors subsidized schools and began to set written examinations. This practice continued, and when the imperial structure was reinvigorated under the T'ang dynasty (A.D. 618–907), the examination system became firmly established as the main avenue to office. For more than a thousand years, down to 1905, this imperial institution produced administrators who had established their qualifications for official life by thoroughly indoctrinating themselves in the official orthodoxy—surely another of the great political inventions. . . .

Individualism, Chinese Style

To Western observers, China has presented a puzzling contrast: a great richness of human personality but little tradition of civil liberties. As in all countries, the creative Chinese writer, artist, or craftsman expressed his individuality, while the hermit or recluse could become a private individualist outside his community. But what was the degree of individualism in the sense of individual rights within the old society?

Instead of simply applying a legalistic Western yardstick, we may well . . . appraise the actual concerns and solutions of Chinese philosophers. The individual, first of all, had to claim his status or rights within the social scene, among his fellow men. Confucius had said, "If I am not to be a man among men, then what am I to be?" Second, the Confucian emphasis on the individual's conduct supporting the social order was only the outward half of the story. The other, inward half stressed the individual's self-cultivation. But this had meant from early times the fulfillment of his personality by living as "a man among men," in proper relations with those around him and so according to moral principles. Selfishness was to be curbed by duty, and duty defined in social terms. Mencius said, "Between father and son there should be affection; between sovereign and minister, righteousness; between husband and wife, attention to their separate functions; between old and young, a proper order; and between friends, fidelity." Thus Chinese man defined his "self" by his relations to others and to the Tao or Way which made them all interdependent through the "web of reciprocal obligations." This by no means diminished the importance of conscience and morality. On the contrary, trying to stay within the bounds of orthodoxy might intensify the individual's moral problems, but these problems were perceived as "situation-centered," . . . not "individual-centered" as in America.

In the sixteenth century a new school of Confucian philosophy arose that gave the individual more scope. Wang Yang-ming (1472–1529), a high official whose thinking was to have great influence in both China and Japan, led a revolt against the Neo-Confucian orthodoxy by asserting that men have a common moral nature and therefore each individual has intuitive moral knowledge within his own mind. The possibilities of sagehood lie within him. Thus his task is to achieve a moral self-reformation. This is to be done mainly through study, but study must include thought, reflection, and the unending search for truth, not as mere verbal formulas but through personal experience. While it did not attack the traditional social order, Wang Yang-ming's subjective approach urged the individual to achieve a disciplined unity between learning and conduct, thought and action, or in today's terms, between theory and practice. This was a quite restricted form of individualism; in the end, as de Bary remarks, it may be "more adaptable to a socialist society than modern Western types of individualism."

Human rights in China are today a wide-open subject—first in our American need to define "human rights" in operational terms of welfare as well as politics; second in the need to find what alternative or equivalent ideas are valued in China. The expected difference in Western and Chinese values makes this study urgent. . . . Tracing the stages through which Chinese children used to be fitted into their society, [we may note] the Confucian stress on acceptance of parental authority, the repression of aggressiveness and selfishness, and the following of rituals and emulation of models, all disciplining the child to avoid disorder and depend upon authority at the same time that he resented it. . . . Modern students of Neo-Confucianism . . . [conclude] that the old anxiety due to dependence on authority was tempered by the gratification of self-assertion and Confucian self-fulfillment. [They] believe that the Confucian individual faced a constant predicament: the possibility or even probability of failure but the need to persevere in moral endeavor nevertheless. Neo-Confucian values, in short, once internalized as authoritative, produced a continual and anxious moral concern for correct behavior. Such studies indicate that we are only beginning to understand the Confucian way; certainly it involved faith, and still underlies Chinese thinking.

2

Sung Society: Change within Tradition

E. A. Kracke, Jr.

E. A. Kracke, Jr., was, until his recent death, a leading American scholar of the Song (Sung) dynasty (A.D. 960–1279). In the following article, he deftly summarizes what made the Song one of the most exciting periods in Chinese history. It was a time of important and innovative change, and in some respects anticipated by many centuries similar changes in the modern West which produced the commercial, industrial, and urban revolutions. In China these changes grew, however, out of the traditional context, as he points out, including the impressive expansion of iron and steel production (not part of Kracke's treatment here) to a level not equalled in Europe for another six hundred years. The Song achievement was cut off by the Mongol conquest of China, completed in 1279, and with the expulsion of the Mongols by the Ming in the fourteenth century, China returned to more traditional patterns. But many of the trends begun under the Song continued and are of special interest now that China is set in a new pattern of economic and social change.

When we speak of social change in China we most often have in mind one or the other of two pictures. The first is the change that we see today [1955], when radically new ideas, techniques and forces from foreign countries have shaken the traditional social order, altering the old patterns rapidly and sometimes violently. The second picture is that of the dynastic cycle, a concept that we have inherited from the traditional Chinese historian, sometimes adding a few embellishments of our own. The political fortunes of a ruling house are often reflected (and perhaps affected) by a characteristic cycle in the whole political and economic order of the nation: from successful adjustment and control to maladjustment and chaos. The end of each cycle, if we focus our attention only on those factors, leaves Chinese society much as it was at the end of the cycle before. But this perspective tends to omit qualitative changes that occur in Chinese society on a different plane.

The kind of social change to be considered now differs from both of these. It is the long and continuous process of social development that in China as in our own civilization has accompanied the interplay between the traditional ideas and ways of life and the new concepts, techniques, and patterns of activity that evolve at home or enter from abroad. While at times this process of development moved slowly, and at times even retrogressed in some respects, the Chinese way of life nevertheless underwent through the centuries a cumulative alteration that was essentially irreversible. At times the forces of change so interacted that their gathered momentum was almost revolutionary in its social impact. An outstanding example of such rapid and far-reaching change is supplied by the Sung period, from the tenth century to the thirteenth.

The beginnings of the movement that attained so dramatic a tempo in the Sung period can be traced back, in some respects, through several centuries. Perhaps the first clearly perceptible aspect of the movement is the striking shift in the mass of China's population, from the northern plain country to the valleys of the mountainous south and southeast coast. This migration had begun in the early centuries of our era, impelled both by economic difficulties and by foreign invaders of the old homeland; but as late as the middle of the eighth century the Yangtse valley and the areas further south still held only some forty to forty-five percent of China's people. By the end of the thirteenth century this area reported no less than eighty-five to ninety percent of the nation's population, and no less than twenty percent were established in the valleys of Fukien and eastern Chekiang along the southeast coast.

The rich new delta lands of the South became the chief suppliers of China's granaries. Some of the economic consequences of this are already well known, and need only be recapitulated here. To feed the armies guarding the northern border, and to provision the capital in the

North, the central administration undertook to expand the canal system and subsidiary land communications from the South on a mammoth scale. Aided by the new facilities, private commerce grew rapidly. The Chinese now living along the remote southern coast no doubt found it necessary to import tools and other goods from the older settlements, and exchanged for these the new products native to the semi-tropical land in which they found themselves, as well as products from the South Seas and the countries of the Indian Ocean. Easier contacts by sea with Persia and Arabia encouraged the growth of foreign commerce, soon bringing to the growing coastal cities settlements of Hindu and Arab merchants. The Chinese also . . . turned to the sea and assumed a leading place among maritime peoples. Internal commerce among the regions of China, at first confined for the most part to luxury items for the few, now expanded in variety and in its significance for larger groups of the nation.

With the growth of inter-regional trade, money came into its own, for many purposes rapidly superseding the old transactions in kind. By the eleventh century, a system of regulated paper currency was in operation, and the coinage of copper money reached proportions never again approached in Chinese dynastic history. Facilities for the transfer of funds and the provision of credit also developed. The various regions of China were no longer self-sufficient economically, but increasingly specialized in their produce—foods or goods or services—and therefore interdependent. These developments brought into being, by the eleventh century, a Chinese economy apparently far more complex than any of earlier times.

Of the social change that accompanied this economic development we have as yet only a very incomplete picture. But certain of its aspects stand out strikingly in the records. One aspect—perhaps of key significance—is the changing role of the great city. In earlier periods the few outstanding cities had achieved their greatness and economic importance only after designation as national capitals. Their symmetrical and regular plan, centered on the principal imperial palace, gave visible evidence of their origin and purpose. From the tenth century to the thirteenth this was not so. In this later period the cities chosen as capitals had already achieved importance as trade centers at strategic points on the lines of communication.

K'ai-feng, the first Sung capital, exemplified this particularly well. Originally a regional administrative seat at a main transfer point on the arterial canal from the South, its access to southern rice supplies recommended it during the troubled years succeeding the T'ang. The city had grown with its commercial importance, as successive new walls enclosed the suburbs that grew spontaneously beyond the older city gates. Within the sixteen-mile circuit of the outer walls, space was at a premium. The second Sung emperor renounced the planned expansion of his palace because it would have forced the demolition of private dwelling quarters. As a result of this history, although the city lay in the level valley of the Yellow River, it lacked the symmetry that had marked earlier national capitals and would later distinguish Peking (also primarily political in its character).

The later Sung capital of Hang-chou was also an important trade center at the time of its political elevation in 1135. Its population was huge: the numbers within its walls during the later years of the dynasty have been estimated as 900,000, and those in its suburbs as some 600,000 more.

While the capitals of the eleventh to thirteenth centuries had thus grown strongly commercial in character, their supremacy among Chinese cities was challenged by other urban centers still more reliant on business activity. By the year 1100 at least four urban areas far surpassed the capital area in population. We have no exact data on the numbers living within the walls of these cities or in their immediate suburbs, but census reports suggest that each of the urban areas held a million or more people within the borders of its prefecture—a space very roughly comparable to the greater metropolitan areas of London or New York. Such population concentrations would seem to outdistance by far the largest urban agglomerations of that time in Europe, even by the largest estimates of the latter.

During the next two centuries the urban growth continued, and in several instances the prefectural populations apparently doubled, tripled, or quadrupled by 1290. Among the most dramatic increases, three were on the southeast coast (Hang-chou, Su-chou, and Fu-chou), and one (Jao-chou) near the inland trade route from the Yangtse to Canton. The prefecture of Fu-chou in 1290 reported approximately 3,875,000 people, suggesting an urban concentration of impressive proportions.

It was just around this time, soon after the Sung downfall, that Marco Polo visited these places as an agent of the Mongol conqueror Kubilai. His descriptions of the magnificence of Hang-chou, the capital, and of the trade metropolis Ch'üan-chou, are well known. But he also observed another phenomenon that is suggested by contemporary census figures—the growth and multiplication of smaller cities and towns. In describing the journey from Hang-chou to Fu-chou (less than three hundred miles as the crow flies), he tells of no less than six "large, noble, and beautiful" or "noble and great" cities, and in the stages of his journey between these he notes no less than seven times "always finding cities and villages enough, very beautiful and very great"; on one two-day ride he remarks that these are "so frequent and continuous that you seem as you ride to go through the middle of a single city." Allowing for the colorful exaggerations we must permit to this oldest of China-hands, the regions that Polo saw along the southeast coast must certainly have been advanced in urban development compared with his native Italy—the most urbanized part of Europe in that day. While most of the terrain was mountainous and poorly adapted to farming, the few lands available had been fully exploited. A Sung writer notes that intensive cultivation had transformed once worthless acres to the most fertile in the empire, and while Marco Polo refers occasionally to the livestock he saw (oxen, buffalo, cows, goats, swine, and fowl) and to certain special plant products, he speaks not of fields but of "fine gardens."

But rich as the fields were, they were still too few. The coastal regions still depended for their prosperity on the income from their mines, commerce, manufactures, tea, and sea produce, and beyond the narrow valley floors must have preserved some of the air of an unsettled borderland. On four stages of his journey Polo mentions the "hunting and chase enough of beasts and birds" and refers as many times to the great and fierce "lions" (tigers?) that molest travellers, to such an extent that in one part of the route at least, "it is very dangerous to pass through those regions unless people go in great numbers." In an area seeming thus sparsely settled over much of its extent, and developing rapidly in industry and trade, typifying the new trend, it is difficult not to suspect analogies with the frontier of opportunity that played a vital role in the development of our own civilization.

Who were the people that lived in the growing cities of this area? We have no clear picture of them, but there are at last some clues to their character. As in earlier times, there must have been a considerable number of civil and military officials, stationed there for limited terms by the central government, along with a more or less permanent corps of clerks and official underlings. There were the army garrisons usually stationed in all large places. There were no doubt well-to-do scholars without official employment, and poorer scholars who lived on their earnings as teachers, or from such miscellaneous employments as public letter-writing or story-telling. And there were the merchants and artisans, great and small, blending at the lowest economic level with the unskilled laborers. Considering the indicated sizes of the cities, the last three occupations must have constituted the preponderant group of inhabitants in most cases. The composition of the Sung populations cannot have differed too greatly from that observed by Marco Polo only around a decade after the dynasty's fall: in all his comments on the six larger cities he saw between Hang-chou and Fu-chou, and in four of his comments on the places between, he notes that the inhabitants "live by trade and by crafts," and implies mercantile activities indirectly by repeated references to the "abundance of all things for life," which he notes were very cheap. (To other activities he makes very little reference.)

What was true of this area was probably true also, to a more limited degree, of the great cities more widely scattered in other parts of China at this time. All were joined by the same commercial links, and often frequented by the same far-travelling merchants.

Surviving records tell us of the merchants' activities and mode of life chiefly at the capitals, but in these respects too different regions may have presented a rather similar picture.

The merchants, artisans, and providers of services were organized in guilds, which had powers of discipline over their own members, although these organizations had no apparent role in the general administration of the cities. The guild members had to some extent emancipated themselves from the close official supervision that existed during the T'ang. Their business activities were no longer confined within the great walled markets, or limited to the hours in which the government permitted the opening of the market portals. Commerce and manufacture were now carried on in shops scattered throughout the city or beyond the city gates, though establishments of the same trade tended to group together.

Long and persistent governmental efforts to regulate trade and control prices were matched by equally persistent and largely successful evasion on the part of the merchants. Attempts of the state to monopolize certain profitable industries had been costly and only partly successful. But in the Sung the state had learned to apply its taxes more flexibly and to restrict its monopolies to certain key operations of an industry;

through such policies the state diverted what was perhaps the lion's share of the profits to its treasuries.

Such state controls may well have retarded significantly the growth of commercial activity and power. At the time, however, there must have been little evidence of this. The more successful merchants accumulated great wealth, and their style of living vied with that of the imperial princes. Sumptuary laws had always, before this, restricted the colors that should be used by each class of society. By 995, however, sumptuary laws were unenforceable, and all were repealed but the ban on a certain shade of deep purple reserved for the imperial house and the highest officials. There is evidence that even this color was taken over by commoners within a few years. We read that the families of great merchants wore pearls and jade. Their carriages thronged the roads, and in the words of a contemporary "rubbed hubs with those of distinguished families." In the T'ang, we are told, even a servant who had served in an aristocratic family scorned a master who haggled in person with a merchant. By the eleventh century, even important officials had discovered the attractions of commerce, and many augmented their income by combining business operations with their official journeys. Merchants were socially accepted in elite circles. Through such connections, or through their wealth, some of them secured government office, and served in positions of some importance.

But the professional trader still found certain barriers to his social advancement. He still lacked the approval of more conservative scholars. His indulgence in luxuries elicited complaints very much like those that had been evoked by a more modest commercial expansion a millennium earlier. His pursuit of money was felt to be unworthy. The officials criticized his disposition to make profits by cornering the market, because this was at the expense of the poor—and no doubt because the official preferred that the state monopolies should garner such profits. The grumbling of the conservatives, however, may have been in itself another indication that power of commerce was recognized as a potential threat to the supremacy of the bureaucrat; in fact, specific complaints of the growing influence that merchants exercised over officials are not lacking.

The new social environment created by the cities surely had its impact on the evolution of Chinese culture. The operation of any but the simplest business naturally required at least a certain minimum of literacy, and the city environment gave better opportunities for even the poorest to gain a smattering of the written character. The successful and ambitious tradesman would naturally hope that education would win for his sons an entree into the bureaucracy. When the new urban reader competed with the older scholar for written texts, a new demand for books was created. In the century after 950 the technique of wood engraving, long used to multiply Buddhist charms and texts, suddenly found new uses, and in a short time the art of printing was applied to practically all the existing varieties of literature.

For the relatively unlettered, a multiplicity of entertainments was also devised, ranging from troops of acrobats and displays of fireworks to puppet shows, shadow plays, and simple theatrical presentations. Through the stories that served as themes for such public performances, some parts of the sophisticated culture could reach the illiterate, and facilitate a sharing of the great tradition with larger groups. Particularly important in this respect was the role of the story-teller: unemployed scholars frequently made their living by recounting some of the dramatic episodes of history to audiences in the market place. Through the prompting-books some of them wrote to aid their confreres, they created the prototypes of the later great fictional themes. At the same time the old themes were presented in the language of the people and transmuted to appeal to a more popular audience, until the content itself reflected their viewpoint and their tastes. It could scarcely be accidental that the Chinese popular novel traces back to this period.

The influence of the new city life also had its impact on society beyond the city walls. The growing importance of a money economy must surely have contributed a significant share to the increasing complications of the farm problem. The crops of different regions were becoming more specialized, leaving the farmer often less self-sufficient, and more vulnerable in years of crop failure. While the farmer probably relied little on the cities for his basic necessities, it seems that travelling merchants from the cities already came to the country fairs to sell such things as salt, and buy for the city market. The glamor of the city had its weakening effect on the old rural patterns of life in other ways. The wealthy peasant, we are told, tended to emulate the merchant's style of living, and we hear repeatedly that the rewards of commerce tempted the poor farmer to abandon the hard and often unrewarding work on his lands, sell his farm implements, and engage in trade.

Finally, we must note the change that came about in the bureaucratic class itself. It was also in this period that new recruitment procedures opened a governmental career to far wider numbers than before. Competitive recruitment examinations were regularly used from the beginning of the eleventh century on a scale far greater than ever before. Improved through the development of elaborate techniques to make the examinations more objective, the new system helped to break the power monopoly once held by a small group of northern aristocratic families. The social origin of the newcomers who replaced them is not entirely clear. The broader distribution of opportunity was certainly made possible by the increase in literacy and the wider availability of books that we have already noted. Several hundred candidates commonly passed the final stage of the triennial examinations, and we are told that for each of these some hundred candidates had attempted the local preliminary tests. The competition was wide indeed. But the fiercest rivalry and the most numerous successful candidates during most of the dynasty came from the southeast coast, where we have seen the rapid pace of urbanization at this time.

How many of these men came from the great cities? How many traced their educational opportunity to families of ultimately mercantile origin? It is still impossible to say. But data from two lists of graduates that have come down to us from the twelfth and thirteenth centuries show that the regions with more and larger urban concentrations tended to supply not only more graduates in proportion to their area, but also more graduates per family, so that they clearly dominated the field. Moreover the largest proportion of apparently new blood tended to appear in the circuits of most rapid population growth, if we may judge from the numbers of graduates counting no officials among their direct paternal forebears. Conspicuous among these regions of growing population were those containing the great coastal cities and those on the main inland trade routes. We have here, then, a seeming link between the broadening social base of the bureaucracy and the social mobility that probably characterized the great cities in their period of most rapid expansion.

The political importance of this changing character of the bureaucracy is obvious. Its cultural effect, while less tangible and less calculable, was perhaps none the less real. For while the Sung was a time of beginnings for the more popular literary forms, it was also a time of great vigor, and in some ways a time of culmination, in the intellectual activities practiced or patronized by the bureaucrat: the fine arts, the more sophisticated literary forms, and critical scholarship. In government, it was a time of imaginative reform schemes and experiments. It saw great advances in several fields of technology. In all of these realms the contribution made by men of the Southeast was outstanding.

Thus we have evidence that a genuine alteration of Chinese social patterns accompanied the rise of the great city. The influence of the city extended beyond the bourgeois to the farmer and the bureaucrat. Despite the inhibiting pressures of official conservatism, and at times in disregard of laws and decrees, the merchant had expanded his influence and breached many of the barriers that surrounded him when the period of change began.

The limits of his rise are also apparent. If he achieved a place in government, it was by transforming himself into a bureaucrat; as a merchant he still enjoyed no active political role. The professional official remained supreme, and steadfastly unsympathetic toward the development of private economic interests.

The history of Chinese urbanization after the thirteenth century, and the reasons why the movement failed to go further than it did, are beyond the scope of the present topic. As we contemplate the situation of the thirteenth century bourgeois, however, it is difficult to discern any single insuperable barrier to his further social rise. Most of his disadvantages were also faced by some at least of his European confreres during the later Middle Ages or the Renaissance. In the thirteenth century, the Chinese bourgeois had demonstrated by his will and his resourcefulness that under favorable conditions, the traditional Chinese social patterns could be significantly modified through the operation of internal forces.

3

Traditional China at Its Peak: Achievements and Problems

John K. Fairbank

This selection from John K. Fairbanks' magistral survey, The Great Chinese Revolution, *assesses the traditional system under the Qing (Ch'ing) dynasty as it had developed by the early nineteenth century. It describes a China that still impressed contemporary European observers. The commercialization and domestic trade that had begun to grow under the Song (Sung) and Ming had reached far higher levels. In 1800, and perhaps as late as 1850, China was still, all in all, probably more prosperous than Europe; average welfare levels were probably higher. But China by then was rapidly falling behind technologically as Europe forged ahead with its industrial revolution. The system had begun to run out of steam, with no new technology boosting production to support a still growing population that had more than doubled since the seventeenth century. In other respects too, the traditional system proved incapable of adjusting adequately to the mounting population pressures. The imperial administration, always a thin layer, was stretched beyond its ability to deal with both local and national problems. Official and private corruption became a growing problem, and there were the beginnings of widespread dissatisfaction, demoralization, and even revolt. Fairbank here adroitly summarizes recent scholarship on this period and gives us a vivid picture of the Great Tradition as it approached its steep decline after about 1850.*

When we look at China in 1800 the first thing that strikes the eye is a remarkable paradox: the institutional structure of the society, especially the government, was showing little capacity for change, but the people and therefore the economy were undergoing rapid and tremendous growth. Until recently this paradox remained largely unnoticed. It may well be called a contradiction between substructure and superstructure. China's modern history began with the Opium War of 1840 both in the thinking of the Western powers that invaded China in the nineteenth century and also in the thinking of the Marxist revolutionaries who have represented the latest phase of that invasion. Early foreign observers noticed that the structure of government from Ming to Ch'ing had hardly altered, the tribute system for handling foreign relations remained active at least in the ritual forms of the Ch'ing court, and the government had not noticeably expanded or developed in comparison with what the Jesuits had reported three hundred years earlier. The result was a European impression of an "unchanging" China.

Recent research has made it plain that this was a very superficial judgment that applied only and mainly to institutional structures like the bureaucratic state and perhaps the family system. The facts of Chinese life were far otherwise. As of 1800 the Chinese people had just completed a doubling in numbers that was even more massive than the contemporary growth of population in Europe and America. With numbers came trade. Aside from some petty exactions by imperial customs collectors, the vast Chinese empire was a free-trade area, more populous than all of Europe. Production of crops for comparative advantage was far advanced: the Lower Yangtze provinces specialized in rice production while the provinces just to the north produced cotton for exchange. Craftsmen in many centers produced specialties recognized all over the country: chinaware at Ching-te-chen, iron cooking pans in Canton, silk brocade from Hangchow and Soochow. Enormous fleets of Chinese sailing vessels (junks) plied the highway of the Yangtze River and its tributaries, while thousands of others sailed up and down the China coast, taking southern fruit, sugar, and artifacts to Manchuria and bringing back soybeans and furs. One early British observer was amazed to calculate that in the 1840s more tonnage passed through the port of Shanghai at the mouth of the Yangtze than through the port of London, which was already the hub of Western commerce.

Exuberant growth and lethargic institutions bear upon one of the great conundrums of modern Chinese history—China's failure in spite of her high level of technology and resources to achieve a breakthrough into an industrial revolution comparable to that in contemporary Europe. This great contrast between China and the Atlantic community in the nineteenth century has given rise to various explanatory theories. One of the most widespread has been the "we was robbed" notion, that China's growth into capitalism was impeded by Western imperialism and its jealous and baleful repression of Chinese enterprise. This theory except among true believers has been exploded, not least because it assumes the primacy of China's foreign trade in her productive processes. To be sure the imperialism of the unequal treaty system after 1842 held China back in that a protective tariff was prevented by treaty while foreigners lorded it over Chinese in the sanctuary of the treaty ports. Amassing the numerous details of imperialist iniquity creates a quite adequate basis for patriotic humiliation and anger. But this by no means settles the economic problem. The non-emergence of capitalism in the Chinese economy goes back much further than the Opium War and the era of imperialism. The basic fact was that China could not increase her productivity per person and so break out of what has been called the "high-level equilibrium trap," the situation where a high level of pre-steam-engine technology remained in balance with a circular-flow of production and consumption that inhibited investment in industrial development. One part of this trap was the enormous muscle supply that made machinery unnecessary. Another reason was that there was little creation of credit or accumulation of capital available for investment. The dynasty and ruling class lived by tax gathering more than by trade.

In effect the China that entered modern times a century and a half ago had achieved a high degree of homeostasis, the capacity to persist in a steady state. Like a human body whose self-righting mechanisms maintain levels of temperature, blood pressure, respiration, heartbeat, blood sugar, and the like within small ranges of normal variation, China's body politic and social had institutionalized a whole series of practices that would tend to keep it going along established lines: salt distribution seasoned the cereal diet, night soil fertilized the vegetables, pigs were raised on human offal, dikes prevented floods, government granaries ensured against famine. The mutual-responsibility system automatically policed the neighborhood, performance of family obligations gave security to its members, the doctrine of the Three Bonds tied the individual into the family and the family into the state, while the examinations inoculated the new talent with orthodoxy. The "law of avoidance" (that no official could serve in his native province) kept down nepotism. Rebels founded new dynasties only to perpetuate the system. This old China was an artful structure, full of local variety within its overall plan, decentralized in material ways but unified by a ruling class with a sense of form and a self-image created by history.

Let us begin by getting a picture of life in the village. The "average" peasant in the 1800s, if we guess from the data of later times, probably had a family of five, including two unmarried children and a parent. A big house with several courtyards, sheltering the nuclear families of two or three sons, was only for the affluent. A peasant dwelling had a beaten earth floor and thatched roof in the North, stone and tile in the rainy South. Northerners might all sleep on a wide mat-covered brick bed with flues within it for warming in winter. Universally windows were covered with paper, not glass. The latrine was next to or above the pig pen. Water came in buckets on a shoulder pole from a village well. Clothes were washed without soap by beating in well water or beside a stream, canal, or pond.

This "average" farmer probably was part owner-cultivator and part tenant. In any case he and his family worked three or four small strips of land at some distance from one another, carrying hoes or sickles back and forth, producing mainly for their own subsistence. Near cites and trade routes they might add cash crops. Their life was lived mainly in the village among neighbors from day to day, punctuated by regular trips to the market town, say, one hour's walk away, where seasonal festivals, itinerant storytellers, or a theater troupe would enliven the year.

Not having been peasants, we are hard put to imagine their inner consciousness. We know the rational-superstitious balance was different and the horizon of concerns vastly more limited, but while the peasant's basic human feelings would no doubt be intelligible to us, there were other attitudes, social drives, and values that would be hard for us to grasp or accept. Supposing "human nature is the same everywhere," still its social manifestations may differ enormously.

Village neighbors, being fixed and lacking automobiles, played larger roles than city or suburban neighbors do with us. Communal activities included not only wedding and funeral ceremonies and the attendant feasts but also mutual arrangements for crop watching against thievery, and defense against bandits. In fact Chinese villagers formed associations, made contracts, and organized collective activities in many lines without reference to officialdom. These arrangements were normally among households and by being collectively accepted formed a legal structure. Thus families who claimed a common ancestor formed a lineage, and a lineage often held property to maintain graves and rites of ancestor veneration, or to keep up instruction in a school available for lineage offspring. Farm households might also join in irrigation projects and agree contractually on the allocation of water rights. They might agree to support religious worship in a temple or enter into a business enterprise to mine coal or sell sugar. A lot went on among the people beneath the notice of the state.

Another thing we know is that villages as units had a lively sense of self-interest, and violent feuds with neighboring villages often resulted, sometimes over water rights, boundaries, or other tangible issues, sometimes from more abstract causes of sectarian faith or accidents of personality or history. Sporadic warfare might result, one community, sect, or confederation against another. Such struggles focused on purely local issues far beneath the provincial, to say nothing of the national level. In short, violent strife, in regions so far studied, seems to have been built into the agrarian social system. The resulting slaughter of enemy villagers might be accompanied by pillage, rape, barbarous torture, and wholesale destruction. The bucolic life was often far from peaceful.

Like any human structure, Chinese society existed in tension, and by the nineteenth century the equilibrium of its parts had grown precarious. First, the balance between land and people was upset by increase of numbers.

The mechanism of population growth in eighteenth-century China, when numbers more than doubled, is still largely unknown. Long-continued domestic peace had helped. So did quicker-ripening rice strains from Southeast Asia and new crops of maize (corn), peanuts, and sweet potatoes from America. The faster-ripening rice permitted more double-cropping. The American crops could grow in sandy margins where rice could not. Moreover, migrants from the eastern provinces opened up new land in the Northwest and Southwest, terracing hilly regions not formerly cultivated. The population as it grew produced more night soil to be used as fertilizer for the fields. Possibly diseases were better controlled, as by variolation to prevent smallpox. Other factors may still be discovered.

Behind the enormous further increase to about 430 million by 1850 lay the fact of a broad base of perhaps 150 million to start with about 1700, so that a very modest rate of growth was quite enough to crowd the landscape. Long-term motives included the Chinese love of children and investment in them as old-age insurance. It was a sacred duty to beget sons to carry on the family line and the pious reverence for its ancestors at the household shrine and in the clan temple. The well-to-do invested in secondary wives and progeny instead of the motorized equipment of today's household. More people meant more hands in the family economy. Thus conscience and calculation both led to more births. It was an uninhibited procreation like the spawning of fish in the sea, since marital sexuality was the last refuge of privacy and still (unlike today) the least-regulated activity in community life.

This growth of numbers was naturally accompanied by growth in the commercial economy. All sorts of economic indicators showed this: more junks plying along the coast; more banks set up by wealthy Ningpo families in the new port of Shanghai; more business for the remittance bankers of central Shansi, who almost monopolized the transfer of official funds; more exports of Fukien teas and Chekiang or Kiangsu silks by way of Canton; and more imports of opium to meet a craving for the drug that was in itself a symptom of demoralization.

Increase of trade, however, did not break out of the pattern of government licensing of commercial monopolies and the limited aim of collecting tax quotas without encouraging investment for growth. Let us cite examples.

If one tries to name one commodity almost universally needed by the American people today it would, I suppose, be gasoline. In the old China it was salt, a dietary necessity for eaters of cereals and vegetables who seldom saw meat. To pursue the analogy (for what it is worth), the American oil barons of Dallas today would find their eighteenth-century counterparts in the salt merchants of Yangchow, whose opulent lifestyle was the envy of the age. Since the Yangchow merchants differed in being under the government, not independent of it, their history may be instructive.

To begin with, the government salt monopoly had come down from ancient times. In the early 1800s salt was produced variously by evaporation of sea water on the coast, by boiling brine lifted from hundreds of deep salt wells in Szechwan (some went a thousand feet down, with bamboo tubing), or from certain inland salt mines or lakes. Salt production was handled by monopoly merchants, whose hereditary rights supported wealthy families. These rights or *kang* allowed the monopolists to sell the product to distribution merchants, who managed the actual business of transporting salt under license. A shipment so licensed and registered could be delivered only to the point specified, where government depots handled the complex local distribution to the populace. Salt intendants in each province, in a complex, self-sustaining bureaucratic network, collected license fees and sales taxes at the main points of production and distribution. The Board of Revenue at Peking got about a sixth of its total receipts from this monopoly. As late as the 1890s, when the land tax and Maritime Customs duties were estimated at 32 million taels each, the salt revenue was estimated at 13 million.

The salt monopoly was a great device for accumulating merchant capital and at the same time for corruption between merchants and officials. One index to the vitality of the system is the reform urged by the scholar-official Wei Yuan in the producing region of North Kiangsu. In the 1832–33 reform the large monopoly rights of the *kang* merchants were supplemented by smaller shipments sold by a ticket system *(p'iao)*, so that smaller purchasers with less capital could function in the trade. Even so, by the time official salt reached its consumption market, its price had been raised by the successive commission, transport, and handling charges, including the official peculation normal to such operations. This made a considerable incentive for smuggling. Perhaps half the total salt was illegally produced and distributed by smuggling gangs on more difficult, roundabout routes, but the cost of preventing this smuggling would have eaten up any gain in receipts. On the other hand, the smugglers could never take the government's basic profits away from it. So officials and smugglers coexisted.

In their heyday the salt merchants, organized in their own guild and with their own temple, were the leading social class in places like Yangchow or Hankow. As the most wealthy merchant stratum, they increasingly supported philanthropies and were called upon for contributions to flood control, defense, and other public enterprises. The reform represented by the ticket system in the early nineteenth century of course opened the door for private enterprisers on a smaller scale than the big hereditary monopolists. Bureaucratic control was reduced during the Taiping war, after which came what Rowe calls the "privatization" of the salt trade, part of a general trend.

Suppose your family firm *(hang)* had belonged to the Ningpo tea guild in the second quarter of the nineteenth century. Your best supply of teas would come from the Bohea Hills on the upper waters of the Min River upstream from the port of Foochow. Tea of course was produced in many parts of South China. A family farm might have its own tea bushes. But the combination of soil and climate in the Bohea Hills, plus the traditional skill of nimble-fingered young women in picking, sorting, roasting ("firing") and otherwise processing black and green teas (differently processed), allowed export to fastidious customers all over China as well as to the European East India companies at Canton. Batches ("chops") from local producers would be purchased by traveling buyers ("guest merchants," *k'o-shang*), who arranged for export from the region. In season, the long lines of tea bearers would have poles attached to their burdens so that, when they stopped to rest, the tea packages would never touch the ground. This was the scene explored in disguise by the pioneer botanist Robert Fortune, who in the 1850s collected tea plants for British India, where government quality control eventually let Indian tea eclipse Chinese tea on the world market.

Suppose your Ningpo tea firm had established its base of operations in the rapidly growing port of Shanghai. Ningpo was a much older emporium, a port for tributary trade with Japan in medieval times. Like Canton, Foochow, Shanghai, and Tientsin, Ningpo was situated several miles up a river so that its port could not easily be raided by pirates. As the trade expanded, the Ningpo tea guild, like Ningpo bankers, became prominent in Shanghai's domestic trade.

If you were shipping a tea cargo five hundred miles up the Yangtze to a trade center like Hankow, you would probably get a berth on one of the Lower Yangtze types of trading junks. Arriving in Hankow after many days, you would find a very busy port on the peninsula formed by the Yangtze and its tributary the Han River coming in from the northwest. Opposite across the Yangtze on the south would be the provincial walled capital of Wu-ch'ang, part of what is now called Wuhan. In Hankow you would deal with agents or brokers to sell and distribute your tea. The export of teas through Canton grew to twenty million pounds a year in the last days of the East India Company monopoly. Yet one could hardly conclude that the foreign export trade was more than one area of growth. Supposing a pound of tea supplied an affluent person for a year, the Chinese domestic market certainly had many more than twenty million affluent customers for the Bohea product.

One secret of China's domestic trade after the eighteenth century was water transport. Water routes north from Canton, for example, went over one or the other of two passes, with short portages to reach the river systems of Kiangsi and Hunan. Even in the arid North the Han River route went several hundred miles toward Sian, while in East China the Grand Canal became an artery of private commerce as well as official foodstuffs. China's muscle-power resources, used with the greater efficiency of water transport, could obviate the comparatively high cost of moving goods long distances by land.

Study of Hankow, the most commercial part of the three Wuhan cities, illustrates commercial development, since Hankow was a focal point of exchange on trade routes coming from all parts of China: (1) The route by the Hsiang River in Hunan brought spices and other tropical products that reached China through Canton, as well as some of the woolens that the British East India Company was obliged to unload on the Hong merchants, who found little use for them in the local heat. In return down this route, Canton received rice from Central China. (2) The Upper Yangtze route above Hankow used different vessels, and so the rice from Szechwan for the Lower Yangtze was often transshipped at Hankow if not Ichang. The timber production in Szechwan eventually gave way in the late nineteenth century to Szechwan opium destined for Shanghai. (3) Up the Han River to the Northwest went brick tea for the overland trade to Russia. The lower reaches of the Han were a cotton-growing area. (4) Hankow's major trade, of course, was down the Yangtze shipping Hupei and Hunan rice to help feed the Lower Yangtze cities and contribute to the rice shipments that went up the Grand Canal to Peking. From the Lower Yangtze came the salt shipments collected at Yangchow from the coastal producing area north of Shanghai. Rice and salt were both essential to the Chinese diet.

The extensive exchanges through Hankow argue for the thesis that by the middle of the eighteenth century if not before China had a genuine national market, in which supply from any sector might meet demands from anywhere else. Of course this applied only to certain commodities. The cellular self-sufficiency of local areas still characterized most of the economy. Like the beginning of the Renaissance in Europe or the onset of a commercial revolution in China, the date when a national market emerged depends on what weight you give to what evidence. The rise of China's national market can be measured by the growth of specialized merchant groups, such as wholesalers, retailers, itinerant peddlers, all overlain by a stratum of brokers and commission agents, who offered their services to principals at a distance in the inter-regional trade.

One symptom of the rise of commerce had been the proliferation in the eighteenth century of native-place associations, generally known as guilds, which were set up primarily to facilitate merchants' activities. Most guilds represented counties or prefectures (groups of counties) rather than whole provinces. Other guilds were devoted to certain trades, and sometimes the two were combined, as in for example the Ningpo teamen's guild. The guild provided the facilities of a hostel, a meeting place, an acknowledged membership, and a capacity to represent group interests, as in organizing a boycott or registering complaints. Another guild function was arbitration of commercial disputes, and trade guilds also of course provided warehouse facilities. They were entirely unofficial agencies, though the officials might acknowledge their existence.

A guild hall would be a series of buildings surrounded by a compound wall, not unlike a *yamen*. The formal entrance would lead through the major halls for meetings and observances, while smaller quarters along the sides provided work and living space. The cultural functions of guilds included religious veneration of the patron deity or historic figure reverenced by the guild. The Hui-chou Guild at Hankow had as its patron Chu Hsi while the Shao-hsing Guild had Wang Yang-ming. Thus the merchants honored these idols of the scholar-class.

The facilities might include not only dormitories for people passing through but also schools for education in preparation for examinations, and possibly an opera stage. Guilds took on the regulation of commerce in place of the local government. In certain matters the entire guild might act as a unit, for instance in setting regulations or in guild boy-cotts. In fact guilds did about everything except industrial production. Both Rotary and Kiwanis, if they had functioned in the old China's commercial centers, would have been considerably impressed.

Guilds were financed by entrance fees. They would also make investments in real estate, and money might be raised by a bond issue. Rent from shops and other properties might be considerable. The Shen-si-Shansi Guild at Hankow had a fine temple and hostelry and rebuilt a section of the city, from which it collected valuable rents. After the Taiping Rebellion the entire complex was rebuilt.

Guilds served the community in a variety of ways. Philanthropic activities were important—providing food for the poor, taking care of public thoroughfares, building bridges and improving the water supply, assisting in firefighting, including the construction of fire lanes where buildings would be removed (the firemen would use water-pumping equipment). In time of need they contributed to local defense. All of this represented Confucian "public-mindedness." Thus the guild organization moved toward providing municipal services as a responsibility. They were still another symptom of the strength of the private merchant community.

Between organization by place and organization by trade, the guild system presented an extremely complicated and internally differentiated structure. During the nineteenth century the creation of trade guilds was the major area of growth in the system. As time went on the combination of native-place guilds with others from the same general area produced larger structures. The spurt in growth of guilds, for example at Hankow, in the late nineteenth century was a new phase in a domestic development long under way.

Naturally the whole guild structure sought official recognition and patronage. In fact the cultivation of official connections was essential for their welfare. Many merchants acquired gentry status by purchase of degrees if not by examination. Inevitably the major guild organizations in a city might band together in a larger organization by a system of linkages or confederations. Guild alliances proved most useful in affecting economic policy, if necessary by boycotts. All this verged upon a kind of municipal government, especially in a time of common need as in the Taiping Rebellion (1850–64).

From this background it is easy to see that the Chinese chambers of commerce that were put together in the 1900s as innovations were little more than a further stage in the kind of merchant-gentry municipal organization that had already grown up. Thus we can conclude that, while the Western impact gradually mounted to become unsettling in the 1890s, before that time there had been a natural domestic growth of private commercial-social organization. This trend included the increasing dependence of the state on revenues from commerce together with less-stringent regulation of it. This latter relaxation of regulation was part of the provincial officials' effort to raise greater revenues from an expanding local trade.

In the nineteenth century the organization of trade was getting beyond the family firm, and true partnerships suggestive of joint stock companies were being set up. Their trading operations had to pay great attention to the multiform Chinese currency system, in which each locality and each trade might have its own unit of account, the differential ounce of silver (tael), that required a lot of bookkeeping. Economists, to be sure, revel in aggregate data, but such are unavailable for 1800. While we can cite evidence of tendencies toward a national market, we lack overall statistics to position it on a scale between medieval and modern.

Not unnaturally the British and American merchants at the new treaty ports (which entered into their heyday after the Taiping Rebellion had been quelled in 1864) attributed the growth of trade to their own influence as an arm of the world market. This view was no more wrong than the usual foreigner's preoccupation with his own small picture of China. In fact, however, the rise of treaty-port trade in the late nineteenth century was in large part a revival of the vigorous communal life already present in pre-Rebellion China.

For example, the brick-tea trade to Russia in the modern centuries was only a continuation of the tea-for-horses exchange with the Mongols set as early as the Sung period. In short, tea had been a principal export to the barbarians long before the arrival of the East India companies by sea. As a commodity produced in some regions but consumed in all, tea had at one time lent itself to government monopoly. The natural instinct of Chinese officials in late imperial times was to get it under some sort of license control by setting up monopoly merchants who could collect an official tax. Chinese licensed monopolists were of course anathema to the foreign traders of the new free-trade era and were the subject of much consular correspondence with local officials. The actual regulation of the trade, in which tea samples might greatly vary from the consignments received and quality control was therefore a principal task, was undertaken by the tea guilds themselves. One of their functions was to maintain standards in the trade and ensure its regularity in opposition to the get-rich-quick operations of Western entrepreneurs. The failure of the Chinese government to step in and ensure nationwide quality standards for the tea trade led by the twentieth century to Japan and India taking the world market away from China. But in retrospect this failure looks like a result of the decentralization of China's economic life, in other words the domination of trade by the private merchants organized in their guilds. In any case the maturity of merchant organization under guilds did not produce entrepreneurs intent on investment in industrial production. Quite the contrary, it was probably a disincentive to European-type capitalism.

One essential for industrial investments is the availability of credit, but here again China's undoubted development had its limitations. The credit structure that facilitated China's domestic commerce began at the lowest level with the pawnbroker and usurer, sometimes the same person, who provided small sums to people in need. At the top level before the arrival of foreigners, the transfer of credit as well as of official funds interregionally was handled by the remittance banks that centered among families in the Fen River Valley in Central Shansi. By establishing nationwide branches, often tied in by bonds of kinship, a Shansi bank in one region could receive funds and issue an order on a branch bank in another region, where the funds in question would be made available at a slight discount for the transfer charge.

In between these top and bottom levels were several categories of large and small money shops or "native banks," as the foreigners called them *(ch'ien-chuang)*. The small ones might serve merely their local residential communities, but the large ones were usually connected with chains of native banks extending along trade routes or between major cities. Such chains could, of course, be most easily set up by the natives of one place, such as Ningpo or Shao-hsing in northern Chekiang, whose banking connections stretched up the Yangtze from Shanghai and along the coast. These intercity banking networks expanded with the growth of trade. In the open competition among them, many banks might issue their own bank notes in the absence of legal tender of the realm authorized by Peking. In other words, the native banks created credit by issuing their bank notes to merchants and even officials. They knew, of course, that a certain portion of specie must be held in reserve, but the amount of the bank notes they issued to a customer might be far greater than his deposit with them. The bank notes' value was stated usually in terms of silver or copper cash and they were payable to bearer. Of course this system led to the evil of speculation on credit and possible bankruptcy of the creditor as well as the speculator. But, in this era of premodern conveniences, city residents were not numbered and ticketed by a watchful government, and a defaulting banker might simply close shop and disappear in the crowd. Efforts to police the banking system and punish defaulting speculators were regularly made by government officials in the light of their duty to respond to citizens' complaints. One major device for regulation was the requirement of guarantors in the traditional Chinese manner, men of substance who stood surety for a given banker as they did also for merchants. At the same time the bankers' guilds in common self-defense tried, through their members, to curb fraud. Along with this the banking guilds took on the supervision of credit, including the setting of the local rate for different kinds of units of accounts or taels. Thus the effort was made to regulate the anarchy of the credit market.

In this way Chinese commerce by the early decades of the nineteenth century was being facilitated "through such innovative services as bills of exchange, deposit banking, book transfers of funds between depositors, overdraft credit and ... negotiable and transferable credit instruments." Banking was another of those "old Chinese customs" that was undergoing rapid development before the treaty ports were opened.

However, this growth of production and consumption seems not to have appreciably changed the productivity per person, the increase of which is a key to the development process. The withdrawal of capital from current consumption and its allocation to purposes that would improve productivity might have begun with the infrastructure, like the building of telecommunications, roads, and eventually railroads, or it might have been put more directly into heavy industry, which requires a large initial investment. This is the kind of investment that the developers of Meiji Japan were able to achieve, but it was not achieved by the late Ch'ing Government or even the provincial leaders, much as some of them tried. One can only conclude that China was too stuck in her old ways, which were marked by growth in volume of people, product, and exchange, but not in the efficiency which constitutes productivity per worker, which in turn amasses capital for investment in the modern mechanized type of economy. The growth of population and of commerce began by simply producing more of the same. There is much evidence of the increased activity of the private sector in economic life and of the development of a credit system which would later be susceptible to a centralized use for investment. But meanwhile more people meant more muscles to use instead of machines—cheap labor power— which was probably a disincentive to radical innovation. To the availability of cheap muscle power was added the widespread incidence of monopolies, corruption, and ostentatious consumption as alternatives to productive investment.

If we compare China with Europe in the early 1800s, strong contrasts at once emerge. The eighteenth century, to be sure, had seen rapid population growth accompanied by an increase of trade in both areas. But, while Europe in the 1790s was in the throes of the French Revolution and its militantly innovative aftermath, the Chinese empire was chiefly beset by the White Lotus Rebellion of 1795–1804, a purely traditional peasant-based rising that foreshadowed dynastic decline but nothing new. Contemporary Europe had also accumulated the ingredients of the Industrial Revolution, when machines greatly increased the productivity of capital and labor. Some have tried to find a process at work in China comparable to Europe's "proto-industrialization." But evidence does not support this search for China's equivalence. The "putting-out system" for cottage production of commercial goods for a merchant, for example, was far from a new development in early modern China, and at all events it would not necessarily lead to a higher stage of economic organization, namely capitalism. On the contrary, China remained stuck in its labor-intensive circular-flow economy at a high level of pre-modern, muscle-powered technology. In the course of time commercialization might conceivably have led on into industrialization, but it had not yet begun to do so.

However, recognition of the growth of commerce and of the private sector in China, before the foreign incursion under the unequal treaties of the 1840s and '50s, is a significant finding. It puts the Western "opening" of China in a new light. It cuts the foreign invader down to size, reduces the importance of the long-assumed "Western impact," and gives late imperial China its due as a society not static but in motion. The primary fact was that economic growth was principally if not wholly in the private sector, leaving the government behind and more superficial than ever. As we have always suspected, China's center of gravity lay within, among the Chinese people, and that is where the ingredients of revolution accumulated. . . .

Economic growth naturally had its social and political effects. These were evident in the increase in unemployed literati, peasant migration, official corruption, military weakness, and social cleavages among the people. Out of all this came a generation of rebellion.

One contribution to the Ch'ing Government's downfall was its failure in the early nineteenth century to keep up with the growth of population and commerce by a commensurate growth of government structure and personnel. For example, the government did not raise the provincial quotas of successful degree holders who could emerge from the examination system. Originally these quotas had been set to maintain some kind of geographical balance, so that the great preponderance of the degree holders would not be from the Lower Yangtze provinces— not unlike arranging membership in the U.S. Congress so that all areas would be included. But, as the number of talented men capable of achieving degree status increased, the rigidity of the quotas closed the door to many of them in their effort to join the government ranks. One result was an increasing effort to attach such talent to the government in the form of advisors *(mu-yu)*, deputies *(wei-yuan)*, and expectant officials *(hou-pu*, "waiting to be appointed"). But this only increased the competition for preferment without increasing the efficiency of administration. The institutional structure of government failed to expand until later in the century.

One effect of this limitation of upward mobility was that a myriad of young literati seeking office became frustrated hangers-on of the government offices or *yamen*, where staffs were swollen and job competition induced all sorts of bribery and corruption. Personal favoritism began to skew the procedures of administration and deny the Confucian ideal of devotion to principle. Personal cliques and patronage networks began to upset the impartiality of the examinations, taxation, and justice. Squeeze took over. Since provincial officials were normally tax farmers, expected to produce established quotas of revenue and keep the surplus for their own expenses and profit, whenever the officials' morale was low, they would gouge the people unmercifully. This official rapacity, inflicting hardship upon the common people, began to rouse rebellion.

Growth of trade did not mean peasant livelihood improved. On the contrary, numbers of the destitute and unemployed from crowded areas migrated to marginal lands in the mountainous West and Southwest, where government was thinly spread. The famous but little-studied White Lotus Rebellion is one example of this trend. China's population explosion had led farmers to move into marginal areas as well as into the new frontier of cultivation in Manchuria. In the mountainous regions where Hupei, Shensi, and Szechwan meet, settlers from Central China had newly established themselves, extending the scope of Chinese rice cultivation in a comparatively unproductive peripheral region. The White Lotus Rebellion that arose in this area had certain classical features: it was inspired by a secret Buddhist folk religion that believed in the Eternal Mother. However, the various leaders (some of them women) who headed the armies and decentralized assemblies by which followers were organized were unable to agree on a Buddhist savior or Maitreya incarnate or on a pretender to lead a revival of the Ming dynasty. The White Lotus sectarians thus remained disunified as well as decentralized, forming a tenuous network of communities. They built defensive stockades around their mountain villages and defied the Ch'ing tax collectors. One of their slogans was the well-known "the officials force the people to rebel." The rising was of course nativist and anti-Manchu. However, the White Lotus does not seem to have been a rising among oppressed peasants on account of heavy tax collections. County magistrates and their underlings were comparatively few and weak in resources. To some undetermined extent the White Lotus seems to have arisen to take the place of an inadequate government, which had not yet developed in this frontier region its usual functions of public works, ever-normal granaries, and examinations for the ambitious. By 1800 the Manchu banner forces, partly because so many commanders profited from the funding of their military complex, were unable to suppress these rebels. The rebellion was ended only after the new Chia-ch'ing Emperor found incorrupt Manchu commanders. They also used Chinese militia, who now excelled the vaunted Manchu bannermen as a military force. To discerning scholars versed in the lore of the dynastic cycle, the fortunes of the Ch'ing dynasty seemed to be turning downward.

The hard crust of corruption in the best-documented imperial institutions has been abundantly described. Take for example the massive Grand Canal transport network, which took Lower Yangtze rice north to feed Peking. Khubilai Khan in the late thirteenth century had extended the Grand Canal on a northern course to his newly built capital at Peking; and the Ming and Ch'ing had used it ever since as a great artery of north-south trade, safer from storms and pirates than the sea route around the Shantung peninsula. A large administration under two governors-general handled the grain transport and managed the thousands of grain boats that every year tried to get through the canal locks (a Chinese invention) in Shantung en route northward. Grain boats 30 feet long with crews of 10 men were annually poled and hauled some 1,100 miles, traversing a high point 140 feet above sea level in order to supply 400,000 tons of rice to the Peking granaries. They carried private cargo too.

One of the problems of canal traffic was that it had to cross the

Yellow River. Over the centuries the director-general of the Yellow River Conservancy had built up a bureaucracy comparable to that of the two directors-general of grain transport. Dikes along the river were mended by engineers so competent that they could use comparatively vast imperial allocations of funds to build dikes that would look good enough but last only a few years. The point was that the officialdom made great profits from the imperial expenditures.

Meanwhile, the Grand Canal transport was handled by a large bureaucracy plus thousands of bargemen. Ancestors of these bargemen had been assigned to their functions some generations before and had often by a sort of subinfeudation arranged for the actual work to be done by nonhereditary gangs of boatmen. From all this paraphernalia of officials, boatmen, and their barges the imperial officials derived considerable profit, which they would not lightly forgo. As breakdown and silting of the canal impaired its efficiency in the early nineteenth century, the old idea arose that transport of rice by sea around the Shantung promontory would be cheaper and more efficacious. In a crisis in 1826 such transport was actually arranged by hiring merchant vessels, but the vested interests of the Grand Canal system were so strong that this improvement was promptly given up. Inefficiency won out.

The population explosion did a great deal more than weaken the government. In economic life the superabundance of human muscles made labor-saving devices uneconomical. Why dam a stream for waterpower, as the Europeans were doing, when labor was dirt cheap and could continue to be used instead for textile spinning and weaving? Indeed, why use mules and a cart when porters were so available? Porters needed only paths to follow, not roads laboriously graded at odds with the contour of rice terraces. The stern oar *(yu-lo)* to move a sampan used manpower very efficiently, as did the Chinese barrow balanced over its centered wheel. On land or water, mechanical transport by steampower would face stiff human competition.

Even animal power was at a disadvantage. The human hoe still outdid the traction plow, and consequently China remained less prepared to make the shift that came so naturally to Western farmers, from animal traction to automotive traction. As a result, seeders, cultivators, reapers, binders, and the whole Caterpillar family remained unfeasible, as they are even today. Production was locked into a muscle-power technology.

Socially, the flood of people was even more deleterious because life was reduced more and more to a grim struggle for survival. Generosity and philanthropy became luxuries that family members could ill afford. As the primary units for survival, families had to watch every rice grain. Some evaded taxes by enlisting as clients of more powerful landowners, and became peons supplying girls, workmen, and guards for their patrons. The self-sufficient owner-farmer had a harder time, needing protection against the officials' *yamen* runners, the big house's bullies and enforcers, and the bandits who emerged from the unemployed and destitute.

Not only local order but also personal morality declined as people proliferated. Natural calamities of flood, drought, famine, and pestilence became more severe because greater numbers were affected. People lost confidence in the future as well as in the work ethic. Virtue brought uncertain rewards. Those who lived by their wits survived better. Sycophancy, cheating, prostitution of boys and womenfolk, smuggling, violence, all had their uses in the struggle. Confucian conduct often became a public sham. After 1800 popular demoralization evidenced in opium smoking set in first amid the minor officials, *yamen* underlings, and troops of the establishment, but as poppy production spread within China, peasant producers took up the habit too.

These evils that flowed so largely from numbers changed the quality of Chinese life. Inevitably it became more brutish and uncertain. Honest officials who died poor became illustrious paragons because their example was so rare. A society that in Sung and even Ming had accepted the individual often on his merits now became suspicious of all seemingly worthy motives, fearful of strangers, and ungenerous. The struggle for survival meant that all ideals were risky, like daily life itself. Such fluctuations in welfare and morale had occurred before, but now in the late Ch'ing comparison with the West revealed more basic and systemic weaknesses.

4

China's Response to the West

Edited by Ssu-yu Teng and John K. Fairbank

The following documents, collected by Ssu-yu Teng and John Fairbank, show the slowly changing Chinese attitudes toward the "Western sea barbarians" who sought trade and then conquest in China. The first is the Emperor Qian Long's (Ch'ien Lung) letter to King George III of England, answering his request, made through his envoy Lord Macartney in 1793, for trade and diplomatic representation. It is a masterpiece of crushing condescension—imperial Chinese style. Forty-six years later, in 1839, the court sent an Imperial Commissioner, Lin Zexu (Lin Tse-hsü), to suppress the illegal opium traffic at Canton. Lin felt it proper to admonish Queen Victoria about her subjects' misbehavior (document 2). When England easily won the ensuing Opium War (1839–42), Lin drew at least some of the right conclusions about Chinese defense (document 3). Also in 1842, Wei Yuan, another Chinese official, recommended a change in strategy and the adoption some Western technology (document 4). But traditional attitudes died hard; Lin's and Wei's advice was ignored, and most Chinese continued to consider Westerners as mere savages, targets rather than models. Document 5, part of a placard posted near Canton after British forces had withdrawn in 1841, vividly expresses this view—one which was to last among many Chinese into the twentieth century, as manifested in the Boxer Rebellion of 1900 and even later anti-foreign riots. Qi Ying (Ch'i Ying), the high official who negotiated the Treaty of Nanjing (Nanking) ending the Opium War, drew on his experience with Westerners in a set of recommendations (document 6) in 1844 which, while still despising Western crudity, urged China to learn from Western military

67

technology. This split attitude toward the West bedeviled China's slow efforts at modernization for the ensuing century (as discussed further in Part 4), and is not yet entirely gone in the China of today.

(1) An Imperial Edict from Ch'ien Lung to King George III of England

You, O King, are so inclined toward our civilization that you have sent a special envoy across the seas to bring to our Court your memorial of congratulations on the occasion of my birthday and to present your native products as an expression of your thoughtfulness. On perusing your memorial, so simply worded and sincerely conceived, I am impressed by your genuine respectfulness and friendliness and greatly pleased.

As to the request made in your memorial, O King, to send one of your nationals to stay at the Celestial Court to take care of your country's trade with China, this is not in harmony with the state system of our dynasty and will definitely not be permitted. Traditionally people of the European nations who wished to render some service under the Celestial Court have been permitted to come to the capital. But after their arrival they are obliged to wear Chinese court costumes, are placed in a certain residence, and are never allowed to return to their own countries. This is the established rule of the Celestial Dynasty with which presumably you, O King, are familiar. Now you, O King, wish to send one of your nationals to live in the capital, but he is not like the Europeans, who come to Peking as Chinese employees, live there and never return home again, nor can he be allowed to go and come and maintain any correspondence. This is indeed a useless undertaking.

Moreover the territory under the control of the Celestial Court is very large and wide. There are well-established regulations governing tributary envoys from the outer states to Peking, giving them provisions (of food and traveling expenses) by our post-houses and limiting their going and coming. There has never been a precedent for letting them do whatever they like. Now if you, O King, wish to have a representative in Peking, his language will be unintelligible and his dress different from the regulations; there is no place to accommodate him. . . .

The Celestial Court has pacified and possessed the territory within the four seas. Its sole aim is to do its utmost to achieve good government and to manage political affairs, attaching no value to strange jewels and precious objects. The various articles presented by you, O King, this time are accepted by my special order to the office in charge of such functions in consideration of the offerings having come from a long distance with sincere good wishes. As a matter of fact, the virtue and prestige of the Celestial Dynasty having spread far and wide, the kings of the myriad nations come by land and sea with all sorts of precious things. Consequently there is nothing we lack, as your principal envoy and others have themselves observed. We have never set much store on strange or ingenious objects, nor do we need any more of your country's manufactures. . . .

(2) Lin Tse-hsü's Moral Advice to Queen Victoria, 1839

A communication: magnificently our great Emperor soothes and pacifies China and the foreign countries, regarding all with the same kindness. If there is profit, then he shares it with the peoples of the world; if there is harm, then he removes it on behalf of the world. This is because he takes the mind of heaven and earth as his mind.

The kings of your honorable country by a tradition handed down from generation to generation have always been noted for their politeness and submissiveness. We have read your successive tributary memorials saying, "In general our countrymen who go to trade in China have always received His Majesty the Emperor's gracious treatment and equal justice," and so on. Privately we are delighted with the way in which the honorable rulers of your country deeply understand the grand principles and are grateful for the Celestial grace. For this reason the Celestial Court in soothing those from afar has redoubled its polite and kind treatment. The profit from trade has been enjoyed by them continuously for two hundred years. This is the source from which your country has become known for its wealth.

But after a long period of commercial intercourse, there appear among the crowd of barbarians both good persons and bad, unevenly. Consequently there are those who smuggle opium to seduce the Chinese people and so cause the spread of the poison to all provinces. Such persons who only care to profit themselves, and disregard their harm to others, are not tolerated by the laws of heaven and are unanimously hated by human beings. His Majesty the Emperor, upon hearing of this, is in a towering rage. He has especially sent me, his commissioner, to come to Kwangtung, and together with the governor-general and governor jointly to investigate and settle this matter.

All those people in China who sell opium or smoke opium should receive the death penalty. If we trace the crime of those barbarians who through the years have been selling opium, then the deep harm they have wrought and the great profit they have usurped should fundamentally justify their execution according to law. We take into consideration, however, the fact that the various barbarians have still known how to repent their crimes and return to their allegiance to us by taking the 20,183 chests of opium from their storeships and petitioning us, through their consular officer [superintendent of trade], Elliot, to receive it. It has been entirely destroyed and this has been faithfully reported to the Throne in several memorials by this commissioner and his colleagues.

Fortunately we have received a specially extended favor from His Majesty the Emperor, who considers that for those who voluntarily surrender there are still some circumstances to palliate their crime, and so for the time being he has magnanimously excused them from punishment. But as for those who again violate the opium prohibition, it is difficult for the law to pardon them repeatedly. Having established new regulations, we presume that the ruler of your honorable country, who takes delight in our culture and whose disposition is inclined towards us, must be able to instruct the various barbarians to observe the law with care. It is only necessary to explain to them the advantages and disadvantages and then they will know that the legal code of the Celestial Court must be absolutely obeyed with awe.

We find that your country is sixty or seventy thousand *li* [three *li* make one mile, ordinarily] from China. Yet there are barbarian ships that strive to come here for trade for the purpose of making a great profit. The wealth of China is used to profit the barbarians. That is to say, the great profit made by barbarians is all taken from the rightful share of China. By what right do they then in return use the poisonous drug to injure the Chinese people? Even though the barbarians may not necessarily intend to do us harm, yet in coveting profit to an extreme, they have no regard for injuring others. Let us ask, where is your conscience? I have heard that the smoking of opium is very strictly forbidden by your country; that is because the harm caused by opium is clearly understood. Since it is not permitted to do harm to your own country, then even less should you let it be passed on to the harm of other countries—how much less to China! Of all that China exports to foreign countries, there is not a single thing which is not beneficial to people: they are of benefit when eaten, or of benefit when used, or of benefit when resold: all are beneficial. Is there a single article from China which has done any harm to foreign countries? Take tea and rhubarb, for example; the foreign countries cannot get along for a single day without them. If China cuts off these benefits with no sympathy for those who are to suffer, then what can the barbarians rely upon to keep themselves alive? Moreover the woolens, camlets, and long ells [i.e., woolen textiles] of foreign countries cannot be woven unless they obtain Chinese silk. If China, again, cuts off this beneficial export, what profit can the barbarians expect to make? As for other foodstuffs, beginning with candy, ginger, cinnamon, and so forth, and articles for use, beginning with silk, satin, chinaware, and so on, all the things that must be had by foreign countries are innumerable. On the other hand, articles coming from the outside to China can only be used as toys. We can take them or get along without them. Since they are not needed by China, what difficulty would there be if we closed the frontier and stopped the trade? Nevertheless our Celestial Court lets tea, silk, and other goods be shipped without limit and circulated everywhere without begrudging it in the slightest. This is for no other reason but to share the benefit with the people of the whole world.

The goods from China carried away by your country not only supply your own consumption and use, but also can be divided up and sold to other countries, producing a triple profit. Even if you do not sell opium, you still have this threefold profit. How can you bear to go further, selling products injurious to others in order to fulfill your insatiable desire?

Suppose there were people from another country who carried opium for sale to England and seduced your people into buying and smoking it; certainly your honorable ruler would deeply hate it and be bitterly aroused. We have heard heretofore that your honorable ruler is kind and benevolent. Naturally you would not wish to give unto others what you yourself do not want. We have also heard that the ships coming to Canton have all had regulations promulgated and given to them in which it is stated that it is not permitted to carry contraband goods. This indicates that the administrative orders of your honorable rule have been originally strict and clear. Only because the trading ships are numerous, heretofore perhaps they have not been examined with care. Now after this communication has been dispatched and you have clearly understood the strictness of the prohibitory laws of the Celestial Court, certainly you will not let your subjects dare again to violate the law.

We have further learned that in London, the capital of your honorable rule, and in Scotland *(Su-ko-lan)*, Ireland *(Ai-lun)*, and other places, originally no opium has been produced. Only in several places of India under your control such as Bengal, Madras, Bombay, Patna, Benares, and Malwa has opium been planted from hill to hill, and ponds have been opened for its manufacture. For months and years work is continued in order to accumulate the poison. The obnoxious odor ascends, irritating heaven and frightening the spirits. Indeed you, O King, can eradicate the opium plant in these places, hoe over the fields entirely, and sow in its stead the five grains [i.e., millet, barley, wheat, etc.]. Anyone who dares again attempt to plant and manufacture opium should be severely punished. This will really be a great, benevolent government policy that will increase the common weal and get rid of evil. For this, Heaven must support you and the spirits must bring you good fortune, prolonging your old age and extending your descendants. All will depend on this act.

As for the barbarian merchants who come to China, their food and drink and habitation are all received by the gracious favor of our Celestial Court. Their accumulated wealth is all benefit given with pleasure by our Celestial Court. They spend rather few days in their own country but more time in Canton. To digest clearly the legal penalties as an aid to instruction has been a valid principle in all ages. Suppose a man of another country comes to England to trade, he still has to obey the English laws; how much more should he obey in China the laws of the Celestial Dynasty?

Now we have set up regulations governing the Chinese people. He who sells opium shall receive the death penalty and he who smokes it also the death penalty. Now consider this: if the barbarians do not bring opium, then how can the Chinese people resell it, and how can they smoke it? The fact is that the wicked barbarians beguile the Chinese people into a death trap. How then can we grant life only to these barbarians? He who takes the life of even one person still has to atone for it with his own life; yet is the harm done by opium limited to the taking of one life only? Therefore in the new regulations, in regard to those barbarians who bring opium to China, the penalty is fixed at decapitation or strangulation. This is what is called getting rid of a harmful thing on behalf of mankind.

Moreover we have found that in the middle of the second month of this year [April 9] Consul [Superintendent] Elliot of your nation, because the opium prohibition law was very stern and severe, petitioned for an extension of the time limit. He requested a limit of five months for India and its adjacent harbors and related territories, and ten months for England proper, after which they would act in conformity with the new regulations. Now we, the commissioner and others, have memorialized and received the extraordinary Celestial grace of His Majesty the Emperor, who has redoubled his consideration and compassion. All those who within the period of the coming one year (from England) or six months (from India) bring opium to China by mistake, but who voluntarily confess and completely surrender their opium, shall be exempt from their punishment. After this limit of time, if there are still those who bring opium to China then they will plainly have committed a willful violation and shall at once be executed according to law, with absolutely no clemency or pardon. This may be called the height of kindness and the perfection of justice.

Our Celestial Dynasty rules over and supervises the myriad states, and surely possesses unfathomable spiritual dignity. Yet the Emperor cannot bear to execute people without having first tried to reform them by instruction. Therefore he especially promulgates these fixed regulations. The barbarian merchants of your country, if they wish to do business for a prolonged period, are required to obey our statutes respectfully and to cut off permanently the source of opium. They must by no means try to test the effectiveness of the law with their lives. May you, O King, check your wicked and sift your vicious people before they come to China, in order to guarantee the peace of your nation, to show further the sincerity of your politeness and submissiveness, and to let the two countries enjoy together the blessings of peace. How fortunate, how fortunate indeed! After receiving this dispatch will you immediately give us a prompt reply regarding the details and circumstances of your cutting off the opium traffic. Be sure not to put this off. The above is what has to be communicated. [Vermilion endorsement:] This is appropriately worded and quite comprehensive (*Te-t'i chou-tao*).

(3) A Letter of Lin Tse-hsü Recognizing Western Military Superiority, 1842

The rebels' ships on the open sea came and went as they pleased, now in the south and now suddenly in the north, changing successively between morning and evening. If we tried to put up a defense everywhere, not only would we toil and expend ourselves without limit, but also how could we recruit and transport so many troops, militia, artillery, and ammunition, and come to their support quickly? . . .

When I was in office in Kwangtung and Kwangsi, I had made plans regarding the problems of ships and cannon and a water force. Afraid that there was not enough time to build ships, I at first rented them. Afraid that there was not enough time to cast cannon and that it would not be done according to the regulations, I at first bought foreign ones. The most painful thing was that when the Hu-men [the Bogue or "Tiger's mouth," the entrance to the Canton River] was broken into, a large number of good cannon fell into the hands of the rebellious barbarians. I recall that after I had been punished two years ago, I still took the risk of calling the Emperor's attention to two things: ships and guns. At that time, if these things could have been made and prepared, they still could have been used with effect to fight against the enemy in Chekiang last fall [1841]. Now it is even more difficult to check the wildfire. After all, ships, guns, and a water force are absolutely indispensable. Even if the rebellious barbarians had fled and returned beyond the seas, these things would still have to be urgently planned for, in order to work out the permanent defense of our sea frontiers. Moreover, unless we have weapons, what other help can we get now to drive away the crocodile and to get rid of the whales? . . .

But at this time I must strictly observe the advice to seal my lips as one corks the mouth of a bottle. However, toward those with identical aims and interests, I suddenly spit out the truth and am unable to control myself. I extremely regret my foolishness and carelessness. Nevertheless, when I turn my thoughts to the depth of your attention to me, then I cannot conceal these things from myself. I only beg you to keep them confidential. By all means, please do not tell other persons.

(4) Wei Yuan's Statement of a Policy for Maritime Defense, 1842

.... The Japanese barbarians [who raided China in the sixteenth cen-
tury] were strong in land fighting and weak in water warfare, because
the pirates who came were all desperadoes from poor islands, who had
no means to build large ships and big guns, but relied upon sheer courage to cross the ocean, and depended upon their swords and spears to
invade China. Therefore, whenever they went ashore it was impossible
to resist them. But when the Japanese ships met the junks of Fukien and
Kwangtung, then they were like rice on a grindstone. If the Japanese
ships met big cannons and firearms, they would be like goats chased by
wolves.... In general, the strength of the Japanese was on the land. To
attack them on the open ocean was to assail their weak point. The
strength of the British barbarians is on the ocean. Wait for them in the
inland rivers. Wait for them on the shore and they will lose their
strength. Unfortunately, the Ming people, in warding off the Japanese,
did not know how to oppose them on the ocean, and nowadays those
who are guarding against the British do not lay ambushes in the interior.
Thus, the really effective ideas in the world must necessarily be contrary
to the opinion of the multitude of mediocre minds....

.... The British ships and guns are regarded in China as due to
extraordinary skill, in the various countries of Europe they are considered as quite ordinary. In Canton international trade has been carried
on for two hundred years. At first the products of their strange skills
and clever craftsmanship were received, and then their heterodox religions and poisonous opium. But in regard to their conduct of war and
the effectiveness of their weapons, we are learning not a single one of
their superior skills. That is, we are only willing to receive the harm and
not ... the benefit of foreign intercourse.

Let us establish a shipyard and an arsenal at two spots. Chuenpi and
Taikoktow outside of the Bogue in Kwangtung, and select one or two
persons from among the foreign headmen who have come from France
and America, respectively, to bring Western craftsmen to Canton to take
charge of building ships and making arms. In addition, we should invite
Western helmsmen to take charge of teaching the methods of navigating
ships and of using cannon, following the precedent of the barbarian
officials in the Imperial Board of Astronomy. We should select clever
artisans and good soldiers from Fukien and Kwangtung to learn from
them, the craftsmen to learn the casting of cannon and building of ships,

and the good soldiers to learn their methods of navigation and attack.... In Kwangtung there should be ten thousand soldiers; in Fukien, ten thousand; in Chekiang, six thousand; and in Kiangsu, four thousand. In assigning soldiers to the ships we must rely on selection and training. Eight out of ten should be taken from among fishermen and smugglers along the sea coast. Two out of ten should be taken from the old encampments of the water forces. All the padded rations and extra rations of the water force should be ... used for the recruiting and maintenance of good soldiers. We must make the water forces of China able to navigate large (lit., "storied") ships overseas, and able to fight against foreign barbarians on the high seas....

(5) Cantonese Denunciation of the British, 1841

The thoroughly loyal and patriotic people of the whole province of Kwangtung instruct the rebellious barbarian dogs and sheep for their information. We note that you English barbarians have formed the habits and developed the nature of wolves, plundering and seizing things by force.... In trade relations, you come to our country merely to covet profit. What knowledge do you have? Your seeking profit resembles the animal's greed for food. You are ignorant of our laws and institutions, ignorant of right principles.... You have no gratitude for the great favor of our Celestial Court; on the contrary you treat us like enemies and do us harm. You use opium to injure our common people, cheating us of our silver and cash.... Although you have penetrated our inland rivers and enticed fellows who renounce their fathers and their ruler to become Chinese traitors and stir up trouble among us, you are only using money to buy up their services—what good points have you? ... Except for your ships being solid, your gunfire fierce, and your rockets powerful, what other abilities have you? ...

We patriots have received the favor of the Celestial Dynasty in nourishing us for two centuries. Today, if we do not exterminate you English barbarians, we will not be human beings. You have killed and injured our common people in many villages, and seriously hurt the universal harmony. You also completely destroyed the coffins in several places, and you disastrously damaged the Buddhist statues in several monasteries. This is properly a time when Heaven is angered and mankind is resentful; even the ghosts and spirits will not tolerate you beasts....

Our hatred is already at white heat. If we do not completely exterminate you pigs and dogs, we will not be manly Chinese able to support the sky on our heads and stand firmly on the earth. Once we have said this, we will never go back on it, even if frustrated ten thousand times. We are definitely going to kill you, cut your heads off and burn you to death! Even though you ask people to admonish us, we will not obey. We must strip off your skins and eat your flesh, and then you will know how tough *(li-hai)* we are. . . . We ought really to use refined expressions. But since you beasts do not understand written characters, therefore we use rough, vulgar words to instruct you in simple terms. . . .

(6) Ch'i-ying's Method for Handling the Barbarians, 1844

. . . . The barbarians commonly lay great stress on their women. Whenever they have a distinguished guest, the wife is certain to come out to meet him. For example, the American chief Parker and the French chief Lagrené both brought their foreign wives along with them, and on occasions when your slave has gone to the barbarians' storied residences to discuss business, these foreign wives have rushed out and saluted him. Your slave was confounded and ill at ease, while they on the other hand were deeply honored and delighted. Thus in actual fact the customs of the various Western countries cannot be regulated according to the ceremonies of the Middle Kingdom. If we should abruptly rebuke them, it would be no way of shattering their stupidity and might give rise to their suspicion and dislike. . . .

With this type of people from outside the bounds of civilization, who are blind and unawakened in styles of address and forms of ceremony, if we adhered to the proper forms in official documents and let them be weighed according to the status of superior and inferior, even though our tongues were dry and our throats parched (from urging them to follow our way), still they could not avoid closing their ears and acting as if deaf. Not only would there be no way to bring them to their senses, but also it would immediately cause friction. Truly it would be of no advantage in the essential business of subduing and conciliating them. To fight with them over empty names and get no substantial result would not be so good as to pass over these small matters and achieve our larger scheme. . . .

(7) On the Manufacture of Foreign Weapons, by Feng Kuei-feng, a Ch'ing Official, 1860

.... Why are they small and yet strong? Why are we large and yet weak? We must try to discover some means to become their equal, and that also depends upon human effort. Regarding the present situation there are several major points: in making use of the ability of our manpower, with no one neglected, we are inferior to the barbarians; in securing the benefit of the soil, with nothing wasted, we are inferior to the barbarians; in maintaining a close relationship between the ruler and the people, with no barrier between them, we are inferior to the barbarians; and in the necessary accord of word with deed, we are also inferior to the barbarians. The way to correct these four points lies with ourselves, for they can be changed at once if only our Emperor would set the general policy right. There is no need for outside help in these matters. . . .

Funds should be assigned to establish a shipyard and arsenal in each trading port. Several barbarians should be invited and Chinese who are good in using their minds should be summoned to receive their instructions so that they may in turn teach many artisans. When a piece of work is finished and is indistinguishable from that made by the barbarians, the makers should be given a *chü-jen* degree as a reward, and be permitted to participate in the metropolitan examination on an equal footing with other scholars. Those whose products are superior to the barbarian manufacture should be granted a *chin-shih* degree as a reward, and be permitted to participate in the palace examinations on the same basis as others. The workers should be double-paid so as to prevent them from quitting.

Our nation has emphasized the civil service examinations, which have preoccupied people's minds for a long time. Wise and intelligent scholars have exhausted their time and energy in such useless things as the eight-legged essays [highly stylized essays for the civil service examination, divided into eight sections], examination papers, and formal calligraphy. . . . Now let us order one-half of them to apply themselves to the pursuit of manufacturing weapons and instruments and imitating foreign crafts. . . . The intelligence and wisdom of the Chinese are necessarily superior to those of the various barbarians, only formerly we have not made use of them. When the Emperor above likes something, those below him will pursue it even further, like the moving of grass in the wind or the response of an echo. There ought to be some people of extraordinary intelligence who can have new ideas and improve on Western methods. At first they may learn and pattern after the foreigners; then they may compare and try to be their equal; and finally they may go ahead and surpass them—the way to make ourselves strong actually lies in this. . . .

5

Modern China in Transition, 1900–1950

Mary C. Wright

Mary Wright, an outstanding American scholar of modern Chinese history, shows her characteristic brilliance in the following selection, which brings clarity to a confused and confusing period. She rightly emphasizes the evolution and impor- tance of nationalism, China's governmental weakness which nationalism sought to correct, and the two major rival political vehicles of nationalism, the Guomindang and the Communist Party. Her analysis of these fifty years during which Chinese struggled to find answers to their country's weakness provides an excellent foundation for understanding why and how it was the Communists whose answers won the widest support. In acquiring the leadership of Chinese nationalism, the Communists won not only the country but its united and organ- ized efforts toward the nationalist goal of modern development, Chinese style.

Most Americans had little occasion to think seriously about China until Communist China began to emerge as a major power. Even those who were especially interested in China seldom gave systematic attention to the current scene. Scholars nearly all studied periods before—usually very long before—1900. Missionaries, government officials, business- men, and military personnel were absorbed in pressing daily tasks. Most lacked the training, even if they had the time and inclination, to observe perceptively and to gauge accurately the momentous changes occurring around them. A handful of journalists made outstanding efforts to find out what was really happening, to set it in its epochal context, and to report it in readable English. Yet even among these, a working knowledge of the Chinese language and a familiarity with recent Chinese history were rarities. No one doubted that a grasp of the background was essential, but the background grasped was a strange blend of conflicting myths that have remained to block our comprehension of contemporary China.

Collapse of the Middle Kingdom

Everywhere in the world the headlong changes that marked the first half of the twentieth century dwarfed the slower changes of earlier centuries, but nowhere did these changes so stagger the imagination as in China. The longest lived and most populous polity in world history had changed so slowly over millennia that sometimes it seemed not to have changed at all. Certainly there had been nothing remotely comparable to the steady and accelerating transformation of European life beginning in the late Middle Ages. Then suddenly and nearly simultaneously China was struck with equivalents of the Reformation, the French Revolution, and the Russian Revolution. Marx and Darwin were new, but no newer than Aristotle and Rousseau. Young Chinese discovered them all at the same time.

This unprecedented telescoping of history was at first obscured by the continued and obviously vigorous persistence of the many ancient ways that so delighted all visitors. In the midst of a living antiquity unparalleled in the modern world, the signs of the progressive stages of a great revolution were generally discounted. Our experience had not prepared us for a society marked both by strong tradition and by powerful revolutionary drives. The signs of tradition were plain to see and comforting. The signs of revolution could be dismissed as superficial. There were such very wide troughs between the waves that at the time we could not see that there was any cumulative buildup. Today in retrospect, the classic French and Russian sequence is clearly outlined. The Chinese timetable, however, was so different that by the time we began to suspect that we might be seeing the beginning of a great social revolution, the revolution was already far advanced.

The basic thread of Chinese history during the first half of the twentieth century was the search—sometimes ebullient, often heartbroken—for new institutions in every sphere of public and private life, institutions which would connect the pride in a great past to high hopes for a great future. In the tumultuous controversies of fifty years, the Chinese centered their attention on one or another facet of a few great questions: What of the old is worth keeping? Can we keep it and survive in the modern world? What of the new is desirable? Must we take the undesirable too in order to survive? Or can China make a future for herself on lines not yet tried elsewhere? These questions were of mounting urgency, for the Chinese state was prostrate and Chinese life seemed to be disintegrating.

The Force of Nationalism

Because vigorous nationalism provides built-in incentives which a successful government can use to spur and control its people, the growth of nationalism was one of the most significant features of China's recent history. When the twentieth century opened, the power of the Chinese Empire was a very recent and live memory. Hence the shattering series of stunning defeats at the hands of the Western powers and Japan was especially galling. We did not give enough attention to the sharp and swift rise of fighting nationalism. Daily observation of the polite and humorous Chinese, plus a little dabbling in Chinese philosophy, led to the myth that the Chinese were only interested in their own families, that they had no conception of country. Everyone could tell a story to illustrate the point, from the embassy to the kitchen level. Opposite conclusions were drawn from this alleged basic characteristic of twentieth-century China: The Chinese were venal and lacking in decent feeling for the public good, or the Chinese were charming sages happily free of the lusts for power that had wrecked what had been European civilization until 1914. But in either case, the basic analysis was dreadfully faulty.

There was in fact a genuine ground swell of Chinese nationalism during the first half of the twentieth century, and for its element of xenophobia there were clear historic roots. So much has been written lately of Chinese popular good will toward foreigners until they were brain-washed en masse that, at the risk of gross oversimplification, something should also be said of Chinese bitterness and hatred toward Americans and Europeans in recent decades. The crude fear of the white peril that the last imperial dynasty had been able to exploit in the

Boxer Rebellion of 1900 had been submerged but not overcome, and the expanding special privileges of foreigners were irritants in increasingly wide spheres of Chinese life. These fears and irritations provided a mass sounding board for what might otherwise have been rather arid denunciations of imperialists. It is well to remember that both Nationalists and Communists have struck this note; that Chiang Kai-shek and Lenin described the tangible effects of imperialism in remarkably similar terms.

The Search for Political Stability

The increasingly patent ineffectiveness of political leadership and institutions was a no less important characteristic of twentieth-century China. This phenomenon was obvious to all, but it was misinterpreted because we did not attach enough importance to the fact that political decline was accompanied by repeated efforts to reconstitute a powerful central government. When government was weakest, the pressures for strong government were greatest, for it was then that both traditional culturalism and modern nationalism were most offended. The various movements and programs that expressed these pressures struck us as rather silly, and the myth grew that Chinese politics was horseplay among warlords with silver bullets. Warlordism was, of course, a fact, but we were wrong to conclude from this that the Chinese people opposed strong government or that no central power could be effective throughout so vast and underdeveloped a country. The imperial tradition of strong central government never died, and now in retrospect one is struck by how much authority the central government did in fact retain until 1917. Even the "warlord period," 1917–27, was no era of general collapse of centralized authority, for the warlords themselves operated effective political machines over substantial territories. More important, the major contenders for power aimed consistently at the reconstitution of a powerful central state. As external dangers and internal crises mounted, the population of the country did not remain as apathetic and cynical as was thought in Treaty Port circles. On the record of performance it is clear that increasingly wide sectors of the population were prepared to throw their support to whoever gave most promise of effective central government.

The terrible strains of the period notwithstanding, the country remained vigorous, and tremendous new potentials were created in spite of war and inadequate leadership. We were too given to pity for a suffering and downtrodden people, and the pity irked. Widespread suffering there was indeed, but at its lowest point twentieth-century China was no beaten and stagnant country. Rather it offered the world the remarkable spectacle of a people whose ancient institutions had retained great vigor and effectiveness until very recent times; a people with a well-justified pride in the record of a great and prosperous state as well as in their intellectual and artistic heritage; a people who were learning modern skills rapidly and well and yet who with all this promise felt themselves in danger of national extinction because they had found no way to mobilize this latent strength for defense against aggression and foreign special privilege, for raising the standard of living, for a cultural renascence.

Agrarian China: Peasants and Politics

During the first half of the twentieth century, China remained an overwhelmingly agricultural country. Although the proportionate position of the agrarian sector of the economy declined somewhat, the peasant's produce remained the chief source of revenue, and his tax burden increased steadily with the rising cost of more elaborate arms, proliferating government offices, and the service of foreign loans. The terms of rural credit were devastating and tenancy increased, especially in the vicinity of modernized cities. The increased acreage planted in cash crops undermined the traditional self-sufficiency of the village, and cottage industries, once an important source of supplementary income, either disappeared or were bought by merchants. The self-employed artisan all but disappeared, and there was little to mitigate the harsh consequences of the imbalance between the high market value of manufactured goods and the low market value of agricultural products.

No patriotic Chinese could remain insensitive to the plight of the peasant base of society, even if the interest was only theoretical. The programs of the warlords regularly mentioned the need for reforms. The Kuomintang, which came to power in 1927, also had an elaborate rural program; its implementation was unfortunately delayed until threats from the Chinese Communists and from Japan could be removed. Perhaps more important as a symptom of the same kind of guilty uneasiness that drove prerevolutionary Russian intellectuals into populist movements, there was a rash of local experiments in rural reconstruction, sparked mainly by liberals of the minor parties whose programs lay somewhere between the Kuomintang and Communist poles. These efforts were important signs of the times; yet the country was so vast that major accomplishment could not really have been expected without strong government support. They were obliterated in the holocaust of the Japanese invasion.

One barrier to the implementation of the Kuomintang land reform program was the landed wealth of its members. There were exceptions of course, especially among Kuomintang members from the modern business and professional classes. Even among these, however, there was fear that a land reform program, once launched, might gain too much momentum and turn against the Kuomintang. After 1937, with the loss to Japan of the modern cities these men represented, the Kuomintang became increasingly dependent upon the rural economy and thus upon the support of ultraconservative landlords in the hinterland.

Meanwhile, the Chinese Communist Party, founded in 1921, moved rather quickly away from the classic Marxian distrust of the peasantry. The party line shifted tortuously on this as on other points, yet within a few years Mao Tse-tung and others were demonstrating their skill in peasant agitation. Kuomintang realization that peasants when aroused would almost certainly swing to the Communists was a major cause of the breakup of the first Kuomintang-Communist united front and of the Kuomintang's swing to the right after 1927. Driven back into the countryside by the victorious Nationalist armies, the Communists began a long series of land reform experiments, varying according to circumstances from moderate rent reduction to wholesale confiscation. By degrees the Communist party learned how to mobilize peasant support. The Chinese peasant loved his land, but by the third and fourth decades of the twentieth century it could no longer keep him alive without radical changes, and only the Communists offered these.

During the civil war, 1946–49, the Communists succeeded in using land reform as a major political and military weapon. The national government, threatened on all sides, was not prepared to take any very drastic steps. The Chinese-American Joint Committee on Rural Reconstruction struggled manfully to improve agrarian technology in the hope that, with an increased harvest, the peasant's plight could be eased without damage to landlord interests. The conclusion of the outstanding Chinese official chiefly responsible for the effort was that nearly everywhere technological change proved impossible without fundamental institutional change; that indeed without social reform, the peasant could not take advantage of improved methods, and his position often actually deteriorated.

Urban Developments

Before 1950, the modern sectors of the Chinese economy lagged so far behind the West, Japan, and even India that one did not usually notice how great the development had been between 1900 and 1950. Beginning in the 1890s, Chinese of a new type, scholar-officials who were also entrepreneurs, began to build substantial modern factories. Mining, railroads, and shipping developed rapidly. The physical plant, the labor force, the managers and technicians required for a modern economy began to appear in increasing numbers. The potential was there for anyone to see, and yet it could not be realized. To the Chinese, this was infuriating. The chief barriers seemed to be inept and predatory government, fragments of traditional social institutions, drainage from the country of the profits from the enormous foreign investment in China, and the special protection that the unequal treaties provided for foreign interests, often directly against Chinese interests. Many Chinese businessmen, who enjoyed a boom while privileged Western competition was deflected by World War I, became in a sense revolutionaries, precisely because they were patriots and businessmen. They supported the Kuomintang in its bid for power, 1924–27, because of its program to abolish imperialism; to create an effective, modern, centralized government; and to campaign relentlessly against the shreds of the Confucian order.

During this period, strikes and other signs of labor unrest were widespread, especially in foreign-owned enterprises. The foreigners' customary retort that their labor was at all events much better paid than other Chinese labor was irrelevant. Chinese peasants coming to work in factories for the first time suddenly saw much greater gaps between poverty and wealth than they had ever seen before. The poverty, and it was still extreme poverty by any standards, was theirs; the wealth belonged to foreigners and to a few Chinese who could readily be labeled "running dogs of the foreigners," and it was often displayed in a manner that could scarcely have been better calculated to offend.

This frustration was felt in many spheres of Chinese society. The professional diplomats of China, skilled though many of them were, made only limited and gradual progress toward abolishing the unequal international status that outraged Chinese of every political persuasion. The Japanese invasion of the mainland struck at the very core of China's national integrity, and the international complications of the war period left a tangled legacy of misapprehensions and misunderstanding. Western relinquishment of extraterritorial privileges during the war came far too late, and the continuing major role of the United States in the postwar period convinced many Chinese that the national government was incapable of independent action. To these Chinese, the situation seemed further proof that diplomatic resources, like economic resources, were useless to a weak government and that military power was essential to political effectiveness.

The Key Role of Military Power

The new importance attached to military power was another major characteristic of modern Chinese history. Chinese had never been the pacifists that we often fondly imagined them to be, and it had been clear to them since their first contact with the military power of the West that only a country with strong armed forces could elect its own policies. For a century there was a steady sequence of military reorganization programs. Every program failed; never was the required fighting strength achieved; never was a war won. Yet what was accomplished in inadequate bits and pieces convinced nearly all Chinese that China need not forever be a pawn in world politics; that there were no insuperable obstacles to genuine great power status. Experience had shown that Chinese peasants could be trained to use modern weapons efficiently and that they could on occasion fight with unsurpassed valor. Why was the opposite so often the case? Experience had shown that the country had the natural resources and the technological aptitudes needed for a modern arms industry. Why had one not developed? China had a small number of skilled strategists and effective line officers. Why were they not better deployed, and why had not many times their number been trained? The popular feeling as defeat followed defeat was less one of despair than of anger at the waste of opportunity. To a desperate government, massive outside aid seemed the only answer. To many Chinese, so much foreign aid to so weak a government seemed bound to lead to spiraling dependence. The suggestion that this was the intention of the aid fell on ready ears.

Education

Some observers insisted that the Chinese attitudes described above were limited to a tiny and powerless fraction of the population. They failed to note how rapidly political awareness was spreading through education and propaganda. It would be difficult to find any period in the history of any country where education was expected to work the miracles it was expected to work in twentieth-century China, and very nearly did. The dominant Chinese tradition, in marked contrast to Western tradition, had always held that men are by nature good and that although their talents vary, the variation has nothing to do with class. Hence education, on which an enormous value was placed, was theoretically as desirable for the lower classes as for the upper. It had always been gratifying rather than terrifying to see the son of a peasant attain a high education with all its consequent rewards. His chance to do this was slim indeed, but the barrier was economic only.

With the twentieth century, the peasant's chance at education began to improve rapidly. The missionary schools and the new government schools provided only a fraction of the facilities that would have been required for universal public education. Even so, they were closer to such a system than they were to the traditional system of tutors and academies. The way seemed open in the not too distant future for every Chinese to be given a basic education and for the ablest Chinese to be given the highest education. But to attain this end, vigorous government action was needed. Successive governments made some contribution, but only under heavy pressure from the leaders of public opinion. Education had a low priority on all budgets, and as new ideas mushroomed, some of those in power came to cherish an illiterate population. Mass education movements found contrived obstacles rather than the support they needed. Too many schools remained under foreign control, and it was humiliating to realize how dreadfully the foreign schools were needed. There was almost no field in which China offered full advanced training, this despite the world renown of many of her scholars, once they were trained abroad.

The Chances for Democracy

Thus in education as in other fields, progress led not to stable satisfaction but to a sharpening awareness of how much more had to be done, and, it was believed, could be done, if China had an effective and efficient government. There were fifty years of controversy over the kind of government China had and the kind of government she needed. The trends were frequently confusing, for in China political characteristics that the West regarded as inevitably associated were often in conflict, and others that the West regarded as mutually incompatible were sometimes fused.

During the first half of the twentieth century, the trend toward democracy was strong in China—in some senses of the word. Legally privileged classes had already disappeared, and as the upper classes continued to expand rapidly in size, there were in China millions of families of some little importance rather than a few hundred very powerful ones. The open classes of the traditional society became highly fluid during a period of such rapid change. The country had since early times been culturally homogeneous, vertically as well as horizontally. Of course there were popular cultures, elite cultures, and subcultures, but nothing resembling the cultural cleavage between classes that until recently characterized much of Europe. With the spread of modern public education, few cultural stigmata of class origin remained. Traditionally, popular opinion had been taken seriously by the government, and after 1919 the media for its expression expanded like the burst of a Roman candle.

In all these meanings—and they are valid meanings—twentieth-century China was democratic, and increasingly democratic. Yet this trend toward democracy lacked two elements considered essential in the West. There was no trend toward the establishment of civil liberties and there was no trend toward government by majority decision.

Neither of the two major political movements—the Nationalist and the Communist—showed any real interest in civil liberties, or even comprehension of what they were. As in traditional China, whatever purported to be the interests of the group remained paramount. In the 1920s there were flurries of talk about civil liberties, mainly among intellectuals, but these were crushed from both left and right. In the 1930s and 1940s, internal crises and foreign aggression seemed to require unfettered action by a powerful government if there was to be a viable future for anyone Chinese. In such circumstances, it is not surprising that a demand for civil liberties came to seem a demand for a right to willful self-indulgence. There was no thought that individual Chinese ought to be guaranteed some small but irreducible minimum of privacy and originality, an area that the state could never touch, however great the alleged public interest.

Nor was there any trend toward representative government in the first half of the twentieth century. In Chinese tradition there had never been any notion that the wisest decision could be reached by counting heads, even in a select group. Statesmanship had been the art of selecting, training, and indoctrinating a small corps of able men who could then be trusted to run every aspect of the public life of a vast empire. To secure popular assent to official decision was essential; to ask the people what the decision should be never remotely occurred to anyone. Within the official hierarchy there were intricate checks and balances, impeachments, conferences, and compromises, but no idea of majority decision. After 1912, the few efforts at a façade of parliamentary government were fiascoes, and most Chinese of all political persuasions saw the main problems as the creation of a competent new political elite to fill the gap left by the collapse of the imperial system. The idea of military tutelage followed by political tutelage meant exercise of power on behalf of the people by a nonhereditary, authoritarian political corps. It was as basic to Nationalist as to Communist political thought. During the first half of the century, neither party relinquished its control to popular elections. In 1950, the promise of ultimate full democracy offered by either seemed remote.

Geographic and Ethnic Diversity

6

The Chinese Scene

John K. Fairbank

One can only applaud John Fairbank's tour de force in sketching in some ten pages most of the basics of China's geography, including the density and distribution of its population, and at the same time providing vivid word portraits of its agricultural system, the values which that system engendered, and the country's major regions. He makes real the dramatic contrasts between the green, hilly, humid south, the dry brown plains of the north, the great river valleys, the steppe frontier areas of the northwest, and the mountainous and remote but locally productive southwest. China's uniquely crowded landscape provides the setting, as he implies, for its structured system of social organization, the rules by which its people live.

The Chinese people's basic problem of livelihood used to be readily visible from the air: the brown eroded hills, the flood plains of muddy rivers, the patchwork of green fields and hives of simple huts that formed the villages, the intricate silver network of terraces and waterways that testified to the back-breaking labor of countless generations—all the overcrowding of too many people upon too little land, and the attendant exhaustion of the land resources and of human ingenuity and fortitude in the effort to maintain life.

Today in the People's Republic the fragmented strips of cultivation have been efficiently consolidated into bigger fields, millions of trees have been planted along new roads and on the mountains, and electric pumps fill the new ponds and irrigation ditches. The face of China has been transformed. But the population has doubled: it is now roughly a billion people.

The Contrast of North and South

To any traveler who has flown through the vast gray cloud banks, mists, and sunshine of continental China, two pictures will stand out as typical, one of North China and one of the South. On the dry North China plain to the south of Peking where Chinese civilization had its first flowering, one sees in summer an endless expanse of green fields over which are scattered clusters of darker green, the trees of earth-walled villages. It is very like the view of our Middle West, where farmsteads and their clumps of trees are dispersed at rough half-mile intervals. But where our corn belt has a farm, on the North China plain there is an entire village. Where one American farmer's family lives with its barns and sheds among its fields in Iowa or Illinois at a half-mile interval from its neighbors roundabout, in China an entire community of several hundred persons lives in its tree-studded village, at a half-mile interval from neighboring villages. The American people in spite of their farming background have no appreciation of the population density which subtly conditions every act and thought of a Chinese farmer.

In South China the typical picture is quite different, and like nothing to which we are accustomed. There during much of the year the rice fields are flooded and present a water surface to the airborne observer. The green terrain is hilly and the crescent-shaped rice terraces march up each hill almost to the top and on the other side descend again from near the crest, terrace upon terrace in endless succession, each embankment conforming to the lay of the land like the contour lines of a geographer's chart. In fact the curving pattern of the rice terraces seen from above is a visual index to the slope of the valleys in which they are built—narrow concave strips of paddy field touch the hilltops, and lower terraces grow broader and longer and bulge out as they descend to the valley floor. Gray stone footpaths are built on many of the embankments and the latter form intricate patterns like the product of some giant's doodling. When the sun is out one sees it from the air reflected brilliantly in the water of the rice fields. The sun seems in fact to be shining up through the fields from below, so that the whole ornate network of the embankments and paths and hilltops appears to rush beneath one

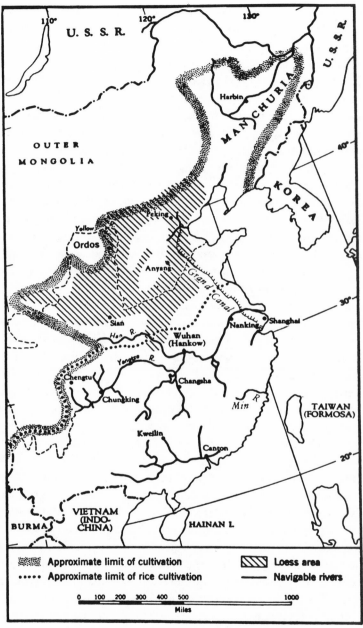

Approximate limit of cultivation	Loess area
Approximate limit of rice cultivation	Navigable rivers

0   100   200   300   400   500   1000
Miles

GEOGRAPHIC FEATURES

as though on a great rolling screen, a black lacework moving across the bright silver of shining water.

No one can fly over the rugged green hills of the South without wondering where the billion or so people of China live and what they eat—such vast reaches of mountain and valley seem largely uncultivable and sparsely settled. One's picture of a big empty landscape is mirrored statistically in the estimate that six sevenths of the population have to concentrate on one third of the land. The really inhabited part of China, at a rough estimate, is only about half as large as the really inhabited part of the United States, yet it supports four times as many people. This is made possible only by crowding some 2000 human beings onto each square mile of cultivated earth in the valleys and flood plains. The United States has some 570,000 square miles under cultivation and could greatly increase this area; China has perhaps 450,000 square miles of cultivated land (less than one half acre of food-producing soil per person) with little prospect of increasing this area by more than a small fraction, even if it is used more intensively.

Little is known in statistical terms about the life of the Chinese people upon their crowded land, but sampling studies, in which American investigators once took a leading part, give us some general indications. The great contrast is between the dry wheat-millet area of North China and the moist rice land of the South. These economic regions divide along a line roughly halfway between the Yellow River and the Yangtze on the thirty-third parallel. Let us look at the factors of rainfall, soil, temperature, and human usage which create this striking contrast.

First of all, the rainfall depends upon the continental character of the Chinese climate and the seasonal air flow to which it gives rise. To put it very simply, the Asiatic land mass changes temperature more readily than the Western Pacific and its currents, and the cold dry air which is chilled over the continent in the wintertime tends to flow southeastward to the sea, with minimum precipitation. Conversely, the summer monsoon of moisture-laden sea air is drawn inward and northward over the land mass by the rising of the heated air above it, and precipitation occurs mainly during the summer. This southerly wind of summer crosses the hills of South China first, and they receive a heavy rainfall, which remains relatively dependable with a variation of only about 15 percent in the amount of precipitation from one year to the next. North China, being farther from the South China Sea, receives less rainfall, and moreover, the amount of precipitation over the decades has varied

ANNUAL RAINFALL

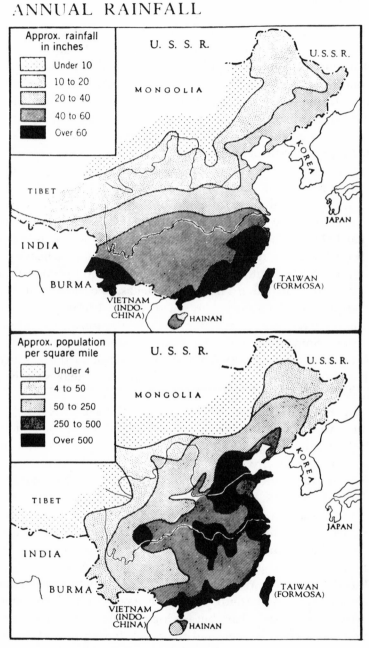

Approx. rainfall in inches

- Under 10
- 10 to 20
- 20 to 40
- 40 to 60
- Over 60

U. S. S. R.

U. S. S. R.

MONGOLIA

KOREA

TIBET

JAPAN

INDIA

BURMA

TAIWAN (FORMOSA)

VIETNAM (INDO-CHINA)

HAINAN

Approx. population per square mile

- Under 4
- 4 to 50
- 50 to 250
- 250 to 500
- Over 500

U. S. S. R.

U. S. S. R.

MONGOLIA

KOREA

TIBET

JAPAN

INDIA

BURMA

TAIWAN (FORMOSA)

VIETNAM (INDO-CHINA)

HAINAN

POPULATION DENSITY

as much as 30 percent from one year to the next. Since the average rainfall of the North China plain is about 20 to 25 inches, like the rainfall of the great American dustbowl, it is hardly more than sufficient to maintain cultivation at the best of times. This high degree of rainfall variability from year to year is a most serious problem. North China is normally on the subsistence margin as regards its water supply, and the periodic failure of rainfall threatens to produce drought and famine. In water supply, South China has the better of it.

As regards soil, however, South China suffers by comparison, for the constant seepage of water through its warm earth has dissolved and leached away mineral foods of great importance for plant life. The leached soil resulting is relatively unproductive, and the situation is saved partly by the fact that the constant run-off from the hills brings down new deposits for the cultivated lowlands. Even so, the heavy population centers of the South are to be found mainly on the alluvial flood plains along the Yangtze or on the river deltas, like those inland from Shanghai or around Canton. The soil of North China, on the other hand, thanks to the relative lack of water, remains unleached and richer in minerals. Sometimes, indeed, as in Mongolia, mineral salts are brought to the surface by evaporating water and, in the absence of rainfall to wash them away, form a saline crust which makes cultivation impossible.

Temperature plays its part in preserving the soil of North China, since the severe continental winters, not unlike those of the American Middle West, limit the growing season to about half the year. In southernmost China crops are grown the year around and rice is double-cropped and even triple-cropped. Too easily we forget that Shanghai is in the latitude of New Orleans and Suez, while Canton is in that of Havana and Calcutta, well into the tropics. This explains why the greater part of the Chinese people live in the more fecund rice economy of the South. Rice culture, with its greater inputs of water and labor, yields more than twice as much food as wheat growing.

Thus the factors of rainfall, soil, and temperature are in a rough balance both North and South, the North having soil which is highly fertile when water is sufficient, but having too often an insufficiency of water and much cold weather, and the South having no lack of water and favorable temperatures but generally infertile soil. In both cases the resources of nature are supplemented by unremitting human endeavor, of which the night soil (human excrement) industry is but one of the more spectacular forms. Without the redolent returning to the land of human waste or equivalent fertilizers no region of China could sustain its present population. It is no accident that Chinese cities from the air can be seen surrounded by a belt of dense green crops which fade out at the periphery. Each urban center sustains its surrounding truck gardens.

A population map will show that the Chinese people are packed into four main regions, which include but a small part of the total area of the country. The first region is the North China plain, the second is the mountain-locked plain of Szechwan in the west, the third is the lower Yangtze valley from the Wuhan cities to Shanghai, including the Hunan rice bowl south of Hankow, and the fourth is the Canton delta in the south. Early travelers compared China to Europe in the variety of dialects and the size of different provinces. For example, three regions along the course of the Yangtze in Central China—Szechwan province in the west, the twin provinces of Hupei and Hunan north and south of Wuhan, and the lower Yangtze delta—are each of them comparable to Germany in area and each bigger in population.

Trade and transport routes in South China have followed the waterways, and the great modern cities—Canton, Shanghai, Wuhan, even Tientsin—have grown up where sea trade can meet the waterborne commerce of the interior. Yet China's foreign trade has never lived up to the foreign merchant's great expectations. Stretching so far from north to south, from the latitude of Canada to that of Cuba, China remains a subcontinent largely sufficient unto herself. As George Washington's contemporary, the great Ch'ien-lung Emperor, put it in his famous edict to King George III, "Our celestial empire possesses all things in prolific abundance and lacks no product within its own borders. There is therefore no need to import the manufactures of outside barbarians."

In spite of the immensity and variety of the Chinese scene, we need not be surprised that this subcontinent has remained a single political unit where Europe has not; for it is held together by a way of life even more deeply rooted than our own, and stretching even farther back uninterruptedly into the past.

China's Origins

.... In racial stock the Chinese have a deceptive homogeneity which does not stand up under anthropological inspection. Peoples from North and Central Asia have continually entered the Chinese scene and have sometimes ruled over it, although never in sufficient numbers to overwhelm Chinese civilization. The arid steppe land north of the Great Wall has been a breeding ground of nomad invaders who could never displace the dense population of agrarian China but who made it more diverse. Consequently the so-called Mongoloid racial type is made up of very mixed strains in which flat noses and hawk noses, black hair and some red hair, beards and lack of beards, all appear, and supposedly common denominators such as the Mongolian eye fold are by no means universal.

The Harmony of Man and Nature

No matter what elements of civilization—peoples or cultural traits— came to China, they all became integrated in a distinctly Chinese way of life, nourished, conditioned, and limited by the good earth and the use of it. To cite but one example, from neolithic times the people of North China have made pit dwellings or cave homes in the fine, yellow, windborne loess soil that covers about 100,000 square miles of Northwest China to a depth of 150 feet or more. Loess has a quality of vertical cleavage useful for such a purpose. Many hundreds of thousands still live in caves cut into the sides of loess cliffs. They are cool in summer, warm in winter, and secure against everything but earthquakes.

The loess of Northwest China seems never to have supported forests. Where forest land occurred, the Chinese, like other early peoples and recent American pioneers, achieved its deforestation. The consequent erosion through the centuries changed the face of their country and erosion today is still a major problem. Through its waterborne loess deposits the Yellow River has built up the broad flood plain of North China between Shansi province and the sea, and the process still goes on. Nothing can so vividly convey a feeling of man's impotence in the face of nature as to watch the swirling coffee-colored flood of the Yellow River, flowing majestically within its dikes across, and 20 feet above, the crowded plain 200 miles from the sea; and to realize that this vast yellow torrent is steadily depositing its silt and building its bed higher above the surrounding countryside until the time when human negligence or act of God will allow it again to burst from the dikes and inundate the plain.

Deforestation, erosion, and floods have constantly been met by human efforts at water control. The planting of trees and damming of tributaries in the limitless western watershed of "China's Sorrow" is a recent achievement in the People's Republic. In all previous periods the rulers of China have been periodically confronted with a fait accompli in the debouching of the Yellow River upon the North China plain in full flood and have lacked the scientific knowledge and the means to get behind this pressing fact. In the earliest period, however, flooding of the plain was less of a problem than the reclamation of it from its primitive swamp and fen condition; techniques of water control were developed for drainage purposes as well as for irrigation and the prevention of floods. Thus many generations of labor have been spent upon the land to make it what it is today, protected by dikes, crossed by canals and roads worn into the earth, irrigated by streams and wells, divided by paths and occasional remnants of grave land in their groves of trees, and all of it handed down from generation to generation.

This land which modern China has inherited is used almost entirely for human food production. China cannot afford to raise cattle for food. Of the land which can be used at all, nine tenths is cultivated for crops and only about 2 percent is pasture for animals. By comparison, in the United States only four tenths of the land which is used is put into crops, and almost half of it is put into pasture.

The human implications of intensive agriculture can be seen most strikingly in the rice economy, which is the backbone of Chinese life everywhere in the Yangtze valley and the South. Rice plants are ordinarily grown for their first month in seedbeds, while subsidiary crops are raised and harvested in the dry fields. The fields are then irrigated, fertilized, and plowed (here the water buffalo may supplement man's hoeing) in preparation for the transplanting of the rice seedlings. This transplanting is still done by human hands, the rows of planters bending from the waist as they move backward step by step through the ankle-high muddy water of each terrace. This goes on in the paddy fields of a whole subcontinent—certainly the greatest expenditure of muscular energy in the world. When the rice has been weeded and is mature, the field is drained and it is harvested, again by hand. Given an unlimited supply of water and of human hands, there is probably no way by which a greater yield could be gained from a given plot of land. In this situation land is economically more valuable than labor, or to put it another way, good muscles are more plentiful than good earth. The Chinese farmer could not afford to put his labor into extensive agriculture, which would yield only half as much per acre. He lacked both the land and the capital for mechanized or large-scale methods. Obliged to rely on his own family's labor power, he was obliged to rely on intensive hand gardening in order to feed them. The effort to mechanize farming in the People's Republic today confronts the serious problem of finding alternative employment for the farm population.

The heavy application of manpower and night soil to small plots of land has had its social repercussions, for it sets up a vicious interdependence between dense population and intensive use of the soil whereby each makes the other possible. Population density provides both the incentive for intensive land use and the means. Once established, this economy developed its inertia and set its own human standards, whereby the back-breaking labor of many hands became the accepted norm and inventive efforts at labor saving remained the exception. Early modernizers of China, in their attempts to introduce the machine, constantly ran up against the vested interest of Chinese manpower, since in the short run the machine appeared to be in competition with human hands and backs. Thus railways were attacked as depriving carters and coolies of their jobs, and there was no premium upon invention.

This is only one of many ways in which the ecology of the Chinese, their adaptation to physical environment, influenced their culture. Life on the great river flood plains has always been a hard life, in which man is dependent upon nature more than upon his own initiative. "Heaven nourishes and destroys" is an ancient saying. On the broad stretches of the plain the patient Chinese farmer was at the mercy of the weather, dependent upon Heaven's gift of sun and rain. He was forced to accept natural calamity in the traditional form of drought, flood, pestilence, and famine. This is in striking contrast to the lot of the European, who lived in a land of variegated topography. Western man, either on the Mediterranean or on the European continent, was never far from a water supply and could usually supplement agriculture by hunting or fishing provided he exercised initiative. From ancient times seaborne commerce has played an immediate part in Western man's economy. Exploration and invention in the service of commerce have exemplified

Western man's struggle against nature, rather than a passive acceptance of it.

A different relation of man to nature in the West and in the East has been one of the salient contrasts between the two civilizations. Man has been in the center of the Western stage. The rest of nature has served as neutral background or as his adversary. Thus Western religion is anthropomorphic and early Western painting anthropocentric. To see how great this gulf is we have only to compare Christianity with the relative impersonality of Buddhism, or a Sung landscape and its tiny human figures dwarfed by crags and rivers with an Italian primitive in which nature is an afterthought.

And yet, paradoxically, Chinese man has been so crowded upon the soil among his fellows that he is also a most socially minded human being, ever conscious of the interplay of personalities and social conventions around him; for he is seldom in all his life beyond earshot of other people.

7

Man and Nature in China

Rhoads Murphey

Picking up where Fairbank leaves off, the excerpts from "Man and Nature in China" (by one of his many students) show how Chinese attitudes toward the natural world reflected and reinforced the values of the traditional society, and then how they have been stood on their heads as an important part of the Communist revolution. The article from which these excerpts were taken was written at the beginning of the Cultural Revolution (1966–76), when the radical wing of the Party was in full control and pursuing what now seem extreme rather than normal policies. Nevertheless, the about face in such a basic aspect of Chinese values may still be a useful measure of the changes in China since 1949, and of the now acknowledged excesses of the Cultural Revolution decade. And although most policy has become more rational since 1978, a general disregard for the environmental consequences of rapid industrialization remains a worrying aspect to many observers of China's contemporary development.

. . . . The most persistent and orthodox traditional view saw man as an integral part of a cosmos dominated by nature. Contentment as well as material success could come only through acceptance of the rightness of man's adjusting himself to the greater natural world to which he belonged. This was of course to some degree an attitude common to many agrarian societies elsewhere, but in traditional China it was enshrined as a central part of a philosophical and moral system. In this classic agrarian society, the Chinese saw the land and the agricultural system which made it yield as the *summum bonum,* both materially and symbolically, the source of all value and of all virtue. The bulk of imperial administration was devoted to its care, directly or indirectly, and agriculture was the support of state and society probably to a greater degree than in any other civilized tradition since ancient Egypt. The emperor's most important ceremonial function was the yearly rites at the Temple of Heaven in the capital, where he ploughed a ritual furrow and interceded with heaven for good harvests. Any farmer must be sensitive to the physical environment, even as he necessarily manipulates and alters it, but the Chinese agriculturists, or at least most of the gentry-literati who wrote about the process, were not merely aware of the vagaries of weather and climate or the properties of soils. They supported a deep respect, even a reverence, for a natural order conceived as grander than man and more to be admired. Admittedly, this frequently had didactic overtones: a man should respect and admire nature as he must respect and admire his human superiors, specifically his parents and the official hierarchy which was symbolically viewed in surrogate parental terms. The proper attitude in both cases was filial. To question or attack nature was to contradict a broader natural order, sometimes labelled "heaven" *(t'ien),* and hence was potentially disturbing to the profoundly hierarchical social order of traditional China.

It was however explicitly recognized that man was a far more active and effective agent in his relation to nature than such sentiments suggested, and implicitly acknowledged that if he were not so, state and society would have no economic base. The legendary histories of the origin of Chinese civilization glorified as culture heroes the first five emperors whose contributions were all part of the transformation of nature: the invention of fire, agriculture, animal husbandry, irrigation and flood control, and other means for man's manipulation of the environment. But in the historical period, the conflict between official theory and peasant action, like the actual conflict between man and nature, was officially and literarily repressed. Harmony must be preserved.

The Chinese have in fact altered their environment, over three millennia of close and intensive occupancy, probably on a greater scale than has been the case in any other part of the world until the present century. Harmonious adjustment, whether the peasant understood or accepted it or not, did not in practice mean inaction, as is clear from the record of Chinese land management and the manipulation of nature— irrigation, terracing, highly intensive cultivation, deforestation, and the progressive occupation of an originally difficult or resistant southern landscape. But such activities were not in doctrinal terms seen as pitting man against nature, nor as destroying a basic official or orthodox attitude of respectful stewardship, of cooperation with a natural order which could, like society, benefit man only if he accepted the limits it was seen to impose and of which he was himself a part. The enormous productivity of agrarian China must certainly have reinforced all these ideas. With the sort of stewardship, manipulative as it may have been, which the Chinese gave it, their environment became without question the most productive agricultural area in the world, until perhaps as late as 1850. It is not surprising that the society as a whole valued it, or that the official belief in the rightness of the particular harmonious system of cooperation which had been worked out was confirmed. It was a demanding environment, especially in its water balance, from a farmer's point of view and given the importance of rice in his cropping patterns, but it returned munificent rewards for the kind of sensitive attention which the Chinese lavished on it.

There is discernible in traditional Chinese poetry and philosophy, the exclusive domain of the literati, also a genuine love of nature, of the sort which has appeared only recently in the postclassical West.... The same values and images ... can ... still be seen in the pavilions for viewing nature which dot the actual landscape, designed and placed so as to maximize the rewards of gazing and meditation from an especially admired site: a lake, the moon, mountains. Mountains are a recurrent poetic and philosophical theme, used as a symbol of natural grandeur, in part because they had not been significantly altered by man, and as a welcome place of retreat where it was possible to achieve a closer touch with ultimate reality, as well as simple peace of mind, than in the hurly-burly of man's activities. The sages invariably lived in the mountains, and there tired officials would repair to restore not merely their vigor but their vision of the good and the true. Many of these attitudes can of course be read in traditional Chinese painting, so much of it portraying the natural world, where mountains sympathetically viewed are perhaps the commonest single element but where birds, animals, flowers, water, or trees, are portrayed in the same admiring context. Nature was rarely painted "in the raw," and never, as in the Western phrase "red in tooth and claw," but treated as man's other and greater self, a world seen through the eyes of a lover rather than those of an antagonist or of an alien observer.

The modern West enthroned man, and cast him in the role of the conqueror of nature. Western man, the king of creation, had indeed a duty to subdue nature, to "wrest from it its secrets," so that progress might continue through the continual assault on every present harmony to produce a better tomorrow. In China, the past was far more important than the future as the guide for present behavior. From the Chinese point of view, the ancients had developed to perfection a set of ideas and a system of action, centered on the notion of harmony in personal relations and in collective relations to man's wider context, which not only worked effectively but had raised the Middle Kingdom to the pinnacle of human greatness. It was an unargued assumption that the greatest achievements and the finest models for human action were to be found in the past; it had been all worked out long ago, specifically in the development of an agricultural system of unparalleled effectiveness which was the predominant base of China's unrivalled material greatness. Modern Western ideas of progress were totally alien, and were indeed correctly seen as implying the disruption of a harmony, with the past and with things as they existed, which the Chinese so carefully cultivated and preserved. It was perhaps understandable that agriculturists, necessarily empiricists, should seek their models in what had been proven over time, and should even believe in effect that innovation does not pay. But this in itself, given the dominance of agrarian values and the wider Chinese vision, to which it belonged, of the rightness and indeed the sanctity of the natural order, suggest a perception of the environment fundamentally different from that of the modern West.

. . . The presence of potentially rich mineral resources and the obviously high level of traditional technology did not produce a scientific or industrial revolution. This came in the end as an import from the modern West to an originally resistant China, concerned about such matters as the threatened disruption of the harmonics implicit in the doctrine of *feng-shui,* the quasi-deified spirit of a natural landscape which must be preserved from the kind of violation which railways, mines, and factories wrought. In sum, traditional China tended, by no means irrationally in the economic terms of its own time, to devalue resources which could not be made to serve agriculture, and to shield the land from other uses. Land which was not agriculturally rewarding—on the steppe margins or in the mountainous areas of the south—was conquered but not occupied by Chinese, a decision which may still make considerable economic sense. By comparison with Europe, the sea was relatively little used as a commercial resource. It was nature's most direct and obvious gift—the agricultural productivity of the soil—which was mainly prized, and which primarily shaped man's attitudes.

Nineteen forty-nine has brought an abrupt about-face. With the dialectic installed as the preeminent guide, conflict, contradiction, and struggle are seen not only as the proper condition of human society but as its most important dynamics, the chief means to the progress in which China now fervently, almost mystically, believes, as the West has begun seriously to question it with the collapse of the splendid self-confidence of the nineteenth century under the varied blows of the twentieth. Traditional Chinese patterns of compromise, adjustment, and harmony are specifically attacked. Work has become a good in itself, needing no reward beyond increased production—for someone else's brighter tomorrow. Leisure is condemned as counterrevolutionary sloth. The past is invariably "the bad old days," and its models are rejected. Nature is dethroned, and man—a confident, pioneering, creating, Communist man—put in its place. "It is man that counts; the subjective initiative of the masses is a mighty driving force." And "It is always the newcomers who outstrip the old. . . ."

As an illustration of what simple determination can accomplish, the story of the villagers of Tachai, in Shansi province, is told and re-told in the press. Tachai was a small and especially indigent mountain village, miserably exploited by landlords and with its thin, poor arable land scattered in isolated bits over slopes and ravines. The Communist Party freed the villagers from the shackles of the past, and then collectivized agriculture. "The peasants had stood up. Nature's harshness failed to dishearten the Tachai people; on the contrary, it aroused their revolutionary will to fight. They drew up a grand project to change nature. The ravines were challenged and conquered." In successive "battles," "they were beaten twice in their campaign to subjugate the Wolf's Den Ravine. (But) the undaunted Tachai people marched on the Wolf's Den again." Finally they "conquered the most stubborn obstacle nature had confronted them with. Steeled in many battles, they refused to be slaves to nature. They lived deep in the mountains, but they had never had their line of vision blocked by the Taihang peaks. . . . They said 'We want to show other people the broad future of socialism and the strength of a collective economy. . . .' They did not sit idly by waiting for the mechanization of agriculture, nor did they simply rely on government aid . . . but resolved to maintain a spirit of enterprise based on hard work." With enormous labor, the villagers converted the ravines into solid fields by constructing terraces and stone retaining walls, and levelled several hundred acres of steeply sloping land to establish a "rich grain-producing area in place of their poor mountain gullies." Tachai became a famous model, held up for villagers everywhere to emulate by developing a "Tachai spirit," becoming "Tachai men," and constructing "Tachai fields" in self-reliant attacks on nature. *Mass participation* and *local initiative,* two recurrent themes sounded in the press and exemplified in this story, are the high roads to economic growth. This is of course the spirit of the Great Leap Forward, preached in industry, in education, and even in scholarship, as in agriculture. The urgency, and the radicalism, which it manifests are related to China's sense of damaged pride over the humiliations and revealed backwardness of the century preceding 1949:

> So many deeds cry out to be done,
> And always urgently;
> The world rolls on,
> Time passes.
> Ten thousand years are too long,
> Seize the day, seize the hour!
> . . .
> Our force is irresistible. . . .

The war against the environment stems in part from two additional factors: the need which the planners see to maintain full mobilization and employment for the entire population, and the need further to dramatize the revolutionary break with the past and its acceptance of things as they are. Revolutionary ardor may cool, and underemployed agricultural workers may become restive if energies and enthusiasms are not continuously committed. One may deduce that an important reason for many projects, for example the drive during the height of the Great Leap to collect wild animal manure—or the Great Leap itself—has been to keep rural labor fully controlled and engaged. The military terminology so commonly used is an understandable part of the campaign. The war against nature, specifically contrasted in official statements with the compromise and adjustment of the bad old days, is also glorified as the gospel of the new age, the dramatic symbol of China's awakening.

As suggested at the beginning of this essay, there is no sharper discontinuity between pre- and post-1949 than in attitudes towards the natural world, and it is not strange that it should be emphasized as the essence of the revolution. The Red Guards are specifically charged with continuing the struggle against "the four olds": the old ideas, culture, customs, and habits of the degenerate past. Such a confrontation is especially clear and far-reaching between the traditional harmony with nature and new China's assault upon it; the contrast is often used as a hallmark of the revolution, a recharger of radical fervor, and a goad to greater efforts in all sectors. China's drive for national development will not be deflected by any obstacles, and will never submit to things as they are. From the point of view of the men in power, it is also important to show that something concrete is happening in the less developed countryside where over 70 percent of the people still live, as well as in the industrializing cities. As the men of Tachai have shown, conflict pays. . . .

For all of the undoubted dividends of the war on the environment, it carries with it the kinds of risks associated with totalitarian planning: decisions tend to have mushrooming consequences. Such risks are augmented by the messianic fervor which is so striking a feature of this Chinese battle, and are increased still further by the largely ineluctable decision to keep capital investment in agriculture at the barest minimum and to substitute for it with mass labor. Nature is now not only to be the servant of man, but agriculture must be the servant of industrialization. There is no denying the truly awesome force generated and channelled by the war against nature, especially in its apparent success in converting individual interests into the sacrifices of an austere campaign whose rewards are predominantly ideological or even mystical. There is more than a shadow of Calvin, Knox, and Cromwell in contemporary China, and also of the frightening *volonté générale* of Robespierre. Mountains are indeed being moved, but there is often a question whether rational economic goals are being served. The present economic margin is perilously thin, and this increases the need for optimum resource allocation. What has sometimes been described as a longstanding characteristic of both Chinese and of Communists generally, fascination with the "big gamble," may also be involved in many of the planning decisions, not only in the Great Leap. Like most gambles, these may be made out of desperation. There simply is not enough capital to support both the industrial and agricultural drive on the scale which the planners want, which China obviously needs, and which national ambition dictates. The temptation is strong to take the chance of ordering headlong assaults on both fronts and damn the risks of proceeding with bets uncovered. All of this, in a totalitarian system, multiplies the consequences of any planning errors, which may reach mammoth proportions before they can, at enormous expense, be corrected.

The most striking instances are of course the Great Leap and the over-extension of the commune system. . . . Communes in many parts of the country were ordered to grow crops for which climate or soils were unsuited or even impossible, and often their complaints were re- plied to by further exhortations to subdue nature. The commune system was also intended to advance agriculture and industrialization simulta- neously, to make steel as well as grow crops, but with little attention to technical skills, capital equipment, raw material sources, or other local conditions. The sparrows of Peking were exterminated by a frighten- ingly effective mass campaign in which crowds of people would follow every sparrow with shouts and gongs until, unable to alight, it dropped dead of exhaustion; the obvious was realized too late: the sparrows, accused of eating grain, were of course far more important as insect eaters, and local agricultural production paid for the mistake. But the Great Leap merely illustrates a continuing theme: mass participation and local initiative must make up for capital shortages, and sweep away the ifs and buts of the more rationally cautious. Agriculture must be at once squeezed and expanded, and nature transformed to pay for indus- trialization.

Mobilization of previously underemployed labor is in itself a clear gain, especially in the agrarian sector, but it may be used more or less productively—and as suggested above, sometimes counterproductively. Most of the series of mass labor projects, beginning in the early 1950s, have produced significant net benefits in purely economic terms, in addition to their revolutionary-political value. . . .

But the absolute control over labor and the momentum of the cam- paign to change nature may lead to irrational as well as rational uses. Many projects seem to be of little or no benefit, or to be accomplished at a cost, including an opportunity cost, which outweighs their value. . . . Even in China labor is not unlimited and opportunity costs have to be considered. The campaign to expand cultivated acreage in northern Manchuria and in Sinkiang, "in defiance of Western experts," is open to similar criticism. These are by any measure marginal areas; little can be done to lengthen the north Manchurian growing season or amelio- rate its soils, except at prohibitive cost; in the Tarim Basin of Sinkiang it would appear that the irrigation necessary to make cultivation possible on the amount of new farm land projected exceeds the groundwater resources of the area; soot has been scattered by plane over the ice and snow fields on the surrounding Tien Shan range in an effort to speed their melting and augment water supplies for irrigation, but this too involves a dangerous gamble, especially with the future. In China, as elsewhere, the most favorable capital/output and labor/output ratios are to be found not in the marginal areas where so much investment of both is being lavished, but in the most favored areas. This applies equally on the smaller scale of village efforts to level mountains and fill rocky ravines with soil, often transporting earth bodily to cover formerly bare or rocky areas, instead of concentrating their total resources on the raising of yields from existing better quality land. Even in terms of unaided labor, it is expensive to transform nature, when more productive labor allocations are sacrificed to less productive ones. It is perhaps not accidental that the "transformation" scheme in which the greatest amount of capital as opposed to labor investment has been made, the immense Yellow River project, where machinery, steel, and concrete were allocated, as well as armies of workers in an effort to control the river, and to produce power and expand irrigation from it, may be the most rationally conceived and planned. Capital must be distributed with care, whereas the seemingly endless supply of labor and the state's complete control over it may the more easily lead to excesses or to rash decisions. As pointed out above, the continuous commitment of labor may be an additional desideratum, and the degree of rationality of the project less important than the maintenance of momentum, the demonstration of new and exciting action against the environment instead of merely increasing the efficiency of existing cultivation. . . .

And yet the economic accomplishments since 1949, which are impressive, and the greatly accelerated and expanded pattern of resource use are not conceivable without the revolution in attitudes about man's relation to his environment, just as the re-making of Chinese society and state in the same period is inconceivable without the Communist revolution. "Let politics take command" remains the most dominant of all slogans. "Expertness" is sacrificed to "redness"; unwise planning decisions are taken and ill-conceived projects mounted. But this may be the inevitable price, or part of it, for the victory of a revolution whose power is awesome and which has been able to galvanize the Chinese people for an all-out assault on the world around them. Economic growth requires a critical momentum, made up in the last analysis of individual and collective commitment. Contemporary China does not do things by halves; if it has made short-run economic errors in some respects, its overall and long-run successes in confronting China's problems, and in creating commitment, is much more important. The immensity and the messianic quality of the crusade against nature, suspect in many instances from a Western cost-accounting point of view, does in fact move not only literal mountains and hence produce some palpable economic gains, but moves the mountain of apathy which is an even greater obstacle in most developing societies, and thus gives China what most scholars agree is a better prospect than most of breaking through the barrier of economic backwardness. China's experience may demonstrate that human drive, called into being and manipulated by an all-powerful revolutionary state, is the most vital resource of all. For all the continuities with the pre-Communist past, the sharp discontinuity in attitudes about man's relations to the physical world may be more important still. "It is man that counts. . . ." But this is not Western "economic man" and, precisely because it is not, China remains distinctive even in its search for wealth and power in the modern world.

8

Patterns of Nature and Man

R. R. C. de Crespigny

This more nuts-and-bolts selection by the Australian geographer Rafe de Crespigny, written in 1970 and hence slightly outdated in its population figures and data on petroleum resources (both have increased), is a basic factual survey. The excerpts here are part of a larger treatment; we have omitted material on soils and climate which duplicates the coverage in Fairbank, and also some more technical sections. Agriculture is still the largest sector of the Chinese economy, and this survey provides useful detail on crop patterns and their physical basis in the various regions of China, plus summary information on industrial resources. It concludes with a reminder that the huge and highly varied area that constitutes China has been unified politically only by governments which have been both strong and effective in serving national needs.

. . . . The present government in Peking now controls an area greater than any single Chinese empire of the past, and it does so through an administrative structure that owes a great deal to the institutions of its predecessors.

China south of the Great Wall, commonly referred to as China Proper, was divided in imperial times into eighteen provinces. The present government has generally continued this arrangement, excepting only the south-western province of Kwangsi, which is not an Autonomous Region, and the centrally administered metropolitan districts about the great cities of Peking and Shanghai. The territory of Manchuria in the north-east, fully incorporated to the empire by the Ch'ing dynasty, is now divided into three provinces, with equivalent organization to those of China Proper. Below the provincial organization, the local government units are counties (*hsien* in Chinese), some 1,500 through the whole country, and about 150 cities. Since 1958, administration below the county level has been controlled by communes, of which there are now some 26,000 throughout the countryside and in the cities.

Outer China, from Inner Mongolia through Sinkiang and Tsinghai to Tibet and Chambo, is administered largely by Autonomous Regions and Autonomous Districts which, like those of south-west China Proper, are established under close central control to protect the rights and interests of minority non-Chinese peoples. However, if a line is drawn from the far north of Manchuria to the Burmese border against Yunnan in the south-west, though only two-fifths of China's land area would be east of the line, the territory is inhabited by more than 90 percent of the population. The Autonomous Regions of Outer China occupy almost two-thirds of the country's area, but the minorities who comprise the bulk of their population are not more than 5 percent of the national total.

Population density in China thus varies from uninhabited regions and those with less than ten people to the square mile over large areas of Mongolia, Sinkiang and Tibet, to urban settlements with a density estimated in one district of Shanghai at well over 300,000 to the square mile. Sixteen cities—all, except Canton, in the Yangtze valley or further north-east near the coast—have a population over a million, and there are some 125 with 100,000 inhabitants or more. The total urban population is some 100,000,000, almost all in China Proper and Manchuria; Urumchi in Sinkiang, with about 350,000 people, is the largest city in the west.

One hundred million people, however, is less than 15 percent of the whole population of China, and the bulk of her people live on intensively-cultivated farmland in China Proper, with population densities perhaps even more striking than the figures for the cities. Chungming Island in the Yangtze estuary has one thousand or more people to the square mile, and some of the hill farmlands of the Yangtze basin and Kwangtung Province in the south may have figures even higher. Not even the Indian province of Bengal can compare with such dense rural settlement, and average densities over the southern coastal lands, the

Yangtze valley and North China Plain regularly exceed a thousand to the square mile.

In such a country, whose economy through history has been based on subsistence agriculture, and whose present government must still be greatly concerned with food production for increasing numbers of people, it is only to be expected that population patterns will follow those of agricultural and industrial development, which in turn are related to landform, climate and mineral resources. This essential interaction must long continue to affect the people of China and their opportunities for development....

The topography of China today is dominated by the mountain ridges running eastwards from Tibet. The effect is much like that of the fingers of a spread right hand, with the palm occupying the position of Tibet, the splayed little finger pointing south along the ridges of Yunnan towards the mountains of Laos and Vietnam, the third finger following the line of the Nan Ling south of the Yangtze, the second finger the Chin Ling Shan and its secondary extensions between the Yangtze and the Hwang Ho, and the index finger leading along the high ground of the Ala Shan, the Ordos and the Yin Shan on the north of China Proper towards the great Khingan Mountains on the borders of Manchuria and Mongolia. The hook of the thumb represents the Tien Shan ridge which separates Dzungaria and the Tarim Basin on the north of Tibet, and the east-west pattern is continued on the north of the great Gobi Plateau by the Altai, and other mountain ranges on the borders of Soviet Russia and Outer Mongolia. In the far south-east, the Wuyi Shan of Fukien run parallel to the coast, following the trend of the Cathaysian geosyncline.

Within these ridges of mountains and hills lie great plains: the Manchurian Plain in the north-east, the North China Plain, the level ground along the middle and lower course of the Yangtze Kiang and the Szechwan Basin, but further south even the lower ground is broken by hill country. The total area of China may be divided in half between the two classification groups of mountains and hills against plains, river basins and plateaux, but much of the flat terrain is represented by steppe country in Central Asia or by alpine desert in the high ground of Tibet.

China has five rivers with a length of more than a thousand miles completely within her borders, the Yangtze, the Hwang Ho, the Si Kiang, the Tarim and the Sungari, while the Liao Ho, in southern Manchuria, is nine hundred miles long. All the streams have had considerable effect on the topography of their basins, but the scouring of the Hwang Ho in the loess soil of Shensi and Shansi, and its wide deposit in an immense alluvial fan and delta, have driven back the sea, joined Shantung to the mainland, and covered connecting mountain ridges and the coal deposits of past ages with a layer of alluvium more than three thousand feet thick. In the North China Plain there is evidence of isostatic sinking, as the underlying rock strata are pressed downward by the immense weight of sediment dropped from the Hwang Ho....

Land Use and Agriculture

Following the patterns of climate and influencing those of soil, the natural vegetation of Outer China varies from the highland steppe and desert of Tibet, through the dry steppe and desert of Sinkiang and Mongolia, to the temperate grasslands and steppe of Manchuria, Loessland and the frontier region between Mongolia and China Proper. In the more settled areas of China Proper, the natural vegetation is broadleaved forest in the north, sub-tropical forest in the Yangtze valley and the south, with tropical forest in the far south and south-west, and temperate mountain forest in some of the high country of the Khingan Mountains in Manchuria, the Central Mountain Belt, and the lower ridges of the Tibetan Massif about the Chamdo Region, Yunnan and Kweichow. Almost every type of tree known in the northern hemisphere can be found in China, and the adaptable bamboo grows in the country south of the Yangtze, but save for the most inaccessible areas of China Proper the natural forest cover has been destroyed to form farmland, or waste ground with dangerous accelerated erosion. So complete is this work of man that vegetation may be best considered through the cultivation regions of rice and wheat.

In all China, fully half the area is waste, unsuitable for cultivation or for anything more than light and occasional grazing. A tenth of the land is forest, largely on the hill slopes in China Proper and Manchuria, 28 percent is useful pasturage, but only some 10 percent, about 300,000,000 acres, is cultivated. In the far north of China Proper and Manchuria, in areas with generally less than 15 inches annual rainfall, spring wheat is sown in April for harvest at mid-summer in July. In southern Manchuria and all north China as far as the Yangtze valley, winter wheat is sown in September for harvest in June. The dry climate of north China raises a hard wheat, like the Australian or Canadian, suitable for bread or for noodles. (Besides gunpowder, printing and paper, one of the less well-appreciated inventions of the Chinese is the noodle, believed to be the forerunner of Italian spaghetti and introduced to Europe through the agency of Marco Polo or some other medieval traveller.) In the Yangtze valley, where rice and wheat may be grown together, the wheat variety is softer, more suitable for cakes and biscuits.

Wheat is the predominant crop in the North China Plain. It is important in every cultivated region of north China, but a wide variety of other grains are grown as well. Millet plantings cover much the same area as those of wheat, and there is evidence from the earliest Chinese legends, which refer frequently to the god-like Prince Millet and to divination by means of millet-stalks, that millet was formerly more important. Kaoliang, which is a tall plant with a strong stalk six or eight feet high and a bushy head somewhat resembling maize, is grown chiefly in the North China Plain and southern Manchuria. The grains in the head are used for food and for animal fodder, and are sometimes fermented into wine, while the stalks are valuable for fences, walls, roofs, dam-building and for fuel. Both millet and kaoliang have the advantage of being drought-resistant, with a short growing season, and their cultivation side by side with wheat is an insurance against large-scale famine in the north.

Two crops which are grown both in the north and in the south are maize corn and soybeans. Maize is grown in a broad belt from Manchuria in the north-east to the Yunnan Plateau in the southwest, and soybeans, which can be treated to supply oil for cooking, oil for paint and soap-making and fodder for animals, is grown in almost every province, but particularly in Manchuria. Soy sauce is the common flavoring of Chinese cookery, and bean curd, frighteningly unattractive to the average Western palate, is the universal Chinese breakfast dish. In the rice-wheat region of the Hwai Ho and the lower Yangtze, barley is a useful crop, with a short growing period to harvest in May and an ability to resist wet conditions better than wheat.

Rice, however, is by far the most important single grain, with an annual production equal by weight to that of wheat, millet and kaoliang combined. To the Chinese peasant, rice is the staple grain, preferred to any other, despite claims that wheat is more valuable as a food.

Rice-growing occupies almost half the cultivated land of the whole country. South China is the major area for rice, but there are patches of rice cultivation even in the unfavorable conditions of the North China Plain and Manchuria. In most regions the growing season is from April to September, but in the far south, in Kwangtung and Fukien Provinces and on the island of Taiwan, two crops are harvested, one in June and the other in November. Besides the wheat and barley of the Yangtze valley, no other grain can compare with the dominance of rice in south China, and only sweet potatoes, introduced by the Europeans from the Philippines in the sixteenth century, have gained a strong position as an alternative food crop in the seaboard regions of Kwangtung, Fukien and Taiwan, in the basin of the Yangtze, and in the North China Plain.

Far the most common method of rice cultivation is by freshwater paddy, a system which requires intensive irrigation by a network of small canals with detailed attention to dikes. . . . One of the factors which encouraged Chinese cultural expansion from the lands of the Hwang Ho to the Yangtze valley and beyond was the ready adaptability of techniques of water control, first used to irrigate Loessland and keep the Hwang Ho within its banks, to the different but equally useful requirements of rice cultivation and the draining of marshes in the humid and tropical south. A present-day map of irrigation areas differs little from any that could be made of the past, showing flood control and irrigation works over the north of China Proper, with more intensive detail in the rice region of the south, particularly around the lakes and rivers of the Yangtze Basin, and, far out to the north-west, oasis settlement near the Ordos Region, in Kansu and in Sinkiang. Flood defenses, the corollary to irrigation, have long been established, and are now maintained and intensified along all the rivers of China Proper and Manchuria. . . .

With such great areas under cultivation and so many people to feed, China is the world's largest producer of food, holding first place in the specific grains of rice, millet, barley and kaoliang, and also in sweet potatoes, soybeans, peanuts and tea. Wheat production is close to that of the United States and the Soviet Union. Most of China's production, however, goes to feeding her own population, and calculations based on Communist statistics appear to indicate that farm production is at best only holding its own with the steady increase in population.

The grains listed above form the basic diet, supplemented as often as possible by vegetables, either grown near the houses of the people, or sometimes market gardens, or as a catch crop between the major harvests. Sweet potatoes, in particular, sown in June and harvested in November, are an important reserve of food for poorer people. Since they grow on vines spreading low to the ground, their foliage tends to keep moisture in the soil and renders them comparatively resistant to drought. In food value, however, the sweet potato is inferior to any grain, and its high moisture content can make storage difficult.

Meat is not a large part of the diet. The meat that is eaten is obtained chiefly from domestic pigs, chickens and ducks, supplemented by fish from the sea or from inland rivers, lakes and ponds. Meat, however, and the vegetable oils used for cooking, are valuable as a means of balancing a diet which would otherwise be heavily overweighted with carbohydrates. Cattle, mainly water-buffalo in the south, are used for draught animals, but there is no room in China Proper to breed them for meat. Mutton, staple food of the herding tribes in Mongolia and the northern steppe country, is regarded with distaste by the Chinese, while it is only in recent years that the value of milk has been appreciated. Some dairy herds are now maintained around the larger cities, but Chinese children are traditionally weaned on soybean curd, a rich source of vitamins, not cow's milk.

Besides these essential foods, however, several crops are grown for cash, for industrial processing and for export. Tea, which has long been used as a medicine and as a beverage, is grown chiefly in the hill territory of the Yangtze Basin, and is sold throughout the rest of the country and all over the world. Many kinds of fruit can be grown in every part of China, from the melons of the oasis regions in Sinkiang to the pineapples, bananas and mangoes of Hainan Island in the south of Kwangtung. Fruit, however, has seldom been regarded as an important crop, and it is only in recent years, both on the mainland and in Taiwan, that its value has been realized and it has been developed as a major food supplement and a crop for export. Sugar, which is grown as beet in Manchuria and the north-west, and as cane in Szechwan and the south, has long been a crop of great potential but little interest. The average annual consumption of sugar in Australia is more than 125 pounds per head, whereas in China it is 6 pounds per head, and to a Westerner, this small use of sugar is one of the most striking differences between Chinese cooking and his own. A week in the Far East on local food rapidly develops a sense of sugar starvation which can only be eased by sticky sweet buns and large quantities of fruit cordial.

Taiwan, under Japanese occupation through the first half of this century, early developed sugar-cane production and a refining industry for the export trade, and the example is now being followed on the mainland. Though all these crops except tea are outside the main tradition of Chinese diet, they are grown increasingly for export revenue, and their processing, packaging and transport supply useful employment for the cities and towns.

Industry and Communication

Among the working population of China as a whole, between 80 and 85 percent are employed in agriculture, and the processing of agricultural produce, whether for export or for home consumption, has accounted for a great proportion of industrial development. Besides the food crops described in the preceding section, three major industrial crops are cotton, silk and tobacco, and the first two of these supply textile mills in neighboring centers of population. Cotton is grown chiefly in Manchuria, the North China Plain and the Wei Ho valley in the north, and in the Yangtze valley, Szechwan, and the hill country of Yunnan in the south. Silk, which is essentially a domestic industry, has its chief centers of production among the major settled regions of southern Manchuria, the North China Plain, Szechwan, the Yangtze valley and the delta country about Canton. Tobacco is grown in some regions of Manchuria and the North China Plain, and in south China it shares the hill country with tea plantations. The island of Taiwan grows both tea and tobacco. Of the major fibrous plants, rami flax is grown thoughout the Yangtze valley, hemp is cultivated in Mongolia and the north of China Proper, and palm fibers come from the far south.

With her primary need to feed the vast population, and with the great majority of her people necessarily tied to agriculture, it will be a very long time before China's industrial and trading patterns become sufficiently developed to encourage the large-scale import of raw materials from abroad for processing and re-export. For the time being, her industrial expansion must depend on material at hand or obtainable within her own borders, and heavy industry in particular is controlled by the availability of iron ore, coal, and other sources of power.

Coal is the chief material of industrial power in China. The main centers of production are in Manchuria, near Tatung in the north, and at Kailan and Hwainan north and south of the North China Plain. There is very likely coal under all the North China Plain, but in much of the area the carboniferous rocks are deeply buried beneath the sediment laid down by the Hwang Ho. The greater part of known reserves is in north Shansi, with other important deposits in Szechwan and the southwest still largely undeveloped. Oil has been found in the west of China Proper and in Sinkiang.... [A] major field, with ancillary works, has been ... developed at Taching in Heilungkiang Province of northern Manchuria. Thermal electric power stations have been built at industrial centers throughout China, a great number of hydroelectric schemes are either planned or at various stages of completion and production, and a few short stretches of railway line, around Peking and Tatung in the north and between Paoki on the Wei Ho and Chengtu in the west, have been electrified....

Of the non-ferrous minerals, China's full reserves are not yet explored but present knowledge indicates that there are comparatively abundant supplies of those most important in present world markets. China is one of the world's largest producers of tungsten, antimony and tin, and is probably self-sufficient in bauxite, the essential raw material of aluminum, and in molybdenum. There are deposits of manganese, bauxite, molybdenum, lead, zinc and copper in southern Manchuria, but most other known reserves of all these minerals are in the territory south of the Yangtze, particularly in the Nan Ling dividing range and the high ground of Yunnan. Because of their situation, they are difficult to work and transport to processing centers, and large-scale production of aluminum, for example, will almost certainly have to wait for the introduction of cheap and plentiful hydroelectric power....

Key Economic Areas

In 1936 the Chinese scholar Chi Ch'ao-ting published a book entitled *Key Economic Areas in Chinese History,* an analysis of the succeeding dynastic empires of China in terms of their dominant areas of control and their economic encouragement of these political bases. In Dr. Chi's theory, to a large extent borne out by the evidence of Chinese texts, the earliest empires were controlled from the base region, the Wei Ho valley and Loessland, the area of the modern provinces Shensi and Shansi, but political power in north China over the centuries moved down the Hwang Ho to the North China Plain, first in the center, about Kaifeng, and later, with increasing interest in the northern borders, to Peking. In times of division, the great centers of power in south China were close to the Yangtze estuary, at Nanking or Hangchow, for this region controlled communications along the Yangtze and had a forward defense line in the north on the Hwai Ho. Szechwan in the west, a fertile plain surrounded by mountains, several times held a balance of power, but it was not until very recent times that the central Yangtze Basin about Wuhan, and the far south about Canton, developed sufficient economic and political influence to rival the other great areas.

The factors which went to establish the influence of these Key Economic Areas are still effective today, though the present century has seen the addition of the Manchurian Plain and the Canton hinterland to their number, and Loessland has long declined in economic importance. In time of peace and unity, any strong government is concerned to maintain its links of administration and supply, particularly from the Hwang Ho to the Yangtze and across the Nan Ling to the far south, but in times of war or internal division, it is upon these lines that China may separate into rival states, and in the early period of the Republic ephemeral war-lord states and their armies struggled for power among the regional fragments of the former empire. Though China may appear monolithic on the map, her unity is an achievement of good government and careful administration, and every ruler, past and present, has had to work to maintain it. One belief that is unlikely to disappear is the concept of the Mandate of Heaven, which grants no divine right to any one regime, but which expects the ruler to prove himself by his ability and service to the people, and which makes rebellion lawful and justified against government that fails.

9

Regional Urbanization in Nineteenth-Century China

G. William Skinner

All China scholars agree that regions have been and remain basically important factors in the national mosaic, and that China has been held together (most of the time) despite the counter-tendencies of its major regions, most of them larger and more populous than any European country. It remained to the anthropologist G. W. Skinner to pin down this important concept in the following short essay by defining explicitly each of the eight "macroregions" into which he divides the country, and arguing that these units make far more effective analytical tools than do the provincial administrative divisions. Most China scholars have accepted Skinner's schema for most purposes, and not only for the analysis of urbanization which is the focus of this selection.

What proportion of China's population was urban in late imperial times? The attempt made in this paper to provide an answer starts with the assumption that the question must be specified rather precisely in both time and space. On the temporal side, my concern is with the nineteenth century, and the specific objective is to develop estimates for two dates fifty years apart—1843 and 1893. On the spatial side, the position taken here is that in premodern times urbanization rates for China as a whole are very nearly meaningless and that the question should be reformulated in terms of regions.

The Regional Approach

Fairly early in my research on Chinese cities it became clear that in late imperial times they formed not a single integrated urban system but several regional systems, each only tenuously connected with its neighbors. In tracing out the overlapping hinterlands of the cities in each one of these regional systems, I came to the realization that the region they jointly defined coincided with minor exceptions to a physiographic unit. In short, it appears that each system of cities developed within a physiographic region. I eventually came to conceive of urban development—the formation of cities and the growth of their central functions—as a critical element in regional development—the processes whereby regional resources of all kinds, social and cultural as well as economic and political, were multiplied, deployed with greater effectiveness, and exploited with increased efficiency.

In imperial times regions differed from one another not only in resource endowment or potential, but also in the timing and nature of the development process. And just as each developing region was distinctive, so was the system of cities that provided its skeletal structure. Thus it is that one would expect the degree of urbanization and the very characteristics of urbanism to have varied systematically from one region to another. Accordingly, I have ordered my data on cities regionally, approached urban history in the context of regional development, and analyzed urbanization separately for each physiographic region.

First-order regional units are depicted on Maps 1 and 2. Without exception they are defined in terms of drainage basins. All regional boundaries follow watersheds (except in the few places where they cross rivers) and more often than not follow the crests of mountain ranges. . . .

Together the nine regions include virtually all of agrarian China, i.e., that part of the empire where sedentary agriculture as traditionally practiced by the Chinese was feasible. In the west, regional boundaries were defined to exclude the arid and otherwise inhospitable basins of six rivers upstream from the cutting points shown on Map 1. The Yun-Kwei region, a plateau in which virtually no rivers are navigable and all official and commercial transport moved by land, was defined to include the upper reaches of the Hung-shui (a tributary of the West River), of the Wu (a tributary of the Yangtze), and of the Chin-sha (as the Yangtze is known along its upper course) from approximately the point where each becomes unnavigable even for small junks.

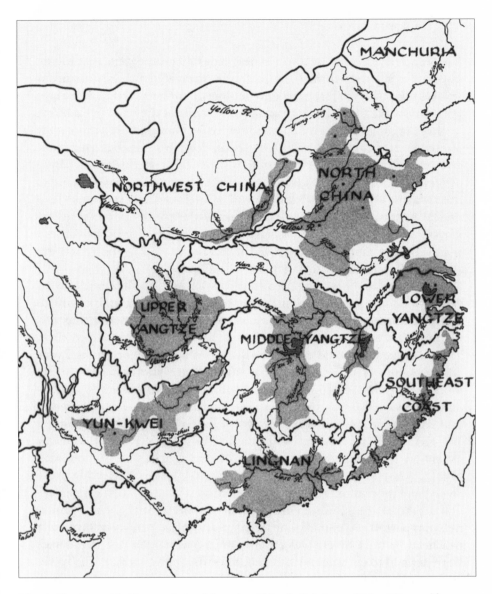

Map 1. Physiographic Macroregions of Agrarian China in Relation to Major Rivers, with Regional Cores Indicated by Shading

For the rest, regional definitions presented few problems. Lingnan is the drainage basin that includes the West, North, and East rivers. The Southeast Coast includes the basins of the myriad rivers that flow from the Wu-i Mountains to the sea. The Lower Yangtze, whose core is the fertile Kiangnan area that figures so prominently in the literature of imperial China, includes the basins of the Ch'ien-t'ang and other rivers that flow into Hangchow Bay. The Middle Yangtze region includes the great basins of four major tributaries—the Han, Kan, Hsiang, and Yüan rivers. The Upper Yangtze region has as its core the fertile Red Basin of Szechwan. Northwest China, consisting in large part of the upper basin of the Yellow River, has been extended, as is customary, to include the internal drainage systems in which the chief oases of the Kansu corridor are situated. North China includes the lower basin of the Yellow River plus the drainage areas of the Huai, the Wei, and the host of smaller rivers that cross the North China Plain.

Manchuria, the ninth region of agrarian China, is excluded entirely from my analysis. . . . The chief reason is that settlement of the region by Han Chinese got under way on a large scale only in the last decade of the Ch'ing period. Thus Manchuria was little developed by the 1890s, and its urban system was embryonic or at best emergent; the rapid changes that were to transform Manchuria into China's most highly urbanized region were all twentieth-century developments. . . .

Though the eight regions treated here are equivalent in physiographic terms, they are by no means commensurate. Table 1 shows for each the approximate area, the estimated population, and the population density as of 1843 and 1893 (1953 data are given for comparison). Regional differences in area and population were reflected in the number of cities at any given level in the urban hierarchy that were "supported" by the region's resources or, to turn it around, the number required to perform the region's central functions at a given level. For instance, from Map 2, which plots all metropolitan cities as of 1843, it may be seen that the Southeast Coast had only one such city, whereas at the other extreme North China had seven. . . .

In human geography, the term region refers to any partition of activity-space made according to one of two criteria: (l) the homogeneity of things to be considered, producing a set of *formal* or *uniform* regions; or (2) the interrelatedness of things to be considered, producing a set of *functional* or *nodal* regions. The regions just defined are of the second type, and if Map 1 appears novel to most readers it is because we are

Table 1. The Macroregions of Agrarian China, Excluding Manchuria: Areas, Estimated Populations, and Population Densities, 1843, 1893, and 1953

Macroregion	Area (sq. km.)	1843		1893		1953	
		Population in millions	Density	Population in millions	Density	Population in millions	Density
North China	746,470	112	150	122	163	174	233
Northwest China	771,300	29	38	24	31	32	42
Upper Yangtze	423,950	47	111	53	125	68	160
Middle Yangtze	699,700	84	120	75	107	92	131
Lower Yangtze	192,740	67	348	45	233	61	316
Southeast Coast	226,670	27	119	29	128	36	159
Lingnan	424,900	29	68	33	78	47	111
Yun-Kwei	470,570	11	23	16	34	26	55
Total	3,956,300	406	103	397	100	536	135

used to regionalizing China according to the homogeneity criterion, producing uniform regions about which generalizations can be made, whether the subject be soil, climate, agriculture, or ethnicity. In contrast to uniform regions, functional regions are internally differentiated and constitute systems in which activities of many kinds are functionally interrelated. In the regions of China under discussion here, cities are the nodes of the systems, the "command posts" that serve to articulate and integrate human activity in space and time.

We are now in a position to account in general terms for the fact that in each of the major physiographic regions there developed a reasonably discrete urban system, i.e., a cluster of cities within which inter-urban transactions were concentrated and whose rural-urban transactions were largely confined within the region. We start with the key fact that each region was characterized by the concentration in a central area of resources of all kinds—above all, in an agrarian society, arable land; but also, of course, population and capital investments—and by the thinning out of resources toward the periphery. . . . Ecological processes, natural as well as technological (e.g., the transfer of fertility through erosion, on the one hand, and the use of irrigation and of fertilizer, on the other), boosted agricultural production in the lowland cores. An indication of where regional resources were concentrated, Manchuria aside, is given on Map 1, where each region's area of highest population density is shaded.

It will be noted that, with the exception of Yun-Kwei, these regional "cores" are river-valley lowlands, which almost by definition had major transport advantages vis-à-vis peripheral areas. Because of the low unit cost of water as against land transport, navigable waterways dominated traffic flows in all regions except Yun-Kwei and the Northwest; and even where rivers were unnavigable their valleys typically afforded the most efficient overland routes. Thus the transport network of each region climaxed in the lowland cores, where most of the transport nodes were situated. River systems aside, the less rugged terrain of the core areas made it relatively inexpensive to build roads and canals.

For these reasons it is hardly surprising that the major cities of each region grew up in the core areas or on major transport routes leading into them, and that all cities within a physiographic region developed hierarchical transaction patterns culminating in one or more cities in the regional core.

Transactions between the centrally located cities of one region and those of another were minimized by the high cost of unmechanized transport and the great distances involved. It cost as much to transport grain 200 miles on the back of a pack animal as it did to produce it in the first place, and the corresponding figure for coal was less than 25 miles. Transport costs of this order of magnitude effectively eliminated low-priced bulky goods from interregional trade. Moreover, we have to take into account the increased expense of transport in the more rugged terrain that characterized most portions of the regional peripheries; even the most advantageous routes between adjacent regions often traversed mountain passes or hazardous gorges. It should be emphasized that systematic differences in transport efficiency affected politico-administrative and social transactions no less than commerce: interregional intercourse was depressed in all spheres.

Insofar as these general arguments can be sustained, it follows that physiographic macroregions are the proper units for analyzing urbanization. To consider units that cover only part of a macroregion is to wrench out of context a more or less arbitrary portion of a systemic whole....

These principles may be illustrated with reference to provinces. Map 2 shows nineteenth-century provinces in relation to physiographic regions. Though provincial boundaries run fairly close to regional

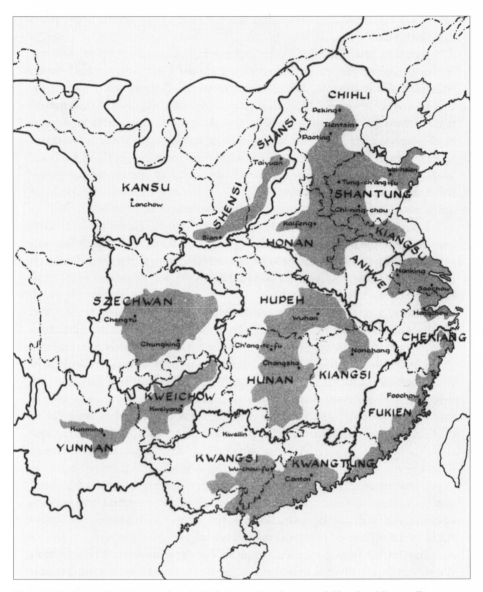

Map 2. Physiographic Macroregions in Relation to Provinces, and Showing Metropolitan Cities, 1843

boundaries in several important stretches, even the closest fits—Szech-wan with the Upper Yangtze region, Kwangsi and Kwangtung with the Lingnan region—are grossly imperfect. Several provinces lie directly athwart regional boundaries, the most striking cases being Shensi, Shansi, Anhwei, Kiangsu, Chekiang, and Kweichow. Thus, it is metho-dologically indefensible and generally misleading to compare provincial urbanization rates, for the explanation of differences found is a func-tion not of what the characteristics of the provinces as systems were but simply of how the boundaries happened to be drawn. . . . Urbanization aside, it is simply inefficient to describe spatial variation in China's ur-banism in terms of provinces. The only way to go about making an accurate description of cities in Chekiang, or Anhwei, or Kiangsu would be to start with the basic regional dichotomy within the province and to repeat the ways in which one part of the province more closely resem-bles the adjacent portions of neighboring provinces than it does the other part. One can specify in the descriptions of Honan, Shensi, Kweichow, Kwangsi, and so on that a certain portion of each province falls within the maximal hinterland of the Wuhan conurbation, but the ultimate significance of these facts is lost when they are presented sepa-rately in provincial context.

Let me adduce, finally, two important reasons why a dynamic ap-proach to urbanization and urbanism requires separate analysis by re-gions rather than aggregate treatment by the empire as a whole. One is that the major catastrophes that have punctuated Chinese history, the late imperial era included, were almost always limited in scope. Disas-trous floods were particularly frequent in the lowland cores of North China and the Middle Yangtze. Disastrous droughts affected Northwest and North China more severely than other regions. Invasions from Inner Asia repeatedly laid waste North and Northwest China, whereas regions in the Yangtze Valley and farther south rarely suffered compa-rable depredations. Internal disturbances seldom wreaked havoc in more than one or two regions at a time. Chang Hsien-chung's rebellion in the 1640s, which had only minor repercussions in the Northwest and the Middle Yangtze, seriously disrupted the Upper Yangtze region and precipitated a sharp population decline there. The Taiping Rebellion in the 1850s and 1860s affected primarily the Lower Yangtze region and the Kan basin in the Middle Yangtze region. The Moslem rebellions in the 1860s and 1870s were limited to Yun-Kwei and the Northwest.

Other uprisings during late imperial times were for the most part even more narrowly localized.

The second reason for eschewing an empirewide approach to urbanization, ironically enough, is that critical decisions by the *imperial* court typically induced or retarded cycles of *regional* rather than empire-wide development. The shift of the imperial capital from Ch'ang-an to Kai-feng at the beginning of Northern Sung marked the onset of devolutionary decline in the Northwest even as it accelerated the regional development of North China. The selection of Hangchow as the Southern Sung capital affected development primarily within the Lower Yangtze region. The monopoly of overseas trade granted Canton in 1757, which accelerated development in the Lingnan region, doomed the economy of the Southeast Coast to nearly a century of stagnation.

Thus, despite a general tendency for the upswing phases of regional development to coincide with the dynastic heyday and for the downswing phases to coincide with dynastic decline and interdynastic disruption, the development cycles of the various regions had their own distinctive rhythms. The relevant point here is that cycles of economic development and decline, of urban development and devolution, and of population growth and reversal within each region were closely interrelated. We can define a more developed regional economy as one in which areal specialization in production, a differentiated occupational structure, and a hierarchical system of credit supported a coordinated network of intraregional trade, and in which prevailing levels of technology were translated through myriad cumulative investment decisions into region-wide social-overhead construction (roads, bridges, canals, dikes, and irrigation works). Such achievements were inseparably intertwined during the upswing of regional cycles with population growth and urban development—i.e., with growth in the size of particular cities, with the rise of new central places, with the development of hierarchical patterns in intercity transactions, and with increased centrality at all levels. Whereas the upswing of a regional cycle invariably saw progress toward a more integrated urban system, the effects of the downswing on the urban system were of variable severity, ranging from a mere slowing of growth as intercity transactions were restructured to the physical destruction of the cities and of the transport infrastructure on which their integration depended. Thus the history of each region was marked by distinctive cycles that affected both the total population and the urban population, i.e., the numerator as well as the denominator of the urbanization formula.

10

City as a Mirror of Society

Rhoads Murphey

Although China, past or present, falls far short of modern Western levels of urbanization, the city has played a critically important role throughout Chinese history, and does so now in a new context. Incorporating the geographer's concern with spatial patterns and the human imprint on the landscape, the following excerpts from a somewhat longer essay trace the changes in urban roles, functions, and values from traditional to contemporary times. As a "mirror of society," the Chinese city has indeed reflected faithfully the changing values, trends, and goals of the larger whole. The city itself is now the chief center of modern change; in it are thus concentrated many of the problems and tensions, as well as the potentials for growth, which characterize China as it strives to achieve "modernization" by the end of this century.

The Traditional Chinese City

The traditional-imperial Chinese city lasted, essentially unchanged, well into the present century in many parts of the country; many of its outlines are thus still observable, in Peking of course, but also in former capitals such as Sian, in other provincial centers which were never part of the treaty-port system (for example, Chengtu, Kunming, Taiyuan), and even in most of China's other cities, where the foreign treaty-port imprint was merely grafted onto a traditional urban base which continued to function as before. These traditional cities were primarily centers of imperial authority imposed in a uniform plan on a varied landscape, symbolic monuments of the power and majesty of the Chinese state and of Chinese culture over which it presided. Functionally, they were in most cases predominantly agents of the imperial bureaucracy; directly or indirectly, the largest sector of the urban workforce was employed in that administrative enterprise. This workforce included officials, clerks, scribes, garrison troops, teachers of the classics to aspirant generations of examination candidates, merchants employed by the state in the management of official monopolies of trade or manufacture, artisans whose output went predominantly to the offices and households of all the foregoing, and the vaster army of shopkeepers, coolies, servants, transport workers, butchers, bakers, and candlestick makers, whose service livelihood depended on the city's basic industry, which was most importantly administration. All of these cities included also a commercial and a manufacturing function, apart from the official and state-run monopolies in salt, iron, copper, weapons, tax or tribute grain, and foreign trade. In a few, these functions were more important than official and administrative functions, but in none above the level of local market town was the hand of the state not apparent, or its business not prominent.

The imperial bureaucratic imprint reached down the urban hierarchy to the level of the county seat (or its equivalent)—the capital of the administrative district, called the *hsien*; the population of the *hsien* as a whole averaged (very roughly) about 200,000 (with considerable temporal and regional variations), while that of the *hsien* capital city might average perhaps 10,000–15,000.[1] In most *hsien*, the capital would be the only real city; in other, more commercialized parts of the country, for example the lower Yangtze valley, there might be one or more as well.

But the *hsien* capital was nearly always the largest, and the only base for the official bureaucracy. There the imperial magistrate, through his court and assistants, was officially responsible for everyone and everything in the *hsien*, but in practice it was not possible to carry out close administration of so large a population, the great majority of it rural-agricultural, in an area (again a possibly misleading average) roughly

---

1. Averages are, as usual, misleading, and especially for a country the size of China over a 2000-year period, not to mention the grossly approximate nature of the population data, but it may be worth giving these estimates as at least a gesture toward fixing a scale. The average *hsien* population in Han times was probably closer to 50,000 and, by late Ch'ing, with a national total three or four times greater, about 300,000.

equivalent to an eastern American county. Unofficial, but often powerful, local gentry and peasant village elders or clans managed the bulk of rural, and hence of *hsien*, affairs. It was a closely ordered society, but not as any direct result of intervention by the bureaucratic state. Although "the emperor (was) far away," in the traditional peasant assertion of independence from imperial control, as, for all practical purposes, was his vicar, the magistrate, in the *hsien* capital, the combined force of family, clan, gentry, and nearly universally accepted Confucian morality kept order remarkably well in what we may call a largely self-regulating society.

But the *hsien* capital played a crucial *symbolic* role in insuring such an outcome, not least through its institutional and iconographic assertion of the Confucian virtues of order, and its manifestation of the state power which, however symbolically, supported that order. All *hsien* capitals were walled, the feature which instantly distinguished them from other lesser urban centers, and were planned in detail. The walls were as imposing as the rank and size of the city dictated, but in every case were designed to awe and affirm, only secondarily to defend, although of course they might be useful in troubled times. The Chinese word for *city* means also *wall,* further underlining the urban function as a symbol of power and of the concentration of authority. City walls were built in a regular and consistent pattern, with great gates at each of the cardinal compass points from which broad, straight avenues led to the opposite gate. These, of course, intersected in the middle of the city, where there was a ceremonial center with a plaza, a drum tower, a cluster of official buildings (including the magistrate's offices and court), or a Confucian temple. The major streets, fixing the main axes of the gridiron pattern, divided the city into major quarters, which were sometimes also enclosed by their own walls, whose gates, like the city's main gates, were closed at night. Each quarter tended to be functionally specific: transport termini, warehouses, and commercial offices or banks in one sector, retailing (often segregated by street according to commodities) in another, manufacturing in another, and others for academies, universities, booksellers, theaters, the military establishment and its garrison troops, public food markets, and so on. Most people lived in the same structures which housed their work activities, and within each quarter there were regular lanes organized into neighborhoods, a system often used for the control of urban populations. The emphasis, as in the ideology of the Confucian state, was on order and on planned management.

Most cities were founded explicitly by the state, as centers of imperial control, although occasionally (especially in the early imperial period under the Han), a pre-existing urban center of trade might be designated as an administrative center, and provided with the planned monumental accoutrements. But the imperial imprint was unmistakable in all walled cities, and in their striking uniformity as part of a master plan, imposed on the landscape for the creation of order. . . . While the *hsien* city was, of course, the commonest, it reflected, on a smaller scale, the superior hierarchical models of the provincial and national capitals, whose managerial and cosmic roles were exercised over progressively larger spheres, until, in the case of the imperial capital, it encompassed "all under heaven," the name by which the Chinese called their empire and its surrounding, but far lesser, tributary states. Within each *hsien*, the capital city was usually located near the middle of the territory, whose areal size varied (naturally enough) inversely with the density of population, but which was ideally designed as much as possible so as to constitute a coherent geographic region of trade, production, and movement. Where the physical landscape and population density permitted, this might be a stream watershed or confluence region, or a basin surrounded by hills. The capital city was responsible for the defense as well as administration of the *hsien* as a whole, and not merely with the defense of its own walled base. It was truly a *center,* not an isolated or discrete intrusion.

This, in turn, was related to the perceived relationship between city and countryside. Traditional China was an overwhelmingly agrarian society; there was no question as to what the source of wealth was, including the means for the support of the state and its apparatus. Cities were designed to control and tax the countryside, but more importantly to serve it, as the basic reason and sustenance of their existence. Trade and merchants flourished in all Chinese cities, but most commodities were of agricultural or rural origin. The primary responsibility of officials was to ensure the productivity as well as the orderliness of the agricultural countryside, since it was this which sustained the empire, its power, its cultural grandeur, and its bureaucratic structures. . . . The close interdependence of city and countryside was far more explicitly recognized, and indeed welcomed, in China than elsewhere. In the West, in particular, when commerce and later manufacturing became proportionately important, the symbiotic tie between rural and urban worlds tended to be obscured, or even forgotten. New classes arose in cities—which, of course, is what the word *bourgeoisie* means; they and the new class of urban proletariat became divorced from the rural context, as different kinds of people with different goals and values. They often scorned rural people as "hicks," or regarded them merely as servants of the city, providers of food, raw materials, or cheap labor. The city, as our word for it suggests, *was* civilization, the mover and shaker—the maker of the modern world.

In China, there was no such split between urban and rural worlds, and no place in either traditional or contemporary China (despite its avowed Marxism) for Marx's mirroring of Western attitudes in his contempt for the "idiocy of rural life." Urban elites may often have exploited the rural sector, but it was universally recognized that the city's chief function concerned the services it provided for the good ordering and productivity of the countryside which fed it, both literally and metaphorically. The state's predominant source of revenue, the land-and-grain tax, was in effect sustained by urban-based elite investment, and management of irrigation and water-control projects, roads and waterways, the dissemination of improved techniques, and the protection of rural areas from disorder. The intensive hand agriculture of traditional China, especially wet-rice agriculture with its heavy cumulative investment in dikes, terraces, and irrigation projects, required consistent order, and organization, to remain as highly productive as it was. The same was true of the social system, with its orderly stress on "right relations" throughout its hierarchy, and on the companion Confucian precept of model behavior. Disorder—chaos, absence of officially sanctioned and enforced rules (all incorporated in the Chinese word *luan*)—was seen as the greatest evil to be prevented, an effort in which urban and rural areas worked together for a recognizable common good.

Urban elites were drawn in the first instance, in each new generation, as much from the countryside as from the cities, and retained close ties with their rural origins. There was a continuous flow of people moving in both directions, officials in the course of their duties or on furlough or retirement, and rural recruits moving into the commercial or bureaucratic world of the city. There was no denigration of rural circumstances and values, but rather, on the part of many of the urban elite, a longing for the countryside, to which they would retreat whenever they could, and to which they almost invariably retired—a theme prominent in Chinese poetry, as in these lines from the Sung poet-official Su Tung-p'o (although, in this version, really from Arthur Waley):

> Layered blue hills make a ring where the brook runs east.
> On a white moonlit sandy shore a long legged heron roosts;
> And this is a place where no dust comes.
> [Dust was the accepted symbol of cities and bureaucracy.]
>
> An old man of the stream says to himself:
> What is your little reason for wanting so much to be a bureaucrat?
> You have plenty of wine and land—
> Go on home to your district, enjoy your share of leisure.

The rural sector was recognized as the source of at least as much wisdom and virtue as the city: Su Tung-p'o was by no means alone in his view, nor was it limited simply to the admiration of nature. The Chinese record is full of conscientious officials or members of the rural gentry, whose careers centered on maintaining and enhancing rural prosperity, and who found rural virtues more important than urban. As an imperial official in the mid-seventeenth century put it:

> Goodness develops only in the village, evil in the city. The city is the place of commerce and trade. People relate to one another only with the aim of making profits. They are superficial and pretentious. As a result, the city is a sink of iniquities. The village is different. These people are self-reliant and have deep emotional ties with each other.

Rural people were better attuned to the world of nature and its rhythms, and therefore better understood the universe and man's place in it. Especially in Confucian logic, this gave them a better moral character and a simple goodness. In the cities, where people disregarded nature, truth was clouded and virtue weakened. Only the continual interchange with the countryside kept the city viable. The great sages did not live in cities, nor did the happiest people. The Chinese version of the good and the true had a strongly rural, even anti-urban, bias. . . . The remarkably high degree of social mobility characteristic of traditional China, whereby something like a third of the gentry-literati group in each new generation were people from originally humble (dominantly rural) origins who had passed the imperial examinations, continued to inject rural people and rural values into the urban world. Rank could not be inherited; the openness of the system had no doubt a lot to do with its long survival, and, for the present point, with its continued reaffirmation of the importance of the rural base for all cities.

Change was not, of course, absent in the long span of 2000 years of imperial Chinese history. But, especially after about the twelfth century, it was not primarily focused in cities, which instead were seen as presiding over the "Great Harmony," a persistent Chinese ideal in which disruptive change was to be minimized, all groups worked together for the common good, and cities served the countryside as part of a single symbiotic order. What pressures there were for change came far more often from rural areas, as protests against arbitrary city-based power, or the exploitative accumulation of urban wealth at the expense of peasants, as corruption and self-seeking became more prominent in the last decades of each dynasty. The rural areas were often seen as the base for correcting the excesses of the city, including the overthrow of urban-based power which often had significant peasant or rural origins. Urban merchants, the spearhead of change in the early modern West, were, in traditional China, too closely involved with and nurtured by the official system to fight against it. . . .

Cities were centers of action in great variety, but in general not of institutional change, which indeed their major efforts were directed toward preventing. They were splendid places, probably the most splendid in the world, as well as the largest and richest, as Marco Polo tried to persuade an unbelieving Europe, which nicknamed him "Millione," a Venetian Baron Munchausen. By the nineteenth century, when Westerners could again travel more or less freely around China (and were able to confirm what were reported to be Polo's dying words to a confessor anxious to relieve his soul of the burden of all those "lies": "I have not told the half of what I saw"), China's now more tarnished cities were no longer so impressive in the heady context of Western industrialization and the booming, though different, splendor of merchant capitals in London, Paris, Berlin, Hamburg, and New York. By then, the whole of the traditional Chinese system was in deep trouble. Cities increasingly became targets of rural outrage, as in the great Taiping Rebellion from 1850 to 1864, which nearly toppled the dynasty, and in many subsequent uprisings. The cities were no longer able to keep agricultural output in pace with population increases, nor to maintain order. . . . Trade and, later, manufacturing increased their proportional shares of the economy, and created some new rich, based in now rapidly growing cities, including the new treaty ports, but the lot of peasants and rural areas deteriorated, until, by the twentieth century, there were many areas of severe suffering, chronic disorder, and periodically catastrophic famine.

The Western Presence

The almost 40 years which have elapsed since the Pacific War, the end of Western colonialism in East Asia, and the rise of a new, dynamic, and unmistakably Chinese revolutionary order, have given us new perspectives on the short period of Western dominance in Asia. Briefly, it no longer seems so important, in the context of the modern world or that of the far longer span of Chinese history. As we can now (with the wisdom of hindsight) survey the scant century of the China treaty ports, they appear more clearly as specks on the far vaster, and far more significant, Chinese landscape.... The treaty ports were seen by their Western masters as beachheads, agents of the transformation of China into a Western likeness through the yeasty power of the commercial and industrial revolutions which had made the West the arbiter of the modern world. The treaty ports were indeed explicitly referred to as "model settlements," and it was expected that their example would of itself convince China to follow the Western path toward wealth and power, rejecting its own clearly inferior and "backward" tradition. Surely no one would *choose* to remain "backward" once he had been exposed to the advantages of railways, power-driven factories, joint stock companies, modern banking, Western medicine, Western learning—and, of course, Christian/Victorian morality, whose superior virtues were plain in their association with the unquestionably superior *success* of the post-1850 West. All of this was consciously encapsulated in the treaty ports. Altogether, about 100 Chinese cities were classified as treaty ports, although less than a dozen (primarily, of course, the biggest coastal or riverine ports) were or became major centers of foreign trade or of foreign involvement and presence. They did acquire the dominant share of China's expanding foreign trade, and of the newly developing industrial sector, and they also attracted as they grew large numbers of Chinese, who remained the overwhelmingly dominant inhabitants of all the treaty ports.

The foreigners hoped that these included a new kind of Chinese, quick to follow Western ways (as the Meiji Japanese had been), and hence to fulfill the treaty-port goal of transforming China in the Western image. These treaty-port Chinese, although a tiny minority within the country, were indeed apt pupils. By the twentieth century, they owned the largest share of treaty-port factories, founded Western-style banks and steamship lines, lived (many of them) in Western style, and formed the most important wing of the new Nationalist Party, the Kuomintang, which at least in part was committed to more such Western-style modernization. Foreign control in the treaty ports also meant that many dissident Chinese, including outright revolutionaries, fled there for refuge from official persecution, and these cities became the main centers of new intellectual ferment. Those who lived in the treaty ports, and were most directly exposed to this challenge to China, were concerned about their country's weakness, its inability to resist foreign pressures, and its technological underdevelopment compared with the modern West or Japan. In the political sanctuary of the treaty ports, they groped for solutions, goaded by the arrogant example of Western success; it was there that the ultimately successful movement was founded for the overthrow of the old dynasty in 1911, and there that Chinese nationalism, in the Western sense, was born, primarily as a reaction to the humiliation of foreign imperialism. The Chinese Communist Party was founded in Shanghai, the biggest treaty port, in 1921, by a group of revolutionaries convinced that China could never be strong again without radical change, but also determined to resist, and eventually to expel, the foreign model in the treaty ports and all it stood for.

The treaty ports offered an alternative model, as Western-style commercial/industrial centers totally different from traditional Chinese cities, where private enterprise and property protected from state control were enshrined, and where traditional Chinese values were stood on their heads. It was a positive model for its demonstration of new technological power, and of wealth for a few, but a deeply negative and bitter one in its affront to Chinese pride. Most of the treaty-port Chinese were not wealthy entrepreneurs, but poor and exploited workers; all treaty-port Chinese were subjected to foreign racism and discrimination—in their own country. Those who profited from the new business conditions in the treaty ports were cut off by their own careers from their traditional roots, and committed to a new and foreign kind of world. Conservatives and radicals alike called them simply traitors, running dog collaborators with the alien forces who were destroying the soul and nibbling at the body of China. The treaty ports never built effective ties with the vast rural hinterland of China, most of which was negligibly affected, except to drain a few goods from it for export abroad, to foreign profit. . . . These cities meant alienation, humiliation, slums, pollution, a new group of urban poor, and foreign control, not "progress." Most of China was materially unchanged by a century of vigorous treaty-port efforts and increasingly shrill preaching, in part because its rural mass, larger than Europe or the United States, was simply too huge to be moved by marginal foreign contact in a few spots on the coast; and partly because the treaty-port formula, born and bred in the urban-commercial West, was profoundly unsuited to China's very different circumstances and needs; most of all perhaps, it was *foreign,* and the deep Chinese pride, buttressed by millennia when China led the world, could not and did not accept it.

The Communist Revolution and After

China remained, as it has always been and still is, a peasant country. Its body, if not its soul, was now seriously sick, but any successful treatment would have to recognize that most of that body was rural, to identify the main problems and find solutions to them there. The treaty ports were important only as a goad—and as a counter-example. China now badly needed new technology, but not through their agency or through their kind of city. In the end, it was a *peasant* revolution, based in the countryside and reaffirming peasant and rural virtues, values, needs, and goals, whose peasant armies won power *against* the cities, and celebrated their victory in Shanghai as in Peking in 1949. Communist-led uprisings in several cities in the 1920s had failed, wiped out by the superior forces of the Kuomintang, whose major bases were in the treaty ports. The industrial proletariat, key to revolution in the Soviet model which the Party tried to follow, were too few, but in any case were unwilling to join the struggle, apparently corrupted beyond redemption by the bourgeois setting of the treaty ports, or with their supposed revolutionary vision blurred by that contamination. Defeated, almost annihilated, in the cities, the communists retreated to the countryside, where, under Mao's leadership, they built a political base among the peasants, who had not been exposed to the corruption of cities or treaty ports. Here was the *real* China, largely untouched by alien influences. Only in the countryside could a genuinely *Chinese* answer to the Western challenge, and a *Chinese* solution to the country's problems, be generated. . . .

Having won political power, with so clear and bitter an anti-urban legacy, the new government's early efforts were directed to deemphasizing the cities—especially the former treaty ports which accounted for nearly all of the large cities—attempting to reduce their size, and to remake them in the socialist image. . . . At the same time, new cities, of the approved sort, had to be built in the rest of the country as necessary bases for the urgently needed economic and technological development of China, most of which had been touched hardly at all by what had happened in the treaty ports.

How well has a revolutionary China succeeded with these goals? In the first flush of revolutionary success, there was talk of actually dismantling much of the industrial structure of Shanghai, and other major treaty ports, so as to build new inland centers, but it was soon realized that development depended on the fullest and most efficient use of the existing base. The development of inland and rural China, and the construction of new industrial cities there, could come only with the help of the former treaty ports, and it made little sense to dismantle them, or to starve them of new investment. However, the largest share of new investment went to the growth of industrial centers in the formerly neglected inland areas, some of them older cities which were now transformed (Loyang, Sian, Lanchow, Chungking, Kunming, all in the neglected west), some wholly new establishments keyed to newly discovered local resources: the steel city at Pao T'ou in Inner Mongolia, the oil city of Ta Ch'ing in northern Manchuria, or the industrial complex at Urumchi in distant Sinkiang. These, and especially the new centers, were extolled as models, socialist cities of socialist man. At the same time, the former treaty ports were used to provide the skilled labor, technicians, and much of the equipment and high-technology components for these new cities, while their own growth was restricted. Shanghai, by far the largest city, was apparently actually reduced in size, through controls on in-migration and the assignment of Shanghai workers to rural or inland urban jobs. Although all other older cities have grown, and especially Peking, as the national capital, with its immense new administrative responsibilities in this planned economy, there has been some success in controlling urban "giantism," as it is called. In a country of about a billion people, there are probably only about 25 million-class cities, and probably only six of those are over 2 million, all, except for Peking, major former treaty ports: Shanghai, Tientsin, Shenyang (Mukden), Wuhan, and Canton.

If it has thus not proved possible to reduce the *absolute* size of these and other former treaty ports (except for Shanghai), their *relative* urban dominance has certainly been reduced as inland centers have grown disproportionately, and have at least begun to correct the lopsided spatial pattern of manufacturing. And if this must be judged only a qualified success in terms of early goals, it looks far more impressive in the context of urbanization in the developing world as a whole. There, in India, South-east Asia, Africa, the Middle East, and Latin America, the growing pains of urban-centered change seem mirrored most sharply in what is often called "over-urbanization," a term poorly defined and quite possibly misleading, but clear enough in its commentary on the urban scene: gross overcrowding, high unemployment, inadequate housing, sewage facilities, transport, water supply, schooling, health services, and other basic minimum support for millions who live in shanty towns or slums, on the edge of an urban promised land to which they are still denied entry.... This was ... the nature of urbanization in the developed world too, in the course of the nineteenth and early twentieth centuries, and there is nothing surprising about it. We forget, with the short historical memories of Americans in particular, what life in New York and Chicago in the 1880s was like for most of their inhabitants, even if we still understand their attraction nevertheless for farm boys from Vermont or Iowa. Urban conditions were probably worse then than in contemporary Calcutta, Djakarta, Lagos, or Lima, judging from accounts of each or from life-expectancy figures. But the waste and suffering of humanity in the often squalid cities of the modern developing world now are undeniable. China has paid a heavy price in minimizing such problems through controlling the growth of its cities;[2] perhaps it has been worth it? One cannot measure the human cost of the controls on travel, employment, housing, and consumer goods which have kept Chinese cities from the extremes of unplanned growth.

What one can see more clearly, especially now that some of the control measures have been eased a little, is that most Chinese, too, despite the official extolling of rural and peasant virtues and priorities, would choose the urban alternative. Those "sent down" earlier from the

---

2. Hardly preventing; they are present in Chinese cities too.

cities to the countryside are massively unhappy and try to use any means to return. It is all very distressing to those, Chinese and outsiders, who found and still find the Maoist vision inspiring: build the new China squarely on its peasant base, get rid of the poison of the cities, "take agriculture as the foundation," and transform the rural body of China through diffusing new industrial technology to it, in the service of the great rural majority. This was to be done not only by dispersing urban industrial centers through each province (as has largely been accomplished), but by bringing modernization and industrialization to the countryside, in small-scale local production units in the rural communes. It was an idea which many people found appealing, an alternative to the undoubted evils of the Western model of industrial concentration in a few big cities with their special privilege, corruption, alienation, pollution, de-humanization, and drearification of life. Instead of depending on technical and professional elites in the big cities, and the unsatisfactory process of "trickle-down," especially for a country as huge and as rural as China, get rid of elitism (something which traditional China had notoriously suffered from), and let the peasants be their own modernizers, technicians, and industrialists. This would also produce development immediately where it was most needed, rather than continuing to concentrate it in the already developed cities. Such a minutely dispersed pattern would also avoid the problems of cities, the pollution, the alienation, the particularism and selfishness, and would at the same time achieve the twin Maoist goals: remove the differences between city and countryside, and between mental and manual labor, peasants and urbanites.

However inspiring this vision, it has run into increasing practical trouble. The problems of economic development are tough, much the same everywhere, and cannot really be solved by slogans or revolutionary fervor. The small-scale rural industrial plants, which at one time produced perhaps half of China's cement and fertilizer and important shares of total output of iron and steel, electric power, and consumer goods, proved, in nearly all cases, to be far more expensive in unit costs than large urban-based plants, and also made much less efficient use of scarce materials. In the end it seems to have been recognized, as now, that China simply cannot afford high-cost development strategies, whatever their political, revolutionary, or just plain human appeal. Small-scale commune-based industry will probably remain, but as a shrinking proportion of national industrial output and increasingly as a symbolic gesture. Agriculture is still (rightly) given priority, but it will have to depend on large urban-based factories for fertilizers, pumps, cement, tools, and equipment—as it will have to depend on urban-based research centers and agro-technicians ("experts") to develop and diffuse the improved crop strains which form the other vital component of the drive to raise output. Far from eliminating the elite, or putting more stress on "redness" than on "expertness," China is now obliged to acknowledge, increasingly openly, that urban elites and experts are essential to successful development, and to planning and management. . . . China is a poor country, and the urgency of development for a billion people is too great to permit the luxury of any other goals which work against maximum economic rationality, as the Maoist vision, however inspiring, clearly does. . . .

Nor does the implanting of modern industrialization on the commune, and the development of new peasant "experts," remove the differences between city and countryside. Rural work is still hard, and the excitement and variety of urban life are missing. There is just no way to create on the communes the equivalent of the city's world. Even in immediately practical terms, rural wages are about half the urban average, and living standards, including health and education facilities, correspondingly lower. In the cities, there is a far wider range of career opportunities, and the possibility of upward mobility which is, it seems, as appealing to Chinese, despite the Maoist vision, as to anyone else. . . . These are all more than sufficient reasons for the pressures for urban migration long held in check by controls, and for the efforts especially of urban youth to avoid rural assignment. With the degree of political relaxation since 1978 (far from complete), more and increasingly vigorous protests against these and other devices to limit upward and centripetal mobility have been voiced. In these terms, China is sitting on a powder keg, re-encouraging education and post-high-school training with one hand, with its built-in expectations of upward mobility in an urban focus, and with the other trying still to prevent runaway urban growth and to curb the manifestations of new expert-based and urban-centered elitism. . . .

What can be salvaged of the original vision? Will China's growing cities become just like those in the West, or in the rest of the developing world? That is surely too pessimistic. There may be no cheap or quick rural-based alternative to the Western model of industrial development concentrated in cities, for all its dreadful flaws, but, for a long time to come, China will remain a dominantly peasant society, and a genuinely revolutionary one, even as the sharp edges of radicalism soften or are adjusted to pressing economic realities. The Maoist vision will continue to inspire, and, even as symbol or lip service, will go on affecting policy and behavior. Its formula for China is too apt, too closely rooted in China's history and circumstances, and too ideologically appealing to even a nominally revolutionary country, to be wholly discarded or ignored. There is little attraction for China, especially with its immense traditional and now revolutionary pride, in becoming merely a second-class and belated follower after a flawed Western model. If China can no longer lead the world as it did for so long, at least it can offer a distinctive new path, one forged in the Chinese context, perhaps a model for other developing societies, but in any case never just an inferior echo of the West. Technology can be decultured, but its application and its urban bases must fit both China's circumstances and her ideological goals. At the least, those goals, changing over time as they may, but necessarily different from those of other societies, are certain to make an impact on policy, planning, and implementation, especially in so politically conscious and controlled a society as China's. There seems no chance that "free enterprise" Western style will, in the foreseeable future, play any major role in shaping China's development, as opposed to planning in a socialist context.

The cities will play a far more important role in that development than the Maoist formula provided, and the greatest challenge may therefore be changing and controlling their *nature,* limiting their bourgeois character, preventing at least the excesses of elitism, ensuring that their growth and functions serve the needs of the country as a whole (primarily rural), and curbing the other evils of urban concentration (pollution, overcrowding, alienation, and so on) by continued careful management. . . . There is not space here to discuss the details of urban planning in China, or the partially successful efforts at spatial re-ordering and rationalization of both older and new cities, but enough has been accomplished to suggest, that, in these respects too, Chinese cities will remain distinctive, and that the effort will continue to make them into cities for "socialist man."

However, the greatest problem may well be what happens to people and their values, as more of them live in cities, and as urban-centered development gathers momentum. Mao was right to identify what he saw as the corrupting qualities of cities and of urban-based elitism as the greatest of all threats to his revolutionary vision. Already, urban people, a privileged minority, live better than rural people, the peasant heroes of revolution who comprise 80 percent of the population. Urbanites use "connections" to advance their status, and to ensure status opportunities for their children. They are in the forefront of the new consumerism, perhaps the greatest single contradiction to revolutionary goals. Urban department stores (but not rural communes) sell a wide variety of consumer goods, many of them nonessential luxuries—watches, cameras, radios, even TV sets; demand far outruns supply, and status is increasingly demonstrated by possession of scarce consumer items. Now there are even hairdressing establishments and fancy clothing stores in the bigger cities. Can the revolution survive such trends? In the face of them, how far can the state continue to hold the lid on migration to the cities? Americans are the *last* people to comment critically on other people's addiction to consumerism, and one must recognize that people everywhere are pretty much the same: they want a better life, and they tend to define that mainly in terms of more goods and services—in some ways, the more nonessential, the better to demonstrate their material success. Urban Chinese are now behaving in these respects like the rest of us, and like upwardly mobile urban Indians, or Africans, or Latin Americans.

But Chinese society will remain distinctive, and so will the cities it builds and shapes. The forces generated by economic change, and the urgency of development, are indeed in many respects in conflict with China's revolutionary or ideological goals. But is there a society anywhere which is not ridden with such conflicts, or where economic forces are not frequently at war with supposed political or moral values or objectives? Of course not, but this does not mean that all societies are the same in other respects. China's cities will, as cities everywhere have always done, reflect the forces at work in the larger society of which they are the expression. As the society moves along the time spectrum of development from its peasant-rural base toward an increasingly urban emphasis, and as its ideological goals continue to adjust to the realities and needs of that development, its cities will mirror those changes, as the traditional city mirrored the values and the grandeur of imperial China.

Part 2

Politics

Edited by Steven M. Goldstein

Introduction

Steven M. Goldstein

China has a political tradition of more than two thousand years. Indeed, before its fall in 1912, the imperial Chinese system was the longest lived political system in human history. This essay provides a brief overview of this rich political tradition in China and introduces the readings which follow. Our approach derives from that developed by Professor Albert Feuerwerker of the University of Michigan in his studies of the traditional Chinese political system. The traditional and contemporary systems are discussed from three perspectives: the political norms and philosophies of each system; the nature of the national institutions—the view from the top; and the interaction between the individual and the state—the view from the bottom.

Political Ideology in Traditional China

The core principles of traditional China's political philosophy took shape during a period of political disunity from the sixth to the third century B.C. known as the era of "hundred schools of thought." Although there would be numerous accretions and developments in the centuries that followed, it was the interaction of two of the "hundred schools of thought" which had the most important—but by no means exclusive—influence on the substance of traditional Chinese political thought. These were the Legalist school and the thought of Confucius as interpreted by his disciple Mencius. Two more different ideologies can scarcely be imagined. And yet it was precisely their contrasting assumptions and political prescriptions that gave life and vitality to the Chinese empire.

Most political philosophies begin with assumptions about human nature. Confucianism, as interpreted by Mencius, argues that individuals are by nature moral and thus have the impulses that make social life possible (see chapter 11). Non-social behavior—civil war, social conflict, etc.—is caused by an environment that discourages them from behaving in accord with their moral instincts.

Specifically, Mencius believed in the importance of a correct environment. The role of government was to provide for the material needs of its people. No person, Mencius believed, could be expected to behave in a morally correct manner unless he was clothed and fed. With these material needs provided for, the state should be ordered in a way that is consistent with the moral, social, impulses in human beings.

Confucius had used the term *li* to denote these principles. Although sometimes translated as "rites," this term is best understood as rules that regulate "the behavior of persons related to each other in terms of role, status, rank, and position within a structured society."[1] In the years after his and Mencius' death, these statuses and ranks were shortened to the famous five relationships: ruler/ subject; father/son; husband/ wife; older brother/younger brother; and friend/friend, with their attendant rules of proper behavior. The message of Confucius and his disciples was a simple one: if society were ordered according to these principles, then its citizens would be moral and truly human, the social order would be harmonious, and the state would be strong.

The most obvious point about these relationships is the prominence of the family. For Confucius, the family comes first in time and is the model for good government. As Professor Benjamin I. Schwartz of Harvard University has noted, the kind of authority exercised by the father in a patrilinear family constitutes the ideal of political rulership. In the family authority is accepted not because it is based on brute force, but through shared moral sentiment. *Li* is the agent that will create a similar moral solidarity in the political order.

Viewed as a system of political governance, Confucianism exemplifies what Victor Li in chapter 18 calls the "internal model" of obedience.

---

1. Benjamin I. Schwartz, *The World of Thought in Ancient China* (Cambridge: Harvard University Press, 1985), p. 65.

Societies adhere and people live together not because of fear of punishment, but rather because they have internalized the norms of social behavior *(li)* and agree with them as does a child in the family.

The Confucian aversion to rule by law is exemplified by the quotation in chapter 11 where the Master calls for government to lead by "virtue" and not "law." This passage states the two elements of Confucius' argument against external law. It does not, in the first place, make us "good." It just punishes us. Humans are not improved by having lived under rule of law, and a basic function of the state—moral improvement—is lost. Second, as Benjamin Schwartz notes, Confucius suggests that such a legal system is not efficient. It might not work without constant surveillance. Although different levels of moral development of the people will always require some law in a Confucian state, law should never be the primary means of control.

But how to achieve this ideal state? Confucius' statement that the people be led by "virtue" suggests the answer. The ordering of society—ruling—is to be the work of those individuals whose thinking and behavior is most in tune with the rules of proper conduct. Confucius believed that ruling was a skill that had to be practiced by the wise and virtuous ruler at the top. However, as one scholar has noted, Confucianism is very much the ideology of the adviser to rulers, the "gentleman" whose knowledge of proper rules of behavior could assist a ruler to have a morally ordered, but also strong, kingdom.

Indeed, Confucius believed that it was the obligation of the "gentleman" to use the power of his moral example to reorder society along the correct lines. His virtue would be like the "wind," causing the people ("weeds") to "bend." Impersonal laws were unnecessary. As the readings make clear, the task of the "gentleman" is to make this world a better, more moral place to live: "He cultivates himself so as to be able to bring comfort to other people." Thus, while serving a ruler, he might be forced to criticize particular actions of that ruler. His ultimate loyalty goes beyond the state to a higher standard of right and wrong.

The high moral tone and this-worldliness of Confucius sparked many responses. One such response was the philosophy of Daoism. It reacted to the intensely political, interventionist thrust of Confucianism by treating human social conventions such as *li* as the problem, rather than the solution. Civilization had moved human beings further from their unspoiled state of nature, according to the Daoists, who counselled withdrawal from this world and a spiritual unity with the natural world.

This protest movement was a corrective to the intense this-worldliness of Confucianism and provided relief and religious sustenance for the weary Confucian administrator. It can be viewed as a primitivist critique of the high culture that lay at the heart of Confucianism.

"Man tends to self-interest as water tends downwards." Thus came the challenge from the Legalists to the Confucians. This school of thought, associated with the names of Han Fei and Lord Shang, sees human beings as self-seeking. The ruler who would seek to govern such individuals should have no illusions that they could be improved or stimulated to be good. As Han Fei writes in chapter 11, the ruler does not "count on people doing good of themselves," rather he seeks to "keep them from doing any evil" by use of strict laws and harsh punishment.

As the readings reveal, the Legalists, like the Confucians, make extensive use of the family analogy, but they draw different conclusions. To them, the Confucians were like doting parents whose insistence on the goodness of their children and emphasis on caring only created spoiled, unruly children. The Legalists saw themselves as strict parents who felt that punishments, while painful in the short-run, were ultimately beneficial in civilizing their children's behavior and creating submissive children/citizens. The principles of rulership were thus simple: use severe punishments to put an end to behavior found unacceptable; use rewards as incentives to promote behavior considered useful. These were the "handles" by which the sovereign would rule.

The embodiment of rewards and punishment was, of course, the law which stood at the center of the Legalist system—a law that would be not only severe, but also "uniform" in application and known throughout the realm. According to the Legalists, laws work only if they are known to all and if they are applied in a uniform and almost mechanical manner with no exceptions made for extenuating circumstances—not even filial piety. The law takes precedence. This is what Victor Li calls the "external model" of obedience. There is no attempt made to reform or even to change attitudes; all that is sought is compliant behavior.

But toward what end? The goal of the Confucian state is to create a truly moral social order, and the political realm is judged against this higher set of values. The Legalist goal is a strong state. There is the suggestion that service to the goals of a strong state is the ultimate criterion of judgment for political actions. There was no allowance for conflicting religious or family values.

Like the Confucians, the Legalists emphasize the importance of rulership. However, the emperor is not a "sage king" who seeks to educate or nurture his people as in the Confucian system. Rather, he is to be a shrewd and ruthless politician who is concerned with harnessing the efforts of the populace towards achieving the unity, wealth, and security of the empire. Below him are bureaucrats, sharply different from the Confucian bureaucrats. Rather than being "gentlemen" who put their loyalty to principle above loyalty to their ruler, the Legalist bureaucrats were to be cogs in a powerful and centralized administrative machine. Rather than ruling in a flexible manner according to an unwritten code of *li*, their job is to obey instructions from above and apply law to those below in a impersonal, efficient manner.

China was united by an Emperor whose rule was informed by Legalism. Qin Shihuangdi (Ch'in Shih Huang Ti), in the short span of eleven years (221 to 210 B.C.), used the ruthless, centralizing principles of the Legalists to create the first semblance of a united China since the decline of the Western Zhou (Chou). Although his dynasty was shortlived and Qin Shihuangdi came to epitomize the evil Chinese ruler, he left behind him the outlines of a nation as well as of a centralized bureaucratic structure capable of governing that nation. These Legalist institutions were retained when the successor Han dynasty adopted Confucianism as the official ideology of China. These sharply contrasting political philosophies thus became a permanent part of the political landscape as Confucianism was made the ruling ideology of political institutions created by Legalists.

Political Institutions: The View from the Top Down

In the Chinese empire, which lasted from the Qin (Ch'in) dynasty in the third century B.C. until 1912, dynasties, boundaries, even capital cities, changed. But two institutions remained constant: the emperor and the bureaucracy.

Both institutions were the marvel of visitors to traditional China: the emperor because of his great power and the majesty that surrounded his office, and the bureaucracy because of its apparent efficiency, national scope, and much-heralded examination system which sought to recruit the very finest minds of the empire into government service on the basis of merit rather than heredity. Indeed, one Western historian has seen the competitive civil service bureaucracy as China's distinctive contribution to world civilization. Both were essential to the proper ordering of the empire.

The emperor, as Rhoads Murphey pointed out in Part 1, was regarded as the "son of heaven" who, as mediator between heaven and earth, had total responsibility for the affairs of the realm. Of course, the power of the office depended very much on the skills of its occupant. However, most historians agree that while the dominant position of the emperor had its roots in the Tang dynasty (A.D. 618–906), it was during the Ming dynasty (1368–1644) that the Emperor emerged as a genuine autocrat. The only possible countervailing power to the Emperor had been in the office of prime minister, which was abolished by a Ming emperor. Also during the Ming, the Office of the Censorate, which was charged with criticizing an emperor who was in error, withered under imperial attack. Gradually, by forming around him reliable cronies in the inner court, depending on the reports of loyalists below through the so-called "palace memorial system," and playing off factions within the bureaucracy, the emperor became a true autocrat.

For the conscientious monarch, power brought with it a tremendous workload. Since the very operation of the system depended on him, the emperor had to keep his finger on much of the work of the empire—he was no figurehead. Within the space of ten days, one Ming emperor read 1,660 memorials dealing with 3,391 separate matters, probably ranging from personnel questions to issues of war to criminal justice appeals.

In performing his job, the emperor was, in theory, assisted by the bureaucracy. But like bureaucrats throughout the world they were concerned with their own interests and secretive, and they sought to blunt the power of the emperor. However, the skillful emperor was able to control and use the bureaucracy to rule his empire. It was indeed a marvellous institution for its times, able to place the far-flung Chinese empire under a seemingly unified system of rule from the capital.

The civil bureaucracy, described in chapter 12 by John K. Fairbank, was headed by six functional "boards"—Civil Appointments, Revenue, Rites, War, Punishments, and Public Works—which oversaw roughly 30,000 civil servants. Below Beijing (Peking) were viceroyships which controlled two or more provinces; provinces (fifteen to eighteen) which were in turn divided up into prefectures (averaging eleven per province); and districts (averaging one hundred per province) which were the lowest rung in the bureaucracy with populations of up to 300,000 towards the end of the empire. The lifeblood of the empire—edicts, taxes, criminal justice appeals, etc.—circulated up and down this bureaucratic system.

Individuals were recruited into this bureaucracy by means of a series of examinations; the first was given at the county level, the next at the provincial level and the final and most important administered under the emperor's supervision in Beijing. Some aspirants to office would spend their entire lives seeking to pass these exams, which were largely based on the Confucian classics. In theory, almost anyone was eligible to sit for the exam and there are many Horatio Alger stories to be found in the annals of Chinese history. However, only a very small percentage of the candidates were successful in passing the final examination hurdle. For most, the examination system represented a life of failure and frustration. But even then the system performed an important political function for China's rulers—that of social control of the intellectual class by channeling their energies into the examination effort.

Let us consider this view from the top in light of the Confucian/Legalist dichotomy discussed earlier. Many scholars of China would argue that in two thousand years the empire had come full circle and was showing many characteristics of the Qin legalism which created it. The emperor was dominant. Few seemed willing to challenge his power or question the morality of his actions. China was ruled by a bureaucracy which emphasized the importance of hierarchy and uniformity. Law, often quite harsh, was clearly in evidence, in regulating the behavior of bureaucrats and the actions of the populace.

Yet, one should not rush too quickly to such a conclusion. Elements of Confucianism were also evident throughout the empire. Some historians would argue that it provided elements of flexibility to the system, permitting it to operate in situations not covered by statutes. Others claim that Confucianism provided the crucial sense of public-spiritedness that made individuals devote such enormous energies to the governance of the empire. Finally, as can be seen in the legal cases in chapter 19, imperial Chinese law was never applied as the Legalists would have it. There were always extenuating circumstances to be considered. Yet, Confucianism also had its pernicious influences. The continued valuation of norms relating to friendship or family intruded into the political system and created personalistic networks and extensive nepotism. Much corruption was the result of bureaucrats placing other values ahead of political ones.

Still, when viewed from the top down, the mature imperial system did seem decidedly Legalist. However, as Professor Feuerwerker has written elsewhere, while the view from the top down might make it seem that imperial China was ruled more by law than by men, when the system is viewed from the bottom up, from the perspective of the villages of China, it looked very much like a Confucian rule of men rather than laws.

Traditional Political Institutions: The Citizen and the State

If one were to stand in a village of traditional China, one would be hard pressed to find any signs of the elaborate and sophisticated bureaucratic empire described above. It was almost as if one were living in another world. In imperial China, there were no government offices in the villages.

Although taxes were paid and goods entered into a national economic network, the villages of rural China in traditional times were largely self-sufficient economies with peasants providing one another with food and traditional handicrafts (see Part 4 for a further discussion of the rural economy). As in all traditional societies, social, economic, and political power was in the hands of a local elite—called the "gentry" in China. These individuals, whose status was based on a combination of economic power and accomplishment in the civil service examinations, effectively ran the localities.

As the reading from Fairbank explains, the gentry did everything from running the local schools to managing the vital irrigation systems to mediating the innumerable personal and economic conflicts that were rife in the Chinese countryside. It was in this respect that the locality seemed most like what Feuerwerker has called "general will Confucianism." A local elite, whose standing and prestige was accepted by the populace, provided instruction in the proper rules of behavior as well as benevolent political rule.

For the ordinary Chinese peasant, preoccupied with pressing family and economic matters, politics was a distant matter of little immediate concern. "Heaven is high and the emperor is far away," went the aphorism. Indeed, for the ordinary citizen politics was not simply distant, it was dangerous. There were references to the "tiger world of politics" and most ordinary Chinese, like Mr. Ch'en in chapter 20, would do anything to avoid contact with the authorities. Better to rely on the local notables to handle such affairs. The traditional political culture of the Chinese commoner was one of passivity and dependence on one's "betters." Local clans were usually managed by the gentry, and even the peasant rebellions of traditional China were often led by gentry.

The common folk were not the only ones who depended on the gentry to keep local order; so did the imperial government. Historians have often commented on the remarkable "thinness" of the imperial government which ruled China with roughly thirty thousand civil servants. The small scale of the imperial bureaucracy is explained by the fact that it did not penetrate below the district level and into the villages of China.

The job of the district magistrate was, thus, not an enviable one. He was a stranger in the area. The "father-mother official" was expected to care for the spiritual and material needs of the people even as he kept order and saw to it that the imperial demands— primarily in regard to taxation—were met. In carrying out this task he was "assisted" by a local office staff of underpaid and often corrupt clerks who frequently created more local problems than they solved. Although there was also a system of registration and mutual-surveillance called the *baojia (pao-chia)* system, which was to assist in keeping local order, it was a weak structure compared to local elite networks. In short, the overworked, understaffed magistrate had no choice but to rely on the local elite to assist him in his work. As Wakeman's story of Mr. Ch'en and Mr. Wang makes clear, the imperial office holder thought of the gentry as "his people," and he freely consulted with them and depended on them to keep the political and economic order of the locality.

Anthropologists thus see the gentry as a "broker" or "hinge" group having standing in, and mediating beween, the particularistic locality and the universalistic national bureaucracy. The gentry were able to represent the interests of the locality to the national bureaucracy even as they represented the national system in the locality. Some historians argue that the strength and longevity of the Chinese empire can be traced to this flexibility and balance that the gentry maintained between centralism and localism. The empire was rarely so centralized as to be brittle, nor so decentralized that it lost its essential unity.

Although much of the credit for this integration must go to the gentry, their role should not be idealized. Whether representing the locality or the nation, they always considered their own social and economic interests. The gentry were capable of being tireless governors moved by a sense of noblesse oblige. But they could also be self-seeking venal landlords. Usually, the truth was somewhere in between and the empire did well. At other times their venality could erode the system at its roots.

Thus, as sociologist C. K. Yang has noted, China for centuries persisted as a unique amalgam of centralized homogeneity and localistic heterogeneity. Its Legalist/Confucian roots persisted and gave the system great vitality. However, by the end of the eighteenth century, this marvellous and complex edifice showed signs of fundamental decay.

The causes of this decay were both domestic and foreign in origin. In the late eighteenth century, there was a population explosion in China; numbers almost doubled between 1770 and 1840. The "thin" system of governance was strained, as was the nation's food supply. There is also evidence of a decline in the quality of the Chinese rulers from the emperor, overworked by the responsibilities of autocracy, right down to the local gentry. Nation-wide rebellions signaled a fundamental crisis in the system even before the Western invasion and occupation of parts of China. The Opium War and its aftermath thus added another burden to a system already in crisis. The dynasty tried to reform itself, but new reforms often created greater crisis. In 1912, the last emperor abdicated.

In chapter 5 Mary Wright makes clear the partial quality of this revolution in government. The dynasty fell, but there was no force to take its place. However, as Wright shows, the platform for success was set. Nationalism was the order of the day in China. Victory would go to that political force that would expel the foreign imperialists, unify the country with effective political structures, and implement some socioeconomic reform.

For the next three or four decades, China was in political decay awaiting a political force that could deliver on the nationalist platform. At times, there was no real national government as local warlords carved up the nation and venal gentry exploited the localities. During the 1930s the Nationalist Party sought to meet the challenge of nationalism. It had a promising beginning, but was unable to create political order in China. The Japanese invasion of China in 1937 was a coup de grace for a hopelessly inept and corrupt regime, and it was the Communists who emerged as the dominant party in the years following the war.

Political Ideology in Contemporary China

There has not been a single Communist ideology in China during the twentieth century. Rather, different Marxists have developed dissimilar ideologies. Even the official ideology has dramatically changed over time.

These changes in Marxist theory result, in part, from the fact that the Chinese Communist revolution did not occur in the kind of society anticipated by Karl Marx. Marx expected revolution to occur in advanced industrial societies, where a mature working class would restructure a developed industrial system to serve the interests of all. In China, Marxist theory had to be adapted to the conditions of a nationalist revolution against foreign interference and invasion in an overwhelmingly rural country. After the revolution, the problem was not simply to restructure industrialization. It was to create an industrial system—to do the work of capitalism—even while advocating a socio-political system superior to capitalism.

The man who had the most prominent role in making these adjustments and in seeking to juggle such conflicting priorities was Mao Zedong. Mao led the Chinese Communist Party from the mid-1930s until his death in 1976, setting the tone and direction of Marxism in China. The many twists and turns of Chinese Marxism during these years were, in large part, a reflection of his restless mind. However, running through Mao's Marxism and that of his successors have been certain central themes, including the role of domestic class struggle and the relative emphasis to be placed on economic growth in relation to the revolutionization of society. In this section we will discuss how the treatment of these and other questions have influenced the evolution of official Communist ideology.

After the Japanese invasion of China, Mao devised the theory of the "New Democratic" revolution. The major tasks facing the Chinese nation, he argued, were the defeat of the foreign powers impinging on China; the overthrow of the most reactionary elements at home; and the creation of a broad united front, led by the Communist Party, of the workers, peasantry, and sections of the middle class. Such a coalition would seek independence for China, the development of private enterprise in the cities and the countryside, and the construction of a truly "democratic" government.

This platform, with its promise of politico-economic reform and resistance to foreign invasion, was clearly responsive to the nationalist mood of the times. Moreover, the apparent prowess and honesty of the Communist armies, as well as the Party's amelioration of some of the worst exploitation of the peasants in rural China, suggested that there was substance behind the promise. Although the Communists made clear their ultimate objective of socialism for China, Marxism took hold in China during the late 1930s and early 1940s emphasizing anti-imperialism, honest government, and socio-economic reform while generally deemphasizing class struggle.

In the early years, Communist ideology stayed very close to its winning revolutionary formulae as it created post-revolutionary policies. Until 1953, its ideological platform was essentially a continuation of the earlier program of "New Democracy" outlined by Mao in chapter 13. Mao proposed to follow through on the promises of the earlier period. The emphasis was on economic growth and limited government intrusion into the private sector. He proposed a mixed economy in which the government would control most of the important industries and financial institutions while private capitalists would be allowed to operate in other sectors of the urban economy. In the rural areas, the holdings of the large landlords were confiscated, but private landholding was allowed, as was the emergence of a middle-class farmer. Only in the political realm was there no sharing of power; the Communist Party was in control despite the window dressing of a coalition government.

After 1953 both theory and ideology changed. The process of ending the mixed economic system gathered momentum. The Chinese announced that henceforth the task would be to build socialism through state management of the economy. First, businesses were nationalized and then farms were collectivized. Chinese ideology borrowed heavily from Soviet Marxism during these years. Socialism came to mean high rates of economic development concentrated in heavy industry and urban areas, with agriculture and living standards sacrificed in the process. As in the Soviet Union, there was little attempt to achieve any of the egalitarian goals of Marxism. Rather, differences in the social, economic, and political power of individuals were all justified as necessary if the economic goals were to be reached. Only after economic growth had been achieved could "higher" social goals be realized. The focus was on what Marxists call the economic substructure, rather than the socio-political superstructure.

In the late 1950s Mao began to rethink the strong emphasis on economic growth. He became concerned about social and political questions. He returned to his theorizing about contradictions, identifying the tensions that exist between an unresponsive bureaucracy and a dissatisfied population. Mao was concerned that the rulers in a highly bureaucratized, socialist country could become a new ruling class. After the bitter criticism leveled at the Communist Party during the Hundred Flowers campaign of 1957, Mao also began to see elements developing within society that sought to overthrow socialism in China. Mao's ideology, and hence the official ideology of the regime, soon shifted; it focused on the dangers of revolutionary degeneration due to bureaucratic complacency and the growth of class enemies within society. China's revolution had to push forward or else it would certainly slide backwards.

As chapter 13 demonstrates, Mao's response to the dangers of revolutionary degeneration was "permanent revolution." This would rekindle the revolutionary enthusiasm of the masses, prevent the emergence of class enemies, and keep the bureaucracy responsive to the needs of the revolution. After 1958, Mao's ideology seemed more concerned with class struggle, politicization of the population, and maintaining revolutionary momentum than it was with the purely economic considerations of the early 1950s. His writings criticized Stalin for ignoring the socio-political superstructure as he developed the Soviet economy. Mao was determined not to make the same mistake. Many commentators saw a return to decidedly traditional Confucian values in Mao's revolutionary approach as attitudinal change and spiritual power returned to center stage in the polity.

During the Great Leap Forward of 1958–60 these ideological concerns were translated into policies that sought the reorganization of the rural population into communes, the mobilization and politicization of the masses, struggle against intellectuals or technical specialists, and a general emphasis on revolutionary egalitarianism. Mao was concentrating his attention on the way society was organized. But that didn't mean he ignored economic growth issues. For Mao these objectives were not inconsistent. A mobilized populace could achieve economic miracles. A revolutionized citizenry would ensure that economic growth would not compromise revolutionary ideals.

In the early 1960s, there was little change in ideology, but much change in practice. The Great Leap Forward was an economic disaster; practically every economic indicator declined and a largely man-made famine killed as many as twenty million. Mao stepped back to the "second line," and although much of the ideological rhetoric stayed the same, Party administrators returned to a system much like that of the 1950s: bureaucratically managed economic growth came to the fore while class struggle and political work were minimized. Their policies proved short-lived. By the mid-1960s, an older Mao, even more concerned over the fate of the revolution in China, and driven by the negative example of Khrushchev's Russia, once again unfurled the banner of permanent revolution and class struggle.

During the Cultural Revolution, Mao's concerns once again set the tone for Chinese ideology. The emphasis was on revolutionizing society. Constant warnings about class enemies turned political differences into civil and class warfare. Those who sought to promote economic growth were suspected of putting "economics in command" and thus sabotaging spiritual revolution in China. The mood was anti-intellectual and anti-bureaucratic. Mao sought to bind the state together with a socialist moral unity achieved through spiritual change. Strict orthodoxy in the arts was required to preserve this unity. Spartan life-styles at home would maintain revolutionary purity. Near economic autarky kept out foreign influences. And, finally, emphasis on moral rather than monetary incentives assured that revolutionary values would not erode. These policies, together, became the essence of Mao's last formulation of Marxism.

In the years since Mao's death, Marxism has undergone yet another reformulation under the aegis of Deng Xiaoping. At the center of Deng's Marxism has been a phrase borrowed from Mao: "Seek Truth from Facts." This has been interpreted as stressing the importance of a critical examination of all formulations inherited from Mao in light of reality.

Under this template, Mao's successors initially moved to dismantle most of his post–1957 ideological innovations. Specific policies associated with Mao's last years, such as suspicion of intellectuals and strictures regarding economic incentives and the use of profit indicators and markets, were reversed. As the excerpt from the 1982 constitution in chapter 14 demonstrates, the regime's new ideological emphases seemed centered on questions of national unity and economic growth. It was as if the post-Mao leadership was returning to its earlier themes of nationalism and economic betterment. Marxist ideology was being associated with the achievement of an economically strong and respected China in the world and improved living conditions and economic development at home.

However, while downplayed, Mao's concerns with preserving socialist values and preventing ideological erosion never entirely disappeared after 1976. As the readings in chapter 14 (including the 1982 constitution) suggest, in the years after Mao's death, references to class struggle persisted, and calls for ideological vigilance resurfaced periodically. And in the period after the April–June events at Tiananmen, such exhortations became particularly strident as China's leaders saw socialist ideology threatened by developments at home as well as in other socialist countries. At the end of the 1980s, the themes of economic development and ideological struggle still coexisted uneasily in Chinese Marxist ideology. A post-Mao ideological consensus continued to elude the nation's leadership.

Contemporary Political Institutions: The View from the Top

In 1949, the Communists found themselves heir to a political system in which national unity was mostly a memory. Since the fall of the Qing (Ch'ing) dynasty in 1912, the nation had experienced nearly four decades of invasion and civil war. In the immediate post–1949 period, the Communist Party ruled through its army.

However, in the mid-1950s a new set of political institutions, modeled after the Soviet Union, was introduced. This was the dual Communist Party/state government described in chapter 15. The major attraction of the Soviet model was its ability to control society in a highly centralized manner. After decades of disorder, the new leadership sought to reestablish order and to harness society towards its new goals of economic development. From the center down through the provinces, the counties and—for the first time in Chinese history—right to the village and the neighborhood, Party and government offices were established.

The principle behind this complex system is straightforward. The Communist Party, as the vanguard of the nation, is charged with formulating the policies for China's socialist development. As chapter 15 suggests, Party members are chosen by a system of co-optation that goes from the Politburo at the top to the Party cell at the bottom. Most major political decisions are made within Party organs by this narrow, self-selected elite.

The state apparatus is expected to implement these decisions under the supervision of the Party. From the ministries in Beijing to the offices at the provincial or county level, China maintains a formal government apparatus. However, as the diagram in chapter 15 shows, a separate, staffed Party organization runs parallel to this state structure.

Party leaders recognize that it is not enough to simply issue instructions and expect them to be carried out. There has to be ongoing supervision via a standing Party organization. Herein lies the great difference between the concept of Party in the West and in China. Although we speak of "Party government" in the United States, it does not really exist. Party organizations are thin affairs that have organizational strength only at election time. There are no real full-time party offices to supervise policy making, and certainly no American party has the right to remove a Supreme Court justice or a member of Congress. In China, Party government means a standing organization to supervise state work of paid, fulltime staffers in specialized Party offices with the power to remove any official whose work is unsatisfactory.

Yet like everything else in China, this dual system has undergone a constant process of change and development since its emergence in the mid-1950s. The dynamic behind this evolution has been the leadership's different policies in regard to five issues basic to the operation of the system: the proper relationship between the Party and the state; the nature of civil-military relations; the proper balance between centralized and decentralized rule; the nature of decision-making at the top; and the kind of individual who is to be recruited into the party/state administration. The nature of today's political system has been decisively shaped by more than three decades of constant experimentation in these five areas.

In the early 1950s, using the Soviet model, China's leaders emphasized highly centralized, *state* direction of the nation. Since much of the business of politics was economic growth, the most powerful political institutions were the state ministries, which controlled large economic empires. Except for the Politburo, the ruling body of the Communist Party, Party offices were of secondary importance. In the Politburo, although Mao was clearly first among equals, he and his colleagues made policy in a largely consensual fashion. Mao was even outvoted on occasion. Finally, the type of Party recruit reflected the new era. Previously, the average recruit was a rural organizer-activist. Increasingly after the mid-1950s, urban administrators were recruited into the Party. Although the emphasis was on both revolutionary background and technical qualifications—both "red and expert"—the latter seemed favored.

Still, the legacies of the revolutionary period were in evidence. As we shall see in the next section, popular mobilization remained an important hallmark of Communist policies. In addition, China's new rulers sought to turn the military from the governor of China to the servant of its civil administration. During these years the emphasis was on demobilization and professionalization of the army.

By the late 1950s fundamental changes occurred in the Chinese polity. The leaders found that centralization was difficult in a country the size of China. Beginning in 1957, large parts of the economy were handed over to the provinces to manage. Because of its strength at the lower levels, the Party benefited from this weakening of centralized ministerial power. More and more, the Party became the everyday manager of the nation's economic and political system, blurring the lines between it and the government. At the same time, the military began once again to play an active role in society and politics, contributing in such areas as economic construction.

Meanwhile, as Mao became more concerned about the future of socialism in China, relations among the elite became more difficult. Although decisions were still made at the highest levels of the Party, Mao tended to go off on his own to a greater extent and to bully or purge his opponents. Within the Party, the movement towards bureaucratization continued as the Party sought to recruit individuals capable of playing its new managerial role. But differences appeared over this issue of recruitment as Mao's distrust of intellectuals caused him to favor revolutionary enthusiasm—"red"—over expertise.

The Great Leap Forward of 1958–60 was a watershed in the development of the Chinese political system. After two years of starvation and administrative chaos, the Party bureaucrats took control of the system in the early 1960s. Although there was some centralization and some yielding of greater powers to state offices, Party dominance continued. Mao became suspicious of his colleagues. He perceived them as growth-oriented, stability-favoring bureaucrats intent on turning the Party of experts into a new ruling class. Disenchanted with the Party, he increasingly looked to the army, which was promoting political study and loyalty to Mao's thought. The political prominence of the military grew once again.

Mao's colleagues, on the other hand, distrusted him. In their eyes he was capable, at any moment, of disrupting their carefully forged bureaucratic stability by launching one more drive towards revolutionary transformation. For the first time since 1949, there were fundamental differences within the leadership over the very nature of the polity.

In 1966, Mao, supported by his allies in the military and by the propaganda apparatus, mobilized idealistic and disaffected youth to attack and demolish the Party establishment. The political goal was to replace the bureaucratic Party with a truly revolutionary political organization staffed by a new generation of cadres who were fervent revolutionaries sensitive to the needs of the masses of China. The actual results of the movement were quite different—chaos and near anarchy. In 1967, Mao was forced to call on the military to restore order. China was under virtual martial rule during the late 1960s. In 1971, Lin Biao, the Minister of Defense and Mao's heir apparent, was killed in a plane crash after an abortive coup attempt. The military's influence was diminished somewhat. However, it remained an important political force in the early 1970s even as the general outlines of the old party/state hierarchy showed signs of re-emerging and many of the old cadres returned.

However, this political system did not have the regularity and stability of the earlier periods. At the top, Mao continued his capricious style of rule. Much like the emperors of old, he prevailed by a policy of bureaucratic divide and rule as well as factional manipulation, though at times it seemed as if Mao was being manipulated. At the middle levels, the degeneration of bureaucratic norms created an administrative hierarchy rife with factional disputes, nepotism, and arbitrary power. With Mao insisting that more and more spheres of everyday life be regulated, governance in China seemed to have evolved towards the worst of all possible worlds: one where all powerful bureaucrats ruled subject to few popular or legal checks. When Mao died in September of 1976, he left the legacy of a political system in disarray.

Mao's immediate successor, Hua Guofeng, began to address this situation. However, it was only after Deng Xiaoping emerged as China's paramount leader and began to place his mark on the post-Mao reform movement that the elements of a strategy for political reform became apparent. In the years between 1978 and the April–June 1989 events at Tiananmen, it became clear that this strategy was based upon a vision of political change in China far more modest than that proposed in the economic realm. In chapter 16 Harry Harding describes the major elements of political reform as they unfolded during that decade. We will only touch on a few of the themes he raises.

A major thrust of political reform under Deng was to put to rest the memory and ideology of the Cultural Revolution period. In 1981, the Party issued its official judgment on these years, condemning most of the policies and placing primary blame for them upon Mao himself. Even as they discarded much of the ideology of the Maoist period, China's leaders sought to find a new ideological basis for the regime by emphasizing the Party's accomplishments and its central mission of economic growth. By 1987, Zhao Ziyang, since deposed as Party General Secretary, had placed China's developmental stage in Marxist terms by using the concept of the "primary stage of socialism" (see chapter 14).

The centrality of economic development was also apparent in the reforms of the political structure. There was an attempt to relax the grip of the administration over the economy and to permit greater initiative at the enterprise level. The planning and distributive powers of the central economic bureaucracies were to be lessened and more power was to be given the various economic enterprises so as to better respond to market forces. For those bureaucracies that continued to function, the reformers had three goals: streamlining; the replacement of old and ineffective cadres with younger, better-educated individuals; and the reimposition of discipline. Lean, well-staffed, and honest bureaucracies were seen as a necessary prerequisite to China's economic development.

Clarifying the precise balance of power among bureaucracies was another goal of the 1978–89 reform movement. In regard to civil-military relations, Deng worked to bring the military under the control of civilian authorities and to lessen defense expenditures, even while building the basis of a modern, professional army. With respect to party-state relations, there was some talk of getting the Party out of the day-to-day management of society, while ceding greater authority to such state structures as legislative bodies. There were even proposals made in 1987 to diminish the staffing powers of the Communist Party. In the fall of that year Zhao Ziyang proposed the creation of a civil-service system to appoint "those doing professional work." Of course, little real diminution of Party power was anticipated. The Communist Party would still maintain overall "political leadership" and appoint crucial cadres.

Finally, Deng sought to address two remnants of the Maoist era. First, there was the issue of succession, which had proven so vexing for

Mao. In contrast to his predecessor who chose—and then rejected—at least two successors, Deng sought to create procedures to assure that his death would be followed by a smooth political succession as well as continuity in policy. Second, there was the capricious nature of the decision-making process bequeathed by Mao. In the decade of reform, Deng sought to cultivate a regularized leadership style characterized by extensive consultation and consensus.

In 1988–89, after nearly a full decade of reform, the limited nature of these reforms, both in their conception and accomplishments, became apparent. In respect to their accomplishments, before the demonstrations in Tiananmen it was apparent that *even by their own criteria,* the reforms had achieved only limited success. There were widespread reports of corruption and of bloated bureaucracies. Attempts to yield greater authority to enterprises were thwarted by local political machines, which took advantage of increased economic decision-making power to promote wasteful and inflationary local development. Finally, in 1986–87, in the wake of student demonstrations, Hu Yaobang was removed as Party leader. This was reminiscent of Maoist times in two respects: not only was a prominent expected successor to Deng removed, but his removal was achieved by a rump meeting of conservative retired officials.

In regard to the scope of reform, the limits to the vision were also obvious. Deng was seeking to create a more efficient, Party-dominated authoritarian system. While decision-making would become more open and regularized, it would remain the privilege of a self-selected elite. Deng and his colleagues were not prepared to cede to society the right to set the political agenda or to choose its leaders. As we will see in the next section, "socialist democracy" had little to do with human rights or popular choice. Rather it meant creating institutions that facilitated participation consistent with the goals of the state as defined by its leaders. Indeed, as Deng himself suggested in 1986, strong Communist Party leadership was essential to successful economic reform and the maintenance of China's international position.

Both types of limitations were highlighted by the Tiananmen demonstrations of April to June 1989. The demonstrators were not protesting only the limited or negative results of the reform—corruption, nepotism, inflation, etc. They were also protesting its narrow conception. The ostensible cause of the demonstrations, the funeral of the reformist leader Hu Yaobang, suggested the dissatisfaction that many felt with the continuing authoritarianism of the government. However, as his decision to use force demonstrated, Deng was determined to stand by his limited vision of reform.

The events surrounding the tragedy at Tiananmen seemed to undo—or perhaps more precisely, expose the superficiality of—much of the reform of the previous decade. The purging of Party General Secretary Zhao Ziyang, who took a more conciliatory stance towards the demonstrators, meant that Deng's succession arrangements had failed again. The prominent role played by elderly leaders holding no official position in that removal once again belied claims of regularized political procedures, and the prominence of the military called into question Deng's new scheme for civil-military relations. Finally, the protests themselves raised questions regarding the success of reform efforts in building new popular bases for political legitimacy.

Tiananmen was also the occasion for a virtual halt to the modest political reform efforts of the previous decade. In the year that followed, development of China's political institutions took a very different turn—one reminiscent of the pre-reform period. In ideology, there were reminders of the dangers of emphasis on economic growth at the expense of socialist values (see Li Peng, chapter 14). In order to assure the inculcation of such values in the Chinese people, political education resumed, accompanied by a return to prominence for the Chinese Communist Party. And, finally, as we shall see in the next section, while there was no return to the intrusive state of the Cultural Revolution, the boundaries of popular participation and of permissible political dialogue were considerably narrowed.

Contemporary Political Institutions: The Citizen and the State

As we have seen, citizenship did not have much meaning in traditional China. Ordinary Chinese viewed contact with the political system as dangerous—better to rely on the gentry to deal with political matters and concentrate on the affairs of one's family. This attitude was not discouraged by the imperial regime, which made no attempt to control the everyday life of its citizens. The traditional Chinese system relied on the gentry and the social organizations they controlled—clans, for example—to keep order. (For a more extensive discussion of this issue see the sections on "Ideology and Organization" and, in Part 3, "The Chinese Family.")

The Communist leaders set out to change the nature of citizenship. As we shall see in the readings that follow, they were convinced that one of the weaknesses of the old system was precisely its lack of control over the populace and the failure to utilize their energies by engaging them in the political system. After 1949, the new leaders of China established a complex social control system revolving around neighborhood and work units, which is described in Part 3.

However, they sought more than simple control. The Communist leaders wanted the enthusiastic and voluntary involvement of the people in the process of creating a new China. They endeavored to change the masses of the Chinese people from nonparticipants to participants in China's political system. But, as James Townsend stresses in chapter 23, participation in China is different from participation in Western democratic systems. In the United States we consider "participation" to involve influence over the choice of politicians and policies. In China the ordinary citizen has not had this kind of influence. Participation has meant taking part in the implementation of policies made by others.

Such participation, while different from our Western notion, is considered essential by the Chinese leadership. By taking part in political and social campaigns, individuals will mobilize their energies for the benefit of the state. Secondly, the participants become educated in the goals and aspirations of the regime. Finally, such participation becomes an effective way of identifying potential new leaders who might be recruited to Party or state positions. The regime has sought a motivated citizenry which has come to accept the basic policies of the regime through participation in their implementation.

How successful has the Communist leadership been in reaching these goals? Has participation captured the minds and energies of the Chinese population? There have been both successes and failures. One apparent success was the land-reform campaign of the late 1940s and early 1950s. In this case, the new leaders sought the participation of the masses in the genuinely popular policy of land-distribution. What resulted was apparently enthusiastic participation and increased Communist popularity. At the other end of the spectrum are cases that have been widely reported of youthful participants in the Cultural Revolution, who voluntarily took part in a movement for their own, often idealistic, reasons, only to find a few years later that their goals and the shifting objectives of the regime did not quite mesh. In the end, such participation yielded not commitment, but disillusionment. (One example is provided in the story "The Wounded" in Part 5.)

In general, however, it would seem that the results of nearly four decades of citizen participation in China have fallen somewhere between these two extremes. In the 1950s the regime launched a number of campaigns, and popular participation seemed to achieve the goals set by the leadership. However, over time, as the Chinese were called upon to participate in more and more exhausting and time-consuming campaigns, and as the objectives of one campaign were repudiated by subsequent ones, something between apathy and cynicism began to set in. Many people went through the motions, saying and doing what was expected of them, but harboring feelings ranging from weariness to indifference to secret opposition.

After Mao's death, the new leaders seem to have sensed this mood within the population. The Cultural Revolution had been a period of nearly continual turmoil. Political campaigns intruded into the lives of most Chinese. What made matters worse was that many were not participants; rather they were victims for reason of class, politics, or simply personal vendetta. The population seemed tired. It desired a return to "normalcy."

Life did, indeed, change for the ordinary Chinese citizen in the years after Mao's death in 1976. Government regulation of everyday life diminished. In areas ranging from dress to the arts to hobbies, permissible bounds were expanded. Moreover, as Harding notes (chapter 22), the reformers sought to ameliorate popular cynicism about politics by strengthening legal safeguards against bureaucratic abuses and by stimulating participation in multi-candidate local elections. In the words of one Western observer, China seemed to be "coming alive."

Despite these widened boundaries, it was clear from the beginning of the reform movement that some things had not changed with respect to the relationship between the individual and the political system. Mao's successors shared his conviction that leadership had to set limits to assure that popular participation served the interests of the nation as they defined them. In early 1979, Deng Xiaoping defined these boundaries by asserting that only those statements and activities that adhered to the "four cardinal principles"—keeping the socialist road, upholding the dictatorship of the proletariat, upholding the leadership by the Communist Party, and upholding Marxism-Leninism/Mao Zedong Thought—would be permitted. To allow the populace to determine what the political agenda was and how it might be addressed, he maintained, would only result in the unraveling of socialism in China—"bourgeois liberalization." In Deng's view, authoritarian Communist Party leadership was necessary if China's economic reforms were to succeed. While he was prepared to allow a limited marketplace for the exchange of economic goods, there would be little marketplace for the exchange of unsanctioned ideas.

Yet, as the reform decade unfolded, a growing number of Chinese were expressing their unwillingness to operate within such constraints. Their views were quite diverse and often inchoate. Some, seeing themselves as loyal opposition, were sympathetic to the regime's socialist goals, but differed over the pace or extent of reform. Others, such as the astrophysicist Fang Lizhi (see chapter 24), were more critical of the Party and its goals, looking, instead, to Western notions of human rights and democracy. But they all shared the belief that Chinese citizens had the right to raise issues in a manner and with a content unbounded by leadership conceptions of what was consistent with China's development.

This dissident movement became prominent in 1978–79, gained momentum with the student demonstrations of 1986–87 and found its most dramatic platform in the Tiananmen demonstrations of April–June 1989. These events, which began as a show of support for the idea of political reform, soon became the vehicle for the expression both of grievances against the results of past policies and of aspirations for the future (see chapter 24 and the discussion in Part 6). It would be impossible to capture the full range of these views here. What is important to note, however, is that it was as much the *fact* of the demonstrations as their content that posed a challenge to Deng Xiaoping's concept of sanctioned popular participation.

Although at crucial junctures in 1986 and 1989 certain of his colleagues counseled moderation, Deng was unyielding in his conviction that such activities could not be tolerated. The political initiative, he believed, had to remain with the Party. The boundaries defined by its leaders would be strictly enforced. In 1979–80, citizens who sought to use the "democracy wall" in Beijing and local elections for unsanctioned goals were dealt with harshly. Deng's comments during the student demonstrations of 1986–87 (see chapter 25) are a frank expression of the attitude that lay behind the ugly suppression of the protest movement in Tiananmen and of the dissidents who supported it.

In the months that followed Tiananmen, many dissidents fled the country or went into hiding, while others were arrested. Although the rest of the nation did not experience a return to the regimentation of the past, the boundaries of permissible dialogue and behavior were narrowed, even as political education was resuscitated as a way of dealing with "bourgeois" ideas (see Li Peng, chapter 14). The leaders had made their point: they would allow only such citizen participation as was consistent with the goals of the state as they, themselves, defined them.

The punishment of non-sanctioned participation brings us to a discussion of the final way in which the individual comes in contact with the state in China: through the legal system. As the readings in this book make clear, the influence of traditional China has been quite obvious in the post–1949 legal system. The pervasive use of mediation and the emphasis on what Victor Li calls the "internal model" of law, all suggest the Confucian roots of the system. The regime has sought to gain the concurrence of the population with the values of the system. When conflicts occur, the goal often is not to punish the offenders but to educate them.

In general, this process has been carried out through the informal mediation process. But it is also apparent in the more formal, criminal justice proceedings that emphasize "reform through education." Chinese prisons seek to reform criminals into contributing, conforming citizens. Their success is difficult to assess. Chinese prisoners, like their counterparts throughout the world, have learned to behave as their captors wish and to feign reform in order to be released. This is the lesson in chapter 21 by Frolic.

Although informal processes and reform-through-labor remain prominent aspects of the Chinese criminal justice system, the more formal, "external model" came into greater prominence in the post-Mao period. During the Cultural Revolution, citizens were subject to arbitrary interference and to punishment by official and semi-official organs. In part, this was the result of informal mechanisms being used irresponsibly. After Mao's death, an effort was made to rebuild the legal profession, draft legal codes, and review past cases so to assure the population that the rules and regulations to which they would be subject would be applied in a consistent and impartial manner. However, for Chinese as well as Western observers, the credibility of such efforts was undermined by the blatantly political uses to which the judicial system was put in the months after Tiananmen (see chapter 25).

Finally, the executions that followed Tiananmen were a reminder that the Chinese legal system has its harsh side as well as its reformist side. The death penalty has been widely used in China. Indeed, its use increased under Deng Xiaoping, who seemed determined to make an example of a wide range of offenders. Thus, not all prisoners are re-educated in China. Some are executed for the edification of others.

Ideology and
Organization

11

Sources of Chinese Tradition

Confucius / Mencius / Han Fei

Many of the core issues of traditional Chinese political philosophy are to be found in the debate between the Legalist school and the Confucians. Part 1 introduced some of the basic Confucian principles. In this selection we have included excerpts from the Analects *of Confucius (551–479 B.C.) as well as from the writings of his famous disciple, Mencius (ca. 372–289 B.C.). In the long history of the Chinese empire, Mencius' interpretation of Confucius proved to be the most influential. Representing the Legalist point of view are excerpts from the writings of Han Fei (died ca. 233 B.C.). Han Fei was an advisor at the court of the first Qin emperor. He was executed, apparently the victim of court intrigue.*

The *Analects* of Confucius

. . . . The Duke of She observed to Confucius: "Among us there was an upright man called Kung who was so upright that when his father appropriated a sheep, he bore witness against him." Confucius said: "The upright men among us are not like that. A father will screen his son and a son his father—yet uprightness is to be found in that. . . ."

The Gentleman

. . . . Confucius said: "The gentleman reaches upward; the inferior man reaches downward."

Confucius said: "The gentleman is always calm and at ease; the inferior man is always worried and full of distress."

Confucius said: "The gentleman understands what is right; the inferior man understands what is profitable."

Confucius said: "The gentleman cherishes virtue; the inferior man cherishes possessions. The gentleman thinks of sanctions; the inferior man thinks of personal favors."

Confucius said: "The gentleman makes demands on himself; the inferior man makes demands on others."

Confucius said: "The gentleman seeks to enable people to succeed in what is good but does not help them in what is evil. The inferior man does the contrary."

Confucius said: "The gentleman is broad-minded and not partisan; the inferior man is partisan and not broad-minded. . . ."

Government by Personal Virtue

Chi K'ang Tzu asked Confucius about government. Confucius said: "To govern *(cheng)* is to set things right *(cheng)*.[1] If you begin by setting yourself right, who will dare to deviate from the right?"

Confucius said: "If a ruler himself is upright, all will go well without orders. But if he himself is not upright, even though he gives orders they will not be obeyed."

Tzu Lu asked about the character of a gentleman [man of the ruling class]. Confucius said: "He cultivates himself in reverential attention." Tzu Lu asked: "Is that all there is to it?" Confucius said: "He cultivates himself so as to be able to bring comfort to other people." Tzu Lu asked again: "Is that all?" Confucius said: "He cultivates himself so as to be able to bring comfort to the whole populace—even [sage-kings] Yao and Shun were dissatisfied with themselves about this."

Confucius said: "Lead the people by laws and regulate them by penalties, and the people will try to keep out of jail, but will have no sense of shame. Lead the people by virtue and restrain them by the rules of decorum, and the people will have a sense of shame, and moreover will become good."

---

1. This is more than just a pun. Confucius was trying to get at the root of the matter by getting at the root of the word.

Chi K'ang Tzu asked Confucius about government, saying: "Suppose I were to kill the lawless for the good of the law-abiding, how would that do?" Confucius answered: "Sir, why should it be necessary to employ capital punishment in your government? Just so you genuinely desire the good, the people will be good. The virtue of the gentleman may be compared to the wind and that of the commoner to the weeds. The weeds under the force of the wind cannot but bend."

The Duke of She asked about good government. Confucius said: "[A government is good when] those near are happy and those far off are attracted."

When Confucius was traveling to Wei, Jan Yu drove him. Confucius observed: "What a dense population!" Jan Yu said: "The people having grown so numerous, what next should be done for them?" "Enrich them," was the reply. "And when one has enriched them, what next should be done?" Confucius said: "Educate them."

Tzu Kung asked about government. Confucius said: "The essentials are sufficient food, sufficient troops, and the confidence of the people." Tzu Kung said: "Suppose you were forced to give up one of these three, which would you let go first?" Confucius said: "The troops." Tzu Kung asked again: "If you are forced to give up one of the two remaining, which would you let go?" Confucius said: "Food. For from of old, death has been the lot of all men, but a people without faith cannot survive."

Duke Ching of Ch'i asked Confucius about government. Confucius replied: "Let the prince be the prince, the minister be the minister, the father father and the son son." "Excellent!" said the duke. "Indeed if the prince is not the prince, the minister not minister, the father not father, and the son not son, then with all the grain in my possession shall I ever get to eat any?"

Mencius

.... Kao Tzu[2] said: "The nature of man may be likened to a swift current of water: you lead it eastward and it will flow to the east; you lead it westward and it will flow to the west. Human nature is neither disposed to good nor to evil, just as water is neither disposed to east nor west." Mencius replied: "It is true that water is neither disposed to east

---

2. Kao Tzu was a critic and possibly a former pupil of Mencius. In general, Kao Tzu held human nature to be neutral, while Mencius insisted it was good.

nor west, but is it neither disposed to flowing upward nor downward? The tendency of human nature to do good is like that of water to flow downward. There is no man who does not tend to do good; there is no water that does not flow downward. Now you may strike water and make it splash over your forehead, or you may even force it up the hills. But is this in the nature of water? It is of course due to the force of circumstances. Similarly, man may be brought to do evil, and that is because the same is done to his nature. . . ."

The disciple Kung-tu Tzu said: "Kao Tzu says that human nature is neither good nor bad. Some say that human nature can be turned to be good or bad. Thus when [sage-kings] Wen and Wu were in power the people loved virtue; when [wicked kings] Yu and Li were in power the people indulged in violence. Some say that some natures are good and some are bad. Thus even while [the sage] Yao was sovereign there was the bad man Hsiang, even a bad father like Ku-sou had a good son like [the sage-king] Shun, and even with [the wicked] Chou for nephew and king there were the men of virtue Ch'i, the Viscount of Wei, and the Prince Pi-kan. Now, you say that human nature is good. Are the others then all wrong?" Mencius replied: "When left to follow its natural feelings human nature will do good. This is why I say it is good. If it becomes evil, it is not the fault of man's original capability. The sense of mercy is found in all men; the sense of shame is found in all men; the sense of respect is found in all men; the sense of right and wrong is found in all men. The sense of mercy constitutes humanity; the sense of shame constitutes righteousness; the sense of respect constitutes decorum *(li);* the sense of right and wrong constitutes wisdom. Humanity, righteousness, decorum, and wisdom are not something instilled into us from without; they are inherent in our nature. Only we give them no thought. Therefore it is said: 'Seek and you will find them, neglect and you will lose them.' Some have these virtues to a much greater degree than others—twice, five times, and incalculably more—and that is because those others have not developed to the fullest extent their original capability. . . ."

Humane Government

. . . . Mencius said: "It was because Chieh and Chou lost the people that they lost the empire, and it was because they lost the hearts of the people that they lost the people. Here is the way to win the empire: win the people and you win the empire. Here is the way to win the people: win their hearts and you win the people. Here is the way to win their hearts: give them and share with them what they like, and do not do to them what they do not like. The people turn to a humane ruler as water flows downward or beasts take to wilderness. . . ."

The Economic Basis of Humane Government

Mencius said to King Hsüan of Ch'i: . . . "Only the true scholar is capable of maintaining, without certain means of livelihood, a steadfast heart. As for the multitude, if they have no certain means of livelihood, they surely cannot maintain a steadfast heart. Without a steadfast heart, they are likely to abandon themselves to any and all manner of depravity. If you wait till they have lapsed into crime and then mete out punishment, it is like placing traps for the people. If a humane ruler is on the throne how can he permit such a thing as placing traps for the people? Therefore, when an intelligent ruler regulates the livelihood of the people, he makes sure that they will have enough to serve their parents on the one hand and to support their wives and children on the other, so that in good years all may eat their fill and in bad years no one need die of starvation. . . ."

Han Fei

. . . When the sage rules the state, he does not count on people doing good of themselves, but employs such measures as will keep them from doing any evil. If he counts on people doing good of themselves, there will not be enough such people to be numbered by the tens in the whole country. But if he employs such measures as will keep them from doing evil, then the entire state can be brought up to a uniform standard. Inasmuch as the administrator has to consider the many but disregard the few, he does not busy himself with morals but with laws.

Evidently, if one should have to count on arrows which are straight of themselves, there would not be any arrows in a hundred generations; if one should only count on pieces of wood which are circular of themselves, there would not be any wheels in a thousand generations. Though in a hundred generations there is neither an arrow that is straight of itself nor a wheel that is circular of itself, yet people in every generation ride carts and shoot birds. Why is that? It is because the tools for straightening and bending are used. Though without the use of such tools there might happen to be an arrow straight of itself or a wheel circular of itself, the skilled carpenter will not prize it. Why? Because it is not just one person who wishes to ride, or just one shot that the archers wish to shoot. Similarly, though without the use of rewards and punishments there might happen to be an individual good of himself, the intelligent ruler will not prize him. The reason is that the law of the state must not be sidetracked and government is not for one man. Therefore, the capable prince will not be swayed by occasional virtue, but will pursue a course that will assure certainty. . . .

Now, when witches and priests pray for people, they say: "May you live as long as one thousand and ten thousand years!" Even as the sounds, "one thousand and ten thousand years," are dinning upon one's ears, there is no sign that even a single day has been added to the age of any man. That is the reason why people despise witches and priests. Likewise, when the Confucianists of the present day counsel the rulers they do not discuss the way to bring about order now, but exalt the achievement of good order in the past. They neither study affairs pertaining to law and government nor observe the realities of vice and wickedness, but all exalt the reputed glories of remote antiquity and the achievements of the ancient kings. Sugar-coating their speech, the Confucianists say: "If you listen to our words, you will be able to become the leader of all feudal lords." Such people are but witches and priests among the itinerant counselors, and are not to be accepted by rulers with principles. Therefore, the intelligent ruler upholds solid facts and discards useless frills. He does not speak about deeds of humanity and righteousness, and he does not listen to the words of learned men.

Those who are ignorant about government insistently say: "Win the hearts of the people." If order could be procured by winning the hearts of the people, then even the wise ministers Yi Yin and Kuan Chung would be of no use. For all that the ruler would need to do would be just to listen to the people. Actually, the intelligence of the people is not to be relied upon any more than the mind of a baby. If the baby does not have his head shaved, his sores will recur; if he does not have his boil cut open, his illness will go from bad to worse. However, in order to shave his head or open the boil someone has to hold the baby while the affectionate mother is performing the work, and yet he keeps crying and yelling incessantly. The baby does not understand that suffering a small pain is the way to obtain a great benefit.

Now, the sovereign urges the tillage of land and the cultivation of pastures for the purpose of increasing production for the people, but they think the sovereign is cruel. The sovereign regulates penalties and increases punishments for the purpose of repressing the wicked, but the people think the sovereign is severe. Again, he levies taxes in cash and in grain to fill up the granaries and treasuries in order to relieve famine and provide for the army, but they think the sovereign is greedy. Finally, he insists upon universal military training without personal favoritism, and urges his forces to fight hard in order to take the enemy captive, but the people think the sovereign is violent. These four measures are methods for attaining order and maintaining peace, but the people are too ignorant to appreciate them.

The reason for the ruler to look for wise and well-informed men is that the intelligence of the people is not such as to be respected or relied upon. For instance, in ancient times, when Yü opened the rivers and deepened them, the people gathered tiles and stones [to hit him]; when the prime minister of Cheng, Tzu Ch'an, cleared the fields and planted mulberry trees, the people of Cheng slandered and reviled him. Yü benefited the whole empire and Tzu Ch'an preserved the state of Cheng, but each incurred slander thereby. Clearly the intelligence of the people is not to be relied upon. Therefore, to seek for the worthy and the wise in selecting officials and to endeavor to suit the people in administering the government are equally the cause of chaos and not the means for attaining order.

. . . . According to the nature of man, none could be more affectionate than one's own parents. And yet in spite of the love of both parents not all children are well brought up. Though the ruler be warm in his affection for his people, how is that necessarily any assurance that there would be no disorder? Now the love of the ancient kings for their people could not have surpassed that of the parents for their children. Since we could not be certain that the children would not be rebellious, how could we assume that the people would definitely be orderly? Moreover, if the ruler should shed tears when a penalty was inflicted in accordance with the law, he might thereby parade his humanity, but not thus conduct his government. Now tearful revulsion against penalties comes from humanity, but necessity of penalties issues from the law. Since even the early kings had to permit the law to prevail and repress their tears, it is clear enough that humanity could not be depended upon for good government. . . .

Now take a young fellow who is a bad character. His parents may get angry at him, but he never makes any change. The villagers may reprove him, but he is not moved. His teachers and elders may admonish him, but he never reforms. The love of his parents, the efforts of the villagers, and the wisdom of his teachers and elders—all the three excellent disciplines are applied to him, and yet not even a hair on his shins is altered. It is only after the district magistrate sends out his soldiers and in the name of the law searches for wicked individuals that the young man becomes afraid and changes his ways and alters his deeds. So while the love of parents is not sufficient to discipline the children, the severe penalties of the district magistrate are. This is because men become naturally spoiled by love, but are submissive to authority. . . .

That being so, rewards should be rich and certain so that the people will be attracted by them; punishments should be severe and definite so that the people will fear them; and laws should be uniform and steadfast so that the people will be familiar with them. Consequently, the sovereign should show no wavering in bestowing rewards and grant no pardon in administering punishments, and he should add honor to rewards and disgrace to punishments—when this is done, then both the worthy and the unworthy will want to exert themselves. . . .

. . . . There was in Ch'u an upright man named Kung, who, when his father stole a sheep, reported it to the authorities. The magistrate said: "Put him to death," as he thought the man was faithful to the ruler but disloyal to his father. So the man was apprehended and convicted. From this we can see that the faithful subject of the ruler was an outrageous son to his father. Again, there was a man of Lu who followed his ruler to war, fought three battles, and ran away three times. Confucius interrogated him. The man replied: "I have an old father. Should I die, nobody would take care of him. " Confucius regarded him as virtuous in filial piety, commended and exalted him.[3] From this we can see that the dutiful son of the father was a rebellious subject to the ruler. Naturally, following the censure of the honest man by the magistrate, no more culprits in Ch'u were reported to the authorities; and following the reward of the runaway by Confucius, the people of Lu were prone to surrender and run away. The interests of superior and subordinate

---

3. This story about Confucius is not recorded anywhere else and evidently is fabricated out of Confucius' teaching on filial piety.

being so different, it would be hopeless for any ruler to try to exalt the deeds of private individuals and, at the same time, to promote the public welfare of the state. . . .

. . . Now the sovereign occupies a position of authority over his subjects and possesses the wealth of a state. If only he will make rewards great and punishments severe, intensifying thereby the searching light of his statecraft, then even ministers like T'ien Ch'ang and Tzu-han, wicked as they may be, will not dare to deceive him. What need does he have of men who are not deceitful? Today one cannot count even ten men of devotion and faithfulness, yet official posts in the country are counted by the hundreds. If only men of devotion and faithfulness were appointed to office, there would be an insufficiency of candidates, and in that case guardians of order would be few, while disturbers of peace would be many. Therefore the way of the enlightened sovereign consists in making laws uniform and not depending upon the wisdom of men, in making statecraft firm and not yearning after faithful persons, so that the laws do not fail to function and the multitude of officials will commit neither villainy nor deception. . . .

12

The Political Tradition

John K. Fairbank

Bureaucracy—along with gunpowder, printing, paper, and the magnetic com-
pass—is often considered one of the great Chinese inventions. The workings of
the bureaucracy and the role of the "scholar-gentry" class, which were essential
to the administration of the vast imperial system, are detailed by John K. Fairbank
in the following excerpt from his classic study The United States and China.

The Gentry

The gentry dominated Chinese life increasingly during the last thousand years, so much so that sociologists have called China a gentry state
and even ordinary people may speak of the "scholar gentry" as a class.
But do not let yourself be reminded of the landed gentry with their roast
beef and fox hunts in merry England, for "gentry" in the case of China
is a technical term with two principal meanings and an inner ambiguity.
It requires special handling.

Non-Marxists generally agree, first of all, that the gentry were not
a mere "feudal landlord" class, because Chinese society was not organized in any system that can be called feudalism, except possibly before
221 B.C. While "feudal" may still be a useful swear word, it has little
value as a Western term applied to China. For instance, an essential
characteristic of feudalism, as the word has been used with reference to
medieval Europe and Japan, has been the inalienability of the land. The

medieval serf was bound to the land and could not himself either leave it or dispose of it, whereas the Chinese peasant both in law and in fact has been free to sell and, if he had the means, to purchase land. His bondage has resulted from a press of many circumstances but not from a legal institution similar to European feudalism. Nor has it been maintained by the domination of a professional warrior caste. Avoidance of the term feudal to describe the Chinese peasant's situation in life by no means signifies that it has been less miserable. But if the word feudal is to retain a valid meaning for European and other institutions to which it was originally applied, it cannot be very meaningful in a general Chinese context.

The Chinese gentry can be understood only in a dual, economic and political sense, as connected both with landholding and with office holding. The narrow definition, following the traditional Chinese terminology, confines gentry status to those *individuals* who held official degrees gained normally by passing examinations, or sometimes by recommendation or purchase. This has the merit of being concrete and even quantifiable—the gentry in this narrow sense were degree-holders, as officially listed, and not dependent for their status on economic resources, particularly landowning, which is so hard to quantify from the historical record. Moreover, the million or so men who held the first level degree under the Ch'ing must be seen ... as "lower gentry" barely removed from commoner status, whereas the small elite who after further years of effort went on up through the rigorous week-long examination rounds at the provincial capital and at Peking formed an "upper gentry" of great influence.

The gentry as individuals were public functionaries, playing political and administrative roles. Yet they were also enmeshed in family relations, on which they could rely for material sustenance. This political-economic dualism has led many writers to define the term gentry more broadly, as a group of *families* rather than of individual degree-holders only. Both the narrow and the broad definitions must be kept in mind.

The gentry families lived chiefly in the walled towns, not in the villages. They constituted a stratum of families based on landed property which intervened between the earth-bound masses of the peasantry, on the one hand, and the officials and merchants who formed a fluid matrix of overall administrative and commercial activity, on the other. They were the local elite, who carried on certain functions connected with the peasantry below and certain others connected with the officials above. . . .

For the officials of the old China the gentry families were one medium through whom tax collections were effected. By this same token they were for the peasantry intermediaries who could palliate official oppression while in the process of carrying it out. The local official dealt with conditions of flood or famine or incipient rebellion and the multitude of minor criminal cases and projects for public works, all through the help of the gentry community. It was the buffer between populace and officialdom.

A poor man, by his educational qualifications alone, could become a member of the gentry in the narrow sense used above, even though he was not connected with a gentry family. Nevertheless, the degree-holding individuals were in most cases connected with landowning families, and the latter in most cases had degree-holding members. In general, the gentry families were the out-of-office reservoir of the degree-holders and the bureaucracy. The big families were the seedbed in which officeholders were nurtured and the haven to which dismissed or worn-out bureaucrats could return.

In each community the gentry had many important public functions. They raised funds for and supervised public works—the building and upkeep of irrigation and communication facilities such as canals, dikes, dams, roads, bridges, ferries. They supported Confucian institutions and morals—establishing and maintaining schools, shrines and local temples of Confucius, publishing books, especially local histories or gazetteers, and issuing moral homilies and exhortations to the populace. In time of peace they set the tone of public life. In time of disorder they organized and commanded militia defense forces. From day to day they arbitrated disputes informally, in place of the continual litigation which goes on in any American town. The gentry also set up charities and handled trust funds to help the community, and made contributions at official request to help the state, especially in times of war, flood, or famine. So useful were these contributions that most dynasties got revenue by selling the lowest literary degrees, thus admitting many persons to degree-holding status without examination. While this abused the system, it also let men of wealth rise for a price into the upper class and share the gentry privileges, such as contact with the officials and immunity from corporal punishment.

The local leadership and management functions of the gentry families explain why officialdom did not penetrate lower down into Chinese society. . . .

In this way the imperial government remained a superstructure which did not directly enter the villages because it rested upon the gentry as its foundation. The many public functions of the local degree holders made a platform under the imperial bureaucracy and let the officials move about with remarkable fluidity and seeming independence of local roots. Actually, the Emperor's appointee to any magistracy could administer it only with the cooperation of the gentry in that area. All in all, in a country of over 400 million people, a century ago, there were less than 20,000 regular imperial officials but roughly one and a quarter million scholarly degree holders. . . .

The Political Tradition

The imperial system survived until 1912, the year Woodrow Wilson was elected President of the United States. The leaders of Republican China grew up under the empire. Those who dominate the Chinese scene today need think back only fifty years to recall the imperial splendor of the old Empress Dowager, the lavish trappings of despotism, the eunuchs, concubines, and court attendants, palace guards and palanquins, formal audiences, kowtow and lesser rituals, within the high red walls and gold-tiled roofs of the palace at Peking. These things have barely passed away. To look at modern China without seeing them in the background makes no more sense than to look at the United States without any recollection of Washington and Jefferson, Dan Boone and Abe Lincoln, manifest destiny, or the rise of the common man and John D. Rockefeller.

Bureaucracy

One key to the understanding of the People's Republic of China today is the fact that the old imperial government was a bureaucracy of the most thoroughly developed and sophisticated sort. To the American who has confronted the problems of bureaucracy only recently, the effort of modern Chinese to escape from the evils and capitalize upon the good points of their own bureaucratic tradition is a matter of absorbing interest.

The old government centered in the capital. Without question the vast symmetrical plan of Peking made it the most magnificently ruler-centered of all capital cities. Paris and London are more diffuse. Washington and Moscow are creations of yesterday and do not attest, in a balance of gate against gate and avenue against avenue, the omnipotence of oriental despots who created their capital city as an outer cover to their palace. Although the great city wall and gate towers were torn down in the 1960s, Peking still centers upon the moated red walls of the Forbidden City. Within it the yellow-roofed throne halls rising from their marble platforms form the main axis of the whole metropolis. Behind them a great man-made hill of earth protects them from the north. Before them were broad avenues, and today a great square stretches south to the old front gate of the city. No Western capital is so plainly a symbol of centralized and absolute monarchy.

At Peking, for the greater part of thirteen centuries the civil administration of China was divided among the famous Six Ministries (or Boards) of civil office (appointment of officials), revenue, ceremonies, war, punishments, and public works (such as flood control). This structure, adumbrated in the first imperial system of the Ch'in and Han, had been formally established under the T'ang. In addition to the Six Ministries there were two other independent hierarchies of administration, the military establishment and the Censorate, as well as a number of minor offices: the imperial academy of literature, a court to review criminal cases, a historiographer's office, the imperial stud, and offices in charge of banquets and sacrificial worship. At the apex of everything the Ming had created the Grand Secretariat, in which high officials assisted the Emperor in his personal administration of affairs. One of the few Manchu innovations was to add in 1729 a less formal body, the Grand Council, which handled military and other important matters and so became the real top of the administration.

Spread out over the eighteen provinces of China under the Manchu dynasty was a network of territorial divisions. Each province was divided into several circuits *(tao)* and below them into prefectures, departments, and *hsien* or counties in descending order. The mandarins in charge of these divisions with their ubiquitous assistants and subordinates formed the main body of the territorial magistracy. Like civil servants trained in the classics at Oxford and Cambridge, they were supposedly omnicompetent, responsible for the collection of revenue, maintenance of order, dispensing of justice, conduct of literary examinations, superintendence of the postal service, and in general for all public events within their areas. Theoretically, they stood *in loco parentis* to the people and were called, or rather called themselves, the "father and mother officials."

The imperial civil service was divided into nine ranks, each of which was divided into upper and lower grades. Each rank was entitled to a particular and very fine costume, including a colored button on the cap and insignia such as "mandarin squares" embroidered on the front and back of the gown. Prerogatives, titles, and dignities were minutely set forth in the statutes. High officials might be rewarded with the right to wear a peacock feather or bear the title of "Junior Guardian of the Heir Apparent."

Intervening between the hierarchy of local officials and the government at the capital stood the higher administration in each province. This consisted of a governor-general who was in most cases responsible for two provinces and, as his junior colleague, a governor responsible for a single province. These two officials were of course so placed as to check each other, for they were expected to act and report jointly on important matters. Under the Ch'ing (Manchu) dynasty, frequently the governor-general was a Manchu and the governor Chinese. Beneath them were four provincial officers who exercised province-wide functions: a treasurer, judge, salt comptroller, and grain intendant (who supervised the collection of grain for the capital).

Official business over the far-flung Chinese empire was conducted as in all bureaucracies by a flow of documents of many kinds. In their special forms and designations these multifarious communications mirrored the elaborate proliferation of red tape. A governor addressed his imperial master in certain prescribed forms and addressed his subordinates in others. Every communication began with a clear indication of its nature as a document to a superior, an equal, or a subordinate. Similarly there were special forms for memorials submitted to the Emperor and edicts issued from him. Each document also went through a certain procedure of preparation, transmission, and reception. Hundreds of thousands of brushwielding scriveners were kept busy year in and year out transcribing, recording, and processing official communications. In the imperial archives of the Peking palace are more than one hundred different types of documents which were in common use.

The flow of paper work was maintained by an official post which reached to all corners of the empire but was limited to the transportation of official mail, official shipments (as of funds), and persons traveling on official business. This postal system was made up of some two thousand stations stretched out along five main and many subsidiary routes which ran into Manchuria, across Mongolia, westward to Turkestan and Tibet, southeastward through the coastal provinces, and southward through the interior of Central China. Couriers and travelers on these routes were provided with official tallies entitling them to the use of the transportation facilities, which in different areas might be horses, camels, donkeys, chairs (palanquins), or boats. In time of crisis couriers could cover 250 miles a day.

Such speed was achieved by the use of horses in relays, a system which the Mongols had developed to cover the distances of Central Asia. In the early nineteenth century this pony express regularly transmitted messages from Canton to Peking in less than three weeks and from Shanghai to Peking in one week.

Central Controls. Given this network of officials, connected by a flow of documents and persons along the postal routes, it was the problem of the capital to stimulate the local bureaucrats to perform their functions and yet prevent them from getting out of hand. This control was achieved by the application of techniques common to bureaucracies everywhere, in addition to the special measures (noted above) whereby the Manchus sought to preserve their dynasty.

Among these techniques the first was the appointment of all officers down to the rank of district magistrate by the Emperor himself. This made them all aware of their dependence upon the Son of Heaven and their duty of personal loyalty to him. Circulation in office was another device. An official was seldom left in one post for more than three years or at most six years. Ordinarily when moving from one post to another the official passed through the capital and participated in an imperial audience to renew his contact with the ruler.

Thus Chinese officialdom was a mobile body which circulated through all parts of the empire without taking root in any one place. In this it was aided by its reliance upon the Mandarin (Peking) dialect as a lingua franca of universal currency in official circles. Frequently an official would arrive at his new post to find himself quite incapable of understanding the local dialect and therefore the more closely confined to his official level. One means to prevent officials taking local root was the "law of avoidance" according to which no mandarin could be appointed to office in his native province, where the claims of family loyalty might impair devotion to the imperial regime.

Another custom which interrupted an official's rise to power was the rule of three years' mourning (actually some twenty-five months) after the death of his father, during which an official retired to a life of quiet abstention from worldly activities. As Arthur Waley says, this was "a sort of 'sabbatical' occurring as a rule toward the middle of a man's official career. It gave him a period for study and reflection, for writing at last the book that he had planned … for repairing a life ravaged by official banqueting, a constitution exhausted by the joint claims of concubinage and matrimony."

In general the bureaucratic principle was to set one official to check upon another. This was done particularly through the system of joint responsibility. The Six Ministries each had two presidents, one Manchu and one Chinese, who watched each other. It was common to appoint one man after he had gained prominence to several offices so that he was not able to master any one of them, and at the same time to appoint many men to perform one job so that no one of them could completely control it. Indeed many offices were sometimes created to carry on the same function, checking each other through their duplication of activity. The result of this duplication of offices and mutual responsibility was to hedge each official about with a multiplicity of commitments in each of which others were concerned. It was something like the unlimited liability of a partnership in which there were dozens of partners. Over and above all these immediate checks created by the involvement of many officials in a common responsibility, there was a system of the Censorate. Under it some fifty-six censors selected for their loyalty and uprightness were stationed in fifteen circuits through the provinces with the duty of keeping the emperor informed upon all matters concerning the welfare of the people and the dynasty. The early Ch'ing rulers even invented an eyes-alone type of "palace memorial" by which designated officials could send secret reports, to be opened only by the emperor and returned with his comments only to the sender. The ruler thus had his informers throughout the bureaucracy.

The evils inherent in bureaucracy were all too evident. All business was in form originated at the bottom and passed upward to the emperor for decision at the top, memorials from the provinces being addressed to the emperor at the capital. The higher authority was thus left to choose alternatives of action proposed, and yet the proposal of novel or unprecedented action was both difficult and dangerous for the lower official. The greater safety of conformity tended to kill initiative at the bottom. On the other hand the efficiency of the one man at the top was constantly impaired by his becoming a bottleneck. All business of importance and precedent were established by his edict. Modern China still suffers from this tradition.

In view of the complete and arbitrary power which the imperial bureaucracy asserted over the whole of Chinese life, it is amazing how few and how scattered the officials were in number. The total of civil officials for whom posts were statutorily available, both at the capital and in the provinces, was hardly more than 9000. The military officials were supposed to number only about 7500. It is true, of course, that there was an increasing number of supernumerary or "expectant" officials who might be assigned to various functions without receiving substantive appointments. There was also the vast body of clerks and factota necessary for the copying, recording, negotiating, and going and coming in each Chinese official's establishment or yamen. Down to the gatemen, runners, and chairbearers, these human elements in the official machine no doubt totaled millions. But if we look for the men of genuine official status who could take official action and report it in the hierarchy as representatives of his imperial majesty, we find them few and thinly spread, totaling at a rough estimate hardly more than 30 or 40 thousand "officials" at most, ruling over a country of about 200 million which grew to perhaps 400 million by the middle of the nineteenth century. Of the nine ranks, for example, the seventh rank near the bottom of the scale began with the county magistrate who was responsible for a population on the order of 300,000 persons. This relative smallness of the imperial administration reflected the fact that it depended upon the gentry class to lead and dominate the peasantry in the villages. . . .

13

The Chinese Revolution

Mao Zedong

Mao Zedong led the Chinese Communist Party from the mid-1930s until his death in 1976. During these years he made the most important contributions to the formulation of Marxist theory in China. The excerpts below illustrate two very different periods in his thinking. The first excerpt, written in 1947, represents Mao's early thinking on the challenges of the Chinese revolution. In this report Mao downplays the revolutionization in Chinese society and emphasizes the importance of economic construction. The next three excerpts are from the "later" Mao. In these statements he emphasizes revolutionization. Here we see the concerns that came to preoccupy him for the rest of his life: distrust of expertise and the necessity for "permanent revolution."

The Present Situation and Our Tasks

The Chinese people's revolutionary war has now reached a turning point. That is, the Chinese People's Liberation Army has beaten back the offensive of several million reactionary troops of Chiang Kai-shek, the running dog of the United States of America, and gone over to the offensive.... This is a turning point in history. It is the turning point from growth to extinction for Chiang Kai-shek's twenty-year counter-revolutionary rule. It is the turning point from growth to extinction for imperialist rule in China, now over a hundred years old....

After the Japanese surrender, the peasants urgently demanded land, and we made a timely decision to change our land policy from reducing rent and interest to confiscating the land of the landlord class for distribution among the peasants. The directive issued by the Central Committee of our party on May 4, 1946, marked this change.... But there should be no repetition of the wrong ultra-left policy, which was carried out in 1931–34, of "allotting no land to the landlords and poor land to the rich peasants." Although the proportion of landlords and rich peasants in the rural population varies from place to place, it is generally only about 8 percent (in terms of households), while their holdings usually amount to 70 to 80 percent of all the land. Therefore the targets of our land reform are very few, while the people in the villages who can and should take part in the united front for land reform are many—more than 90 percent (in terms of households). Here two fundamental principles must be observed. First, the demands of the poor peasants and farm laborers must be satisfied; this is the most fundamental task in the land reform. Second, there must be firm unity with the middle peasants, and their interests must not be damaged.... In carrying out equal distribution of land in different places, it is necessary to listen to the opinions of the middle peasants and make concessions to them if they object. During the confiscation and distribution of land and property of the feudal class, the needs of certain middle peasants should receive attention. In determining class status care must be taken to avoid the mistake of classifying middle peasants as rich peasants. The active middle peasants must be drawn into the work of the peasant association committees and the government. With respect to the burdens of the land tax and of supporting the war, the principle of being fair and reasonable must be observed. These are the specific policies our party must follow in carrying out its strategic task of uniting solidly with the middle peasants. The whole party must understand that thoroughgoing reform of the land system is a basic task of the Chinese Revolution in its present stage. If we can solve the land problem universally and completely, we shall have obtained the most fundamental condition for the defeat of all our enemies. ...

Confiscate the land of the feudal class and turn it over to the peasants. Confiscate monopoly capital, headed by Chiang Kai-shek, T. V. Soong, H. H. Kung, and Ch'en Li-fu, and turn it over to the new democratic state. Protect the industry and commerce of the national bourgeoisie. These are the three major economic policies of the new democratic revolution. During their twenty-year rule, the four big families, Chiang,

Soong, Kung, and Ch'en, have piled up enormous fortunes valued at ten or twenty thousand million U.S. dollars and monopolized the economic lifelines of the whole country. This monopoly capital, combined with state power, has become state monopoly capitalism. This monopoly capitalism, closely tied up with foreign imperialism, the domestic landlord class and the old-type rich peasants, has become compradore, feudal, state monopoly capitalism. Such is the economic base of Chiang Kai-shek's reactionary regime. The state monopoly capitalism oppresses not only the workers and peasants but also the petty bourgeoisie, and it injures the middle bourgeoisie. This state monopoly capitalism reached the peak of its development during the War of Resistance and after the Japanese surrender; it has prepared ample material conditions for the new democratic revolution. This capital is popularly known in China as a bureaucrat-capital. This capitalist class, known as the bureaucrat-capitalist class, is the big bourgeoisie of China. Besides doing away with the special privileges of imperialism in China, the task of the new democratic revolution at home is to abolish exploitation and oppression by the landlord class and by the bureaucrat-capitalist class (the big bourgeoisie), change the compradore, feudal relations of production and unfetter the productive forces. The petty bourgeoisie and middle bourgeoisie, oppressed and injured by the landlords and big bourgeoisie and their state power, may take part in the new democratic revolution or stay neutral, though they are themselves bourgeois. They have no ties, or comparatively few, with imperialism and are the genuine national bourgeoisie. Wherever the state power of new democracy extends, it must firmly and unhesitatingly protect them. . . . The new democratic revolution aims at wiping out only feudalism and monopoly capitalism, only the landlord class and the bureaucrat-capitalist class (the big bourgeoisie), and not at wiping out capitalism in general, the upper petty bourgeoisie or the middle bourgeoisie. In view of China's economic backwardness, even after the country-wide victory of the revolution, it will still be necessary to permit the existence for a long time of a capitalist sector of the economy represented by the extensive petty bourgeoisie and middle bourgeoisie. In accordance with the division of labor in the national economy, a certain development of all parts of this capitalist sector which are beneficial to the national economy will still be needed. This capitalist sector will still be an indispensable part of the whole national economy. The petty bourgeoisie referred to here are small industrialists and merchants employing workers or assistants. In addition, there are also great numbers of small independent craftsmen and traders who employ no workers or assistants and, needless to say, they should be firmly protected. After the victory of the revolution all over the country, the new democratic state will possess huge state enterprises taken over from the bureaucrat-capitalist class and controlling the economic lifelines of the country, and there will be an agricultural economy liberated from feudalism which, though it will remain basically scattered and individual for a fairly long time, can later be led to develop, step by step, in the direction of cooperatives. In these circumstances the existence and development of these small and middle capitalist sectors will present no danger. The same is true of the new rich peasant economy which will inevitably emerge in the rural areas after the land reform. It is absolutely impermissible to repeat such wrong ultra-left policies toward the petty bourgeois and middle bourgeois sectors in the economy as our party adopted during 1931–34 (unduly advanced labor conditions, excessive income tax rates, encroachment on the interests of industrialists and merchants during the land reform, and the adoption as a goal of the so-called "workers' welfare," which was a short-sighted and one-sided concept, instead of the goal of developing production, promoting economic prosperity, giving consideration to both public and private interests and benefiting both labor and capital). To repeat such mistakes would certainly damage the interests both of the working masses and of the new democratic state.... To sum up, the economic structure of new China will consist of: (1) the state-owned economy, which is the leading sector; (2) the agricultural economy, developing step by step from individual to collective; and (3) the economy of small independent craftsmen and traders and the economy of small and middle private capital. These constitute the whole of the new democratic national economy. The principles guiding the new democratic national economy must closely conform to the general objective of developing production, promoting economic prosperity, giving consideration to both public and private interests and benefiting both labor and capital. Any principle, policy, or measure that deviates from this general objective is wrong.

The Vision of the Great Leap

Speech at the Supreme State Conference

Now our enthusiasm has been aroused. Ours is an ardent nation, now swept by a burning tide. There is a good metaphor for this: our nation is like an atom.... When this atom's nucleus is smashed the thermal energy released will have really tremendous power. We shall be able to do things which we could not do before. When our nation has this great energy we shall catch up with Britain in fifteen years; we shall produce forty million tons of steel annually—now we produce only just over five million tons; we shall have a generating capacity of 450,000 million kwh of electricity—at present we can generate only 40,000 million kwh, which means increasing our capacity ten times, for which we must increase hydroelectric production and not only thermoelectric. We still have ten years to carry out the Forty Point Program for Agricultural Development, but it looks as if we shall not need ten years. Some people say five years, others three. It would seem that we can complete it in eight....

I stand for the theory of permanent revolution. Do not mistake this for Trotsky's theory of permanent revolution. In making revolution one must strike while the iron is hot—one revolution must follow another, the revolution must continually advance. The Hunanese often say, "Straw sandals have no pattern—they shape themselves in the making." Trotsky believed that the socialist revolution is complete. We are not like that. For example, after the liberation of 1949 came the land reform; as soon as this was completed there followed the mutual aid teams, then the low-level cooperatives, then the high-level cooperatives. After seven years the cooperativization was completed and productive relationships were transformed; then came the rectification. After rectification was finished, before things had cooled down, then came the technical revolution....

It is possible to catch up with Britain in fifteen years. We must summon up our strength and swim vigorously upstream.

Talks at Chengtu

In the period following the liberation of the whole country (from 1950 to 1957), dogmatism made its appearance both in economic and in cultural and educational work. In economic work dogmatism primarily manifested itself in heavy industry, planning, banking and statistics, especially in heavy industry and planning. Since we didn't understand these things and had absolutely no experience, all we could do in our ignorance was to import foreign methods. Our statistical work was practically a copy of Soviet work; in the educational field copying was also pretty bad, for example, the system of a maximum mark of five in the schools, the uniform five years of primary school, etc. We did not even study our own experience of education in the liberated areas. The same applied to our public health work, with the result that I couldn't have eggs or chicken soup for three years because an article appeared in the Soviet Union which said that one shouldn't eat them. Later they said one could eat them. It didn't matter whether the article was correct or not, the Chinese listened all the same and respectfully obeyed. In short, the Soviet Union was tops. . . .

On Uninterrupted Revolution

Permanent revolution. Our revolutions follow each other, one after another. . . . We must now have a technical revolution, in order to catch up with and overtake England in fifteen years or a bit longer. Because China is economically backward, and its material foundation is weak, we have hitherto been in a passive position. Mentally, we feel that we are still fettered; in this respect, we have not yet achieved liberation. We must summon up our energies, and in another five years, we may be in a somewhat more active position. After ten years, we will be in a still more active position. After fifteen years, when we have more grain and more iron and steel, we will be in a position to exercise yet greater initiative. Our revolution is like fighting a war. After winning one battle, we must immediately put forward new tasks. In this way, we can maintain the revolutionary enthusiasm of the cadres and the masses, and diminish their self-satisfaction, since they have no time to be satisfied with themselves even if they wanted to; new tasks keep pressing in, and everyone devotes his mind to the question of how to fulfill the new tasks. In calling for a technical revolution, we aim to make everyone study technology and science. The rightists say we are petty intellectuals, incapable of leading the big intellectuals. There are also those who say that the old cadres should be "bought off," paid a bit of money and asked to retire, because the old cadres do not understand science and technology, and only know how to fight and to carry out land reform. . . . We must learn new skills, we must really understand professional work *(yeh-wu)*, we must really understand science and technology. Otherwise, we will be incapable of exercising good leadership. . . . Once attention is shifted to the technical side, there is also the possibility of neglecting politics. We must therefore pay attention to integrating technology with politics.

The relation between redness and expertness, between politics and professional activities *(yeh-wu)*, is that of the unity of two opposites. We must definitely criticize and repudiate the tendency to pay no attention to politics. On the one hand, we must oppose empty-headed politicians; on the other hand, we must oppose pragmatists who lose their sense of direction.

Those who pay no attention to ideology and politics, and are busy with their work all day long, will become economists or technicians who have lost their sense of direction, and this is very dangerous. Ideological work and political work are the guarantee that economic and technical work will be carried through, they serve the economic basis. Ideology and politics are the supreme commander; they are the soul. Whenever we are even slightly lax in our ideological and political work, our economic and technical work will certainly take a false direction.

At present, there is on the one hand the grave class struggle between the socialist world and the imperialist world. On the other hand, as regards conditions within our country, classes have not yet been finally wiped out, and there is still class struggle. . . . During the period of transition from capitalism to socialism, there are still hidden among the people some anti-socialist hostile elements, such as the bourgeois rightists. In dealing with such elements, we also adopt basically the method of solving the problems by letting the masses air their views. It is only toward serious counterrevolutionary elements and saboteurs that we adopt the method of repression. After the transition period has come to an end, and classes have been completely abolished, then, as far as conditions within the country are concerned, politics will consist entirely of relationships among the people. At that time, ideological and political struggle among man and man, as well as revolution, will definitely still continue to exist, and moreover cannot fail to exist. The law of the unity of opposites, the law of quantitative and qualitative change, the law of affirmation and negation, exist forever and universally. But the nature of struggle and revolution is different from what it was in the past. It is not a class struggle, but a struggle between the advanced and backward among the people, a struggle between advanced and backward science and technology. The transition from socialism to communism is a struggle, a revolution. Even when we have reached the era of communism, there will definitely still be many, many stages of development, and the relationship between one stage and another will necessarily be a relation leading from quantitative change to qualitative change. Every mutation or leap is a revolution, and they must all go through struggle. The "theory of no clashes" is metaphysical. . . .

14

Ideology after Mao

CCP Constitution / Deng Xiaoping
Zhao Ziyang / Li Peng

After Mao's death in 1976, Deng Xiaoping and his colleagues set about reversing much of Mao's revolutionary theorizing. In general, they sharply criticized his emphasis on class struggle, the distrust of the intellectuals, and the ascetic tone which they thought permeated Chinese life during his last years. However, they did not abandon all of Mao's concerns. In the preamble to the 1982 Communist Party Constitution we see the post-Mao focus on national unity and economic betterment, but the references to class struggle persist, along with exhortations to promote ideological education. The two emphases have coexisted uneasily since then. In the excerpt from Deng Xiaoping's comments during student unrest in 1986, we see his powerful commitment to eliminating dissidence. A year later, Zhao Ziyang, the General Secretary of the Communist Party who would be purged in the midst of the Tiananmen demonstrations, touched on the issue of class struggle, but stressed the importance of economic growth by using the term "initial stage of socialism" to describe China's condition. During such a period, he argued, the development of a diversified economy was a central task of the nation. However, in the wake of Tiananmen, preoccupation with ideological erosion returned, as illustrated by the report presented by Li Peng, the Premier of China, who declared martial law during the demonstrations.

The Constitution of the Communist Party of China, 1982

The Communist Party of China is the vanguard of the Chinese working class, the faithful representative of the interests of the people of all nationalities in China, and the force at the core leading China's cause of socialism. The Party's ultimate goal is the creation of a communist social system. . . .

The Chinese Communists, with Comrade Mao Zedong as their chief representative, created Mao Zedong Thought by integrating the universal principles of Marxism-Leninism with the concrete practice of the Chinese revolution. Mao Zedong Thought is Marxism-Leninism applied and developed in China; it consists of a body of theoretical principles concerning the revolution and construction in China and a summary of experience therein, both of which have been proved correct by practice; it represents the crystallized, collective wisdom of the Communist Party of China.

The Communist Party of China led the people of all nationalities in waging their prolonged revolutionary struggle against imperialism, feudalism and bureaucrat-capitalism, winning victory in the new-democratic revolution and establishing the People's Republic of China—a people's democratic dictatorship. After the founding of the People's Republic, it led them in smoothly carrying out socialist transformation, completing the transition from New Democracy to socialism, establishing the socialist system, and developing socialism in its economic, political and cultural aspects.

After the elimination of the exploiting classes as such, most of the contradictions in Chinese society do not have the nature of class struggle, and class struggle is no longer the principle contradiction. However, owing to domestic circumstances and foreign influences, class struggle will continue to exist within certain limits for a long time, and may even sharpen under certain conditions. The principal contradiction in Chinese society is that between the people's growing material and cultural needs and the backward level of our social production. The other contradictions should be resolved in the course of resolving this principal one. It is essential to strictly distinguish and correctly handle the two different types of contradictions—the contradictions between the enemy and ourselves and those among the people.

The general task of the Communist Party of China at the present stage is to unite the people of all nationalities in working hard and self-reliantly to achieve, step by step, the modernization of our industry, agriculture, national defense and science and technology and make China a culturally advanced and highly democratic socialist country.

The focus of the work of the Communist Party of China is to lead the people of all nationalities in accomplishing the socialist modernization of our economy. It is necessary vigorously to expand the productive forces and gradually perfect socialist relations of production, in keeping with the actual level of the productive forces and as required for their expansion. It is necessary to strive for the gradual improvement of the standards of material and cultural life of the urban and rural population, based on the growth of production and social wealth.

The Communist Party of China leads the people, as they work for a high level of material civilization, in building a high level of socialist spiritual civilization. Major efforts should be made to promote education, science and culture, imbue the Party members and the masses of the people with communist ideology, combat and overcome decadent bourgeois ideas, remnant feudal ideas and other non-proletarian ideas, and encourage the Chinese people to have lofty ideals, moral integrity, education and a sense of discipline. . . .

Take a Clear-Cut Stand against Bourgeois Liberalization

Deng Xiaoping, December 30, 1986

The recent student unrest is not going to lead to any major disturbances. But because of its nature it must be taken very seriously. Firm measures must be taken against any student who creates trouble at Tiananmen Square. The rules and regulations on marches and demonstrations promulgated by the Standing Committee of the Municipal People's Congress of Beijing have the force of law and should be resolutely enforced. No concessions should made in this matter. In the beginning, we mainly used persuasion, which is as it should be in dealing with student demonstrators. But if any of them disturb public order or violate the law, they must be dealt with unhesitatingly. . . . It is essential to adhere firmly to the Four Cardinal Principles; otherwise bourgeois liberalization will spread unchecked—and that has been the root cause of the problem. But this student unrest is also a good thing, insofar as it is a reminder to us.

... We have to admit that on the ideological and theoretical front both central and local authorities have been weak and have lost ground. They have taken a laissez-faire attitude towards bourgeois liberalization, so that good people find no support while bad people go wild. Good people don't dare to speak out, as if they were in the wrong. But they are not in the wrong at all. We must stand up for the Four Cardinal Principles and especially the people's democratic dictatorship. There is no way to ensure continued political stability and unity without the people's democratic dictatorship. People who confuse right and wrong, who turn black into white, who start rumors and spread slanders can't be allowed to go around with impunity stirring the masses up to make trouble. A few years ago we punished according to law some exponents of liberalization who broke the law. Did that bring discredit on us? No, China's image was not damaged. On the contrary, the prestige of our country is steadily growing.

In developing our democracy, we cannot simply copy bourgeois democracy, or introduce the system of a balance of three powers. I have often criticized people in power in the United States, saying that actually they have three governments. Of course, the American bourgeoisie uses this system in dealing with other countries, but when it comes to internal affairs, the three branches often pull in different directions, and that makes trouble. We cannot adopt such a system. . . .

Without leadership by the Communist Party and without socialism, there is no future for China. This truth has been demonstrated in the past, and it will be demonstrated again in future. When we succeed in raising China's per capita GNP to $4,000 and everyone is prosperous, that will better demonstrate the superiority of socialism over capitalism, it will point the way for three quarters of the world's population and it will provide further proof of the correctness of Marxism. Therefore, we must confidently keep to the socialist road and uphold the Four Cardinal Principles.

We cannot do without dictatorship. We must not only affirm the need for it but exercise it when necessary. Of course, we must be cautious about resorting to dictatorial means and make as few arrests as possible. But if some people attempt to provoke bloodshed, what are we going to do about it? We should first expose their plot and then do our best to avoid shedding blood, even if that means some of our own people get hurt. However, ringleaders who have violated the law must be sentenced according to law. Unless we are prepared to do that, it will be impossible to put an end to disturbances. If we take no action and back down, we shall only have more trouble down the road. . . .

This time, we have to take action against those who openly oppose socialism and the Communist Party. This may make some waves, but that's nothing to be afraid of. We must resolutely impose sanctions on Fang Lizhi, Liu Binyan and Wang Ruowang, who are so arrogant that they want to remold the Communist Party. What qualifications do they have to be Party members? . . .

The struggle against bourgeois liberalization will last for at least twenty years. Democracy can develop only gradually, and we cannot copy Western systems. If we did, that would only make a mess of everything. Our socialist construction can only be carried out under leadership, in an orderly way and in an environment of stability and unity. That's why I lay such emphasis on the need for high ideals and strict discipline. Bourgeois liberalization would plunge the country into turmoil once more. Bourgeois liberalization means rejection of the Party's leadership; there would be nothing to unite our one billion people, and the Party itself would lose all power to fight. A party like that would be no better than a mass organization; how could it be expected to lead the people in construction? . . .

The struggle against bourgeois liberalization is also indispensable. We should not be afraid that it will damage our reputation abroad. China must take its own road and build socialism with Chinese characteristics—that is the only way China can have a future. We must show foreigners that China's political situation is stable. If our country were plunged into disorder and our nation reduced to a heap of loose sand, how could we ever prosper? The reason the imperialists were able to bully us in the past was precisely that we were a heap of loose sand. . . .

Advance along the Road of Socialism with Chinese Characteristics

Zhao Ziyang, October 25, 1987

. . . Building socialism in a big, backward Eastern country like China is something new in the history of the development of Marxism. We are not in the situation envisaged by the founders of Marxism, in which socialism is built on the basis of highly developed capitalism, nor are we in exactly the same situation as other socialist countries. So we cannot blindly follow what the books say, nor can we mechanically imitate the examples of other countries. Rather, proceeding from China's actual conditions and integrating the basic principles of Marxism with those conditions, we must find a way to build socialism with Chinese characteristics through practice. Our Party has explored ways of doing this and has achieved major successes. but the road it has traversed has taken many twists and turns, and this has cost us dear. Beginning in the late 1950s, under the influence of the mistaken Left thinking, we were too impatient for quick results and sought absolute perfection, believing that we could dramatically expand the productive forces by relying simply on our subjective will and on mass movements, and that the broader the scale and the higher the level of socialist ownership, the better. Also, for a long time we relegated the task of expanding the productive forces to a position of secondary importance and continued to "take class struggle as the key link" after the socialist transformation was basically completed. Many things which fettered the growth of the productive forces and which were not inherently socialist, or were applicable only under certain particular historical conditions, were regarded as "socialist principles" to be adhered to. Conversely, many things which, under socialist conditions, were favorable to the growth of the productive forces and to the commercialization, socialization and modernization of production were dubbed "restoration of capitalism" to be opposed. As a consequence, a structure of ownership evolved in which undue emphasis was placed on a single form of ownership, and a rigid economic structure took shape, along with a corresponding political structure based on over-concentration of power. All this seriously hampered the development of the productive forces and of the socialist commodity economy. This state of affairs has taught us that it is of prime importance to have a clear understanding of China's basic conditions and of the present stage of socialism in China.

What, then, is this historic stage, the primary stage of socialism in China? It is not the initial phase in a general sense, a phase that every country goes through in the process of building socialism. Rather it is, in a particular sense, the specific stage China must necessarily go through while building socialism under conditions of backward productive forces and an underdeveloped commodity economy. It will be at least 100 year from the 1950s, when the socialist transformation of private ownership of the means of production was basically completed, to the time when socialist modernization will have been in the main accomplished, and all these years belong to the primary stage of socialism. This stage is different from both the transitional period, in which the socialist economic basis was not yet laid, and the stage in which socialist modernization will have been achieved. The principal contradiction we face during the present stage is the contradiction between the growing material and cultural needs of the people and backward production. Class struggle will continue to exist within certain limits for a long time to come, but it is no longer the principal contradiction. To resolve the principal contradiction of the present stage we must vigorously expand the commodity economy, raise labor productivity, gradually achieve the modernization of industry, agriculture, national defense, and science and technology and, to this end, reform such aspects of the relations of production and of the superstructure as are incompatible with the growth of the productive forces.

In short, the primary stage of China's socialism is one in which we shall gradually put an end to poverty and backwardness. It is a stage in which an agricultural country, where farming is based on manual labor and where people engaged in agriculture constitute the majority of the population, will gradually turn into a modern industrial country where non-agricultural workers constitute the majority. It is a stage in which a society with the natural and semi-natural economy making up a very large proportion of the whole will turn into one with a highly developed commodity economy. It is a stage in which, by introducing reforms and exploring new ways, we shall establish and develop socialist economic, political and cultural structures that are full of vitality. Lastly, it is a stage in which the people of the whole country will rise to meet the challenge and bring about a great rejuvenation of the Chinese nation. . . .

Report on the Work of the Government

Li Peng, March 20, 1990

In late spring and early summer last year a handful of people, taking advantage of the student unrest, organized, planned, and plotted political turmoil, which later developed into a counterrevolutionary rebellion in the country's capital, Beijing. In essence, it manifested the sharp conflict between bourgeois liberalization and the four cardinal principles [keeping to the socialist road, upholding the people's democratic dictatorship, leadership by the Communist Party, and Marxism-Leninism and Mao Zedong Thought—*Trans.*] and an acute struggle between infiltration and anti-infiltration, between subversion and anti-subversion, and between the forces for and against peaceful evolution. The sole purpose of both domestic and foreign hostile forces in creating such disturbances was to overthrow leadership by the Chinese Communist Party, subvert the socialist system and turn China into a bourgeois republic and a dependency of developed capitalist countries. At that crucial moment, when the fate of the state and the nation hung in the balance, the proletarian revolutionaries of the older generation, represented by Comrade Deng Xiaoping, did all they could to turn the tide, playing the important role of mainstay. With the support of all nationalities in the country, the heroic Chinese People's Liberation Army, the Armed Police and the Public Security Police succeeded in quelling the turmoil and the rebellion. Here, let us once again express our highest respect for them. . . .

In 1989 the people of all nationalities in China managed to hold fast to the socialist position in the complicated and constantly changing international situation and accumulated valuable practical experience that will prove to be important to our country's stable political, economic and social development in the days ahead.

. . . In order to carry on socialist modernization and reach our strategic goal in three steps,[1] we need a peaceful international environment and domestic political stability and unity. The disturbances of last year showed us once more than when turmoil prevails in the country and grave anarchy engulfs society, it is impossible to carry on economic development and the programs of reform and opening to the outside world or to safeguard people's normal life and protect their lives and property. The Chinese people have suffered enough from the turmoil and will allow no one to stir it up again, turning socialist China, full of promise for a bright future, into a chaotic and turbulent China. Preservation of China's stability and the great unity of all our nationalities is in the fundamental interest of the Chinese people and represents the aspirations of the people and the general trend of the times. Now, as

---

1. The three steps are: first, to double the 1980 GNP and solve the problem of food and clothing for the Chinese people; second, to quadruple the 1980 figure by the end of this century, thus enabling the Chinese people to lead a fairly comfortable life; and, third, basically to accomplish the modernization drive and reach the per-capita GNP of moderately developed countries by the middle of the next century, thus enabling the Chinese people to enjoy a relatively affluent life.

we confront pressure from abroad and difficulties at home, preservation of the country's stability is a matter of paramount importance. Every citizen of the People's Republic of China should cherish the hardwon political stability and unity as he would treasure his own life.

. . . It was a necessity of historical development that the Chinese people choose the socialist road. The entire history of the Chinese nation, fighting for national liberation, state independence and the people's happiness for over a century, attests to the truth: Only socialism can save China; only socialism can help develop China. In our country, if we did not keep to socialism but, instead, as some people advocate, turned back to take the capitalist road, a wide gap between the rich and the poor and a polarization of classes would inevitably arise, the overwhelming majority of people would sink into poverty and social unrest would prevail for a long time to come. Fraud, degeneration and crime, inherent in a society of exploiting classes, would spread unchecked.

Under such circumstances economic development would be out of the question and the country could not be truly independent; instead, it would only be reduced to a dependency of the developed capitalist countries. Only by upholding socialism can we attain common prosperity, enable all the people of the country, who share the same fundamental interests, to work together for common ideals and goals, and safeguard the country's independence and the nation's dignity. Only thus can we realize modernization and can China show promise. Upholding socialism is inseparable from upholding leadership by the Communist Party. The leading position of the Chinese Communist Party has been acquired through protracted struggle and accepted by the people of their own accord. In China, if we do not uphold socialism and leadership by the Communist Party, we can expect no stability in the country, no unity among the people and no rejuvenation of the Chinese nation. . . .

We must conscientiously learn the lesson from previous years' neglect of socialist cultural and ideological progress and, along with economic development, reform and opening to the outside world, redouble efforts to improve ideological and political work. Among people throughout the country, particularly young people, we should conduct intensive education in the need to uphold the Four Cardinal Principles and oppose bourgeois liberalization and in patriotism, collectivism, socialism, communism, self-reliance, hard work, revolutionary traditions and professional ethics. We should urge people to take the interests of the whole into account and devote their all for the public good, and we should work hard to raise the quality of the entire nation, training new socialist builders who have lofty ideals and moral integrity, who are better educated and have a strong sense of discipline.

The spirit of Lei Feng exemplifies the Chinese nation's traditional virtues combined with lofty Communist ideology. Recently a vigorous campaign to learn from Lei Feng was launched anew throughout the country, achieving initial success. We should carefully analyze experience in this regard and warmly commend advanced collectives and individuals learning from Lei Feng on different fronts. We should publicize their exemplary deeds in conducting the drive to learn from Lei Feng extensively, thoroughly, persistently and in a down-to-earth manner. This constitutes an important part of building socialist culture and ideology.

Marxism-Leninism and Mao Zedong Thought must prevail in the ideological field. Departments of theoretical studies, literature, art, the press, publishing, film production, television, etc., must be oriented towards serving socialism and the people, adhering to the principle of letting a hundred flowers blossom and a hundred schools of thought contend, giving wide publicity to the fine culture of the Chinese nation and learning whatever is useful from alien cultures. In the ideological field our work should both be rectified and flourish. . . .

15

China after Mao

Steven M. Goldstein, Kathrin Sears, and Richard C. Bush

In the mid-1950s, the Chinese Communist Party adopted the Soviet-style party/ state system. Except for a period during the Cultural Revolution, this basic structure has defined the constitutional outlines of China. The following excerpt and charts are an introduction to the system as it existed in the 1980s. They seek to provide some sense of the relative influence of the various institutions and levels of administration in the Chinese political system. They also provide the context for the discussion of reforms in the next chapter.

.... To implement its policies the Chinese leadership chooses to rely on a Soviet-style dual structure of Party and state hierarchies that reach from Beijing to every city and township. It is within this huge, complex bureaucracy that the fate of the new leadership's policies will be determined. Victory at the Politburo level by no means assures implementation in the villages. Deng Xiaoping and his colleagues have quickly come to realize that they must gain control of this bureaucracy if they are to change the nation's agenda.

The formal Party structure (see Chart 1) is modeled on the Soviet Communist Party. It combines two different types of institutions: members' meetings and representative congresses on the one hand, and leaders (called secretaries) and executive committees on the other. Despite attempts to enhance the power of the representative bodies, the latter

Chart 1. Structure of the Chinese Communist Party

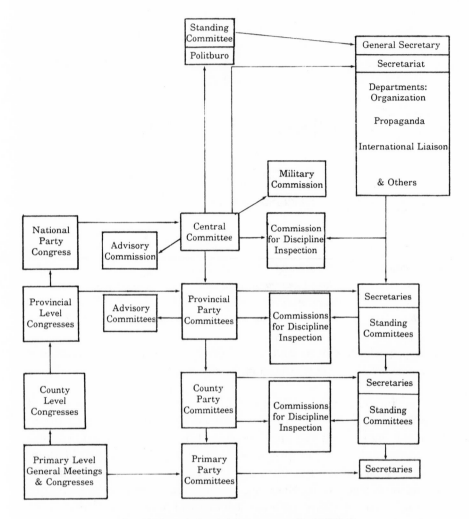

County-level organizations include congresses and committees at the regimental level and above in the PLA. Primary-level organizations include branches, general branches, or committees which are set up in factories, mines and other enterprises, communes, offices, schools, shops, neighborhoods, PLA companies and other such units.

institutions are more important than the former. In addition, power has flowed from the top down rather than the other way. Formally, Party congresses—held at national, provincial, and county levels—and general membership meetings of the primary organizations elect the committees and secretaries to be the executive bodies at that level. In practice, they meet infrequently, largely to ratify the work of their committees. Moreover, higher levels have a large say in the scheduling of congresses, their composition, and the election of the committees and secretaries.

At the national level, for example, the Central Committee of the Party, the most important representative body in China, delegates key decision-making powers to its Politburo, whose power is further centralized in the Standing Committee. The Politburo exercises its executive power through a central Party bureaucracy consisting of the Central Committee Secretariat—re-established in 1980—and its various specialized departments. This body, headed by Hu Yaobang [Hu died in 1989], is thus second only to the Politburo as the most powerful institution in China. Central Committee departments play a dual role. They supervise state ministries and also oversee local level state organs and CCP organizations that conduct the daily work of the Party. The Party runs China. But the Secretariat, under Hu Yaobang, runs the Party.

Underlying this Party structure is the basic organizational principle of "democratic centralism." This principle combines "inner-Party democracy" in the discussion of issues and election of leading bodies, and "centralist discipline" once a decision is made, subordinating the individual to the organization, the minority to the majority, the lower level to the higher, and the entire Party to the Central Committee.

The state structure (see Chart 2) roughly parallels that of the CCP in two respects. First, there is a similar division of administrative units among central, provincial, county, and basic levels, facilitating Party supervision of state organs at the same level. Second, there is a similar distinction between representative and executive/administrative hierarchies. Representative congresses possess formal constitutional authority, but the administrative organs have the actual power. The representative bodies are called people's congresses; administrative bodies are known as governments (a change from the Cultural Revolution era when they were known as "revolutionary committees"). At the central level, the key administrative unit is the State Council, a sort of large cabinet. With an array of commissions and ministries under its control, it is an important

Chart 2. Structure of the PRC Government

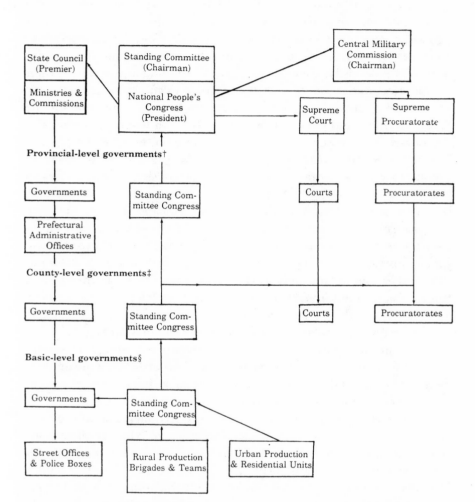

Note: Terms for people's congresses are five years at the national and provincial levels, three years at the county level, and two years at the basic level.
†Includes: 21 provinces, 5 autonomous regions, 2 directly administered cities.
‡Includes: 2,000 counties, 230 cities, 100 autonomous counties and prefectures.
§Includes: municipal districts, towns.

agency of the centralized governmental structure, even though it is subordinate to central Party directives and subject to Party supervision.

As suggested earlier, this immensely complex bureaucracy was copied from the Soviet Union where Lenin believed that only Party supervision of government at all levels could assure loyal service by former Czarist officials. In theory, the Party is to simply decide broad policy guidelines and supervise their implementation. The government is expected to do the actual day-to-day governing. In practice, these functions have never been easily separated. Bureaucratic expansion, overlapping jurisdictions, and complaints of Party meddling are endemic to the Chinese system.

The post-Mao leadership has, to some degree, tried to deal with these problems. It has sought to define the role of the Party, to allow greater freedom from bureaucratic interference for certain institutions, and to streamline the number of Party-government offices. However, in recent years *organizational* changes have largely taken a backseat to attempts at *personnel* change.

Put simply, it has become clear that Deng and his colleagues doubt that the Party-state bureaucracy as currently staffed is either willing or able to implement the new economic policies. In part, the problems are those common in any large bureaucracy: caution, nepotism, corruption, exploitation of privilege, etc. But there are also problems peculiar to China. The sudden reversals of past years suggest to many bureaucrats that caution in implementing new policies might be advised. The bureaucracy is also aging. The old revolutionaries do not have the vitality or the skills to rule a China undergoing rapid economic transformation. Moreover, of the nearly 40 million party members, perhaps 18 million joined during the Cultural Revolution. This group is poorly trained and generally considered to be ill-disposed toward much of the post-Mao platform pursued by Deng and his colleagues.

Deng and his supporters have pursued a number of tactics in their effort to discipline the bureaucracy and infuse it with new blood. Both the carrot and the stick are being used. Older cadres are provided with pensions, nominal posts on advisory commissions, and are in other ways encouraged/pressured to make way for younger, better trained men and women. Disciplinary commissions and formal trials are used to deal with corrupt or more recalcitrant cadres.

Since the Twelfth Party Congress in the fall of 1982, efforts have been stepped up. Observers of China have noted that while the top leadership has stayed in the hands of the old guard, a new technocratic leadership has shown signs of emerging at the middle levels. Since the Twelfth Congress, pressure has been intensified for the recruitment of younger, better trained cadres. The launching of an important Party "consolidation" campaign in the fall of 1983 suggests that Deng and his colleagues are intent on rooting out those unwilling or unable to implement their policies.

What the results of all this will be is hard to say. There is evidence that a corps of younger, more skilled bureaucrats is emerging in China. However, the problems of reforming the Chinese bureaucracy are immense. Bureaucrats, after all, are notorious footdraggers when it come to implementing new policies; and they can become even more so when their jobs are at stake.

16

Institutionalizing the Post-Mao Reforms

Harry Harding

Despite the resilience of the Soviet-style party/state system, there was, nonetheless, important institutional change in China in the decade after 1978. In the excerpt that follows, Harry Harding, Senior Fellow at the Brookings Institution, describes the changes in China's political structures that were both implemented and contemplated during these years. In general, we see a political reform movement that seemed more limited and cautious than that in the economic realm. Moreover, Harding's emphasis on the fragility of post-Mao political norms was corroborated by the events surrounding the Tiananmen demonstrations.

... From Deng's perspective, the Chinese political system in the late 1970s and 1980s was characterized by three problems that threatened the long-term survival of his political and economic reforms. First, China was governed by overaged, undereducated, overstaffed, and poorly organized party and state bureaucracies. The policy-making process was in disarray, after the dogmatism and factionalism of the Cultural Revolution. And the rehabilitation of veteran officials who had been purged during the Cultural Revolution had increased both the size of the bureaucracy and the average age of China's leadership. All told, the Party and state organizations were ill prepared to design and implement a program of sustained economic modernization.

Second, the relationships among China's chief political institutions were seriously imbalanced. Thanks to Mao's preference for "redness" over "expertise," the Party had come to exercise tight control over both the government bureaucracy and the nation's state-owned enterprises, with state officials and factory managers alike shunted aside in favor of Party secretaries. As a result of the turmoil of the Cultural Revolution, the military had been able to expand its power over China's civilian affairs, and enjoyed a degree of representation and influence in the Party that threatened civilian control over the armed forces. Moreover, the political orientations of both the Party and the army ensured that these organizations were sources of powerful opposition to the reforms that Deng and his colleagues envisioned.

Finally, there were no clear mechanisms governing the political succession to Deng Xiaoping. Although Mao had been preoccupied with the question of succession for many years, he had failed to create an institutionalized process for handling it. Mao defined the succession in highly personalized terms as the transfer of unlimited power to another individual for life, but he consistently lost confidence in the men whom he selected as his heirs apparent. . . .

Reforming the Political Process

Restaffing the Party and State Bureaucracies

Remolding the bureaucracy to provide a firmer technical and political base for reform has been a principal aim of Deng and his associates, and they have faced difficult complications in the pursuit of their goal. On the one hand, they recognized that the institutionalization of reform would require a major restructuring and restaffing of the nation's major bureaucracies. But at the same time, the reformers also had to reassure the cadres who would be the targets of organizational reform that they would not be purged in a violent or humiliating manner, but would be eased out of office with their dignity and their perquisites intact. Indeed, one of the most remarkable accomplishments registered by the reformers has been to find ways of making wholesale organizational change acceptable to those very officials at whom it is directed.

Transforming the Party and state bureaucracies into highly professional organizations has required, first of all, a massive program of organizational restaffing. The reformers are using a combination of retirement, purge, and recruitment to replace the old with the young, the poorly trained with the better educated, and the more conservative with the more reform-minded. Since the late 1970s, the reformers have tried to remove from office those cadres who are deemed to lack the proper political and technical qualifications, and to replace them with officials who are more skilled, more capable, and more committed to reform. . . .

The net effect of the replacement of older and less-educated officials by younger and better-trained successors has been a great change in the average age and level of education of Chinese officials. By the end of the second round of rotations in 1985, the average age of cadres at nearly every level had been reduced by about five years: the Politburo from 74 to 69, the Secretariat from 66 to 61; the provinces from 64 to 53; the central ministries from 64 to 58; the central Party departments from 64 to 60; and cities and prefectures from 58 to 50. Simultaneously, the percentage of leaders with a college education rose substantially: in the central state bureaucracy from 38 percent to 50 percent; in the provinces from 20 percent to 43 percent; in the prefectures and cities from 14 percent to 44 percent; and in the counties from 11 percent to 45 percent.

It would be an exaggeration to conclude that the Chinese bureaucracy has, because of this personnel turnover, become highly professionalized. The level of education is still much lower than in many other countries and regions in East Asia. Most of the new appointments are political generalists, although with a higher level of education than their predecessors. There has been enormous resistance to the promotion of younger and better-educated cadres, and to the retirement of senior ones. . . .

Rationalizing China's Civil Service

To take greatest advantage of the turnover of administrative personnel, the reformers will have to find more efficient ways of managing China's civil service and of remedying the corpulence and disorganization of the Party and state bureaucracies. Chinese leaders have assigned high priority to developing a rational program of personnel management and reducing the size of the country's administrative apparatus. But progress has been slow, and they have achieved only partial results. . . .

. . . It was only toward the end of 1986 that the state Ministry of

Labor and Personnel and the Party's organization department jointly issued draft regulations on the recruitment and dismissal, promotion and demotion, and assessment and retirement of state officials. No comprehensive civil service law has yet been adopted, and there is still no universal examination to assess the quality of new applicants for service in either the Party or state bureaucracy. This absence of systematic personnel procedures may well reflect the resistance of China's administrative officials to an change in what is familiarly known as their "iron rice bowl": the previous system of complete job security, lifetime tenure in office, and blurred lines of responsibility. . . .

A key feature of the contemporary Chinese policy-making process has been the increasing opportunities for participation by scholars and specialists both inside and outside government, largely through the proliferation of policy staffs and "think tanks" throughout the Party and state bureaucracies. The State Council has created two research centers on domestic policy: one to examine macroeconomic policy and one to conduct feasibility studies of major investment projects. The Party Secretariat has a general policy research office and a second research center on agricultural policy. The State Commission on Reform of the Economic System, which is charged with designing and implementing the restructuring of the country's economic system, has its own research institute, largely composed of younger intellectuals. Most other ministries, from the Ministry of Foreign Economic Relations and Trade to the State Planning Commission, have established or expanded their own research institutes. And a growing number of provinces have created their own policy planning staffs. . . .

Although intended to improve the ways in which central leaders reach decisions, some of the changes in the policy-making process that have occurred in the last decade have created problems. The more relaxed political environment, and the decentralization of the Chinese economy, have exacerbated many of the dysfunctions that originally stemmed from the intellectual size and diffuseness of the Chinese bureaucracy. Studies of decisions in such areas as water policy and energy policy have revealed a lack of coherence and coordination in the formulation of policy, protracted debates among bureaucratic agencies with divergent interests and perspectives, lengthy delays in reaching decisions as disagreements are referred up the bureaucratic ladder, and gaps between the intentions of central leaders and how policies are implemented by administrative agencies. Still, these problems are found in most complex bureaucratic systems. And they are arguably less serious than the "decisions at random" that previously characterized China's policy-making process.

Redefining Organizational Roles and Relationships

Deng's strategy to institutionalize the post-Mao reforms also includes recasting the roles of China's three principal political institutions—the army, the Party, and the government—and redefining the relationships among them. The military has been returned to the barracks, and the officer corps has undergone a gradual process of rejuvenation and professionalization. The Party has been given less responsibility for administrative matters, and the criteria for recruiting new Party members have been revised. More tentatively, the state bureaucracy is being restructured to reduce the size and power of those government agencies responsible for the administration of state-owned enterprises. If these trends continue, the net result will be to reduce the power of the Party over the state, the influence of the military in civilian affairs, and the control of the government over the economy.

The Military

Deng Xiaoping believed that the inflated role assumed by the People's Liberation Army (PLA) in Chinese politics as a result of the Cultural Revolution posed a serious potential threat to the durability of his political and economic reforms. The military was commanded by men who were elderly, poorly educated, and relatively conservative. It had been one of the beneficiaries, and perhaps even one of the architects, of the priority on heavy industry and the emphasis on state planning that had been characteristic of most of the Maoist period. Like much of the Party apparatus, it seemed unconvinced of the need for a sweeping restructuring of the Chinese political or economic system. At a minimum, the military was a powerful interest group largely opposed to reform. And if a crisis over political succession occurred, the military was in a position to intervene in favor of leaders who might attempt to resurrect the policies and institutions of the pre-reform era.

Because of this potential, Deng Xiaoping has concentrated simultaneously on making the Chinese army a more professional organization while also ensuring civilian dominance in Chinese politics. In fact, Deng has given this aim the greatest personal attention since his rehabilitation toward the end of the Cultural Revolution in 1973. . . .

. . . In 1985 Peking announced the demobilization of 1 million troops, from an army of about 4 million men and women. This decrease is to be achieved primarily by transferring some specialized branches of the military (such as the Armed Police and the Railway Corps) to their corresponding civilian ministries, and by reducing the size of the lightly armed and poorly trained local forces. Cuts may also be made in the political department of the PLA. In turn, the savings created by these reductions in force will make possible the modernization of the main forces and the development of the capability to engage in combined land-sea-air operations on a much larger scale than in the past. At the same time, China is making modest but steady progress in the development and production of new weapons, including tanks, artillery, anti-tank weapons, surface ships, submarines, interceptors, and ballistic missiles. Some of the technology for these new weapons systems is being imported from abroad, and some is being developed in China's own ordnance industry. The goal of the restructuring is not simply to build a more efficient and effective military force but to give the PLA a greater stake in, and more sympathy for, the process of technological modernization and economic reform.

The restructuring of the armed forces is also designed to further the demilitarization of Chinese domestic politics. Reducing the size of the local forces will not only increase the military effectiveness of the PLA but will also shrink those sectors of the army that, in the past, have been most important in civilian politics at the local level. At higher levels of Chinese politics, Deng Xiaoping has been able to reduce the level of military representation in civilian politics to the lowest level in the history of the People's Republic. The PLA, which held 45 percent of the seats on the Central Committee elected at the height of the Cultural Revolution in 1969, gained only about 13 percent of those elected at the National Party Conference in 1985. Army officers, who held thirteen of twenty-five positions on the Politburo in 1969, occupied only three of twenty-two Politburo seats at the end of 1986. Military commanders no longer play a significant role in civilian politics at the local level.

Despite the reduction in military representation in the highest levels of the Chinese Communist Party, the PLA remains a powerful force in national politics. The high command still enjoys close personal relations with China's top civilian leaders; and the military retains representation on the National People's Congress, the Central Committee, the Politburo, the Party Secretariat, and (assuming the minister of defense remains a military officer), on the State Council. Moreover, although the rate of turnover of high-ranking military officers has been high, the PLA is still a conservative organization, with interests in preserving a stable political order, ideological conformity, a controlled economy, and an emphasis on heavy industry. . . .

The Party

Beginning in the mid–1950s, the Party became an ever greater force in the Chinese political process as the result of Mao's desire to place power in the hands of ideologically committed generalists instead of technically proficient specialists. The Party increasingly arrogated to itself the task of political administration that had originally been the responsibility of the state. The Party Secretariat and its functional departments superseded the State Council as the principal arena in which policy options were clarified and policy decisions translated into administrative guidelines. Party secretaries at all levels assumed responsibility for day-to-day decision-making, taking power away from government officials and enterprise managers. During the Cultural Revolution, the state apparatus was dismissed as a duplicative and redundant bureaucratic structure, and organizational reforms undertaken in the 1970s transformed the government bureaucracy into little more than the administrative arm of the Party.

The Cultural Revolution also saw a large increase in the size of the Party. Membership rose from about 20 million in 1965 to more than 35 million in 1977. By the time of Mao's death, about half of the Party had been recruited during the decade of the Cultural Revolution. Although it would be incorrect to assume that all of these new Party members were devoted to Maoist values and programs, it is still true that they joined the organization when ideological commitment, as well as class background, were the principal criteria for recruitment. Many members recruited during this period could therefore be assumed to be skeptical about the post-Mao reforms, if not actively opposed to them.

These considerations have led to several serious changes in the Party since the early 1980s: the rectification of the Party organization to bolster support for reform; the recruitment of new Party members from different sectors of the Chinese population and with different political orientations than in the recent past; and, most important, the redefinition of the role of the Party to give other organizations somewhat greater autonomy....

Compared with the rectification movements of the late Maoist period, the rectification campaign of 1983–87 was orderly, moderate, and gradual. It unfolded slowly, from the central and provincial organs in 1983–84, to the middle levels in 1984–85, and finally to local branches in 1985–87. This step-by-step process avoided the disruption that might have been caused if the rectification had been conducted simultaneously at all levels of the Party....

... The final report on the campaign revealed that more than 200,000 members were expelled from the Party or denied the opportunity to renew their membership, and that more than 325,000 others received some lesser form of disciplinary action. Although the total number punished during rectification was large in absolute terms, and although the number expelled from the Party was more than five times as many as had originally been estimated, the victims of the movement still constituted little more than 1 percent of the Party's 47 million members....

If rectification is unlikely to have yielded a major transformation in the composition or attitudes of Party members, then a change in Party recruitment standards may produce somewhat greater results, at least over the longer run. During the Maoist period, the emphasis was placed on the class background and revolutionary commitment of potential Party members. Today, the reformers want to bestow Party membership on those groups that are believed to be among the strongest supporters of their program. To be sure, the Party—like mass communist parties anywhere—still seeks a fairly broad base of recruitment. A forum on Party recruitment conducted by the Party's organization department at the end of 1983, for example, continued to stress the desirability of drawing new members from workers, peasants, and military personnel. But for the first time since the mid–1950s, particular attention is being paid to recruiting intellectual and college students. Of the 6.3 million new members admitted to the Party between 1980 and the middle of 1986, 22 percent were described as "technical professionals." This figure corresponds with reports of Party recruitment at the provincial level, where about one-quarter of new Party members have been described as intellectuals....

Questions can properly be raised, however, about the feasibility of this new recruitment policy. In the past, the Party had little difficulty in attracting new members, if only because it was the most important channel of upward mobility in the country, and because it offered membership to those sectors of society whose low levels of education gave little hope of advancement through other channels. Today, in contrast, Party membership is no longer the sole source of social prestige or economic advancement. Individual and collective entrepreneurship now offers the opportunity for acquiring wealth, and the academic and managerial communities provide chances for gaining status and respect. . . .

Finally, the reform of the Party has included a reduction in its exercise of direct control over administrative matters, particularly at the middle and lower levels of Chinese society. According to the reformers, the growth of the Party's administrative power between the late 1950s and the late 1970s was undesirable for several reasons. The Party was neither large enough, nor skilled enough, to manage all the details of an increasingly complex economy. The concentration of political power in the hands of a closed, hierarchical organization contributed to the growing alienation of the Chinese people from their government and to the "crisis of confidence" of the early 1980s. Furthermore, if the Party was preoccupied with routine administrative work, it would be impossible for Party leaders to devote sufficient attention to more important concerns, such as setting long-term policy and educating the public in socialist values. Indeed, if the Party were directly responsible for all administrative and political decisions, then the problems that Chinese society would inevitably encounter would be blamed on the Party's leadership. The Party should be monitoring and correcting the performance of other organizations, rather than directly assuming their responsibilities.

The reformers say the Party should no longer be the "direct administrator, let alone the ruler," of the country. This formula has implied a growing division of labor between the Party and the government, and between the Party and enterprise management, particularly at the grassroots. The jobs of first Party secretary and government chief executive at each level, held by the same person during most of the 1970s, have again been separated. Party committees are not supposed to administer the day-to-day work of the government or give direct orders to government officials. And provincial governors, factory managers, and university presidents are gaining greater authority to make their own decisions and appoint their own subordinates, without first requiring the approval of the cognizant Party committee or Party secretary.

Nonetheless, if the Party is not supposed to be the "direct administrator" of the country, Chinese leaders still insist that it remain the "leader of national life." As one has put it, China's socialist system requires that "our Party exercise a planned and overall control over all national life, the development of the whole national economy and society, as well as the establishment of material and spiritual civilization." Deng Xiaoping made the same point even more directly in 1980, when he warned that if the principle of Party leadership were eliminated, "China will retrogress into divisions and chaos, and modernization would become impossible." . . .

. . . The Party no longer seeks to maintain direct control over all administrative details in China, but instead limits itself to formulating national policy and identifying and correcting the problems encountered in the course of modernization and reform. The Party no longer regards itself as mobilizing dispossessed and disenfranchised sectors of society, but seeks instead to identify and coopt China's emerging technical and intellectual elites. In short, the Party is now to act as a national manager, seeking to lead the system toward the goals the Party wants to pursue, but doing so after consultation with technical specialists and important interest groups.

The Government

If the PLA and the Party have lost some of their power and standing as the result of the post-Mao reforms, the government bureaucracy has been the principal beneficiary of many of these structural readjustments. Government officials are now much more influential in formulating economic policy than they were in the late Maoist period, and they have even acquired somewhat greater authority in some areas, such as culture and education, which had previously been the exclusive preserve of the Party.

The discussion of radical political reform in the middle of 1986, however, yielded some proposals that, if adopted, would seriously limit both the size of the government's economic bureaucracy and the extent of its control over the Chinese economy. As noted, the radical reformers believed that the autonomy of government agencies and basic-level units could not depend solely on the self-restraint of the Party, but would require the dismantling of many of the Party's grassroots organizations. Similarly, they were also convinced that the autonomy of state enterprises from bureaucratic interference could not rest completely on the self-discipline of government administrators. Instead, the reformers favored a big reduction in the size and power of the bureaucratic agencies responsible for the management of the economy.

Premier Zhao Ziyang explained the general concept behind this aspect of structural reform in his report on the Seventh Five-Year Plan, given at the National People's Congress in April 1986. Zhao said that the state should no longer be responsible for "assigning quotas, approving construction projects, and allotting funds and materials," which were its principal tasks under a system of mandatory planning. Instead, the government bureaucracy should conduct "overall planning, implement policies, organize coordination, provide services, use economic means of regulation, and exercise effective inspection and supervision." In short, as the economy was transformed from a centrally planned system into a regulated market, "the functions of the government departments concerned will have to change accordingly." . . .

Arranging for the Succession

As a final part of his effort to institutionalize the post-Mao reforms, Deng Xiaoping has also devoted much attention to creating a viable set of arrangements for political succession. His aim has been to forestall an intense conflict among contending leaders or a sudden change in national policy, similar to what occurred after the death of Mao Zedong in 1976. . . .

Deng's succession arrangements seemed promising when they were first designed and implemented in the early 1980s. Gradually, however, the scheme decayed, as the leaders Deng tried to ease into retirement resisted their political demise, and as the successors that Deng tried to promote into higher office encountered objections and opposition from powerful groups and individuals. The sudden dismissal of Hu Yaobang as Party general secretary in January 1987 reflected the collapse of a major part of Deng's plan for the succession. It remains to be seen whether Deng can rebuild a viable succession arrangement in his few remaining years of active political life. . . .

Officially, Hu Yaobang was charged with "errors," which were said to require his dismissal. He was accused of neglecting political work, tolerating the spread of liberal ideas in the Party, raising expectations for a rapid improvement in living standards, committing indiscretions in conversations with foreigners, and making decisions on domestic matters without consulting colleagues. Some accounts have suggested that the restructuring and restaffing of the Party were important in Hu's dismissal. Hu offended senior leaders by demands that one hundred more veterans be removed from the Central Committee at the Thirteenth Party Congress and by attempts to limit promotions for children of high-ranking cadres.

More generally, Hu's political travails could be said to reflect a "successor's dilemma," which is inherent in the succession arrangements in most personalistic, authoritarian political systems. On the one hand, Hu was well aware that Deng Xiaoping's active political life was nearing its end. If Hu were to succeed to Deng's position as China's preeminent political leader, he would have to build his own power base within the Party by staffing the Party bureaucracy with trusted followers and by defining his own position on significant policy issues. In doing so, however, Hu ran the risk of alienating the senior generation of Party leaders, including Deng, whom he hoped to succeed. Hu's association with radical political reform, his persistent efforts to win the chairmanship of the Military Affairs Commission, and his attempts to promote the careers of men and women previously associated with him in the Communist Youth League were designed to strengthen his political position in the post-Deng era. But, in the end, these measures were Hu's undoing, as they turned influential Party veterans, and Deng Xiaoping, against him.

The dismissal of Hu Yaobang in early 1987 dramatized the limits to political institutionalization in post-Mao China. The confrontation between Hu and the Party veterans revealed the absence of clear and accepted norms defining the authority of the general secretary, specifying the power of senior Party cadres who had retired into advisory positions, establishing terms of office for high Party officials, or providing for the removal of a general secretary when he had lost the confidence of most of the Politburo. Indeed, the fact that Hu's resignation was accepted by an irregular session of the Politburo, attended by members of the Central Discipline Inspection Committee and the Central Advisory Committee, aroused heated debate among observers in both Hong Kong and the mainland over whether the action was in accordance with the provision of the Party constitution. At a minimum, Hu's ouster before the Thirteenth Party Congress violated the rudimentary norms on fixed terms of office for national leaders, and his replacement as acting general secretary by Premier Zhao Ziyang infringed the embryonic rule requiring the separation of Party positions from government offices. . . .

17

The Origins of China's Pro-Democracy Movement

Yasheng Huang

Many have argued that the demonstrations at Tiananmen were the result of a gap that existed between the limited political reforms described in the last excerpt and the dramatic economic reforms discussed in Part 4. In this reading, Yasheng Huang, a witness to events in Beijing and an assistant professor at the University of Michigan, questions this argument by highlighting the flaws that existed in both the economic and political reforms.

. . . In tracing the origins of the social crisis that led to the events of Tiananmen, a common explanation offered is what might be called the "disjunction theory." This theory holds that the disjunction between political and economic reforms—the progress of political reforms lagging behind that of economic reforms—was largely responsible for the explosion of the pro-democracy movement in the spring of 1989. The argument is that the successes of the economic reforms are marked by the emergence of divergent and pluralistic social and economic forces in Chinese society such as private entrepreneurs and the managerial elite. The emergence of new social and economic forces generated new political demands which the traditional one-party system could not meet.

This explanation must be rejected on two grounds. First, the leaders and the most active participants in the pro-democracy movement of 1989 were not members of new social classes created in the course of reforms, but were students and intellectuals.... Secondly, the themes of the movement—freedom of speech and assembly, greater participation in the political process and respect for human rights—as well as the protest tactics (class boycott and hunger strike, etc.) could all find their precedents in the pre-reform period and therefore were not products of the economic reforms.

An alternate explanation is that the economic and political reform programs themselves were flawed fundamentally from the very beginning and later on generated forces that sowed the seeds of destruction for the reformers themselves. Contrary to conventional wisdom, it was the failures of the economic reforms, rather than their successes, that contributed to a sense of social crisis and political discontent. These failures resulted from the nature of the economic reform programs. Furthermore, the failures of the political reforms, which, like the economic reforms, were due more to the manner of their implementation than to lack of effort, significantly shaped the way the government responded.

Economic Reforms

The most glaring symptoms of the failures of the economic reforms are corruption and rampant inflation. Corruption probably was the issue that featured most prominently in the student demonstrations. According to a survey of the public's attitude toward the student demonstrations, students' anti-corruption slogans received the most enthusiastic support among all the social groups and an overwhelming majority of the respondents (around 70 percent) viewed corruption as the most likely cause of social unrest in China.

Corruption is viewed commonly as a political and legal phenomenon, but first and foremost it is a function of the way economic resources are allocated in the society. Chinese economic reforms started out without a particularly well-defined agenda or clear visions and objectives and proceeded on a trial-and-error basis. The partial, piecemeal nature of the reform measures had the twin effects of undermining disciplinary supervision of economic officials and infusing powerful profit incentives into normal bureaucratic functions. Large-scale corruption became prevalent as a result.

Two examples are relevant here. One is enterprise decision-making; the other is price-setting practices in the Chinese economy. In both areas, the leadership wanted to delegate control to the forces of the market, but were not willing to relinquish control completely. The result is a hybrid economic system that combines the worst aspects of the two worlds: economically the system did not produce efficient outcomes, especially as measured by economic stability; politically the system created the potential for abuses of power that undermined the sense of legitimacy and trust people had in the system in general and the reform process specifically.

What China has attempted so far in both enterprise decision-making and price-setting is known as "administrative decentralization." Administrative decentralization, as opposed to genuine economic decentralization, transfers decision-making powers from a higher level bureaucracy to a lower level bureaucracy, rather than to enterprise managers. Since 1979, in the area of enterprise decision-making powers, the central government gradually has delegated considerable controls over investment, allocation of raw materials and production inputs and personnel appointment to provincial governments, which, in turn, have surrendered another round of controls to county and district governments. In the area of setting product prices, China adopted a "dual-track" system, in which products under administrative allocation orders are sold at state-listed prices and products outside administrative allocation orders are sold at market prices. Since many of these products are scarce raw materials and intermediate goods (or rights to buy and sell premium goods), the discrepancy between state-listed prices and market prices can be huge. . . .

The second symptom of the failures of economic reforms is inflation, which took a significant turn for the worse in 1988. The official cost of living for thirty-two large- and medium-sized cities increased by 18.5 percent between 1987 and 1988. Unofficial sources put it at a much higher rate, possibly in the 40–50 percent range. This was a considerable acceleration over 1987 (7.3 percent), 1986 (6.0 percent) and 1985 (8.8 percent). In China, inflation always has been politically sensitive; the CCP itself often traced the origin of its support to the hyper-inflationary period of the Nationalist government. Economically inflation was also hard hitting because most Chinese urban residents live on fixed incomes. . . .

There were two reasons for the acceleration of inflation in 1988. One was systemic: the economy was operating in a chronic shortage environment and the initial reaction to any loosening of bureaucratic control was a rise in the general price level. In many ways, this kind of price change is necessary and inevitable in the reform process. The second reason has to do with macroeconomic policies that were unduly accommodating to the inflationary pressures generated by the system, for example, expansive monetary and fiscal targets. . . .

Two developments were responsible for enhancing the role of policy-related factors in bringing about the inflationary situation. First, as in the areas of enterprise decision-making and price determination, the partial nature of the economic reforms accentuated rather than alleviated many of the old problems that plagued the centrally planned economic system. One of the major problems in a planned economy is "investment hunger"—the pervasive tendency on the part of economic bureaucrats and managers to acquire and invest in new projects. . . .

Secondly, the central government became more and more accommodating to local governments' appetites for investment projects and adopted relatively loose fiscal and monetary policies when caution and austerity were appropriate. Here Zhao Ziyang was directly to blame. Zhao, largely out of political imperatives (discussed below), was consistently in favor of faster economic growth rates and argued for loose expenditure and monetary policies as a means to stimulate growth. . . . In the first six months of 1988, income expenditures increased 23.7 percent and administrative spending increased 46.5 percent. During the same period, the money supply increased 22.7 billion yuan, even though the increase target for the whole year had been 20 billion yuan. . . .

Political Reforms

There were two periods of political reform programs. During the first period, political reforms were set in place principally in reaction to the traumatic experiences of the Cultural Revolution and were designed to restore the Party's normative framework—rule by collective consensus and intra-Party democracy—that was said to govern the leadership style in the early 1950s. . . .

Between 1982 and 1984, reform programs were under way in earnest to curb the personality cult and concentration of power, starting with the central agencies of the Party and the government and then proceeding with reforms at the local level. . . .

The second period of political reforms was marked by attempts to rationalize government institutions and properly structure the state-society relationship so as to reduce the CCP's excessive interventions in people's lives. The reforms during this period were driven principally by the imperative of economic reforms—the recognition that efficient administration and some degree of political pluralism had to be allowed for the economic reforms to proceed smoothly and rapidly. . . .

The student demonstrations and the government's brutal suppression demonstrated, in a graphic manner, the futility of all these reform efforts. In a moment of crisis, the CCP easily reverted to its old ways; rule by men triumphed over rule by law and the Party's normative framework was revealed to be in as much disarray as it was during the Cultural Revolution. . . .

The troubles with the political reform programs, however, did not start with the student demonstrations and the government's groping for a response; they were fundamentally flawed from the very beginning. Like the economic reforms, the political reforms failed not so much because of their purposes or lack of efforts, but the manner of their implementation.

There were two major problems with the approach employed in the political reforms. First, the reformist leaders, driven by their pragmatic ideology, always emphasized substance over the sanctity of process and the consistency of procedures. In the name of weeding out anti-reform elements in the leadership, reformers successfully engineered large-scale personnel changes. . . . What received scant attention, however, was that these personnel changes were effected before the ground rules for making personnel changes were firmly set in place and therefore the retired leaders were able to negotiate, into their "retirement package," promotions of their relatives and friends into key positions. It was from this date that cronyism and nepotism acquired semi-legitimacy in Chinese politics, which not only had corrosive effects on the reputation of the CCP but also compromised the institution-building efforts of the reformist leaders themselves.

The second major problem with the political reforms was the role of Deng Xiaoping. Although Deng understood the need for and initiated many of the measures to institutionalize Chinese politics, in effect he was the most obstinate barrier to their implementation. He did this by remaining the *de facto* supreme leader without occupying a formal position commensurate with his power. Initially his decision not to seek top Party and government posts was hailed both inside and outside China as his sincere effort to curb the personality cult, but its actual effect was to move the center of power away from the Politburo and the Central Committee where it should have belonged. . . .

The failures of the political reforms to strengthen the importance of the political process and the Party as an institution had disastrous effects on the implementation of the economic reform programs. As mentioned before, Zhao's impatience with the pace of economic growth and reforms led him to adopt loose fiscal and monetary policies that fueled inflationary pressures and social discontent. This economic imprudence originated from the fact that Zhao probably never felt secure in his position, knowing that the real power did not lie with him. His lack of power and legitimacy as ruler despite his position as the head of the Party made him eager to produce results. As he was most closely identified with economic performance, he needed faster growth rates and reform progress to prove his political worth. . . .

The failures of political reforms in restoring the Party's normative framework had an important role in shaping the government's response to the student demonstrations. In the face of the gravest challenge to the CCP's power, no emergency session of the Central Committee and, after mid-May, no full meeting of the Politburo was held. Instead, formulating a response was left to palace intrigues and behind-the-door maneuvering among a small group of people who were not even members of the formal decision-making bodies. . . .

Conclusion

The problem with China's reform efforts during the last ten years was not that there was too much in the economic sphere and too little in the political sphere. The reforms in both areas were substantial and real. The story is far more complicated and has to do with the nature and the manner of the political and economic reform programs.

The halfway house between a planning and market-affected system as a result of ten years of economic reforms was inherently unstable; it fueled open inflation and it made bribery and corruption the requisite oil that greased its operation. Political reforms, used more as an expedient vehicle to advance reformist goals rather than to establish the sanctity of the rules of the game, only compounded the problem. Cronyism and nepotism became a price the reformist leaders paid to institute a more reform-oriented leadership. Deng Xiaoping, himself the proponent of political institutionalization, contributed further to the personalization of the political process, rather than rectifying the damages left over from Mao's era. . . .

The Individual
and the State

18

Two Models of Law

Victor H. Li

How to maintain social control and stability has been a continuing concern of Chinese political philosophy. In an earlier reading we saw the debate between Legalism and Confucianism on this issue. In this reading, Victor Li, a specialist on Chinese law, explores the ramifications of this debate for the post-1949 legal system in China. Two models of law—the one based primarily on formal, written legal codes, the other on moral suasion—continue to coexist, and the tension between them remains at the center of the Chinese legal system.

During the past twenty years, the Communist Chinese have used two separate models of law, each having its own rationale and objectives. Depending on the period, one model or the other has been dominant, but on the whole, they have existed side by side in a combination of harmony and competition.

The first model (for convenience, I will call it the "external model") is based upon the establishment of a formal, detailed, and usually written set of rules, that is, a legal code which defines permissible and impermissible conduct. A governmental organization enforces compliance with these rules, resolves ambiguities, and settles disputes. This organization in turn has regulations of its own that specify the manner in which it should operate and that provide means for members of the public to obtain redress against improper official actions. Generally, the legal system and the rules of law tend to be complicated and difficult to understand. Trained specialists are required to manage the legal bureaucracy and to act as legal advisors to the public.

This model of law is similar to and derives mainly from the Western legal concepts that were introduced into China at the beginning of this century, and reinfused into Chinese life with the adoption of Soviet legal institutions, methods, and thinking after Liberation in 1949. To a lesser degree, this model also is influenced by traditional Chinese legal practices. Some of the early legalist philosophers *(fa-chia)* had similar attitudes toward the role and function of law. More important, in spite of the Confucian disdain for formal coercive law, China has had for many centuries an active and complex legal system, complete with codes, courts, and the like. Thus, as part of their cultural heritage, the Communists possessed some familiarity with a formal legal system and with centralized bureaucratic government.

The adoption of the external model of law provides many advantages for the Chinese. For one thing, it makes the Chinese legal system more recognizable, and consequently more acceptable, to the West and to the Soviet Union. China's past difficulties with Western criticism of the Chinese legal system and with extraterritoriality make this an important consideration. The external model also provides a clear and rationalized system of government and administration to nation builders who are seeking clarity and rationality; and it strengthens central control. Through the establishment of legal rules and procedures, higher level authorities not only can provide guidance for lower level officials, but also can restrict the scope of their discretionary powers. Moreover, through the medium of law, the public can know when an official is acting improperly and can inform the higher level authorities through the various complaint and appeal procedures. The legal system also is an effective means of controlling the public. In addition to maintaining a degree of public order, law can be used to publicize and to enforce new social policies, as well as to monitor the implementation of and response to these policies.

The second model of law (I will call it the "internal model") is quite different. Proper modes of behavior are taught not through written laws, but rather through a lengthy and continuing educational process whereby a person first learns and then internalizes the socially accepted values and norms. Compliance is obtained not through fear of governmental punishment, but from a genuine understanding and acceptance of the proper rules of conduct. Where such self-control fails, social pressure arises spontaneously to correct and to control the deviant. The coercive power of the state is used for enforcement only in the most serious cases in which the deviant is particularly recalcitrant or depraved. Since each individual is deeply involved in the legal process, law must be simple and must be capable of being applied without the help of skilled specialists. And, since enforcement is handled to a great extent by the community at large, the role of the state in legal administration is limited and the size of the legal bureaucracy is small.

This model seems to include many traditional Chinese ideas and practices. Especially striking is its similarity to the concept of *li*. Both rely heavily upon persuasion and education rather than force, and upon the use of social pressure rather than governmental power. Both also stress the importance of internalizing the rules of conduct and point out the ineffectiveness of using fear of punishment to make people behave. Indeed, if one substitutes the term "socialist morality" for "Confucian morality" and the term "comrade" for *chün-tzu* (gentleman), one can use some of the Chinese classics to describe this model of law.

While the traditional influences certainly are present, other factors are not less important. Communist Chinese ideology, for example, calls for the participation and involvement of the masses in all aspects of government, including law. Some degree of decision making and of sanctioning power also is granted to the masses, or at least to a local social group. Ideological commitment to the mass line is reinforced by some practical considerations. To begin with, internalization of the socially accepted values and norms is a more effective means of controlling conduct than the use of coercive force, and self-policing is much cheaper than the employment of a vast state police apparatus. Because of problems such as the size and variety of Chinese society, the difficulties of communication, and the limited amount of available resources, Peking can exercise direct and strict control over local administration only in the most important matters. For routine items, including much of the administration of the legal system, it is more efficient and effective to permit a substantial degree of local autonomy. Furthermore, the Communists have a distrust of and a dislike for bureaucrats and bureaucratism. This results in part from a reaction against the isolation and abuses of power by the traditional and the Nationalist powerholders, and in part from a fear that an entrenched bureaucracy will not heed

Party direction. As a result, the Communists use the masses as a check on official actions and as a counterbalance to official power.

Other aspects of the internal model also reflect a combination of traditional and nontraditional influences. For example, the traditional practice of having members of the community handle most dispute settlement and control most deviant conduct prepared the way for the contemporary belief that legal administration does not require the services of skilled specialists. This traditional influence is reinforced by the Communists' own experiences. In the border and the liberated areas which they occupied before 1949, there was little functional specialization in the government or in the legal system. Cadres tended to be jacks-of-all-trades. This worked fairly well since the areas were small, the societies they contained were simple, and the cadres and the masses were highly motivated by the concerns of revolution and war. In addition, almost no legal specialists were available, even if one wanted to use them. This personnel problem was not alleviated after Liberation, even though the law schools and the holdovers from the Nationalist regime provided a small supply of legally trained persons. Consequently, legal theory and practice had to be adjusted to enable generalists to operate the legal system.

There are a number of areas where the external and internal models of law conflict or, at least, pull in opposite directions. For example, the internal model stresses local initiative and decision-making power, and tolerates considerable variations in norms, methods, and results from area to area. This runs counter to the external model's desire for clarity and certainty and its emphasis on strong central government. The external model's reliance upon a professional bureaucracy and skilled specialists to administer the legal system in an efficient and rationalized manner conflicts with the internal model's commitment to simplicity and mass participation. The internal model also lacks the clear appeal procedures and channels of the external model, and must therefore find very different means to protect a person from arbitrary actions by officials or by members of his peer group.

While the two models are quite dissimilar, some of their differences are more apparent in theory than in practice. Often the two models complement each other, with the external model handling serious matters and the internal model dealing with more routine affairs. Furthermore, the existence of the external model usually does not preclude the simultaneous existence of the internal model. In general, a person does not learn what he can and cannot do by studying or even by referring to the legal codes. Most notions concerning proper and improper conduct are learned as part of the socialization process, a process whose concepts and practices greatly resemble those of the internal model. . . .

19

Law in Imperial China: Cases from the *Hsing-an Hui-lan*

With commentary by Derk Bodde and Clarence Morris

As Li pointed out in the previous section, there was a very active and well-documented formal legal system in imperial China, despite the Confucian aversion to rule by law. Presented below are two cases, as they found their way up the appellate process in Qing (Ch'ing) China (1644–1911). The reader should note that while law figured prominently, Confucianism is also evident in the manner in which that law was applied. Allowances were always made for prevailing social norms; the social context of law was rarely ignored in traditional China.

Destruction of Tools, Crops, and So On

1833. The governor-general of Szechuan has reported a case in which Chou Tzu-tao, a [non-civil service] functionary connected with the civil service examinations, after having been refused a loan by Teng Fa-hsien, was moved by hatred to destroy the stone lining of the channel which carries the water to irrigate Teng's fields.

This Board finds that this subsidiary channel with its stone lining is distinct from the main [government-maintained] dike system, so that Chou, when he destroyed the stone lining of this channel, caused no damage to the main dike itself. Therefore, his offense is not identical with that of someone who deliberately cuts a [government-maintained] river dike. [The penalty for which ... is 100 blows of the heavy bamboo and three years penal servitude. Note here the characteristic emphasis upon the seriousness of destroying public as against private property.]

Chou should be sentenced by analogy to the statute which states that if someone destroys or damages the house, walls, or other property of another person, the cost of restoration will be calculated, and the offender will be sentenced as he would for taking the same amount in squeeze *(tsang)*. . . .

The sum spent by Teng in repairing the stone lining amounts to 160 ounces of silver, which, halved, comes to 80 ounces. This means that Chou Tzu-tao should accordingly be sentenced to 100 blows of the heavy bamboo.

[The reason for applying (the statute) analogously rather than directly is that the statute deals with the destruction of houses and walls, whereas Chou's offense is that of destroying an irrigation channel. *Tsang,* the word here rendered as "squeeze," more generally signifies loot, booty, property acquired improperly. In the present context, however, "squeeze" seems to be the best rendition. . . . In contrast to an ordinary bribe (a sum paid to an official or other person in authority to induce him either to do or refrain from doing a certain action), *tsang* or squeeze is simply what such an official keeps for himself when money or other wealth passes through his hands. . . . [To use the] table of punishment to be given for taking varying amounts of squeeze, . . . it is necessary to divide in half the amount of actual squeeze in a particular case and then to use the resulting figure as the basis for calculating the punishment. The lightest punishment listed, for example, is 20 blows of the small bamboo, which corresponds to a single ounce of silver. Since the single ounce, in turn, represents only half of the amount squeezed, the 20 blows are actually a punishment for having squeezed two ounces. Likewise, the maximum punishment of 100 blows of the heavy bamboo and three years penal servitude is specified for 400 or more ounces, or, translated into actual fact, this is the punishment for having taken 800 or more ounces in squeeze. This table is the basis for the 100 blows of the heavy bamboo given to the offender in our case. . . .]

Homicide Committed during an Affray or with Intent

1826. The governor of Hunan has reported a case in which Wang Ssu and others jointly assaulted Yang Ta-ho and Li Hung-huai, causing their deaths. . . .

This Board finds, according to sub-statute, that if several persons have planned a joint assault resulting in the death of two persons not belonging to the same family, and if the original planner of the assault should die of illness while awaiting sentence in prison, his death will be acceptable as requital for the deaths of the victims, the result being that any of the other assailants guilty of having actually inflicted fatal blows and therefore normally punishable by strangulation [after the assizes] shall have this penalty reduced by one degree to life exile [at a distance of 3,000 *li*].

[To be properly understood, this sub-statute should be read in conjunction with the basic statute on homicidal group affray, according to which the person (or persons) who actually strike the mortal blows in such an affray are to suffer strangulation after the assizes, in contrast to its original planner who, irrespective of whether or not he has physically participated in the fight, is merely to receive life exile at a distance of 3,000 *li*—unless, that is, he too has been one of those striking the fatal blows. (The explanation for this differentiation given in the Shen Chih-ch'i Commentary is that the original planner merely intended to injure his prospective victim, and that therefore if the victim nevertheless dies, this is the fault of those who mortally wounded him and not of the planner.) With this statute in mind, we can now better understand the sub-statute, according to which, should the original planner die in prison while awaiting sentence, his death expiates, so to speak, the capital crime committed by his associates in fatally injuring the victim. Their punishment of strangulation after the assizes is therefore cancelled for them, and in its place they receive the punishment of life exile which otherwise would have gone to the original planner.]

[Despite its comparative modernity (it was promulgated in 1801), this sub-statute embodies a cosmological conception of very early origin. The key term here is *ti ming*, "requital-life" or "requiting a life," the meaning of which is that one life (or death) is to be given as requital for another. The term appears in the clause of the sub-statute rendered freely but accurately above as "his death will be acceptable as requital for the deaths of the victims." To the ancient Chinese, with their insistence upon a basic harmony existing between man and nature, a human crime—particularly a homicide—was regarded as a disruption of the total cosmic order. This disruption could be repaired only by offering or sacrificing adequate requital for what had been destroyed—a life for a life, an eye for an eye. Precisely how this should be done was less important than the fact of requital per se. Thus, in the sub-statute, the death of the original planner of the affray, even though fortuitous, is reckoned as cancelling out the death of the victim or victims, and therefore as releasing the planner's guilty associates from undergoing the retributive capital punishment otherwise required from them. Of course the concept in late times becomes highly symbolic: the penalty for striking the fatal blows, once a straightforward strangulation, has now become mitigated to strangulation after the assizes and thus no longer precisely balances the death of the victim; likewise the death of the original planner is accepted as adequate requital for the deaths of even two victims. . . .]

In the present case, Wang Ssu and Hu Teng-k'o, the latter now a fugitive from justice, accepted the invitation of Tseng Li-fang to join in an attack on Yang Yung-tso because Tseng was angry at Yang for having prevented him (Tseng) from collecting grass in waste lands belonging to the state. The ensuing fight resulted in the death of Yang's son, Yang Ta-ho, and of an unrelated neighbor, Li Hung-huai. Investigation has shown that Hu Teng-k'o was the one who fatally wounded Li Hung-huai, and Wang Ssu was the one who did the same to Yang Ta-ho. Since the attack did not involve any unusual circumstances, the offenders were sentenced under the ordinary statute on assault.

Now, inasmuch as the original planner of the affray, Tseng Li-fang, has subsequently died of illness while in prison, the governor of Hunan has therefore sentenced Wang Ssu under the sub-statute cited above, according to which the death of the original planner while in prison is acceptable as requital for the death of the victim, thereby allowing a one-degree reduction of sentence for the actual striker of the fatal blow. Accordingly, the governor has sentenced Wang to bambooing and life exile instead of strangulation after the assizes. [Presumably the other chief assailant, Hu Teng-k'o, would have similarly benefited had he not become a fugitive.]

As for Tseng Li-fang himself, it happens that he surrendered himself to the authorities on learning that he was wanted. The governor has accordingly reduced his sentence by one degree from the life exile for which he would otherwise have been liable to [three years] penal servitude. In view of his subsequent death, there is no need to discuss his case further.

Both of these verdicts being appropriate, it is proper to request a confirmatory reply.

[.... Note that Tseng's surrender to the authorities, unlike his death in prison, results in no transferal of reduced punishment to the assailant Wang Ssu because only the death itself serves as a requital for another death....]

20

Mr. Wang vs. Mr. Ch'en: A High Ch'ing Parable

Frederic Wakeman, Jr.

Behind the exterior of impersonal bureaucracy in China, personal relationships played a crucial role. In this parable by an eminent historian at the University of California, Berkeley, we see how one individual of better-than-average standing tries to use those connections to his advantage in a legal case. We also see the sense of powerlessness that an ordinary Chinese feels in dealing with this system. In this context, the tendency for ordinary Chinese to avoid involvement with the traditional Chinese political system becomes understandable.

Let us [cite] a property lawsuit as parable. Mr. Wang, a wealthy but untutored peasant of Kiangsu, claimed title to a piece of fertile land next to the villa of Mr. Ch'en, whose great grandfather had been a ministry official sixty years earlier. Mr. Ch'en himself held no office, no titles; but he had been tutored in the Classics as a youth and still spent three hours a day in his small study making modest marginal comments on a text of the *Book of Changes* in his own, rather elegant hand. One afternoon a week, he would meet eight close comrades at a temple near the district capital. Wine would be heated and served, philosophical papers presented, and—as dusk came on—poems exchanged or a friend's painted scroll admired.

As the lawsuit developed, Mr. Wang mulled over his options. They were not many. Like any other peasant claimant, he could present himself at the magistrate's gates and plead for justice. Such temerity would probably earn him only a beating from the yamen runners for having dared to disturb the magistrate's nap. On the other hand, he could pay a large sum of money to one of the official law clerks and hope to get a hearing for his case. Naturally, this would appear most irregular from the viewpoint of the authors of the *Ch'ing Statutes*. A competent magistrate was supposed to prevent such petty corruption by staying alert, knowing his district intimately, keeping his finger on the pulse of the people. And how was a magistrate to get this kind of information? A man of his stature could not walk about the streets accosting congee peddlers, asking if they had heard of any bribery cases lately. That would not only demean the necessary dignity of his office but would leave him open to every crackpot with a minor complaint. Since his routine sources of intelligence, the yamen's petty clerks and policemen, were seldom able to resist the blandishments of the highest bidder, he had no recourse but to turn to the one group in the community that he could approach without tarnishing his badges of rank: the gentry. Unfortunately for poor Mr. Wang, these were precisely the sort of men with whom his opponent, Mr. Ch'en, consorted.

Mr. Ch'en's management of the impending law case was simple, though indirect. First, he paid a call on a fellow member of his poetry club, who also happened to have been a *t'ung-nien*[1] of the local magistrate. This friend was most happy to introduce so cultivated a guest as Mr. Ch'en to the official the following day over tea. Exchanging pleasantries, the two men hit it off well. The magistrate was also enamored of the *Book of Changes* and impressed by Mr. Ch'en's theories about that classic. As Mr. Ch'en was leaving, he asked if he might have the honor of presenting the magistrate with a small painting. ("The antique-dealer claimed it's a Sung scroll. It's not, of course. But it is quite a good forgery, and I thought Your Excellency might enjoy looking at such a trinket from so worthless a one as myself.") The official was happy to accept, and the two men parted on the best of terms.

When Mr. Wang discovered that his opponent in the coming lawsuit was an acceptable guest at the judge's own home, he realized how foolhardy he had been and dropped the matter altogether. Later, he even

---

1. Literally, "same year," referring to men who take the state examinations together. This was one of the closest ties among members of the elite, roughly similar to those between American fraternity brothers at the same college.

paid his own visit to Mr. Ch'en, apologizing for having disturbed His Honor. Fortunately, he obsequiously added, *"Ta-jen pu chi hsiao-jen kuo"* ("A great man does not remember the faults of a smaller man").

This is an entirely imaginary incident, drawn from no specific text but symbolic of thousands of such situations and designed to show two things: first, that gentry status could be reduced to a common denominator—power-holding through office or *access* to power-holders—and, second, that people who spoke or thought in ways we now identify with the high culture of China were better able to protect their local interests than those who did not share this language and way of life with Chinese officialdom. Mr. Ch'en's family may not actually have had a power-holder in its ranks for three generations; he himself would not be found on official gentry lists, and he was perhaps registered only as part of a *fu-chia* ("wealthy household"). But he was nonetheless identified with that local elite. This is not to say that Ch'en's ilk was forever protected from the hard end of the stick. A classical education was an expensive proposition and hard to come by. Once established, a family had to hope that continuing generations would produce at least one kinsman with the aptitude and dedication for classical learning. Besides, living up to the gentry way of life (fine wine, copies of the *Book of Changes*, Sung "trinkets") could fritter away a family's fortune. But the appearances still told. The Ch'ens of China found it easier to accumulate and hold fortunes than the Wangs, for, although "status manner" and capital were intimately related, the former determined the outcome.

Another aspect of this parable remains to be explained. When Ch'en and Wang began struggling for that piece of property, neither acted corporatively. Corporate interest groups did, of course, exist, but they were usually outside the limits of acceptable political behavior. In other parts of China, for example, the two men might have enrolled their kinsmen in the dispute and incited a clan feud. Or Mr. Wang might have turned to a local gang leader and engaged footpads to accost Ch'en some dark night. Ch'en, in turn, might have recruited his own group of vigilantes for self-protection. These activities, however, were criminal examples of corporate behavior, existing because other forms of group action, which are usually regarded as legitimate in the West, were forbidden in Ming and Ch'ing China. For instance, perhaps Mr. Wang could have tried to get together some friends to form a peasants' union. But a petition or two at the yamen and a demonstration protesting bribery in the law courts would probably have been misconstrued as a treasonable riot. Any group of peasants that formed a society for political reasons was automatically suspected by the authorities and likely to be proscribed for inciting revolt. If circumstances were right, considerable pressure might be exerted on a magistrate by threatening a riot, but this was done only in moments of genuine desperation, since the outcome was unpredictable. Besides, even if the magistrate acceded to the threat, Mr. Ch'en would have yet another card to play. Using some other friends, he would try to see that more gifts and pleasantries were exchanged at an even higher level. A prefect or a provincial treasurer, perhaps even a ministry official in Peking, would be approached and the magistrate overridden. Victory would still go to the man with contacts in high places.

Of course, this practice is not unique to eighteenth-century China. How many close friends of the chief of police resist trying to get their parking tickets fixed? The difference lies in emphasis. In China, "fixing," or the use of contacts, was regarded as less of a danger, and therefore as more legitimate, than allowing farmers to form unions. Even Mr. Ch'en—whose poetry club was a perfectly respectable scholastic association above doubt—was not likely to formally summon a gentry committee for help; rather, he would find the one or two liaison men who could put him in touch with a higher bureaucratic figure. Ch'en looked up toward Peking for political help, not around him for potential corporate allies.

In short, the local gentry was not a political estate. But it did, over the hundreds of years of Ming rule, begin to act like a social one. Although the founder of the Ming, Chu Yuan-chang (reign: 1368-98), had tried to destroy the "wealthy households" of the Yangtze basin that he saw as a threat to his control over that important revenue region, his successors felt that such local notables had to be trusted to check the petty despotism of district officials. Therefore, men of local wealth and power were encouraged to supervise rural tax-collection offices in order to prevent clerks and magistrates from growing corrupt. This meant that the power of the gentry itself increased unchecked, and by the late sixteenth century it threatened to become either an interest-seeking political pressure group or a resuscitated feudal elite capable of breaking away from imperial control. . . .

21

The One Who Loved Dog Meat

B. Michael Frolic

B. Michael Frolic, of York University in Toronto, Canada, spent considerable time in Hong Kong interviewing refugees from Mao's China. He collected their stories, told as first-person narratives, in his book Mao's People. *The following excerpt tells the story of a former prisoner in a reform-through-labor camp. Again, we see the double strands of social control through law, as represented by the prison sentence, and through political and moral education.*

. . . . I was taken in a boxcar to Yingde, a huge forced labor camp located 120 kilometers north of Canton. What a place Yingde was, like a miniature country of 25,000 people, all of them prisoners or ex-prisoners! We grew our own food, provided our own entertainment, and produced large quantities of goods for export. I'm sure the state made a big profit from our work. Sulfur and tea were the big exports. The sulfur mine employs nearly 20,000 people and the Yingde "Big Leaf" tea is famous throughout China. We also produced sugar, bamboo, and other forestry products. We had our own schools, farms, repair shops, and small factories. Contact with outsiders was almost nonexistent, and many of our neighbors were ex-prisoners who had been asked to stay on after their sentences had been completed. These people couldn't leave, even though they had served their sentences. The whole area was fenced off by barbed wire and guarded by the Guangdong Province Security Bureau, which operated Yingde in conjunction with the various economic agencies involved in its production enterprises.

They issued me a metal mug which served to hold my food at meal times and also for washing myself. We used a small wooden barrel in the corner of the room for night soil, but we had to piss outside. I was given a vest, shorts, cotton padded tunic, trousers, rubber shoes, bed sheet, and thin blanket. There were forty of us in a brick room with wooden bunks side by side. At night the guards locked the doors from the outside. We got about six ounces of rice per meal, often with pickles and bean curd. Once a month we received a small piece of meat. You began work in the fields at 6:00 a.m. and you worked all day till 6:30 p.m. Each of us had to pick 50 pounds of tea daily, and this required backbreaking work on the steep hillsides. In the evenings we had to attend political study sessions, usually outside our barracks on the basketball court. A large blackboard was placed on one side and we listened to lectures on politics, on the Party, and on how even prisoners could better serve the Motherland.

I was put on a tea plantation within Yingde, which turned out to be a lucky break. It was a small farm of only 300 people and conditions there were pretty good. Once you learned how to pick tea in a squatting position, and once you mastered the techniques of political reeducation, then it was easy to survive. We had enough food, even during the Three Difficult Years when the rest of China was starving. Of course, you had to have your wits about you. If you questioned authority, or if you brooded too much about the injustice of your fate, you could suffer a horrible end. I remember Liao, who had been sentenced to five years for profiteering. He had been repairing a few electric engines on the side for communes. One day a commune refused to pay him and the next thing he knew he was in Yingde. "They never paid me any money," Liao kept saying, "and I was only doing what everybody else was doing." He appealed his sentence even though everyone said that was a waste of time, since the state never admits it made a mistake. "No one gets a reduced sentence," said old Wang who had been at Yingde for four years. "If you appeal then it merely means that you need still more reeducation and obviously need a longer sentence!" But Liao was stubborn and sure he would be proved innocent. One day they told him the bad news: the appeal was over and he had been given an extra five years. So he hanged himself from a hook in the drying shed with a rope made of torn-up cloth strips.

There weren't any other "successful" suicides I can recall. Two prisoners once escaped by smuggling themselves out in a truck. One of them was brought back ten days later, dirty and exhausted. He had managed to reach Canton but no one there would dare help him and he couldn't get food because he had no money or ration tickets. They caught him stealing food, brought him back to camp, and invited us a week later to watch his execution. The other prisoner never came back, but local gossip said he had been killed in a fight, trying to escape his guards. It was foolish to try to escape because the camp was too isolated and, even if you did get out, it was almost impossible to survive.

So the best solution was to flow like water. That's what you had to do to stay alive. I saw that I had to become a model prisoner, because then you get a little leverage and some privileges. I stayed out of trouble, worked hard, watched carefully, and always kept my thoughts well hidden. The trick was to make a full confession of your "sins" and then become an activist in the political studies group. I plunged into politics with a vengeance, surprising even myself with my ability to talk convincingly about the correct political line, fundamental principles of Marxism-Leninism, the Party's role in leading the masses, and so on. Soon Zhang, the cadre responsible for our sessions, came and praised me for my improved thought. "We've been watching you," he said, "and we think you're making progress." This was encouraging. Within a few weeks I was asked to lead some of the political study sessions and there I was, next to the basketball hoop, explaining Party politics to my co-prisoners. It was an easy game to play and, since I had confided in no one, my co-prisoners never knew for certain whether I was serious. Some figured rightly that I was an opportunist and others thought I was an informer.

It wasn't long before the authorities made me a trusty. With this status I could win favors from the guards and could help prisoners get certain things. The guards would do almost anything to have a woman, and many of the prisoners were willing former prostitutes and actresses. Some were just lonely. Others figured they could get extra food, blankets, and other privileges. I knew just about everything that was going on and could use this information to make life easier for myself. My biggest break came when Zhang, the cadre, got me involved in his affair with one of the prisoners. After that I practically had the run of the camp—extra food, easier workload, and free time with my own girlfriend, an actress from Canton who had been sent to Yingde because she spurned the advances of the big-shot political boss in charge of her troupe's activities.

All in all, prison wasn't that bad. You had to learn to accept the permanent smell of piss lingering in the air, the ever-present dirt, and the constant duplicity. No one could be trusted—but then why should a labor camp be any different than the rest of China? Actually in some ways we were better off than many "free" workers. While parts of China were desperately short of food and people were starving, we had food in our rice bowls even in the blackest months. We didn't have to worry about making any political mistakes because we had already been branded (most of us) as political misfits. So we could relax and not worry so much about politics as those on the outside. For me, life at Yingde taught me how to play the game of politics, so that in the future I wouldn't again blunder and get caught unawares.

It wasn't that hard for me to leave the camp. I had been a trusty and managed to walk that tightrope so carefully that I was considered to have been politically reeducated. Zhang had been transferred, but my file now indicated that I had made a remarkable shift in my attitude. In 1961 a few prisoners were released and I somehow got on the list, after just over three years. I left Yingde suddenly one morning, without any tears, along with thirty others. We were given a certificate of release stamped by the authorities, 50 yuan, and were allowed to keep our prison clothes. I was then taken to the train station to begin the trip back to Huizhou. I was told I would be put under three years of surveillance back in Huizhou, which meant I had to report regularly to the local Public Security Office, but in fact nobody bothered with this once I came home. . . .

22

Liberalizing Political Life

Harry Harding

In the decade after Mao's death in 1976, his successors sought to lessen the intrusiveness of the political system on individual Chinese and to end the capriciousness that characterized the last years of Mao's rule. In the excerpt that follows, Harry Harding describes post-1978 reforms aimed at changing the way the state interacted with society in China. As he makes clear, the "liberalizing" of political life did not mean that China took on the characteristics which we associate with liberal democratic systems. Much of the Leninist nature of the system remained and would be later reinforced in the wake of Tiananmen.

By 1980 the reformers associated with Deng Xiaoping were prepared to admit that, despite the purge of the Gang of Four and the restoration of political stability, there was still a serious "crisis of confidence" among sizable segments of the Chinese population. Many young people, they acknowledged, still adhered to Mao's view that a separate class of Party bureaucrats ruled China solely in its own interest. If no measures were undertaken to create a reconciliation between the Party and the people, these reformers warned, then China would risk popular unrest comparable to what was then sweeping Poland. As the reformers saw it, they had to reshape the structure of political life in ways that would create a greater degree of democracy and legality. Only in doing so could popular support for the regime be rebuilt.

The reformers also saw an economic rationale for a transformation of the political structure. Retaining the totalitarian system of the past would be incompatible with the economic reforms that they envisioned. Tight organizational and ideological controls would make it virtually impossible for scientists to innovate, technicians to invent, economists to develop new strategies for development, or entrepreneurs to launch new economic activities. Nor would foreigners, particularly those from the West, find it convenient to interact with a China that remained under rigid administrative controls.

For all these reasons, China's reformers have agreed on the necessity for a relaxation of political life. But most of them, including Deng Xiaoping, remain committed to certain fundamental Leninist principles that limit the political liberalization that has occurred. These principles, in turn, echo deeply rooted Chinese values that give the state the right—even the obligation—to promote moral conduct by educating citizens in an official doctrine believed to be morally valid. The state must also preserve social harmony by prohibiting the emergence of political organizations that would challenge the control of the central government. These Chinese values and Leninist principles permit the state to suppress dissent or heterodoxy in society, preclude the emergence of genuine political pluralism, justify the maintenance of broad Party leadership over all other political and social institutions, and preserve a significant, although attenuated, role for Marxist ideology in political affairs. . . .

The political reforms launched in the late 1970s and early 1980s fall into three broad categories. These include promoting a reconciliation between state and society by reducing the scope and arbitrariness of political intervention in daily life; expanding the opportunities of popular participation in political affairs, although with limits on both the form and content of political expression; and redefining the content and role of China's official ideology to create a new basis for authority in contemporary Chinese politics. Together, the reforms have greatly relaxed the degree of political control over Chinese society, without fundamentally altering the Leninist character of the Chinese political system.

Reducing and Regularizing the Role of the State

In post-Mao China the state has reduced both the scope and arbitrariness of political intervention in social life. The range of activities that the state attempts to regulate has been substantially restricted, and those controls remaining on certain activities have, with some exceptions, become more predictable and less arbitrary.

As a result, ordinary citizens now enjoy much greater freedom of belief, expression, and consumption than was true in the past. The Chinese Communist Party today places less emphasis on securing from non-Party members an active commitment to Marxist ideological principles, and pursues the less ambitious goal of obtaining popular compliance with national policy. Citizens therefore spend less time in political study than they did during the Maoist period, and those study sessions that do take place are more likely to deal with practical policy questions than with general ideological principles. Religion is no longer condemned as superstition: churches and temples in urban areas have been allowed to reopen, there has been a revival of folk customs and local religious practices in the countryside, and the recruitment and training of monks and priests have been resumed.

The scope for expression is greater. In both the arts and intellectual matters, artists and writers are encouraged to revive traditional styles and to experiment with modern techniques. Popular tabloids, widely available in major cities, carry articles and pictures on subjects ranging from crime to romance. . . .

[Another] important aspect of political liberalization since 1976 has been the removal of the pejorative political and class labels that had been assigned to hundreds of millions of Chinese during the Maoist period. Beginning in 1978, political labels, such as "rightist," "capitalist roader," or "counterrevolutionary" were lifted from approximately three million people who had received them during the antirightist campaign of 1957 and the Cultural Revolution of 1966–76. In 1977 discriminatory class labels were lifted from almost all former landlords, rich peasants, and capitalists. . . .

The creation of a legal framework that more fully specifies the substantive and procedural rights of Chinese citizens has been another feature of political reform. The state constitution of 1982 specifies, for the first time, that all Chinese citizens are "equal before the law" and includes new provisions granting citizens the rights of religious belief, the inviolability of the home, privacy of correspondence, and freedom from unlawful arrest. The constitution also stipulates that all government organs and political parties must "abide by the Constitution and the law" in conducting their work. The criminal law and the code of criminal procedure, adopted in 1979, guarantee against torture and arbitrary detention and specify the right to a trial with a courtroom defense. The new legal code also offers a more restrictive definition of "counterrevolutionary" offenses.

Although these changes have been impressive, important limits remain on the extent to which the scope of state control over society has been reduced. Both the state and the Party continue to promote certain kinds of beliefs and to discourage others. The state constitution notes the responsibility of the government to "educate the people" in "dialectical and historical materialism" and, at the same time, to "combat capitalist, feudalist, and other decadent ideas." The Party constitution stipulates that the development of a "socialist spiritual civilization," the struggle against "nonproletarian ideas," and the inculcation of "communist ideology" are all part of the Party's basic program. The state periodically reminds intellectuals and artists of their obligations to maintain a "socialist orientation" and to fulfill their "social responsibilities." The assumption that the state has the obligation to create and maintain public morality in China has justified the periodic movements against various forms of social and political deviance since 1978. . . .

[Finally] there is still no tradition of judicial independence in China. Although the Party seems to intervene less frequently in the treatment of ordinary cases, the handling of more important crimes is subject to review, and often to ultimate decision, by the cognizant Party committee. In addition, no provision is made for independent judicial oversight of the conduct of Party and state officials, except when the Party itself has chosen to bring errant cadres to trial. The process of codification remains incomplete, providing Party officials great leeway in interpreting the law and in acting outside the legal framework. Consequently, the importance of formal legal provisions in shaping the relationship between the citizen and the state should not be exaggerated.

Increasing Opportunities for Popular Participation

The increase of opportunities for political participation at both the grassroots and national levels constitutes a second aspect of political liberalization. The introduction of competitive elections to local legislatures, the expansion of the role of the people's congresses, and growing consultation with various social groups through several institutional mechanisms characterize the post-Mao reforms. Even so, the political participation that is allowed and the views that can be safely expressed are subject to important restrictions.

During the Maoist period, elections in China were highly ritualized affairs. Only delegates to people's congresses at the lowest levels of Chinese society were directly elected by their constituents. The Communist Party controlled the process of nomination and put forward only as many candidates as there were vacancies to be filled. But under the election law of 1979, the use of direct elections was extended to the level of rural counties and urban districts. Even more significant, the number of candidates must now, by law, exceed the number of vacancies, and ordinary citizens may nominate candidates to stand for election.

These elections would have little meaning, of course, if the legislative bodies to which delegates were chosen had only minor functions in the policy-making process. In the past, people's congresses served only to legitimize Communist Party decisions, holding short and infrequent meetings in which laws, policy documents, and personnel appointments were approved by acclamation. Since 1979, however, the role of the people's congresses has been expanded, especially at the national level. The National People's Congress (NPC) holds an annual plenary session, and its Standing Committee meets on five or six occasions over the course of the year. The NPC has established functional committees that specialize in particular aspects of foreign and domestic policy and that have played a more active role in drafting legislation. The meetings of the NPC—and, on rarer occasions, meetings of provincial and county congresses as well—have increasingly served as a forum in which delegates can fairly frankly discuss national and local policy, question government officials, and advance the interests of their regional or sectoral constituencies. By the spring of 1986, some members of the NPC were actually voting against nominations and reports presented to them. . . .

But all these opportunities for political participation remain limited. The implementation of the new election law has encountered serious difficulties at local levels. Some cadres have refused to nominate more candidates than vacancies, harassed truly independent candidates who had not been nominated by the Party, and overturned election results whose outcomes they disapproved. . . .

Similar limits affect the functioning of the people's congresses. Despite the recent increase in the frequency of their meetings, the range of their activities, and the outspokenness of their delegates, the people's congresses in China remain, on balance, consultative and advisory bodies. They have not yet become independent legislatures that can routinely initiate legislation, veto state proposals, or impose accountability on government or Party officials. . . .

Nor has there been much progress toward democratization within the Chinese Communist Party. The Party constitution does provide for competitive elections for delegates to Party congresses and for members of Party committees at every level. But these provisions have not been widely implemented. Only in a few places has the press reported the selection of Party leaders by competitive elections, without direct intervention by higher levels. . . .

Despite the constitutional provisions guaranteeing freedom of assembly, association, and press, there are restrictions on the rights of independent organization and publication. All organizations, especially those that may become national in scope, must receive the sanction of the state, and those that fail to do so are forced to disband. This residual power of the state has been used to prevent the emergence of independent trade unions, rural secret societies, religious organizations deemed to have political ambitions, and even academic organizations.

Journals and newspapers, too, must register with the government. Those not approved are prevented from publishing, and those that later express unacceptable opinions are subject to suspension. . . .

Most important of all, restrictions remain on the content of what can be said, through whatever organizational channel. The Party still holds that the freedom of speech is not absolute, but is constrained by principles of national unity, socialist morality, and, for Party members, Party discipline. The most important guidelines are the "four cardinal principles" identified by Deng Xiaoping in the spring of 1979, which establish the outer limits of political expression. The four principles call for upholding the leadership of the Communist Party, preserving the general structure of the Chinese state, following a socialist course in economic development, and maintaining Marxism as the official ideology of the nation. Chinese are much freer now than in the past to reinterpret each of these four principles. There has been a lively debate over the essential characteristics of socialism and Marxism and growing discussion of how to reform the government and improve the leadership of the Party. But none of the four cardinal principles can be openly rejected or challenged without fear of punishment.

Changing the Basis of Political Authority

... The Chinese are also reevaluating ideology as a source of authority for their political system. To begin with, they have extensively reexamined the content of doctrine. The Party has repudiated many of the ideological concepts associated with Mao's later years: that class struggle is the principal contradiction in socialist society, that "continuous revolution under the dictatorship of the proletariat" should be the basic line of the Party, and that cultural revolutions should be conducted every few years against "party people in authority taking the capitalist road." Other concepts, such as Mao's theory of the three worlds and Lin Biao's "people's war," have been quietly abandoned. Even Leninism has undergone a subtle reevaluation, with some theorists privately denying that Lenin's concepts of imperialism and the vanguard party have much relevance to contemporary Chinese experience, and others publicly extolling the contributions of other communist leaders, such as Rosa Luxemburg, who criticized the dictatorial tendencies inherent in the Leninist model of political organization.

As a result of this sort of reassessment, the content of official doctrine has been transformed along several dimensions. The main task of politics is now seen as promoting modernization and reform, rather than undertaking continuous struggle and revolution. The Maoist vision of a socialist society as one rent with conflict among antagonistic social classes has been replaced by a more consensual vision, in which class struggle plays a relatively minor role. The responsibility of the contemporary Chinese state is increasingly defined as expanding democracy, rather than exercising dictatorship. Accordingly, elements of the Marxist legacy that acknowledge the possibility of the alienation of people from their government even under socialism, and that acknowledge common bonds of humanity that cut across social classes, have been cautiously and gradually resurrected.

Equally important, the Party today admits that many intellectual, scientific, and technical questions can and should be addressed on their merits, without regard to ideological considerations. This attitude presents a stark contrast to the Cultural Revolution period, when all decisions were supposedly taken only after a consideration of the relevant doctrinal principles. The list of socioeconomic policies and political institutions said to be required by a commitment to Marxism has been pared, and some of the most radical reformers believe that being a Marxist should not preclude adoption of any particular policy, so long as it can be shown effective. Increasingly, doctrine is regarded as a set of broad skills for the future and a methodology for analyzing social and economic problems, rather than a list of detailed and infallible solutions to immediate policy problems. Ideology, in other words, no longer requires very many policies, but simply sets limits on those that can receive serious consideration.

As the role of doctrine in Chinese political life recedes, the Party has come to base its substantive legitimacy on the concepts of modernization and nationalism. In early 1984, for example, Hu Yaobang announced that the principal goal of the Party was to "make people rich." Eight months later, on National Day, one of China's two official news services declared that the Communist Party, unlike previous modern Chinese governments, had been able to unify and strengthen the country to the point that no foreigner could call the Chinese people a "sheet of loose sand" or the "sick men of Asia." "The Chinese," the editorial continued, "are no longer targets of attack and insult wherever they go." And a few weeks later, Deng Xiaoping announced that one aim of reform was to turn China into a world power by the turn of the century. In short, the Party is promising to create a powerful nation that will assume leadership in international affairs, raise the living standards of the Chinese people, and create a modern social, economic, and political system that embodies the best of the Chinese tradition. . . .

. . . Although rational-legal authority has become a more important aspect of the Party's procedural legitimacy, it has not totally supplanted charisma in post-Mao China. Although the Chinese political system is no longer organized exclusively around the rule of a single charismatic leader, as it was during the Cultural Revolution, it is still focused on the personal prestige of a single individual, Deng Xiaoping, who is widely regarded as having extraordinary qualities of leadership. Conversely, the development of either rational or legal authority in contemporary China remains limited. Intellectuals are still prohibited from freely investigating and debating certain basic economic and political issues, such as the leadership of the Party or the desirability of socialism. And, despite the development of legal codes, electoral mechanisms, and more powerful legislatures, powerful Party cadres, relatively unconstrained by formal legal procedures, still exercise political authority. . . .

Many aspects of Chinese political life have changed since the death of Mao Zedong in 1976. The reach of the state is less intrusive and less arbitrary than it was during Mao's lifetime. The Party no longer interferes in the details of the daily lives of most citizens. A system of law, which guarantees the Chinese people certain substantive and procedural rights, increasingly constrains the exercise of political power. Greater opportunities have been opened for Chinese outside government, particularly intellectuals, to express their views on national policy. Discussion of political issues, both in private occasions and in public forums, is more lively, frank, and detailed. And the tone of political discourse is less charismatic, more secular, less ideological, and more rational. On balance, the political system is more open and relaxed than at any time since 1949.

At the same time, the political reforms of the post-Mao era have not fundamentally transformed some of the basic Leninist features of the Chinese political system. Chinese politics is not characterized by pluralism in either the organizational or the ideological sphere. The Party may now consult with a larger number of individuals and institutions in its determination of national policy, but it still allows no independent political parties, no autonomous mass media, no independent social or professional associations, and no true contest for political power. The Party has relaxed control over large segments of Chinese society, but it has not yet acknowledged in any binding manner that there are spheres of life in which it has no right to interfere. The government employs administrative regulations and criminal codes to enforce policies in a predictable way, but it has not yet accepted enduring legal procedures that unconditionally protect citizens against the arbitrary exercise of power. The Party may now admit that Marxism is a living doctrine that must evolve in keeping with changing circumstances and may even tolerate the absence of a firm commitment to Marxist ideology among many Chinese. But it still does not tolerate the open competition of alternative social and political philosophies for the allegiance of China's intellectuals.

Thus China in the post-Mao period has become what might best be described as a "consultative authoritarian" regime, a significant departure from the totalitarianism of the recent past, but not a truly pluralistic, or even quasi-democratic, political system. It increasingly recognizes the need to obtain information, advice, and support from key sectors of the population, but insists on suppressing dissent, cultivating its vision of public morality, and maintaining ultimate political power in the hands of the Party. . . .

23

Political Participation in Communist China

James R. Townsend

One of the difficulties for Westerners in understanding China is that similar words mean different things to the Western and Chinese mind. We consider the Chinese system to be "authoritarian"; they speak of their nation as being the most "democratic" in the world. The differences involve more than propaganda points; they also involve dissimilar conceptions of the same term. In the following excerpt, James Townsend of the University of Washington discusses the nature and meaning of political participation in China.

The changing political life of the masses is a recurrent and powerful theme in the Chinese revolution. Many who have studied or witnessed this revolution, in either its past or present phases, have called attention to the rising political consciousness and activity of the Chinese people. . . .

. . . . There is a significant comparative interest in analysis of political participation in China. Most obviously, this interest lies in the study of political development and the related concepts of nation-building and political modernization. Leonard Binder has stated that "political development" is a further specification of the more general term "political change" when political change in any historical period has a particular direction. The conviction that political change in the modern era is in fact moving in a particular direction is widespread. Literature in this field consistently refers to broadly similar political changes that derive from global trends toward industrialization, urbanization, and the spread of organization and technology; it cites increasing specialization in governmental structure and performance, the rational recruitment and placement of political actors, the growth of power and effectiveness of central governments, and the drive for nation-state status with an integrated and nationally conscious citizenry as among the main political characteristics of "development" or "modernization." ... The "participation explosion" that China is now experiencing is not, therefore, an isolated or unique event. Whatever the unique features of China's past and present policies might be, the political awakening of the Chinese people is comparable to similar trends elsewhere, whether recently begun or long established, and is directly relevant to a general understanding of political development.

The fact that China now shares with many other states the experience of the common man's entrance into politics does not necessarily mean that political participation in China is identical to, or even moving toward, varieties of political participation that exist elsewhere. There are, of course, strong similarities between the political process in China and in some other "developing" states that have organized a single-party system with a mass political base. But when we speak of political development it is not sufficient to note similarities among societies at roughly comparable "stages of development." We must also compare societies at different "stages" in an effort to understand the dimensions and dynamics of the "particular direction" that gives political development its meaning. In the specific context of political participation, one of the most critical questions is whether or not the Western democratic style of participation defines the direction that participation in other societies will ultimately take.

.... In China ... there has emerged a style of participation that differs sharply from patterns of participation in the modern democratic state and yet seems certain to endure for a long time to come. A general statement of these differences ... will be useful here.

The Chinese Communist and Western democratic styles of political participation have in common a claim to provide representation of popular interests and a demand for extensive popular participation in political life, but the differences between them far outweigh these common characteristics. First, and most important, perhaps, the Chinese style defines the major function of participation as execution of Party policies, whereas the democratic style defines it as exerting popular influence on political decisions. Second, the Chinese style emphasizes direct contact between cadres and masses as the surest means of eliciting popular participation and keeping political leaders in touch with popular demands. The democratic style relies mainly on representative institutions to transmit popular demands to political leaders and to serve as the arena for political action. Third, the Chinese style insists that popular political action support a supreme, unified national interest as defined solely by the Communist Party; it concedes that partial or temporary interests may conflict with the "true" national interest, and it theoretically allows such interests political expression, but it insists that they must be subordinated to, and ultimately submerged in, the national interest. The democratic style recognizes the existence of a national interest, but sees it as a fluid combination of diverse interests that may legitimately compete, so long as they observe the law, both before and after decisions are made. Fourth, the Chinese style emphasizes the quality and morality of political leaders, rather than legal and institutionalized popular controls, as the guarantee of good government. The democratic style exalts its legal and institutional framework and aims at "a government of laws and not of men." Finally, the Chinese style recognizes no theoretical limits to the extension of demands for political activity and no private obligations can take precedence over public ones. The democratic style values participation highly but insists that the inviolability of private life places limits, however vaguely defined, on public obligations and permits the individual to abstain from political action if he chooses.

While the foregoing statement is a gross simplification open to many qualifications, it demonstrates that the terms of popular political action in China are quite different from those in the Western democracies. . . .

. . . . Political participation includes all those activities through which the individual consciously becomes involved in attempts to give a particular direction to the conduct of public affairs, excluding activities of an occupational or compulsory nature. . . . The individual who becomes involved in the execution of a policy with the understanding that he is thereby committing himself to one political viewpoint in opposition to another is engaged in political participation, even though he may have had no part in the original decision.

The most difficult aspect of a definition of political participation is

the role of voluntarism. . . . Political participation need not be spontaneous, and even the insistence on voluntarism cannot be too rigid, although it must remain one of the categories by which political participation is analyzed. Perhaps the critical factor in voluntary participation is a
willingness to perform certain acts that are perceived to have political significance even when performance is required by law or other pressures.

. . . The form which popular political participation takes in Communist China has a profound importance in Chinese political development and the operation of the Chinese political system. The fact that
Chinese claims about the representative and influential functions of
their institutions for popular participation are not substantiated is, of
course, very relevant to our analysis; we shall try to examine these claims
carefully, taking note of their inadequacies and of the stultifying impact
of Party controls throughout the political system. At the same time,
however, we must recognize that the absence of effective political influence and representation does not exhaust the political significance of
our subject. The political meaning of actions is not determined solely
by the nature of the actions themselves or the institutions that provide
their setting, but involves as well the psychological motivations and interpretations that surround them; that is, it is the way in which actions
are rationalized that gives them a public, or political, character. . . .

We must also take note of multiplicity of function in various types
of social behavior. In his discussion of "manifest" and "latent" function,
Robert Merton points out that the unintended and even unrecognized
consequences of some actions may perform significant social functions.
For example, an Indian rain ceremony may perform the "latent" function of reinforcing group identity, and the American political "machine"
may perform the "latent" functions of assisting the needy, dispensing
political privileges to business, and providing channels of social mobility.
With specific reference to political participation, it is now widely recognized that democratic political practices, though "manifestly" devoted
to exerting influence on decisions or decision-makers, are "latently"
powerful agents for the creation of consensus, the cementing of individual loyalties to the community, and the gratification of individual psychic needs. Clearly, the "manifest" function of the Chinese style of participation—popular execution of Party policies—does not exhaust the
full meaning of the actions involved. . . .

24

China after Mao:
The Emergence of Dissent

*Fang Lizhi / Beijing University Handbill
Workers' Union Handbill*

In this selection we present a sample of some of the dissident thought that developed in China during the late 1980s. The first selection is an interview with Fang Lizhi, an astrophysicist whose views had long been a thorn in the side of China's Communist rulers (see chapter 14). In the aftermath of the Tiananmen tragedy, he sought refuge in the United States embassy in Beijing and was not allowed to leave the country until the following year. The statements reprinted below attributed to Chinese students and workers illustrate the point made in chapter 17—much of the dissidence that surrounded events in Tiananmen was sparked by the perceived inequity and corruption that resulted from the reform movement.

Fang Lizhi: An Interview with Tiziano Terzani

Professor Fang, among Chinese students you are a hero. The international press has hailed you as China's Sakharov. Deng Xiaoping, on the other hand, calls you a "bad element." China's Communist Party maintains you are a victim of the disease called "bourgeois liberalization." What are you really?

A little bit of all of these. But in the first place I am an astrophysicist. The natural sciences are my religion. Einstein once said something of the sort. Previously I did not understand him. Now I know: we scientists have a belief and an aim, we have an obligation towards society. If we discover a truth and society does not accept it, this weighs on us. This is what happened to Galileo. That is when, as scientists, we have to intervene. With this mission I step into society.

What kind of a mission do you have in China?

Democratization. Without democracy there can be no development. Unless individual human rights are recognized there can be no true democracy. In China the very ABC of democracy is unknown. We have to educate ourselves for democracy. We have to understand that democracy isn't something that our leaders can hand down to us. A democracy that comes from above is no democracy, it is nothing but a relaxation of control. The fight will be intense. But it cannot be avoided.

First you have attacked local Party cadres, then the Municipal Party Committee of Peking. Recently you attacked the Politburo. What is your next target?

Next I will criticize Marxism itself.

You go very far.

It is an undeniable truth that Marxism is no longer of much use. As a scientist I can prove it. Most answers given by Marxism with regard to the natural sciences are obsolete, some are even downright wrong. That is a fact. What Marxism has to say about the natural sciences stems from Engels' book *Natural Dialectics*. On nearly every page of this book one can find something that is either outdated or completely incorrect.

For example?

In the 1960s, with the aid of Marxism, the USSR and China repeatedly criticized the results of modern natural sciences. In biology they criticized genetics, in physics they criticized the theory of relativity and extended their criticism from cosmology to the development of the computer. Not even once has their criticism been proved correct. Therefore, how can one say today that Marxism should lead the natural sciences? It's a fallacy.

Have you ever believed in Marxism?

I certainly have! Immediately after Liberation [1949] and in the 1950s I firmly believed in Marxism. In 1955, when I joined the Party, I was convinced that Marxism would lead the way in every field and that the Communist Party was thoroughly good.

When, in 1958, during the Anti-Rightist Campaign, I was expelled from the Party, I made a very sincere self-criticism. I was convinced that I had wronged the Party. Now the Party has expelled me a second time, but this time I know that I was not in the wrong. Therefore I have refused to make a self-criticism.

Deng stated in 1979 that, in conformity with the Chinese Constitution, every citizen should be guided by the Four Basic Principles: the socialist road, the people's democratic dictatorship, leadership of the Party, and Marxism-Leninism and Mao Zedong Thought.

Marxism is a thing of the past. It helps us to understand the problems of the last century, not those of today. The same is true in the case of physics. Newton developed his theory three hundred years ago. It is still valuable, but it does not help to solve today's problems, such as those related to computer technology. Marxism belongs to a precise epoch of civilization and that era is over. It is like old clothing that must be put aside. . . .

You consider a communist system to be reformable—but until now this has never been achieved.

It is difficult, but if any country stands a chance, that country is China.

A better chance than the Soviet Union under Gorbachev?

Of course. We find ourselves in a much better position—for a simple reason: in the Soviet Union the Communist Party has achieved a few successes, for example, in terms of military defense and the sciences. Their intellectuals enjoy much more freedom than we have ever had. In China, on the contrary, the Communist Party cannot boast a single success. It has achieved nothing of value during the past thirty years.

That's why leaders at all levels are worried. That's why even among the highest cadres there are some who admit that nothing of value has been achieved. This couldn't be said as easily in the Soviet Union. . . .

Up to now it has been the Party that has decided on the role of the intellectuals. During the Cultural Revolution they were forced down to the lowest, "stinking ninth" position of the "nine bad categories" of people. Today, under Deng Xiaoping, they have climbed up again to the third position, after peasants and workers. But they are still not independent.

Quite right. Mao described the dependency of the intellectuals with the saying: "The hair clings firmly to the skin." The situation remains unchanged. Intellectuals continue to be looked upon as tools. Now is the time for them to show their strength. No one should be intimidated. That is democracy. If we fail to achieve this, China can hardly expect to become a truly developed, modern country. . . .

What about human rights in China?

It is a dangerous topic. The question of human rights is taboo in China. Things are far worse than in the Soviet Union. Wei Jingsheng is a famous case, but there are thousands of others whose names are not even known. At least in the Soviet Union there are name lists. Not so in China.

Is democracy really a necessary condition for the development of a country? States like Taiwan, South Korea, Singapore and the Crown Colony of Hong Kong have made enormous economic progress without being true democracies.

First of all, in the countries you have named there is far more democracy than in China. Secondly, those countries are under American protection, and the USA wants their economies to develop. Things are different in the case of China. Moreover, it is particularly difficult to separate economic from political democracy in China.

Deng holds a different view. He has told the Chinese: "Get rich; to be rich is glorious. The Party will take care of the rest."

In China the Party wants not only to manage politics. It wants to control everything, including people's lifestyles and thinking. Today, factories are being run by managers, but the real power still lies in the hands of Party cadres. Peasants enjoy a free market system, but the cadres tell them: You still need our rubber stamp and for that you still have to buy us! And here lies the root of the new corruption. In order to create a true economic democracy in China, one ought to abolish political controls. And that is exactly what the Party fears most.

Hasn't Deng Xiaoping with his economic reforms opened a Pandora's box? Doesn't he equally want democracy?

No. In the short term Deng's reforms are intended to stabilize the system. What he wants to do is avert a total collapse of the system. The Party is in a quandary: if it introduces reforms then it has to reduce its own power; if it fails to reform then its power will be undermined even faster.

Deng Xiaoping is the hero of the West. In 1985 Time *magazine elected him Man of the Year. The West views him as an ally on the international stage.*

It would appear that the West has a very superficial understanding of China. . . .

Today China is importing Western technology in order to push forward its own modernization. Do you think this is right?

Certainly. But it is not enough just to import things in a piecemeal fashion, to buy a few big computers. In order to become truly modernized, we have to import the spirit of Western civilization into China. Chinese civilization has achieved many profound insights, but it ignores logic. For the sake of our development, we must adopt the Western spirit.

The Party has accused you of being polluted by Western ideas, and of advocating the wholesale Westernization of China. Is this true?

We must open our country in all directions, then many positive things will come in, while our own values will not be lost. I have never said that we should repudiate those Chinese traditions which are good. However, the feudal relationships of Chinese society are bad and must be done away with. True, Western morality is different from ours, but that doesn't mean it is worse. . . .

Soldiers, Look How Profiteering by Government Officials Is Eating You Up

(Beijing University Handbill)

Dear soldiers, please ask yourselves how come in these days of wild inflation, your food stipend remains at 1.65 yuan. I suggest that you take a look at the profiteering going on among government officials!

What does it mean when people talk about "profiteering by government officials"? To describe it simply, it refers to officials using their power to acquire things such as goods at low state-fixed prices, import and export licenses (or documents), loans, and foreign currency at special low exchange rates, so that they can reap huge profits. These officials do business in the name of their companies. The companies can be categorized into two kinds: those run by the government and those run by the sons and daughters of high-level cadres [officials]. . . . The trading done by these companies can likewise be categorized into two kinds: domestic trade and foreign trade.

Now, let's take a look at the variety of ways these profiteering officials abuse their power to run their operations smoothly and suck the lifeblood out of the people!

First, let's look at domestic trade. Now, our Crown Prince Deng Pufang [Deng Xiaoping's son], travel-worn [from his trips up and down the country], flies into the Northeast. . . . The Heilongjiang Province leadership, upon hearing of his lordship's arrival, wastes no time in taking him on a grand tour to Daqing [a major oil field in Northeast China]. Prince Deng is delighted to find Daqing has some profits he can dredge up: he buys, among other things, some tons of polyethylene and polypropylene at the state-fixed price of about 3,000 yuan a ton, and then, after shipping them through the Shanhaiguan pass down to Beijing proceeds to resell them at 9,000 yuan a ton. Well, what a "piece of cake." Prince Deng has made a killing, doing practically no work while getting a hundred times' return. Money has poured into his pockets. Who wouldn't be gleeful in his shoes?

When it comes to foreign trade, well, things get a bit tougher. There are three conditions for success, and having only two just won't do. The first is the import/export license. The second is the state-granted "right to engage in foreign trade." The third is foreign exchange bought at the official state-fixed rate [in comparison to the market rate, which is nearly double]. Of the three, the import/export license is the most important. But for those government lords, a license is hardly an obstacle. They can always get one from their daddies or brothers who are big officials. And if their company has not been granted the right to engage in foreign trade, they can always find a company that does have the right to act as their agent. As for foreign currency, it's always available at the foreign exchange markets; it's only that they might have to buy it a higher price.

In late 1984 or early 1985, when Kanghua [Deng Pufang's company] had just begun operating, it already occupied as office space a compound on Gongyuan Street and a suite in the Overseas Chinese Hotel. One day a certain businessman went up to one of these offices. There he was met by a Kanghua employee who showed him a thick pile of import/export licenses (800 in all); there were licenses for over a thousand cars and a few thousand color TV sets. The employee offered the licenses to the businessman for a "service charge" of 3 percent. And by international trade custom, Kanghua could also obtain from the foreign manufacturers of those goods a commission ranging from 5 to 10 percent [for helping to arrange their import]. Well, whether in the end this money went into the accounts of Kanghua company, or into the private pockets of Deng Pufang, only the devil knows. In this world of ruthless competition, all you need to know is how to act as the middleman, how to pull the right strings, so why worry that money won't reach your hands? The key to success is you have to hold onto your official's cap; with power in hand, licenses come naturally.

Well, let me tell you, if you have power today, use it. Tomorrow you might not have the chance. And let me tell you, our lord officials are not monks who have taken a vow of abstinence. Who cares that the people are suffering hardships, who cares that there are urgent telegrams from disaster areas? You show them cash, their heads go dizzy. I'll give you another example: when the China National Coal Import/Export Corporation (CNCIEC)—where, by the way, Miss Deng [daughter of Deng Xiaoping] presides—exports coal, businessmen in Hong Kong pay officials a commission of U.S. $2 each ton (the price of coal is U.S. $41–45). And where is this money cached away? In Hong Kong.

Because Shen Tu [the former Director of the General Department of CAAC, the national airline] demanded from the Boeing Company some U.S. $500,000 in bribes for having CAAC purchase their 747s, he was promptly dismissed. Yet he still has three sons in America and a daughter in Europe. One of his sons came back to China just about a month ago, and said that he could obtain import licenses for the following items [all of which are subject to state control and cannot be freely traded]:

1. Fish meal, 20,000 tons
2. Zinc-plated iron sheets, 20,000 tons
3. Fertilizers (including carbamide), 19 tons
4. Polypropylene
5. High-pressure polyethylene, 1,000 tons
6. Cold-rolled thin sheets, 1,000 tons
7. Cold-rolled planks, 1,000 tons
8. Copper plating
9. Palm oil, 6,000 tons
. . .
16. Sodium hydroxide, 1,000 tons
17. Wood, 500,000 square meters
18. ABS resin, 2,000 tons

This Shen Tu junior has already lived in America for ten years, yet he still commands immense power in China. Thus it's small wonder that China's foreign debt has hit such an astronomical level—if only you realize that there are people who are fattening themselves out of all this.

Mind you, these profiteering officials are not nobodies. They have power and extraordinary IQs, and you name it, they know from A to Z the 1,001 ways to make a profit. Even in the area of foreign exchange, they don't miss a chance. For example, during the period 1984–1985, company X (let's not reveal its name here) bought a few million U.S. dollars at the official exchange rate. It then sold this foreign currency at an exchange rate of 1:15 [as opposed to the official rate of 1:3.72— even the rate at the officially sanctioned foreign exchange markets is only about 1:7] to companies that desperately needed it to purchase merchandise from abroad.

Turning your head to one side, you hear people with hungry stomachs complaining, and turning it to the other, you see others squandering money without a second thought. And the general state of economic depression persists alongside the ever-expanding pockets of a few individuals. Why is China's foreign debt so immense? Why is China's economy such a mess? Why does the daily stipend of a soldier remain at 1.65 yuan after all these years, despite rocketing prices? Nowhere else can one find the answer to these questions except in the word "official." One official takes the lead, another follows, and very soon each official acts as a protective shield for another's crimes. Now let me ask, in whose hands shall China crumble? "No corrupt officials, no revolt," as the saying goes. We want to build our country and we want to bring prosperity to the people, but allowing these corrupt officials to have their way will reduce all this to empty rhetoric. Trees must be chopped down when they are rotten, and parasites exterminated. My dear soldiers, let me ask you: if the people say no, if history says no, will you still allow this situation to go on?

Ten Questions

(Beijing Workers' Union Handbill)

We request that the Central Committee answer the following questions:

1. How much money has Deng Pufang [Deng Xiaoping's son] spent placing bets at the horse races in Hong Kong? Where did this money come from?

2. Do Mr. and Mrs. Zhao Ziyang pay the golfing fees when they play every week? Where does the money for the fee come from?

3. What evaluation has the Central Committee made of the [progress of] reforms in the recent past? Premier Li Peng acknowledged during the official Lunar New Year's festivities this year that there had been errors in the current reform process. What were these errors? How can he account for the actual situation of difficult we are in?

4. The Central Committee has promised to take measures to control general inflation and pricing. In fact, prices have risen without respite as the living standards of the people have dropped precipitously. May we ask the reason for this?

5. Beginning next year, [China] must begin to repay its foreign debt. We would like to ask the size of the burden in national per-capita terms.

6. Will the people's basic standard of living be affected? Please answer....

7. How many houses and palatial retreats do Central Committee leaders have scattered about the country? What are the rates of their material consumption and expenditures? May these figures be made public? Please give an answer.

8. Make public the personal incomes and expenditures of Central Committee leaders.

9. What comment does the Central Committee have on the three preconditions for peaceful negotiations set forth by the authorities in Taiwan? How will the Central Committee answer?

10. Please have the Central Committee provide precise explanations of the definitions and connotations of the following three terms: (a) political party; (b) revolution; (c) reactionary.

We request that the Central Committee publish the responses to the above ten questions in the newspapers.

25

China after Mao:
Consequences of Dissent

Deng Xiaoping / Amnesty International

The brutal behavior of the Chinese army in ending the demonstrations in Beijing shocked the world. Although he was rumored to have later regretted the extent of the bloodshed, Deng Xiaoping's earlier comments (see chapter 14), as well as those a few days after the affair, which are excerpted here, suggest that he was not at all inclined to negotiate with those whom he saw as determined to undermine Chinese socialism. On the evening of 3–4 June 1989, troops were sent in to end the demonstrations in Beijing. The Amnesty International reports of August 1989 and April 1990, excerpted below, describe the course of that intervention and the crackdown that followed.

Deng Xiaoping's Remarks to Martial Law Officers on June 9

Comrades, you have been working hard! . . .

This disturbance was bound to come sooner or later. It was determined by the international macro climate and China's micro climate. It was definitely coming and was something that could not be diverted by man's will; it was only a matter of time and scale. For it to occur now is advantageous for us. The biggest advantage for us is that we have a large group of old comrades who are still living and healthy. They have gone through many disturbances; they understand the complexities and

subtleties of matters. They supported taking firm steps against the upheaval. Although there were some comrades who for some time did not
understand, in the end they will understand, and they will support this
decision of the Central Committee

The April 26 *People's Daily* editorial defined the nature of the problem as "turmoil." This word "turmoil" exactly describes the problem.
What some people opposed was this word; what they demanded revised
was this word. [But] as our experience has proven, the judgment was
correct. Subsequently, the situation developed into a counter-revolutionary rebellion; this was also inevitable.... It was relatively easy for
us to handle the present explosion. The main difficulty in handling the
matter is that we have never before encountered this kind of situation
in which a small handful of bad persons were mixed into the masses of
so many young students and onlookers. For a while, we could not distinguish the good from the bad; this made it difficult to take many steps
that we should have taken. If there had not been so many elder comrades in the Party who gave us their support, then even grasping the
nature of the matter would have been difficult. Some comrades do not
understand the nature of the problem and believed that it was purely a
problem of how to deal with the masses. In reality, the opposing side is
not only a mass of people who exchange truth for lies. It also consists
of a group of people who have created an opposition faction, and many
dregs of society. They want to subvert our country and subvert our
Party: this is the [true] nature of the problem....

Was the general conclusion of the Thirteenth Party Congress of
"One Center, Two Fundamental Points" correct? Are the "Two Fundamental Points"—namely, supporting the Four Cardinal Principles and
continuing the policy of reform and opening up to the outside—wrong?
Recently, I have been pondering this question. We are not wrong. Adhering to the Four Cardinal Principles [adherence to socialism, adherence to the "people's democratic dictatorship," leadership of the Chinese Communist Party, and adherence to Marxism, Leninism, and Mao-
ism] was not in itself a mistake; if there has been any error, it has been
our not adequately implementing them. We have failed to make the
Four Cardinal Principles the basic framework for educating people,
students, and all officials and Party members. The nature of this incident is the antagonism between bourgeois liberalism and adherence to
the Four Cardinal Principles....

Was the basic policy of reform and opening up a mistake? No. Had there not been reform and opening up, how could we be where we are today? In the last ten years, there has been a relatively big improvement in the living standards of the people. It should be said that we have climbed up a step; even though inflation and other problems have appeared, the accomplishments of the last ten years of reform and opening up are more than enough. Of course, the policy inevitably brings with it many [negative] Western influences; we have never underestimated this [danger]. . . .

Our basic approaches, from [overall] strategies down to [specific] policies, including the policy of reform and opening up, are all correct. If there is anything that has been insufficient, it is that there is still not enough reform and opening up. We will encounter more challenging problems in the course of reform than in the course of opening up. In the reform of the political system, there is one point that can be affirmed: we will adhere to implementing the system of the National People's Congress rather than the American-style system of the separation of three powers. In reality, Western nations also do not carry out a system of separation of powers. The U.S. condemns us for suppressing the students. But when they handle domestic riots and student demonstrations, don't they send in the police and the army? Aren't there arrests and bloodshed? They suppress students and people; on the contrary, we are putting down a counter-revolutionary rebellion. What credentials do they have for judging us? From today on, when we handle this kind of problem, we must pay attention to see that when unrest appears, we cannot allow it to spread.

Killings, Arrests, and Executions since 3 June 1989

Amnesty International

(August 1989) At least a thousand civilians—most of them unarmed—were killed and several thousands injured by troops firing indiscriminately into crowds in Beijing between 3 and 9 June 1989. According to official reports, several dozen soldiers were killed and over 6,000 injured in Beijing. At least 300 people are also reported to have been killed by troops and security forces on 5 June in Chengdu, the capital of Sichuan Province in central southern China, following student protests there. A number of civilians are also reported to have been killed by security forces in Lanzhou (Gansu Province) in early June.

During the night of 3 to 4 June, hundreds of armored military vehicles escorted by tens of thousands of troops started moving from the outskirts of Beijing toward the center of the capital to enforce martial law, which had been imposed in the city on 20 May following five weeks of peaceful students protests. Government reports say that the aim of this massive military operation was to "clear" Tiananmen Square in central Beijing, which had been occupied peacefully for several weeks by thousands of students, and to "restore order" in the capital.

The student protests, which started in Beijing in mid-April, spread in May to most major cities in China's provinces. The students originally demanded an end to official corruption and called for political reforms. Their demands drew wide popular support and the protests developed into a pro-democracy movement.

On 13 May several hundred Beijing students started a hunger-strike in Tiananmen Square to press for a dialogue with top Chinese officials. During the following days, hundreds of thousands of people started congregating in the Square, at the time when Soviet leader Mikhail Gorbachev arrived in Beijing for his first visit to China. On 18 May an estimated one million people demonstrated in Beijing to express their support for the students on hunger-strike and to demand democratic reforms and freedom of the press. The demonstrators included people from various sectors of society: workers, government employees, members of the police and of the armed forces, journalists, intellectuals and representatives of various government departments.

On 19 May Party General Secretary Zhao Ziyang and Prime Minister Li Peng visited the students on hunger-strike, and Li Peng reportedly acknowledged the students' "patriotic enthusiasm" and their "good intentions." The students decided to end their hunger-strike later that night. The next day, however, an order to impose martial law in "part of Beijing" was issued in the name of the State Council. The order was signed by Prime Minister Li Peng and was to be implemented by the Beijing Municipal Government. Martial law was effective from the morning of 20 May and applied to all of urban Beijing and most of the rural districts. The stated aim of martial law was to "firmly stop the unrest," to safeguard public order and to "ensure the normal function of the central departments and the Beijing Municipal Government."

During the following days hundreds of thousands of people took to the streets again to demonstrate against the imposition of martial law. Similar large-scale demonstrations took place in China's major provincial cities. There had never been such large-scale popular demonstration of discontent in the history of the People's Republic of China.

On 25 May Premier Li Peng acknowledged on television that many people—the majority of them "young students"—had been taking part in demonstrations. He said that "many of their views are identical with those of the party and the government. There are no fundamental contradictions between them and the party and government." However, he reaffirmed the need to enforce martial law as "a precautionary measure to firmly stop disturbances." On 21 May the official New China News Agency (NCNA) also stated: "The troops are by no means targeted at the students. Under no circumstances will [the troops] harm innocent people, let alone young students." Similar reassurances were issued by other official sources during the following days. By that time, however, the official press had also started denouncing a "handful of people with ulterior motives" who were exploiting the unrest for their own ends.

After the massive military intervention in Beijing on 3 to 4 June, the authorities justified their decision to use lethal force by saying that a "counter-revolutionary rebellion" had occurred in the capital on 3 June and by accusing a "tiny handful" of people of exploiting the student unrest to launch "organized and premeditated political turmoil" with the aim of "overthrowing the leadership of the Chinese Communist Party and the socialist system" in China. The government's justification for the extensive killings that did take place must be seriously questioned. Indeed, by 2 June the number of students occupying Tiananmen Square had considerably decreased and the large-scale demonstrations had stopped. The authorities, however, do not seem to have attempted to restore order by traditional crowd control methods. Furthermore, the period since 4 June has seen a continuing wave of repression, including mass arbitrary arrests, summary trials, and executions.

Since early June, at least 4,000 people are officially reported to have been arrested throughout China in connection with pro-democracy protests, but the total number of those detained is believed to be much higher. Those arrested include students, workers, peasants, teachers, writers, journalists, artists, academics, military officers, and unemployed people. They are held on a variety of charges, including involvement in "counter-revolutionary" activities; disrupting traffic or public order; attacking soldiers or military vehicles; "sabotage" and looting. Some of them belonged to independent organizations formed by students, workers and residents during the student protests in Beijing and other cities. These organizations have now been banned and declared "illegal." Denunciations are openly encouraged by the authorities: citizens who fail to report people involved in banned organizations or other "counter-revolutionary" activities are themselves liable to be arrested and imprisoned.

Those arrested are believed to be held incommunicado, without access to relatives or lawyers. Chinese law does not permit access to lawyers until a few days before trial—or in some cases until the trial starts. It is also a common practice in China not to allow visits by relatives until after the trial. The relatives of some of those detained have said that they were denied information by the authorities as to the whereabouts of their imprisoned relatives. Some of those arrested in June are reported to have been severely beaten by police or soldiers and it is feared that detainees may still be put under strong pressure—and, in some cases, beaten or tortured—to confess to crimes or to denounce others involved in the protests.

Some of those arrested have already been sentenced to imprisonment after trials which fell far short of international standards for fair trial. Some have been executed after summary trials: many more executions than those officially reported are believed to have taken place. No details have been issued by the authorities about the fate of many detainees charged with offenses punishable by death, other tan a few prisoners involved in publicized trials in June and July. However, the authorities have called on local courts to "try quickly and punish severely" people involved in the "counter-revolutionary" rebellion. Legislation adopted in 1983 provides for expedited trials under summary procedures in the cases of people regarded as "criminals who gravely endanger public security" and who are charged with offenses punishable by death. This legislation is applicable to many of those arrested recently. In the past, those sentenced to death under this legislation have been tried, sentenced and executed within a few days of arrest. . . .

(April 1999). . . Serious human rights violations continue to occur in China. Amnesty International has not recorded any significant improvement in the human rights situation there since August 1989. Although the authorities have released some prisoners, thousands of people continue to be imprisoned throughout China for their participation in the

1989 pro-democracy protests. Arbitrary arrests, incommunicado detention without charge or trial, unfair trials and executions have continued. Though martial law was lifted in Beijing in January 1990, the laws which permit the occurrence of such human rights violations remain in force.

Since August 1989 the Chinese authorities have sought to publicize widely their version of events in Beijing on 3 and 4 June, when heavily armed troops and thousands of military vehicles stormed into the city to clear the streets of protesters. The authorities have produced videotapes and individual testimonies in an attempt to suggest that the army not only exercised "great restraint," but also suffered many casualties because of violence provoked by "rioters."

Official accounts have included selected testimonies supporting claims that no one was killed during the final evacuation of Tiananmen Square. Official documentation, however, provides only a partial version of what occurred. The authorities have completely failed to consider numerous, well-attested incidents in which soldiers deliberately shot unarmed civilians and military vehicles crushed people during the course of their operations. Eye-witness testimonies published and broadcast since the events of early June amply document these incidents. The authorities still have not explained why they chose to use lethal force against unarmed civilians and why they failed to use conventional crowd control methods before 3 June to disperse protesters. . . .

A large number of summary executions were reportedly carried out in secret following the military crackdown. Some sources indicate that several hundred people were secretly executed in Beijing between June and August. At least two execution grounds were reportedly used: one located in the northwest of Beijing, the other near the Marco Polo Bridge in the southwestern suburbs of Beijing. According to one source at least eight groups of up to 20 people were executed before dawn near the bridge between June and mid-July.

The Chinese authorities have not disclosed the total number of people detained, tried or executed throughout the country since the June crackdown on pro-democracy protesters. At least 6,000 arrests have been officially reported throughout China, but the real number of detainees is reportedly in the tens of thousands. The majority of arrests took place in June and July. Between 8,000 and 10,000 people have been arrested in Beijing alone, according to sources, although some 4,000 detainees were apparently released after varying periods of interrogation. Arbitrary arrests continue to occur in many areas of

China. Numerous students, academics and others have been arrested for their alleged activities in connection with the pro-democracy protests. Official sources, however, have confirmed few of the arrests. . . .

Secret trials of students active in the protest movement reportedly began in Beijing in November 1989. Reports received that month indicated that people accused of leading the protest movement would soon be tried on "counter-revolutionary" charges, some of which may carry the death penalty. Proceedings against four students from the Foreign Affairs College in Beijing reportedly started in November. The defendants were accused of "counter-revolutionary" crimes, but their names and details of their cases were not known. The trials were apparently held in secret and even the families of the accused were not allowed to attend.

Official sources have reported few trials held in connection with the protest movement. Some defendants were charged with "counter-revolutionary" offenses solely because they peacefully exercised basic human rights. Zhang Weiping, a 25-year-old student at the Zhejiang Fine Arts Institute in Hangzhou city, was sentenced in August 1989 to nine years' imprisonment for "counter-revolutionary propaganda and incitement." According to official reports, Zhang Weiping was prosecuted for telling the Voice of America radio station in Washington D.C. on 6 June that the Zhejiang provincial government headquarters had flown the flag at half mast in commemoration of people killed in Beijing on 4 June. He is the first student officially reported to have been tried and sentenced in connection with the pro-democracy protests. . . .

Part 3

Society

Edited by Martin K. Whyte

Introduction

Martin K. Whyte

In any society as large, diverse, and poor as China, maintaining cohesion and order is not an easy job. Chinese rulers down through the centuries have feared the chaos and conflict they sensed always lurking beneath the surface of Chinese social life, and they adopted strategies to promote social order that are in many ways different from those that evolved in the West. When the Chinese Communists came to national power in 1949, they intended to introduce revolutionary changes. Yet at the same time they also had to be concerned about social order. For if they miscalculated and destroyed too much of the cohesion of Chinese society, chaos could erupt and undermine their new accomplishments. Chinese society in the Maoist and post-Mao years is the result of a shifting balancing act between construction and destruction, between the new and the old, with the proper balance subject to continuing debate.

The three sections of Part 3 describe basic patterns of social organization in both Imperial China and the People's Republic: "The Chinese Family" examines the basic unit of social life; "Creating a Broader Community" explores the ways in which individuals and families are linked to others; and "Cleavages and Social Conflicts" examines some of the divisive forces that may weaken the effort to promote community and social order. Together these chapters provide some idea of the bonds that have united Chinese, and the cleavages that have divided them, both in the past and at present. In this essay we will stand back and look at the general assumptions that Chinese rulers have made about the nature of a well-ordered society, and how they have tried to bring such a society into being.

Late Imperial Social Order

Chinese society in late imperial times was shaped by a set of Confucian assumptions and values about the ideal society. As the previous sections have illustrated, in this Confucian framework, the cement that held society together was supposed to be moral consensus, and the building blocks that were held together by this cement were human bonds and mutual obligations arranged in a vast hierarchy—from emperor and ministers down through local officials and local gentry, and finally to the immediate family—the bonds between father and son, husband and wife, brother and brother, and so on. It was assumed that a uniform, "correct" set of values and rules of behavior could be specified for all of the links in this complex human chain of relationships; in the ideal society, systematic instruction in these proper rules, and group pressure to comply with them, would produce social harmony and prosperity. As the selections in Part 2 of this volume have already made clear, this sort of emphasis led to a very different view of politics and the role of the state from that which developed in the pluralist, competitive West, a view in which officials were as much preachers as administrators.

These themes in the Chinese tradition did, in fact, lead to a variety of interesting attempts at moral indoctrination that anticipate the study of Mao Zedong's thought in contemporary China. For example, during the Qing dynasty local officials were required to have lectures on Confucian moral homilies given regularly in market towns throughout the realm, and righteous individuals and virtuous widows were publicly honored, sometimes with memorial arches to commemorate them. Still, officials and political philosophers did not think that social order could be maintained simply by preaching to the population. Most people were not educated or enlightened enough to understand and obey the dictates of Confucian principles, but they could be expected to conform to the demands of their parents, their teachers, and their employers or patrons. Thus, ideally Chinese society should have no autonomous individuals or deviant subcultures. Instead, all individuals should be members of one or more groups or social networks which would lock them into a chain of obligations that linked them ultimately to the state. Political order would rest not upon a sense of citizenship, but upon this hierarchical chain of personal ties and mutual obligations.

In many ways the Chinese family was viewed as the key to a good society, since for most of the population family interactions and obligations far outweighed any other social bonds. Many traditional writings on social order in China used family images for the entire imperial hierarchy, from the emperor as the "son of heaven" through the "father-mother officials" *(fumu guan)* down to the actual families in local communities. In a very loose sense, then, the entire society was seen as one vast, extended family ruled over by a paternalistic emperor, and only if family bonds and socialization were developed properly throughout China could social harmony reign. A passage from the *Great Learning,* one of the "Four Books" that formed the core of Confucian learning, conveys this set of assumptions:

> By inquiring into all things, understanding is made complete; with complete understanding, thought is made sincere; when thought is sincere, the mind is as it should be; when the mind is as it should be, the individual is morally cultivated; when the individual is morally cultivated, the family is well regulated; when the family is well regulated, the state is properly governed; and when the state is properly governed, the world is at peace.

The form of family life that had evolved in China by late imperial times conformed to this imagery of strict, hierarchical role relationships and was thus in many respects different from family forms in the contemporary West. Individuals were born into not only a family but a patrilineal kin group, and in some parts of China entire rural villages of several thousand people belonged to a single lineage (sometimes called a Chinese "clan"). Both patrilineages and the families that comprised them were organized hierarchically, with younger members and females expected to show deference and respect for elder members and males. From infancy onward Chinese were instructed in obedience to the family and "filial piety," an ethic of worshipful deference toward one's parents. (This extreme emphasis on respect toward one's elders extended even beyond the grave in the form of ancestor worship rituals at graves and in lineage halls.) All members of the family were expected to defer to the will of the family patriarch who, as the representative of the patrilineal line and the head of the corporate family, was supposed to make binding decisions that would promote the interests of the family as a whole. Although most Chinese spent much of their lives in nuclear family units, rather than in the multigenerational, extended families that form most Westerners' image of China, still a small family could be a fairly authoritarian place in comparison with Western families as we know them today.[1]

Perhaps nothing better illustrates the strong emphases on group loyalty and the internal hierarchy of the Chinese family than the dominant set of marriage customs in late imperial times. Marriages were customarily arranged by parents with the aid of hired marriage go-betweens. In many if not most cases the result might be termed "blind marriage"—the bride and groom did not even meet until the day of the wedding. Since the maturity, compatibility, or consent of the couple were not required, marriages were sometimes arranged between children or between a boy and a mature woman, or vice versa. And since divorce was strongly discouraged, the couple, never having met and often poorly matched, were expected to endure each other to the end of their days. These customs sound strange to Westerners oriented to romantic love, relative freedom of mate choice, and husband-wife companionship, but to the Chinese they were quite reasonable. The new wife was not seen as a romantic partner for her husband, but as a new recruit for the existing, corporate family. (In the great majority of cases the bride moved into her husband's family, rather than he moving into hers or the couple going off to start a new family of their own.) So it made perfect sense that the parents, rather than the young man, did the choosing. In fact, previous acquaintance and romantic involvement could create problems, since a groom too enamored of his bride would not show the required respect and obedience toward his parents, and might even respond to his bride's unhappiness by wanting to leave their home. If the bride was an intimidated stranger, her husband could be expected to fulfill his required role—to help bring her into line so that she would become a dutiful and deferential daughter-in-law, devoted to the interests of her new family.

In sum, Chinese families in the past were characterized by an unusually strong sense of loyalty and obligation to a family unit that was

---

1. Families in Western societies were, to be sure, more authoritarian in the nineteenth century than they are today. But even in that period there was generally less emphasis on family hierarchy and subordination of the individual to the family than was the case in China.

seen as extending back many generations and that would persist long into the future—if family affairs were properly managed. Managing family affairs consisted of socializing family members into strict patterns of obedience and deference. To aid in this project, down through the ages literati and kin groups produced family advice manuals which laid down, sometimes in excruciating detail, the proper forms of behavior and family role obligations. (See the Ming-dynasty family instructions excerpted in chapter 26.) If instruction failed, strict measures, including beatings and even expulsion, could be used against disobedient family members, and the state generally approved of such harshness. These distinctive emphases in Chinese family life created strong family bonds and a sense of security as well as indebtedness; such sentiments could be a powerful force in motivating individuals to work hard, study diligently, and take risks—all for the welfare of the family. But these features were achieved at some cost, primarily in the unhappiness and frustrated aspirations of individual members whose needs and feelings might be overridden by the demands of the family and its patriarch.

Families were not, of course, the only groups in the social landscape. A variety of other groups and social networks linked individuals and families together and provided some degree of social cohesion. In rural areas individuals belonged not only to families and perhaps lineages, but often also to mutual help groups with other peasants (for crop-watching, sharing of tools, and for pooling burial funds, for example), and to groups that worshiped at a variety of religious temples and shrines. (Chinese religion involves an eclectic variety of deities and cults that can be worshiped according to need and preference, with no unitary church or national hierarchy.) This religious activity drew villagers to market towns and nearby cities and into contact with non-kin; marketing activity and the search for marriage partners had the same effect. Where possible, peasants tried to cultivate personal "connections" *(guanxi)* and networks of mutual obligation with non-kin, rather than to deal with strangers on an impersonal basis. Thus beyond the confines of the family and village, something like the Confucian picture of local society as a complex network of human bonds and obligations often materialized.

In Chinese cities in imperial times similar patterns of association were found, although kinship was less central than in the countryside. Sometimes urbanites would bond together in "same surname associations," but more important were various kinds of non-kin groups: native place associations, temple associations, and guilds. Native place associations united people of one locale who went off to seek a living in a distant city. They were the result of a process of "chain migration" in which earlier migrants from some locality would help later migrants get established in the city. Van der Sprenkel in chapter 31 briefly describes how guilds and local temple associations worked. As in the countryside, these forms of association expressed the belief that individuals (and families) needed to seek support and protection in groups based on personal ties. Cities were definitely not seen as places in which rugged individualists competed in the impersonal marketplace. Elsewhere van der Sprenkel comments,

> Probably few commercial transactions of any consequence in traditional China were either impersonal or casual. At their heart, as a necessary condition, was the prior establishment of a personal relationship. In the case of routine purchases of any commodity, purchaser and vendor usually maintained a continuing relationship.... For a service to be performed for another, or for any deal involving trust and credit, the parties to the transaction entered it as *persons in relationship*, normally using an intermediary to arrange the terms of the agreement. And the same would apply to taking on staff or apprentices and to borrowing a sum of money. One got nowhere until a relationship of trust had been established.

The government's control over grassroots social life in late imperial times was minimal and largely indirect. The authorities did, over the course of most of the last millennium, attempt to institute a system of mutual responsibility groups in localities to assist the government in meeting its primary goals—maintaining order and collecting taxes. These groups tried to make other families liable to penalties if group members—their neighbors—did not pay their taxes or if they engaged in criminal or rebellious activity. The government also, as mentioned earlier, regularly made attempts at moral instruction of the people and, through the examination system used to select officials, provided powerful incentives for local communities to organize their own efforts to tutor the young in Confucian ideas. In addition, imperial authorities were quite willing to use force to suppress forms of associational life that were deemed a threat to central rule—heterodox religious sects, secret societies, feuding lineages, and so forth. Still, the imperial bureaucracy was quite small both in numbers and resources, and it could not hope, nor did it attempt, to control directly grassroots social life. Instead, officials were generally content to allow autonomous social groupings to manage their own affairs as long as they did not challenge the system. And well into the twentieth century many activities that we associate with modern governments—running schools, caring for the poor, and even organizing local police and fire protection—were often carried out by lineages, guilds, and other relatively autonomous social groups, rather than by the state.

The Dilemmas of Reform

In the nineteenth and twentieth centuries, as China's weakness in competition with foreign powers became increasingly clear, voices in favor of reform and revolution were raised. Although the distinctive patterns of social organization we have sketched might have helped to promote stability in dynastic times, now, the reformers argued, fundamental changes were needed. Critics could for the most part agree on what was wrong with Chinese social organization, but not on the solution.

China was weak, many argued, precisely because of the legacy of basing state power on personal ties and group membership. Individuals were socialized to be loyal primarily to their own family and kin group, and secondarily to neighborhood cults, guilds, groups of former schoolmates, and so forth. This form of social organization, however, inhibited the development of nationalistic sentiments and loyalty to the central government and made it difficult to develop broader sentiments of solidarity based on class consciousness or a sense of citizenship. Government efforts to foster general laws and principles were constantly frustrated by the built-in tendency for people to use their personal ties and connections to try to arrange special treatment for their group. Loyalty and kind treatment to those in one's network of mutual obligations went hand in hand with callous indifference or even vicious cruelty toward strangers or rivals. The nature of grassroots social life made not general harmony, but factional disputes, lineage feuds, and even open warfare between linguistic and ethnic groups endemic in late imperial China (see chapter 36.) Early in the twentieth century, Sun Yat-sen, from the viewpoint of a frustrated leader, characterized Chinese social life as a "sheet of loose sand." In truth, however, it was not simply that the grassroots groupings would not stick together, but that they were often at one another's throats.

Traditional forms of social organization were criticized as harmful in other ways as well. The strong emphasis on obedience, deference to hierarchical superiors, and reverence for traditional ways were said to foster a conservative and passive mentality in the population at large, obstructing new ideas, technical innovations, and progress in general. Change would also be impeded by expectations of nepotism and personal favoritism in other forms, which made it difficult to select the most qualified people for available posts in industry or government. Entrepreneurship might be encouraged, insofar as it served the interests of one's family, but innovative behavior that went beyond these limits would unleash hostile social pressure, thus fostering timidity and fatalism.

Perhaps most important, the predominant emphasis on loyalty to the corporate family was seen by critics as leading to both widespread personal unhappiness of family members and harm for the society as a whole. Young people and women seemed especially oppressed by China's patriarchal family life. Again the custom of arranged marriage shows the problem particularly vividly. The excerpt in chapter 27 from Ba Jin's famous 1933 novel, *The Family*, gives a poignant view of how the hopes and aspirations of the hero were dashed against the unchallengeable plans for his marriage and employment made by the family patriarch. And it is perhaps not unimportant that one of Mao Zedong's first appearances in print, in 1919, involved a series of newspaper articles denouncing an incident in which a young woman committed suicide to escape an arranged marriage. Widespread personal unhappiness, however, was not the only consequence of the imperious demands of family elders. Behavior that might serve the interests of the immediate family might be harmful to society if replicated on a broad scale by other families. For example, families benefited by having many sons, who could labor and produce income and support their parents in old age— roles that daughters could not fulfill since they usually married into the husband's family. But this preference for large families, when followed throughout the realm, threatened to overpopulate the country.

By the Republican period (1912–49) these criticisms of traditional social life had coalesced into two rival agendas for change. Although it has been customary to refer to these as reform versus revolution, those labels are somewhat misleading for, as we shall see, the "revolutionary" option that came to power with the Chinese Communist Party in 1949 was in some ways more "traditional" than the agenda offered by the

Western-oriented "reformers." We will therefore refer to the alternatives as the "liberal" and "statist" options.

Those Chinese influenced by the Western liberal tradition advocated the development of a modern state machinery, a well-developed legal system, an extensive marketing system, and the freeing of individuals from the excessive demands of, and loyalties to, their families and other social groups. They argued that individuals free to make their own marriage and career choices would join into more "modern" forms of association—trade unions and professional organizations, for instance—which would not be based on hierarchical and personalized social bonds. The liberals argued that, as in the West, the liberation of individuals from traditional group bonds and obligations would not only permit greater personal happiness and fulfillment, but would also unleash much greater initiative and energy in all spheres of life and would thus benefit society in general. The weakening of traditional bonds and the development of new forms of association would also make it possible to develop broader sentiments of citizenship and national loyalty. Individual behavior would be regulated not so much by a hierarchy of personal obligations, but by a strong and impartial legal system, markets, commercial law, and other institutions that would allow the government to influence citizen behavior more directly, while still leaving ample room for individual choice. The liberal reformers hoped, then, that the weakening of group bonds would not produce chaos, but in fact would lead to a strong state and an aroused citizenry.

While on the surface the "statist" solution, particularly as developed by Chinese Marxists, seemed to be advocating many of the same changes, such as freedom of mate choice in place of arranged marriage, in reality this solution was quite different. And since this statist vision of the ideal society was the one that guided the Chinese Communist Party in power after 1949, we need to be clear on its distinctive features. Whereas the Western liberals viewed the freeing of individuals to pursue their own interests and happiness as the solution to society's problems, the Chinese Communists, in contrast, shared with their dynastic predecessors the belief that individual freedom from group constraints was very dangerous, with chaos the likely result. If the demands of families and other personalistic groups on their members constituted a major impediment to progress and national strength, the proper solution was not to free individuals from such demands, but to change the nature of these groups so that they would work to the benefit of society.

It is in this sense that the statist solution is less "revolutionary" than the liberal solution, since it aims to realize an age-old Chinese dream of a unified hierarchy of solidary groups. The crucial innovation, however, was that the Chinese Communists would have the power and resources to try to realize this dream, things their dynastic predecessors never had.[2]

The liberal alternative was most widely debated and discussed during the 1920s. After the Chinese Nationalists under Chiang Kai-shek achieved nominal national unity in 1927–28, liberal voices increasingly lost influence. Locked in a bitter struggle for power with the Chinese Communists as well as Japanese invaders (from 1937 to 1945), Chiang presided over a shift toward authoritarian doctrines, both of traditional Chinese and foreign origins. By the time Mao and his forces vanquished the Nationalists on the mainland in 1949, liberal arguments were heard mostly from a few academics and intellectuals, people who had had little influence over the Nationalist leaders and would have even less over Mao and his comrades. Only after Mao's death would it again become possible to raise liberal arguments.

Social Transformations in Maoist China

What did this statist solution mean in practice in Maoist China—i.e., in China in the period 1949–76? It meant that thoroughgoing attempts were made either to gain control over, or to suppress and replace, existing forms of grassroots groups and thus produce collective units that would be directly controlled by the new government. In other words, China's new rulers recognized that control of factories, banks, railways, schools, the mass media, the military and other basic institutions would not be enough to remedy the ailments of China's social order. The revolution would also have to transform the nature of grassroots social organizations and the ways in which they were linked to the larger society.

More specifically, in rural areas lineages were attacked and deprived of their land and lineage halls during the land-reform campaign of the early 1950s, and outside "work teams" organized poor peasants

---

2. One other crucial difference from the traditional social order was that the hierarchical bonds in the new society were supposed to be based not upon personal ties and obligations, but upon loyalty to the country, to the Party, and to Mao Zedong.

to band together against their rich kinsmen. Out of these struggles new local organizations were formed—peasant associations, local Party organizations, and so forth—and a new group of leaders who owed their power to the Party were placed in charge of village affairs. During the mid-1950s these new leaders directed the amalgamation of scattered family plots into collective farms (called agricultural producers' cooperatives), and in 1958 these in turn were amalgamated into still larger units called people's communes. In the course of the various transformation campaigns most local shrines were desecrated, local temples were closed or converted to other uses, and in general forms of community solidarity that might have rivaled the new organizations were eliminated. The new organizational forms of the commune system, which are described by Whyte in chapter 32, did provide some economic security and social solidarity, and peasants benefited from improved access to schooling and health care. But at the same time they were made much more dependent upon their leaders, and ultimately on the state, than peasants had been in earlier times. For example, national migration restrictions prevented peasants from moving to other areas and into the cities in search of a better life, and even permission to engage in local peddling or construction work required the "chop" of local cadres. (See chapter 37 for a description of these restrictions.) Many crops could be sold only through official channels at state prices that were kept artificially low, and at the same time state planning and procurement practices sometimes forced peasants to stop growing the crops that were most suitable to the locality.

In urban areas much the same transformation occurred, but the specific organizational forms differed. As in the countryside, the aim was to eliminate any autonomous social groups. Some organizations, such as secret societies and religious sects, were attacked and suppressed, while others were co-opted or replaced by new organizational forms. With the transition to socialism in the mid-1950s, private ownership and private enterprise were for the most part eliminated, and the government tried to limit or suppress markets for labor, housing, and other resources. As a result, urbanites became extremely dependent upon two organizational systems. Much stress was placed upon one's work "unit" (*danwei*). Work units not only organized the daily work activities of their employees, but they also often provided housing, nursery schools, health clinics, dining halls, and recreational facilities. They also organized political study sessions, supervised leisure time activities, ran cleanliness campaigns, mediated disputes, and regulated the marriages and childbearing not only of employees, but of their entire families as well. (See the account of life in one such *danwei* in chapter 33.)

For those employees who did not live on the premises in work unit housing there was another form of organizational life—neighborhoods and their residents' committees. These were not voluntary associations of the sort that spring up in some Western cities, but rather organizations established and run by the government according to regulations passed in the early 1950s. As with work units, they had a dual role: to provide services and to exert control. The appointed officers of the residents' committees might help to run clean-up campaigns, establish nursery schools and first aid clinics, organize reading rooms for the retired and elderly, run small-scale sewing and bicycle repair workshops, mediate disputes, and keep an eye on local "latch-key" children; they also organized political study meetings, reported strangers to the police, organized crime patrols, and pressured local families to accept the state's birth control targets. (Chapter 34 is an account of the experience of one former residents' committee leader.) Many urbanites, of course, fell under both organizational systems, as they lived in one neighborhood and had family members perhaps employed in several work units elsewhere. Above the grassroots level there were other organizations—trade unions, the Women's Federation, associations of artists and writers, the Communist Youth League, and so forth; these also were very far from being voluntary associations.

Where does the Chinese family fit into this organizational system? Some outside observers have argued that the Chinese Communist Party tried to destroy the family so that individual members would be released to give total loyalty to the Party and to Mao. Although there have been some instances of encouraging conflict within families, for the most part this has not been the approach adopted. On the contrary, the post-1949 changes were not intended to destroy the family but simply to eliminate its autonomy, so that the family would be a strong, compliant group serving the interests of the state rather than its own "narrow" interests. Families have been buffeted by demands for change, it is true—to eliminate emphasis on filial piety, to allow young people to choose their own mates, to pressure women to work outside the home, to eliminate nepotism, and so forth. But for the most part the goal of such changes has not been to weaken families and liberate individuals from them, but instead to transform families so that they will mobilize their members to serve state interests. In some respects the state has even made family stability a legal requirement. For example, young people are required by the Marriage Law (in both its 1950 and 1980 versions) to provide support for their elderly parents, and divorce has been made very difficult to obtain, as illustrated in chapter 30.

Flaws in the New Social Order

In many respects the social changes introduced after 1949 were quite successful. The nation was politically unified under a strong government that could stand up for China in world affairs. The new regime was able to mobilize human energies on a vast scale to confront the nation's problems, and local conflicts between lineages and language groups were kept largely under control. The "sheet of loose sand" image no longer applied to China's body politic, and the authorities were able to gain an impressive degree of control over grassroots social life. As a result, sentiments of nationalism and loyalty to the new regime and its leader, Mao Zedong, became widely shared.

But the new system had a number of inherent flaws, which became particularly apparent during the Cultural Revolution decade from 1966 to 1976, when Mao and his radical followers tried to realize more fully their vision of solidary socialism. Regarding the family, official goals proved to be contradictory. As noted earlier, the authorities wanted strong and cohesive families, but families that would be egalitarian rather than patriarchal. In practice, the stress on family cohesion and stability reinforced the corporate sense of solidarity of Chinese families and undermined the calls for equality within families. Families remained quite autocratic, and women and young people continued to have to defer to their elders and to males. The account of "the lady of the sties" in chapter 29 portrays an instance of this, in which a talented and well-educated rural woman was unable to realize her ambitions and desires. The following reading about Yu Luojin deals with another variation on this theme: a woman who, in her search for personal happiness, sought to end two arranged or convenience marriages and thereby created a scandal. Personal unhappiness of family members was perhaps not of great concern to China's leaders, but the fact that cohesive families did not always do the bidding of the government was. Particularly in the countryside, where the state's control was less direct and effective than in the cities, peasant families often ignored calls for free choice marriage, simple weddings, cremation, and other "socialist" customs and persisted in following traditional ways—with arranged marriages, huge wedding feasts, and "superstitious" burial rituals. In such cases vital state interests were not challenged, but when peasant families saw their interests served by ignoring the state's birth control campaign and trying to have more children, the stage was set for a protracted conflict. (This conflict is vividly portrayed in the rural study by Steven Mosher in chapter 39.) Increasingly the authorities were concerned that in a number of ways Chinese families were working against the interests of the state, rather than for them.

The tendency of families to work in their own interests and subvert the goals of the state was accentuated by the widening gap between the state's paternalistic proclamations and social reality as it was experienced during the Cultural Revolution decade. Mao and his followers tried to eliminate all private enterprise, market competition, material incentives, and vested interests, and to substitute a benevolent bureaucracy that would provide the population with their basic needs and reinforce their group and national solidarity. The premise was that by relying on the paternalistic state, people would experience security and rising living standards and a sense of commitment to the system.

Most Chinese in Mao's last years saw their social environment in very different terms. Urbanites found themselves locked into low and fixed-wage jobs in organizations filled with political tensions. Growing families had to be squeezed into increasingly tight housing, and the search for food, clothing, and other needs was frustrated by shortages, tight rations, long lines, and other difficulties. In a society that was production- rather than consumption-oriented, most urbanites had to struggle and spend long hours just to meet the basic needs of their families, as described in the Chinese "time budget study" in chapter 28. In addition, families confronted a situation in which the schooling of their children was disrupted and most secondary school graduates ended up in agricultural labor in the countryside, rather than in college or an urban job. Large numbers of alienated youths who had been so exiled sneaked back into the cities illegally, contributing to a growing juvenile delinquency problem that made urbanites feel increasingly unsafe. In rural areas the situation was somewhat different, since peasants could grow crops to meet more of their own basic needs and were not so totally dependent on the state. Even there, however, state interference in farming, the rising overhead expenses of rural bureaucracy, and the inability of peasants to seek better opportunities elsewhere led to a situation of declining living standards and frustrated aspirations in many locales.

Popular disillusionment with the paternalistic promises of the system led increasingly to perceptions of inequity and to social conflict. In some cases social cleavages developed as unintentional consequences of the rigid organizational structures of the new society; Potter, in chapter 37, argues that the widening gap between peasants and urbanites under Mao fits this situation. In other instances, however, the authorities created and magnified social conflicts in a way that suggests that they wanted to encourage "scapegoating" as a method of dealing with the failings of the new society. (This sort of argument is advanced by Unger in chapter 38 to account for the maintenance of a discriminatory system of "class labels" under Mao.) But in any case, many Chinese came to believe that they wouldn't have their basic needs met if they simply relied on the system, and that therefore they had to try to figure out ways to "beat the system." These efforts led, as the sociological essay by Zheng in chapter 35 argues, to a strong revival of the custom of relying on personal ties and connections to get things accomplished "through the back door," rather than waiting for the bureaucratic system to dispense its grudging benefits. This tendency, and the organization of society into a rigid set of bureaucratic cells to which it was a reaction, in turn helped to undermine any general sense of citizenship and community obligation, and fostered a strong sense of group competition instead.

As Zheng argues in his essay, this reliance on connections also undermined faith in the system even more, since it became increasingly clear that one had to use connections to get anything accomplished. Since it was obvious to all that high-ranking bureaucrats were in the best position to use connections for personal benefit, the frustrations of life in the Cultural Revolution decade produced a growing sense of "us versus them" conflict between the population and the state itself. (This sense of conflict between the people and the state is particularly apparent in Mosher's account in chapter 39 of enforcement of the birth control campaign.) Clearly aware of these flaws in the Maoist system, the post-Mao leadership has moved to introduce reforms in China's social order.

Chinese Society in the Post-Mao Years

The reforms implemented under the leadership of Deng Xiaoping after 1978 are complex and dramatic, and no attempt will be made to summarize them all here. We will focus simply on the way in which those reforms have attempted to alter the nature of grassroots social life in China. (Part 4 discusses the impact of the reforms on economic life.)

At the core of the post-Mao social changes is the argument that the attempt under Mao to eliminate all markets, competition, and mobility and make all social groups pawns of the bureaucratic state had more in common with feudalism than with socialism. The state should withdraw somewhat from its attempt to control all social groups and activities, thus allowing individuals and groups to exert their own efforts to meet their needs and pursue advancement.

In the cities the reform effort draws at least in part on the liberal strategy that had long been rejected. This approach is expressed in an emphasis on meritocracy, with individuals competing with one another in revived markets. The government has declared that it will no longer assign all individuals to jobs, and youths are encouraged to compete through examinations and other means for the best state jobs, or to set up their own private enterprises. Lifetime service at the pleasure of the state is supposed to be replaced by a restored labor market, so that individuals can change jobs and seek opportunities most suited to their skills. A new system of labor contracts of limited duration is advocated in place of permanent assignment to jobs. (There is also a negative side to this attempt to destroy China's system of permanent employment— termed the "iron rice bowl." The reformers also want to make it possible both to close down inefficient enterprises and to have managers demote or fire unproductive employees, thus creating job insecurity and unemployment and forcing individuals to reenter the competition for jobs.)

Similar reforms are advocated for other realms. For example, no longer will all housing be allocated by government offices and work units. Instead, individuals can pool their funds and build cooperative apartments and rent and sell housing to other individuals, thus restoring a market in housing as well as labor. All such reforms, then, are aimed at making urbanites less totally dependent upon bureaucratic allocation and stimulating them to compete for desirable opportunities. Efforts to introduce these reforms on a systematic basis after 1984 encountered considerable resistance from both bureaucrats and working people.

Even before the Beijing massacre, many of these urban reforms remained frozen at the trial or experimental stage, while others, such as the attempt to marketize urban-housing distribution, were being quietly abandoned. The events of 1989 threw into question even more the future of such systematic reform efforts. As a result of the stalling of the reforms, most people in China's cities in the 1990s remain oriented toward their neighborhoods and work-unit cells, rather than having become individual competitors in new markets. Within those cells, most urbanites remain subject to the decisions and whims of their local leaders. Richard Terrill's memoir of teaching in China in chapter 40 conveys the frustration many college students felt in the late 1980s when confronted with the gap between reform slogans and bureaucratic realities. That frustration was, of course, a key ingredient in the political explosion of the Beijing Spring in 1989.

In China's countryside major reforms began earlier, in the late 1970s, and have gone much further. The rural reforms embody less a liberal strategy than a partial return to the patterns of China's past, in which the state rests more lightly on the countryside and allows peasant families some autonomy in pursuing their own interests. As the readings in the "Agriculture" section of Part 4 describe, this has been accomplished through dismantling the communes, China's system of collectivized agriculture, and substituting a system of contracting land and production targets to peasant families. No longer subject to day-to-day direction of their work by village leaders, peasant families are encouraged to find ways to increase their incomes by better farming and by off-farm activities such as handicrafts, construction, hauling, and peddling. To succeed in this reformed system does not require as much cooperation with one's neighbors as in the collectivized system, and instead depends increasingly upon making contacts and seeking opportunities outside of the village. Although the system of migration restrictions remains in effect and peasants are not supposed to be able to establish permanent residences in China's cities, nevertheless the government is now actively encouraging part of the rural labor force to move into non-agricultural activities and into rural towns. The rural reforms have gone further than those in the city, then, in weakening the local corporate groups used in the Mao period to promote social order. But it is not so much the individual as the strong peasant family that has gained from this change, and, in some villages, related families are merging to form multi-generation extended families that can organize their labor power to take better advantage of these new opportunities. In some places lineages have revived as well, complete with newly constructed ancestral halls and annual processions by all family members to the graves of lineage founders.

The post-Mao reforms helped initially to alleviate some of the problems inherited from the Mao era. Income and consumption levels went up dramatically, and fewer goods were subject to strict rationing. Broken careers and separated families were made whole again, and a wide range of new opportunities for advancement were created. The state withdrew somewhat from trying to control all aspects of social life, allowing more variety in dress and customs, as well as a limited revival of religious activity and traditional rituals at weddings, funerals, and other occasions. The revived incentives and opportunities unleashed a powerful spurt of effort and entrepreneurial activity in both city and countryside. The post-Mao leadership took comfort in the fact that the tensions built up in Mao's final years had been at least partly defused.

However, producing social order in Chinese society remains a difficult task, and toward the end of the 1980s social tensions and antagonism between ruled and rulers increased once again. The post-Mao reforms had not moved China very far away from its status as a bureaucratically and group-organized society, one that remains quite different in most respects from market societies in the West or in Japan. But even the limited changes introduced in the decade after Mao's death produced a new set of problems and revived old ones. Economic competition and partial price reform led to renewed inflation; new economic activities in combination with the remaining power of bureaucratic agencies fostered blatant corruption; fear of losing income or jobs under the reforms led to anger toward new rich elements as well as toward those pushing the reforms; the restoration of family farming led peasant families to mobilize the labor of all available hands, producing a sharp reduction in secondary-school enrollment; the growing visibility and special privileges of foreigners produced ambivalence or outright hostility among many patriotic Chinese; and students, intellectuals, and entrepreneurs—supposedly primary beneficiaries of the reforms—grew increasingly restive at the controls exerted over them by China's bureaucrats. In addition, the behavior unleashed by even limited reforms led some Party leaders to fear that the people were using their new-found autonomy in undesirable ways—engaging in superstitious activities, launching lineage feuds, having more babies, developing "decadent" tastes for pornography or traditional adventure stories, or simply thinking unorthodox thoughts. Conservative elements within the leadership made several aborted attempts during the 1980s to turn back the clock and return to a simpler, bureaucratically managed social order. The political conflicts of 1989 provided an opportunity for such leaders to regain influence. As China entered the 1990s, it was unclear whether the liberal alternative had lost out again to the bureaucratic vision embedded in both Confucianism and Maoism, or whether the halt in the effort to reform China's social order was only temporary.

The Chinese Family

26

Family Instructions

Edited by Patricia B. Ebrey

In many parts of rural China, families still live in communities among kinsmen who are organized into lineages. Traditionally, such lineages often held ancestor worship rituals and owned property, and they also served as higher authorities on family matters. Family disputes about such issues as inheritance could be referred to the lineage elders, who might also help parents to discipline unruly or disobedient children. In general, lineage leaders were committed to keeping the lineage and its member families strong through proper observance of the correct forms of behavior. To this end, lineages often compiled lists of rules for proper behavior and advice on how to maintain family harmony. The following are excerpts from one such advice manual, a late Ming-dynasty document (sixteenth-seventeenth century) from the Miu lineage in Guangdong province. Its precepts show the way in which Confucian moral views were spread to local communities.

Work Hard at One of the Principal Occupations

1. To be filial to one's parents, to be loving to one's brothers, to be diligent and frugal—these are the first tenets of a person of good character. They must be thoroughly understood and faithfully carried out.

One's conscience should be followed like a strict teacher and insight should be sought through introspection. One should study the words and deeds of the ancients to find out their ultimate meanings. One should always remember the principles followed by the ancients, and should not become overwhelmed by current customs. For if one gives in to cruelty, pride, or extravagance, all virtues will be undermined, and nothing will be achieved.

Parents have special responsibilities. *The Book of Changes*[1] says: "The members of a family have strict sovereigns." These "sovereigns" are the parents. Their position in a family is one of unique authority, and they should utilize their authority to dictate matters, to maintain order, and to inspire respect, so that the members of the family will all be obedient. If the parents are lenient and indulgent, there will be many troubles which in turn will give rise to even more troubles. Who is to blame for all this? The elders in a family must demand discipline of themselves, following all rules and regulations to the letter, so that the younger members emulate their good behavior and exhort each other to abide by the teachings of the ancient sages. Only in this way can the family hope to last for generations. . . .

2. Those youngsters who have taken Confucian scholarship as their hereditary occupation should be sincere and hard-working, and try to achieve learning naturally while studying under a teacher. Confucianism is the only thing to follow if they wish to bring glory to their family. Those who know how to keep what they have but do not study are as useless as puppets made of clay or wood. Those who study, even if they do not succeed in the examinations, can hope to become teachers or to gain personal benefit. However, there are people who study not for learning's sake, but as a vulgar means of gaining profit. These people are better off doing nothing.

Youngsters who are incapable of concentrating on studying should devote themselves to farming; they should personally grasp the ploughs and eat the fruit of their own labor. In this way they will be able to support their families. If they fold their hands and do nothing, they will soon have to worry about hunger and cold. If, however, they realize that their forefathers also worked hard and that farming is a difficult way of life, they will not be inferior to anyone. . . .

---

1. The *Book of Changes [Yijing]* and *Book of Rites [Liji]* were ancient texts that became incorporated into the Confucian classics.—*Ed.*

Observe the Rituals and Proprieties

1. Capping [coming-of-age rituals for young men] and wedding ceremonies should be carried out according to one's means. Funerals and burials, being important matters, should be more elaborate, but one should still be mindful of financial considerations. Any other petty formalities not found in the *Book of Rites* should be abolished.

2. Marriage arrangements should not be made final by the presenting of betrothal gifts until the boy and girl have both reached thirteen: otherwise, time might bring about changes which cause regrets.

3. For the seasonal sacrifices, the ancestral temple should be prepared in advance and the ceremonies performed at dawn in accordance with [Chu Hsi's] *Family Rituals* and our own ancestral temple regulations.

4. For burials one should make an effort to acquire solid and long-lasting objects to be placed in the coffin; but one need not worry as much about the tomb itself, which can be constructed according to one's means. The ancients entrusted their bodies to the hills and mountains, indifferent to whether their names would be remembered by posterity; their thinking was indeed profound.

5. Sacrifices at the graves should be made on Tomb-Sweeping Day and at the Autumn Festival. Because the distances to different mountains vary, it is difficult to reach every grave on those days. Therefore, all branch families should be notified in advance of the order of priority: first, the founding father of our lineage; then ancestors earlier than great-great-grandfather; next, ancestors down to each person's grandfather. Established customs should be followed in deciding how much wine and meat should be used, how many different kinds of sacrificial offerings should be presented, and how much of the yearly budget should be spent on the sacrifices. All of these should be recorded in a special "sacrifice book" in order to set standards.

6. Not celebrating one's birthday has since ancient times been regarded as an exemplary virtue. An exception is the birthdays of those who are beyond their sixty-first year, which should be celebrated by their sons and grandsons drinking to their health. But under no circumstances should birthdays become pretexts for heavy drinking. If either of one's parents has died, it is an especially unfilial act to forget him or her and indulge in drinking and feasting. Furthermore, to drink until dead-drunk not only affects one's mind but also harms one's health. The

numbers of people who have been ruined by drinking should serve as a warning.

7. On reaching five, a boy should be taught to recite the primers and not be allowed to show arrogance or laziness. On reaching six, a girl should be taught *Admonitions for Women* and not be allowed to venture out of her chamber. If children are frequently given snacks and playfully entertained, their nature will be spoiled and they will grow up to be unruly and bad. This can be prevented if caught at an early age.

8. When inviting guests to dinner, one should serve not more than five dishes or more than two soups. Wine and rice should also be served in the right proportion. . . .

Prohibit Extravagance

1. All our young people should wear cotton clothes and eat vegetables. Only on special occasions such as ancestor worship or dinner parties are they to be allowed to drink wine, eat meat, and temporarily put on new clothes. They are fortunate enough to be sheltered from hunger and cold; how dare they feel ashamed of their coarse clothing and coarse food! Also, they should do physical labor. As long as they are capable of carrying loads with their hands and on their backs, they have no need to hire servants. They are fortunate enough not be ordered around by others; how dare they order other people around! They should learn to cherish every inch of cloth and every half-penny, thereby escaping poverty.

2. Among relatives, presents should not be exchanged more than twice a year, and the gifts should not cost more than one-tenth of a tael of silver. Relatives should agree to abide by the principle of frugality and refuse any gift exceeding this limit. This rule, however, does not include celebrations and funerals, for which custom should be followed.

3. Ordinarily, custom dictates the foods to be offered guests. However, relatives and friends who visit each other often can be served just a dish of fish and another of vegetables. . . . Whenever a guest comes to visit, we should not have many dishes and should not force the guest to drink too much. Our aim should be to have the congenial mood last a long time, and the host and the guest enjoy it together.

Since our branch of the family has many members, when a visitor comes, it is difficult to have everyone present for dinner. Instead, only some members of the family will be asked to share the company of the guest. This is designed to save expense. The members will all have their turns at being invited and should not compete among themselves, lest jealousy or suspicion arise.

Exercise Restraint

1. Our young people should know their place and observe correct manners. They are not permitted to gamble, to fight, to engage in lawsuits, or to deal in salt privately. Such unlawful acts will only lead to their own downfall.

2. If land or property is not obtained by righteous means, descendants will not be able to enjoy it. When the ancients invented characters, they put gold next to two spears to mean "money," indicating that the danger of plunder or robbery is associated with it. If money is not accumulated by good means, it will disperse like overflowing water; how could it be put to any good? The result is misfortune for oneself as well as for one's posterity. This is the meaning of the saying: "The way of Heaven detests fullness, and only the humble gain." Therefore, accumulation of great wealth inevitably leads to great loss. How true are the words of Lao Tzu![2]

A person's fortune and rank are predestined. One can only do one's best according to propriety and one's own ability; the rest is up to Heaven. If one is easily contented, then a diet of vegetables and soups provides a lifetime of joy. If one does not know one's limitations and tries to accumulate wealth by immoral and dishonest means, how can one avoid disaster? To be able to support oneself through life and not leave one's sons and grandsons in hunger and cold is enough; why should one toil so much?

3. Pride is a dangerous trait. Those who pride themselves on wealth, rank, or learning are inviting evil consequences. Even if one's accomplishments are indeed unique, there is no need to press them on anyone else. "The way of Heaven detests fullness, and only the humble gain." I have seen the truth of this saying many times.

4. Taking concubines in order to beget heirs should be a last resort, for the sons of the legal wife and the sons of the concubine are never of one mind, causing innumerable conflicts between half brothers. If the parents are in the least partial, problems will multiply, creating

---

2. Lao Tzu was the founding figure of Daoism.—*Ed.*

misfortune in later generations. Since families have been ruined because of this, it should not be taken lightly.

5. Just as diseases are caused by what goes into one's mouth, misfortunes are caused by what comes out of one's mouth. Those who are immoderate in eating and unrestrained in speaking have no one else to blame for their own ruin.

6. Most men lack resolve and listen to what their women say. As a result, blood relatives become estranged and competitiveness, suspicion, and distance arise between them. Therefore, when a wife first comes into a family, it should be made clear to her that such things are prohibited. "Start teaching one's son when he is a baby; start teaching one's daughter-in-law when she first arrives." That is to say, preventative measures should be taken early.

7. "A family's fortune can be foretold from whether its members are early risers" is a maxim of our ancient sages. Everyone, male and female, should rise before dawn and should not go to bed until after the first drum. Never should they indulge themselves in a false sense of security and leisure, for such behavior will eventually lead them to poverty.

8. Young family members who deliberately violate family regulations should be taken to the family temple, have their offenses reported to the ancestors, and be severely punished. They should then be taught to improve themselves. Those who do not accept punishment or persist in their wrongdoings will bring harm to themselves.

9. As a preventative measure against the unpredictable, the gates should be closed at dusk, and no one should be allowed to go out. Even when there are visitors, dinner parties should end early, so that there will be no need for lighting lamps and candles. On very hot or very cold days, one should be especially considerate of the kitchen servants.

10. For generations this family has dwelt in the country, and everyone has had a set profession; therefore, our descendants should not be allowed to change their place of residence. After living in the city for three years, a person forgets everything about farming; after ten years, he does not even know his lineage. Extravagance and leisure transform people, and it is hard for anyone to remain unaffected. I once remarked that country living has all the advantages, and that the only legitimate excuse to live in a city temporarily is to flee from bandits.

11. The inner and outer rooms, halls, doorways, and furniture should be swept and dusted every morning at dawn. Dirty doorways and

courtyards and haphazardly placed furniture are sure signs of a declining family. Therefore, a schedule should be followed for cleaning them, with no excuses allowed.

12. Those in charge of cooking and kitchen work should make sure that breakfast is served before nine o'clock in the morning and dinner before five o'clock in the afternoon. Every evening the iron wok and other utensils should be washed and put away, so that the next morning, after rising at dawn, one can expect tea and breakfast to be prepared immediately and served on time. In the kitchen no lamps are allowed in the morning or at night. This is not only to save the expense, but also to avoid harmful contamination of food. Although this is a small matter, it has a great effect on health. Furthermore, since all members of the family have their regular work to do, letting them toil all day without giving them meals at regular hours is no way to provide comfort and relief for them. If these rules are deliberately violated, the person in charge will be punished as an example to the rest.

13. On the tenth and twenty-fifth days of every month, all the members of this branch, from the honored aged members to the youngsters, should gather at dusk for a meeting. Each will give an account of what he has learned, by either calling attention to examples of good and evil, or encouraging diligence, or expounding his obligations, or pointing out tasks to be completed. Each member will take turns presenting his own opinions and listening attentively to others. He should examine himself in the matters being discussed and make efforts to improve himself. The purpose of these meetings is to encourage one another in virtue and to correct each other's mistakes.

The members of the family will take turns being the chairman of these meetings, according to schedule. If someone is unable to chair a meeting on a certain day, he should ask the next person in line to take his place. The chairman should provide tea, but never wine. The meetings may be canceled on days of ancestor worship, parties, or other such occasions, or if the weather is severe. Those who are absent from these meetings for no reason are only doing themselves harm.

There are no set rules for where the meeting should be held, but the place should be convenient for group discussions. The time of the meeting should always be early evening, for this is when people have free time. As a general precaution the meeting should never last until late at night.

14. Women from lower-class families who stop at our houses tend

to gossip, create conflicts, peek into the kitchens, or induce our women to believe in prayer and fortune-telling, thereby cheating them out of their money and possessions. Consequently, one should question these women often and punish those who come for no reason, so as to put a stop to the traffic.

15. Blood relatives are as close as the branches of a tree, yet their relationships can still be differentiated according to importance and priority: parents should be considered before brothers, and brothers should be considered before wives and children. Each person should fulfill his own duties and share with others profit and loss, joy and sorrow, life and death. In this way, the family will get along well and be blessed by Heaven. Should family members fight over property or end up treating each other like enemies, then when death or misfortune strikes they will be of even less use than strangers. If our ancestors have consciousness, they will not tolerate these unprincipled descendants who are but animals in man's clothing. Heaven responds to human vices with punishments as surely as an echo follows a sound. I hope my sons and grandsons take my words seriously.

16. To get along with patrilineal relatives, fellow villagers, and relatives through marriage, one should be gentle in speech and mild in manners. When one is opposed by others, one may remonstrate with them; but when others fall short because of their limitations, one should be tolerant. If one's youngsters or servants get into fights with others, one should look into oneself to find the blame. It is better to be wronged than to wrong others. Those who take affront and become enraged, who conceal their own shortcomings and seek to defeat others, are courting immediate misfortune. Even if the other party is unbearably unreasonable, one should contemplate the fact that the ancient sages had to endure much more. If one remains tolerant and forgiving, one will be able to curb the other party's violence.

Preserve the Family Property

.... 6. In order to cultivate the moral character of the young, one must severely punish those who are so unruly that they have no sense of righteousness or who so indulge their desires that they destroy their own health. One should also correct those who have improper hobbies, such as making too many friends and avoiding work, indulging in playing musical instruments and the game of Go, collecting art and valuables, composing music, singing, or dancing. All these hobbies destroy a person's ambition. Those who indulge in them may consider themselves free spirits: yet little do they know that these hobbies are their most harmful enemies.

7. If among patrilineal and affinal relatives and fellow villages there are people who give importance to propriety and are respected for their learning and ability, one should frequently visit them to request advice and offer one's respects. Then, in case of emergencies in the family, one will be able to obtain help from them. Besides, receiving frequent advice is good in itself. By contrast, to make friends with the wrong sort of people and join them in evil deeds is to set a trap for oneself. If one is jealous of upright gentlemen and avoids upright discourse, misfortune will strike, the family will be ruined, lives may even be lost. Then it will be too late for regrets.

8. Scholars, farmers, artisans, and merchants all hold respectable occupations. Scholarship ranks the highest; farming is next; and then craft and business. However, it should be up to the individual to measure his ability against his aspirations as well as to find the most suitable occupation for himself. In these family instructions, I have given first place to the profession of scholarship, but have also devoted a great deal of attention to the work of farmers, artisans, and merchants. These family instructions attempt to show the correct procedures to be followed in everyday life. If one truly understands them and fulfills the duties appropriate to his way of life; if one upholds public and private obligations; if one can in good conscience invite Heaven's favor, then misfortune will stay away and bliss will enter without conscious effort on one's part. In this way, a person can face his ancestors without shame and instruct his posterity; there are no other secrets to having good and capable descendants.

Translated by Clara Yu

27

The Family

Ba Jin

The May Fourth Movement, which was sparked by anti-Japanese protest in 1919, initiated a prolonged period of cultural ferment and political argument in China. Liberalism, pragmatism, Marxism, and other political creeds were debated, and new styles of writing were published in an explosion of new journals. This same spirit led to a prolonged debate about Chinese family traditions, and to conflict about the old ways of family life and the new. In what is perhaps China's most famous twentieth-century novel, The Family, *originally published in 1933, Ba Jin (Pa Chin) vividly portrays the kind of conflict between genera-tions in a wealthy family that typified the May Fourth period. Ba Jin survived the many turmoils that characterized literary politics in China after 1949 and was, after Mao's death, the grand old man of Chinese letters.*

To Chueh-min and Chueh-hui, Chueh-hsin was "Big Brother." Though born of the same mother and living in the same house, his position was entirely different from theirs. In the large Kao family, he was the eldest son of an eldest son, and for that reason his destiny was fixed from the moment he came into the world.

Handsome and intelligent, he was his father's favorite. His private tutor also spoke highly of him. People predicted that he would do big things, and his parents considered themselves fortunate to be blessed with such a son.

Brought up with loving care, after studying with a private tutor for a number of years, Chueh-hsin entered middle school. One of the school's best students, he graduated four years later at the top of his class. He was very interested in physics and chemistry and hoped to go on to a university in Shanghai or Peking, or perhaps study abroad, in Germany. His mind was full of beautiful dreams. At that time he was the envy of his classmates.

In his fourth year at middle school, he lost his mother. His father later married again, this time to a younger woman who had been his mother's cousin. Chueh-hsin was aware of his loss, for he knew full well that nothing could replace the love of a mother. But her death left no irreparable wound in his heart; he was able to console himself with rosy dreams of his future. Moreover, he had someone who understood him and could comfort him—his pretty cousin Mei, "mei" for "plum blossom."

But then, one day, his dreams were shattered, cruelly and bitterly shattered. The evening he returned home carrying his diploma, the plaudits of his teachers and friends still ringing in his ears, his father called him into his room and said:

"Now that you've graduated, I want to arrange your marriage. Your grandfather is looking forward to having a great-grandson, and I, too, would like to be able to hold a grandson in my arms. You're old enough to be married; I won't feel easy until I fulfill my obligation to find you a wife. Although I didn't accumulate much money in my years away from home as an official, still I've put by enough for us to get along on. My health isn't what it used to be; I'm thinking of spending my time at home and having you help me run the household affairs. All the more reason you'll be needing a wife. I've already arranged a match with the Li family. The thirteenth of next month is a good day. We'll announce the engagement then. You can be married within the year. . . ."

The blow was too sudden. Although he understood everything his father said, somehow the meaning didn't fully register. Chueh-hsin only nodded his head. He didn't dare look his father in the eye, although the old man was gazing at him kindly.

Chueh-hsin did not utter a word of protest, nor did such a thought ever occur to him. He merely nodded to indicate his compliance with his father's wishes. But after he returned to his own room, and shut the door, he threw himself down on his bed, covered his head with the quilt and wept. He wept for his broken dreams.

He had heard something about a match with a daughter of the Li family. But he had never been permitted to learn the whole story, and so he hadn't placed much credence in it. A number of gentlemen with unmarried daughters, impressed by his good looks and his success in his studies, had become interested in him; there was a steady stream of matchmakers to his family's door. His father weeded out the applicants until only two remained under consideration. It was difficult for Mr. Kao to make a choice; both of the persons serving as matchmakers were of equal prestige and importance. Finally, he decided to resort to divination. He wrote each of the girls' names on a slip of red paper, rolled the slips up into balls, then, after praying for guidance before the family ancestral tablets, picked one.

Thus the match with the Li family was decided. But it was only now that Chueh-hsin was informed of the result.

Yes, he had dreamed of romance. The one in his heart was the girl who understood him and who could comfort him—his cousin Mei. At one time he was sure she would be his future mate, and he had congratulated himself that this would be so, since in his family marriage between cousins was quite common.

He was deeply in love with Mei, but now his father had chosen another, a girl he had never seen, and said that he must marry within the year. What's more, his hopes of continuing his studies had burst like a bubble. It was a terrible shock to Chueh-hsin. His future was finished, his beautiful dreams shattered

He cried his disappointment and bitterness. But the door was closed and Chueh-hsin's head was beneath the bedding. No one knew. He did not fight back, he never thought of resisting. He only bemoaned his fate. But he accepted it. He complied with his father's will without a trace of resentment. But in his heart he wept for himself, wept for the girl he adored—Mei, his "plum blossom."

The day of his engagement he was teased and pulled about like a puppet, while at the same time being shown off as a treasure of rare worth. He was neither happy nor sad. Whatever people told him to do, he did, as if these acts were duties which he was obliged to perform. In the evening, when the comedy had ended and the guests had departed, Chueh-hsin was exhausted. He went to bed and slept soundly.

After the engagement, he drifted aimlessly from day to day. He stacked his books neatly in the bookcase and didn't look at them again. He played mahjong, went to the opera, drank, and went about making the necessary preparations for his marriage, in accordance with his father's instructions. Chueh-hsin thought very little. He calmly awaited the advent of his bride.

In less than six months, she arrived. To celebrate the marriage, Chueh-hsin's father and grandfather had a stage specially built for the performance of theatricals in the compound.

The marriage ceremony turned out to be not as simple as Chueh-hsin had anticipated. He too, in effect, became an actor, and he had to perform for three days before he was able to obtain his bride. Again he was manipulated like a puppet, again he was displayed as a treasure of rare worth. He was neither happy nor sad—he was only tired, though roused a bit by the general excitement.

This time, however, after his performance was over and the guests departed, he was not able to forget everything and sleep. Because lying in bed beside him was a strange girl. He still had to continue playing a role.

Chueh-hsin was married. His grandfather had obtained a grand-daughter-in-law, his father had obtained a daughter-in-law, and others had enjoyed a brief period of merry-making. The marriage was by no means a total loss for Chueh-hsin either. He had been joined in wedlock with a tender, sympathetic girl, just as pretty as the one he adored. He was satisfied. For a time he reveled in pleasures he had not believed possible, for a time he forgot his beautiful dreams, forgot the other girl, forgot his lost future. He was sated, he was intoxicated, intoxicated with the tenderness and love of the girl who was his bride. Constantly smiling, he hung about her room all day. People envied him his happiness, and he considered himself very lucky.

Thus one month passed.

One evening his father called him into his room and said:

"Now that you're married you should be earning your own living, or people will talk. I've raised you to manhood and found you a wife. I think we can say that I've fulfilled my duties as a father. From now on you must take care of yourself. We have enough money to send you to a university, downriver, to study, but in the first place you already have a wife; secondly the family property has not yet been shared out among me and my brothers, and I am in charge of the accounts. It would look like favoritism if I advanced money from the family funds for your university education. Besides, your grandfather might not agree. So I've found you a position in the West Szechuan Mercantile Corporation. The salary's not very large, but it will give you and your wife a little spending money. Moreover, if you do your work diligently, you're sure to advance. You start tomorrow. I'll take you down myself. Our family owns some shares in the company and several of the directors are my friends. They'll look after you."

Chueh-hsin's father spoke in an even voice, as if discussing something quite commonplace. Chueh-hsin listened, and assented. He didn't say whether he was willing or unwilling. There was only one thought in his mind—"Everything is finished." Though he had many words in his heart, he spoke not a one.

The following day after the midday meal his father told him something of how a man going out in the world should behave, and Chueh-hsin made careful mental notes. Sedan-chairs brought him and his father to the door of the West Szechuan Mercantile Corporation. Entering, he first met Manager Huang, a man of about forty with a moustache and a stooped back; Chen, the accountant, who had a face like an old woman; Wang, the tall, emaciated bill-collector; and two or three other ordinary-looking members of the office staff. The manager asked him a few questions; he answered simply, as if by rote. Although they all addressed him very politely, he could tell from their actions and the way they spoke that they were not the same as he. It occurred to him with some surprise that he had seldom met people of this sort before.

His father departed, leaving Chueh-hsin behind. He felt frightened and lonely, a castaway on a desert island. He was not given any work. He just sat in the manager's office and listened to the manager discuss things with various people. After two full hours of this, the manager suddenly noticed him again and said courteously, "There's nothing for you to do today, Brother. Please come back tomorrow."

Like a pardoned prisoner, Chueh-hsin happily called a sedan-chair and gave his address. He kept urging the carriers to walk faster. It seemed to him that in all the world there was no place more wonderful than the Kao family compound.

On arriving home, he first reported to his grandfather, who gave him some instructions. Then he went to see his father, who gave him some more instructions. Finally, he returned to his own apartment. Only here, with his wife questioning him solicitously and at great length, did he find peace and relaxation.

The next day after breakfast he again went to the corporation and did not return home until five in the afternoon. That day he was given his own office. Under the guidance of the manager and his colleagues, he commenced to work.

Thus, this nineteen-year-old youth took his first big step into the world of business. Gradually, he grew accustomed to his environment and learned a new way of life. Gradually, he forgot all the knowledge he had acquired in his four years of middle school. He began to feel at home in his work. The first time he received his salary of thirty-two dollars, he was torn between joy and sorrow. It was the first time he had ever earned any money, yet the pay was also the first fruits of the sale of his career. But as the months went by, the regular installments of thirty-two dollars no longer aroused in him any special emotions.

Life was bearable, without happiness, without grief. Although he saw the same faces every day, heard the same uninteresting talk, did the same dull work, all was peaceful and secure. None of the family came to bother him at home; he and his wife were permitted to live quietly.

Less than six months later, another big change occurred in his life. An epidemic struck his father down; all the tears of Chueh-hsin and his brothers and sisters were unable to save him. After his father died, the family burdens were placed on Chueh-hsin's shoulders. In addition to looking after his stepmother, he also became responsible for his two younger sisters and his two young student brothers. Chueh-hsin was then only twenty years of age.

Sorrowfully, he wept for his departed father. He had not thought that fate could be so tragic. But gradually his grief dissipated. After his father was buried, Chueh-hsin virtually forgot him. Not only did he forget his father, he forgot everything that had passed, he forgot his own springtime. Calmly he placed the family burdens on his own young shoulders.

For the first few months they didn't seem very heavy; he was not conscious of any strain. But in a very short time, many arrows, tangible and intangible, began flying in his direction. Some he was able to dodge, but several struck home. He discovered something new, he began to see another side of life in a gentry household. Beneath the surface of peace and affection, hatred and strife were lurking; he also had become a target of attack. Although his surroundings made him forget his springtime, the fires of youth still burned in his heart. He grew angry, he struggled, because he considered himself to be in the right. But his struggles only brought him more troubles and more enemies.

The Kao family was divided into four households. Originally Chueh-hsin's grandfather had five sons, but the second son had died many years ago. Uncle Ke-ming and his Third Household were on fairly good terms with the First Household, which Chueh-hsin now headed. But the Fourth and Fifth Households were very unfriendly to Chueh-hsin; the wives of both secretly waged a relentless battle against him and his First Household, and spread countless rumors about him.

Struggling didn't do the least bit of good, and he was exhausted. What's the use of this endless strife? he wondered. Those women would never change and he couldn't make them give in. Why waste energy looking for trouble? Chueh-hsin evolved a new way of managing affairs—or perhaps it would be better to say of managing the family. He ended his battle with the women. He pretended to go along with their wishes whenever he could. Treating them with deference, he joined them in mahjong, he helped them with their shopping. . . . In brief, he sacrificed a portion of his time to win his way into their good graces. All he wanted was peace and quiet.

Not long after, the elder of his two young sisters died of tuberculosis. Although he mourned for her, his heart felt somewhat eased, for her death lightened his burden considerably.

Some time after, his first child was born—a boy. Chueh-hsin felt an immense gratitude towards his wife. The coming of his son into the world brought him great happiness. He himself was a man without hope; he would never have the chance to fulfill his beautiful dreams. His only function in life was to bear a load on his shoulders, to maintain the family his father had left behind. But now he had a son, his own flesh and blood. He would raise the child lovingly, and see in him the realization of the career he had lost. The boy was part of him and the boy's happiness would be his own. Chueh-hsin found consolation in this thought. He felt that his sacrifices were not in vain.

Translated by Sidney Shapiro

28

Urban Workers' Housework

Wang Yalin and Li Jinrong

The discipline of sociology was officially abolished in China in 1952. In the post-Mao period, however, it was decided that sociology could provide useful information about Chinese society and social problems. The field was therefore officially rehabilitated in 1979, and a large number of local researchers started trying to conduct empirical studies and to learn how Western sociologists conducted their research. The following article is based on replicating the international time budget study reported in Alexander Szalai, ed., The Use of Time, *in which respondents were asked to keep daily logs of the amount of time they spent on various tasks. The authors used their data to recommend a variety of measures to lighten the unusually heavy burden of domestic chores on Chinese families. One of their recommendations—that women be allowed to withdraw from the work force for extended periods—set off a spirited debate in the Chinese press. Critics argued that encouraging some women to be housewives would undermine the effort to promote sexual equality.*

Housework may appear to be a very ordinary and trivial affair, but it is not. Housework is an integral part of each person's everyday life. The state of housework, the amount of time spent on it and the intensity of that labor directly affect the amount of time and energy which a person has left over for physical, intellectual and cultural growth. . . . Therefore, today as our whole country is engaged in the work of socialist modernization, research on housework, clarification of the actual situ-

333

ation and theoretical problems, is very important.

With the cooperation and assistance of local chapters of the Women's Federation and research institutes, from November 1980 to March 1981, we made a survey of housework in Harbin and Qiqihar, two large cities in northeast China. Using random sampling by classification for 28 work units, we investigated over 60 items related to the structure of sparetime and housework for urban workers. Altogether we investigated 2,293 people (1,632 in Harbin and 661 in Qiqihar), including 1,165 adult males and 1,128 adult females, a sampling of over 3 percent of each work unit. . . .

Time Spent on Housework

. . . . How do Chinese urban residents spend their time? Table 1 shows the daily time structure of urban workers. We can use this table to analyze the composition of sparetime. The greatest portion is spent on physiological needs: Chinese men and women workers daily spend 9.4 and 9.1 hours respectively, not an excessive amount when compared to other countries. The amount of time spent on physiological needs by urban residents in the U.S.A., the Soviet Union, France and Czechoslovakia ranges from 9.9 to 10.9 hours for men and from 9.5 to 10.7 hours for women.

The next largest category is housework. The time spent on housework by Chinese urban workers is very great, for men 3.9 hours and for women 5.2 hours daily, women spending 1.3 hours more than men (or, on a yearly basis, about 470 hours more than men). If the time spent on work doesn't change, the more time spent on housework, the smaller proportion left each day for free time. From Figure 1 we can see that the time spent on housework each day by Chinese men workers is 2.5–2.8 hours more than in other countries and for Chinese women workers 0.7–1.9 hours more. Male workers' free time is 1.6–2.3 hours less than in other countries and women workers' 1.3–2.4 hours less. Calculated on a yearly basis, male workers in China spend 1,387–1,496 hours more on housework than in other countries and have 584–840 hours less free time; Chinese women workers spend on housework 329–693 hours more than in these other countries and have 475–876 hours less free time. If we eliminate the factor of how different social systems condition the composition and content of free time, the free time of Chinese workers is much less than that of workers in some developed countries.

Table 1. Timetable for Workers in Harbin and Qigihar (Average Hours per Day Each Week)

		Time classification				
Sex	Work	Traveling to and from work	Physio-logical needs	House-work	Child-care	Free time
Male	7.1	0.8	9.4	3.9	0.3	2.5
Female	6.9	0.9	9.1	5.2	0.2	1.7

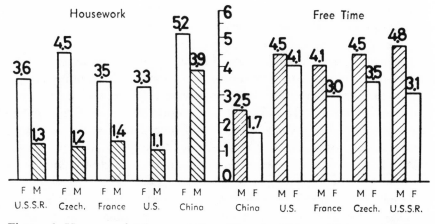

Figure 1. Housework Time and Free Time in Chinese Cities and Other Countries (Hours per Day)

Of course, there are other factors which affect the amount of free time available to Chinese workers, such as the length of the working day and the time spent traveling to and from work, but housework is undoubtedly the main reason behind their paucity of free time.

It is important to recognize that these statistics do not completely reflect the actual amount of time spent on housework. For example, workers may use work time to buy groceries and do other household chores. In the autumn many work units in northern cities schedule from 10 to 20 work days to distribute and store fall vegetables. Before the Spring Festival many workers use several work days to prepare for the holidays—buying food supplies, preparing clothes, washing quilts and padded clothing, cleaning up and so on. If we were to include all of the time spent on housework each year by urban workers, the total figures would exceed those in the table. . . .

Once a worker has married and set up an independent household, the burden of housework becomes very heavy. Some young women report that after getting married and having children, they have almost no time for reading. The original idea behind Sundays, of course, was that they should be mainly for rest and recreational activities. But in some Chinese cities, Sunday has become "housework day," with men spending six to eight hours and women as many as eight to nine hours. For many workers, Sunday housework is an all-day affair—washing the week's laundry, cleaning out storage spaces and vegetable cellars, lining up at the grain store to stock up for the week, running around town to line up to buy those hard-to-get items or take care of other chores which have been put off for too long. The common saying, "uptight Saturdays, fighting Sundays, exhausted Mondays," gives a pretty clear picture of the situation. And within each working day again, "fighting mornings, frantic middays, exhausted evenings." Many workers year after year fritter away huge amounts of precious time on endless household chores. . . .

Why So Much Housework

. . . . In this section we will focus on the excessive unreasonable expenditures of time of housework and make a preliminary analysis of the direct social causes of this problem. . . .

According to incomplete statistics for early 1980, in eleven of Heilongjiang's cities, there were 137,000 households without housing;[1]

181,000 households which either had three generations crowded into one room or shared a kitchen with several other households; and 257,000 households living in extremely crowded conditions of which 115,000 households had housing which allowed only two square meters per person. In the city of Qiqihar in 1979, the average amount of living space per person was only 2.86 square meters. The quality of housing is also poor: 80 percent of the housing is either traditional courtyard-style or mud brick buildings. The total amount of water needed for everyday use in Qiqihar is 150,000 tons, but the present maximum capacity of the city's water supply system is only around 50,000 tons. About 54 percent of the population has running water. Only about 10 percent of the city's districts have drainage facilities and in some court-yard districts there aren't even enough toilets. In Harbin about 71 percent of the population has running water but several hundred thousand people are still without it.

In the last few years great efforts have been made to improve housing and public facilities but these problems cannot be solved overnight. Poor housing and public facilities directly affect the everyday lives of urban workers forcing them to spend huge chunks of their free time on household chores. For example, a household without a kitchen has a lot of running around to do just to prepare a meal; insufficient water supplies increase the amount of time required to do the laundry and prepare meals; going out at night after work to stand in line for water and bring it back in buckets even cuts in on sleeping time. A woman working in a commercial establishment in Harbin describes her every-day life: "It's really a pain in the neck not to have plumbing. Every day we need about four or five buckets of water. To get them from the house to the water station takes about three minutes. But then each time I fill a bucket I have to stand in line for a long time. Every day it takes more than an hour just to get the water, and then once we've used it I have to get rid of it! By the time I go to work in the morning, I'm already exhausted, and by the time I get home at night I'm not interested in reading or studying or anything."

---

1. For example, some married couples who already have a baby or are expecting one live separately in dormitories for single persons; others live in their respective offices or workshops or find temporary shelter with a friend or relative; others rent a room in the suburbs, paying a relatively high rent and spending hours going to and from work; still others live in hotels or hostels, for which the very high monthly rent—running sometimes into hundreds of yuan—is of course paid by their units.—*Trans.*

According to our random sample surveys in Harbin and Qiqihar, for every 1,000 households, only 261 have kitchens, toilets, running water, plumbing and heating; the other 739 lack all or some of these facilities. In households with all of these facilities, workers spend 3.65 hours each work day on housework: workers in households which lack some of these facilities spend 4.71 hours each work day, a difference of more than an hour.

Second, the social organization of urban residents' everyday life is poor. Social service facilities are far from sufficient. During the last twenty years the urban population has soared and the rate of employment has continually increased. Facilities for the urban people's everyday lives should have developed correspondingly, but in fact the trend of change was the reverse.

Comparing 1957 with 1980, the population of Heilongjiang increased by 120 percent. Both the number of non-agricultural workers and society's purchasing power increased by more than 300 percent, but the number of commercial retail outlets decreased. In 1980 there were 31,000 state-owned and collective commercial, catering and service retail outlets, 8,000 less than in 1957. In 1957 each commercial retail outlet on the average served 640 people, increasing to 1,374 by 1980. In Qiqihar, the second largest city in the province, ... childcare, repair and processing facilities far from meet the demand. There is not only insufficient quantity of social services, the quality is poor too. The distribution of retail outlets is uneven and the mode of service is backward and not suited to the pace of life in a modern city. In terms of the whole country the total number of urban workers is over 100 million, of whom only a little over 10 million are engaged in commercial, catering or service trades. This proportion is not only less than in the industrially advanced countries, it is even less than in some developing countries. This has created a situation where, on [the] one hand, huge numbers of young people are waiting for job assignments, and on the other hand, the convenience services and labor exchanges which consumers want and need are not available....

When China established a people's government in 1949, the level of productive forces inherited from the old society was very low. China's economic backwardness objectively limited the participation of women in social productive labor. Furthermore, since education was not widespread, many women lacked the necessary cultural level and job training required for participation in social labor. In approaching the problem of women's employment, we should have proceeded from these realities, taking into account the necessary and the possible and gradually making arrangements according to different situations. But with the Great Leap Forward and the movement to set up communes in 1958, many women who were not in a position to participate in social labor were mobilized with unrealistic leftist slogans to "get out of the house and make revolution," as though all Chinese women could be liberated overnight. Consequently, the number of non-agricultural workers soared, creating serious problems for economic development. In the following decades, because economic growth was sluggish and wages did not increase, real wages dropped and the average number of people which a family could support correspondingly fell. As long as wages do not change, a family's income is mainly conditioned by the rate of employment within the family. . . .

Compared to other countries, China's rate of employment within the family is exceptionally high. Practically every member of the family with labor power is employed. Meanwhile, however, the amount of housework has not decreased. Although there has been substantial economic growth since liberation, we are still not able to produce enough commodities to renovate home equipment and improve the conditions for housework. Also, the degree of socialization of housework is still very low. Thus, families with both husband and wife employed are frantic: both men and women workers spend huge amounts of their "leisure" time on housework. Families not only have "female housewives" but also "male housewives," with the heaviest burden of course falling on the women.

29

Zhao Xiuyin: Lady of the Sties

Mary Sheridan

In spite of China's post-Mao "open-door policy," very few Westerners have been able to live and conduct research for extended periods of time in Chinese rural communities. Mary Sheridan, a sociologist trained at Cornell University, made several visits to a mountain village outside of Chongqing (Chungking) over the course of a decade (1973–83), and lived there for two years, from 1979 to 1981. This prolonged exposure allowed her to become personally close to many of the villagers and makes the following account of the life of one of these families particularly vivid.

Introduction: The Village in 1981

Jingang Brigade—my village—is composed of scattered hamlets which nestle among the bristly pine ridges and stepped paddy valleys of Gele Mountain. A few hours from Chongqing, one of the largest cities in China and the industrial center of the southwestern province of Sichuan, the village maintains its rural charm in relative obscurity. This mountain retreat is blessed with gentle winds to sweep its air clean and springwaters to nourish its unpolluted soils; it does not suffer from industrial sprawl like other villages on the lowlands. One can still find villagers here who in their lifetime have never been to a city. . . . .

The people I describe here are very special to me, but they are quite representative of the best qualities to be found in any Chinese village. I

340

have changed names and altered some details to protect privacy, but all the people are real, and events are told as they happened. The Li family members are Old Li (father, age 52); Zhao Xiuyin (Li's wife, 48); Popo (Li's mother, 73); an eldest son and daughter, both married and living away from the house; Second Son (25) and his wife, Yin (Xiuyin's daughter-in-law, 22); Simei (daughter, the fourth child, 22) and her fiancé, Xiao Hao (25); and the youngest son (17).

The father, Li Dazhi, is an admirable man of complex character. He is one of the production leaders of the village—intelligent and bold and sensitive, reflective yet decisive in action, full of anger and sweetness and humor, a talker and a thinker and a late-night reader, completely modern in his attitudes toward science and the wider world yet self-professedly old-fashioned in some (but not all) of his attitudes toward women. Other people say that he is good to his wife and family.

Old Li's character dominates the household—provoking it while fiercely but gently holding it together. The women move in counterpoint to him and to one another. His sons strive one by one to find their own orbits. Because the father loves his own independence, he has gradually let the sons find theirs. The case of the women is somewhat different. I have taken up their stories as I learned them in 1981.

A Day in July

.... Although I've been coming to live in this home and others on and off for over a year, this is the first time Xiuyin has talked about the past. Usually we are too interested in discussing our work and life in the present. . . .

"I got married at the time of Spring Festival in 1950, just after Liberation. If there had been no Liberation, I probably couldn't have married Li, because my family was better off than his. But we had been classmates, and because of Liberation, we could decide the matter ourselves. Of course, in those days, young people were very shy and proper. So we asked a matchmaker to do all the talking and to go around to settle with our parents, who agreed. Even today, it is often done that way." (Xiuyin glances at Simei, whose schoolteacher-fiancé has been "introduced" by the village school's headmistress. Simei blushes.)

Xiuyin continues: "When I was young, I went to elementary school. To go to school, we paid in unhusked rice [because of the worthlessness of money during high wartime inflation]. I went to elementary school for five years, then for another two years to a school which tutored us in the Confucian classics. Compared to my seven years of schooling, my husband had only five. Of my age group, I had the most schooling on the mountain, and my marks were not bad [actually very good]. I am better at writing and the abacus than my children.

"After I finished those seven years, I took the examination for three middle schools and did well on all of them. But my family opposed my going to middle school—it cost a lot, and they were uneasy about my being so far away. [The school was only about an hour's walk to the foot of the mountain, and many village boys and girls study there today. In the old days, however, families were reluctant to let a young girl out of their sight.] Before Liberation, few people had any book learning. In our hamlet, there was only one who had ever been to middle school. Because I loved school so much, I'd hoped my children would go on to a university. But they all made a poor showing on the difficult entrance exams. In our village, few have ever passed.

"Just after Liberation, the village was quite feudal. At that time—about 1950—everyone elected me to be the leader of the women's work. But my husband didn't want me to go [to] the women's meetings and scolded me about it all the time. He didn't understand as much as I did. Just after Liberation, it was possible to take a literacy examination to become a cadre. I could have become a cadre even without the examination, because I had high marks in school and had a graduation diploma. If I had presented these to the leadership, I would have been given work immediately. But my husband opposed it. He scolded me and scolded me. I cried and cried—for years."

Popo goes into the kitchen to wash dishes. Simei is off to her job across the hill in the brigade noodle factory. Xiuyin pauses for a while, and I pause too, thinking of the old framed photos on the wall of the next room. One shows Xiuyin as a young girl just after her marriage; she is hoeing, towel around her neck over her flower print jacket, with a glowing smile—the most beautiful girl in the village then, still robust and lovely now. A snapshot shows her husband as a stocky youth, and a formal portrait poses the young family—Popo, Xiuyin, and Li, together with their first baby. In this household, Popo is an exceptionally independent, energetic character, and Xiuyin's husband Li is a brilliant farmer, perhaps the most intellectually enlightened man in the village. A talented, strong-willed older generation, they are united by genuine admiration and affection. Yet each has confided to me a private sorrow or a failed ambition that is partly the result of conflicts between character and sentiment insoluble within the family structure. I mull this over silently until Xiuyin picks up the thread of her thought and goes on.

"In those days, things were just too feudal. Now things have gotten much better. At that time, though, I couldn't do anything about the situation; I couldn't go to work as a cadre. Even now, when I think of it, it still makes me unhappy. I'm not stupid. It's just that my husband interferes so much—always trying to control me. In 1954, the brigade leadership asked me to study the new methods of midwifery. But by then I already had two children. I studied for a month, but because of the children, it was very troublesome. The brigade said just to forget it.

"The next year, the brigade leadership again sent me to study, this time at a special training school for nursery teachers. [This school is at the foot of the mountain—about an hour away by bus.] But I was pregnant with Simei. I had to carry this burden while I was trying to study. After a year, I had to come home without finishing the two-year program. Back in the village, I worked in the brigade kindergarten.

"At that time, my husband's mother was running the kindergarten. In those days, the kindergarten had both half-day and full-day charges, but all ate lunch in the school whether they came from near or far [to ensure proper nourishment]. I worked there for a year, but my husband thought it was inconvenient, so I had to give it up and just do agricultural labor in our team. That way I was always near our house to cook for him and mind our children.

"It wasn't long before the brigade leadership called me for another training program, but my husband was still opposed. I remember one time after he had been berating me, I thought I must certainly leave home. I got up very early and made breakfast. Then I told his younger sister: 'I can't stand it. I'm going.' But his mother heard me and ran out to block my way. She did not want me to go and told me to be a good daughter-in-law—that a family should not quarrel.

"Nowadays it's different. If my husband tried to control me that way now, I could run away. But then it wasn't in my character to fight him. I just cried. He's a good man, but he didn't understand. Men are more feudal than women. Before Liberation and just afterward, women were terribly oppressed. Of course, at that time, there were some women who did run away. One woman whose child had died did not want to stay in her mother-in-law's household. Because she had milk, she ran away to work for other people as a wet nurse. Her husband's household went out to search for her and dragged her back. There were also some who did not return and some married ones who ran away and later married another man.

"Now I don't think about the past so much. But even though life is better, things do not go well in my heart. Every day I go to work and then come home to do housework. I can't study, and I don't know much about important things in our country. If my husband hadn't controlled me, then I'd probably be working in a different place today—"

Xiuyin stops abruptly in mid-sentence, because Popo comes into the room and exclaims: "What? You haven't gone to work yet? It's already past nine o'clock!" Jumping up, Xiuyin grabs her broad-brimmed straw hat from the hook on the wall and runs out. I gather my notebook, straw hat, and towel and rush out to catch up with her.

She is 48 and I am 43, but we go off together like girls—slipping and sliding down the steep path, sloshing and laughing through puddles in our plastic sandals. The moist gray haze has lifted, and the paddies are spotted with dabbling white ducks which scold us as we pass. We turn off the road at a long building of packed earth with a small center courtyard. It stands slightly apart from a cluster of family houses. Xiuyin unlocks the doors, and we enter. This is the pigsty of her production team, and she is the keeper.

She checks the pens and starts a fire in the huge stove which fills one corner of the sty's kitchen. The fire is fueled with straw and pine branches which she has carried in towering bundles on her back from the forest slopes an hour away, then stacked along the outside walls of the sty under the eaves. The fire begins to heat the water in the giant iron *guo* (also called a *wok,* a curved iron cauldron shaped like the smaller Chinese frying pans in my own kitchen at home). Xiuyin puts chopped leaves and vines into the water to simmer, adding mash from rice bran and a few sweet potatoes. We go back to sweep out the pens, talking as we work. When the watery swill is hot, we ladle it into large wooden buckets to carry to the pens.

The pigs are a white variety—long and lean at the moment. It is the custom here to raise pigs lean and full size "so their bones will grow strong." This is why they get the watery diet of cooked greens, with bran added for nourishment. Only in the last few weeks before sale are the pigs fattened up quickly, mostly on sweet potatoes.

The animals in this sty are very clean—no sores on their backs, no nervous rubbing against the stones of the pens. Every day, following their afternoon meal, Xiuyin hoses them down (there is piped-in running water), and the pens are washed out morning and evening. The stone floors of the pens slope outward and drain into fertilizer pits, the grounds of the sty are swept up twice a day, and lime is used so that there is no odor. I comment to Xiuyin: "Your sty is so clean. I've been around to the sties of other production teams, and yours is the cleanest one!"

She replies: "Ah Mali [her pronunciation of my name], pigs are like people. They don't like dirt. Right now we have 26 pigs in this sty. In the winter, we had over 50, and last year there were many more than that. Because of my work, the brigade elected me to go as a representative to the district meeting of advanced producers."

"Why aren't you raising so many pigs now?"

"It's too tiring for one person to do so much. Last year, I took care of the sty alone, but this year the production team appointed a half-time person to help me. Last year, the jobs were undertaken by contract, and I earned over 8,000 work points, which are distributed according to the profits made for the team. But afterward people said I got too many work points. So now I'm just paid according to the hours I spend at work. It comes to eight work points each day."

I say, "But I met a man in the Tingzishan production team who earns 20 points a day just for looking after four plow oxen. When I saw him, he was just sitting around on the grass smoking comfortably, while the oxen cooled off in the reservoir. Surely your work is as heavy as his."

"It's very hard to look after oxen."

"So—just because it's a bit harder physically, which seems doubtful anyway, he gets more than twice as much as you do for raising over 50 pigs? How can that be?"

"Ahh—his work points are set by job contract."

Silently I contemplate Xiuyin's modesty and understatement in accounting for her tasks. From other quarters in the village, I've heard that she is considered outstanding in pig-raising. When she took over the work of the sty, it had been losing money, but she turned it around and made a huge profit for the team. In spite of these profits, from which everyone benefited, the large number of work points she earned aroused jealousy. Some people felt it unfair that one person could earn so much. So she was cut back to an hourly pay rate. Now she will be paid the same whether she raises 20 pigs or 50. Under her present pay scheme, even if she shirks on the job, she will still earn her hourly wage. But she continues as conscientiously as before.

To spread income opportunities (there is hidden underemployment on this overpopulated mountain), another woman was assigned to help Xiuyin for half a day each day. Throughout China, it has been more or less standard to assign women a maximum of six to eight work points per day, according to individual strength and skill. For men, the work point range has been seven to ten. The ox herder therefore does well at 20 work points a day.

At this point in our morning tasks, a young woman of about 35 comes to join us. This is Xiuyin's *tangmei* (female cousin on her paternal side). She is the additional half-day laborer assigned to the sty. Xiuyin comments that having a helper from the family makes work a little more convenient. The two women can sometimes swap tasks or working hours to help each other when illness or special occasions like weddings call them away, without having to make troublesome arrangements through the team leaders. This doesn't affect their efficiency or output. In some work groups which are based on family relationships, the kinship ties seem to have a negative effect on reporting and accounting. For this reason, teams have tried not to allow kinship to be the basis of work groupings. Of one work group whose members were all relatives, other people said, "That group is unmanageable. You can't tell them a thing. They stick together against everyone else, but among themselves it's nothing but constant squabbling."

I ask the cousin about the crumbly reddish-brown granular feed piled in a *guo* in the corner of the kitchen: "What kind of feed is this?"

"It's the roughage left over from making soy sauce. We buy it from Ciqikou, the peasant free market at the foot of this mountain. It's good because it has some salt in it."

Xiuyin adds, "Every pig gets three or four *liang* of fodder a day—corn or sweet potatoes, depending on the season. If we feed them wheat bran or rice bran, then we figure that two *jin* of these are equal to one *jin* of grain. Fresh green fodder or fermented greens are used just to fill up the pigs [to assuage their appetites without actually fattening them] and are not figured at any certain amount per day. When the production team members harvest vegetables in the team's fields, they strip off the outer waste leaves in the fields before bringing the vegetables to the loading platform for weighing and trucking into the city. If there is a lot of waste left in the fields, we ask the team to send it over; if not, the two of us just collect it ourselves. The fermenting greens here in the courtyard are cabbage leaves. We pile them up, water them, and trample them down with our feet. Ten days later, they are ready to use as fodder. It takes a year to raise a pig until it is fat enough to sell."

While Xiuyin is talking, she has started to make a long-handled broom from a large dried plant. She wraps the springy branches tight with a long supple strip of bamboo and ties them to form a suitable sweeping shape. I ask her about this.

"I'm making a broom from a kind of wild plant called *tiesiaoba*—iron broom plant. When I took over this job in the sty, I went up the mountain slopes and brought back some seedlings to plant here in front of the sty—these bushes in front here. They are easy to use. I just pull up a bush, let it dry out in the storeroom, then bind it up with bamboo this way. The other teams haven't thought of this method—just us. So we don't waste money on bamboo brooms."

Xiuyin thus saves money for her team by her ingenuity and thrifty management. It takes her extra effort yet brings no additional remuneration for her. I begin to understand the difference in work attitudes and how difficult it is to arrive at fair remuneration for any effort in a farming village, because individual character, production skill, and physical strength are inevitably uneven, and social relationships further influence such complex factors. Our tasks are done by eleven o'clock, and Xiuyin locks up the sty. The cousin takes my hand, and we three walk home in the light drizzle which has started to cool off the day. It is peaceful and pleasant, like many such days which Xiuyin and I have shared together.

Between 1979 and 1981, when I lived in the village, there were no women on Gele Mountain who did not work. Whoever wanted to work could do so, and suitable jobs were found for women and old or handicapped people. Many men over 70 still like to earn work points in the fields whenever the weather is not too formidable. (Extremes of summer heat and winter cold, intensified by high humidity in both seasons, keep most older folk indoors.) Some young women have husbands with salaries as rural factory workers, truck drivers, or small cadres, so often they go to the fields less than others, but they don't stop altogether. The women say that their situation is better here than in some other parts of China. Some villages have sent their women back to the hearth because of overpopulation and hidden underemployment, saving the jobs that earn work points for men. When this happens, the women lose their economic independence.

The women's relative equality of work opportunities in this village sometimes has its negative side. Sturdy girls vie with men for jobs at the gravel works, where they lift, haul, and breathe the harmful dust. They choose these jobs because they get equal pay for equal work (unlike the work point system in the fields). On the other hand, chemical spraying of crops (done with small backpack hand pump strayers) is done mostly by women, because they themselves demand it as "light" labor. Pregnant women especially want this task. The leaders of the village strenuously and continuously warn against such hazardous practices. But at the level of the small work groups, where tasks are actually assigned, the women get their way. Neglecting safety instructions, they spray without masks, even on windy days. (One sees the same thing in Japan and throughout Asia—farm women walking the fields in a halo of chemicals.)

In this village, the use of the work point system contributes to the women's choice of spraying as a "light" task. The task is considered an eight-point day, the same eight points which Xiuyin receives for the much greater labor and management skill she puts into running her team's pigsty. These inequities are very difficult to adjust, and no one method is satisfactory for all situations. This is one reason why a variety of forms of work accounting are now being tried. Of these, the most important are work points set per person per day, set tasks for set points, productivity and profit incentives, and responsibility systems.

Work points are a labor value per person per day assigned on the basis of the individual's strength. The work points have no intrinsic monetary equivalent, because their value is determined at the end of the year when the production team's total profits are divided between its membership. If the team's entire profit has increased over the previous year, then each work point is worth more, and vice versa. Thus Xiuyin's sty may earn a huge profit, but if other team enterprises lose money, the value of her work points decreases according to the final average.

Set tasks may be assigned a set work point value. Whether the task is done quickly or slowly, by a woman or a man, the pay is the same. Sometimes this leads to hasty or sloppy work, so it provides an incentive for some tasks and is appropriate to others. The ox herder who earns 20 work points per day is paid in this way.

Productivity and profit incentives may be fixed so that work points are earned according to the profits made by an enterprise. This is how

Xiuyin earned over 8,000 work points in 1980, arousing the envy which brought about a change in the method by which she is paid. If she had done a poor job and had lost money on the sty, her team might have kept her pay tied to profits and losses. If she were a less conscientious person, she might have slacked on the job when her pay was reduced to eight work points per day. But because of her strong character and her own fairness, she worked as hard under one system as the other.

Responsibility systems include a variety of new methods for contracting tasks. Intended to reward higher productivity and penalize lower productivity, these were being introduced gradually but did not affect Xiuyin's work in 1981. . . .

30

Courtship, Love, and Marriage: The Life and Times of Yu Luojin

Emily Honig

Most sociologists would argue that when arranged-marriage systems are changed into free-choice marriage systems, certain other changes will probably follow. For instance, it is likely that premarital sex will increase, and it is also likely that marriages will become more brittle, with an increase in divorce rates. Official family policy in the PRC favors freedom for young people to pick their own mates and search for conjugal companionship, but at the same time it actively tries to prevent both premarital sex and divorce. The result is that many Chinese end up married to people they know only superficially, and yet they are expected to remain faithful and married until the end of their days. Thus the quest for truly fulfilling marriages, which began in the May Fourth era, continues, and individuals who challenge the established ways by demanding a divorce to escape an unfulfilling marriage face many obstacles. Yu Luojin, whose case is described here by historian Emily Honig, did this not once but twice, thereby creating a public scandal.

Yu Luojin achieved instant notoriety in 1980 with the publication of her scarcely-fictionalized autobiographical story "A Winter's Fairy Tale" in a Peking literary magazine. The story created a sensation among university students, who cut classes and abandoned homework when their turn came to read one of the hard-to-find copies of the issue, which had sold out almost as soon as it was published. For several weeks after the story appeared, heated arguments about Yu Luojin's life dominated conversations at universities throughout China. Almost everyone took sides: some sympathized with her as a social victim; some heralded her as a "liberated woman"; some denounced her as a morally bankrupt opportunist.

"A Winter's Fairy Tale" is essentially the story of Yu Luojin's—and her family's—tragic experiences during the Cultural Revolution, the circumstances under which she married, subsequently fell in love with someone else, and finally divorced her husband. The story itself is remarkable not as literature, but as a social document, for it is a uniquely candid record of a young woman's experiences with and attitudes towards love, marriage, sex, and divorce. Perhaps even more remarkable than the story itself is the debate it triggered—a debate about the nature of love, marriage, and the morality of divorce. It was in the context of discussing Yu Luojin's story that, for the first time in over a decade, many of these private issues became the subject of public discourse.

The debate was not restricted to the contents of the story itself, for almost everyone knew that after the divorce she describes in her story, Yu had remarried and was in the process of requesting a second divorce. This second divorce trial coincided with the implementation of the new marriage law of 1980—a law which specified that the absence of "mutual affection" between a husband and wife was grounds for divorce. For almost a year, China's major legal journal, *Democracy and the Legal System (Minzhu yu fazhi)*, devoted its section on "how to handle divorce cases" to a presentation and analysis of Yu Luojin's case. . . .

After the debate had gone on for almost a year, Yu Luojin published a sequel to "A Winter's Fairy Tale," called "A Spring Fairy Tale." Again, it was a semi-fictionalized autobiographical account, supplementing the first with more details of her family's history, her marriages, and divorces, giving a painfully intimate account of her romantic involvement with an older, married man. . . . Before taking a more detailed look at the questions Yu Luojin's story brought up for public discussion, let us look briefly at some of the experiences that have shaped her life.

Who Is Yu Luojin?

Yu Luojin was born in Peking in 1946. Her mother was a factory director; her father, who had studied in Japan, worked as a construction engineer. Both were labeled rightists in 1957. They were divorced when her father had an affair with a younger woman, but were reunited several years later. In the meantime, Yu Luojin attended the Academy of Industrial Arts in Peking. When she graduated in 1959, she was assigned a job in the design section of a toy factory, where she worked until the beginning of the Cultural Revolution.

The experiences of Yu's family during the Cultural Revolution were similar to those of many urban intellectuals. Shortly after the Cultural Revolution began, both of her parents lost their jobs. Yu's older brother, Luoke, a student activist who had gained some notoriety for essays he had written criticizing Cultural Revolution policies at a time when it was suicidal to do so, was arrested. On the basis of his diary, which was found by Red Guards after he had entrusted it to Yu Luojin to hide, he was sentenced to death and executed. Yu's two younger brothers were sent to a very poor part of Shanxi Province. Yu Luojin herself was accused of being a reactionary, and was sent to a labor-reform camp in the Peking suburbs. Three years later, she was moved to a state farm and was finally assigned to a production team in the Lin Xi district of Hebei Province.

From the time she arrived in Hebei, she found herself under increasing pressure to marry. The pressure came first from the leadership of the production team. Assuming that Yu would marry and, according to custom, move into her husband's house, the team used the 150 *yuan* it had been given for Yu's "settling in" expenses to purchase tools and equipment which it needed. When Yu asked what she should do about housing, the surprised Party Secretary replied, "You'll get married sooner or later and then move anyway, so you certainly do not need to fix a house now.... You're already twenty-three. It's high time you found a husband for yourself! You can't live alone." In the meantime, she was instructed to board at another team member's house.

More acute pressure to marry came from her family. In 1970, Yu's parents, still living in Peking, heard that they were to be sent to the countryside as well. They calculated that their only hope of avoiding the fate of being sent to a very poor village rested on Yu's marriage. If she could marry someone in a richer area, then the official residence of her parents and brothers could be transferred there. It was under these circumstances that her parents located a potential husband for her in the Northeast; and, for the sake of her family's survival, Yu married him. "I never would have dreamed that I, who was so full of lofty ideals, would make such a casual decision to get married," Yu later wrote of her marriage to Zhao Zhiguo.

> Even if there had been a brothel I would have been willing to go. All I cared about was that my family could live well. . . . I had become completely numb to everything else.

Yu was only one of many members of her generation whose marriages were arranged for the benefit of their families rather than for their personal fulfillment. Yu never loved her husband, and in fact refused to sleep with him after their wedding night, but she remained married to him for several years. Then she met another educated youth from Peking, who also lived in the Northeast, and fell in love with him. Hoping to marry him, Yu requested—and was granted—a divorce from Zhao Zhiguo. She did not, however, succeed in marrying the man she loved, for his parents refused to allow their son to marry a woman who was not only an alleged "counter-revolutionary," but a divorcee as well.

After the divorce, Yu was transferred from one production team to another and, as a divorced woman, found herself treated as an outcast wherever she went. She resolved to return to Peking, where the rest of her family lived. Once again, marriage was the only way in which Yu could transfer her official residence from the countryside to the city. Someone introduced her to Cai Zhongpei, a worker in Peking who had also been recently divorced, and Yu married him in 1977.

One year later, Yu once again fell in love with someone else—this time, a newspaper editor named He Jing, a married man more than twenty years her senior. She loved him, she said, because he had delivered a speech demanding the posthumous political rehabilitation of her brother and because he "was the first person who could truly understand me." In 1979, when the political charges which had been made against Yu during the Cultural Revolution were cleared, she was able to return to work. She then informed her husband that she was in love with He Jing, and moved out and rented a room of her own in a peasant's house.

In May 1980, Yu filed for—and was granted—a divorce by the district court in Peking. . . . The district-court judge decided that this particular divorce raised issues worthy of public discussion, and wrote an article in the news magazine *The New Observer (Xin Guancha)*, explaining why he had decided to grant the divorce. This touched off the explosion of articles debating the case. . . .

The Debate

The debate about Yu Luojin's case actually consisted of two simultaneous debates: a legal debate over how to interpret and implement the marriage law of 1980, and a popular debate over the relationship between love and marriage, and the morality of divorce. . . .

For the courts, Yu Luojin's application for a second divorce provided the first major test of how to interpret the new marriage law of 1980. This law specified that in cases such as Yu's, in which only one partner requests a divorce, "the people's court should try to bring about a reconciliation between the parties. In cases of complete alienation of mutual affection, when mediation has failed, divorce should be granted." The tricky question for the court was how to define "mutual affection" *(ganqing)*, a term which throughout the legal discussion was used interchangeably with "love" *(aiqing)*.

Yu's case pitted legal officials who believed that love's meaning was derived from politics and class struggle against those who insisted that love was a matter of emotions and feelings between two people. These opposing positions are most bluntly summarized in an angry exchange between two judges involved in the case:

[Guo Jie]: The words of our revolutionary teachers are forever inscribed in the heavens—love has a class character! It does not matter whether or not the two people are close. The question is one of class. There is no such thing as abstract love nor is there abstract hatred. When we judge divorce cases we must use the criterion of class struggle to observe, analyze and manage everything.

[Da Ji]: Engels has said, "Marriages which have no love are the most immoral of marriages." When we judge divorce cases we always neglect to examine whether or not there is love in the relationship. Some people even turn the corrupt ideas and values of feudalism into a weapon of Marxism-Leninism. By treating the question of love or feelings as a capitalist element, they make their decision, and the result is that feudalism even more deeply penetrates our thinking.

Guo Jie's view represents the one that had prevailed in most divorce cases since the beginning of the Cultural Revolution. It meant, for instance, that a divorce would be granted to persons who wanted to "draw a clear line" between themselves and a spouse who had been labeled a counterrevolutionary. However, couples who simply claimed to no longer "love" each other had little hope of obtaining a divorce from the courts. It appears that a group of judges (and perhaps the government as well) hoped to use Yu Luojin's case to discredit what they considered an ultra-leftist definition of love. "In trying Yu Luojin's case," wrote the judge Li Yongji,

> we want to grasp the principle of "deciding on the basis of feelings." . . .
> We hope that legal officials can be educated by this case, and will give a correct and prompt decision to those who filed for divorce ten or twenty years ago. These people should be liberated from their spiritual suffering so that they can concentrate wholeheartedly on the Four Modernizations.

Li Yongji was the first to publicize Yu's case and, throughout the legal discussion, it was clear that he hoped to use Yu's case to establish a precedent for deciding divorce cases on the basis of what he himself called "bourgeois love." . . .

The key question for the public, as for the court officials, was how to define love. For the popular audience, however, the question was not simply whether or not love was "political," but rather what sentiments constituted "love." Was a marriage that was voluntary inherently based on love? Was love automatically present after two people had shared their lives for a number of years?

To many people, the desperate circumstances under which Yu Luojin had married both times, and the fact that she had had no alternatives, made the question of love almost irrelevant. Yu herself argued that she had not loved Cai when she married him, but had hoped that their marriage could demonstrate the maxim, "first get married, then fall in love."

By the time she wrote "A Winter's Fairy Tale," Yu had developed a more radical definition of love. For Yu, "love" required an intellectual, if not a spiritual bond between two people, and she concluded that her marriage to Cai held no potential for the development of such a bond. Cai did not appreciate literature, nor did he like the movies she liked. When they went to the Fragrant Hills outside of Peking, instead of expressing appreciation of the autumn foliage, he could only talk about where one could buy the cheapest fish in Peking. At home Cai liked to play the radio at full volume, while Yu longed for tranquility so that she could read and write. "I cooked for him every day, and we very democratically put our wages together," Yu admitted to her opponents.

> But there was no love! There was no content to our relationship other than eating and sleeping together.... Unfortunately it seemed that I was surrounded by couples who could "make do." Of course I could not say they were wrong if they wanted just to "make do," but why did they have to be so accusing of those who did not want simply to "get along"?

Yu Luojin thus became a spokesperson for those who insisted upon their right to "spiritual love." To them, she was a heroine, struggling to challenge feudal traditions.

The meaning of "spiritual love" becomes more clear when contrasted to the definition of love used by Yu's opponents. They argued, first, that Yu's marriage to Cai was technically voluntary, not arranged, and hence was based on "love." Furthermore, they found substantial evidence to show that love had developed even more during the period in which Yu and Cai were married. "In fact after marriage they took care of each other, lived in harmony and democratically shared their earnings," one person wrote in a letter to *Democracy and the Legal System*. "They not only established the sentiments of 'husband and wife,' but also implemented the principle of 'equality of men and women.'" Their marriage, this writer implied, could be cited as exemplary.

To many, the fact that Yu's husband had spent his own money and a great deal of effort to transfer Yu's residence from the Northeast to Peking, sought "back doors" through which to arrange temporary work for Yu before her political problem was resolved, persistently badgered the Public Security Bureau to expedite the rectification of her older brother's name, and bought her birthday presents, all proved that Yu and Cai "spoke a common language." That Yu took care of Cai when he was in the hospital was seen as additional evidence of the love that had developed between them.

In other words, if a husband and wife could "get along" and help each other meet the needs and demands of their daily lives, their marriage satisfied the requirements of "love" specified by the marriage law. To Yu's opponents, the kind of love Yu demanded was ridiculous:

[Yu] hopes that her love life can consist of discussing the successes and failures of movie actors, strolling on the big avenues at night when the lights are glistening, together discussing *The Dream of the Red Chamber.* Her husband must be able to understand how to play with her fingers; he must understand the pleasure of kissing her in daylight. As soon as questions such as "What will we eat today?" or matters such as coal, rice, oil and salt enter her "love life," then it is no longer lofty. In fact it is the "unlofty love," and cause for separation.

It is important to note that Yu's notion of love, which comprised emotional, intellectual and physical intimacy, is likely held by only a small minority of China's urban, intellectual population. On the other hand, the concept of love articulated by Yu's critics—that is, mutual affection which develops between a husband and wife who help each other meet the needs of their daily lives—represents a much more popular notion of love, and one with a much longer historical tradition in China. . . .

Given this public discussion, Yu's case obviously put the courts in a very awkward position. If they granted the divorce, did it mean that all those who claimed that their marriages were loveless could also win divorces? Did it mean that anyone who had married during the Cultural Revolution, under circumstances in which there was no alternative but marriage for survival, could demand a divorce? In a society in which marriage remains one of the few ways in which a person can hope to change his or her status, and in which gaining access to material goods is often one of the major factors in the choice of a marriage partner, would granting Yu's divorce imply that everyone was free to marry, collect their goods, and then request a divorce?

Court officials found themselves caught between conflicting demands. On the one hand, judges had to make a decision which would not sanction such "bourgeois" notions as "liking the new and hating the old," or "changing one's mind the moment one sees something better." On the other hand, they had to make a decision which would oppose such "feudal" ideas as the belief that a woman must be faithful to her husband her entire life, or that "a good woman does not marry twice." Finally, there was the law itself, which said that in cases where "mutual affection" had been destroyed, a divorce must be granted. If the court denied Yu's request for divorce, what would it mean for the future of the new marriage law and public confidence in the law? The decision would certainly have been simpler had Yu's case not become so famous.

The pressure the courts were under was evident in the decision of the middle-level court. While the judge made it clear that he was vehemently opposed to Yu Luojin, he dared not make the actual decision. Instead, his verdict scolded Yu for her irresponsible behavior, but returned the case to the district court for further investigation. He obviously did not want to be the one to bear the burden of responsibility for the decision. Ultimately, in May 1981, Yu was granted the second divorce. . . .

Not for Public Debate

. . . . Yu Luojin's demand for a kind of love that embodies both emotional and physical fulfillment, and her demand for the freedom to pursue love both within and outside the confines of marriage, are perhaps reminiscent of feelings expressed by an earlier generation of women writers—particularly Ding Ling in her story "The Diary of Miss Sophie." Yu Luojin herself drew on the precedent of Ding Ling to justify writing stories which explored women's experiences with love, sex, and marriage.

What is particularly interesting and ironic, however, is the way in which Yu's opponents drew on the analogy of Ding Ling to deny the legitimacy of bringing these private issues into the realm of public discourse. When Ding Ling wrote about these issues, they said, it was the 1920s and 1930s, and it was therefore progressive to create characters who pursued personal liberation, struggled against dependence on men, and opposed the traditions which made women subservient to men.

> However, the author of "A Spring Fairy Tale," has forgotten one thing; that is, Miss Sophie was a product of the 1930s, and Yu belongs to the 1980s. . . . In today's society which has already undergone a radical transformation, the thinking, pursuits and spiritual life of youth have also changed. Not to create characters which reflect today's youth, but instead go back to Miss Sophie—isn't that taking the wrong path?

In other words, it was legitimate to raise these issues in the context of pre-revolutionary society; but after thirty years of revolution, these questions have become obsolete.

That the questions raised by Yu Luojin's stories are far from obsolete is suggested by the unusually widespread public response they provided. These private issues are obviously far from resolved for those who have grown up during the times of Yu Luojin.

Creating a
Broader Community

31

Urban Social Control

Sybille van der Sprenkel

Westerners have long been fascinated by what seem to be distinctive styles of behavior and interpersonal relationships that characterize Chinese society. Although these are sometimes explained in terms of Chinese culture or Chinese "national character," it is possible to argue that they are based upon the distinctive ways in which society was organized in Imperial China. Sybille van der Sprenkel, a sociologist who specializes in the study of legal institutions in China during the Qing dynasty, describes here the particular forms of social organization that were common in nineteenth-century Chinese cities. Although such grassroots groups helped to provide order and a sense of community, they also inhibited the development of a sense of generalized urban citizenship which, historians argue, had arisen in Europe centuries earlier.

. . . . It must be stressed at the outset that in traditional China "urban" was not a category to be sharply distinguished from "rural." . . . Town and country were alike governed by a blend of two different kinds of organization: the first, the territorial network of the centralized imperial authority reaching from the top downward to the family or household at the base, the seat of whose administration was merely located within one city in the *hsien;* and the second, the customary unofficial organization of overlapping groups and associations, which arose not by design or by explicitly established right but spontaneously wherever and whenever groups of people associated regularly and shared neighborhood, activities, cult practices, common interests, or general interdependence. . . .

Imperial law [on trade] never having developed beyond the concern to enforce ethical norms and safeguard the public interest, people were left to pursue their activities locally with a minimum of interference—so long as they did not flagrantly contravene the statutes—and without benefit of court adjudication. In other words, much was left to unofficial social organization.

This organizing of activities locally went on mainly in the particularistic groups and ad hoc associations for which Chinese everywhere have shown such outstanding talent. . . . The structure, membership, and leadership of these associations were quite formal, and they had their own rules and sanctions that were well known to their members. (The unorganized or unincluded, it will be seen later, were at a certain practical disadvantage, so the implicit sanctions of expulsion or loss of reputation were always in reserve if no particular sanctions were specified.)

The extent to which the imperial administration exercised real control locally depended on how much power it could command. It is commonly asserted that its power was felt more in towns than in the countryside and of course in the capitals and garrison cities more than in other towns. In the countryside, where land was the chief means of production, the landowning function of the kinship group gave it significant power to control members' lives. In towns and cities, the lineage was less significant in this respect. Though business at both the merchant and the artisan level was organized on family lines (and of course within the family discipline was exercised by senior family members over their juniors, as was general in China), kinship organization was not the machinery by which business was regulated.

A large part of what went on in towns and cities had to do either with temples or with trading. . . . Apart from family occasions, i.e., weddings, funerals, and private ancestor worship (and guilds also served as proxy family in the case of funerals and burials of deceased sojourners), temples and guilds probably covered the activities that were most significant in the lives of urban residents: neighborhood temples were associated with street markets, festivals, and processions; guilds with the practice of crafts and trade; and both with such recreations as theatricals, jugglers, and feasts.

A good many towns, perhaps most, possessed religious foundations—Confucian temples, lama temples, Buddhist monasteries, mosques, and so on—more important than those based on purely local cults, and the rituals associated with them punctuated the year and enhanced the lives of the area residents. Temples located in towns were sometimes also connected with secret societies, which, by their nature, tended to overlap with heterodox sects. Leong and Tao mention temples built by ephemeral societies through public subscription led by someone well-to-do. "When the work is completed, nothing but the temple with the monks remains. Yet the utility of these temples, which are found everywhere in China, is manifold, as the site of festivals, the warehouse of goods, the classroom of private tutors, the meeting-place of poor artisans, the dining-room of feasting parties, etc." These indications of overlap of clientele and ambiguity of function—at times religious, political, economic, and social, perhaps changing cyclically—warn against making too sharp a distinction between temples and other types of organization.

Neighborhood religious associations formed the focus of a sort of local self-government. The pervasive beliefs in spirits associated with places, and the consequent needs that premodern Chinese, urban as well as rural, seem to have felt, gave rise to practices which, as they were shared by people in the neighborhood, had somehow to be organized and financed; and presumably the association took on other functions by accretion, like the parish in Western cities. . . .

The organization of townmen's workaday lives was in the hands of guilds. . . . They varied in their structure—some were relatively democratic and others hierarchical—but they were alike in adopting rules or standards appropriate to the particular business of their members and in providing effective machinery for intragroup adjudication and sanctioning. They were both inclusive and exclusive. Membership offered benefits without which the individual trader could not hope to survive (protection against official demands that went beyond what was usually exacted, against unfair or improper practices on the part of fellow members or competitors, and against the hostility experienced by sojourners at the hands of the host community), but these were bought at a cost. The cost was obedience to the guild's own authority, which rested on its indispensability to members. Guilds also offered their members certain other attractions such as conviviality, assistance in time of need, and the opportunity to participate in the most immediate political processes and to share in the exercise of some authority. They were of course particularistic and sectional in their interests and not directly concerned with the welfare of the general public, though insofar as they kept up the quality of goods and the standards of work and helped to maintain order they could be said to have served the public interest also. Their existence was recognized by the authorities, with whom guilds were in regular communication—merchant guilds through their secretaries, craft guilds through their leaders—and magistrates were frequently called on to approve guild rules, in the hope perhaps of avoiding charges under the statute on monopolies or under other government regulations.[1] The context in which they operated, we must remember, included not only the imperial administration (concerned as described above with controlling the economy) but also the prevailing intellectual climate in which the economic philosophy of the limited good was generally accepted, and the actual existence in the Chinese countryside of a permanent reservoir of surplus labor, among whom many would have been ready to leave the hardships and insecurity of the rural scene for work in the towns unless some deterrent had been placed in their way. The premise on which guilds were based (or perhaps one should say on which most of them were based) was the belief in trade as a stagnant pool. Each group watched jealously to preserve its position and to maintain the status quo between its members through such methods as putting barriers in the way of alienating another member's customers and restricting the numbers who might be taken on for training. For porters within a city, for example, additional rules delimited areas within which members might operate. The regulations of various guilds dealt directly or indirectly with the subject of debt—stipulating how and when accounts were to be settled, or setting out measures to prevent anyone who did not pay up from continuing in the trade. Guilds were concerned to avoid friction between members because group solidarity was indispensable to the pursuit of their primary objectives; and, no doubt for this reason and also in order to preserve both their strength and their "public image," the rules of some guilds ordered members not to take disputes to the yamen without first bringing them before the guild for a hearing. . . .

Adjudication is said to have been informal, and the sanctions the guilds imposed, ranging from small fines to expulsion or worse, were

---

1. Analogously, beggars had their own association rules, as did the blind. These associations would not have owned their own hall but would have met in a temple.

practical. Presumably on account of both the rotation of duties that was the practice in many guilds and the personal familiarity that existed in most, it seems likely that there may have been a "there but for the grace of God . . ." atmosphere about the proceedings. The fact that the guild premises were the scene of the occasional ritual to the patron deity no doubt added strength to any reprimand received there. Perhaps it is worth noting that whereas the diffuse character of the functions of the imperial administration militated against the usefulness of the yamen for judicial purposes (the magistrate being responsible for tax collection, the census, and land registration besides legal work), the reverse was true of the guild. The diffuseness of its activities made it more effective for purposes both of control and of adjudication: continuing personal familiarity opened up many opportunities for exerting pressure or influence, on which the effectiveness of informal adjudication rests. . . .

The control guilds exercised over their members gave them strength in conducting their external power struggles with the public, their competitors, and the imperial administration. The stance they adopted toward administrative authority varied at different times and in different instances: at some times complying with yamen demands, at others resisting, and sometimes one guild petitioning against others for a decision or action in its favor, i.e., manipulating the power of the administration for its own ends. . . .

32

The Commune
as a Social System

Martin K. Whyte

In 1955–56 China carried out collectivization throughout its rural areas. In 1958, during the Great Leap Forward campaign, the resulting collective farms were amalgamated into much larger units, the rural people's communes. Although initially the commune system was poorly organized and unwieldy, and helped to bring on a famine in which millions died, by 1962 a modified and much more manageable commune organization had been devised. With a variety of minor changes, this commune system formed the structure in which Chinese peasants operated until the early 1980s. At that point the rural reforms initiated in 1978 led to a nation-wide decollectivization, with a dismantling of much of the commune organization and a return to a modified form of family farming. In this selection Martin Whyte, a sociologist at the University of Michigan, gives a "nuts-and-bolts" account of how the people's commune system was organized.

. . . . There were 50,000 plus people's communes in China in 1980, which means each had an average size of about 15,000 people, or roughly 3,000 families. This is a somewhat smaller unit than the initial communes of 1958, but still today's communes cover a dispersed area and several dozen villages and hamlets. The commune headquarters is usually situated in the largest of these villages, often one that was a traditional market town for that area. The commune is the highest of three administrative levels, being divided into production brigades, which are in turn divided into production teams. (The average commune has about fifteen brigades and 100 teams.) The commune level of this structure has both governmental and economic functions. In terms of rural government, the registry of births and marriages, postal services, police headquarters, and other facilities are located there. Each commune also has a clinic and generally a middle school which are used by people in the surrounding villages. The commune also runs a broadcasting station, which sends its own messages as well as programs transmitted from provincial and national stations out over a spiderweb of wires to loudspeakers in each village and in many individual peasant homes.

On the economic front, the commune plays an intermediate role in agricultural planning, taking targets sent down by county authorities, dividing these up among subordinate brigades and teams, and negotiating their approval. The commune also plans and carries out projects that are too large for smaller units to run, such as dam-building and irrigation projects, and figures out how many laborers and other resources should be provided by various brigades and teams in order to complete these projects. Communes are also encouraged to set up factories to produce simple farm machinery, fertilizer, cement, and other useful products, and these enterprises provide employment for some peasants in surrounding villages. Commune authorities also supervise the procurement of grain and other crops from brigades and teams in order to meet the state's agricultural delivery obligations, and they maintain granaries where grain is stored to guard against famine. Finally, there are a variety of small shops and service facilities available in the commune town and generally at least one "free market" where peasants can sell output from their private plots and household sideline activities.

The commune is also the locus of political leadership in the countryside, featuring a commune management committee and party committee supervising all aspects of commune operations. The personnel who serve in these commune-level posts are a mixture of outsiders and natives from the local area, with outsiders more often appointed to serve in the leading positions. Most of the others employed at the commune level, including teachers, doctors, shop sales personnel in the commune town, and so forth, are classified as nonagricultural personnel and receive fixed salaries, unlike the local peasants. Even though commune cadres are supposed to spend obligatory periods engaging in agricultural labor alongside of the peasants, still the nature of these people and the way they are paid makes the commune the level at which the state's interests are most strongly considered.

There are many activities, however, that are not directly controlled by commune authorities but are managed by the subordinate brigades and teams. This fact is the basis of the relatively decentralized operation of commune administration. A production brigade encompasses about 1,000 people or 200 households on the average and will be subdivided into five to twenty teams. Brigades and teams are organized on a territorial basis rather than being specialized units engaged in particular agricultural tasks. Often a brigade consists of a large existing village or several small adjacent villages, along with the surrounding land area. A production team generally has twenty to fifty households or 100–250 people and is based upon a small hamlet or a neighborhood within a larger village, again with its adjacent land area. In general the people organized together into teams and brigades are the descendants of peasant families who have lived in a locality for centuries, and many of them will be closely related. Thus age-old solidarities and conflicts underlie these "new" farming structures.

The brigade, like the commune, has multiple functions. Often it runs a primary school and sometimes lower-middle school classes as well. It also generally has a brigade medical station staffed by "barefoot doctors," who are individuals with short-term medical training who provide simple medical care and refer cases up to the commune clinic. The brigade is also where the basic-level political organizations are located. The brigade party branch supervises the activities of the brigade management committee and takes charge of the political activities and indoctrination of all party members in the brigade. In the brigade one will also find a Communist Youth League (CYL) branch as well as basic-level units of the militia and the women's federation. . . .

The brigade also provides for a whole range of economic activities. Again an intermediate role is played in negotiating agricultural production and delivery plans between teams and higher authorities. The brigade may organize labor and other exchanges between teams to assist them in meeting their targets. Farm machinery may be purchased by the brigade and then loaned or rented out to subordinate teams as needed. Some small brigade factories may provide a few jobs for local people, as well as useful manufactures, and it is common for brigades to run grain husking mills and tool repair shops. Some brigades also have established specialized farming units—orchards, collective pigsties, and so forth—which recruit laborers from subordinate teams. The leaders of the brigade are virtually always local people, and they are not paid fixed salaries but earn "work points" whose value depends upon the incomes and work points values of the subordinate teams.

Production brigades are not, however, the organizers of daily farming in most of rural China. This is the task of the production team level of the commune, and as a consequence the activities of the team are more exclusively focused upon economics. Sometimes political study and other kinds of meetings are held, but teams are mainly concerned with organizing agricultural production. The team is led by a management committee of six to twelve members, e.g., production team head, assistant heads, work point recorder, accountant, cashier, warehouse keeper, women's leader. These leaders are all local villagers, and they are elected by the team membership, with higher level supervision and approval. These leaders also earn work points rather than fixed salaries, so their incomes are tied to the success of the team's production efforts. Teams are supposed to agree to annual plans specifying cropping patterns, expected yields, crop deliveries, and so forth, and at times these plans may deviate from the pattern of crops that local peasants think would be most suitable. But once the agricultural plan is set, the decisions about day-to-day farming are made by team leaders rather than by higher authorities. Team cadres decide which tasks need to be performed each day on the team's fields and assign individual members of work groups to perform those tasks.

Members of the team have work points recorded in their names as they perform particular tasks, and these are graded in terms of the difficulty of the job, the skill of the laborer, and other factors. In this fashion the most skilled males in their prime may earn, for instance, ten to twelve points a day; women and less skilled men may earn seven to nine points; and old, young, and sickly members may earn four to six points. These work points are totaled up in the books of the team's work point recorder and then used to determine the shares of the collective income to be paid to each family in the team. The amount of team income available for distribution in cash and in kind, which is affected by the team's yields, investment burdens, and other factors, is divided by the total number of work points earned by all members of the team to determine the value of each work point unit. This figure is then multiplied by the total number of points accumulated by all members of a family to determine the income to be distributed to that family. Thus a family's collective income is affected both by the efforts of its members and by the overall farming success of the team, and neighboring families and teams can differ very substantially in their earnings. The team is termed the "basic accounting unit," which means that the fruits of its success (or failure) in farming affect team members but not the people in other teams nearby. Cooperation is clearly involved in the team's operations, but there is not much in the way of communal sharing.

Since the early 1960s there have been shifts back and forth in the emphasis on incentives versus equality within the commune system, and each attempt to promote one of these goals has meant sacrificing the other to some extent. During the 1968–71 and 1974–76 periods, for instance, egalitarianism was the order of the day. This took several forms. In some localities the unit of accounting and management was raised up from the team to the brigade, which meant that this larger unit would be the one within which the fruits of member efforts would be shared. Some localities eliminated private plots and closed peasant free markets also, in an attempt to encourage maximum devotion to the collective economy (farming the team's fields) and reduce the income disparities private sources of income produced. Localities were also pressured to grow grain even when local conditions were suited for cash crops, and higher authorities in some places tried to place upper limits on the incomes peasant families could earn. These efforts were apparently motivated by the conviction of radical elements in China's leadership that more emphasis on collectivism and equality were necessary to develop agriculture and check capitalist tendencies in the countryside. The result, however, was growing peasant discontent and stagnating agricultural production.

Since 1976 these policies have been repudiated, and by 1980 the pendulum had swung all the way back to a predominate emphasis on incentives and rural differentiation. Team autonomy and private plots and free markets were to be protected and expanded, and attempts to limit peasant incomes were denounced. Localities were being encouraged to specialize more in crops suitable for their locality and to think of new activities that would enable them to "grow rich." In terms of rural social structure, the most important changes involved modifications in the incentive system and a willingness to view some fundamental features of the commune as alterable rather than sacrosanct. In many localities permanent work groups within the team have been formed and given responsibility for farming specific areas of the team's land. These work groups are given production targets to fulfill, and if they surpass these they can distribute a proportion of the excess to work group members as rewards. In Sichuan and some other localities this "contracting down" has even extended to the level of the household. Individual families are assigned to farm a plot of land (or to raise a number of pigs, or tend fruit trees) and again are able to earn rewards for overfulfilling the contracts they receive from their teams. These reforms seem to threaten team solidarity and promote income differentiation within the team, and they remain quite controversial. A similar kind of family sharecropping within the framework of collectivized agriculture was practiced in the early 1960s, and it was later denounced as a dangerous deviation from socialist principles. . . .

There is a final level of rural social organization yet to consider: the peasant family. In spite of occasional political rhetoric about putting the interests of the state before one's own family, in fact the family remains the basic unit of rural life. The general pattern has already been noted. Peasants live in family units alongside others with whom they have relationships of kinship and neighborliness stretching back over centuries. Almost everywhere the housing they live in is privately built and owned, and building a new home requires a lengthy period of saving and often assistance from relatives. Families also still have a corporate economic identity even when contracting down to the household is not practiced in the locality. Work point incomes from the team are paid to the family head rather than to each individual laborer. The family also carries out a variety of private moneymaking activities: growing produce on the family's private plot, raising pigs and fowl, engaging in household handicrafts, marketing these goods in nearby free markets, and so forth. Together these activities are likely to yield 30 percent or so of the family's total income and a higher proportion of their disposable cash income. (Much collective income from the team is distributed in kind—in the form of grain rations.) Families may also have members working in commune factories or engaged in short- or long-term labor outside of the commune and sending remittances back to the family. Families thus have complicated economic management tasks to engage in even though the organization of day-to-day farming is carried out by the team and not individual families. Team leaders realize they have to take family interests into account if they are to receive motivated efforts by peasants in the team's fields, for they know that discontented peasants can always reduce their efforts for the team and devote themselves more exclusively to these private moneymaking activities.

Families remain central to rural life in still other ways. Meals are prepared and eaten in the home in family units. Most young children are cared for by grandparents rather than being raised in collective nursery schools. There is also no general system of old age pensions except on an experimental basis in some wealthy suburban communes. So support of the aged falls upon the family as well. In general, then, in important ways peasants still depend heavily upon their families and not solely upon their commune or the state.

How then has socialism transformed rural social organization? First, the fact that the commune organization is built on top of preexisting village and family units means that the success of the commune depends upon its fit with these traditional social forms. The state, in attempting to bring about change, must work through local leaders who are not paid by the state, people who are bound by obligations and loyalties to the peasants they are supposed to be leading. Because of this somewhat indirect form of CCP rule in the countryside, it is difficult to implement changes that do not accord with peasant perceptions of village needs and interests and family obligations. This does not mean that changes do not occur and that peasants preserve all their traditional ways intact. Rather, change occurs in many areas of rural life in an indirect fashion, as the changing economic, health, and other environments of peasants undermine some old customs while sustaining and preserving others. At times the state has become frustrated with the slow pace of change in the countryside and has tried to speed things up by demanding compliance and by sending in outside work teams to enforce new policies. In most such instances more problems have been created than solved, and the state has had to back off and mend its fences with the peasantry. In sum, in recent years the commune organization has taken on a fairly stable institutional form that allows peasants to pursue the interests of their families and their villages, but as a consequence the state has not been able to force the pace of further change.

A further implication of commune organization and the system of migration restrictions mentioned earlier affects the mobility prospects of rural youths. Since there are such limited chances of mobility into the towns, most rural males end up settling down in their native villages, and this helps to sustain the solidarity of rural families. (Rural females move at marriage into the home of their husbands in keeping with traditional practice.) This fact of rural life also helps to prevent the draining of young talent away from the countryside, but by the same token it deprives most talented and ambitious rural youths of the chance to compete for positions in the larger society, which may be a source of personal frustration. The limited mobility out of or between villages also prevents poor localities from gaining relief from excess population pressure. The relative stability and closure of rural populations also contributes to a strong sense of corporate interest on the part of individual teams and brigades which inhibits broader cooperation and may even contribute to rivalry and conflict between such units. So the current structure promotes solidary families, teams, and brigades, but the consequences of this solidarity are not all favorable.

33

A Chinese Hospital

Gail E. Henderson and Myron S. Cohen

Although a number of in-depth accounts of village life in the PRC are now
available, we have very few comparable descriptions of what daily life is like in
Chinese urban neighborhoods and work organizations. Gail Henderson, a soci-
ologist, and her husband, Myron Cohen, a medical researcher, were able to live
for half a year in a provincial hospital in the city of Wuhan in central China in
1979–80. This excerpt, from their larger monograph on hospital organization
and the medical-care system in China, provides a rare look into one Chinese work
organization.

The *Danwei* and China

The importance of the work unit *[danwei]* lies primarily in its unique
combination of social, political, and economic life—much like an "urban
village." During the first decade of Communist rule, all workplaces in
urban China (factories, schools, hospitals, stores, government offices)
were organized into administrative units. This move was accompanied
by the restriction of free migration into urban areas, the socialization
of Chinese industry and commerce, and the centralization of job and
housing assignment by the state. Each work unit was placed under the
jurisdiction of its appropriate occupational bureaucracy—a hospital under the Ministry of Health, a university under the Ministry of Education. Units also are under the authority of other administrative bodies

concerned with the allocation of personnel, the provision of services, and the maintenance of public security. . . .

Work units are thus firmly embedded both in the economic hierarchy of a socialist government and in the parallel political administration of the Chinese Communist party. They are characterized by a fairly stable staff population, and the larger *danwei* also provide housing and other services. These factors combine to produce an intense and unique environment in which many functions of society and of family life take place. . . .

Danwei are isolated from each other in relatively closed systems, dependent upon higher levels for the source of their power and authority over members. The *danwei* system is, of course, not the sole force affecting the lives of work unit members. Other factors include the family, relationships with people outside the *danwei*, membership in neighborhood organizations, the power of the professional within a bureaucratic organization, constraints on middle-level leaders, and the influence of the Communist party and other national organizations. Nevertheless, the *danwei* has an extraordinary influence on its individual members and (in our case) on the formal and informal relations among the hospital administrators, doctors, nurses, and patients. . . .

Daily Life in the *Danwei*

The hospital complex, its staff dormitories, and various auxiliary buildings are located by a lake on the outskirts of the fifth largest city in China, Wuhan.[1] As a teaching hospital, it serves the needs of the medical college, which is adjacent to the hospital grounds. As a provincial-level hospital, it treats patients referred from fifteen counties in the province, with a combined population of some 7 million. The total population of the province is 33 million.

There are several entrances to the hospital *danwei* from the main road, which winds along the lake. Unmarked gateways and some well-trodden dirt paths lead to apartment buildings of varying style, height, and age. Farther down the road, the main entrance gate exhibits a black and white sign, "SECOND ATTACHED HOSPITAL OF HUBEI PROVINCIAL MEDICAL COLLEGE UNDER THE ADMINISTRATION OF THE PROVINCIAL BUREAU

---

1. Wuhan comprises the three cities of Wuchang, Hankou, and Hanyang, located at the junction of the Han and Yangzi rivers.

OF HEALTH." Heavy wrought-iron gates hang on either side of an eight-foot wall that gives the impression of encircling the entire hospital complex.

From the front gate, a short road ends in a circular driveway in front of the main hospital building. A tall pine tree in the center of the driveway obscures the view of a four-story, Soviet-style hospital constructed of graying cement during the fifties. Jeeps, Shanghai-brand sedans, white ambulances, bikes, hand-pulled carts containing produce or patients, and a variety of people dressed in either white coats or the ubiquitous dark-blue, gray, or army green populate the drive at all times. The pace is unhurried. In warm weather, benches are brought outside for hospital staff to sun themselves on the steps. Peasants arrive to sell their vegetables or fruit, and news of unusual items for sale quickly spreads through the hospital. Except on the coldest days, an old vendor stands beside the front door offering visitors a final chance to purchase bread, cookies, and cigarettes.

Outside the front gate, more people wait at the bus stop to be taken to the city or to the nearby countryside. The buses are white and blue, and often two are joined by an accordionlike black material that looks as if it should expand and contract as the crowds push in and out in massive numbers. Behind the bus stop are a green post office, housing its worker and his family in the back, and a small food store. In front of this store, a tiny old woman with few remaining teeth sets up a fire pot and wok to sell a kind of deep-fried bread *(mianwo)* that is a local speciality. When it rains, she cooks with one hand and holds her umbrella with the other.

The hospital is surrounded by low bushes that often function as natural clotheslines for patients or their relatives to dry freshly washed clothes. Occasionally the garments are little more than tatters, but they are repeatedly washed and dried until the last bit of usefulness is pounded out of them. The hospital grounds consist of packed dirt and low-lying shrubs or small pine trees. Near the medical college are several wooded sections in which medical students pace back and forth with books in hand. At the slightest rain, the grounds become impassable. Cement sidewalks and narrow roads wind around the hospital and back by all the staff apartments so that a jeep or truck can reach most sections.

As one faces the hospital, the staff apartments are to the left, specialized or newly constructed facilities at the back, and the medical college on the right. Bricks lie in large and small piles in every empty lot, tangible evidence of the constantly changing physical environment. In the midst of the bricks, chickens scratch, children create makeshift platforms for table tennis, and construction teams are rarely absent. The apartment buildings are brick and cement. The older ones are one story high, with communal kitchens and baths for several families in individual three-room apartments. The newest buildings are four- and five-story cement structures housing one hundred families. In addition to housing, the unit includes a dining hall, a day-care center, a bathhouse attached to the hospital boiler room, an administrative office, a garage for unit cars and jeeps, and shops for the maintenance and repair staff (plumbers, carpenters, electricians). Behind the hospital, construction of a new pharmaceutical factory is under way. From this point it takes no more than five or ten minutes to walk to the front of the unit.

The medical college facilities are spread over a campus slightly larger than the hospital grounds. They include several teaching buildings, a library, student dormitories, a dining hall, an athletic field, administrative offices, and several small college-run industries. Because land is scarce even on the outskirts of the city, the housing, dining hall, food store, day-care center, and primary school for the medical college staff are all located on the other side of the hospital grounds, beyond the hospital staff apartments.

Not all of the approximately 830 people who work at the hospital live in the *danwei*. Some live with parents or spouses in other work units and travel each day by bus or bicycle, sometimes commuting as much as an hour each way. Likewise, not all the people in each household work in the *danwei*. Some spouses or children leave the unit each morning for employment elsewhere. However, approximately two-thirds of those who work in the hospital live in the hospital's apartments or single staff dormitories, and many spouses and even some children are employed by the *danwei*. The walls and gates and the close proximity of most services create an atmosphere of people working and living together in a somewhat closed community. The profusion of shared experiences, the necessary cooperation, and the routines performed by all sharpen the sense of community.

The daily rhythm of routine events creates a backdrop for the larger dramas of life and work. Very early each morning, the individually and collectively raised chickens combine their voices in a discordant chorus calling all to rise. For breakfast, most people send one member of the family out to the dining hall to pick up steamed bread, oil cakes,

or dumplings. Those too late for a family meal will munch their breakfast on the short walk to the hospital. People carrying kettles and ther-
moses line up at the hospital boiled-water faucet, which is directly attached to the boiler room. A sign over the faucet praises the hospital for
providing such a convenience to its staff. Occasionally a woman waits
with a metal pan and tiny stool or chair, preparing to wash out some
clothes or perhaps quickly wash her own hair in the hot-water drain,
which runs alongside the drinking-water faucet. After breakfast, mothers and fathers carry their tightly bundled children to the day-care
center. Even in mild weather, the children are wrapped in several layers
of blankets, quilts, and padded clothing. Toddlers are led by the hand,
and school-age children dressed in colorful jackets walk with playmates
and neighbors to the primary school, which serves the families of both
the hospital and the medical school staff. The local high school is a
ten-minute walk down the main road that runs along the lake.

By eight, everyone has disappeared except the logistics or service
staff *(houqing)*, who are getting food and laundry ready for the day, and
a few grandparents tending young children in an apartment courtyard.
Periodically, the morning silence is broken by the sounds of construction
teams moving bricks from their stacks in empty lots to some new project
in the unit. These unskilled workers are often young men and women
waiting for job assignments by the state. Their main task is to pile bricks
into wheelbarrows and push, pull, or run downhill with them in an
effort to keep them under control and moving toward the construction
site. As they pick up speed, the wheelbarrows sometimes get away from
the young workers, overturning in a crash of bricks at the bottom of the
hill. Everyone knows to keep out of the path of the speeding wheelbarrows.

At noon, people pour out of the buildings and stop by the dining
hall to purchase a square-shaped portion of rice or several squares for
a family. The portions never seem to fit well into the rectangular metal
containers used as food plates, and the large rice squares protrude precariously as people rush out. To avoid the ten- or fifteen-minute wait
for lunch, some carry their rice home and cook vegetables in their own
kitchens. Others, for convenience and to save home fuel, buy their lunch
and either take it home or eat it at the dining hall. Food coupons are
sold by the dining hall accountant each month for use only at a prescribed eating place, and only this currency can be used. In addition,
government ration coupons for items such as wheat and sugar are re-

quired at dining halls and stores. An individual may eat modestly at the dining hall for 20 yuan a month (U.S. $13.20) or very well for 30-40 yuan.[2] Most agree that home cooking is better and a little cheaper, but the dining hall is chosen for convenience.

Directly after the noon meal, everyone not on duty lies down for an hour's rest *(xiuxi)*. In the heat of summer, this nap may extend to two hours. Primary school children are home, but the day-care youngsters take their naps at the center from noon until three. The *danwei* is very quiet until about half past one, when people begin to stir and get ready to go back to work or school by two. People who live in other nearby work units usually ride their bicycles home for lunch and a rest. Those who live too far away may lie down in the on-call room or visit with friends. Some take noon duty more frequently so that they can leave earlier in the afternoon.

Except for those people on evening or night shifts, the work day ends around five or half past five. At that time, the hospital staff stroll back to their homes. Parents pick up their babies and young children from the day-care center, where the older ones are dressed in their coats and hats, sitting in neat semicircles. A long line forms at the hot-water faucet. Families with a newspaper on order send one member to the front gate office, where unit mail, journals, and newspapers are received. If the weather permits, children play on the sidewalks until they are called for dinner. Evening meals are often prepared at home, especially in families in which a mother or mother-in-law is home to begin preparations early. Those with busy schedules or night duty take advantage of dining hall services, and staff working all night are given another meal at ten. Children whose parents are away for the night often stay at home alone. There are some "latchkey" children in the unit, but neighbors are at most only a shout away, and from the age of eight or ten, children are left alone.

After supper things quiet down. In pleasant weather, families may go for a walk or sit out on their balconies. Children are put to bed, and many adults engage in some sort of studying. When there is an outdoor movie, families can be seen at twilight, each member carrying a stool or chair to sit on during the show. Families with television sets are visited by those without. In general, evenings are uneventful, and people are

---

2. An exchange rate of $1.00 U.S. = 1.50 yuan is used.

in bed between ten and eleven. The only sound ever to disturb our night's sleep (besides our own daughter's cries) was the screeching of a wild cat in heat. . . .

Housing and Family Life

Even when one is assigned to work in an urban *danwei*, housing at that work unit is not guaranteed. Many *danwei*, particularly in crowded cities such as Shanghai or Guangzhou (Canton), have simply run out of room for staff dormitories. In these cases, people live in urban neighborhoods and commute to work. Housing in our *danwei* is said to be typical of factories, schools, and city and county hospitals in less congested urban areas. Approximately two-thirds of the hospital staff live on the grounds, and it is estimated that 70 to 80 percent of all hospital and medical staff are married to each other.

It is certainly more efficient for the work unit to house couples who work for the hospital or its parent and neighbor organization, the medical college. Physicians and researchers who meet in school can logically be assigned to the same type of work unit. Likewise, among staff such as low-level administrators, service personnel, or workers in the unit's auxiliary organizations, a strong attempt is made to find work for both spouses or to give them both training for jobs in the same *danwei*. It is not uncommon for single people assigned to the unit to pair off and marry. There seemed to be a feeling that, as one person put it, it was "not appropriate for people of unequal education to marry." This sentiment was borne out in our observations of young people with similar occupations and educational degrees pairing up, as well as the very common occurrence of husbands and wives having the same or similar occupations.

In many countries, the size and location of one's housing is testimony to one's status. In China such distinctions may be true to some extent, but they are complicated by several factors. First, the only immediately apparent segregation in our *danwei* was that between single and married people. In a family-oriented society such as China, unmarried people may be its most disadvantaged minority. Their dormitories are sex segregated, with up to three persons living in a rather small room at a cost of about one yuan per person per month. A new staff member who is bringing a family, even if the spouse also works at the unit, must wait years to be assigned housing, in some cases as much as ten years.

In the meantime, the couple may live in the spouse's unit, find a room with parents, or occasionally live separately until housing is found. In our *danwei*, the major determinants in obtaining an assignment to "nice" housing seemed to be length of association with the unit, luck, a policy to restore those persecuted during the Cultural Revolution to the equivalent of their previous quarters, and probably connections with the *danwei* leadership or housing office. Thus it was not at all uncommon to find doctors living next door to cooks or hospital maintenance workers. The director of the hospital, for example, lived in an apartment below a garage mechanic. Perhaps in response to earlier abuses by officials, the *danwei* administrators maintained a low profile in terms of housing. While we were there, they even moved out of their offices and worked in temporary structures in order to provide more space for unit members who had been waiting years to be assigned housing.

We were often told that living conditions in our *danwei* were better than those of other urban settings. Most of the apartment buildings have been constructed since 1949, and two new apartment buildings had just been completed. The standard apartment, for which families pay about five yuan per month, consists of an eating area, two bedrooms, and a small kitchen and bathroom.[3] The parents' bedroom usually doubles as a living room. An attempt is made to place larger families in more substantial apartments, but because most apartments have the same number of rooms, people with many children simply devise means to accommodate them within limited space. When children are young, they sleep with their parents. As they grow older, children may share beds; one family we knew with three boys in one room constructed bunk beds. When the eldest children are old enough for job assignment, they may obtain housing in other *danwei* or live with relatives. As children begin to find their own mates, the second bedroom often becomes the room for a married son and perhaps a grandchild. . . .

---

3. Of the five yuan, two are for rent and three are for utilities.

34

My Neighborhood

B. Michael Frolic

B. Michael Frolic is a Canadian political scientist who has done research on urban organization in both the Soviet Union and China. The following excerpt from interviews conducted in Hong Kong with a woman who had served as an officer in a residents' committee in Shanghai illustrates both the rewarding solidarity and the oppressive control that this distinctive form of urban organization can achieve at the same time.

I am fifty-two years old and have three children, all of them married. My husband is a machine tool operator and makes a good salary, 78 yuan a month. I used to work in a textile factory when I was younger, but I stopped in 1963 because of my health. I suffer from high blood pressure and got dizzy while working at the machines. Also the noise was affecting my hearing. Luckily my two eldest children were already working, so the loss of my income wasn't a burden on the household. Only one of them was still living with us. The others had their own families, and my number-one son lived far away in Xian, where he was a teacher. After I retired from work (I had been working since I was twelve years old), the Party decided to recommend me for membership in our local residents' committee. I'm not a Party member, but that doesn't matter a bit. Actually most members of the residents' committee are just housewives like myself or pensioners.

I guess they chose me because I had lived in that neighborhood, in the same building, since 1956. I knew most of the people in our building by name and all about their personal backgrounds and problems. Not that I'm a snoop or gossip, mind you, but I like to talk with people and find out about them. When the Party first asked me about becoming a member of the residents' committee, I was hesitant; I replied that I wanted to wait a while to see about my blood pressure and also to catch up on a few household matters. I also expressed concern that I was almost illiterate—I really could only read a few slogans that I knew by heart and could only draw a few simple characters. "Never mind," the Party cadre said, "it's not your fault that you can't read and write very well. You've worked hard for thirty years and when you were little, you didn't have the chance. Now that you've retired, the Party will help you, so don't worry." His words were reassuring because I was embarrassed about my illiteracy. The Party cadre did ask me to make up my mind soon, because the woman now responsible for our building was in bad health and couldn't continue much longer. Well, after three months I decided I wanted the job, and within a month it was mine.

For the next nine years I was a member of that residents' committee, and it was like a full-time job. There were eighteen members on the committee and I was responsible for my building, containing forty-seven households and totaling over two hundred people. You can imagine that with this many people there were always things to do and problems to settle—there were many days where I was so busy that I didn't have time to take care of my own household. Fortunately my husband was a modern man and was willing to help out. Many days after his shift ended at 4:00, he did the afternoon shopping and helped prepare the evening meal. My daughter-in-law (second son's wife) also helped occasionally, but she worked the evening shift at her factory and slept in the dormitory there. So she usually only stayed with us one or two nights a week. It wasn't so bad, really, and I loved my new work. At the beginning I wasn't sure whether my friends in the building would change their feelings toward me, now that I was a member of the residents' committee. It was no secret that the people didn't always welcome our presence. We had called my predecessor Old Snoop, Meddler, and other such nicknames behind her back. Most residents felt that the committee spent more time poking its nose into personal business and prying into people's lives than in acting on behalf of the residents. One of my neighbors asked me bluntly before I took the job, "Do you really want to do this? Your relations with your friends won't be the same anymore. They'll never speak their minds when you're around. They'll always think of you as someone who is going to cause them trouble. You know how people feel about the residents' committee: it's like a little policeman always checking up on us."

Actually the job turned out better than I had expected. True, my neighbor was right: my relations with old friends had changed. Nothing I could point to with any certainty, mind you, but they were more reserved in my presence now and we didn't do much gossiping together anymore. On the other hand, I was so busy that I didn't have much time to bring out my little wooden stool and sit around gossiping. Now I was either at meetings, organizing some sort of activity, or solving a problem. With over two hundred people in one building, I just couldn't keep an eye on everything, and I had help from four activists who were each responsible for one of the entranceways into which the building was subdivided. These activists weren't members of the residents' committee, but they were our eyes and ears in each of the entranceways. You know that in Shanghai, as in other large cities, the four-story apartment building built in the fifties is really a separate housing unit with four separate entrances and staircases. People don't just have an address such as "No. 10 building, such and such neighborhood," but you must add, "No. 10 building, No. 2 entranceway" as well as the neighborhood and street. Each entranceway has twelve apartments, divided into one, two, and three bedrooms (the three-bedroom apartments are only on the ground floor, and they are the most desirable). The activist in each of these entranceways was an older woman, who was either widowed or retired and who enjoyed organizing and checking on residents. Three times a week I met with my activists at my place to discuss problems and to assign them their duties. I got on well with them, although I knew that the residents didn't care for them because one of their main duties was to check up on illegal residents and to settle household arguments. The activists were the ones who showed up at night with the local police, not me, so the residents didn't like them. I had some problems for a while with the residents of No. 3 entranceway because the activist there, a retired worker, was too zealous in her job. But eventually she was right: through her vigilance we caught two illegal residents, one of them a bad element, and during the Cultural Revolution she was one of the leaders in the neighborhood struggle against revisionism and class enemies.

In fact most of the work of the residents' committee had little to do with snooping on other people's affairs or with looking for class enemies. We devoted a large part of our time to public health and sanitation. For example, we conducted campaigns to get rid of flies, cockroaches, rats, and mice. In June and July we gave everybody powder to burn in their apartments. I think it was called 666. This smoked up the apartment and killed all the pests. We made sure people did it properly and that they stayed out of their apartments for six hours afterwards. We ran campaigns to tell parents to get their children vaccinated against chicken pox, small pox, measles, and scarlet fever. Sometimes it took a lot of persuasion—many parents were still reluctant to trust vaccinations and others simply had no time to spare. So we knocked on doors and held special meetings and hung up posters that told residents about vaccinations. In the summer we warned everybody about encephalitis, what its symptoms were and how you could catch it from mosquitoes. We urged people to report any serious sickness like that at once so it wouldn't spread. Once we had three cases of encephalitis in one entranceway. We sprayed the place with disinfectant and got rid of all the mosquitoes. Then we inoculated all the children at the local clinic with a special encephalitis vaccine.

In 1964 we began a major birth control program, holding meetings in which we talked about the need to plan family growth. Actually it wasn't much of a problem in our neighborhood, since families weren't that large. Mine was one of the largest, but then I had my children before Liberation. We were mainly trying to get younger couples to postpone having children for a while, so that the wife would work longer and there would be fewer children per household. This wasn't difficult to do in Shanghai because families weren't as large as in some other cities, and certainly much smaller than in the countryside. We talked to the women and gave information about contraception, what devices to use and how to use them. During the Cultural Revolution, we dispensed birth control pills free of charge to all married women. First we held a mass meeting, usually of all women in a building, to explain about birth control and the possibilities involved. Then the entranceway activists visited individual families to talk with them, especially with the husbands who, though fairly enlightened, didn't pay much attention to our efforts. We often brought along the doctor from the local clinic to explain birth control methods. We didn't talk much about vasectomies because the men didn't want to listen. Abortion was available on demand, however. Also, for 5 yuan you could get fitted with an IUD. We persuaded one woman to have her tubes tied after she had her fourth child, despite preventive methods. I think our efforts were successful because over the next decade the number of children in our neighborhood did drop.

The residents' committee kept the neighborhood clean and secure, and that was an important duty. I went around personally from time to time on inspection trips or on special clean-up campaigns. Each entranceway had to be swept up, and any garbage had to be put away daily. We checked for fire hazards and in the winter made sure residents remembered to keep a supply of fresh air coming into their rooms while they had the stove on. Each year hundreds of careless people in China are asphyxiated because of the fumes from their coal stoves. We tried our best to make the neighborhood look nice and clean; that wasn't always so easy, however, because the city Housing Administration was responsible for maintaining and repairing the buildings and they wouldn't give us any money for painting or repairing. Sometimes we used extra supplies from political campaigns to do some painting or patching. When there was a real emergency and the Housing Administration refused to come (for example, if a ceiling had fallen down), we put pressure on the street committee to get the Housing Administration to do something. We weren't always successful, but at least we tried.

We also kept a sharp eye out for unwelcome strangers lurking around our neighborhood. If you didn't do that, you'd find sooner or later that something important was missing. I remember that in 1969 a bicycle was taken from the courtyard. It just happened that the activist who normally kept an eye on that courtyard was at a meeting. Someone had seen a young man passing through from the street entrance. It was probably a "black youth" who stole the bike for cash so he could survive a bit longer in the city.[1] That bike wouldn't stay for long in Shanghai; it would quickly be sold to a gang of thieves, who would then resell it in the countryside where second-hand bikes didn't have to be licensed.

We locked our doors when we were away and at night cleared the courtyard of personal belongings. The activist on duty always called out around 10:00: "Come and take in your bicycles. It's ten o'clock." Only a fool would leave anything out after that. When we were at home around the building, however, we didn't lock our doors and even left them wide

---

1. "Black youth" are sent-down youth who have returned to the city illegally from the countryside. They do not have a residence permit and cannot legally obtain ration cards or a job.

open while we were outside talking, doing the laundry, or eating on the stoop. We wouldn't steal from each other, but you had to be on guard against "outsiders," and I don't mean class enemies either, but just ordinary thieves and bad people *(huai ren)*. During the Cultural Revolution you had to be particularly vigilant because you couldn't be sure that a so-called revolutionary wasn't simply a thief in disguise. Between 1966 and 1971 we were especially careful about people coming into the neighborhood from outside. Once a group of Red Guards burst in looking for trouble, but we managed to send them on their way since we didn't have any class enemies living in our building and most of us were factory workers or pensioners. So after we read each other quotations from Chairman Mao's Thought, we sent them on their way to continue "raising high the banner of revolution."

During the Cultural Revolution I had plenty to do. The residents' committee was constantly relaying the latest instructions to the neighborhood, mobilizing people in support of new policies, and organizing political study sessions, sometimes two or three a day. So much political pressure soon took its toll: my health deteriorated and I had to stay in the hospital for several weeks. Luckily my daughter-in-law had given up her dormitory room and was now living with us, so she helped out with the cooking and shopping. I recovered quickly, however, and was soon back at my job. . . .

Life in our neighborhood settled down after the Cultural Revolution. Less of my time was spent on political campaigns. . . . The residents' committee again was doing a lot of public hygiene and sanitation work, as well as maintaining the security of the neighborhood. We also spent a great deal of time in settling disputes among the residents. As a matter of fact, it seemed as if our building was always erupting into quarrels and arguments. . . .

In my thinking about my work as a member of the residents' committee, I would say that I enjoyed it a lot. What I lost because my former friends no longer trusted me, I gained in understanding how different people behave and how they respond to authority. I left China feeling that we try too hard to control people's lives and we keep too tight a rein on what they do after work in their homes. Here in Hong Kong, however, neighborhood life is so impersonal that I wonder if my Shanghai experience couldn't somehow be applied here. Maybe we should try to organize some type of Hong Kong residents' committee—not to snoop on people or to mobilize them politically, but just to help them keep the place clean, to take pride in their surroundings, or simply to get them to know one another. What's missing in Hong Kong is people in the neighborhood feeling part of some group. In Hong Kong almost everyone is a stranger. As a result there is dirt and chaos, and people don't care about each other. In China there's too much control and in Hong Kong there's not enough; at least that's how I feel right now after a year of living in Hong Kong.

35

Connections

Zheng Yefu

This essay by Zheng Yefu is another product of the newly revived sociology in China. Zheng, a researcher in the Sociology Office of the Beijing Social Sciences Institute, offers here not an empirical study, but a theoretical analysis and critique of a disturbing social tendency. In his view, recent developments in China have revived and reinforced a traditional tendency for Chinese to rely on personal connections to get ahead or simply to cope with life. (Chapter 20 provides a vivid example of how such connections have worked in the past.) The proliferation of what Chinese call "connections networks" (guanxi wang) undermines community solidarity and faith in the system and orients Chinese to compete against their neighbors and colleagues in the effort to gain special favors.

Over the long history of Chinese feudal society, the atmosphere of "stressing human feelings and emphasizing personal connections" (*jiang renqing, zhong guanxi*) has prevailed in every realm—among officials and scholars, within secret societies, and in villages. Although in almost every dynasty there were honest officials, such as Bao Zheng and Hai Rui, they could never counter this general tendency.[1] For thousands of years, reliance on connections continued to exist from generation to genera-

---

1. These two individuals earned fame in Chinese history as officials who sacrificed their power in order to challenge corrupt emperors. Hai Rui is especially significant in the history of the PRC because his name was invoked to legitimize criticism of Mao Zedong in the early 1960s. The Cultural Revolution was launched in 1965 with an attack on a play whose hero was Hai Rui.—*Trans.*

tion. In feudal society, *guanxi* were the talisman used by people to manage their lives, and by officials to get promoted; they were both the morality and the law of society—they were the underpinning of all of social life. With the establishment of the new China, we were for a time successful in sweeping away this rubbish, and thus we went through the "naive" 1950s and the "devout" 1960s. However, as a result of the ten years of chaos of the Cultural Revolution, the tendency of stressing human feelings and private connections has, like the genie in *The Arabian Nights,* reemerged from the bottle and grown in an instant from a small wisp of smoke into an uncontrollable monster. Now once again it has penetrated every corner of our society—in all realms, for big things and small things, for public and private things, if you don't rely on *guanxi* nothing gets done. Of course greedy people are delighted to use connections, but even upright people can't get by without relying on them—through looking for "a way," and studying some "connections-ology." Of course, calls for justice never end, and by their day-to-day joking and cursing of the reliance on connections people reveal their hatred of it. But they can do nothing to stop it, and in fact they are controlled by this atmosphere to a great extent. What a bizarre phenomenon! This phenomenon has a basis in our history and in our current society. It is both contradictory to the spirit of our times and indicative of current social problems; it is both hated and utilized by all. Our writers have already exposed this phenomenon with detailed and vivid descriptions. It is time for us sociologists to make an analysis of it based upon its historical origins, its contemporary reality, and its theoretical basis. This article presents a brief analysis of reliance on connections in the hope of arousing public attention and stimulating discussion of this major social problem.

Poverty and Reliance on Connections

This sort of "reliance on connections" is inseparable from poverty. Some popular sayings of recent years reflect this phenomenon. For example, "A stethoscope, a steering wheel, and a sales clerk are three precious things. " The three kinds of people referred to in the saying were at the center of connection activities not because they were so important, but because people made demands upon them. Shop clerks had the petty power to control the selling of goods; drivers had the ability to travel to other places and markets, and in the situation of general scarcity, this became a very valuable resource. As for doctors, people sought them out for a variety of reasons. But for many it was not because they were ill, but rather because they wanted a certificate of illness. "Educated youths" who had been assigned to the countryside needed certificates of illness to be able to come back to the cities, and other people had a variety of similar motives. If we study what it was that gave these occupations their special powers at the time, we see that in many cases during the Cultural Revolution period connections were used to cope with the basic necessities of life—getting back to the cities, getting employment, and so forth. The extensive poverty and the difficulties of the period were one of the important reasons for the change in social atmosphere. If it had not been for these real difficulties in livelihood, then the butcher in Mo Yingfeng's short story would not have become an "emperor,"[2] and doctors, drivers, and sales clerks could not have become so important in the hearts of citizens, or at least connections would not have become so dominant in daily life. In a society with poverty it is easy for corruption to grow, and on the contrary in a wealthy society it is easy to eliminate this atmosphere. Marx said,

> The reason there must be a development of production forces is also because if there is not such development poverty will be widespread, and in this kind of extreme poverty, people must struggle anew for all the basic necessities of life, and in this situation all the old and decayed things will revive.

It goes without saying that the poverty that characterized the Cultural Revolution years is one of the reasons for the revival of that outworn thing, reliance on connections. Imagine if the pork supply was unlimited—who then would be willing to seek help subserviently just for a few pounds of pork? And if bicycles were freely sold, there is no chance that the son of the cadre in charge of bicycle distribution would get arrested for selling a bicycle coupon.[3]

Poverty encourages unhealthy tendencies. But on the other hand,

---

2. This story, entitled "The Butcher Emperor," describes how the shortages of pork enabled a butcher to become arrogant and overbearing.

3. Pork, grain, bicycles, and dozens of other items were rationed during the Cultural Revolution decade, and a black market trade in ration coupons sprang up.—*Trans.*

when unhealthy tendencies abound, the economy cannot prosper. When connections penetrate the education field, they interfere with the selection of the best talents to be trained; when connections permeate the personnel field, the selection and promotion of officials depends upon personal relations; when connections penetrate into production, they interfere with payment according to contributions and harm labor enthusiasm; when connections permeate into commerce, those who have connections are like fish in water, but the money of those who don't have connections might as well be scrap paper.[4] All of these outcomes imply to people that working hard isn't necessary—the important thing is to build a network of connections. This is the highly corrosive effect on our social life of reliance on connections. This atmosphere is incompatible with social progress and the Four Modernizations. As for the question of whether poverty causes the emphasis on connections, or vice versa, this is something like the question of "the chicken and the egg." But the difference is that the chicken and the egg are linked together in mutual causation by evolution, whereas the relation between poverty and reliance on connections is a vicious circle. The less of the unhealthy atmosphere of relying on connections there is, the more society and the economy can progress; and the higher the level of economic development, the more there is the desire and ability to stop this reliance, so that over a period of time this problem can be basically eliminated.

Reliance on *guanxi* and poverty are inseparable, but economic development is still not a sufficient condition for the elimination of this phenomenon. Since social interests can never be totally egalitarian, and since the desires of some people know no limits, if there are no institutions and laws to put limits on power, then power will continue to be affected by personal relationships and will be used to serve selfish interests.

---

4. The metaphor used by the author here immediately brings to mind the short story, "The Big Fish," by Chen Jo-hsi, from her collection, *The Execution of Mayor Yin* (Bloomington: Indiana University Press, 1978). In that story an old man goes out to buy a fish to cook for his ailing wife. He makes a purchase but is then forced to give his big fish back when it is determined that the sale was a "mistake." The fish are "display items" kept out to impress foreign visitors.—*Trans.*

The Legal System and Reliance on Connections

Thus the reliance on connections is also a product of the lack of development of our legal system. In societies with a well-developed legal system, it is difficult for personal relations to penetrate into the realms of the economy and administration. Without a doubt personal relationships are a source of warmth, and social life without them is impossible. But they are antithetical to a rational legal system. In all of public life they should be kept under institutionalized constraints and be held in check by definite norms, so that taking advantage of personal relationships and weaving connections, if carried to an extreme, will be seen as violations of discipline and law. Unfortunately, the reliance on connections is generally seen as legal, or at least not illegal. For example, most of the educated youths sent to the countryside have now returned to the large cities, and many of them used connections and took advantage of personal relationships to open the door to get back. But who among them in the last analysis did not have the proper procedures followed, in order to make their transfer "legal?" In work units where employees complain that too many children of cadres and of families connected to them have been given jobs, the leaders may try to pacify them by announcing, "If you can find one who was hired by the back door, then that person will be immediately fired." It should be understood that the distinctive characteristic of this "new" reliance on connections is its "legality," since it is legitimized by going through the required procedures. The people in power can take good care of those connected with them and still be within the boundaries of what is "not illegal." That is to say, relying on connections includes both acts that are illegal and acts that can be considered "legal." Most such acts are between the extremes of legality and illegality and can go on occurring because of the gaps in our legal system. In sum, both poverty and the weakness of the legal system are breeding grounds for reliance on connections.

Traditional Morality and Reliance on Connections

When the reliance on connections is like wild seeds growing on Chinese soil, with great vitality and persistence, it is also because this reliance has a deep basis in China's traditional morality. From ancient times, our family-based small agricultural producer society provided a social basis for a morality based upon human relations and human feelings. And as these concepts of human relations and human feelings acquired some autonomy, they spontaneously developed into a strong social force. The distinctive feature of this traditional Chinese morality is that it is a personalized ethic—that is, one stressing treating people differently depending how closely or distantly they are related to you. Several decades ago Fei Xiaotong in his analysis of Chinese traditional morality said,

> There are different lines in the treatment of other people. The most basic is for family members, between parents and children and among brothers, where the morality requires piety toward parents and respect for older siblings as the hallmarks of humaneness. The next line is for friends, and there the moral element stresses loyalty and trust: "When working for someone you must be loyal, with friends you must be trustworthy." The tenets of Chinese morality and law all change in accordance with the degree of intimacy of the personal relationship. Because of this, in this sort of society general models of behavior have no utility. You first evaluate who it is you are dealing with, and then you can decide what standards to use.

Mencius reproached the Mohists: "Generalized love means you don't acknowledge your parents." So you can see that what Confucianism emphasizes in morality is making distinctions based upon intimacy.

The great Western sociologist Max Weber also made a comparison of Chinese and Western ethics. He said that Chinese lacked a sense of impersonal rationality, and that all behaviors were seen solely in personalized terms. "Confucian personalized ethics is undoubtedly an obstacle to the development of a sense of impersonal rationality, since it keeps lumping individuals under kinship contexts. Whatever the circumstances, working in a specific post is always seen as working for a particular person." In Western countries it was the emergence of capitalism that dealt feudal morality a death blow, and the ideological preparation occurred in the occupational ethics and the ethics centered on money that emerged during the Protestant Reformation. [Marx and Engels wrote:]

> The bourgeoisie, wherever it has gotten the upper hand, has put an end to all feudal, patriarchal, and pastoral relations. . . . It left nothing else between man and man than the naked self interest expressed in cold cash. . . . The bourgeoisie has torn away from the family its sentimental veil and has reduced its relationships to a simple money matter.

When money as a marker of general value replaces other measures and dominates social life, then a universal morality will replace special treatment based upon personal ties, and occupational esteem will surpass sentiments of friendship. In regard to the role of the Protestant ethic in the West, Weber said, "From the economic viewpoint, it meant basing business confidence on the ethical qualities of the individual revealed in his impersonal work in his vocation." In capitalist societies, where self interest can be realized with the aid of money, one does not need to rely on kinship and friendship relations, and moreover a large scale division of labor develops that works to exclude these relationships. It is not that in traditional societies interests are not important, but that they are expressed in terms of kinship and friendship relationships, and it is very easy therefore to develop factions and cliques. For thousands of years these ethics spread to all corners of Chinese society and expressed themselves in a variety of forms: Factions became important among officials, teacher and student bonds were emphasized in the world of education, and in secret societies you got masters and disciples and blood brother relationships. The fact that this outmoded ethic can be so vigorous today is because as in the past it is bound up with the people's pursuit of their interests and because it is connected to traditional outlooks that have penetrated into people's hearts. Therefore, in such a society that stresses human feelings, a person who wishes to handle a matter impartially will find himself in a very difficult and embarrassing situation among his relatives and friends.

The Causes of the Rise and Fall of Reliance on Connections over the Last Thirty Years

But stressing human relations and relying on personal connections has not been an unvarying tendency. The good social order and atmosphere of the 1950s leads people even now to look back fondly on that time. If we say that capitalism used money and law to destroy feudal special privileges and personal connections, then what mechanisms did the newborn people's China use to eliminate this reliance on personal connections, and how was it possible for this bad atmosphere to revive itself? The reason that the Qing dynasty and the Republic of China were overthrown and replaced by the new China was because they were corrupt societies, in which the bureaucratic strata and exploiting classes suppressed the people. The Communist Party led the revolution to overthrow this system, and the Chinese people were willing to follow the revolutionary road because they suffered a lot under its corruption. And when the new China was established, the destruction of the old system cleared out the atmosphere of the old ways. At the time everything was fresh and pure. But we need to see that the good social atmosphere of the 1950s was only based upon a spiritual force—the people's hatred of the old system and the old atmosphere, and their trust in the new society and communist morality and their support for the new rules of this society. Our social structure had not produced any force which could thoroughly eliminate the reliance on connections, and neither had it produced anything like the reliance on money that in the West provided a force to give human feelings and connections a fatal blow. Therefore we did not totally eliminate from our system the possibility of "going by the back door" opening up again. In other words, it is not that people in the 1950s didn't have opportunities to go by the back door, or that there were no gaps where this behavior could penetrate, but rather that at the time the great majority of people would have been ashamed to do it. The hopes people had for the new China purified people's morality. And so the evil spirit of relying on connections was squeezed into the genie's bottle. But the plug which sealed the bottle was not some impenetrable legal system, nor was it a material force such as money. Instead it was a spirit, a faith, a morality that people voluntarily obeyed. Without a set of forces to replace the reliance on connections, and without a legal system to place limits on this phenomenon, the new social ethic was based upon a spiritual force, and so this basis was inherently weak. Once the situation had changed, the revival of the "monster" of old customs was almost inevitable. The ten years of chaos provided such a changed situation—the economy stagnated, living standards went down, and the imperfect legal system was smashed. People lost faith in communist thinking, and they were also affected by some of the absurd reforms that were tried, such as using recommendations to select workers, peasants, and soldiers to fill the universities.[5] All of these things smashed the faith and morality that

---

5. The Cultural Revolution reforms prevented young people from going directly from secondary school to college, but instead required them to go to work or to join the army. Then people were recruited to attend college through work unit recommendations, rather than by their academic records or entrance exams. In theory this was supposed to foster educational opportunities for youths from worker and peasant backgrounds, but in prac-

people had developed in the 1950s and 1960s, and so the social atmosphere changed, and relying on connections reared its ugly head again.

The Two Main Forms of Connections Today

The kinds of making connections and going by the back door that exist today vary and can be classified into two forms. One of these is connected to sentiments of "face." To stress face and emphasize establishing feelings has such a long history and such a deep basis that it is hard for people to avoid its influence. One should say that some people use connections not to serve their own interests, but simply because of "face"—they surrender before the "bullets" of human feelings. The other form is people using connections to directly serve their own interests. These people are more deeply infected by the poison of relying on connections, and they use them to seek selfish profit and take advantage of their positions. In traditional Chinese morality obligations are adjusted to the people they apply to—with strangers there may be little obligation felt, but in regard to parents, siblings, and friends, there is loyalty, piety, and trust without calculating one's profit or loss. These sentiments have the appearance of self-sacrifice, so they can be viewed as a sincere old custom (which is, of course, backward). But in the second type of relying on connections, "human feelings" become the bargaining chip in a naked trade.... In this kind of trade of "human feelings," power then becomes the basis, and people are really exchanging power for favors. Of course, the kinds of power that can enter into such exchanges are very broad, and include power over personnel decisions, the power of recruiting employees and students, power over providing medical certificates, power to allocate housing, and even power to sell goods in shops. But naturally enough in relying on connections those who have the most power have the most capital to use in such exchanges. Since it is an exchange, there will be bargaining and a comparison of values. And since the social status of people is not equal, the weaker side will have to pay tribute money to the stronger side. In this fashion the last drop of the simple old custom of "human feelings" is squeezed out, and what is left is the stink of cash that makes people vomit.

---

tice powerful families often used their connections to get their own offspring recommended.—*Trans.*

Simple Suggestions for Eliminating Relying on Connections

The ten years of chaos were the last struggle of feudal politics in China. By the same token, relying on connections is the last gasp of feudal morality. But old institutions die hard, and we should not underestimate the influence of this one. If we want to make progress in the Four Modernizations, then we need to clean out this decayed old custom. Historical experience teaches us that being a recluse such as Tao Yuanming or an upright official such as Hai Rui will not solve the problem, just as keeping oneself clean will not clean up a polluted river. If you shut one back door that is still only one, while the entire system has to be eliminated. It is high time that the cycles of Chinese history were ended, and this can be done when the new generation of revolutionaries establish changed institutions. People are still human, so there will still be the possibility that some will fall prey to the "bullets" of human feelings. But institutions and laws must be impartial, not recognizing bosses and kin. Only when we have these will we have the dams and embankments for a new morality and a guarantee of success in the Four Modernizations. We don't wish to deemphasize the importance of the moral quality of individuals, but those who are intent on reforms should keep their eyes on the question of the system and use all of their energies in order to establish solid institutions in all areas. This is what the several thousand years of Chinese history and the experience of the last thirty years have taught us. . . .

Finally, I wish to talk a little about what will take the place of traditional morality. Many Western writers feel that when capitalism took the stage in history, money replaced the sentimentality of kinship and friendship; when people in the West are immersed in pursuing their interests, they lose that which is most precious in life—the human feelings between individuals. Thus although the economy in Western societies is developed, people there become the slaves of money and machinery, and so spiritually they are impoverished. On the other hand, traditional societies for the most part emphasize human feelings, and among kin and friends there is great warmth. Especially in our five-thousand-year-old civilization, human feelings have been cherished from ancient times. It should be noted that in our tradition, human feelings include both a calculating side and an altruistic side. But those in our society today who stress human feelings and connections are only developing the base side of the Chinese tradition, and they have lost the beautiful and lofty side. This beautiful and lofty side was cherished from ancient times in our society, and socialism should provide a means for it to be expressed even more. As we proceed on the road to modernization, we should draw lessons from the earlier experience of the West. We should establish principles of rationality suitable to our socialist economic and political life, and not allow relying on connections to be a part of this. At the same time we should establish our own spiritual civilization. Our people in studying, working, living, and engaging in recreation together should preserve human feelings in their lofty form. Respect for elders, teachers, parents, and older siblings and esteem for friends—these are part of the good essence of several thousand years of Chinese society, and they should stand as spiritual treasures among world civilizations. Only if the rubbish of relying on connections is discarded can we absorb the essence of our own motherland's civilization and enjoy the fruits of real human feelings.

Translated by Chen Jieming and Martin K. Whyte

Cleavages and
Social Conflicts

36

Subethnic Rivalry

Harry J. Lamley

Particularly in periods when imperial power was in decline, the image of Chinese society as ruled by moderation and social harmony gave way to a reality of intense competition between rival groups. This competition could be between families, lineages, language groups, ethnic groups, or other rivals for power and wealth. Harry Lamley, a social historian, describes here one such endemic conflict, that between rival Chinese language groups on Taiwan, during the period of dynastic weakness that preceded the downfall of the Qing dynasty.

. . . . Taiwan's Chinese subcultural groups differed primarily in dialect and provenance. In Ch'ing times, most of the island's Chinese inhabitants were Hokkien and Hakka speakers, whose dialects remained mutually unintelligible. The Hokkien speakers, locally referred to as "Hoklo" *(Fu-lao),*[1] hailed mainly from Ch'üan-chou and Chang-chou prefectures in southern Fukien and areas peripheral to these prefec-

---

1. Hokkien speakers who migrated from southern Fukien to coastal areas farther south probably as early as the ninth century (and eventually to areas overseas) became known as "Hoklo"—i.e., "People of Fukien." In eastern Kwangtung as well as in Taiwan, other speech groups referred to these people as Hoklo in Ch'ing times. The Hokkien (i.e., "Fukienese") originally hailed from Honan and other regions of North China, and first began to settle southern Fukien extensively during the seventh and eighth centuries.

tures. The Hakka *(K'o-chia)*,[2] by contrast, came chiefly from eastern Kwangtung. Thanks to a further division of the Hokkien speakers into rival Ch'üan-chou and Chang-chou subgroups there developed in effect three, extensive, mutually exclusive subcultural groups in Taiwan. Within these groups, especially the Ch'üan-chou group, there was a further tendency to divide into communities based on county *(hsien)* origins. Except among some Ch'üan-chou communities, however, competition among county-level subgroups never seems to have been intense. . . .

. . . . [A] phase of exceptionally severe subethnic strife lasted from the 1780s to the 1860s. . . .

Subethnic Feuds and Government Response

In several important respects, Taiwan's subethnic feuds seem to have been patterned after the home region's feuds among lineages and surname aggregates. For one thing, feuds in both areas were highly organized—in fact, almost with the formality of ritual. For another, temples commonly served as headquarters for feud preparations. Moreover, the armed bands issuing forth from Taiwan's community temples and *i-min* shrines (with banners, images of local deities, etc.) reflected community and temple influence in much the same way that the armed bands issuing forth from the home region's lineage temples manifested the strength of local lineages or of larger buildups of surname aggregates. Then, too, temples in both areas were important in financing feuds. In Taiwan, funds from local ancestral estates *(chi-ssu kung-yeh)*—formed by kinship groups to support ancestor worship—were frequently used for feuds. In the home region, proceeds from nearly identical "sacrificial land" *(cheng-ch'ang-t'ien)* associations were misappropriated for the same purpose. This form of support was less substantial in Taiwan than it was in the home region because Taiwan's kinship groups had less corporate

---

2. *K'o-chia* means "guest families," indicating that the Hakka were latecomers in regions of southeastern China. Like the Hokkien, the Hakka originally came from North China, began to advance southward in the seventh and eighth centuries, and started to enter eastern Kwangtung at the end of the Southern Sung. Chiaying, the chief center of Hakka culture in Ch'ing times, became a purely Hakka area during the latter half of the fourteenth century when heavy concentrations of emigrants from T'ing-chou (in southwestern Fukien) and southern Kiangsi converged there.

wealth. Nevertheless, local lineages with common property ... supplied funds and leaders for feuds, as did Taiwan's great families and surname aggregates.

However, *chi-ssu kung-yeh* did not become numerous in Taiwan until well into the nineteenth century. The extensive subethnic feuds of the eighteenth and early nineteenth centuries appear to have been financed largely by local religious societies *(shen-ming-hui)*. These societies were usually organized to support the worship of particular deities and to finance the upkeep of these deities' altars and temples, although some served as organizations for supporting ancestor worship or as professional or artisan associations. By and large, the versatile *shen-ming-hui* provided a network of mostly non-kin connections in communities lacking extensive agnatic ties.

The support that temples and religious associations provided for feuding groups was not limited to men and money but extended to supernatural aid from gods, ghosts, and ancestors. In Taiwan, for example, the ghosts of local braves who had fallen in previous subethnic feuds (or in battles against rebels or aborigines) were cared for in *i-min* shrines and called upon by shrine communities for help against common enemies. More often, gods and ancestors were appealed to for their aid and blessings and requested to "witness" oaths and contracts made in preparation for armed forays.

Taiwan and the home region differed, however, with respect to those who participated in the fighting. In the turbulent areas of southern Fukien and eastern Kwangtung, where lineage feuds were frequent, the fighting often led to the development of a professional mercenary class dependent on feuds for a livelihood. In some counties, powerful rival bands of mercenaries were able to extort vast amounts of lineage wealth, with a ruinous effect on the feuding lineages and on local society in general. Nineteenth-century accounts, for example, cite many cases of lineage leaders who were unable to control or stop the feuds that they had started: reportedly, wealthy lineage members became impoverished and powerful lineages grew weak as a result.

Feuding was most destructive, of course, when entire villages or market towns were plundered and burned, and the survivors killed or forced to flee. In Taiwan, feuds on this scale were sometimes incited by bandits and vagrants merely anxious for an opportunity to pillage. Taiwan's authorities were appalled by the ease with which feuds could begin, intensify, and spread to distant areas with similar alignments of subethnic rivals. This matter was particularly serious because large-scale feuds posed a direct threat to governmental authority. Sometimes, in fact, subethnic feuds gave rise to rebellions, although more often rebellions (dependent on subethnic alliances) gave way to feuds. Taiwan's most serious rebellions of the Ch'ing period—those of Chu I-kuei (1721), Lin Shuangwen (1786–87), Chang Ping (1832), and Tai Ch'ao-ch'un (1862)—all involved ethnic strife....

Government response. Ch'ing authorities acted harshly, though not always effectively, to suppress subethnic feuding in Taiwan whenever armed affrays spread and threatened to engulf entire localities. In the eyes of the government, such feuding was tantamount to local rebellion. The precedent for dealing with large-scale feuding was established in 1782 in response to the first major outbreak of fighting between Ch'üan-chou and Chang-chou settlers. Officials quickly dispatched troops to pacify troubled areas and ordered the execution of rival leaders. The onset of extensive Hoklo-Hakka fighting in 1826 provoked a similar response, even prompting the governor-general, stationed in Foochow, to tour Taiwan and to devise a plan for bolstering local defenses in the northern half of the island.

Military efforts, however, proved insufficient to curb local violence, largely because such efforts did nothing to lessen the intense animosity that gave rise to the violence. In fact, this animosity was sometimes exacerbated by local civil and military functionaries who regarded Hakka settlers as "outside provincials" from Kwangtung. Moreover, the actions of the Green Standard troops stationed in Taiwan constantly posed a problem. These rotated troops shared backgrounds and traits with the island's Ch'üan-chou and Chang-chou inhabitants and were therefore apt to take sides in feuds rather than act impartially to stop the fighting. Furthermore, officials, officers, and yamen runners often tried to extract bribes or fees by offering to intervene in feuds or in litigation following outbreaks of violence. With unreliable subordinates and underlings, even the best officials were unable to maintain order, much less devise means of reducing subethnic tension.

The makeshift solution to which local officials most frequently resorted was to pit rival groups against each other, "using the people to control the people" *(i-min chih-min)*. The government's formal recognition of armed Hakka bands as a legitimate militia in southern Taiwan and the awards bestowed on these "righteous commoner" *(i-min)* forces for their stand against rebels during the Chu I-kuei Rebellion provide a notable instance. Thereafter, Hakka forces were deployed as far north as Chia-i in later engagements with Hoklo rebels.

Spurred in part by the fear that internal disorder might invite foreign intervention, Taiwan's authorities experimented with other forms of local control during the early nineteenth century. Local directors *(tsung-li)* and overseers *(tung-shih)* were selected from commoners living in rural communities, charged with keeping the peace, and reprimanded whenever subethnic fighting took place in their localities. The authorities also began to introduce collective security measures based on the existing *pao-chia* system under which registered households were organized into small units and the inhabitants held accountable for each other's actions. In 1833, a united *chia (lien-chia)* system was briefly established in central areas of the island to unite "law abiding people" *(liang-min)* within much larger units made up of towns and nearby rural localities. In other parts of Taiwan, officials initiated "united village compacts" *(lien-chuang yüeh)* that embraced entire rural districts. Under these compacts, large villages were required to protect small villages, and powerful kinship groups were obliged to defend weak ones. United militias were also formed to guard against local uprisings, banditry, and feuding.

These early experiments in collective security were not very successful in curbing subethnic strife. United *chia* and united village systems functioned only as long as dedicated officials were on hand, and even then were introduced in only a few areas. Furthermore, in most instances such security measures called for the inclusion of rival communities within the same units. During the latter half of the nineteenth century, however, local officials assumed a more realistic view of Taiwan's deep-rooted subethnic rivalry and allowed separate Hoklo and Hakka confederations and militia bands to maintain order within their own territories. . . .

The feud seems to have been an appropriate form of conflict for rival communities contending in an insecure environment plagued by disorder and weak government. Communities at feud tended to balance off each other, thus allowing for a relative status quo and for brief periods of peace. Moreover, feuding brought about a high degree of community organization and cooperation under "closed" conditions, factors that enabled local economic development to proceed. However, intermittent feuding also intensified and perpetuated local tensions and consolidated the boundaries between contending communities and enclaves, thereby enabling subethnic rivalry to become an enduring and deeply rooted phenomenon in Taiwan. . . .

37

The Position of Peasants

Sulamith Heins Potter

Mao Zedong led a peasant revolution to power, and he himself had grown up in a village in South China. It has often been assumed that factors such as these made the Chinese revolution much more favorable to peasants than the Bolshevik Revolution in Russia. Yet it is increasingly clear that peasants in China suffer from a set of disabilities and restrictions that seem ironic, given the nature of the Chinese revolution. In the following selection, Sulamith Potter, an anthropologist who lived in a village in southern Guangdong province in 1979–80 with her anthropologist husband, Jack Potter, presents a picture of how the peasants living there viewed such restrictions.

It is plain that relationships between rural and urban dwellers have been an important subject of concern for Chinese administrators, at least since the third century B.C. when the philosopher-administrator Xun Qing said, "The duty of the local official is to adjust matters between town and country, to harmonize clashing interests." At the present time in the People's Republic of China, the distinction between rural and urban dwellers is still a matter of the greatest administrative concern. Furthermore, this distinction has acquired a legal meaning and structural importance that are of immense significance in China's social order. Every citizen of China is classified at birth as rural or urban personnel. This classification is inherited from the mother and can be changed only in exceptional cases. Since classification as rural personnel is not

valued equally with that as urban personnel—the former being regarded as inferior—what has been created is clearly a system of birth-
ascribed stratification. . . .

The historical context for the division of the population into urban
and rural personnel was the effort in the late 1950s to avert the national
emergency which threatened to result from a massive exodus from the
countryside to the cities, which could not provide a living for so major
an influx of the rural population. In discussing this period, Selden refers to

> the rush of peasants to the cities in search of jobs, higher incomes, and the
> promise of urban life. . . . Despite government restrictions, the urban popu-
> lation swelled from 57 million in 1949 to 89 million in 1957. Rural migrants
> accounted for two-thirds of the increase, more than 20 million people. The
> capital intensive strategy of the first 5-year plan, however, produced only
> one million new nonagricultural jobs a year, while agricultural employment
> increased only slightly.[1]

The administrative solution to these grave problems was the for-
malization of the distinction between the people who lived in the cities
and were responsible for nonagricultural production, and the people
who lived in the countryside and were primarily responsible for producing the vital food supply; the latter were forbidden to leave the land.
This formalized distinction became law throughout China. It was closely
tied to the household registration system, which is the bureaucratic basis
for finding employment and being provided with rations and thus was
most effectively enforced. Today, the existence of the formalized distinction between urban and rural personnel is an indubitable social reality. . . .

The Meaning of the Category "Rural Personnel"

In order to understand what it means to be classified as rural personnel,
it is first necessary to understand in some depth the social organization
and cultural significance of the category. My analysis is based upon
anthropological fieldwork carried out in 1979 to 1980 among the people

---

1. *The People's Republic of China: A Documentary History of Revolutionary Change*, ed. Mark
Selden (New York: Monthly Review, 1979), p. 55.

of Zengbu Brigade, Chashan People's Commune, Dongguan County, Guangdong Province. These rural personnel think of themselves as peasants and refer to urban personnel under the broad classifying term "workers." Urbanites are, of course, vividly aware of the status gradations within the category urban personnel: the social meanings of working in a bath house or crematorium, being a factory worker, a high-ranking cadre, or a member of the tiny group of intellectuals. But from the peasants' point of view, all members of the category urban personnel are classed together in structural opposition to themselves. I shall share this terminology to facilitate the expression of the point of view of peasants.

The peasants of Zengbu Brigade express the distinction between peasants and workers in terms of the source of a person's rice. A person who eats rice supplied by the state is, in these terms, a worker, and a person who eats rice supplied by the production team is a peasant. One would not ask, "Is so-and-so classified as rural or as urban personnel?" but rather, "Does so-and-so eat the state's rice?" This way of expressing the situation dramatizes the structural distinction between peasants and workers. Peasants have a fundamentally different relationship to the state: a relationship in which the rice they eat is not provided for them under the terms of their employment. And this specifically peasant type of relationship to the state is maintained in practice by specifically peasant forms of bureaucracy and social organization that are not used by workers who have differing specific forms of their own. These peasant forms of social organization reflect the assumption that the relationship between peasants and the means of production is different from the relationship between workers and the means of production; this may be seen in the systems according to which peasants are paid, and in the economic risks that they are required to assume.

It must be said at the outset that peasant forms of social organization in China exist in a remarkable state of flux, and specific organizational elements assume different degrees of importance, depending on governmental policy and on local level choices within policy guidelines. But despite variations in emphasis on the importance of one specific aspect of organization or another, two underlying structural principles persist: that peasants are rewarded in direct proportion to the success of the lowest relevant social unit, and that peasants bear the losses if the social unit fails, whether as a result of incompetence or of natural disaster. In 1979–80, the lowest relevant social unit—the primary level of specifically peasant social organization—was the production team. (By late 1981, many of the economic functions of the production team had been taken over by the households as delegates of the team, but the two principles I have just mentioned continued to operate, applying now to the household instead of the team.)

One joins the peasant category at birth, deriving membership from the mother; one joins the household at birth, deriving membership from the father in the traditional way; and one joins the production team at birth—team membership is inherited. One's team is always located in the village in which one dwells, and since marriage is patrilocal, it is the father who passes on the team affiliation which will be his child's. A male peasant is automatically a member of his father's team—or in rare cases where the father has been reclassified, of the team that his father would have been a member of had his status not been shifted. A female peasant is a member of her father's team until she marries. At marriage, a woman leaves her father's team and is registered to work in her husband's team. She has no further obligation to the team into which she was born, and it has none to her. (If she should seek a divorce, the team will be reluctant to take her back, so she has no rightful place in the structure unless she remains with her husband.) . . .

Workers' units provide a clear contrast to peasant households, teams, and brigades. Workers do not use the household as a level of production responsibility. They are not assigned to their units at birth but instead when they finish school. Workers' units are not called teams, nor organized like teams, nor grouped into brigades. Obviously, the village is not a relevant level of organization for workers. Workers know in advance what they will be paid for their services. They do not have their salaries figured as proportions of the actual profits of their units. They can count on their earnings, and they are cushioned from the economic vicissitudes their units may encounter. Since workers' units are not producers of grain, workers receive a grain ration from the state as a condition of employment. It is this which has been taken by the peasants themselves as the key indicator of the distinction between peasants and workers. . . .

Social and Governmental Attitudes and Values

. . . . It was not until 1958 . . . that definitive regulations implementing the peasant-worker distinction were brought into being, with a revised version of the "Regulations for Household Registration of the People's Republic of China," signed by Mao Zedong to indicate his approval and published in 1959. Briefly, the household registration system acts as a means of identifying every citizen, registering all changes in status, controlling all changes of residence—whether temporary or permanent—and providing the basis for the distribution of rationed foods and goods—without valid registration documents, rations are unobtainable. Nor could an unregistered person find regular employment. Changes from rural to urban residence status require elaborate documentation. Urban and rural residents follow somewhat different registration rules. (For example: "In the city, each household should be given a [registration] booklet. In rural areas, the booklet is given to a collective unit.") In Zengbu, the records are maintained by the brigade, and they are impressively careful, accurate, and complete. It may be seen that the system as a whole is a formidable instrument of social control. . . .

During the Cultural Revolution, the official attitude toward peasants underwent a change of emphasis, and it became part of the current political morality to emphasize the ideological importance of learning from poor and lower-middle peasants. This was to be accomplished by going down to the countryside to live and work among them. However, being sent down to the countryside to learn from peasants came to mean receiving stern punishment, rather than being ideologically strengthened in any desirable sense. This was because the change from worker to peasant had such devastating social consequences, of which participation in productive labor was among the least; more important were loss of status, loss of economic security, loss of access to urban life, separation from family, and the knowledge that this painful new status would be inherited by one's children.

Any high social ideals originally present in the Cultural Revolution's emphasis on learning from peasants faded as the idea of going down to the countryside took on a complex of secondary meanings. Urbanites experienced it as a humiliating penance of indefinite, perhaps permanent duration: to live like a peasant was a punishment. This in itself illustrates the gulf in status between peasants and workers. For peasants, the influx of untrained and resentful young people—who had to be supported by taking shares of the team's profits when they themselves were not fully capable of pulling their weight—created reciprocal resentment and strain; and mutual resentment reinforced mutual prejudices. Rather than closing the gap between peasants and workers, the program tended, in my opinion, to open it wider. And in spite of propaganda efforts, and sending people from the cities down to the countryside, the mechanism for enforcing the structural distinction between the two—that is, the household registration system—remained in effect, and there was no suggestion that it be changed.

The Household Registration Regulations have provided some of the elements that have become symbolically significant in publicly demonstrating the status distinctions between peasants and workers. The possession of the ID card of an urban resident is an important mark of status. In Zengbu Brigade, I have seen visiting workers display their ID cards with pride and I have heard peasants speak of them with envy. The ID card of an urban resident gives a greater freedom of movement; it validates the person's right to be present in a city. Peasants have no right to be present in a city. If they go, they have to have a letter of introduction from their brigade to produce on demand, explaining the justification for the trip. This is experienced as a public symbolization of lower status, and hence humiliating.

Another status marker tied to the Household Registration Regulations has to do with the closely allied rationing system. Different kinds of food are available for urban residents that peasants are not permitted to buy: the food available to peasants is not so high in quality. The people of Zengbu resent seeing others eating better than they do, as, for example, when business visitors from Hong Kong who might be able to offer the brigade a lucrative contract arrive and must be welcomed with a banquet; the contrast with daily village fare is painful. . . .

Another culturally understood status marker is the wearing of city clothes which easily identify the wearer as a worker rather than a peasant. The ability to speak Mandarin, and holding a job that requires the speaking of Mandarin are also indicators of status—at least in areas like Guangdong Province where Mandarin is not the vernacular. I have seen peasants pointedly and effectively excluded from participation in social gatherings when higher ranking urban cadres chose to switch from Cantonese to Mandarin in front of them. . . .

Enforcement of the Distinction at the Local Level

. . . . The communities of China are ranked in order, along a scale that has peasant villages at the bottom and Beijing at the top. So, every household is registered in a community with a rank. People are only allowed to transfer their registration to a community of the same rank as their original one, or to a community of a lower rank. A person registered in a rural, grain-producing village can transfer only to another, as a woman does when she marries or as a man does in the exceptional case when he marries into his wife's family and takes up residence with them. A worker registered in a commune town such as Chashan could transfer to another commune town, but not to a town of higher rank, like the county town of Dongguan. People of Dongguan could transfer to another town of similar importance, like Taiping or Shilong, but not to a major city like Guangzhou. Since Beijing has the highest ranking, a worker from Beijing could move to Guangzhou, but not vice versa.

One can move laterally or down at any level, but there are restrictions against moving up. Even permitted moves are rare and difficult to achieve. They may involve waiting until a person with a similar job in the desired town is willing to arrange a trade. Most often, the application to move is rejected outright. But in any case, the ramifications of town ranking do not matter to a peasant, whose only choice is remaining in a peasant community.

The regulations have important implications for marriage. For example, if a man who was a worker married a woman who was a peasant, she would not be permitted to change her household registration to go and live with him. She could, in theory (but this would present serious practical difficulties) stay with him temporarily in the city, without a job or food rations. (This possibility was the suggestion of the cadre in charge of civil affairs.) She could, in theory, stay in her own team and live apart from her husband. However, team leaders we spoke with tended to express resentment at the idea of a married woman becoming once more the responsibility of the team into which she was born. If the man had peasant parents and had recently become a worker for special reasons, the woman could live with the man's parents in his native village. (This is the solution that occurs most commonly in Zengbu.)

The cadre in charge of civil affairs told us that when a man was born a worker, he was most unlikely to marry a peasant woman; it had happened no more than once or twice in his experience. He suggested that it would only happen if there was no other possible marriage partner for the man, or if there were exceptionally good feelings between the two. This second possibility is unlikely to arise, because young peasants have few opportunities to meet young workers, and when young people do meet, their behavior is regulated by very strong customary patterns of modesty, shyness, and puritanical decency. In cases where the woman was a worker and the man a peasant, the woman would be faced with the prospect of shifting her household registration out of a workers' community and into a peasant community, if she were ever to live with her husband.

So, marriages between peasants and workers are almost impossible for practical reasons. The regulations have produced the unintended effect of creating two endogamous groups crosscutting all of Chinese society. . . .

The system I have described is an extraordinary one, and full of paradoxes. It is a deliberately created system of birth-ascribed status, in the context of a modern socialist state, enforced by bureaucratic methods rather than by custom. It is a system that, in spite of being based on birth-ascription, is intended to be temporary, rather than perpetual. It is a system in which status is inherited from the mother, in the context of a social order that has always been characterized by strongly patrilineal institutions. Considered separately, each of these features is striking enough, and taken together they form a remarkable structural complex. Yet the importance of this system transcends its own inherent qualities, for this is the system that shapes the lives of the 800 million members of the largest meaningful category in the study of social structure—the peasants of China.

38

The Class System
of Rural China

Jonathan Unger

Marxists engage in heated debates over whether classes exist in socialist societies, or only in capitalist societies. If socialist societies still have classes, can there also be class struggle among them? China under Mao differed from most other state socialist societies, such as the Soviet Union, in insisting that classes and class struggle continue to exist after the revolution and the elimination of private ownership, and in carrying out a nation-wide effort to pigeon-hole families into various social-class categories. Much of the grassroots social discord in Mao's later years revolved around induced conflicts between the groups which these class labels created. Jonathan Unger is a sociologist who has worked with a team of scholars studying the post-1949 history of a particular Chinese village, and in the following selection he describes the impact of the class label system on that small corner of the Chinese social world.

For the first three decades after the establishment of the People's Republic, class labels strongly influenced the life chances of each and every Chinese. A class label did not refer to a person's current income nor to his or her relationship to the means of production. It did not, in short, denote class membership in the existing socio-economic structure. Rather, a class label had been affixed to each household in the early 1950s after the revolution's victory, categorizing the family's economic position under the *ancien régime*. During the next thirty years these capsule designations weighed heavily in determining social and political statuses; and nowhere was their impact more strongly felt than in the countryside. . . .

Illustrations of how this "class system" operated shall be drawn from a community called Chen Village, in South China's Guangdong Province. . . .

With a population of slightly more than 1,000, Chen Village is somewhat larger than the average community in the region. It contains a single lineage, as do many of the villages in its immediate district. By Guangdong standards its residents are neither rich nor poor. It is not an outstandingly progressive village (Chen Village has never been designated a model for its commune) but neither has the village gained a reputation as politically backward. Interviewees from the village felt that its internal "class" stratification was typical of the villages in the surrounding district. . . .

The "Class" Structure in Chen Village

During land reform in 1950, a workteam of cadres sent by the Party had carried out careful investigations to determine how much property each Chen family had owned on the eve of the revolution. The apex of the village's socio-economic pyramid had been occupied by a small number of landlords and rich peasants. Below them was a considerably larger number of middle peasants who owned enough land to be basically self-sufficient. But the bulk of the village population had consisted of tenants who owned only small plots (or no land at all) and landless laborers. All of those at the bottom of the pyramid subsequently were grouped together under a "poor-peasant" label.

During land reform this traditional pyramid was shattered. Economic exploitation was eliminated from Chen Village and the rest of the Chinese countryside. But in the process new socio-political distinctions were created. The pre-revolutionary class designations were stored in dossiers, and eventually a new system of the caste-like rigidity was devised on the basis of these files.

The former poor peasants were placed officially at the top of a new inverted pyramid, on the grounds that they could be counted upon to support revolutionary change. But the government wanted to broaden its popular appeal beyond this category and eventually granted almost the same privileged status to the former lower-middle peasants (who make up approximately a quarter of Chen Village's population). Before Liberation, the main source of the lower-middle peasants' earnings had been their own small landholdings, but they had had to supplement their income by renting additional land or by hiring themselves out as part-time laborers. They, too, had benefited from land reform.

Together, during the decades to come, they and the former poor peasants were to comprise the village's "good-origin" *(chengfen haode)* families. . . .

Between 80 and 85 percent of the families in Chen Village belonged to this privileged stratum of former poor-and-lower-middle peasants. Another 10–12 percent belonged to the middling stratum of former middle and upper-middle peasants.

During and after the land reform, there had been fears in Beijing that the old village elites might informally retain influence over local affairs. This fear had prompted repeated official efforts through the mid-1950s to discredit and isolate the overthrown classes. Landlords were targeted during land reform, and the rich peasants were stripped of their property and residual influence during the organization of cooperatives and collectives. But . . . the temporary measures employed against the former village elites became transformed into permanent fixtures of village society. By the mid-1960s, all of the "bad-class" households in Chen Village (4–5 percent of the village population) had been consigned to an outcaste status.

The Village Outcastes

A household was bad class when it was headed by a "four-bad-categories element" *(si lei fenzi),* defined as a landlord, rich peasant, counter-revolutionary (none in Chen Village), or "rotten element" *(huai fenzi).* Among these, the true pariahs were the village's two former landlords: "They were treated like lepers. If you greeted them your class standing was considered questionable. They had no friends. They didn't dare to talk to each other, either." The former rich peasantry, though facing stiff discrimination, never suffered this degree of isolation and unremitting contempt.

As the titles connote, the remaining two types of "four-bad elements" (the rotten elements and counter-revolutionaries) were not categories based upon economic class origins. They included people who, even if poor peasants before land reform, had been designated village bullies *(e-ba)* in the employ of the Guomindang or landlords. More significantly, these categories also covered people who had committed serious felonies or political errors after the Party came to power. A good origin peasant thus had to bear in mind that the punishment for a major transgression could be a permanent four-bad-element "hat." The prime example from Chen Village was a former bandit-turned-guerrilla who had been rewarded after Liberation with a petty post in urban government. Caught in an act of theft, he had attacked and injured his supervisor. The offender was officially branded a "rotten element" and sent back to Chen Village to face lifelong discrimination.

As a symbol of polluted status, during the 1960s and 1970s the dozen or so elderly "four-bad elements" (the designations included their wives and widows) had to sweep dung from the village square before mass meetings were held there. To symbolize further that most of them were irredeemably among the damned, they were not permitted to attend any political sessions or participate in Mao Study groups. If a production team was caught concealing the size of its harvest in order to reduce the government's grain quotas, a four-bad member of the team could expect to be pinned with part of the blame; he or she was deemed to be a corrupting influence on better-class teammates. In most of the various political campaigns of the 1960s and 1970s, bad-class villagers became the targets of struggle sessions, to remind the audience of past exploitation and the persistence of "bad-class" hostility toward the new order. During the Cleansing of the Class Ranks campaign of 1968–69 (by far the fiercest campaign in Chen Village since land reform), fifteen out of the twenty campaign victims who spent time in the village jail were either "four-bad elements" or their close relatives. A number were beaten in the highly emotional climate of the struggle sessions.

The poor and lower-middle peasants' suspicions of the "bad elements" were, if anything, fuelled by this maltreatment. Many of the good-class peasants reasoned that if they themselves had been so miserably treated they would want to seek vengeance. This rationale allowed some villagers to indulge in a hysteria that conveniently reconfirmed and underscored the bad elements' status as "class enemies":

> After a period in which they'd been struggled against, we became very careful when walking in the lanes at night. Who knows? If they couldn't

get over the humiliation might they not club you down in the dark? It's a custom in the village at such times to put some fish in the wells, to test whether there's any poison in the drinking water.

The young people from bad-class homes were not themselves "elements." The government had never given them political "hats" placing them under the "dictatorship" and supervision of the masses. They have always held the various rights of citizenship; they could vote in team elections and attend Mao Study sessions. The official rhetoric consistently has held that these young people, like those from all other class categories, were politically "educable" and could be "united with." Alongside this rhetoric, however, the government implicitly endorsed the argument that world views were hereditary: that the thinking of bad-class children had been dangerously contaminated by their parents. "Actually," commented a former Chen Village cadre, "you should be more on guard against the landlord's son. The old landlord himself is already just a useless old stick." Official discrimination was invited against all bad-class descendants by noting their father's class origin label prominently in their personal dossiers. In keeping with traditional Chinese practices, class origin labels are hereditary only in the patriline, and the sons of the bad-class sons (but not the children of bad-class daughters) bore the stigma in turn. Even had they left Chen Village, the dossiers and labels of the bad-class grandchildren would follow them through life.

Many of the bad-class descendants grew up burdened by confused feelings of inferiority. . . .

Most bad-class young people quietly kept to their own kind. A good-class peasant from another village observed in 1976:

Ordinarily, the young children of the four-bad elements get together in the evenings. Those of good-class background separately get together. They make up different social sets. The poor-peasant kids don't hate the others, but they're worried to visit with them. . . .

Examples of Good-Class Advantages

The "class line"—a Chinese term meaning privileged access to goods and services on the basis of one's class status—was pushed most strongly in rural China in the years between the end of the Cultural Revolution in 1968 and Mao's death in 1976. But during these years, the application of the class line varied noticeably from one village to the next. The reason was that the class line was brought to bear precisely where local shortages in goods and services were most pronounced. Interviews with former schoolteachers from six Guangdong villages indicate, for instance, that villages which could not provide enough primary-school places enacted a strong class-line admissions policy. This policy gradually weakened as primary schooling expanded, but in these same villages a strong class line in admissions was again applied as the competition to get into local middle schools increased.

In the same fashion, in some villages class-line decisions began to affect even the selection of teachers. In the 1950s, at a time when there was no real contest for middle-school places, many former landlord and rich-peasant families pushed their sons through the educational system as the only means of providing for their futures. Where their services were needed, they became primary-school teachers without any local protest. But as education expanded in the 1960s and early 1970s, large numbers of good-class peasants began to qualify to teach primary school. For the first time, teachers of unsavory class origins were suspected of spreading bad ideas among their poor and lower-middle peasant pupils. A good class background soon became the indispensable qualification for new teachers. In fact, the incumbent bad-class teachers in some villages were dismissed *en masse* to make room for good-class candidates. But in areas where teacher shortages still existed, a very different perception of the bad-class teachers sometimes prevailed. An interviewee from Canton who had been sent to settle in the countryside was recruited to be a teacher even though his father was a former capitalist:

> Nobody cared about that, because they had a shortage of teachers in the village junior middle school. Even after I tried to run off to Hong Kong and got caught, the village leaders still wanted me to go back to teach in the school. They told me, "Don't worry about that little incident. The poor and lower-middle peasants still trust you."

In short, the class line could be turned on or off, depending on the local needs of the good-class peasantry.

They gained benefits from the class system in other respects as well.

The privileged status of good-class men gave them an advantage in acquiring brides. This could be even more important to them than access to schools or jobs.

Peasant bachelors often needed this advantage. There is evidence of a demographic imbalance (with more young men than young women of marriageable age) in certain parts of rural China, including Chen Village, well into the 1970s. (This imbalance may be due to a persistence into the 1950s of the traditional strategy of female infanticide or neglect when food supplies were limited.) In these circumstances, young men were more than willing, if need be, to accept a bride of questionable class heritage. Since the official policy decreed that class labels are passed only through the patriline, these good-class bachelors knew that their children would inherit good credentials irrespective of their mother's origin.

Notwithstanding this, a woman's class status still made some difference to a prospective groom. Accordingly, women who married hypergamously did not usually rise very far above their origin. If a poor or lower-middle-class peasant family could not find a satisfactory bride for their son within the circle of good-class households, they normally approached a middle-peasant family. Middle peasants who could not find marriage partners within their own category would look for brides among the bad classes.

Though the shortfall of rural woman was only a few percentage points, this was enough to dim very substantially the marriage prospects of the bad-class men. Such men came, after all, from the least marriageable 5 percent of the rural population. Bad-class parents faced the prospect that none of their sons would be able to marry. This situation, ironically, was the converse of pre-Liberation times, when it was the poor peasants who did not always have the financial wherewithal to see their sons married.

To keep the family line alive, bad-class households began resorting to a special strategy. "Just about the only way a landlord son can get married," noted a Chen Villager, "is through a swap with another household.... Both families sacrifice their daughters to keep the incense burning [i.e., to sustain the male line]." Normally such exchanges were arranged with other bad-class families. But this was not always the case. One of Chen Village's landlord families traded brides with an impoverished poor-peasant family whose only son was dim-witted and ugly. This

exchange of sisters between two categories of despised grooms was practiced often enough to warrant a special derogatory title—a "potato skin/
taro root exchange. . . ."

Post-Mao: The Destruction of Class Barriers

Following Mao's death in 1976 his political successors moved to abandon
the Party's policies of class discrimination. They evidently were aware
that the old system no longer constituted an effective means of appealing to the majority of peasants. But more than this, the new leadership
believed China needed a new era of social stability and economic progress, grounded in a new set of political premises. They wanted to end
the sense of conflict which "class struggle" purposely had induced and
the growing political disaffection among those who had lost out.

In particular, Party officials wanted to defuse the resentments of
China's middle-class constituencies. . . . But above all, the leadership
needed to win back the support of the urban intelligentsia and the
middle-class technocrats who had been alienated by the intense class
policies of the 1960s and 1970s. The success of the Four Modernizations
campaign depended upon regaining their confidence.

Thus, for reasons partly tied to a new rural political strategy but
partly also to the new drive to modernize China, Beijing made a series
of sweeping announcements in late 1978 and 1979. To symbolize an end
to class struggle throughout the nation, it was declared that most of
China's four-bad elements, including the great majority of the old landlords, had "remolded" themselves over the past three decades. Though
their class-origin labels would remain in dossiers, the Party central committee directed that their "hats"—the official stigmata—be permanently
removed.

Already weakened, beliefs in the immutability of class labels collapsed in Chen Village in the wake of these pronouncements. Some of
the older peasants were displeased initially, but their opposition soon
subsided. Much as if rigid discrimination had never existed, the bad-
class households eased back into the village's social and political life. For
example, within two years one of the production teams elected a former
rich peasant to serve as its team head, while a second team elected the
son of the ex-guerrilla "rotten element" to serve as head. Remarkably,
interviews in early 1982 revealed that class origins were no longer taken

much into account even in marriage decisions. Bad-class youths could now obtain brides on almost equal terms with the young men of good-class backgrounds.

In short, in a period of less than three years, a structure of discrimination based on class labels had simply disappeared, with scarcely a trace remaining. Interviews in 1982 regarding other villages in Guangdong suggest the same rapid disappearance of class distinctions. I would suspect that this pattern has been widespread throughout rural China—for reasons basically similar to those of Chen Village. From Chinese media reports it is clear that in the 1970s much of the Chinese countryside had experienced similar troubles and bureaucratic impositions, with a corresponding erosion of faith in Party policies.

In earlier decades, the men who currently run China had been firm adherents of the rural class policies. The reasons are apparent given the historical circumstances. The Party had been unable to live up to its economic promises of the collectivization "high tide" and Great Leap Forward; throughout the 1960s and 1970s most of the countryside remained impoverished. In lieu of prosperity, the Party could provide the majority of good-class peasants with marginal advantages (both material and non-material) offered by the class line. These gave the peasants the satisfaction of an honored status; the belief that they were bearers of a noble mission; and the feeling that they were innately superior to the scapegoats in bad-class households.

When these beliefs, along with their faith in the Party, began crumbling in the 1970s, a new means for appealing to the peasantry became necessary. By the late 1970s, national leaders wagered that peasant loyalties could be retained by introducing new material gratifications which would supplant the earlier symbolic rewards. It was clearly felt that a program of economic liberalization (with expanded free markets, larger private plots, and better prices for agricultural produce) would bring noticeable improvements in the peasantry's standard of living. Full food bins would render obsolete some of the political functions which the class system had served.

In Chen Village, that is exactly what happened. In 1980 the communities near Hong Kong were allowed to sell food directly to buyers from the colony's booming markets. At the same time, under a new government program which, in effect, decollectivized agriculture, the fields surrounding Chen Village were parcelled out to individual households to be tended—independently—as family enterprises. The peasants quickly reconverted rice paddies into lucrative vegetable plots and commercial fishponds. Incomes rose several fold in just two years. By 1982 a household's success at its private endeavors had become a major source of its status. As an emigrant from Chen Village commented in 1982: "It's not class origin which counts any more; what counts now is making money. . . ."

39

Birth Control:
A Grim Game of Numbers

Steven W. Mosher

China has long had the largest population of any nation in the world, more than one billion people according to the 1982 national census. For much of the period after 1949 the Chinese population continued to grow at roughly 2 percent a year. This large population and continued growth posed severe problems for China's planners, who saw economic gains eaten up by all of the new mouths that had to be fed. Yet the government's attempt to enforce birth control as a state policy after 1970 often ran up against considerable opposition. In the following excerpts from his book, Steven Mosher, an anthropology student whose expulsion from his Ph.D. program at Stanford University created a controversy, describes how the birth control campaign was being enforced in the South China village in which he lived for a year in 1979–80. It should be noted that at the time that he made these observations the official "one child" campaign, which aimed to reduce birth rates even further, had not yet begun to be implemented locally.

The Chinese government, it turns out, is deadly serious about birth control. That is not what you would think from the sheer mass of the Chinese population, numbering over 1 billion, or one-fifth of the world's population, at last count. And that is not the way it seems when you enter the main gate of the Yuexiu Park in the northern section of Guangzhou City on any day of the week to be confronted with a one-million-square-meter carpet of people of all ages. Nor is that the impression left by walking through the narrow alleyways of a Chinese village and encountering band after band of little urchins playing in front of their high-walled brick homes. But it is what I found when I attended a family-planning meeting at Equality Commune.

Family-planning meetings, which all women who were pregnant with their third or later child were required to attend, or who had had their first child within the last four years, had already been in progress for four days in each of the commune's twenty brigades, and over 300 women had agreed to terminate their pregnancies under urging from local cadres. An equal number of village women had not acceded to the cadres' demand, however, and the commune revolutionary committee had decided to move the meetings to the commune headquarters, where their progress could be more carefully monitored and senior cadres placed in charge. . . .

From Sandhead Brigade there were eighteen women, all from five to nine months pregnant, and many red-eyed from lack of sleep and crying. They sat listlessly on short plank benches arranged in a semicircle about the front of the room, where He Kaifeng, a commune cadre and Communist Party member of many years' standing, explained the purpose of the meeting in no uncertain terms. "You are here because you have yet to 'think clear' about birth control, and you will remain here until you do. . . ."

Then he began to reason with the women about their concerns. "We know that you want a son in order to be secure in your old age. But remember that you are still young. As the country develops, it will create welfare programs. By the time you are old, you will not have to worry about who is going to support you. The government will support you." Speaking directly to the several women present who had brought along their girl children, he said, "You must remember that some girls can be as filial as boys. And you can always call in a son-in-law. I know one in Sandhead Brigade who treats his mother- and father-in-law as if they were his own parents. I hope that everyone will think more clearly about this problem, discuss this problem with relatives, and agree to an abortion."

. . . . Looking coldly around the room, he said slowly and deliberately, "None of you has any choice in this matter. You must realize that your pregnancy affects everyone in the commune, and indeed affects everyone in the country." Then, visually calculating how far along the women in the room were, he went on to add, "The two of you who are eight or nine months pregnant will have a caesarean; the rest of you will have a shot which will cause you to abort." Several of the women were crying by this point, and Comrade He Kaifeng apparently decided that his words had had the proper impact, for he went back to the table at the end of the room and took his seat with the other cadres.

There matters were left for half an hour or so, in order, He Kaifeng told me afterwards, to allow the women time to think about what he had said. "They must be made to realize the seriousness of this matter before they will think clear about abortion," he explained. At the end of this intermission, Chen Shunkui, the assistant Party secretary of Sandhead Brigade, strode to the center of the room and began to talk to the women. In contrast to He Kaifeng, who had been stern and authoritarian, even threatening the women, Chen Shunkui was relaxed and easygoing, and joked with the women at several points. . . .

"We aren't forcing you to abort," he said, taking the edge off of He Kaifeng's concluding remark. "The decision to undergo an abortion has to be made by you yourselves. But in making this decision, you have to consider not only yourselves but the country and the collective as well. Obviously the country needs to control its population for the sake of the Four Modernizations. The collective, as well, needs to limit its population."

This was, as I knew, perfectly correct. At the time of the 1952 land reform Sandhead Brigade had had only 3,480 residents all told. The 1979 annual census registered a total of 8,010 brigade members, for an increase of 130 percent in twenty-seven years. Like most other collectives, Sandhead had already brought all available land under cultivation, and further population expansion would only lower per capita resources to even more marginal levels. . . .

Chen Shunkui spoke in a light and rather matter-of-fact fashion, befitting the fact that he was talking with friends and neighbors. "The commune Party committee is quite concerned about you. They have even"—here his tone brightened even further—"arranged to have cars pick you up and take you to the commune clinic for the operation and back to the village when it is over." Several of the women laughed out loud at the outrageous thought of riding in a car, a Cinderella-like fantasy for peasant women, some of whom have never even ridden on a bus. The laughter broke the ice, and one woman, voicing a concern of many, called out, "What about safety?" Chen Shunkui had a ready answer: "The commune has arranged for two doctors from the Red Wind People's Liberation Army Hospital in Guangzhou to take charge of the operations. The abortions will be done properly. You will be safe and secure. The doctors are experts." Chen Shunkui paused momentarily to gain the women's full attention before continuing with his next line: "Mosquito nets have even been brought over from the commune reception center [a kind of hotel used by visiting cadres] for your use while you are in the clinic."

This the women found amusing as well, but their bemused chatter stopped as Chen Shunkui brought the meeting back to its main point with a question. His query, "Who would like to undergo an abortion?" was greeted with silence. After a pause, a woman flanked by two young daughters raised a question that was on all of their minds. "Will we be allowed to go home tonight? If not, then we have to go home to fetch our blankets." The women had been told during the earlier round of brigade meetings that once the commune meetings began, they would have to stay in a commune dormitory until they agreed to an abortion. Hoping to have an excuse to go home at least briefly on the evening of the first day, they had agreed among themselves not to bring bedding. The atmosphere grew tense as the women waited for Chen's answer.

"Well, we aren't going to make everyone stay here," he began in a conciliatory fashion, but he quickly went on to make clear what the price of going home was going to be. "We will allow you to go home, but only to convince your husbands, mothers-in-law, or fathers-in-law, or others at home that it is best that you have an abortion. You must first tell me that you agree to an abortion and are going home to convince others. If not, then you must stay here tonight." He ended on this note, stepping back to the table and taking a seat. Again the women were left to mull over his remarks among themselves.

Except for a break for lunch, the meeting continued in this fashion throughout the day, with Comrade He Kaifeng, Chen Shunkui, and Sandhead Brigade's woman's work cadre taking the floor in turn. The commune cadre would usually take a hard line, while the two brigade cadres just as often took a more amiable approach. Although the atmosphere of the meeting was less tense when the brigade cadres were speaking—they were, after all, fellow villagers—the gist of their argument was identical to that of the commune cadre: the women must agree to an abortion. After each cadre spoke, there would follow a half-hour break to allow the women to consider what had been said.

Finally, late in the afternoon, Chen Shunkui strode again to the center of the semicircle of benches and announced that it was time for the women to decide whether to stay overnight at the commune or go home. Taking out a small notebook, he began to read out the names of the women one by one.

"Lin Xinlan," he called out. Everyone in the room swung around to regard the woman flanked by two small daughters who had earlier raised the question about going home. Her face remained expressionless. "Do you want to go home?" Chen Shunkui pressed, deliberately avoiding the use of the word "abortion." The woman's control suddenly broke, and she cried out that she would "never abort."

Ignoring her outburst, Chen Shunkui smoothly read out the next name on his list. "Su Shaobing." A very young and very pregnant woman replied in a small, hesitant voice that she wanted to go home. "Good," the cadre said quickly. "Go home and convince your parents-in-law that you should have an abortion. Remember that you have already agreed."

Chen Shunkui continued down the list, reading one name after another, noting each woman's reply to the question "Do you want to go home?" Although one other woman, whose one child, a lad of two and a half, was severely retarded, shouted out that she was going to bear her child regardless of the consequences, the rest of the women responded quietly and fatalistically. Of the twenty-four women whose names were read out three agreed to abortions, all of which were scheduled for the following day, five agreed to go home to convince their families that they should abort, and ten refused an abortion. Six of the twenty-four who had been instructed to attend that day were not present, and would each have 2 *rmb* deducted from their family's income, a fine what would continue to be levied each day they did not attend.

Overall, that first meeting brought jarringly home to me certain realities of China's effort to control its population growth. Although the program is officially described as planning births it might more appropriately be entitled "restricting births," for its goal is to limit births to the lowest number possible. The technique of reeducation in public meetings adopted to achieve this goal is similar to that used in China's numerous earlier sociopolitical movements. Alternately threatening and cajoling, persuading and reasoning, the cadres explain over and over why it is necessary to follow the Party line, applying a steady psychological pressure that deadens reason and gradually erodes the will to resist.

Experience has taught the Chinese that arguing back at authority will only make matters worse, and so they listen passively and finally come to agree to whatever is being demanded of them. The whole process is reminiscent of the Chinese proverb "Water drops can pierce a rock. . . ."

Since 1974 the principal method of encouraging smaller families has been to hold annual or biannual family planning "high tides." At meetings and during home visits, women are barraged with all kinds of propaganda, from the reading of family-planning regulations and directives about rewards and sanctions for those who accept and reject birth control, to arguments advanced by cadres against having large families and against simply letting nature take its course.

Women are not paid their regular work points for the days that they are in meetings. This amounts to an enforced idling of, in most cases, one-half of the family work force and acts as a strong prod toward the alacritous acceptance of family planning. "It seems harsh," a local brigade cadre admitted to me, referring to the meetings-without-pay principle, "but the collective had no choice. If we were to continue to give them work points for not working, they would never 'think clear' about contraception." What keeps the women in the meetings and out of the fields is that women who miss meetings are fined 2 *rmb* a day for each day they are absent, an amount equivalent to more than a day's wages.

Chinese peasant women have never been given to vague, romantic statements about fulfillment through motherhood and the like. They were led during the course of family-planning "high tides" to rethink their reasons for wanting children in an even more hardheaded way, and the younger women that I spoke with no longer gave the continuation of the family line as the primary reason for having children. Mencius may have believed that "there is no behavior more unfilial than to have no male descendants," but young rural Chinese women are no longer so sure. "Though my mother-in-law says that you have to have a son to carry on the family name and lineage, I really don't think that this is a very good reason," one young woman, pregnant with her third child, told me. "I have already agreed to have a tubal ligation performed immediately following delivery, regardless of the sex of the child." She paused momentarily and then added with a wan smile, "I hope it is a boy."

Many women now say that they would be satisfied with two children, that this would be their ideal number of children, but only if both turned out to be boys. Otherwise they would continue to bear children until they reached this number of sons, even if it meant having a string of girls in the process. "Many sons mean a happy and prosperous household" and "Boys are precious, girls worthless" are among the traditional proverbs that rural women for hard, practical reasons, still quote when cadres are not around. Jwang Yaguan, the secure mother of two teenaged boys, told me that "a woman needs a manchild because without one she will be poor and picked on in her old age. Families with only girls have little voice in village affairs. Everyone knows that the girls will sooner or later marry out. A son will stay by your side until you pass away."

Sons are the only social security system known to peasant parents, for the vast majority of rural collectives are too poor to provide for the welfare of the elderly. Neither can daughters render long-term assistance, for in the countryside custom decrees that they take up residence with their husband's family upon marriage and sever all economic ties with their natal family. Only sons continue to live at home after marriage, the sole support of aging parents.

Unlike Americans, who see old age as a grim and dreary finale to life, Chinese look forward to it as a relaxed time of leisure and high status. The "entering the ancestral hall" ceremony at age 60 celebrates a man's release from the backbreaking slog of field labor. Thereafter he spends his days in the courtyards of the village ancestral halls, smoking and chatting with the other old men of the village. But whether he actually retires at this point depends on having one son, or better yet two, to slog in his place. I remember seeing a grizzled old peasant at work on a private plot some distance from the village on a dreary winter's day, his hoe rising and falling in a slow, tired rhythm. In his tattered black cotton trousers and coat of coarse burlap, shoeless despite the cold, he made a pathetic figure alone in the fields. I judged him to be nearly 70, and asked my companion in surprise what such an elderly man was doing in the fields. "That's Old Man Wang," he replied. "His wife died several years ago, and his daughters have all married out. He lives alone." Then, after we had gone a few steps farther, he grimly observed, "You see, that is what happens when you have no sons." Wang, dirt-poor and pitied by his neighbors, has no choice but to continue toiling in the fields until he dies. For the Chinese villager there remains no greater misfortune in life than to have no sons to "inherit the ancestral estate and pass along the generations." To his government this is feudal nonsense which hinders the program to bring reproduction under state control, and thus threatens the success of the all-important modernization program. . . .

The birth control plan is quintessential Chinese socialism: the state setting forth a far-reaching blueprint to reengineer society. The people are expected to fall uncomplainingly into line despite the shortcomings of the state plan. The plan in operation exacts from the population a heavy toll to which the state remains largely oblivious.

Though I had gained glimpses of the human cost of birth planning Chinese Communist style while attending meetings and interviewing cadres, I only apprehended the full dimensions of the sacrifice being demanded of Chinese women during a visit to a commune clinic during the 1980 "high tide." I found that this facility had been transformed into an abortion clinic for the duration of the campaign, an impression confirmed by Dr. Chen Buozhen, one of four clinic codirectors (and the only one of the four with any medical training). "At this early stage in the high tide we have been giving priority to abortions over sterilizations," he explained as we sipped tea in the clinic office. "Our seventy beds are currently all occupied with women undergoing abortions, our surgical staff has been organized into special abortion teams, and our two operating theaters are in use throughout the day performing caesarean sections and induced abortions. We have even called up four barefoot doctor midwives from the brigades to help with the patient load."

Despite the concentration of all available medical resources, the clinic had averaged only a dozen abortions a day the first four days of the "high tide," and the waiting list of 170 women was growing longer with each day of meetings. One reason for the slow pace was a lack of space: as a concession to the women's fears, they were accompanied by family or cadres during their three-to-four-day stay in the hospital. But the main reason, Director Chen confided, was that the commune cadres, worried lest premature births spoil their drive for 100 percent compliance, had directed that all pregnancies of seven or more months be terminated first. "On a woman seven or eight months pregnant, performing an abortion is a complex and time-consuming procedure," Chen pointed out. "We begin by injecting Rivalor, an abortifacient, into the uterus to destroy the fetus and cause birth contractions to begin. The fetus usually expires within twenty-four hours, and is expelled on the second day. In the cases where expulsion does not follow within forty hours, we have no choice but to perform a caesarean." "And if the fetus has not yet expired?" I asked, wondering what the clinic staff would do when faced with the awkward problem of how to dispose of a live baby delivered by caesarean. "We always wait until the fetus expires," he answered firmly. While passing quickly for the harried clinic staff, this death watch can seem interminable to the women themselves. . . .

Although it is the peasants whose security, privacy, and family continuity are most threatened by the program, they are for the most part politically inarticulate and naive about matters beyond their own rice bowl. Even the young peasant women themselves, who stand to lose the most, mount only individual and passive resistance to the program. They keep their pregnancies secret, telling only their families, and avoid prenatal physicals, knowing the brigade midwife will report their condition to the authorities. They continue to work in the fields as usual, binding up their abdomens under their baggy pants and blouses from the fourth month on so that they will not show. Many in this way avoid detection until they are only two or three months from term, thinking that they have a shorter gauntlet of meetings to run. Those who can afford to pay the fines go away to the hills or to the home of a relative, coming back only after their infant is born. Those women who attended the meetings I witnessed were largely silent, less defiant than resigned, less rebellious than fatalistic, each enduring on her own. On the one occasion when a woman unexpectedly railed bitterly against the cadres, I saw the other women self-consciously look away, distancing themselves from the protester. They seemed as helplessly isolated as their unborn babies, incapable of uniting in even verbal opposition to a policy that each one of them privately opposed. Neither did their husbands or other family members back in the village work to undermine or circumvent the program, or even go so far as to criticize it publicly. To be sure, men grumbled and cursed that the program was taking away their sons and grandsons, but only within their family gates and only to family members and trusted friends.

Yet I did witness several spontaneous outbursts by individuals against the policy, the most striking of which came during the course of a birth control meeting. One of the young mothers present, who had two girls but no boys, had started talking during an interlude about how she had managed to keep her pregnancy a secret until just a few days previous when "they" became suspicious and ordered her to undergo a physical. "They are so strict now," she continued, tears welling up. "I just want to have this one more baby, and then I'll be glad to have a tubal ligation. In the village there is no way to survive when you are old if you don't have a son. Sons are like heavy cotton quilts in the winter; if you don't have one, you will freeze to death."

She was sobbing heavily by this time, and, thinking it best to end the conversation, I stood up to go.

"They won't let me have my baby," she burst out. "I will agree to anything they want if they only let me have my baby."

I was anxious to shut off her torrent of words, but was carried along by her intensity.

"If I talk to you like this, is it illegal?" she asked suddenly, eyeing the two cadres present who had sat with faces averted during our conversation.

"No, it isn't," I answered with an assuredness that I definitely did not feel.

"I don't care if it is," she went on without really listening to my reply. "Vice Premier Deng says that we are to 'tell it like it is.' All I am doing is telling you the truth."

I nodded, noting apprehensively that the cadres were casting glowering sidelong glances at the woman.

But she was not to be cowed. Looking directly at the two cadres, she cried, "They are forcing us to have abortions!"

Occasionally, protest has gone beyond the merely vocal and become violent as well, as happened in a village in the Pearl River Delta where the birth control campaign was pushed with special vigor by a young, ambitious brigade Party secretary. Finally all but one of the village women pregnant with an over-quota child had reluctantly gone to the commune clinic for an abortion. The lone holdout was a woman whose husband, himself an only son, was desperate for a son to continue the family line. They held out against the cadre's harassment and veiled threats for several weeks more before finally caving in. When the woman's seven-month pregnancy was aborted, she was found to have been carrying twin boys. In the eyes of rural Chinese, who prize sons above all else, this was a monstrous tragedy, and word of it quickly spread beyond the hospital walls to the woman's horrified husband. This man went into a black fury and, shrieking that his two sons had been murdered, tore wildly to the Party secretary's home. Seizing the man's two sons, aged 8 and 10, he heaved them into the courtyard well and then leaped in himself. All three drowned.

This household-shattering double murder and suicide, as tragically poignant as it was, touched me less deeply than a quiet ritual I observed, which better exemplified the passive Chinese acceptance of acts of gods, fate, and the state. During the early April *Qing Ming Jie,* the "bright and clear" festival on which Chinese remember their ancestors, I visited a neighbor woman who had gone through a late abortion a month earlier and found her just completing the domestic portion of the memorial ritual. Eight sticks of incense were smoldering on the high mantle before the family's ancestral tablet, clothing, money, and ingots made of paper were being transubstantiated by fire into the nether world for the use of the ancestors, and she was chanting prayers for the peace and prosperity of the household members, both living and departed. But instead of ending the rite at that point as customary, she lit a final length of incense in a corner of the room and briefly stood crooning before it. It was, she explained to me afterwards, for "the unborn one."

40

Saturday Night in Baoding

Richard Terrill

Richard Terrill spent a year teaching English in Hebei University, located in the city of Baoding, in 1985–86, a period in which educational reforms were supposed to have gone into effect. In the following excerpt from his memoir, Saturday Night in Baoding, *Terrill describes the mounting anxiety among his senior students as the time of graduation and job allocations approached. This selection vividly conveys the competition and animosity still reigning between "red" and "expert" students—those who choose to use political versus academic prowess as their route to success. Perhaps more important, in view of the student movement that exploded in Beijing less than three years later, this excerpt shows the bitterness created by the gap between reform slogans and campus realities and the deep resentments felt toward the bureaucrats who still have nearly total control over student fates.*

In conversation class I assign my juniors to prepare for a "prophecy" game the next week. Each student in the class has written his or her name on a slip of paper. The slips are mixed in a hat, then each student draws the name of another student, as if for an office Christmas party.

Then the road takes a turn: each student must write a one paragraph prophecy of the situation fifteen years from now of the person whose name he or she has drawn; the student may discuss family, wealth, health, occupation, education, or anything else that he or she wishes. In class next week, each student will read his paragraph, and the others will have to guess the identity of the person written about.

The juniors seem to like the idea of the game, and when we are talking about it after class outside the classroom building, the interest is strong to the point that younger students stop by to listen, and the juniors explain the exercise to them in English (being allowed to speak only English within my earshot).

Then comes the inevitable fall. Several of the students say it will be quite easy to guess the identity of students from the descriptions—except for the part about occupations.

"That of course is decided by the Party."

I'm aware of this—from my conversations with Jiang Xia, with some of my older seniors, with virtually anyone else including Party members themselves. But I have been led to believe the students have some voice in choosing their future occupation, that their preference will be taken into consideration when job assignments are handed out.

"It's true we can write down a choice," one student says now, "but it will have little affection on what happens" ("*effect* on what happens," I correct him). "There is a committee that chooses ... Dean Liu and the Party secretary and the teacher responsible for our class...."

"Well then it's two teachers and only one Party man. That can't be too bad," I say.

"We are afraid that Dean Liu has little to say. It's mostly the other two."

"Which teacher is it on the committee? One who teaches you intensive reading?" (the course that is most important in the English students' curriculum).

"No. One who works in the office," he says. In Chinese, even those who do clerical or manual labor are referred to as *laoshi,* teacher, if their work unit is an academic department.

"It's not one who teaches a class. It's one in charge of student life." By this he means one involved with political study. "And he's very young and wants to improve his standing in the Party, so he's very strict with the students and none of them like him."

I am sad because I know some of the best students aren't interested at all in politics and do poorly in those courses.

"The very political students have an advantage; they will get better jobs. Those who like nice clothes or popular music will be worse off. The Party leaders don't like them at all. And if two students are boyfriend and girlfriend—which is against the Party's wishes—then they will be aparted...."

"Aparted on purpose?" I ask.

"Maybe. The Leaders are what we call 'old generation.'"

Other students, some just by their silence, confirm that this is the case. A lull falls over our discussion, which has been cheery to this point, with humorous predictions about the future of different members of the class. I almost catch myself meeting the silence with the usual Chinese words of consolation. "Well, there's nothing we can do about it." I've come to despise those words, along with "We are just small fish," "We try not to think about it," and, worst of all, "We're used to it."

All at once there is nothing to say; for a minute each of us looks away from all the others standing there. I feel we're letting time pass so that the injustice, the obstacle in our conversation can be forgotten and we can walk away, each with the appearance of a smile. . . .

Soon students begin to volunteer to me more and more tales of their unhappiness with their lives and of the injustice of the Party on campus and in our department. . . .

I'm in a badminton game with Miss Wang Mei, my loyal dancing partner, when a conversation begins, one similar to the one I had with the junior students after our prophecy exercise. Maybe these subjects come up because job assignments—which is to say politics and the Party—have been on the minds of the seniors day and night lately. As the juniors told me, the foreign language department's Party secretary—an old man who speaks not a word of any foreign language (some Party secretaries in college departments have no more than a high school education)—is in charge of job assignments for all thirty-four Younger Seniors.[1] The consternation of the students is clear.

As we hit the badminton birdie between us, Wang Mei and I are expressing our sympathy for Miss Li Fengyan, my guide to the medical clinic last winter. . . . Miss Li didn't pass her entrance exam to graduate school, thus she won't be allowed to take the test again for at least two years, and this means that like the rest of the students her future will be decided on the whim of the Party Leader. This means, too, that she won't be allowed to go home. Miss Li is from Henan Province, and our school is in neighboring Hebei Province. The Party reasons that if you

---

1. The seniors taught by the author included two groups—individuals sent by their work units for further training in English, and destined to return to those units, and secondary school graduates. Terrill refers to these two groups as "Older Seniors" and "Younger Seniors."—*Ed.*

go to school in Hebei province, you *owe* a debt to that Province (or "to the people" of that Province, they say) and thus should work for it ... for perhaps the rest of your life. In the case of Li Fengyan, no one told her before she came here that she would likely not be allowed to return home.

The saddest part is that Li Fengyan has a boyfriend at home, assigned by the Party to work there. Baoding is a twenty-four hour trip by train from the city where he lives and works. There is no place within Hebei Province close enough to make a meeting between them more than just a twice-a-year occasion—Lunar New Year and summer vacation. This is their lot for the next two years at least. I asked Li Fengyan about the likelihood of her relationship with her boyfriend withstanding the separation. "You're young," I said. "Maybe you will find another." "Oh no," she replied. "We've known each other for years. And there is a good feeling between the families."

There's irony and cruelty to compound the sadness of Li Fengyan's story. It would be possible for a senior student to be assigned to Henan province, but only if the bureaucracy gives our department some positions in that province to assign to students. This in itself is unlikely. What's more, Wang Mei tells me, in wanting to go to Henan, Miss Li "has rivals." The Party has said that not everyone who wants to can be allowed to go home, and there are two other senior students who want to go home to Henan.

And they're both Party members.

So Li Fengyan hasn't a chance. She has the option of going home on her own, but she could only get part-time work, most likely translating, even though she wants to be a teacher and would make an excellent one. She would have no health insurance. And her refusal to submit to the will of the Party would be a black mark on her record always.

Li Fengyan even went as far as to get a letter from a school in her home town saying they would love to give her a job teaching there. The letter bore the chop of the principal of the school, a vital sign of "officiality" here. The job was not a particularly desirable one, nor a high paying one (almost no teaching job in China is), but it's all she wanted.

When she presented the letter to the Party Secretary, he laughed in her face, then criticized her for being selfish.

Li Fengyan is perhaps the most generous, good natured, and sincerely helpful person I've met here. She's incapable of doing harm to others. She's the kind of person you'd like to hug once every day, not to give her support—she doesn't need it, being extremely strong—but to reassure yourself that there is some force of good operating in the world. Besides being remarkably strong, Miss Li is also bright, hard working, and extremely mature for her age—about twenty-three I guess. She's among the favorite students of many teachers here, Chinese and American.

On the other hand is one of her two rivals who are Party members: he's lazy and irresponsible. Except that he's not lazy when it comes to manipulating people and events. He does only what he has to do, then depends on cleverness and guile to get him through, barely. As far as English ability and studiousness is concerned, there's no comparison between him and Li Fengyan. But when it comes to getting a job assignment as teacher or translator, if one exists for Henan Province, he'll win.

I'm learning a great deal during my badminton game with Wang Mei, us talking over the wind, slowly moving away from the others who are lifting weights and standing in circles hitting volleyballs during this after-class sports period. As the wind carries the birdie continually over my head and I hit it back to Wang Mei, short into the wind, we drift farther away from the others, farther away from the warm weather stench of the *cesuo,* the communal toilet for a number of families assigned to work and live at the university. Finally, after a while, we stop playing altogether and stand with rackets in our hands and talk openly, out of earshot of the others.

"There are a few in our class, those who were Party members or wanted to be, who all the time we were freshmen, sophomores, and juniors would run to the Party secretary whenever something good happened to them," Wang Mei says. "If they got a good mark on a paper, or won a prize or did well in sports, they made sure the Party Secretary knew about it. . . . Everybody else hated these students." . . .

"Mr. Sun Je (Li Fengyan's rival for a chance to go home to Henan) was the worst of all in our class," Wang Mei continues, "and he was the first to be accepted into the Communist Party. He always was running to the Party Secretary with good news of something. For three years he reported his own good fortune, as he saw it, and he told the Party Leader bad things about everyone else, personal things so that they'd be criticized every Saturday in the political meeting. If two friends had an argument, just something minor, not anything political, Mr. Sun would tell the Party Secretary, and the two friends would be criticized. They were told they should work together for the people and not be concerned about their own affairs. Mr. Sun told the Party Secretary any secret we might have. If a boy and girl became boyfriend and girlfriend, Mr. Sun told the Party Leader. If someone went off on Saturday night after classes and came back on Sunday night, Mr. Sun had better not find out, or the people would be criticized the next weekend for thinking only of themselves and not obeying their duty to be good students."

"Politics are important in China, for everything," Wang Mei says. "The students all hate the Saturday political meetings. But they dare not miss them. We have to study politics. And many students join the Party just to get a higher position in society. Advancement comes faster to Party members. To be a professor, to maybe get a chance to study overseas. . . ."

"Have you applied to join the Party?"

"No, I haven't . . . not yet." She laughs guiltily.

"I know many students have, even those who think the Party is bad and getting worse. I can understand if you feel you have to."

"I just want to live a peaceful life; I want to live satisfactorily, but . . ."

The sentence remains unfinished.

Just as during my conversation with the juniors, I feel a cloud descend. So often lately: some new anecdote, some new evidence of injustice that is making the lives of people I like very much amount to far less than they should.

To ask what I can do is as pointless as the answer is certain: nothing. More and more my experience here is becoming like that of an otherwise happy man who is plagued by periods of hopelessness that begin without warning. Lately walking on campus, I seem randomly to run across people crying—to a friend maybe, to a classmate off in a corner or under a tree. I see people with long, impenetrable faces, empty stares—people whose expressions are usually brighter, people I know. Though these sights have surely been here all year, I'm seeing them only now because now I understand of the despair that brings them about.

What I see is not American unhappiness, that born of loneliness or isolation. I see here a listless sadness, a sadness of having given up, a sadness that comes from outside the individual and that the individual can thus do nothing to alleviate. It's as though the mind has come to the illogical end of a logical process. There are only walls around it. And the walls can be seen through but not walked through. They can be touched and felt, but not described or talked about. There is no more rethinking or reconsideration to be done. There is only time that can pass so that the mind turns to its other functions—respiration, perception, imagination—and the mind learns of futility, and a time passes before it strolls down that same street again that leads to those same walls, that same blindness. That I am an American and am experiencing this frustration as an outsider no doubt makes me less able to accept it, makes me understand it all the less. . . .

A few days later I see a guy walking down the street carrying a bag full of rolls. The bag breaks and the rolls pour out onto the dirt. There is a moment of surprise, then the guy laughs. So do the others around him. It's not a cruel laugh. Maybe it's a laugh of sympathy. At any rate, the guy's laugh is a sincere one, not one that was meant to cover up some kind of unhappiness.

I've noticed that Chinese people often laugh at their own adversity, just as they laugh at the adversity of others. Someone trips and falls on the street. Hilarious. In a movie—probably a pulpy imported American movie—a guy is brutally shot in the chest. Absolutely side splitting. . . .

One night Yuan Zhenyi, a favorite student of Smith's and mine and one of the Older Seniors, comes by to tell us he has just been to Beijing and has found out why he hasn't been accepted to graduate school. It seems as though some students, actually many students, have "gone through the back door" (*zou houmen* in Chinese) to get in. His test score on the supposedly highly competitive examination was higher than many of the fifty students who were allowed to go on to take the second qualifying examination. He went to Beijing to investigate because he'd heard nothing from the school after taking the test—no notice of passing or failing. Now the reason why he heard nothing was clear—because he had passed the test, but they needed to pretend he hadn't.

I'm having an impromptu party with some of the seniors younger than Yuan when he comes by and tells his story. He speaks quickly and forcefully and in Chinese, and he holds the close attention of his audience with the story of the injustice done to him. It's a story of anger told in a voice of Chinese anger.

Everyone, of course, laughs.

Not cruelly, but in sympathy with Yuan, who is also laughing. I don't think anyone is surprised at the injustice. It happens here as often as not, so there's no reason for anyone to be surprised.

"They invited me to try again next year," Yuan says, then everyone laughs again, even louder.

"Isn't there anyone you can appeal to," I say—sounding no doubt stupidly American—"anything you can do?"

"Nothing. It would be a waste of breath."

More laughter.

Li Fengyan is listening to the story, maybe thinking of the injustice to be done to her. She doesn't know whether or not to take the job assignment we both think is in line for her right here at the university. Her main concern is how to get back to her home, family, and boyfriend in the least number of years. Now, she says, the opinion of Dean Liu is that if she were to take a job assignment here, she should be willing to make a commitment to stay forever. She says her uncle was just last month finally allowed to return to his home in Henan Province after his tenure at Hebei in the "public English department," as they call the office responsible for teaching English to non-majors. His sentence away from home: twenty years. Miss Li fears a similar fate.

But, she concluded, since she had the opportunity to stay here and teach—a good job for her—she would, and she would try to get her boyfriend assigned here also. This would seem to be a great compromise. But for it she was harshly criticized by the Party Leader, who said she was "looking for an excuse to stay at the university." She told him she wouldn't stay here now even if she were asked. On her request form she asked to be sent to a big unit somewhere so that after a few years she could maybe "trade down" to a poorer unit closer to her home. In risking this, she will be at the mercy of the Leader of the unit where she is assigned. If he doesn't want to let her go, he can keep her there until one of them dies.

We also fear that the Party Leader in our department is angry and, flexing his near-absolute power, will send her to the worst of places, which in bleak Hebei Province can be quite bad. It will be up to Dean Liu to stand up for her and try to convince the two politicos that she deserves a better fate—that is, if *he* isn't angry at her for turning down the chance to work under him here at the university. . . .

[Richard Terrill left China before the work assignments were announced, but he received word of some of the results in the following letter from his fellow English teacher who had stayed on.—*Ed.*]

Dick,

Included is the rundown on job assignments for the seniors. The results weren't as bad as we'd feared. Almost no one got sent to the countryside. One of the two long-time "public" couples were sent to the same city, though it wasn't a desirable one—a punishment or not? The other couple were not sent to the same city, and the boy was back in Baoding to try to get his assignment changed. He was also suspected of having thrown a rock through Dean Liu's window. Basically, many students got to go back to their home towns, or the towns of their boyfriends or girlfriends. Li Fengyan got a good job . . . but not one in Henan.

Not much surprising about the bleak array of jobs—the big problem is the waste of motivation that comes from denying people the job they want to do. Ma Jingxian, among all those assigned to be teachers, got the plum job of remaining in our department—too bad because I hear she's not keen on teaching. Similarly, Xie Rong is set for life as a teacher at the school where she will do her graduate work in Beijing. She admits that she's very lucky to go to the capital, but her dream was to be an interpreter.

The other big problem is the impossibility of change. Who knows if this society will ever loosen up to the point where people can go from one job to another without facing a gauntlet of disapproving intransigent cadres.

And there were the expected injustices. Sun Je, the rat fink, got the best job, as an interpreter in the Beijing Water Department. . . .

Smith

Part 4

The Economy

Edited by Robert F. Dernberger

Introduction

Robert F. Dernberger

A universal and fundamental theme in human history is the formation of social units. One purpose of social grouping is to provide the members of the society with ways to utilize resources and technology to furnish their material needs, such as food, housing, and clothing: the society's economic system. In studying how the Chinese have tried, and continue trying today, to solve their economic problems, it is important to understand that the economic system adopted and implemented by a society is a social organization or a part of the total society's social system. The same is true of the society's political system, religious system, cultural system, etc. That is why economics is a social science; it is not the study of the raw materials or the engineering technology or techniques of production that are used to produce goods. Rather, it is the study of how people are organized to produce, distribute, and use the goods. The important point to emphasize here is that not all societies have an economic system similar to our own.

Physical Environment of the Chinese Economy: The Good Earth

A major factor that influences the form, functioning, and success of a society's economic system is, of course, the physical environment with which that society is endowed. Throughout China's long history, the predominant economic activity has been agriculture: the growing of crops. Thus, the most important resource in China's economic development is the arable or cultivable land within China's borders.

As we have seen in Part 1, China is a continental land mass which slopes from the "Roof of the World" in Inner Asia (the Pamir Knot) to the Pacific Ocean, with mountain ranges and river systems running approximately in the same direction. The major areas of China's agricultural land lie along the eastern one-third of the country. Although the quality of the soils in these agricultural regions deteriorates as one moves from north to south, the benefits from weather, which are essential to agricultural production, run in the opposite direction: abundant rainfall and warm, lengthy growing seasons in the south and sparse rainfall and colder, shorter growing seasons in the north. Soil experts judge the average quality of the soil in China's major agricultural regions to be fairly good, i.e., capable of growing most crops. Thus, a major reason why Chinese agrarian civilization has enjoyed such a long history and has been able to support one-fourth of the world's population since 200 B.C. is this large endowment of good agricultural land.

Despite the absolute size of this endowment, the most common perception of China's major economic problem today is that there are too many people working with too little arable land. With its very large area of fertile and cultivable land, China did not always suffer overpopulation. China's demographic history is a story of successive migrations with population pressures building up in the existing agricultural areas leading, in turn, to large migrations along rivers or over mountains into adjacent areas of available agricultural land: a slow and steady process of filling up China's borders. The latest of these great migrations occurred in the last century, when the Chinese peasants migrated into the northeast (Manchuria), the former homeland of the Manchus. While adapting to their new environment, the Chinese migrants retained the basic features of Chinese society which they brought with them.

Two important aspects of China's history of population growth call for emphasis. First, the process of filling up China's borders occurred over a very long period of time and was not due to an "excessive" rate of population growth. Throughout this period, China's rate of population growth, on the average, was similar to that of the world's population as a whole: a high death rate and a high birth rate yielded a net increase in population well below 1 percent a year. Second, as these migrations took place, the migrants did not create new countries. They remained part of China's population. Whereas other empires in history have long since broken up into separate entities, China has remained intact as a single nation, in part because of the strength of its institutional, cultural, and social heritage.

China's current population problem is thus of relatively recent origin, i.e., in the last two centuries, and is due to the convergence of rather simple phenomena: (1) the increase in the rate of population growth experienced throughout the world as death rates fell and birth rates remained relatively high; (2) the settling of all areas of fertile, cultivable land within China's borders; and (3) the failure of China's economy to modernize so as to create sufficient employment opportunities outside of agriculture.

Institutional Evolution of China's Economy

Although China's resource endowment must, on balance, be judged as favorable, the economic problem involves the conversion of these resources into the material products that satisfy the desires and needs of the society. A very important determinant of a society's success in solving its economic problems is the institutional framework—the economic system—which is adopted or naturally evolves for organizing the society for that purpose. Since 1949, the Chinese Communist leadership has attempted to introduce and employ a new set of institutions, a socialist economic system, and new norms of behavior; these new institutions, however, were adopted in the context of a firmly implanted set of traditional economic institutions and norms.

As an economic institution in traditional China, the importance of the family cannot be overemphasized. In contrast to the contemporary American family, the Chinese family as a unit was much more important than the individual in ownership, decision-making, work, and distribution of income. As an economic institution, the Chinese farm family was similar to an American family business, with the head of the family buying and renting land on behalf of the family and seeking out other new opportunities for making more money, allocating family and hired labor for the family's income earning activities, borrowing and lending money on behalf of the family, and distributing and selling output produced to maintain and increase the standard of living of the family members. Not all families, of course, were equally successful, and some sank into poverty. However, they sank into poverty or rose to great wealth as a unit, and each member of the family contributed his or her labor and best efforts to increase the family's well-being. This long history of "family" farming reinforced the strong family ties and allegiance which continue to prevail in China today (see Part 3).

Complementing the development of agricultural production based on the extended family as the unit of production, the institution of private property and its corollary, free markets, have been basic features of China's economy for at least the last eight centuries. The history of private property and free markets in China is emphasized because they contrast sharply with the economic system of slavery and feudalism—prevalent in the history of many other countries—under which the fruits of the peasant's labor in the field belonged to someone else. In China, private property and free markets provided built-in systems of incentives for China's peasant families to increase output even after they had satisfied their own immediate consumption needs. These features of China's traditional economic system were basic to China's success in developing a very sophisticated system of agricultural production with relatively high yields for traditional agriculture by the eighteenth and nineteenth centuries, making it possible to support China's large population.

On the other hand, even with family farming, private property, and free markets, it was likely that more successful peasant families would buy the land owned by those less successful. Thus, in the long run, the result could be one group of wealthy families owning the land and renting it to landless peasants or hiring landless peasants at subsistence wages to work their land for them, thereby considerably reducing the incentives to the peasant producer for innovation and increasing production. A second limit on the incentive mechanism for innovation and growth was the extent or size of the market. As discussed in Part 1, long-distance transportation in traditional China was limited to shipping along navigable rivers, a few important caravan routes, and a major North-South canal, the Grand Canal. The bulk of the commodities transported from place to place in China were carried short distances by human carriers or by animal-drawn carts. This lack of convenient and inexpensive transportation, therefore, limited the size of the market, creating a number of relatively self-sufficient economic regions spread throughout traditional China, each with a major urban center.

In addition, the commercialization of traditional Chinese farming was further limited by the natural tendency of the peasant families to avoid risks and to increase their security by growing and producing for their own subsistence needs as much as was possible. For example, many peasant families spun and wove cloth, raised a few chickens and a pig, grew some vegetables, and harvested a basic grain crop, thereby limiting the extent to which they depended on commodities supplied exclusively by the market for their own needs.

Two other aspects of traditional China which help explain China's economic system are the village and the network of markets which integrated these villages into a national economy. The traditional village economy is described in chapter 41. Unlike traditional farm families in America who lived in the midst of the fields they farmed—these fields being large plots of contiguous land—most Chinese peasant families lived in villages that were surrounded by the individual families' widely scattered, very small pieces of farmland.

As earlier sections have made clear, in traditional times, the bureaucracy of the central government rarely reached down to the village level, and the village leaders represented the villagers in dealings or negotiations with the state. Traditional Chinese farming involved a considerable degree of cooperation among the families in a village, including sharing work during the peak seasons of activity, such as planting and harvesting, when the scattered nature of the small plots owned and worked by each family made cooperative activity essential. These cooperative and kinship ties were important in creating sources of credit, which the individual peasant households needed to tide them over the relatively long periods of time between harvests.

The individual economies of the myriad similarly organized villages throughout rural China were integrated into a market network. Commercial centers or market towns emerged over time and served as the hubs of market areas for the villages in their immediate vicinity (see chapter 42). The important economic function of these market towns was that they tied the peasant households into an economic system larger than their isolated villages and eventually into the nationwide Chinese economy as a whole.

China's Agricultural Evolution

Chinese agricultural history is a story of the continuous introduction of new and higher yield crops or better varieties of existing crops. By the modern era, almost every known crop in the world was being grown in China. The Chinese peasants did not have chemical fertilizer, but they did make extensive use of night soil, manure, fish, bean cakes, river mud, green plants, and so forth. They did not utilize mechanized irrigation, but they had developed both large-scale and small-scale water storage, control, and irrigation networks. Thus, when they entered the modern era, the variety of crops produced and the use of irrigation and fertilizer in Chinese agriculture were as extensive as in any traditional, nonscientific agriculture the world has known.

No greater example of the sophistication of Chinese agriculture can be found than the practice of multiple cropping. Once fertile land became scarce, a peasant family could try to increase yields per unit of land already under cultivation. New crop varieties, irrigation, and organic fertilizer were several ways of increasing yields, but multiple-cropping, or the growing of more than one crop on a single plot each agricultural year, is a truly remarkable feature of Chinese agriculture. Because of the soil characteristics and climate constraints, particular crops are dominant in select areas, yet a tremendous variety of crops are grown in each agricultural region and even on each farm. Inasmuch as single crop growing exhausts the fertility of the soil, in many countries the land is allowed to lie fallow periodically to renew its fertility. In China, however, the extensive use of organic fertilizers and irrigation, as well as the love and sweat put into the topsoil by the Chinese peasant, allowed the Chinese to introduce and use a continuous crop rotation. Although the use of sophisticated agricultural techniques was greatest in the southern region of China, Chinese peasants throughout China have developed traditional farming into a highly sophisticated system.

China's Agricultural Problem in Modern Times

If Chinese agricultural growth by traditional means from the fifteenth through nineteenth centuries was adequate to maintain an ever-growing population at an above subsistence standard of living, what went wrong in more recent times? Although the increase in cultivated land had accounted for one-half of the total increase in agricultural production in the previous five centuries, by the twentieth century China's borders were being filled up. This meant that the expanding population had to lavish more and more labor on a limited amount of land, and that there was a growing need to increase the yield from the labor-intensive means that the Chinese had traditionally relied upon. Furthermore, the very success of past means of increasing production limited their usefulness for increasing future yields. Most known and highly productive crop varieties were already grown in China, irrigation was rather common in areas where adequate rainfall was available, multiple-cropping was already practiced where allowable by the growing season and existing crop varieties, and organic fertilizer was already applied at relatively high levels. This does not mean that each of these traditional sources of growth could not produce some increase in yields, only that it became significantly more difficult to rely upon these sources of growth in the twentieth century.

To compound these technical problems in China's agricultural evolution, the problems of rural poverty, land shortages, and tenancy also became considerably more severe in the late nineteenth and early twentieth centuries. The natural process of economic growth, improvements in transportation, and the opening of China to foreign trade combined to increase the commercialization of the Chinese economy. Most peasant families continued to be relatively self-sufficient, but more and more, the Chinese peasant's livelihood began to depend on the sale of his crops and the purchase of consumer goods. With the spread of market forces, there occurred greater specialization in industrial crops such as cotton, soy beans, tobacco, etc. As more crops could be sold for money, rents were increasingly converted from payments in crops to payments in money, and the value of owning and renting land to others for cultivation increased. With the growing commercialization of agriculture, the extent of unequal land ownership and the number of households relying mainly on working land rented from others increased. Even by the mid-twentieth century, however, most peasant families still owned some land that they worked, supplementing it with land rented from others. Absentee landlords and landless farm laborers were a very small proportion of the rural population. Much more important was the growing inequality in the ownership of land (i.e., wealth), and the small average size of the land owned by a growing majority of the peasant families. There was not enough land to go around—no matter who owned it— and some families were working plots too small in size to maintain a family.

In economies that have already been modernized, institutional reforms and the scientific revolution led to the modernization of agriculture before the population-land ratio reached such a high level, and the industrial revolution, which followed this agricultural revolution, absorbed any surplus labor in urban-industrial centers. In contrast, however, the ability of the Chinese peasants to increase output steadily within the context of traditional means of production was leading them into a dead end. From the individual family's point of view, more children, particularly sons, offered the hope of more income earners and security for elderly family members. From the point of view of the economy as a whole, however, more laborers simply increased the ratio of labor to land and reduced the productivity per worker. Thus, output per worker and the standard of living began to fall. Most experts agree that the solution to this declining labor productivity was the scientific transformation, or modernization, of Chinese agriculture.

China's Industrial Evolution

During the Tang and Song dynasties, China had the most advanced, powerful, and wealthy empire the world had ever known. As one Western observer so aptly remarked about the contrast in China's comparative position in the world, China's peasants "ploughed with iron when Europe used wood," but "continued to plough with it when Europe used steel." It was the steady rise in the ratio of labor to land over the five centuries before the twentieth century, the strength of the self-sufficient village economies, and the difficulties of long-distance transportation which combined to thwart the rise of industrialization in China. Handicraft production using relatively cheap and abundant labor to produce consumer goods and tools for the local market was more profitable. Thus, by the nineteenth century, the Chinese economy was largely an agricultural economy, as described above, permeated with handicraft production in the home and in handicraft workshops in the villages and towns. Modern factory production in industry did not exist; it was brought to China, as the chapters in the "Industry" and "Trade" sections explain, by the Westerner only in the late nineteenth century during the Age of Imperialism.

The Westerner had come to China and other parts of Asia in successive waves, reflecting the changing fortunes of the Western powers in Europe. None of these Western powers was able to make China one of its colonies, not only because of China's size and distance from them, but also because of the competition among themselves. Throughout the last half of the nineteenth century, however, the series of Western military victories over China resulted in treaties that increased Western access to China's economy. Between the middle of the nineteenth century and the early 1930s, foreign businessmen took advantage of these treaty arrangements, developing trade with and investing in China (see chapters 46 and 50).

This episode in China's industrialization is often blamed for many of China's economic problems in the mid-twentieth century. The problem is very complex, and the arguments probably will be debated for some time to come. Attempts by a few Chinese officials and entrepreneurs to create modern industries (such as arsenals, coal mines, and textile factories) in China near the end of the nineteenth century did encounter a host of cultural, political, economic, and international constraints. Some Chinese peasants did suffer economic decline and misfortune because foreign products displaced their handicraft activities and markets, especially those engaged in producing homespun cotton yarn. At the same time, however, others enjoyed economic prosperity due to the creation of new export markets (e.g., silk and tea), or to the demand for their products (e.g., tobacco) as inputs in the foreign-owned factories in China. With the spread of modern transportation, the increase in commercialization, and the growing ties to foreign markets, the peasant became increasingly vulnerable to price fluctuations. Within the context of growing commercialization and modernization, it is difficult to assess blame for who did what to whom, although in any reasonable and rational assessment, the forces of imperialism and the Westerner are due for their share of the blame.

Yet we should not overlook a very important phenomenon that was taking place. Despite the numerous cultural, political, and economic obstacles, native Chinese entrepreneurs were creating industrial facilities, as described in chapter 47. Total industrial production and employment, of course, were still a relatively small share of total economic activity in China. Even so, between 1912 and 1936, Chinese industrial production was growing at an annual average of 9.4 percent. Thus, whatever the unfair advantage enjoyed by the foreigner, or the extent to which his behavior can be described as exploitative of the Chinese, the process of industrialization was taking root and growing in China in the first three decades of the twentieth century.

Economic Development in the People's Republic of China

The New Economic System

China's long-run social, economic, and political problems were not changed by the return of peace following World War II, and the Civil

War between the Communists and the Nationalists, which had been contained within the framework of a United Front against the Japanese during the war, erupted into an open struggle for power. By late 1949, the Communists had gained control of the mainland of China, while the Nationalists withdrew to the island of Taiwan. Once they had rehabilitated the economy, the Chinese Communists launched a program of institutional reorganization that contrasted sharply with China's economic organization of the past.

Immediately upon gaining control of an area, the Chinese Communists implemented a land reform program which essentially redistributed the land from those who owned but did not work it to those who worked but did not own the land. Because the population in rural China was so large in relation to the cultivated land area, this redistribution of land holdings in favor of the poorer peasant households meant that they ended up with scattered plots that were too small in total size to maintain their livelihood. Furthermore, the source of rural credit, so essential to agricultural production, had been eliminated by expropriating the landlords, and no other source had been created in its place.

Thus, when the Communists introduced the transition to collectivized agriculture, the pooling of their land, labor, and capital, as well as risks, appealed to many of the poorer peasant households. Collectivized agriculture also made economic sense in terms of production possibilities, given the special conditions of Chinese agriculture. The individual household in a given area could not mobilize labor for the traditional labor-intensive tasks, such as multiple-cropping, irrigation, and fertilization, as optimally as could a larger unit, i.e., the collective. These larger units also could better utilize large pieces of equipment and undertake more large-scale investment projects than the individual households. Thus, although collectivized agriculture has not achieved a record of great success in increasing output in many other countries, it had obvious economic advantages in China.

Despite these potential benefits of larger scale agricultural production, the Chinese Communists encountered two major problems in their collectivization of agriculture: (1) the determination of the proper size of the decision-making unit; and (2) the creation of an incentive system which would ensure that the individual peasant contributed his best skills and efforts in production. When the commune was first introduced, the Communist leaders hoped it eventually would be the basic decision-making unit in agriculture, allocating work to be done among the brigades and teams it contained and distributing the resulting income among its members somewhat equally. Because of the size of the commune, the distance which separated those making decisions at the top and those engaged in production at the bottom was too great, and this attempt proved to be counterproductive (see chapter 43.) In addition, over the 1960s and 1970s, various attempts were made both to make the peasant household income more equitable and to award work points (i.e., the peasant's share of the collective's net income) on a monthly or annual basis or according to social and political qualifications, rather than on the basis of completing particular work assignments. These attempts, also, did not prove to be very efficient or productive.

In the industrial sector, the institutional reorganization of the economy by the Chinese Communists after 1949 was as sweeping as in the agricultural sector. The new government nationalized the banking system and all modern transportation, while all industrial enterprises of any size soon became either state owned or run by collectives; state owned and operated enterprises dominated the non-agricultural sectors. In general, these state enterprises were operated like their counterparts in most other socialist economies. There was, however, one very important characteristic of the administrative organization of state industrial enterprises in China: the degree of decentralization and control. Each of the state enterprises is owned, controlled, and incorporated in the budget of some unit of the state, but those run by county governments and provincial governments are much more numerous than those directly controlled by the central government itself.

To coordinate and integrate industrial and agricultural production of major products at each level, the Chinese Communists introduced a system of planning to replace most of the functions performed by markets and market prices in economies such as that of the United States (see chapter 48). Although this planning system was also decentralized to a considerable extent, relying more on lower level initiative and control than in most other socialist economies, the central planning authorities exercised considerable control over the allocation of resources, investment, and outputs in China's economy.

To ensure adequate supplies of labor for State industry and, more important, to restrict the number of unemployed workers who would migrate from the rural areas to the cities in hope of finding a job, the state recruited labor for jobs in industry, assigned workers to industrial jobs, and limited the right of those in rural areas to move to the city. A major reason for the need to stem migration to the urban areas is the advantages enjoyed by urban-industrial workers: because of their higher money wages, their many fringe benefits, and the greater supply of social and leisure services made available for this privileged group, the factory worker and urban resident enjoys a real income that is considerably better than that of his average rural counterpart.

Post-Mao Economic Reforms

Following the death of Mao Zedong in 1976, those more moderate or pragmatic economic policy-makers who had been purged during the Cultural Revolution were rehabilitated, once again assuming control over the economy and economic policy. Throughout the remainder of the 1970s, the Chinese engaged in wide-ranging and well publicized criticism of their economic system. The more radical or utopian economic principles of the Maoists have been rejected, and a thorough and persistent program to reform the economic system has been introduced. Foremost among these changes has been the renewed emphasis on material (monetary) incentives and on markets for the production and distribution of some commodities and services. To some observers, these changes signaled the abandonment of what is referred to as the Soviet-type, socialist economic system in favor of a mixed system or "market socialism," i.e., socialism with markets.

By 1990, it had become impossible to predict the exact nature of the future economic system that would result from the program of reforms. From its very beginning in the early 1980s, the more conservative reformers have consistently emphasized their view of the objectives of the reforms: to improve the results of a socialist economy dominated by planning, state enterprises, and government control, but with markets and non-state and non-planned economic activities allowed as necessary complements to the dominant state-sector economic activities.

Peasants have left the collectives and are encouraged to engage in crop production, specialized activities, and side-line occupations and to sell to the state or on the market at market prices (see chapters 44 and 45). Public enterprises are encouraged to use their facilities to provide commodities in demand by consumers on the market, after they have met their assigned target in the plan, state enterprises now being responsible for their own profits and losses. Quite simply, the Chinese are seeking a combination of planning and markets, of central government control and local, low-level initiatives which would improve the efficiency with which resources are mobilized to meet the needs and priorities of both the economic planners and the consumers.

While this may have been what the more conservative of the reformers have always had in mind, at the end of 1984, the more radical reformers appeared to get the upper hand in determining economic policy. From 1985 through most of 1988, the more radical group, under the leadership of Zhao Ziyang and supported by Deng Xiaoping, was able to introduce much bolder and more extensive "experiments" in the marketization and privatization of the economy. By the end of 1988, the rapid growth of the non-state, non-planned market sector of the economy was becoming a challenge to the slower growing state and planned sector, and the loss of central control throughout the economy and the inflation, growing budget deficits, and balance-of-payment problems were easily attributed to these more radical reforms.

In the face of these growing problems, the conservative reformers were able to regain control over economic policy-making at the end of 1988 and soon solidified their position with the overthrow of Zhao Ziyang and his radical reformers in the aftermath of the Tiananmen demonstrations in the spring and summer of 1989. Still trying to regain control over the economy and stabilize it, the new, more conservative coalition leadership in Beijing has yet to announce its economic plans for the future, with the exception of rather vague assurances of its intention to carry on the policy of opening to the outside world and, as soon as they have restored stability and control over the economy, to push forward with the domestic reform program.

Despite developments in Eastern Europe and the Soviet Union, which in some cases have seen public calls for restoring a market system and in others open rejection and abandonment of the Soviet-type economic system, the present Chinese leaders have made clear their intention of retaining a "socialist system with Chinese characteristics." What this appears to mean is that reliance on central planning and controls, with state enterprises run by state-appointed managers, will continue to dominate the industrial sectors of the economy. In short, as the Chinese entered the last decade of the twentieth century, most evidence indicated that the system outlined in this essay as the Soviet type will continue to dominate the economic sector and to mobilize and allocate resources in China for the foreseeable future. The political disturbances and the harsh measures that ended them have led to the reaffirmation of a Leninist-type political system under the control of a single party, with the Party under the control of a few very senior Party leaders. The advanced age of those leaders indicates that a generational change in Party leadership may well occur before the end of the century.

The Record of Economic Growth

Despite the many problems faced by the economic system the Chinese Communists introduced after 1949, the Chinese accomplished considerable economic growth between 1949 and 1988—a period of almost forty years. Estimates would indicate an average annual rate of growth in per-capita national product of about 6 percent. Such a record would place China among the most successful of the developing countries over this period. Statistical and definitional problems, however, limit the confidence one can assign these estimates, and they can serve only as a rough quantitative measure of China's economic development under the Chinese Communists.

The single most important explanation of the high rate of growth for the economy as a whole is the exceptionally high rate of growth in industrial development (13 percent a year in 1949–88), especially in heavy industry, or in the production of industrial products for use in other industries. This concentration on industrial development, however, came at the expense of other sectors of the economy. For example, the failure to invest more in the transportation sector, despite the inadequacies of the system inherited in 1949, means that transportation continues to be a serious constraint on the Chinese Communist developmental efforts. This imbalance between sectoral development over the past several decades has left China's present leadership with the need to restore balance among the various interdependent sectors of China's economy.

Nowhere is this imbalanced record of sectoral growth more serious than in regard to the agricultural sector: the key sector in terms of the total economy and in terms of China's successful economic development in the future. Largely because of remarkable growth after the introduction of the economic reforms at the end of the 1970s, agricultural output increased annually by about 3.5 percent, or 2 percent per capita over the forty-year period 1949–88. While this record, given the historical situation inherited from the past, represents considerable progress, it is a tribute to the skill and effort of the Chinese peasant as much as it is an indication of success for the agricultural programs introduced by the Chinese Communists. More important for the future, despite the start that has been made on the scientific transformation of Chinese agricultural production from labor-intensive traditional technology to modern technology, the low yields and labor productivity associated with traditional peasant agriculture remain typical in rural China. Much has yet to be done to solve China's agricultural problem.

No matter what may happen to a nation's total output of material goods or rates of growth in the different economic sectors, other dimensions of the economic development process affect the individual's well-being much more immediately and directly. Although a few necessities are still rationed in some cities, the supply per capita has increased significantly, especially in the past decade. The standard of living for the majority of Chinese is now well above a minimum level, freeing them of the insecurity of the recurring famines (every three to five years) so prevalent in China's pre-1949 history. Furthermore, necessities are distributed more equitably than in most countries and, at least until the inflationary price rises associated with the economic reforms became a serious problem, were available at relatively stable and low prices. Even though the job insecurity and unemployment accompanying the economic reforms had become serious problems by the end of the 1980s, it is still true that the majority of the world's largest labor force has been given jobs with wages and fringe benefits that compare favorably with the incomes of the rest of the population, and that they enjoy a job security that has been identified as one of the more meaningful benefits of Chinese socialism.

Finally, again as a result of the reforms, the Chinese have built up a significant level of foreign and domestic debt. Nonetheless, when compared with the debt problems of other developing countries, China has achieved its record of economic growth with rather limited dependence on financial assistance from other countries (see the "Trade" section). These are only some of the qualitative features that are part of China's rather remarkable record of statistical growth over the past four decades, but they suffice to depict how China's growth record over that period contrasts sharply with the experiences of other developing nations.

Agriculture

41

The Chinese Peasant Economy

Ramon H. Myers

If one were to select the "typical" Chinese, the probability is very high that the individual selected would be a peasant, and if a male, would be living in a village his grandfather had lived in. Before 1949, the family was the basic unit of economic activity—it was the unit that owned the land and that determined how to use that land and how to allocate the family's income. The village was the peasant's economic and social world. Most of the products produced and consumed were produced and consumed within the village, and there was little reason for the peasant to leave the village. To begin to understand the Chinese economy, we must begin with the peasant and his village.

Under the stimulus of Western social science, Chinese and Western scholars began to carry out empirical village studies only in the twentieth century. One of the most detailed of these studies was carried out by the Japanese during their occupation of North China. After the end of the Second World War, this very large collection of household-by-household interviews was seized and taken as war reparations to the Library of Congress, where it has been used as the basis of studies of the true characteristics of the economy of the typical village on the North China plain.

For example, one scholar, Philip C. C. Huang, used these studies in his book The Peasant Economy and Social Change in North China *to examine the villagers' relations with the extractive policies of the state. He shows how changes in this relationship unleashed pressures within the village that weakened community cohesion, creating a growing class of poor and alienated peasants.*

Mao and the Communists aimed their appeals at these poor peasants and poor villages in the Civil War. Yet, as Ramon Myers points out in the following selection, not all peasants or villages were poor in the 1930s. Myers, a specialist in the study of China's modern economic history and curator of the China collection at the Hoover Institution on the campus of Stanford University, uses the data provided by the Japanese surveys to analyze the economy of the typical village, including all families in four villages at different levels of well-being. This reading was excerpted from Myers' book The Chinese Peasant Economy.

The North China Village

. . . . Differences existed between these four villages in living standards, average size of farm, percentage of households dependent upon non-farm income, and villagers' indebtedness, but these were differences of degree. Sha-ching was the poorest of the four. Although living standards did not deteriorate markedly in this village, at least until after 1938, households possessed few consumer durables, a large percentage had to send labor to work outside the village, and nearly a quarter of the village's income came from nonfarm income. Peasant debt to outsiders was great, and part-tenant households were numerous.

Conditions were quite the reverse in Ling-shui-kou, probably the village with the highest standard of the four. In this village there were shops and artisans; only a small percentage of the village's households dispatched workers outside to earn nonfarm income; most debt was held within the village; and many households possessed some consumer durables such as bicycles.

. . . . Villages were naturally subjected to the influence of similar economic factors, but these differed because of location, resource conditions of the locality, and the frequency and duration of random disturbances such as war and climatic disasters. Therefore, various economic factors, which were in turn influenced by these variables, produced different types of village economic development rather than a single pattern of sequential stages of growth, maturity, and decay.

The economic factors, common to all villages, appear to have operated in the following way between 1880 and 1940. Population increased steadily at an annual rate of about 1 percent. All arable land in the villages was cultivated by the 1920s or 1930s, so that since the late nineteenth century the increase in cultivated land had been only marginal and the average size of farm had declined. There were only slight improvements in farm technology, such as the introduction of the American cotton seed and new corn seeds. Additional wells had been constructed, and the supply of traditional fertilizer was increased. The capital stock of the average farm household remained unchanged. Because the number of households had increased, the supply of village capital stock increased slightly. These economic factors interacted and influenced productivity according to the natural resource base of each village, the village's location to urban centers of development, and random disturbances, such as a natural disaster or war, which inflicted minimal damage on the village.

There is not any evidence that peasant living standards before 1937 declined, and therefore, total farm production increased in order to support the rise in population. Even though household farms gradually diminished in size, average productivity was maintained. Furthermore, the manufacture of village handicrafts, the introduction of industrial crops, and the new opportunities of nonfarm employment in nearby cities enabled peasants to augment their incomes from cereal and vegetable production. If villages were fortunate enough to enjoy these advantages, levels of income could be maintained, perhaps even increased, and peasant living standard need not fall.

If villages suffered a series of poor harvests caused by bad weather, floods, and crop pests or a significant decline in the number of carts, animals, and able-bodied men because of marauding armies, their loss of wealth made it extremely difficult for peasants to regain former living standards. The inevitable consequences were increasing indebtedness, an increase in tenant and landless households, and even emigration. Villages suffered more from some major disaster, natural or man-made, than from any other combination of economic factors.

Five types of village economic development can be derived from these four village studies.... First, villages having a cash crop, handicraft, and an opportunity of off-farm employment earned more than enough income to compensate for any temporary loss in village income. Such a case is Ling-shui-kou which had a higher standard than most villages. Second, villages possessing two or more of the above three sources of income might have experienced a series of poor harvests, but they eventually recovered their former living standards. Furthermore, the number of tenant and landless households had not changed. Such a case was Hou-hsia-chai of En County. Third, villages with two or more of the above alternate income sources, but experiencing poor harvests, suffered a slight decline in living standards, and the number of tenant and landless households increased. Village debt to outsiders rose, and considerable transfer of village land to outsiders took place. This was the case of Ssu-pei-ch'ai. Fourth, villages having only one additional source of income, off-farm wages, might experience few random disturbances. Although their living standards were lower than in the above village types, they had not declined over the past half century. Such an example was Sha-ching. Fifth, villages having only off-farm wages to supplement farm income might suffer from many random disturbances. Living standards declined, tenant and landless households increased, and some households were forced to move away. In the village survey materials I used, there was no example of such a village. However, other rural surveys undertaken in the early 1930s indicate that such villages in north China existed. . . .

It is difficult to say which type approximated the general conditions of north China villages. All types co-existed, and villages of each type could be found in the same county. . . .

Important Village Similarities

. . . . All villages, except Sha-ching, experienced the same shift from paying land rent as a percentage of the harvest to a fixed amount of the harvest. In Sha-ching, money rents had existed as early as the nineteenth century and before. . . . The change in land rents from percentage to fixed amount of harvest was gradual, and both systems could be found side by side in the same village.

The land inheritance system made it impossible for large farms to remain intact for more than one or two generations. Farm land became increasingly fragmented and difficult to farm efficiently. When villages underwent a large number of household divisions at the same time, many households with little land were formed. Thus, more peasants had to leave the farm for short periods to earn nonfarm income.

Village boundaries were undefined until the establishment of village crop-watching associations around the turn of the century and after. Villages had always acquired and lost land depending on harvest fluctuations and village debt, and peasants lacked a strong sense of village identity. After crop-watching associations were formed, the peasants became accustomed to regarding the area of land guarded by these associations as the village proper.

Village taxes in the form of *t'an-k'uan* [special assessments] increased greatly after 1920, and by the late 1930s it was the major source of revenue for local administration. Village leaders had the difficult and disagreeable task of allocating this tax burden and seeing to its payment. They allocated the tax burden by assessing households a fee per unit of land. This was then collected through the village household organization, the *pao-chia*. . . .

Village organizations for agricultural development to construct wells, irrigate fields, produce fertilizer, and increase livestock supply were nonexistent. These matters were left to individual households. However, households cooperated with one another privately to purchase farm capital, share livestock and labor, or rent lands. These arrangements were worked out by informal agreement between household heads of the same lineage group, friends, or neighbors and were specifically intended to overcome scarcities of capital, labor, and land.

The influence of clan management in village affairs and farming was very small. Village leadership consisted of prominent and able owner cultivator household heads capable of dealing with local officials and handling village problems. This elite group's composition constantly changed from one generation to another and was not based upon hereditary succession. Change in village leadership very much approximated the rise and fall of households in the village.

Some General Findings

The household must be considered the basic economic and social unit. Clans were weak organizations in village life, and village leaders devoted their efforts primarily to tax collection, village defense, and settlement of household quarrels. Households were very responsive to farm price changes and attempted to put their land to the best economic use. They weighed the advantages and costs of leasing or renting land. They rationally considered various income alternatives to farming and how much labor to allocate between different tasks to maximize household income. Households were powerfully motivated to earn more income and buy land.

The land tenure system in all four villages functioned to enable households with different land holdings to farm more efficiently and obtain more farm income. Pure tenants made up a very small proportion of villagers, although many households owning land frequently rented plots for short periods. In this land tenure system landholders gave neither guidance nor material assistance to their tenants, and new techniques were not transferred from landholder to tenant. Few large landholders farmed the land, and the absentee landlords living in market towns usually acquired their land through the rural credit system.

The credit system was based upon households using land as security and near money. Households borrowed small sums by pledging some of their land as collateral or, if larger sums were needed, by mortgaging or even selling land. Considerable village credit was provided by households lending to one another. Some credit flowed from market towns to villages, and households used their land as security to obtain it. If loans were not repaid, households mortgaged their land. Creditors, rather than farming the mortgaged land themselves, preferred to have the debtor households rent and farm it until the original loans were repaid and the land redeemed. Risk was the great difficulty in this credit system, but this was reduced by recourse to a third party to provide personal introduction, character reference, and financial guarantee that the loan would be repaid. This made for greater trust and obligation between debtor and lender. Interest rates remained fairly constant at 2 and 3 percent per month over this period except when inflation became serious after 1938.

Technological change and the improvement of the rural infrastructure such as schools, water control systems, and roads were very slow or nonexistent. Local officials were far more interested in collecting taxes and preserving order so as to maintain administrative power than in developing agriculture. Officials successfully taxed villages more heavily by using greater police power to impose frequent levies on villages. Tax revenue was divided between the provincial and local governments, with the latter spending mainly for official salaries and to enlarge the police force. Peasant distress was not apparent during the period in spite of increased taxes and the absence of any government investment to promote rural development.

There is every indication that, over the long run, land distribution did not change, and the inequality of land holding, already very great, did not become more unequal. The reason for stable land distribution was the inheritance system of dividing land equally between the male heirs. . . .

The Peasant Economy

.... Without a thorough understanding of the conditions under which peasants lived, their behavior often appears irrational and devoid of purpose in the eyes of outsiders. The following should correct that impression and show the operating principles which guided peasants in the use of their resources.

The supply of household labor was directly related to the size of the farm. The household allocated its available labor to field work and non-farm employment according to the amount of effort and risk involved to earn the largest income. If farm land and capital were scarce, the household dispatched more labor to work in other villages and market towns. If the farm was large and had capital, more labor was retained for farming. In reality households worked out the combination of these two alternatives which provided the largest income.

Households used their savings from farm and nonfarm income to buy land and increase the size of the farm. Beyond a certain size of farm, households leased land to other peasants and used their wealth for moneylending or investing in handicraft and commerce. The decision to invest less income in farming was determined by the existing technology and the managerial skill of the household. When the rate of return from greater farm capital became unattractive in comparison to the rate of return from alternative investments, more household wealth flowed to nonfarm activities. . . .

The land which the household managed was allocated among different uses. Some land would be allocated for growing high income crops for the market, and the remaining land was used to grow crops vital for the household's consumption. The decision of how much land to allocate between these two categories of crops depended upon the peasants' knowledge of which crops grew best, the existing soil conditions which permitted certain crops to grow better than others, and the opportunities to exchange crops for goods that could not be cheaply produced on the farm. As a result, some districts specialized in industrial crops, and others in food crops. Households also decided which cash crop or combination of cash crops should be grown. Such a choice depended upon the labor supply and household's ability to provide additional capital in order to prevent a decline in soil fertility.

The above decisions were ultimately determined by the foresight, experience and knowledge of the peasants. Some households made better decisions than others and were able to earn more income and accumulate land. In every village a few wealthy households could be found. Households which made bad decisions inevitably became poorer.

The Process of Agricultural Development

Between 1880 and 1940 the average size of the household farm declined. Farms were increasingly fragmented depending upon the rate of population expansion. . . .

Population increased between 60 and 80 percent during this period, and the proportion of the population living in cities by 1949 was probably 5 or 10 percent more than in 1880. Farm output rose slightly more rapidly than the rate of population expansion and it was possible for cities to grow. . . .

. . . . Urban economic growth provided expanding employment opportunity for peasants and enabled households to substitute crops of higher prices for those of lower prices. Because household income rose, small farms survived and living standards did not decline.

In a comparison of the trends of rural wages, land price, and the price of farm capital, the results show that land did not become critically scarce and the rural workforce was not excessively enlarged with underemployed and landless peasants. Rising values should not be interpreted to mean that peasants were prospering. The steady increase in population and the gradual rise in farm production probably just enabled households to maintain their living standards. At no time did production increase rapidly enough to permit large stocks to accumulate. . . .

It was a major triumph for this peasant economy to provide additional labor to the cities, increase the supply of industrial staples and food, and yet maintain living standards comparable to those of the recent past. It was only the rural households that invested in farming, and their managerial decisions alone made this process possible. This is remarkable considering that so little new technology from outside was introduced into agriculture during this period.

Technology and Agricultural Development

. . . . The more usual method of generating technical advance was for peasants to use trial and error methods of selecting better seeds and farming methods suited to the immediate environment. This was a very slow and tortuous way of advancing knowledge and educating successive generations of peasants. . . .

. . . . It was observed that beyond a certain size of farm, output and income per unit of land declined. Associated with this trend was a decline in the percentage of household income invested in variable capital. More household wealth was invested in nonfarming activities or used for consumption, and the household leased more land to other households. Increasing the size of household farm would not have changed household economic behavior or made farming more profitable in terms of raising output and income per unit of land. Improving and raising agricultural production could take place without altering the size of the household farm.

The improvement could be achieved simply through technological change, such as new, high-yield seed varieties, chemical fertilizers, pesticides, improved tools, and a stable water supply. Without improving these inputs and increasing their supply, households were compelled to use age-old techniques and a limited supply of farming inputs. Inadequate knowledge and limited managerial skill restricted investment to a small, fixed percentage of income and limited the size of farm that could be managed efficiently. Without knowledge of more efficient farming, wealthy households found it more profitable to invest outside agriculture and to lease their land to other farmers. . . .

42

Marketing and Social Structure in Rural China

G. William Skinner

The specialists offer many different explanations of why China's agricultural economy failed to achieve a successful transition to the high yields of modern, scientific agriculture, remaining within the limits of traditional, labor-intensive techniques. Ramon Myers, in the previous article, clearly puts the blame on the failure of the government or educational system to make modern technology available to the peasants, leaving them to discover new technology themselves by means of trial and error. This line of reasoning came to be labeled the "technologist" explanation.

Reference was earlier made to other authors' concentration on the poorer classes of peasants and villagers; these authors argue that increased commercialization of agriculture in the twentieth century led to a worsening of the distribution of income between the owners of the land and the tillers of the land and growing tensions between these classes. According to this "distributionalist" explanation, those who had the capital to invest in the technological transformation of Chinese agriculture were using these funds for investment in other sectors or for the consumption of luxuries, while the poorer peasants, the producers, lacked the means to invest in modern technology. Another serious constraint on China's agricultural development was its high degree of subsistence production. The size of the market available to the producer was small because of high transport costs and transactions costs, greatly limiting the degree of specialization and trade that was possible.

Although limited, the Chinese economy was a market economy, with the individual villages and their economic activity somewhat loosely tied into a nascent national economy of market towns, regional trade centers, and major central cities. Thus, residents of the capital and major metropolitan centers could enjoy the products produced in remote villages in the provinces, while the peasants— those with enough money, anyway—could on rare occasions obtain products produced in distant cities, even from abroad. Our knowledge of this marketing system comes largely from the insightful, detailed, and informative research done by a single scholar, the anthropologist G. William Skinner of Stanford University. The following micro-view of this hierarchical system of markets, with emphasis on the local marketing system, is taken from a series of three articles he published in the Journal of Asian Studies, *collectively titled "Marketing and Social Structure in Rural China." We have already seen, in chapter 9, the view of that same system from the macro perspective, with emphasis on the various major economic regions of which these market systems were a part, and their loose integration to form a national economy.*

Marketing Structures as Spatial and Economic Systems

.... In order to set forth meaningful propositions about marketing structures as spatial systems it will be necessary to have recourse to simple models.... Theoretical considerations based on impeccable geometry and tolerably sound economics tell us that ... market towns should be distributed on the landscape according to an isometric grid, as if at the apex of space-filling equilateral triangles. In theory, too, the service area of each market should approach a regular hexagon. These expectations apply anywhere in the world—neither the geometry nor the economics is peculiarly Chinese—and it is therefore of no particular moment to report that in six areas of China where I have been able to test the proposition, a majority of market towns have precisely six immediately neighboring market towns and hence a marketing area of hexagonal shape, albeit distorted by topographical features....

Our model, then, which is diagrammed as the basic pattern of Figure 1, shows a hexagonal marketing area with the market town at the center, surrounded by an inner ring of six and an outer ring of twelve villages. As is empirically typical, the model calls for six paths radiating out from the town.

These paths are at once the arteries and the veins of an economic system whose heart is the market in the town at its center. Along these

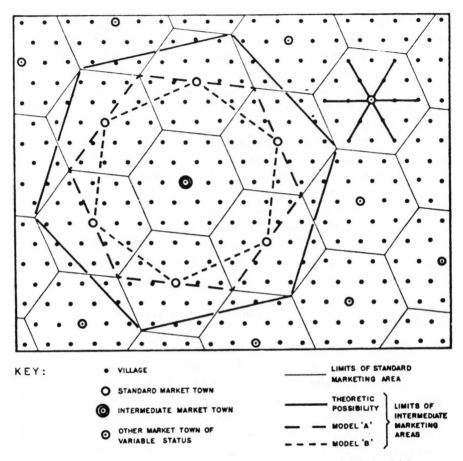

KEY:

● VILLAGE

○ STANDARD MARKET TOWN

◎ INTERMEDIATE MARKET TOWN

⊙ OTHER MARKET TOWN OF
VARIABLE STATUS

_____ LIMITS OF STANDARD
MARKETING AREA

_____ THEORETIC
POSSIBILITY   ⎫ LIMITS OF
                  ⎬ INTERMEDIATE
— — MODEL 'A'   ⎥ MARKETING
                  ⎬ AREAS
– – – – MODEL 'B' ⎭

Figure 1. A Model of the Chinese Standard Marketing Area as a Stable Spatial System, Together with Three Possible Models of Intermediate Marketing Areas

paths, in the early morning hours of every market day, typically pass at least one out of every five adults living in the whole array of dependent villages. . . .

During the few hours of market before the inward flow of villagers is reversed, the meager facilities of the typical standard market town are sorely taxed. Most such towns have only one real street and lack a defined single marketplace altogether. Instead there is a multitude of petty marketplaces, one for each product. The grain market may be held in the temple courtyard, the pig market at the edge of the town, while each of the various items of perishable products and minor crafts produced locally has its customary marketing section along the main street. Even though most sellers at any standard market are likely to be itinerants, the standard market town normally has a certain minimum of permanent facilities. These typically include—in addition to the socially important tea houses, wineshops, and eating places—one or more oil shops (selling fuel for wick lamps), incense and candle shops (selling the essentials of religious worship), and at least a few others offering such items as looms, needles and thread, brooms, soap, tobacco, and matches. Standard market towns normally support a number of craftsmen as well, including most typically blacksmiths, coffinmakers, carpenters, and makers of paper effigies for religious burning. A few crude workshops to process local products may also be located in a standard market town.

The standard market functions in the first instance to exchange what the peasant produces for what he needs. The peasant needs not only goods of the kind already suggested, but also the services of tool sharpeners and livestock castrators, medical practitioners and "tooth artists," religious specialists and fortune tellers, barbers, myriad entertainers, and even, on occasion, scribes. While many of these services are not available every market day, itinerants purveying all of them occasionally visit every standard market.

The standard marketing system also has a modest financial dimension. Shops in the town extend credit to regular customers. Certain shop keepers and landowners lend money to peasants in transactions which may take place in the town on market day. The rotating credit societies of the peasant are also usually organized in the teahouses on market day and are thereby restricted to villagers from within the system. In addition, certain landlords maintain an office in the town which collects rent from tenants.

With regard to transport, village communities normally include a few landless peasants, as they are usually termed, who are regularly for hire as transport coolies. (Not only the local elite but also the stratum of the peasantry which is fully "respectable" eschew such public manual labor as carrying or carting bulky produce.) These men normally cart goods along the village paths serving a single marketing area and thus constitute another element in the standard marketing structure as a spatial-economic system. . . .

It is apparent from what has been described already that the standard marketing system, when viewed in spatial and economic terms, is but a subsystem of a larger structure. In particular, there is a regular movement both of goods and of mobile firms between the standard market town and the intermediate or still higher-level market towns to which it is immediately tied. I use the plural because in the usual case the standard market is dependent on two or three higher-level market towns rather than just one. . . .

This fact points up a crucial distinction between the standard marketing system, on the one hand, and intermediate and higher-level marketing systems, on the other. Whereas the former is essentially discrete with regard to the inclusion or exclusion of component settlements, the latter are not. . . . [Moreover,] peasants attend their intermediate market only occasionally—to make purchases which are out of the ordinary, to obtain some service which peasants do not normally demand, to secure credit on an extraordinary scale, or to attend an annual religious festival. During three months when I lived with a typical peasant family in Szechwan, whose farmstead was three *li* [about one mile] from one market town, Kao-tien-tzu, and five *li* from another, Niu-shih-k'ou, the household head and his wife between them marketed forty-six times at the former, their standard market, and only three times at the latter, their intermediate market. . . .

The situation was rather different in the case of the local elite. Everything which set them apart from the peasantry encouraged their attendance at the intermediate market. They were literate, and in the intermediate as opposed to the standard market they could buy books and stationery supplies. Their style of life was if not exalted at least gentlemanly, and from time to time they needed to purchase foodstuffs, decorative items, or cloth of a quality which for a peasant would be sheer indulgence and hence unavailable in standard markets. They were men of comparative wealth, and the intermediate market town offered a range of opportunities for money lending and investment unmatched in their standard market towns. They were also men of leisure, and it was only in intermediate or higher-level markets that tea- and wine-houses especially equipped to fill the idle hours of leisured gentlemen were available. In short, while the regular needs of the peasants were met by the standard markets, those of the local elite were met only by the intermediate market. . . .

Let us now look over the total complex of nested marketing systems and survey, first of all, the downward flow of merchandise. Exotic goods shipped to the central market town, and other goods produced in it, are distributed in part through the central market itself, in part by itinerants who circuit both intermediate and standard markets throughout the central marketing system, and in part to firms in the six intermediate market towns. Merchandise received by firms in each intermediate market town, together with other goods produced there, are similarly distributed: in part through the intermediate market itself, in part by itinerants who circuit standard markets within the intermediate marketing system, and in part to firms in the six standard market towns. The firms receiving goods in this downward flow consist, in the case of standard market towns, chiefly of small shops; in the case of intermediate market towns they include distributors who supply itinerants as well as dual wholesale-retail establishments; and in the case of central market towns they include most prominently wholesalers equipped with warehouses. Merchandise which is consumed by the peasantry or required by petty craftsmen flows down through the system to every market; consumer goods for the local elite and supplies for artisans move no further down than the intermediate market; while consumer goods of interest chiefly to the bureaucratic elite, together with industrial supplies, normally go no further than the central market town itself.

The flow of goods upward through the marketing system begins when the peasant sells his product in the standard market, either to local consumers, to dealers based in the standard market who process and/or bulk the produce, or directly to buyers who are visiting the standard market from higher-level market towns. Purchasing agents and buyers visit standard markets from central as well as intermediate market towns; they visit intermediate markets from local cities as well as central market towns. Whether the collecting firms are commercial houses or industries which process or consume the local products, these products are drawn up through the marketing system to ever higher-level centers.

. . . . Marketing structures, unlike administrative structures, take the form of interlocking networks. It is the joint participation of standard markets in two or three intermediate marketing systems, of intermediate markets in two or three central marketing systems, and so on, which articulates and unites the local economies centered on each market town into, first, regional economic structures and eventually into a single society-wide economy. . . .

The complexity of the whole, however, should not be taken to imply that the marketing system was either monolithic or tightly structured. Not only was there no one economic apex paralleling the administrative capital, but the flow of goods, which defined the structure, was seldom very heavy by modern standards. . . .

43

The Commune System before Reform

Frederick W. Crook

As a result of the introduction and spread of modern means of transportation, i.e., railroads, and the growth in trade between the major economic regions identified by G. William Skinner, greater specialization and signs of a nascent national economy began to develop in the first half of the twentieth century. Yet, many specialists believe that even today the Chinese economy is best described as a "cellular" economy, or a loosely and weakly integrated cluster of regional economies. In fact, when the Chinese Communists gained control of the national economy in 1949, they administered economic policy through regional governments. In addition, given the long history of private property rights and market relationships then in existence, markets were used as the major means for the allocation of resources and goods during the first few years of the new regime.

To solve the agricultural problem, i.e., the need to increase yields and achieve much larger per capita supplies of foodstuffs and industrial crops, throughout much of the post-1949 period the Communist leaders in China have relied upon a basic institutional reorganization of the traditional labor-intensive pattern of agricultural production. Before they introduced this reorganization, however, they kept their promise to the peasants to carry out an extensive land reform program. Households that did not work the land they owned had their land expropriated and distributed to those who worked the land. Thus, although richer peasants were allowed to keep any land they actually worked, the landlords who lived by the work of others were either killed or classed as non-persons with few rights. Almost 40 percent of the cultivated land in China was thus distributed to the poorer and landless peasants. Unfortunately, there were too many peasants and too little cultivated land, so that the average size of the private farm after the land reform was too small to support the peasant family. The Communists believed that collectivized agricultural production was the solution.

The essential features of the institutional organization of China's collectivized agricultural sector have been described in chapter 32 by Martin Whyte. The following article, prepared by Frederick W. Crook of the U.S. Department of Agriculture for the Joint Economic Committee, U.S. Congress, and published in The Chinese Economy in the Eighties, *assesses how that system functioned as a replacement for private, household farming. This volume is one of a series of collected papers on China's economy that the Joint Economic Committee has published about every three or four years for the purpose of better informing itself, the Congress, "and the interested public."*

The commune system in the period from 1975 through 1979 had stable institutions; output from commune and brigade enterprises grew rapidly; and social services for commune members expanded. But tight controls, rigid planning mechanisms, ill-conceived management rules, a single organization pattern for rural areas, and reduced production incentives retarded growth of agricultural output and per capita income....

The major elements of the commune system will be described briefly. This background information will help readers understand the complex changes which occurred from 1980 to 1984 and continue in 1985....

A Review of the Commune System, 1975–79

In the period 1975–79 the commune system continued to consist of four parts: commune-unit, brigade, team, and households. The size of these units and their organizational patterns paralleled corresponding units in the 1963–74 period. Production teams continued to produce most of rural output, to make economic decisions, and to distribute income. Teams also owned most of the assets in the rural areas. The four parts were fitted into a hierarchy with the commune-unit at the apex and households at the base of the structure....

Ownership of land and fixed assets had three forms in rural areas.

Private ownership did exist but consisted of limited amounts of fixed assets. Land and fixed assets in state farms were owned by the state—ownership by all the people. Land and fixed assets in the commune system were owned collectively by members of teams, brigades and the commune-unit.

Factors of production such as labor and capital were tightly controlled and were not permitted to move freely. The government used administrative regulations and the rationing system to prevent farmers from moving to urban centers. Economic entities such as units in the commune system or commune-unit or brigade enterprises were organized or disbanded by administrative fiat. New entities did not enter and old entities did not exit the system on the basis of strict economic profitability or loss.

Prior to the reforms [i.e., before 1979], economic decision making in the commune system was characterized by strong central controls. These control mechanisms passed orders from Beijing through provincial and county centers to the commune. These orders specified what crops should be produced and marketed. Local self-sufficiency was an important principle embedded in the planning system. Units in the commune system struggled to provide their own basic requirements from resources within their boundaries.

A large part of the output generated by the commune system was consumed locally. The small portion of output moving across commune boundaries did so through the government-owned marketing system. The same marketing system sold inputs and supplies to production units. Grain, edible oil, and cotton cloth and other goods were rationed to consumers through retail stores. Rural free markets, which traditionally had an important place in rural life, were forbidden to operate or functioned for limited time periods under stringent controls.

Both material and non-material incentives were used to motivate commune members to work. A large part of a member's annual income came from production teams in the form of egalitarian grain payment for work done. A small fraction of members' income came from the labor day work payment system which attempted to relate payments to the quantity and quality of work done. A third source of income came from households, working private plots, when these plots were allowed to exist by Party decree. Party leaders taught socialist principles and encouraged farmers to work for the good of the community and the nation.

The commune system was organized in part to implement Mao's vision of the rural economy. Rural cadres, however, quickly found that to increase output, raise income and make the commune system work, it was necessary to rely on relatively small-sized production teams in which the means of production were collectively owned, capitalist-like incentives were employed to induce farmers to work, and some fairly strong autonomous forces were allowed to work within teams. Maoists were fearful that the pursuit of self-interest, capitalist forces, and the relatively uncontrolled initiative generated in teams might get out of control and destroy the socialist system. To prevent such an outburst they constructed powerful mechanisms to control the rural economy. Over the course of several decades from 1958 to 1978 the Party and Government issued regulations and administrative orders, and built institutions to control the initiative of teams and households. . . .

In the period from 1975 to 1979, the commune system brought powerful forces to bear on teams to fulfill state production plans and follow prescribed economic and political behavior. A production team weighing possible consequences of increasing the area sown to cotton and reducing the area of wheat in order to raise income, could well have made the following analysis. If we grow more cotton, party leaders in the brigade *danwei* (basic unit) could remove our trusted team leaders from their posts. Officers in the commune *danwei* such as the state-managed credit cooperative could deny our team a loan to purchase a much-needed tractor. Managers of the commune-operated irrigation system could arrange for our fields to be watered last. Supply and marketing cooperative cadres could deny or slow down deliveries of seed and chemical fertilizers to our team and could down-grade the quality of our cotton and pay lower prices for the cotton we produced in excess of our assigned quota. If we produce less wheat, cadres in the grain station could refuse to sell us the wheat we need to meet our basic food grain rations. Cadres could choose young people from other teams to work in brigade and commune-run industries, to attend high school, and to join the youth league.

Teams and households, surrounded on all sides by entities with coercive power and cadres armed with a host of restrictive red tape, decrees, and orders, bridled their self-interest. Government and party leaders were successful in containing the energy inherent in teams and households which they feared so much, but at the same time they so seriously dampened incentives that output and income growth was sluggish and peasant enthusiasm for the commune system weakened.

Assessment of Strengths and Weaknesses of the Commune System

China's leaders reviewing the strengths of the commune system highlighted the following points. The system with its relatively large size was effective in mobilizing and directing the rural labor force to terrace fields, level plots, and generally upgrade farmland. Communes were also effective in managing irrigation and drainage systems, and in constructing and expanding water control projects. Also the system supported the growth of rural industry. The combining of government administrative and economic management in the commune system did improve collective economic organizations and strengthened rural political organs.

Also it is important for us to recall that in the period from 1958–79 peasants in the commune system saw the following products of commune activity:

- development of strong control apparatus;
- growing importance of commune-unit and brigades as institutions advancing toward socialism;
- widespread electrification;
- development of an extensive rural road system;
- development of an agricultural extension system;
- expansion of rural financial institutions;
- development of a rural health care system;
- expansion of primary and secondary education in rural areas;
- construction of movie theaters, libraries, and sports grounds;
- development of a rural wired broadcast system; and
- development of a disaster relief system.

Given these strong points, could the weaknesses in the commune system have been altered and reformed to improve performance? There were alternative paths which could have been taken, but of course the most important fact is that China's leaders in 1978–79 decided radical changes were required.

The primary criticisms against the commune system were as follows. First, the commune system had one organizational pattern and forced economic organs to fit within administrative boundaries, which resulted in economic dislocations. Some commune economic entities such as supply and marketing cooperatives would have functioned better had they been permitted to cross commune boundaries or even county lines.

Second, the unification of politics, administration and economic decision-making into one entity led to many abuses and errors. Political work in rural areas is reported to have declined during the commune period because rural cadres were forced to spend so much of their time making economic decisions. Furthermore, leading cadres in the commune system were also political cadres and often they did not consult experienced peasants in making decisions. Instead they issued administrative orders to implement production plans. These blind orders often led to declines in production as crops were planted, cultivated, irrigated, and harvested in the wrong way and at the wrong times.

Third, the commune system, characterized by a single system of public ownership, by centralized labor, and by distribution according to the labor day work payment system, did not provide strong incentives. Leading cadres made basic economic decisions in the system but bore limited risks because administrators' primary source of income came from their wages as state employees. Peasants in the teams, on the other hand, had little or nothing to say about the basic decisions affecting their lives, but they bore the risks. A crop failure because of a management decision to use an untested new seed variety resulted in reduced grain rations for peasants but not a commensurate decline in income for cadres who had an "iron rice bowl" from state wage funds.

.... The system failed to motivate farmers to work. To increase output, raise living standards, and to keep peasants loyal to the regime, the vitality, creativity, and energy of 800 million peasants needed to be released....

44

Socialist Agriculture Is Dead; Long Live Socialist Agriculture!

Kathleen Hartford

As suggested in the previous reading, with the death of Mao in 1976, the ensuing change in leadership, and the flood of economic data released by the new leadership, there was a serious reappraisal of the commune system. While aggregate output had gone up, inputs per unit of output had also increased and productivity had declined. Incomes in agriculture had not increased significantly and some communes were suffering a decline in income. In terms of the standard of living, grain consumption per capita was no higher than it had been in the mid-1950s, while per-capita consumption of cooking oils, vegetables, and sugar had declined. In other words, aggregate output had been increased only by a massive increase in inputs and effort, with little return on a per capita basis for the peasants. Some of these negative results obviously were due to mismanagement at the local level, some due to the adoption of inappropriate policies at the national level; not all the poor results can be attributed to the attempt to replace China's traditional system of private farms and village markets as described by Myers and Skinner with the socialist system of collectives described by Crook.

Yet, the new leadership under Deng Xiaoping clearly believed the existing socialist organization of the agricultural sector he inherited was counterproductive and would be an obstacle to the transformation of China's agriculture from traditional, labor-intensive to modern, scientific agriculture. The clear sign for a change in policy was issued by the Third Plenum of the Eleventh Central

Committee in November/December of 1978. The reorganization of agriculture that followed was begun in areas of Anhui and Sichuan provinces, but soon gained a momentum which spread the "restoration of private farming" throughout the rural areas in all of China. The following article assesses the dramatic changes that were introduced in the rural sector in the early 1980s, while warning about the limits to and consequences of these changes, especially insofar as they address the fundamental economic problems in China's agricultural revolution. The author, Kathleen Hartford, is a political scientist who specializes in the comparative study of socialist agriculture. It is interesting to note that, despite her sympathy and interest in socialist organizations in China's agriculture after 1949, she ends with the same emphasis on the need for modern technology to solve China's agricultural problems with which Myers, a strong advocate of private farming, concluded his analysis of China's agricultural problems in the period before 1949.

In the space of only five years, China's agricultural organization has undergone changes of a magnitude matched only by the collectivization process of the 1950s. Most farmland is now contracted to individual peasant households. Private rural commerce in market fairs is flourishing. Peasants and handicraft workers may hire laborers or apprentices, collectives may sell off tractors or tools to individuals, and collectively owned enterprises may be sold to households or small groups. The commune structure is being formally scrapped in favor of a system that "separates economics and politics." Is collectivism dead in rural China?

The general response of most Western observers is a resounding—and generally approving—yes. In this [article], however, I shall present a counterargument. In my view, the architects of reorganization in China's agricultural sector cannot completely dismantle the collective system. We are likely to see in the future, not a "return to capitalism" in the Chinese countryside, but a reaffirmation of several key features of collectivism. . . .

The New Model

Production Responsibility Systems (PRS)

Responsibility systems for agricultural production were experimentally introduced beginning in 1978, and have now spread to include nearly all production teams. The responsibility systems include a wide variety of practices, but generally all involve two common features: first, production contracts, concluded between the team and smaller units below the team; and second, differential compensation distinguishing the work contribution of each producer, thus satisfying the principle of "to each according to his work." Beyond these similarities, responsibility systems vary along several dimensions: in the size of units awarded contracts, in the degree of division of agricultural (or other) tasks, in the degree of team control over production plans and disposal of final product, in the methods used to arrive at team members' compensation, and in the duration of the contracts.

From the time of their introduction nationwide in 1978, the responsibility systems have changed with a rapidity that has apparently bewildered many Chinese nearly as much as outside observers. When the systems were first bruited, then CCP Chairman Hua Guofeng pointed to the fixed-compensation systems as the most desirable arrangement. As of early 1980, this type of contract still accounted for the majority of production teams. Very soon thereafter, however, the other types of PRS—dubbed "compensation linked to output" *(lianchan jichou)*—swiftly gained ground, and, by 1983, accounted for nearly all production teams. An enormous array of such systems were current in 1979–81. . . .

Among these types, there has been a fast-moving change in composition, from those relying more on centralized team planning, unified distribution, and larger work groups, to those awarding contracts on a long-term basis to individual households and which curtail or altogether eliminate unified distribution.

Household Contracting Systems. The "contracting-production-to-the-household" PRSs retain the team's role in centralized production planning and unified distribution, but day-to-day management devolves to individual households. The team assigns plots of land to households by contract; allotments may be made on a per capita basis, or pegged to a combined index of household population and labor-force participation. Contracts generally stipulate the land and other inputs to be provided by the team, the output targets, and the work points to be awarded. (These factors are often referred to as the "three fixed"—costs, output, and compensation.) In addition, contracts generally specify bonuses for better-than-contracted performance, and penalties for substandard performance.

. . . . In the other type of household contracting system, "contracting tasks to the household," individual households receive contracts for fixed plots of land in return for fixed payments to the collective which are supposed to satisfy state and collective requirements (taxes, welfare funds, collective investments, procurement quotas). The household keeps all other produce for its own use or sale. Unlike the other responsibility systems, this method features no "unified distribution" of the team's product. Peasants are basically self-employed and they "compensate" themselves directly with their own output. They are also responsible for providing their own food needs. . . .

The term of household contracts has varied by localities. My interviews in 1983 revealed some localities using annually renewed contracts which reallocated land to allow for changes in households' size or situation; and some in which the duration was unstipulated but assumed to be long term. In the latter, land allocations were to remain unchanged regardless of household situations ("births or deaths, you don't change it" *sheng si bubian*). The Chinese press has recently hailed explicit long-term contracts, and even "land-use certificates" granted through county offices and good for fifteen years, as the latest fruitful development in the responsibility systems—"joyously received" by the peasants! . . .

Further Organizational Changes in China's Agricultural System

. . . . *Surplus Labor and Development of the Private Sector.* Given China's high population-to-land ratio, efficiency gains occasioned by the responsibility systems were likely to be reflected in an overt rural labor surplus. *Ex ante* estimates by officials had put this surplus at one-third to one-half the rural labor force of 300 million. Studies of local experiences have confirmed the expectations. The labor surplus is supposed to be absorbed within the rural sector.

Several policies are aimed at speeding this absorption. First, rural cadres were urged to begin by arranging contracts with those whose special productive skills require little or no land inputs (beekeeping, livestock-raising, and so forth), thus reducing the numbers needing access to land for their livelihood. Second, official policy now permits independent economic activity by "private individuals" who may enter small-scale production, repair work, or commerce, using their own investment funds, retaining their earnings; they are responsible for their own costs, and not subject to state or collective plans or assessments. Third, in areas not using household contracting systems, up to 15 percent of the production team's land may be assigned to individual households as private plots. Households may, in addition, retain any wasteland they have reclaimed. All households are encouraged to develop "household sidelines" to use surplus household labor and supplement their incomes from "agricultural" (crop-growing) pursuits.

Recent information suggests that these moves have brought about a significant shift in the pattern of the economic activity in the countryside. This is apparent in the growing number of "specialized and key-point households" producing a wide variety of commodities, and in the general burgeoning of commerce in the rural market fairs.

. . . . "Specialized households" are those in which all or nearly all labor is applied to specialized production, while in "key-point households," only "supplemental labor" (that is, labor by women, children, and the elderly) engages in specialized production. All specialization does not, however, stem from the same origins. Some "specialized households" have been assigned to the work and awarded contracts by the team; others have developed through intensification of what began as household sidelines. Whatever their origins, these households have been lauded by analysts who stress their high commodity rate (generally over 70 percent, sometimes as much as 90 percent, of the household's production is for sale), high labor productivity, and cost effectiveness. Because of their contribution to the overall rise in rural prosperity and the national supply of agricultural commodities, they are entitled to state-supplied "award grain" (grain supplied, with or without charge, in return for sale to the state of specified quantities of a given commodity), to team allocations of fodder land or feed-grains, and to bank loans.

Chinese policy-makers and scholars have increasingly focused their attention on the development of specialized and key-point households, and some point to them as harbingers of the future. However, it should be noted that the specialized households have also excited hostility among some cadres and peasants. Specialized households concentrating, as they generally do, on high-value products with high commodity rate, tend to earn whopping incomes relative to the rural Chinese average. The vast majority of peasants now and for the foreseeable future will be required to concentrate on growing low-value grain in order to ensure local and national food supplies. . . .

The Emerging New Model

The organizational formula for Chinese agriculture is still very much in flux. On the one hand, the leadership asserts that the responsibility systems—and therefore household-based production—will remain unchanged for "a certain time," that is, for an uncertain but supposedly lengthy period. On the other hand, there has been a growing emphasis on building up more cooperative or collectivized organizational forms, whether in specialized production, in small-scale manufacturing, in commercial activities, or in agricultural infrastructure investments. Just how the "centralized" and "decentralized" forms will interact, and which will be paramount, is anyone's guess. Any informed guess based on past practice, however, would at least point to an enforcement from above of a definite model once the leadership has winnowed out of the welter of local initiatives something it thinks fits together as a workable, dynamic combination.

. . . . Increasingly, the Chinese commentaries have pointed toward a new model of socialist agricultural organization which departs from the Maoist one in virtually every respect except for collective ownership of the basic means of production. While maintaining the necessity of centralized planning, the new model points to scientific and economic planning rather than mere planning in physical quantities without regard to regional comparative advantage. Most production is to be organized on a household basis, with increasing specialization and rising commodity rates providing dynamism needed for growth. "Socialization" of production may progress as household producers themselves recognize the greater gains made possible by combining capital and coordinating specialized labor—or merely as they become more specialized and more deeply involved in the commodity economy. The self-sufficiency of territorially defined units will be jettisoned in favor of exchange relations voluntarily entered into by all concerned parties. All production and provision of essential services will be organized for maximum efficiency and high rates of return, through contractual arrangements between the relevant parties—be they state purchasing agencies and the team (perhaps renamed a "cooperative") or households or "economic combinations"; or between household producers and specialized service "companies" or individual service vendors. Collective ownership of land and planned allocation of contracts will ensure access by all peasants to some means of making a livelihood, and will guarantee the careful husbanding and development of agricultural resources.... We have, in effect, a new model of agricultural socialism, knit together by contract rather than by collectivist vision.

We see, with the emergence of this new model, a determination by China's new leaders to bury the Maoist model once and for all. In the space of only four years, they have moved from tentative tinkerings to massive dismemberment of the basic features of the former collectivized system.

On the surface, it would seem that the reforms are working well.... Agricultural output and rural incomes have both increased substantially since implementation of the rural reforms. These increases have been explained by many Chinese commentators as due in large part to the new responsibility systems. In my view, however, much of the success cannot be traced directly to the organizational reforms. Other factors that may have played a role include a jump in producer prices, increased private marketing opportunities, a rise in fertilizer application, and a pronounced shift in cropping patterns to capture comparative advantages. The point is not that reorganization has had no effect on productivity, but that the total increase in output owes much to other circumstances.

What of the difficulties ahead for the organizational reforms? Like the Maoist model, the new model's coherence in theory must be matched in practice; all parts must be in place and playing their assigned roles if the model is to work as envisioned. Here the problems are likely to arise from a paradoxical situation: that the reforms will go too far, and that they will not go far enough. Four features of the model probably cannot be taken far enough, and two already give signs of going too far.

Of the reforms that will not go far enough, the first is the separation of political and economic functions.... Thus, local political cadres should not be able to interfere with the administration of economic units or use their funds at will. While some improvement in accounting methods in local units might come out of this reform, it is unlikely that economic management can be liberated from Party interference. Quite apart from the overlap in personnel at the local level, one need only note the irony of the CCP Central Committee (which still maintains for itself the prerogative of proclaiming the major national agricultural policies) insisting upon local Party cadres' non-interference in economic management—while maintaining that Party members are responsible for implementing Party policies. If politics becomes truly separated from economics at the grassroots level, it will be because politics has lapsed entirely, something the Central Committee is by no means anxious to see happen.

Second, under the new model, all management of economic relations is to be done through contractual agreements, in which the responsibilities of all parties are spelled out, the exchange to be made is quantified, and penalties are stipulated for nonperformance. This may be workable where only two parties are involved; or where the contracting parties have a choice among contractual partners, so that poor performance by one does not force the second party into defaulting on the contractual obligations. The former situation obtains only in the most backward of areas; as for the latter, very few alternative suppliers or buyers are available in the Chinese countryside.

Third, agricultural restructuring in line with comparative advantage has already encountered major obstacles. These may be due largely to the inherent contradiction between comparative advantage and planning. By early 1982, the state placed a three-year freeze on "both the level of resales of grain to rural producers of non-grain crops and the level of inter-provincial cereal transfers." This decision, stemming from policy-makers' concern for ensuring national food supply and holding down food subsidy costs (often defined in terms of limiting non-urban demands for marketed grain), places severe restrictions upon the capture of regional comparative advantage. . . . Finally, the current policy of concentrating state investments in "commodity bases" (especially for grain) may only skew development greatly toward areas which have significant, but not overwhelming, natural advantages to begin with, without developing *any* of the comparative advantages of the areas less blessed.

Fourth, there are already apparent difficulties for establishing more "organic" commercial ties. The restraints placed on interprovincial grain transfers are but one indication of the resistance, at all levels of the economic system, to dilution of the state marketing system's virtual monopoly control over commercial transactions. . . .

Thus, the Chinese system remains considerably more rigid than the reform rhetoric would lead us to suppose—and these rigidities are often safeguarded in practice by the very policy-makers who have ostensibly approved the rhetoric. But residual rigidities are not the only stumbling block for implementing the new model. In some respects, the organizational reforms may have gone too far. . . .

There remain severe limitations on the autonomy of peasant producers in the present system. . . . But many households are now freed of such restrictions—either by their access to grain or inputs in rural free markets or by their opportunities to move out of the rural community—and can afford to make their own decisions regardless of team plans or procurement quotas. Planners have to deal with the undesired consequences of this new autonomy: the abandonment of agricultural land while peasants pursue higher incomes outside of agriculture, the unauthorized shift out of grain into cash crops, the violation of the planned-births policy. The threats that such trends pose for ensuring national food supply and maintaining demographic control are not yet critical, but they are obvious, and of deep concern to policy-makers.

These trends beyond autonomy to what the planners consider anarchy may be encouraged as the specialized households develop. The encouragement of specialized households spells a strong possibility of extreme polarization of incomes in the countryside, not between localities, but within them. Curiously, while the specialized households' arrangements have been touted as particularly suited to those with special skills or talents, some recent information suggests that the opportunities for specialized-household status (which are allocated by the collective) may be disproportionately assigned to team and brigade cadres or former cadres, educated youths, and demobilized soldiers—the very types who were accused of using their positions to benefit at the expense of other peasants in the pre-reform system. Thus, to social polarization there may be added an element of political resentment. . . .

Predicting the future of the reforms necessarily partakes of the nature of crystal-ball gazing, but, if the factors discussed above are given any weight, we must conclude that, *so long as current national development priorities remain unchanged,* the reforms are not likely to proceed according to the blueprint set by the new model. Furthermore, I would contend that the pressures upon the reform process coming from all relevant quarters—national planners and policy-makers, local and regional cadres, and peasants themselves—will lead toward the restoration or reconfirmation of some (not all) of the features of the Maoist model. From the national leaders' perspective, concerns with the costs of food subsidies, security of national food supply, and demographic control seem decisive. For regional and local cadres, the concerns focus more on issues such as local growth prospects, the capacity to respond effectively to demands from above, and, of course, their own power and welfare. For peasants, guarantees of basic needs and prospects for continued increases in incomes and living standards may be taken as strong concerns. . . .

This does not mean that the Dazhai [Maoist] model will be back. Certain features of the old model, especially the tendency to large-scale production organizations, are not likely to be welcomed back. Nor does it mean that the restitution of the old model will perfect the agricultural system. A hybrid will probably emerge that avoids major shortcomings of both models, but that still will not solve China's problems of agricultural development. If Americans characteristically turn to a "technological fix" to solve problems, the Chinese leadership has tended to resort to an "organizational fix." The new model for agricultural organization, for all its distinctiveness from the Maoist approach, may be traced to the same root assumption that reorganizing human activities will free latent energies to permit natural, spontaneous development. That such an assumption runs counter to certain other basic assumptions, such as the primacy of Party leadership, is obvious. But what is more important is that no purely organizational formula will break through China's development impasse. And, more particularly, no amount of organization and reorganization will substitute for the improved technology, the massive investments, and the other concrete resources that Chinese agriculture so sorely needs.

45

China's New Rural Reform Experiments

Francis C. Tuan

Many of the unfavorable consequences of the contract responsibility system in agriculture, i.e., the restoration of household farming, worried about by Hartford in the previous reading, did prove to be troublesome. Furthermore, as Hartford suspected, the significant increase in agricultural output in the early 1980s did turn out to be a one-time shift in productivity due to non-repetitive changes in the peasant's environment: the restoration of the land to the control of the household and the increase in prices paid for the output produced on that land by the peasant. Statistical analyses of China's agricultural output since 1949 indicate that increases in prices paid for the peasant's output are the surest way to obtain increases in output. Desiring to keep prices of agricultural products low for urban consumers, however, the Chinese leadership has been unwilling to secure sustained growth in the agricultural sector by means of continuous increases in the prices paid for that output. Thus, in the last half of the 1980s, crop production stagnated for several years, and grain output did not regain its peak level of 1984 again until 1989. In other words, sustained growth of agricultural production will depend, as most of the authors in this section have argued, upon technological change, modern inputs, and large-scale irrigation projects; all activities that were promoted more within the framework of the traditional system of cooperative agriculture than has been true within the framework of small-scale, household farms. In fact, the same statistical analyses of China's agricultural produc-

tion since 1949, mentioned above, indicate that the contribution to agricultural growth of technological innovation has been negative since the household responsibility system was introduced at the end of the 1970s.

Yet, the agricultural reforms initiated in the early 1980s have been interpreted by the Chinese leadership as having been very successful; so much so that the early 1980s are now viewed by the current Chinese leadership as the golden age of the reform program. Thus, they continued the process of reforming agriculture in the last half of the 1980s. In fact, by the time of the conservative retrenchment in the reform program at the end of 1988, the rural sector was the most reformed sector in China's economy, with a large share of economic activity within what could be called a private and market sector. Moreover, despite the removal of the radical reformers and their patrons from positions of power following the crushing of the Tiananmen demonstrations in June of 1989, there was no attempt to recollectivize agriculture or to dismantle the rural reforms that had already been introduced. Perhaps the reason for this was that the reforms were very popular with the peasants, and they constitute the largest group of popular support for the current, more conservative leadership. In addition, despite the economic reforms in the direction of creating an extensive degree of private (household) and market activities in the rural sector, the state still retains significant controls, and there remain many constraints on these private and market activities.

The reading that follows consists of extracts from a report by Francis C. Tuan, U.S. Department of Agriculture, of a briefing on the status of China's rural reforms given to a visiting U.S.D.A. delegation by a Chinese official at the end of the 1980s. As indicated in the briefing, these reforms in China's rural sector are still unfolding, although any attempt to return to a collective system of farming becomes more and more difficult with the passage of time and the continued reliance upon household production and market distribution of agricultural products. As indicated at the end of Tuan's report, however, the more conservative leadership was likely to proceed much more cautiously with the economic reform program.

In general, agricultural reforms implemented since the end of 1978 have revitalized China's rural economy.... However, China is at a turning point, in that the country now has to deal with even more difficult reforms in order to keep its economy growing and meet more diversified demand for agricultural output.... In its No. 5 Document issued in 1987, the central government proposed to establish reform experiments in rural areas to examine possible outcomes—success or failure—for future adoption or improvement.... The initial experiments were planned to last for two years ... [and the] experiment results can be summarized according to the 5 major types of reforms, which are as follows: 1. grain procurement and marketing system; 2. land tenure system; 3. township and village enterprise development; 4. rural cooperative system; and 5. rural financial and credit system.

(1) Grain Procurement and Marketing System

[Despite markets for most crops, the State still dominates or controls the purchase of key crops from the peasant and their sale to the non-peasant households or sectors—*Ed.*] China's grain prices—both government procurement and resale prices—are relatively low compared to market prices. On the one hand, low government purchasing prices reduce farmer's enthusiasm to sell to the state, and on the other hand, lower resale prices by the government make State subsidies necessary. The low retail prices also directly and indirectly encourage higher consumption and use of grain, both in food processing and livestock-raising. In the past few years, sharp increases in grain use put heavier burdens on the government budget.

Two types of reforms related to the grain purchasing and marketing system are being carried out in the experiments: (a) grain procurement prices are being increased to about the market price; and (b) subsidies on inputs are being reduced and the agricultural tax is being increased. The two experimental areas are ... in Henan province and ... in Guangxi autonomous region.... Based on the evaluation [of these reforms], the government will plan future nationwide reforms of grain procurement and marketing. Overall, it would seem easier to carry out the grain procurement and marketing system reform nationwide. The free market prices of grain are very similar in various regions, and inter-regional grain movements are possible. However, the government has to consider the possibility of consumer dissatisfaction and reactions ... [to higher grain prices. Nonetheless,] regional experiments are being carried out not only in Henan and Guangxi, but also in Guangdong, Fujian, Shanxi, and Jiangxi provinces....

(2) Land Tenure System

Land resources in rural China are recognized as the most important input in farming. The stability of the land tenure system has become critical in order to increase land productivity continuously. Currently, China faces several land tenure problems. First, the implementation of the responsibility system in rural areas has resulted in cultivated land being dispersed and plots being small. The average land holding per family is about 0.6 hectare. According to a survey of 20,000 households, each family works on nine plots of land on average. Second, the policy on contracted land use is unstable, which together with grain's disadvantage owing to lower net profits results in farmers being unwilling to make longer term investments in the land. Third, there is no legal binding on contracted land use [i.e., no legal document covering the points at issue exists, or the means for enforcing an existing contract have not been agreed upon.—*Ed.*] and many disputes among rural families are related to land use.

Also, changes in farm household labor force in the last few years have created a situation in which many households still hold a relatively large piece of contracted land but do not have enough laborers to work it, while some families with a larger labor force work only on a small piece of land. In recent years, about 80 million farmers have transferred to nonagricultural jobs, but less than 2 percent of the land [has been] transferred. In the coastal areas, about 60 percent of farmers have shifted to nonagricultural work and 80 percent of incomes come from nonfarm activities. All these [developments] indicate that the government is in urgent need to establish a better land tenure system.

. . . . An experiment has been carried out to improve the land tenure system. A major feature of the experiment is to establish a land bank. The bank provides farmers funds for medium- and long-term investment, and requires land use rights as collateral. A land market will also be developed. . . . Different methods have been used to encourage farmers to expand [the scale of] land [use], including the establishment of organizations to provide funds. In southern Jiangsu province, persons leaving farming retain a piece of the land, called a "ration plot," but give up the remainder of the land to collectives [i.e., the administrative organization that continues to control the allocation of land and capital to the former members of the collectives in the commune system. The communes, of course, have been removed as a result of the economic reforms, and production and income-distribution decisions now are made by the peasant households. Thus, the collective organization has lost many of its former functions and presumably will be phased out as the local government assumes its remaining responsibilities. The peasant households are free to form voluntary cooperatives on their own and are encouraged to do so. See the discussion in section 4 below.—*Ed.*]

Since there has not been a market price on land, price determination is a difficult issue. In [one] county, farmers who acquire land rights turn over about 40 percent of production as compensation to farmers who give up land. Regulations permit this compensation, but the amount is negotiable.... [Whether or not this rent will continue to be collected over the long-run by the household currently renting out the land allocated to it under the contract responsibility system will depend upon laws or regulations that will result from the experiments, such as the one mentioned above, taking place in rural areas.—*Ed.*]

(3) Township and Village Enterprise Development

[With the dismantling of the Commune system, the former township government has been restored, replacing the Commune; the traditional village has taken over most functions formerly performed by the Brigade and the Team in the Commune system.—*Ed.*]

The growth of rural enterprises has been very successful in recent years. It provides a means for farmers to leave their land and increase family income. Currently, there are about 15 million rural enterprises—collective, township, village, and individual. These enterprises employ a total labor force of 80 million in rural China. In 1987, the output value of these enterprises exceeded the value of rural agricultural production. The Chinese government wants to have a continuous and healthy development of these enterprises.

.... Currently, few enterprises have good record-keeping on assets, and property relationships are not clear. Management and profit distribution needs to be institutionalized. The establishment of experimental reforms is therefore meant to improve management of rural enterprises, formulate regulations, build prototype township and village industrial areas, improve marketing channels, establish training centers, and facilitate the healthy development of rural enterprises....

(4) Rural Cooperative Systems

As a result of the elimination of People's Communes and the adoption of the household contract system, individual farmers in rural China have to face the risks of the market on their own. The government hopes that farmers can form their own cooperative organizations to facilitate their production, to gain . . . bargaining power, and to increase their farm income and profit. . . . There are two basic types of cooperatives that have been established: (1) supply or service organizations, called "regional cooperatives"; and (2) commodity organizations, called "specialized cooperatives."

The regional cooperatives . . . operate differently than cooperatives did under the commune system. Farmers now have their own property and management rights. They may also purchase fertilizers together . . . [and work together in] field plowing, plant protection, etc.

The specialized cooperatives include joint operations in production of vegetables, berries, milk, honey, and other products. In [one] county, there are more than 200 of this type of cooperatives [that] . . . operate on the basis of adopting new varieties, technology, processing, marketing, and joint investment. . . .

Other than the above two types of cooperatives, another organizational form is the cooperative company formed by private farmers to integrate production, processing, and marketing. Farmers are shareholders in the company. . . . [While the authorities hope the peasants will voluntarily organize their own cooperatives, now that the "forced" cooperative system has been dismantled in favor of household farming as part of the economic reform program, the suggestions made here are rather vague as to what these new cooperatives may do. The "regional cooperatives" would appear to represent a replacement of the former cooperatives; in other words, they are expected to cooperate in the management of a given area of land, but are to be democratically run by the member households instead of by the state. The specialized cooperatives, also voluntary, would be organized among those producing a single product or engaged in a single service activity, much like cooperatives in the United States (i.e., milk cooperatives). The third type of cooperative mentioned is much more ambitious in scope, making the cooperative members more like stockholders in a holding company that manages the units of production, the units processing the output, and the units that transport and distribute the final product. Each of these suggestions represents not so much a significant real trend as the hopes of the authorities.—*Ed.*]

(5) Rural Financial and Credit System

The financial and credit system of China's rural areas is inadequate for its rapidly developing commodity economy.... More than 40 percent of China's currency circulation is in rural areas. On the one hand, the official financial system is being reformed.... On the other hand, various forms of nonofficial financial organizations are also being established in rural areas as part of the experimental reforms.

In [one] county, for example, experiments include: (1) improving management of the banking system and increasing decision-making authority [at the local level—*Ed.*]; (2) developing rural credit cooperatives by allowing farmers to be more responsible for profit and loss [of the credit cooperative], and by better management and more democratic decision-making; (3) creating more credit instruments and more financial channels; and (4) establishing financial markets... and nongovernment credit and loan systems.... [As in the case of the cooperatives, this discussion of credit for the peasants is quite vague. Having dismantled the former commune system in favor of household farming, the authorities were faced with the problem of creating larger-scale units of production and distribution for the sake of greater productivity and efficiency—hence the call for voluntary cooperatives. The peasant household farmers, no longer being able to rely on the forced savings of the commune system or on the landlords, as before 1949, also need a source of credit to finance their agricultural operations. Thus, the authorities hope that improvements in the management and authority of the local-level banking system will result in better use of existing funds; that voluntary credit cooperatives will increase the amount of credit available to peasants; and that the creation of new, private means for providing credit will make up for any deficit in meeting the peasants' need. While the discussion in both sections 4 and 5 above indicates that the authorities recognize the problems created in rural areas by the economic reforms, it also indicates that they have only weak and rather vague solutions.—*Ed.*]

In general, the government understands the difficulty of the... [rural] reforms, which are closely related to urban reforms, and will proceed cautiously.

Industry

46

The Foreign Establishment in China in the Early Twentieth Century

Albert Feuerwerker

Within the context of the agrarian-market economy, handicraft production and even prototype manufacturing facilities had developed in China's towns and urban centers well before the industrial revolution occurred in Europe. Why, then, was China not the first country to achieve modernization, or why did China fail to modernize even by the middle of the twentieth century? These are complex questions for which scholars have offered many explanations. The author of the following reading has argued that perhaps the failure to modernize is the norm that does not require explaining; rather it is the miracle of the industrial revolution in Northern Europe that is the deviation from the norm which requires explanation. Whatever the true causes of either China's failure to modernize or Europe's success, both Chiang Kai-shek and Mao Zedong, as well as many Chinese intellectuals and political leaders of the twentieth century, agree upon one major explanation—the inability of native Chinese efforts at industrial development to survive in the face of the unfair advantages enjoyed by foreign enterprise created on Chinese soil by the imperialists.

The economic presence of the foreigner within China was concentrated along the seaboard in international settlements, which were ruled by the foreigner, not the Chinese authorities. Some have argued that because foreign enterprise was

511

relatively isolated from the interior of the economy, the impact of the foreigner on the Chinese economy—the rural, agrarian economy—was limited. Albert Feuerwerker, of the University of Michigan, is the recognized dean of economic historians studying the modern period in China. His survey, The Foreign Establishment in China in the Early Twentieth Century, *covers the whole range and variety of foreign participation in China's politics, economy, and society. In the following excerpt, he assesses the types and extent of foreign participation in China's economy during the early twentieth century and its impact upon the indigenous economy. As noted by the author, for good or evil, it was these foreign economic activities that unleashed the forces of modernization in China's economy during this period.*

The foreign economic presence in China in the early twentieth century was a very visible one, but that conspicuousness itself constitutes something of a paradox. Foreign firms, investments, loans, and personnel dominated important parts of the modern sector of China's economy in the early republic. The modern sector, however, although it is prominently recorded both in contemporary sources and retrospective studies, represents only a minute portion of the Chinese economy as a whole. Neither foreign nor Chinese modern enterprise, while both grew steadily, bulked very large before 1949. As late as 1933, 63 to 65 percent of gross domestic product [GDP] originated in agriculture, for the most part organized and operated along traditional lines and entirely without direct foreign participation. The South Manchurian Railway Company operated a number of experimental farms in Manchuria, but in no part of China were there foreign-owned plantations producing even the major agricultural export items (tea, silk, vegetable oil and oil products, egg products, hides and skins, and bristles) not to speak of the rice, wheat, vegetables, and cotton which were China's main crops. Handicraft production, again with no foreign participation, accounted for 7 percent of GDP in 1933 compared to 2.2 percent for modern industry in which the foreign share was significant. Transportation by junk, cart, animal, and human carriers was three times as important (4 percent of GDP) as the modern transportation sector in which foreign-owned or operated railroads and foreign steamships appeared so prominently. China's foreign trade and even her interport trade were carried mainly in foreign vessels, but total foreign trade turnover certainly never exceeded (and probably never reached) 10 percent of gross domestic product....

But the foreign businessman and alien capital were nevertheless present in early republican China. What forms did they assume and what influence did they have? I shall look in turn at trade, banking, manufacture and mining, transport, and public finance.

Trade. Foreign firms ... ranged from such giants as Jardine, Matheson and Company and Carlowitz and Company to the modest Sweetmeat Castle, "pastry cooks, confectioners, bakers, wine and spirit merchants" or the Schlacterei W. Fütterer, butcher to the German community in Shanghai. By trade they encompassed among others, accountants, advertising agents, banks, brokers, commission merchants and agents, engineers, general merchants, lawyers, outfitters, physicians and dentists, printers and publishers, shipowners and shipping agents, undertakers, and wine and spirit merchants. Many were retail establishments or services catering exclusively to the foreign residents of the treaty ports. Some were manufacturers who operated plants in China. The largest and most typical, however, engaged in importing or exporting or in some service ancillary to foreign trade, with which manufacturing operations were sometimes combined.

Their number varied somewhat from year to year. On the margin, for the smaller firms at least, failures occurred, while the total increased along with the expansion of trade. [There were] customs estimates that the number of foreign "firms," head offices, and branches counted separately, in the treaty ports in 1918 was nearly 7,000. Typically, excluding Japanese and Russian firms in Manchuria, the head offices in China of the larger enterprises were located in either Shanghai or Hong Kong, with varying numbers of branches maintained at other ports.... The resident foreign merchant played a critical role in the import-export trade, but in the early republic his function had for some time been largely restricted to that point in the commercial process at which foreign goods were landed in China or Chinese goods loaded on ship for export abroad. There were exceptions to be sure, and they will be noted below, but as I have argued elsewhere, "It is perhaps only a small exaggeration, with respect to the importation and distribution of the major staples of commerce, to describe the foreign trading firms in China as having been gradually transformed into Shanghai and Hong Kong commission agents serving the established Chinese commercial network." ...

[An exception to this pattern of trade was] direct distribution through local Chinese agents who worked on a commission basis [and] was successful mainly with standardized or proprietary goods such as cigarettes, kerosene, dyes, patent medicine, alkalis, and soap.... In the sale of kerosene and of cigarettes—and the manufacture of the latter in China as well—British and American firms other than the large commission merchants in the treaty ports took the lead.

The Standard Oil Company of New York shipped its first kerosene to China in the 1880s where it was sold by firms such as Butterfield and Jardine. In 1894, after the failure of lengthy negotiations with Jardine, Matheson and Company to have that firm become Standard's permanent sales agent in Asia, including China, Standard Oil undertook to establish its own marketing organization. At first it sold its kerosene only at Shanghai to Chinese dealers who handled all the "up-country" distribution. Standard Oil resident managers were, however, soon established in the major ports where bulk storage facilities were erected, who appointed and bonded Chinese "consignees" and closely supervised the sales of these agents and their numerous subagents. "In some places, as in Wuhu, for example, the hand of the New York company extended into street peddling." Specially prepared Chinese-language pamphlets and posters advertised Standard's premium "Devoe" brand and the cheaper "Eagle." The free distribution or sale at a very low price of small tin lamps with glass chimneys (the famous "Mei-foo" lamp) created a market for kerosene. By 1910 Standard Oil was shipping 15 percent of its total exports of kerosene to China. . . .

Standard Oil's chief competitor in China, the Asiatic Petroleum Company (a subsidiary of Royal Dutch Shell, an Anglo-Dutch alliance), operated through a single sales network under its direct control. In spite of such departures from the usual pattern of trade as sending Western salesmen into the interior, erecting storage facilities in many Chinese cities, and maintaining ownership of the kerosene wherever it was transported until the actual retail sale, Standard Oil's and Asiatic Petroleum's success ultimately depended upon utilizing rather than replacing China's existing commercial system. Their Chinese "consignees," i.e., wholesalers or jobbers, were more often than not established merchants who had other commercial interests as well. Even the retail proprietors of Standard Oil's distinctive yellow-fronted shops were usually prominent local dealers. The foreigner's marketing structure was after all a superficial one. . . .

This dependence upon China's traditional marketing structure to reach the final consumer characterized as well the Singer Sewing Machine Company, Imperial Chemical Industries which sold chemicals based on alkalis, dyes, and fertilizer, and the enormously successful

British-American Tobacco Company. BAT was distinctive in that, in addition to importing cigarettes manufactured in England and America, it operated a half-dozen substantial factories of its own in China by 1915, which escaped significant direct taxation because of their claimed extra-territorial status. From 1913 BAT was actively involved in promoting the cultivation of tobacco grown from American seeds by Chinese peasants in Shantung—a foreign intrusion into agricultural production which was as rare in China as it was typical in the fully colonized Asian countries. But its system of distributors and dealers directed by a network of foreign agents was merely superimposed upon existing Chinese transportation and local marketing facilities. And in the distribution of seed and fertilizer in Shantung—long a tobacco-growing area—as well as in its purchase of the crop, BAT relied primarily upon Chinese intermediaries. The direct foreign role was a more modest one than the company's public pronouncements claimed.

Beyond the commercial structure itself, what fundamentally limited the impact of foreign merchants and their goods—the large sales of kerosene, cigarettes, and imported cotton piece goods before these last were ousted by the competition of cloth woven in China were important exceptions of course—was the overall poverty of the Chinese economy. Much has been written about the "myth" of the China market which called many to Shanghai and the other treaty ports, and I shall not repeat it here. Notwithstanding the steady growth of both imports and exports after 1900, even in 1936 the per capita value of China's foreign trade, including Manchuria, was still smaller than that of any other country. If, as some analysts suggest, neither China's share of world trade nor its per capita foreign trade were "abnormally" low for an underdeveloped country of its size and resource endowment, it is still true that foreign demand for China's agricultural and mining exports generated only very weak "backward linkages" (i.e., induced demand for the production of other products in the Chinese economy), while the imported manufactured or processed commodities went mainly to satisfy final demand and consequently generated only weak "forward linkages" (i.e., capital or raw material inputs into Chinese production). The hope of economic gain had brought the foreigner to China, but it was less his specific economic influence than the political and psychological facts of his presence under privileged conditions that directly affected the course of China's modern history.

Banking. In the absence of modern financial institutions in China, the foreign merchant houses undertook to provide for themselves many of the auxiliary services such as banking, foreign exchange, and insurance essential to their import-export business. In time these subsidiary enterprises were replaced or supplemented by newly established specialized firms. The first Western bank in China, the Chartered Bank of India, Australia, and China which opened a Shanghai branch in 1858, was still largely an appendage of the Indian trade. Only with the organization of the Hongkong and Shanghai Banking Corporation in 1864 did the China traders acquire a locally controlled organ designed to meet their particular needs. Although its directorate was a cosmopolitan body, the Hongkong Bank was effectively a British institution. It began operations simultaneously in Hong Kong and Shanghai, and before the 1890s had few serious competitors. By the second decade of the twentieth century, twelve foreign banks were operating in China. . . .

The majority of these banks engaged principally in financing the import and export trade of the foreign firms. Some direct advances were also made to Chinese merchants, but their chief impact on the Chinese commercial structure took the form of short-term "chop loans" to the native banks *(ch'ien-chuang)* who in turn lent to Chinese merchants. These credits to the *ch'ien-chuang*, which ceased with the Revolution of 1911, for a time gave the foreign banks considerable leverage over the entire money market in Shanghai. As they monopolized the financing of foreign trade, the banks in practice controlled the foreign exchange market in China. Fluctuations in the exchange rate between Chinese silver currency and gold which was the world standard were frequently large. The conduct of foreign exchange dealings and international arbitrage provided substantial profits to the foreign banks and in particular to the Hongkong Bank whose daily exchange rates were accepted as official rates by the entire Shanghai market. . . . A more important source, however, resulted from the banks' role in servicing China's foreign debt and indemnity payments which brought an endless inflow of customs and salt receipts and of the working capital of many railroads. The major banks, moreover, were directly involved in the placement of indemnity and railroad loans with European lenders which itself produced large profits. . . .

While the foreign banks lost some of their privileged position to the government-backed triumvirate of the Central Bank of China, the Bank of China, and the Bank of Communications in the 1920s and especially after the establishment of the Kuomintang regime, they continued to be preeminent in the financing of foreign trade. At any time, however, their influence on the Chinese economy outside of the foreign trade and government finance sectors was negligible. Like the traders who were their chief customers, the foreign banks affected China most because they were foreign, privileged, and frequently arrogant.

. . . . Domination of the modern sector, if it could be achieved by outsiders—or even by insiders—hardly constituted control of China as a whole as subsequent history was to show.

Manufacturing and Mining . . . . In 1933 foreign-owned firms produced 35 per cent of the total value of production by manufacturing industries as a whole, but no comparable estimate can be made for 1910–20, at a time when 75 to 90 per cent of modern coal mining and nearly half of the cotton textile industry were in foreign hands. Production figures are not available, but the cigarette industry was dominated by foreigners too, judging by a comparison of BAT's sales of twelve billion cigarettes in 1919 (a large part manufactured in China) with the two billion sold by its chief Chinese competitor, the Nanyang Brothers Tobacco Company. . . .

Yet the caveats that I have already raised against reading large conclusions into statistics about the modern sector, just because they are the only quantitative data available, need to be faced once more. Cigarette sales certainly boomed after BAT was launched in 1902, but there is little evidence that the predominant forms in which tobacco was consumed outside the urban areas did not continue to be in the peasant's long pipe, in water pipes, or as snuff—all of which had been widespread since the seventeenth century. Even as late as 1935, only 19 percent of farm families purchased tobacco of any kind. In the case of cotton yarn, only 18 percent of total consumption in 1905, and 34 percent in 1919, was produced in modern mills, Chinese- and foreign-owned, in China. The comparable figures for cotton cloth are 1 percent and 5 percent in 1905 and 1919 respectively. Handicraft production and imports together accounted for 82 percent of the yarn consumed in 1905 and 66 percent in 1919; and for 99 percent and 95 percent of the cloth. These proportions suggest that China's most developed modern industry, cotton textiles, in which the foreign share loomed so large, did not clothe a substantial majority of the Chinese population. . . .

Of the forty-five cotton mills in China in 1919, fifteen were Japanese- and British-owned. On the average, the foreign mills spun yarn five to seven counts higher than the Chinese-owned mills. This difference had two important implications for the ability of the Chinese firms to withstand very strong competition and to hold their share of the market in succeeding years. Low-count yarn was spun using a more labor-intensive technology than high-count yarn, and therefore fitted the circumstances of more scarce and expensive capital and somewhat lower labor costs which the Chinese producers faced as compared with their foreign competitors. The lower-count yarn was also more readily marketed to handicraft weavers who used it as warp in combination with handspun weft to produce a coarse, long-wearing cloth much in demand in rural areas. There was a tendency, in other words, for Chinese and foreign manufacturing firms to operate in partially discrete markets, the bulk of the foreign output supplying consumers in the treaty ports and other large cities. . . .

. . . . The economic consequences—with respect to both development and distribution—of whether a plant was foreign-owned or Chinese-owned were miniscule as compared with what I have already several times stated to be the primary political and psychological effects of the privileged, and in the case of modern industry sometimes dominant, foreign presence in China. Studies of pre-1949 industry, although faced with substantial data problems, show not only the impressive rate of growth cited above [8 to 9 percent], but also strong evidence that Chinese-owned enterprises grew at least as fast as foreign manufacturing firms. Evidence for the long-term trend in the twentieth century is scanty at best, but—excluding Manchuria after 1931 and occupied China during 1937–45—it suggests a gradual increase for the Chinese share of capitalization and output in foreign trade and banking as well as in industry. . . . In the long-run perhaps the most important (and largely unintended) aspect of foreign manufacturing was its role in the transfer to China of modern industrial technology in the form of machinery, technical skills, and organization. This "demonstration effect" also operated in the commercial and financial sectors where Chinese foreign trading companies modeled on the foreigner began to be significant in the 1920s, and Chinese modern banks and insurance companies became increasingly important after 1911.

. . . . Anti-imperialist sentiment was a growing reality in modern China, but it does not follow that, because nationalist propaganda pronounced it so, foreign industry in China in fact retarded China's modernization, undermined handicraft production (which contradicts the first assertion), prevented the growth of Chinese manufacturing, or exploited Chinese workers any more (or less) egregiously than native capitalists.

Transportation .... That China's overseas trade was carried primarily in foreign vessels is not surprising, but cabotage, i.e., coastal and inland navigation, in international law is generally restricted to domestic carriers. Trade by foreign vessels between Chinese ports and navigation of China's rivers had been imposed upon China by the treaty powers; no reciprocal right, even in theory, was received by China....

It is impossible to assess the precise quantitative effects of foreign coastal and riverine steamer trade on traditional junks and their boatmen. Chinese government opposition to expansion of the scope of steam shipping was based in part on apprehension of possible disorders sparked by unemployed boatmen. On the other hand, on balance Chinese junks probably benefited from an expansion of total inland trade. There were countless places unreachable by steamer which were tied to the growing commerce by 500,000 junks which plied not only the rivers but also extensive networks of canals and creeks. All the quantitative indicators as well as the scattered statistics available for the 1930s suggest that the junk was still the predominant means of transportation in south China in the first decade of the twentieth century....

Transportation accounted for nearly a third (31. 5 percent) of direct foreign investment in China in 1914. The bulk of this third was invested in railroads, the capitalization of the steam shipping companies being relatively small. Foreign railroad interests were a complex amalgam ranging from a fair number of unrealized railroad concessions to several minor lines which were directly controlled by foreign powers. Between these two extremes were lines built entirely or in part with foreign loans under contracts which generally granted the construction of the lines to the lenders (who profited as the purchasing agents for imported materials) and ... placed the management of the lines in the hands of the lenders during the period of the loan....

As of 1918, out of an approximate total of 6,700 miles of railroad lines in operation, including Manchuria, only a few hundred miles of the incomplete Canton-Hankow line, the short Tientsin-Shanhaikwan section of the Peking-Mukden line, and 376 miles of the Peking-Suiyuan line had been built entirely with Chinese capital, and only the last by Chinese engineers. Foreign-owned railroads totalled 2,487 miles.... Between 1913 and 1915 the 4,000 miles of line which constituted the Chinese Government Railways were welded into a national system, so far as accounts and statistics were concerned, with the assistance of Dr. Henry Carter Adams of the University of Michigan and the Interstate Commerce Commission who served as adviser to the Chinese government on the standardization of railroad accounts during 1913–17....

.... The imperialist purposes of the several powers rather than China's economic development as an independent and desirable end from which the foreigner too might profit was what brought foreign capital into China's railroads. As glaring symbols of foreign derogation of Chinese sovereignty and territorial integrity, both the concession lines and those with heavy foreign indebtedness drew the wrath of Chinese nationalism.... But the enormous physical capital construction contributed by the foreigner—while no study has been made of this question, it is probable that as a consequence of wars and political changes in China and abroad a substantial part of the foreign capital invested in railroads was never repaid—played a major role in providing modern transportation facilities in the northern half of China where widely separated economic regions and the absence of substantial water routes were major barriers to economic development....

Public Finance. In the decade 1912–21, at least seventy mostly quite small unsecured loans and advances with a total outstanding balance of perhaps Ch$200 million in 1921 were made to various central government or provincial agencies by a very wide variety of foreign lenders.... Given the deteriorating financial situation of the Peking government, these loans were mainly in default. The outstanding railroad loan balance of about Ch$300 million, in contrast, was regularly serviced from the income of the several lines until about 1925. But the largest part of China's foreign public indebtedness was made up by the Japanese war and indemnity loans, the Boxer indemnity, the Crisp Loan of 1912, and the Reorganization Loan of 1913, which together represented an outstanding balance in 1921 of approximately Ch$1,000 million. These debts were all secured on either or both the Maritime Customs revenue and the Salt Administration revenue, and principal and interest were paid without interruption.

Apart from the railroad loans, these foreign funds contributed nothing to the Chinese economy. The indemnity loans and the Boxer indebtedness represented a net drain while the rest were expended for the largely unproductive administrative and military needs of the Peking government.... Even excluding the Boxer Indemnity, annual payments of interest and amortization on China's foreign debt in the second decade of the century amounted to at least a quarter or a third of the revenue of the impoverished Chinese central government. . . .

About all that can be said in favor of China's foreign indebtedness in the early republic is that on a per-capita basis—perhaps Ch\$3 in 1921—it was low by international standards. Like the modern sector of the economy in which foreign interests were so heavily involved, the political sway of the Peking government extended neither very broadly nor very deeply into Chinese society. . . .

. . . . What I have implied about the foreign economic presence in the foregoing pages is that the foreigner's economic gains, based in part on and multiplied by his privileged position, were not absolute deductions from China's economic welfare. On the contrary, China's indigenous economic modernization—the first ruptures of the "high-level equilibrium trap" which ensnared the Chinese economy at a low level of total output—began only in response to the exogenous shock of imported foreign goods and foreign manufacturing in China. Trade, foreign investment in manufacturing and transportation, and the importation of technology produced absolute gains for the Chinese economy, albeit the growth of national product was slow and its social distribution questionable. In a different political context, i.e., if China had been served by an effective central government, the backward and forward linkages of foreign trade and foreign manufacture with the Chinese-owned sector of the domestic economy could undoubtedly have been greater. The foreign economic presence, however, was only one factor—and not the major one—contributing to the debility of the Chinese polity.

47

China's Transition to Industrialism

Thomas G. Rawski

One of the most important considerations in evaluating China's economic modernization in the recent past and in the future is the sheer size of China's economy. Thus, for the purpose of his argument, Feuerwerker emphasized the almost insignificant scale of the modern sector, where the foreigner was most active, in terms of the economy as a whole. Yet, the creation and expansion of modern industry in a traditional, agrarian economy as large as China's would have to begin and take root in a few local urban centers within the vast expanse of the rural economy. The modernization of China's economy will take a long time, even if the process of modernization or of industrialization (which is only one feature of the much broader process of modernization) is very successful.

As explained in Feuerwerker's selection, the foreign penetration of China's economy occurred on the margin of China's economy; but the important feature of this foreign presence was the demonstration effect it had on native Chinese entrepreneurs, who emulated the foreigner in creating Chinese industrial enterprises. Again, no matter how rapidly these Chinese modernizers acted, their efforts at industrialization were bound to appear small when viewed in the context of the Chinese economy as a whole. If successful, of course, their efforts would finally accumulate a critical mass of modern economic activity that clearly would reveal their progress toward modernization. Unfortunately, well before that could occur, the Japanese occupation of Manchuria in 1932, the Sino-Japanese War in

1937–45, and then the final stages of the Chinese Civil War interrupted and precluded the industrial development and modernization of the Chinese economy under the Nationalist Government.

Professor Thomas Rawski, who has researched economic developments in China during the first half of the twentieth century, has recently published the results of his research in Economic Growth in Prewar China, *presenting evidence of the considerable and successful economic modernization that was occurring under the republic, before the late 1930s and the 1940s. The selection presented below is from an earlier publication of Rawski's devoted specifically to the producer's goods industry, showing that the Chinese were not merely copying the foreigner in developing industries to produce consumer goods and other end products, but were steadily increasing their ability to produce investment goods and acquire greater industrial entrepreneurial and technological skills as well.*

At the time of China's republican revolution of 1911, activity in the producer sector was limited to a handful of isolated units: a few mechanized mines and railway repair shops, railmaking facilities at the Han-yeh-p'ing ironworks, the Ch'i-hsin cement works in the north, and a small number of urban utilities catering largely to nonindustrial users.

. . . . The ensuing decades witnessed substantial growth of producer output. As a result, the outlines of an integrated producer sector, though far from complete, can be discerned by 1937. New industries appeared and were joined to one another by expanding commodity flows linking enterprises managed by men familiar with Western technology and attuned to market opportunities. Even more important were the qualitative changes of these years, which not only altered the character of prewar producer activity, but also provided a foundation that proved essential to the continuing development of China's producer sector after 1949. . . .

Engineering

. . . . The industrial history of many countries shows that the equipment and skills needed to maintain, repair, and manufacture textile machinery, for example, are readily transferable to the production and operation of a wide range of engineering goods. This is because machinery manufacture consists of a sequence of basic operations—design, heat treatment of metals, machining, assembly, and inspection—that can be applied with minimal variation to produce equipment for any sector of the economy. This unique characteristic leads to the expectation that gradual mastery of these basic activities will push individual firms, and eventually the engineering sector as a whole, toward technological thresholds beyond which existing resources of equipment and skill can turn out a vastly expanded range of machines.

The most detailed picture of evolutionary development in Chinese engineering comes from a history of Shanghai's Ta-lung Machinery Works, established in 1902 by Yen Yü-t'ang, an associate of foreign merchants. Yen sensed the profitability of ship repairing and used his foreign contacts to solicit business. A partner managed the actual work, which consisted mainly of general steamship repairs. The small initial capital of seventy-five hundred *liang* [ounces of silver] came from three partners, and the labor force of eleven was recruited from foreign-owned factories and from the Shanghai Dockyard.

Ta-lung's origins are typical of many engineering enterprises. Small machine shops were often established by men with experience in foreign firms and, later, with overseas technical training. T'eng Hu-ch'en, a former apprentice trained to repair German warships at Tsingtao, founded the Hua-feng Machine Works in 1920. Yi Chih-chung, a pioneer in needle- and nail-making, was among many machinery entrepreneurs who had studied abroad.

Formation of new enterprises without recourse to financial intermediaries is another feature common to many firms. The absence of indivisibilities and scale economies in the repair work initially undertaken by engineering firms enabled small groups of friends, relatives, business associates, or classmates to enter the trade with only their personal savings. Company histories show that few private machine shops obtained bank loans in their early years. Although larger firms, including Ta-lung, had developed banking ties by the 1930s, a 1938 survey of Chinese-owned machinery plants in Tientsin reported modern or native bank financing in only two of thirty cases.

Men with factory experience formed a growing pool of skilled labor that new enterprises could tap. As early as 1912, the thirty-five railway factories and arsenals administered by China's communications, army, and navy ministries employed over twenty thousand persons, many in positions requiring some technical skill. At the same time, the Japanese owned South Manchurian Railway employed eighty-nine hundred non-Japanese. Later, the private sector became a fertile training ground: Ta-lung trained an estimated ten thousand apprentices before 1949, many of whom became workers, managers, and owners of machine shops throughout China. Former textile and steel workers also established their own machinery plants.

Ta-lung's growth ... illustrates both the Schumpeterian entrepreneurship of its management and the transferability of technical knowledge and skills among various branches of engineering—features shared with other enterprises whose history is less richly documented. Yen Yü-t'ang bought out his partners around 1906 when Ta-lung's work force had risen to fifty. Faced with growing competition from other shipyards, which threatened Ta-lung's profits, Yen shifted his attention to Shanghai's burgeoning textile industry.

Yen's foreign contacts again proved useful, but it was the skill and experience of his workers, readily shifted from marine to factory repairs, that brought continued success. Mill owners were prepared to offer high prices, but only for swift and competent service that minimized idle time. When an English firm failed to duplicate a broken steam pipe, Ta-lung completed the job, thereby winning the custom of Naigaiwata, a Japanese firm with over a quarter million spindles in the Shanghai area, and of other Japanese mills as well.

Ta-lung's repair work, which included replacement of broken parts, engine maintenance, installation of bearings to increase machine speed, and adjustment of defective imported equipment, gradually created the skills needed for manufacturing. After 1911, the business expanded to include regular production of spare parts for textile machinery. No special materials or techniques were needed; aside from the spindle itself, cotton textile machinery of the day demanded neither close tolerances, high speeds, nor extreme pressures. Once again, the absence of rigid technical requirements and easy transfer of skills facilitated the firm's growth. Similar transitions occurred elsewhere; Yang Ta-chin notes sixteen producers of equipment for textile workshops and factories were established before 1914, most of them in Shanghai.

The isolation of China's textile industry from foreign suppliers and competitors during World War I provided an opportunity to which neither Ta-lung nor its rivals could respond. Despite a combination of soaring textile profits with restricted supplies, and rising prices of foreign equipment, no domestic producer could meet the demand for textile machinery. China's spindle stock stagnated until the postwar resumption of normal foreign trade flows, which brought an immediate spurt of spindle imports to satisfy the pent-up demand for equipment.

At this time, manufacture of textile machinery was simply beyond the skill frontiers of domestic engineering concerns.

This began to change during the 1920s, when growing technical and financial strength enabled Ta-lung and other firms to begin producing textile equipment. At Ta-lung, trial manufacture of components, including looms, picking machines, and bundling and hydraulic presses, was followed by a series of organizational and technical improvements incorporated into a new plant opened in 1926. A new management team led by Yen Ch'ung-ling, a son of Yen Yü-t'ang who had received technical training in Germany, split the workers into specialized groups, formed a design department, and hired a Japanese engineer to improve the plant's casting methods. As a result, modified versions of British spinning machinery were successfully produced for the first time.

The problem of marketing now came to the fore. To avoid a head-on clash with formidable British interests, Yen Yü-t'ang created his own sheltered market by purchasing a bankrupt textile plant in 1927 and stocking it with Ta-lung machines. Yen eventually controlled seven mills, all equipped with Ta-lung machinery and managed by his sons, former Ta-lung apprentices or close friends of the Yen family. The profitability of this combine provided excellent advertising for Ta-lung's products within Shanghai industrial circles.

The outbreak of war with Japan cut short Yen's campaign to penetrate the domestic market for textile equipment. Ta-lung's Communist historians argue that imperialist restrictions on China's trade policies and the irrational preference of both foreign and Chinese managers for imported machinery condemned Ta-lung to a secondary role as supplier to captive firms controlled by the Yen family. This pessimism was certainly not shared by Yen Ch'ung-ling, who anticipated that the low cost and improved quality of his products would open markets in Southeast Asia as well as in China, and accordingly ordered price lists printed in English as well as in Chinese.

The condition of Ta-lung's operations appears to vindicate Yen's optimism. In 1937, Ta-lung was no longer a handicraft enterprise. Its plant was equipped with over five hundred machine tools and staffed by an experienced work force of thirteen hundred men. Trained engineers directed the production process and introduced a stream of innovations in metallurgy, design, and measurement that lowered costs and raised quality. Business decisions rested in the hands of men with a knack for decisive entry into profitable fields and quick recognition of mistakes. With its strong financial base and technically skilled management, Ta-lung could begin to challenge some of its foreign competitors in the textile machinery industry.

Ta-lung's wide range of products, which included machine tools, stoves, engines, and agricultural equipment as well as textile machinery, its subsequent recovery from wartime damage, and its production of large quantities of cotton spindles as well as munitions during the Pacific war all indicate that by 1937 the Ta-lung Machine Works had crossed the technological threshold dividing handicraft and repair activities from modern engineering operations.

Ta-lung's emergence as a manufacturer of machinery was not an isolated event. A nationwide survey from 1932–33 showed that engineering firms accounted for about 4 percent of factory sales and 6 percent of factory employment in China proper, with foreign-owned enterprises accounting for less than one-quarter of the total. Most of this output was the result of a rapid growth spurt which continued until 1937. K. C. Yeh finds that employment in China proper in the manufacture of machinery and parts rose by 141 percent between 1931 and 1936.

A succession of factory surveys offers a more detailed picture for Shanghai, China's foremost industrial metropolis. In 1928, investigators reported 64 machine shops with capital in excess of 5,000 *yuan* [Chinese dollars] and 11 electrical machine shops with assets of over 3,000 *yuan*. These plants employed an average of 58 workers and showed assets of 494 *yuan* per worker. The number of metal-processing and machinery enterprises using mechanical power and employing over 30 persons rose from 82 to 173 between 1931 and 1933 alone, while output, capital, and employment for all firms in these sectors rose by approximately 300 percent, 100 percent, and 60 percent respectively during the same short period. By 1933 there were 306 Shanghai machinery plants registered under China's factory law; they employed an average of 65 workers and showed assets of 833 *yuan* per employee.

Less detailed descriptions indicate considerable expansion of machine shops in Wusih, Hangchow, Chinan, Chungking, and other secondary industrial centers. Engineering developments in Chekiang, for example, followed a familiar pattern: after modern factories were established with machinery procured from Shanghai, local people started repair shops that gradually turned to machine manufacture. By 1933, the larger local plants had already begun shipping their products to Shanghai, Hong Kong, and Szechwan.

Expansion in both the volume and variety of output enabled Chinese machinery to begin displacing imports in a growing range of product lines. In textiles, the largest sector of industry, Chinese equipment was noted in nearly all branches of the cotton, wool, and silk trades. One incomplete survey lists ninety-nine manufacturers of spinning machinery, looms, stocking frames, bowing machines, equipment for reeling and weaving silk, cotton gins, and dyeing equipment.

Domestic machines were increasingly prominent in other expanding consumer industries. A 1935 survey of the match industry, in which Chinese producers had captured the domestic market during World War I and fought off later dumping attacks by Japanese and Swedish rivals, reported that "plants established during the past seven or eight years use only Chinese machines." Nearly one-third of the cigarette-making machines in sixty Kiangsu factories were Chinese. Domestic firms supplied a variety of equipment to rice, oil and flour mills, to canneries and printers, and to producers of ink, leather, glass, candles, and soap.

Engineering firms also contributed to the growth of fixed capital within the producer sector. Larger plants regularly augmented their equipment with machines built in their own shops. Tientsin firms pioneered in commercial manufacture of machine tools, turning out a variety of lathes, milling machines, shapers, and grinders. Te-li-hsing was the largest producer, employing six hundred workers in two shifts and selling up to twenty machine tools each month to small shops in North China and Manchuria. San-i-ch'eng and I-chü-cheng were smaller iron-works that also produced lathes for sale locally and in Manchuria. Chemical plants, cement works, smelters, mines, and railways also purchased a variety of equipment from local producers.

Chinese products rarely matched the capacity, precision, and durability of foreign equipment. When they did, they quickly swept imports from the market, as in 1933–35 when Ta-lung sold ten thousand stoves in North China at less than one-third of the price formerly charged for similar German products.

.... But with high borrowing costs and political instability, chronically underfinanced Chinese businesses often preferred low-cost domestic machines despite their overall inferiority.

The rapid progress of import substitution in China's machinery markets during the 1930s was the outcome of a gradual process of skill development that originated with the introduction of foreign technical knowledge and capital equipment in the latter half of the nineteenth century. The expansion of machine-making capacity owed much to the nature of engineering technology.... Shanghai's engineering firms managed to limit their capital needs to levels that were low even by the standards of other Shanghai industries. This reflects the technical feasibility of pushing forward from repair work into manufacturing without encountering sharply increased capital requirements. The transferability of skills among different branches of engineering was equally valuable to fledgling producers, whose ability to diversify their output even at early stages of development helped them survive under volatile market conditions.

Vigorous entrepreneurship was another essential feature of engineering advances. Although producers of sophisticated machines were few in number, the republican decades showed that many entrepreneurs willingly followed the example of Ta-lung and other leaders in braving the hazards of domestic uncertainty and unrestricted foreign competition. Just as Yen Yü-t'ang's firm had initially occupied a nexus between foreign enterprise and the domestic economy and had gained technical and financial strength by associating with foreign firms, later entrepreneurs often benefited from links with Chinese industrial leaders, beginning their careers as employees, subcontractors, or customers of older firms.

By the end of the Nanking decade [i.e., in 1937], China's few dozen major engineering concerns were backed by hundreds of obscure craft and repair shops whose function as customers and suppliers, as training grounds for mechanics and future entrepreneurs, and as a reservoir of potential expansion should not escape our attention. At the same time the expansion of ironworks and machine shops in areas far removed from the coastal centers of industry meant the start of new and independent development sequences that would parallel the earlier response of Shanghai and other treaty ports to the introduction of Western machinery and transport equipment.

Despite its modest size and limited range of products, China's prewar engineering sector had already embarked upon a process of skill formation and technical development whose momentum ... has continued to the present.... The long-run significance of this initial stage of output growth and import substitution may be anticipated by referring to similar stages in the industrialization of other nations.

Historians have traced the origins of modern machinery manufacture in both the United States and Japan to initially inept efforts to copy and compete with foreign equipment. As in China, American and Japanese machinery output was long dominated by inferior goods whose main selling point was their low price, a feature that appealed to customers who were often perilously near insolvency. Despite these weaknesses, we find that in both America and Japan the repair and manufacture of textile machinery formed an early and vital link in the emergence of engineering skills that were later transformed to the manufacture of many other types of machines. Skills developed to meet the needs of the textile industry were gradually applied to the manufacture of transport equipment, armaments, engines, electrical machinery, and, above all, machine tools, through which the influence of engineering skills eventually penetrated into all sectors of the national economy. The recent history of China's engineering industry supports the present contention that the modest prewar achievements of Ta-lung and other machinery producers represent an early stage of a parallel development process in China. . . .

Conclusion

The development of a dynamic process of output expansion and import substitution in certain producer industries has been the major theme of this [article]. The gradual filling of previous empty input-output interstices provided China in 1937 with the outline of a modern producer sector. Domestic machinery plants offered a growing range of equipment to all sectors of manufacturing. A new chemical industry furnished a domestic base for further expansion of many industries. Manchuria's few large and modern enterprises, although oriented toward Japan, represented a potential source of future industrial strength for China.

. . . . The evolutionary growth of producer manufactures in republican China, combined with Manchuria's state-sponsored projects, launched China onto a path of industrial advance that retained considerable unexploited potential when the process was disrupted by war. The momentum of prewar industrial expansion continued to make itself felt during the 1950s and 1960s. . . .

48

China: The Economic System

The World Bank

The previous reading shows that the Chinese Communists did not have to start from scratch in creating an industrial base when they came to power in 1949; they inherited a non-trivial amount of industrial capacity, skilled industrial labor, and entrepreneurial talent. This inherited base came to play a major role in the development of China's modern industrial sector in the 1960s and 1970s, after the Sino-Soviet split of 1960 caused the Soviet Union to withdraw from active economic assistance to China. Immediately after 1949 and throughout the 1950s, however, the Chinese followed the policy of "leaning-to-one-side" (reliance on the Soviet Union) and literally copied the Soviet model of industrial development.

Under Stalin in the late 1920s and in the early 1930s, the Soviet Union had developed economic policies, strategies, and institutions to cope with its immediate economic problems and to secure industrial development. These policies, strategies, and institutions were not to be found in the classic texts of Marxism, nor did they result from a consistent, theoretically derived model. Rather, they were the result of a host of administrative decisions at all levels of the economy that later became identified as "a model." It is an irony of history that by the post–World War II period, the Soviet model had come to be identified as the model for socialist countries everywhere—to be adopted by any country as soon as the socialist revolution succeeded. China was no exception and by the mid-1950s had carried out successfully the transition from a market economy to a Soviet-style socialist economy. By the 1980s, several socialist countries had begun

*to question the effectiveness of the Soviet model in achieving economic develop-
ment and superior economic performance; they began to seek alternative policies,
strategies, and institutions which would yield better results.*

*The Soviet model essentially calls for the mobilization of a high rate of
savings (low rate of consumption) for the sake of investing in new production
facilities for the heavy industrial sector (producers' goods), while resources and
commodities are allocated according to plans and administrative directives. In
other words, a decentralized, market economy is replaced by a centralized, bureaucratically administered economic system. Benjamin Ward, who has spent most of
his career studying various socialist economies, argues that most economies in the
world can be identified as a variant of one or the other of these two basic types
of economic systems. The following selection, from the World Bank's 1983 report
on the Chinese economy, provides us with a description of the Soviet-type economic
system that has prevailed in China during most of the past three decades.*

Instruments of Management and Control

Basic policy in China is determined by the Communist Party, on the
principle that the Party provides leadership for the state (the administrative organs of government), and the state manages the economy.
Party leadership is exercised both centrally (through the influence of
the Politburo and the Central Committee Secretariat on the State Council and its subordinate ministries and bureaus) and locally (through
Party committees, and Party members at all levels of state government
and in communes, factories and other institutions). Although Party
members comprise only 6–7 percent of the adult population, they occupy most of the responsible jobs.

China's economic management system is, by international standards, extraordinarily centralized and characterized by strict vertical
control, with relatively few horizontal linkages. Commands flow constantly downwards, and information (including large quantities of statistics) upwards. The response of units at the bottom to changes of policy
at the top is remarkably quick and uniform.

The sheer size of the country, however, means that the Government
has to be composed of several levels, among which administrative responsibilities have to be divided (although this division is often complicated by the principle of "dual leadership," whereby a local specialized
agency is responsible both to the local government and to the corresponding specialized agency in a superior level of government). The

typical arrangement consists of three governmental tiers, which for simplicity will be referred to below as the center, the province and the county. The average province has a population of about 35 million; Sichuan has the largest population, with each of its 212 counties containing nearly half a million people.

Annual Plan and Flows of Goods

What is produced, by whom, and the uses to which it is put are all matters that in the Chinese economy are predominantly the subject of administrative decisions. These decisions are centrally coordinated through an annual plan, consisting of several parts, including a production plan, a material allocation plan, a wage and labor plan, etc. At the center, preparation of the plan is the responsibility of the State Planning Commission, while implementation is supervised by the State Capital Construction Commission (large capital construction projects), the State Economic Commission (industry and transport) and the State Agriculture Commission. (Similar institutions exist at the provincial level.)

The core of the annual plan is a set of interlocking material balance tables, one for each major commodity, specifying sources (production, imports and stock depletion) and uses (intermediate inputs, investment, consumption and exports)—all in physical units. The planning bureau in each province and county prepares a similar local plan. County plans are guided and integrated by the provincial planners, provincial plans by the State Planning Commission.

Beneath the general planning umbrella, responsibility for commodity flows is divided among several agencies, chiefly according to the nature of the goods concerned. Most industrial producer goods come under the jurisdiction of the State Material Supply Bureau or (mainly for more specialized items) the relevant industrial ministries. The Food Ministry deals with grain and edible oil, the Commerce Ministry with nonstaple food, other consumer goods and services, and a few producer goods such as wire, paint and gasoline. The supply and marketing cooperatives handle nonfood agricultural output, producer goods for agriculture, and sales of consumer goods in rural areas.

Each of these agencies has subordinate or counterpart units at the provincial and county levels, and in each case the division of responsibilities between the various levels of government is broadly similar. Goods regarded as of national importance—around 1,000 in number—

are initially allocated at the national level among provinces and centrally controlled organizations. The relevant provincial agency then allocates these goods (together with the output of small, provincially controlled enterprises, which is exempted from the national allocation process) among counties and provincially controlled organizations; it does the same for a further range of goods regarded as of lesser importance. Likewise, the relevant county agency then allocates (among communes and county-controlled organizations) its allotment from the province, the output of small county-controlled enterprises, and an additional range of goods regarded as of minor importance.

For each type of good, and at each level of government, the allocation procedure is again similar. For example, the communes, county-controlled enterprises, construction units and departments individually submit requisitions for the coming year to the relevant county agency, which prepares a draft allocation on the basis of preliminary information about the availability of the good concerned from provincial and local sources. This draft is discussed and revised at a conference of local users and producers; it then becomes the basis of the county's requisition from the province, which in turn is discussed at a provincial conference. The process culminates, for important goods, in national conferences of user and producer representatives, where vigorous formal and informal negotiations are followed by revision and finalization of lower level allocation plans. . . .

The conduct of foreign trade is equally centralized. Each of a number (currently 16) of foreign trade companies under the control of the Ministry of Foreign Trade has a monopoly on the import and export of a specific group of goods. Annual plans for trade are drawn up by this ministry and the State Planning Commission; in accordance with these plans, the companies either procure goods domestically and sell them abroad, surrendering the foreign exchange earned to the Bank of China, or procure goods abroad on behalf of enterprises and organizations that have been issued licenses for such imports. A parallel system exists at the provincial level, although these transactions are dominated by the central companies and their branch offices in the provinces.

The Budget and Flows of Money

State Budget. The principal instrument of financial control over the economy is the state budget, through which about 30 percent of GDP [gross domestic product] flows. Provincial and county governments, which have their own budgets, collect more than 80 percent of all revenues and carry out 50 percent of all expenditures. In form, however, the state budget is consolidated, with county budgets incorporated into provincial budgets, which in turn are incorporated into the state budget. In substance, there has likewise consistently been strong central control, not only over tax rates and policies, but also over the level and composition of local expenditures. . . .

During periods of decentralization (such as 1958, 1970 and 1980), the basic principle has been to allow each province to retain a predetermined proportion of the revenues it collects, which then determines its total expenditure, and to give the provincial government substantial freedom in deciding the composition of its expenditure. (These devolutions of fiscal authority have usually been accompanied by a parallel devolution of authority over state enterprises.) At most times, however, the central government has maintained control over both the total and the composition of provincial revenue and expenditure, and there has been little connection between revenues and expenditures in particular localities (except that in many years the provinces have been permitted to retain a proportion of their above-plan revenues or expenditure savings as discretionary funds). Even during periods of decentralization, moreover, the extent of local discretion has remained circumscribed, especially over investment, as the central government has continued to set tax rates and to issue guidelines on the composition of expenditure. And at all times the central government has retained ultimate control through its power to determine the nature of the system itself.

An important and consistent feature of the Chinese budgetary system has been the much smaller share of revenues retained by the rich, industrialized provinces than by the poor, backward ones. . . .

Another distinctive feature of the Chinese budget is that enterprise profits are the largest single source of revenue—partly because profit margins are high, but also because enterprises have generally been obliged to remit virtually all their profits to the state. The second biggest source of revenue is an industrial and commercial tax, which accounts for three quarters of all tax receipts. More generally, industry and commerce serve as the main revenue gatherers: the only agricultural tax— effectively a combination of production and land tax—now accounts for less than 3 percent of total revenue.

On the expenditure side, a distinctive feature—indeed the feature that makes the budget so important as a means of economic control—is the large amount of investment. Over the past two decades, grants for fixed and working capital formation have accounted for about half of total budgetary expenditure. They have financed most investment in industry and commerce, as well as infrastructure, and a significant part of that in agriculture.

Control of investment has been shared between the Ministry of Finance and the State Planning Commission. Disputes have been settled by higher organs, such as the State Council. . . .

Banking System. The other main instrument of financial control over the economy is the banking system, of which the core is the People's Bank of China. The People's Bank has an immense network of branch offices; but it is administratively highly centralized—provincial and county governments, for example, have no control over its operations in their localities. In addition to the normal functions of a central bank, it has three main roles: first, it is the conduit for gathering and disbursing most budgetary funds except capital construction grants; second, it functions as a normal financial intermediary, taking deposits at interest from households and institutions and making loans, mainly short-term advances to producing and trading organizations, which supplement (and in aggregate, substantially exceed) their budgetary flows of money. The last is important because most flows of goods involve monetary transactions. Even where physical allocation is strictly governed by the plan, enterprises and most other organizations pay for their inputs and are paid for their output; they keep accounts; and they must prepare financial plans corresponding to their physical plans. These financial plans must be approved by the People's Bank, which (since inter-organizational financial transfers must be made through its accounts) is also well placed to oversee their implementation.

Two other banks—the Agricultural Bank and the Bank of China—are specialized banks under the leadership of the People's Bank. The Agricultural Bank accepts deposits in rural areas and extends short-term credits to communes and their subordinate units. The Bank of China handles all external transactions of the economy and implements the foreign exchange plan. A fourth bank—the Capital Construction Bank, under the leadership of the Ministry of Finance—does not at present act as a financial intermediary but is essentially a conduit for capital appropriations from the ministry to state enterprises and organizations; it also helps supervise the use of these funds.

Centralized financial surveillance and control have been a crucial element of economic management—more important, perhaps, than physical control. But not all flows of money are directly controlled, even outside the household sector. Counties, for example, levy fiscal surcharges (10 percent of the agricultural tax, 1 percent of the two main industrial and commercial taxes) that do not enter into the consolidated budget and may be spent more or less at their discretion. Similarly, state enterprises have long had some discretion in their use of the bonus, depreciation, major repair and welfare funds—and sometimes also a small fraction of profits. Communes, likewise, have usually been able to decide how to allocate their collective savings with only general guidance from above.

The Price System

Flows of goods are, of course, linked to flows of money by prices. Heavy reliance on administrative direction has caused prices to play only a limited allocative role; even household expenditure patterns have been shaped partly by rationing. But prices have had a major impact on various aspects of income distribution. First, they are one of the main determinants of industrial and commercial profits, and hence of the share of budget revenues in national income. Second, the relative prices of agricultural and industrial goods affect the living standards of farm as compared with nonfarm households. Third, the relative prices of different consumer goods affect the pattern of living standards among households with varying money incomes.

Virtually all prices have been set by the Government, through a hierarchy of price bureaus. The central Price Bureau maintains a book specifying which prices are subject to central, and which to provincial and subprovincial, control. Broadly speaking, the division of responsibility is parallel to that for the flows of goods outlined above. Thus the prices of agricultural and industrial goods of national importance (and accounting for around two thirds of total production) are subject to central control, as are transport tariffs on major national routes. The price of other goods, local transport tariffs, and charges for social services are controlled by provinces or counties.

Under the central price determination procedure, particular ministries or departments submit proposed prices for the goods and services under their jurisdiction to the price bureau (and in important cases also to the State Council) for vetting. More specifically, these are the factory or farm-gate prices (for consumer goods, also the wholesale and retail prices) or specific varieties in specified major producing areas. In other areas, the prices of these goods are set by local price bureaus, which add transport costs to the national benchmark prices. As a result, and with the exception of a few manufactured consumer goods (including matches, salt and books), even "centrally" determined prices are not nationally uniform.

Local price bureaus set prices for other varieties of major commodities and for the output of small, locally controlled enterprises. The division of this responsibility—and of the responsibility for setting the prices of less important commodities—between the provincial and county price bureaus is a matter of provincial discretion and varies from province to province. But there are regular consultations between the price bureaus of neighboring provinces, and indeed also between the central and provincial bureaus concerning prices that are nominally under local control. In addition, since many prices are strongly affected by industrial and commercial tax rates (which are set centrally), there is close consultation between the price bureaus and the Finance Ministry.

The principles on which industrial and commercial prices are set are generally of a cost-plus character. In determining centrally controlled prices, the average cost of production in each major producing area is supposed to be supplemented by a profit margin large enough to permit most or all of the enterprises in that area to make a profit. . . .

In the setting of agricultural prices, the major considerations are concern about "equal value exchange" as well as practical concern about rural living standards. Only recently, however, have attempts been initiated to study the cost of production of agricultural commodities and its evolution over time. . . .

Domestic prices have been insulated from world prices, and the exchange rate has played a very limited economic role. Foreign trade companies sell imported goods to local enterprises at the state-determined domestic price of a similar, locally produced good, with due allowance for quality difference. Only for goods for which there are no domestic equivalents—currently about 20 percent of imports—are the domestic selling prices determined by converting the foreign price at the official exchange rate and adding import duty, taxes and fees. For exports, selling prices abroad are determined by world market conditions, but trading companies buy from domestic suppliers at domestic prices.

Since Chinese prices of most agricultural and mining products converted at the official exchange rate are below world prices, exports of these commodities are generally profitable to the trading companies. So are most imports, since Chinese industrial prices at the official exchange rate are well above world prices. But for the same reason, the companies suffer substantial losses in the export of manufactured goods. . . .

The State Economy

Apart from the communes, the economy is dominated by organizations owned by the state. Private business—including self-employment—is now limited to a small number of service workers. Collectives, which employ a fifth of the urban labor force, are nominally owned by their members (and pay tax on their profits rather than remitting them to the state): but for most practical purposes they are now indistinguishable from state-owned enterprises. More generally, although the state sector spans many different economic activities—farming, industry, construction, transport, commerce and services—the way in which these activities are organized is fundamentally similar.

Production

The internal arrangements of state enterprises and other economic organizations are on the surface quite conventional. Each enterprise is headed by a director, supported by a chief accountant and a chief engineer, beneath whom there is a normal managerial hierarchy with little scope for formal worker participation. Less conventionally, not only the director but also all managerial personnel are appointed from outside, by whichever level of government controls the enterprise—most commonly a province or county. In addition, the Party committee and secretary often exercise an important leadership role.

The activities of each economic organization revolve around its annual plan—sometimes subdivided into periods as short as ten days—which in turn is one element of the larger local and national plan. The organization's plan has usually been summarized in a set of physical and financial targets: value (at constant accounting prices), mix and quality of output; quantities and cost of inputs (including labor); working capital use; investment and innovation; and (for enterprises) profit. Additional directives have specified input sources and the channels through which output (including above-target output) is to be disposed of, as well as the prices to be paid or charged. Profits have been remitted to the state; other working capital has been provided by the People's Bank.

What distinguishes these enterprise plans and targets from those common in businesses in other countries is the degree of external influence and the amount of detail involved. Combined, these factors have tended to allow enterprises, manipulated by the planners and watched over by the economic and capital construction commissions, very little independence. Each organization's relationship with its economic environment has been tightly structured, with information flowing to and from it through vertical channels, and with little scope for establishing independent horizontal linkages with other economic organizations. But this picture of enterprises without entrepreneurship requires qualification in two respects.

First, the enterprise's management has a hand in the formulation of its plan. To what extent is something that has probably varied widely, both over time and among enterprises. But at the least each organization is the primary source of information about its own capacities and requirements. Also, for the larger enterprises, there must be some scope for negotiation of targets with the state bureaucracy, in addition to participation in allocation conferences.

Second, the enterprise plan does not fulfill itself, but requires the exercise of managerial skill and effort, especially in dealing with the consequences of defects in the system. For example, the plan may have provided for insufficient inputs; or the planned inputs may not have been available because designated suppliers could not fulfill their own plans. Managers have thus had to exercise initiative—bringing pressure to bear on the bureaucracy, arranging informal barter deals with other organizations, building up stocks, or developing the capacity to make troublesome inputs in-house (sometimes by quietly diverting money and materials destined for current production or repairs).

The issue of managerial motivation has thus been important. Unlike the system in the USSR, and despite episodic attempts to tie employee bonuses in general to enterprise performance, the Chinese system offers few direct financial incentives for managers to achieve or surpass plan targets. Instead, greater reliance has been placed on non-material rewards (praise and promotion) and to a lesser extent on penalties (criticism and demotion), which have relied for their effectiveness partly on the internal commitment of managers to the service of Party and state. Moreover, emphasis has in principle been placed not on myopic fulfillment and overfulfillment of targets, but rather on understanding and acting to further the broader objectives of the system.

Labor and Wages

Employees of state organizations—who, together with members of urban collectives, are referred to as "workers and staff"—are paid according to centrally prescribed wage scales. These scales, which have remained almost unchanged since 1956, vary from place to place (as a result of early efforts to establish uniform nationwide real wages in the face of regional cost-of-living differences), among industries and occupations in the same place, and within industries according to both the size of the enterprise and the level of government that controls it. The scales for industrial workers all have eight grades with a wage range (from the highest to the lowest grade) of about three to one. There is a 16-grade scale for technicians and engineers, a 26-grade scale for government administrators, and so on, with the widest wage range of the order of 15 to 1.

Young people joining the labor force tend to be paid below the standard scale for the first two or three years, but once on the scale are usually promoted to the second grade within a year or so. Subsequent movement up the scale has in principle been dependent on individual skill and performance, but in practice, since the late 1950s, all movements up the pay ladder have been prohibited except those authorized (for specified numbers or categories of workers) by the central government (promotion in responsibility or position has been permitted). Such exceptions occurred in 1963 and 1972 (when promotion was confined to workers with long service in grades 2 and 3), and in each of the years from 1977 to 1979.

In urban collectives, the original idea that workers would share their enterprise's income has long been superseded by the payment of ordinary wages. The applicable scales are not centrally prescribed, but they must be approved by local labor bureaus and have usually been related to, though somewhat below, those in state organizations.

Both in state organizations and in urban collectives, wages are only part of total remuneration. Except in public administration and social services, a sum equal to 10–12 percent of the total wage bill has been available for bonuses, which have been distributed among individual workers in a variety of ways—but not always according to work performance (by contrast with the USSR, piecework payment systems are rare). The worker's welfare fund (another 11 percent of the wage bill in most state organizations) finances pensions, sickness and disability benefits, construction of housing, and in some instances provision of education and health facilities. But there are no paid vacations, apart from seven public holidays a year (and one day off per week).

Most labor is allocated by central and local labor bureaus, aided (in the case of college graduates) by the Ministry of Education and the State Planning Commission, and (in the case of technical and vocational school graduates) by the localities, ministries or enterprises that run the schools. An annual labor plan, subject to approval by the planning agencies at each level, specifies the disposition of new entrants to the labor force among different organizations and enterprises. It also specifies the permitted amount of migration, if any, from communes to urban areas and (in the past) the number of urban youths to be settled in communes. Managerial appointments are handled by a separate hierarchy of personnel bureaus.

Each enterprise and organization is obliged to employ the number of people specified in the plan (which in principle is based on standard labor input coefficients but in practice also reflects a desire to provide jobs). Employing organizations have likewise had little choice about whom to hire—in general they have simply had to take whomever the labor bureau sent. And once taken on, it has been virtually impossible to discharge a worker, no matter how unsatisfactory his conduct.

For individuals, although their schooling and on-the-job performance are obviously important determinants of their employment prospects, entry into the labor force is a particularly crucial juncture. For at this point they are allocated to a particular enterprise or organization in which they can expect to spend the rest of their working lives. Technical and professional staff are sometimes transferred from one place to another in the service of the same organization. But inter-organizational transfers, though possible in principle, have been extremely rare.

In general, then, there has been no labor market: labor allocations and wage levels have been determined by an administrative process. . . .

Income Support

In principle, all able-bodied urban adults of working age (including women who wish to work) are provided with employment—a policy reinforced by restricted rural-urban migration and at times by compulsory urban-rural migration. Many of those above working age (60 for men, 55 for women) are provided with pensions by their former employers or in recognition of war service—occupational pensions vary with length of service, but can be as high as the pre-retirement wage. Likewise, many of those who are unable to work through sickness or disability are provided for financially through the welfare funds of their employers.

For those who fall outside these categories, and who are not adequately supported by their families, there is, as in rural areas, a social relief system financed through the state budget and administered by county-level governments. The available funds are parcelled out (on the basis of informal surveys of need) among street committees—the lowest level of urban political organization—which in turn distribute the money among needy individuals.

. . . . The prices of necessities—including basic food, clothing, and housing—are kept steady and low. Part of the cost of this policy is borne by commune members via low agricultural procurement prices. The remainder is borne by the budget via reduced profits (or low tax rates) at one or more points in the production and distribution chain. To offset this budgetary burden, however, high prices (with consequent high profits or tax rates) are charged for less essential consumer goods.

Partly because their prices have been kept low, necessities have been rationed. Although there is a considerable stock of private urban homes (mainly small, traditional dwellings), most city housing is publicly owned and administratively allocated—some by enterprises and other organizations to their own employees, the rest by local government. Grain, cotton and edible oil, as well as products derived from them, have likewise always been rationed—as have meat and other nonstaple foods in most years. Grain rations vary according to age and occupation—being larger for those in strenuous manual jobs—while cotton rations vary according to age and occupation—being larger in the colder northern provinces. The ration system also provides a convenient means of regulating mobility: ration tickets can be used only in the city where they are issued.

49

China's Economic Reforms

Robert F. Dernberger

The previous reading clearly described an economic system that differs signifi-cantly from the private enterprise, market economies of the developed countries in the West. Once adopted in the 1950s, the institutions of the centrally planned economic system remained in place, allocating resources, goods, and services in the urban-industrial sector of the economy until the end of the 1970s. By the early 1980s, however, the post-Mao, coalition leadership, dominated by Deng Xiao-ping, began to reevaluate that economic system and search for a more efficient and decentralized system.

Quite simply, the centralized decision-making in the Soviet-type economy relied upon for the purpose of mobilizing a higher rate of investment and direct-ing that investment to the sectors given priority by the planners led to rapid growth—but growth that was unbalanced and produced many bottlenecks, which eventually began to threaten further growth. The excessive centralization of deci-sion-making and bureaucratic means for implementing those decisions also con-strained and eventually began to eliminate any initiative and rational problem-solving at the local level. The results were persistent waste and inefficiencies in industrial production and distribution. Finally, the attempt to assure full employ-ment and equitable income distribution not only gave industrial workers a guar-anteed income regardless of how hard they worked, but also failed to reward those who did work hard.

The Soviet-type economy, however, has proven to be very difficult to reform or remove, once it is adopted as an economy's economic system for any period of time; bureaucratic methods and undisciplined labor assignments provide security to the significant portion of the population made up of bureaucrats and workers in the Soviet-type system, while moving to a system which rewards entrepreneurial management and workers for their efforts and skills is much more risky and difficult. Moreover, the Chinese were "educated" ever since 1949 that market economies cause many social problems and achieve poor economic results, while a socialist economy of state ownership and central planning is far superior in these regards. Nevertheless, stimulated by the economic problems they faced and by the apparent success of their reform efforts in agriculture, the post-Mao coalition leadership under Deng Xiaoping launched a serious and rather sweeping series of experimental and radical reforms in the urban-industrial sector in the decisions of the Third Plenum of the Twelfth Central Committee in October of 1984.

The more conservative members of the coalition leadership undoubtedly did not agree with all of the reforms proposed, and the split between the conservatives and the more radical reformers became more serious over time. The radical reformers gained greater control over policy-making throughout 1985–88, but their policies led to a worsening economic situation, i.e., budget problems, inflation, balance of payments problems, and problems of corruption. Thus, the conservatives regained control of economic policy-making in the fall of 1988 and introduced a program of retrenchment and controls to cool off an overheated economy.

As the last decade of the twentieth century begins, the conservatives remain in power. These leaders repeatedly argue that they are dedicated to continuing the economic reform program, once they have secured stability and balanced growth in the domestic economy. What happens to the reform program in the future obviously depends directly upon the outcome of the unstable political situation in China at the present time, especially at the highest levels of the Party. Given recent developments in Communist countries of Eastern Europe and the age of China's present political leaders, there is good reason to believe there will be a new political leadership in China in the not too distant future and that the new leadership will continue to seek a new economic system—a mixed system of both state and private enterprises and both planned and market allocation of resources and goods.

To summarize the urban-industrial reforms that had been introduced since 1984, as well as the nature of the political forces and their objectives involved in the struggle over the economic reform program, the following reading presents extracts taken from two recent writings by Robert F. Dernberger.

China's Economic Reform Program

With the death of Mao and the overthrow of the Gang of Four, the post-Mao leadership had not only an interest in but the opportunity to make far wider institutional, strategy, and policy changes than mere adjustments to resource allocation priorities. However, as the new leaders were consolidating their political control at the end of the 1970s, their first attempt at reform was to criticize Maoist economic principles and replace them with many of the socialist principles that had governed Chinese economic policies during the 1950s. Fairly early in the economic reform program, the post-Mao leadership also began to question the reliance on a Stalinist or big-push development strategy and attempted to reduce the rate of investment while giving greater priority to agriculture, light industry, and "non-productive" investment, such as schools and housing. In short, the new leaders made a significant attempt to correct economic imbalances by rewarding consumers with a greater share of the pie and basing growth more on increases in productivity and efficiency than in the past.

The rejection of the utopian Maoist economic principles in favor of socialist principles more in keeping with China's level of development and the modification of the previous development strategy and priorities in favor of more consumerism and balanced growth would have significantly improved China's economy. Yet, these economic policy and strategy changes were bound to generate questions about institutional and systemic reform. The existing institutions and economic system had been developed specifically to implement the big-push, high-growth economic strategy and policies. However, the Soviet-type economic system is not well-suited for carrying out programs that promote consumerism, agricultural development, demand-orientated production, exports, infrastructure development, and technological innovations.

Thus, the Chinese economic reform program grew out of the early economic strategy and policy reforms and has gathered intensity as these initial reform moves encountered constraints imposed by the existing economic institutions and system. Since China's current economic reform program encompasses many changes, only a general survey of the major themes are presented here—enterprise ownership, decentralization, and the incentive mechanism.

Rather than all enterprises being state owned and managed, a mixed system of individual, private, cooperative, and state ownership is now accepted as consistent with socialism. Obviously, state ownership is to remain the dominant form of ownership in industry, but individuals are now allowed to create enterprises and hire workers, especially in the service trades. Cooperatives are encouraged in the trade, savings deposit, and food sectors as well as in workshop enterprises.... Small-scale state enterprises, especially those suffering losses, are being leased out to private individuals and cooperatives who operate them for a profit. Other state enterprises are raising funds by selling shares to workers who receive a fixed annual dividend or share of the profits.

To allow the various forms of ownership to play a significant role in the economy, it is now accepted that not all economic activities must be planned. Planning remains one of the key distinguishing features of China's socialist economy, but centralized planning and bureaucratically administered commands now cover a considerably reduced number of commodities. Some output outside the mandatory plan is included in guidance plans. which are given to lower-level authorities as a reference in determining production of commodities [i.e., in factories] under their control. The production of commodities outside the mandatory plan and the guidance plans are determined by the production unit itself. State monopolies under the control of a central ministry are also being broken up to allow for greater decentralization and competition in production and trade, even foreign trade. Thus, the stifling constraints of planned targets and allocations are being reduced, many planning responsibilities are being transferred to lower levels of the bureaucracy, and market transactions between enterprises are being allowed.

These changes in ownership and enterprise functions have been accompanied with changes in incentives. Individual, private, and cooperative enterprises in both the rural and urban sectors are free to produce for the market and, after payment of business and commercial taxes, to retain and distribute the net profits. Enterprises operating within the state-planned sector are now allowed to keep their net profits, after payment of the business and commercial taxes and a new profit tax. Local government units are allowed to retain a share of the revenues they raise and the profits made by enterprises under their control. Fewer investment projects are now funded by unilateral budget grants from the central government; investment now relies more on funds raised by the enterprise and bank loans require interest payments and repayment of the principal.

In short, there has been considerable movement away from production and allocation decisions being made by planners at the top level of the economic bureaucracy and being implemented on the basis of administrative orders. China hopes to achieve a more productive and efficient economy with lower-level initiative and decisions based on economic levers or pricing, taxes, profits, and retained earnings. Furthermore, China's reform program has encouraged competition between the private and collectively owned enterprises, and the market sector and the planned sector. The state enterprises and planned sector may be ahead in the competition, but they now monopolize very few areas. Thus, what began as a local first step in adjusting economic strategy and policy for the sake of restoration and sustained growth has grown into a major economic reform program in search of a new economic system.

The Chinese Economic System Today

.... To what extent has the economic reform program created a new and different economic system? ... Some observers have argued that China already is or soon will be a capitalist, market system or a market-socialist system, while others see the changes as relatively minor and temporary concessions in the face of economic necessity. The changes in China's basic economic institutions and policies, however, have been too significant and cumulative to be regarded as just temporary deviations from the traditional Soviet-type system. On the other hand, many of the most basic institutions remain in place with the role they had in the traditional system.

The four types of ownership—individual, private, cooperative, and state—exist in almost every sector of the economy, but the state sector dominates production for most sectors except agriculture. The mandatory, centrally planned targets also probably dominate economic activity in the state sector, although state enterprises also produce and trade above target output with other enterprises at negotiated prices or sell the surplus on the market at market prices. Almost all commodities are transacted at administered, negotiated, or market prices, and very few are produced and allocated completely within the state sector under mandatory plans. In the factor markets—capital, labor, and land—the erosion of the traditional means for allocating and pricing by the introduction of markets has, thus far, been very limited. In addition, the state's control over long-distance internal trade and foreign trade remains very strong and is readily asserted with vigor whenever relaxation of that control leads to undesired results.

.... There always was considerable slippage between the plans and orders issued in Beijing and activities at the local level.... [However,] the economic reform program has significantly reduced the control of the central planners and enhanced the authority of local officials and cadre. More important, the ... decentralization movement [was] ... a serious attempt to remove some economic activity from the state and planned sectors altogether....

On the other hand, China's leaders assert that they will not allow a capitalist, market economic system to return, and they appear to be serious in their efforts to seek a truly mixed system—a "socialist system with Chinese characteristics." Their present economic system does represent a mixed system, but one in which state-planned or -controlled economic activities still dominate, at least outside the agricultural sector.... Thus, a rather lengthy period of unstable relations between the ... elements of the traditional system and the elements of the ... nonstate sectors may lie ahead.

A major issue that divides the leadership is how much further and how fast they should proceed to achieve a more balanced mix, that is, to reduce the role of the state and the centrally planned or controlled sectors.... Much of the reform movement thus far has involved the removal of constraints imposed on the economy in the past, not the building of a new economic system. When instability or imbalances occur as a result of this liberalization, however, constraints and controls are reimposed.... Yet, several fundamental economic reforms remain to be adopted for the economy to achieve [the reformers'] ... objective [i.e., the creation of a new economic system].

Thus, the past decade represents the successful first stage of economic reform.... The reform of the price system, the creation of factor markets, the significant reduction of subsidies in consumption and production, the closing of unprofitable and inefficient enterprises, and the creation of effective monetary and fiscal policies remain as challenges for the Chinese reformers. These steps in the second stage of China's economic reform will require even more political courage and will than did the first stage and will not yield the instant success experienced in the first [stage]. Furthermore, the second stage will encounter significant opposition by those who lose as a result of these reforms, more so than was true during the first stage of the reform program....

The Future of The Reform Program

Obviously, the economic problems of inflation, instability, budget deficits, domestic and foreign debts, balance of payments disequilibrium, and open and disguised unemployment are of much more immediate concern to China's political leaders than the long-run benefits... [that may be obtained from] the economic reform program.... Moreover, the ... [evidence for] long-run benefits appeared to be declining ... while the seriousness of the [above mentioned] economic problems was becoming worse. In these circumstances, Zhao Ziyang was removed from day-to-day control over economic policy implementation, while Li Peng, Yao Yilin, and other more conservative reformers were put in charge and began implementing greater administrative controls in the latter half of 1988 and early 1989 to try and stabilize the economy and regain control over economic developments.... It is most unfortunate that... the unresolved economic policy problems... [were] answered by the use of military force ... in mid-1989. Before this political crisis resolved the issue, for the time being at least, most members of the leadership program had formed a consensus in support of the reform program. They differed considerably, however, as to the pace and extent of the reforms to be implemented. In the last half of the 1980s, there appeared to be three major groupings among the reformers.

The most conservative group would not turn the clock back to the mid-1950s, but does believe the attempt to reform the economic system has gone quite far and the attempt to continue with further reforms would threaten the basic principles of a socialist economy.... They are willing to have a mixed economy, but privatization and marketization had gone too far and too fast under Zhao and his followers.

A second group wished to move ahead with the reform, but believed the need to stabilize the economy... had a greater priority. They also argued for a better planning of reform strategy, without the wave-like fits and starts of the past. Dedicated to the need for reform, they are very concerned that the reformers may be their own worst enemy by acting too hastily and without appreciating the consequences of their actions before they occur, often to the detriment of the economic reform program....

Finally, there are those who have been most frequently quoted by outside observers as spokesmen for the "reformers" and are now labeled as the "radical" reformers by China's present conservative ... leadership group. This group was dedicated to economic reforms to such an extent that they were often impatient with the wave-like character of the reform movement in the past. Their argument was that the period of transition was bound to be painful and involve costs, but these should not discourage the Chinese or cause them to retreat and reimpose controls. These people had hoped that the Chinese economy would "grow out of the planned economy" as a result of the reforms and achieve something close to a market-socialist economy.

In the effort to restore stability and regain control over the economy at the end of 1988, the shift in control over the reform process essentially involved a reduced role for the third group of reformers and a greatly enhanced role for the first two groups. The demands and open demonstrations for a more open political system, greater individual freedom, and a free press was viewed by the conservatives as but a complement to the rapid growth in the non-state, unplanned, and market economic activities ... [promoted by] the radical reformers.... With the full support of Deng Xiaoping, the conservatives were able to ... [rely on] military force to end the demonstrations, remove Zhao Ziyang and other leaders of the radical reform group from their positions of power, arresting or detaining some of them and isolating and silencing others. Again with the support of Deng Xiaoping, the conservatives were able to formulate a new more conservative leadership group, consisting largely of representatives of the first two groups of reformers, soon after the tragic events of Tiananmen in June of 1989....

Unfortunately, ... the economic reform process [had] contained the seeds of its own destruction—as an economic reform program it was rapidly becoming inconsistent, irrational, and unworkable. It is most likely that economic developments in the late 1980s would have spawned a conservative backlash and attempt to regain control over the economy ... even in the absence of the political crises which brought the struggle between the conservative reformers ... and the radical reformers ... to a head.... [Under the new conservative leadership], the Fifth Plenum [in 1990] that was to determine China's economic policy over the next few years resulted in a broadening and deepening of the retrenchment, which was already breaking the back of the inflation and leading to absolute declines in light and heavy industry and in local small-scale industry sector output. There are now [early 1990] threats to impose greater controls over the private and market sectors and calls for increasing the role of planning and supply allocation by the state....

On the other hand, the new consensus leadership has frequently reaffirmed its dedication to continue the reforms, officially declared to be placed on hold for two more years.

.... As long as the current conservative and moderate... reform consensus in the leadership remains, the reform process in the future would undoubtedly place major emphasis upon trying to reform the planning system, the enterprise management system, the credit system, the fiscal and the monetary mechanism. The move to greater privatization and marketization involved in the [past decade] of reform will not be rejected, but will be placed under greater control and constraint.... Yet, much of this will represent an inevitable and necessary period of pause, retrenchment, and realignment following the [1980s], a sort of interregnum between the Deng era economy and the era that will follow.

.... [Those] among the ranks of the radical reformers think their role in designing and implementing the reform of China's economy is not over. For the present [1990], several subjects are taboo and many suggestions would be reckless to make and politically unacceptable. But after a few years, when the economy has been stabilized and some of the senior members of the leadership finally go to meet Marx, the Chinese will turn again to the search for China's modernization. As current events in Eastern Europe indicate, they then will discover they have not only lost more ground to the capitalist countries, but have fallen behind many of their socialist friends who have accepted and implemented both radical political and economic reforms. In other words, history would appear to be on the side of the radical reformers and should at least give them a second chance to... [help determine]... China's economic reform process in the future.

Trade

50

Foreign Trade and Industrial Development of China

Yu-kwei Cheng

A basic argument of Adam Smith's Wealth of Nations, *which created the modern social science of economics, was that the wealth of a nation, or its national income, depended upon the size of the market; the larger the market, the greater the scale of production for the market and, therefore, the more specialized (i.e., productive) could be the workers and capital engaged in production. China's very large domestic market would be sufficient, it would seem, to support the economic gains from specialized production without the need to search for foreign markets. Foreign trade also benefits national economies by allowing them to take advantage of their different resource endowments; those with relatively more labor can specialize in labor-intensive commodities and trade them for the capital-intensive goods produced by economies with abundant capital. These "gains from trade" are obtained from all exchanges, within a country as well as among countries; foreign trade just adds more units that can participate in these gains. Again, in the case of China, gains would seem to be marginal given the very large size of the domestic market to begin with. Yet, there is a third benefit from foreign trade: obtaining commodities that cannot be produced domestically because the necessary skills and technology are lacking. In other words, by means of foreign trade countries obtain new capital and technology to provide for their industrialization or economic development from more advanced or developed countries. Trade brings new goods, better goods, new machines, better machines, and— finally—new methods for producing new or old goods more cheaply.*

Because China was located at the very fringes of the trade routes plied by the world's major trading countries, China's early foreign trade was very small and had little impact on the domestic economy. Yet, China did engage in foreign trade, and as England began to emerge as the world's most advanced economy in the nineteenth century, trade with China grew. Unfortunately, however, rather than exchange precious metals for Chinese silk and tea, the British found a commodity produced in their colony—India—that had a ready market in China: opium. As the documents in the "History" section of Part 1 illustrate, this stage of Chinese history, in which commercial relations with foreigners provided China with few "gains from trade," has left a legacy in Chinese thinking about foreign trade to this very day. The author of the following selection, however, a Chinese academic in the Institute of Social Sciences, Academia Sinica, before 1949, relates the early history of China's foreign trade but only hints at the more emotional nationalistic feelings of many Chinese about China's "gains from trade" with other nations during this period.

Early Trade

The commercial intercourse between China and the outside world can be traced as far back as the second century A.D., when China traded silk goods with Rome for such precious stuff as spices, pearls, and jade, either along the central Asian caravan routes or by water across the Indian Ocean and Tongking Bay in the South China Sea. Later on, the commodities exchanged between the Chinese and Roman Empires grew to include Chinese furs and metals, in addition to the principal item of silk goods, on the one hand, and glassware, asbestos, medicines, and precious stones on the other. Trade between China and Rome was carried on rather intermittently until the seventh century, when the Arabs controlled Southeastern Asia and seized the trading privileges from the Romans.

Between the seventh and the sixteenth centuries, the principal Chinese trade was with the Arabs. By sea they came to the Chinese coastal cities of Canton, Ningpo, Wenchow, and by land they often stopped at Kansu, then the leading trade center in Northwest China. By the twelfth century, the volume of goods offered by the Arabs—such as spices, pearls, ivory, piece goods, knives and swords—had reached such significant proportions that the Chinese government deemed it profitable to institute agencies to levy duties. In exchange for these goods, China exported principally silks, chinaware, camphor, rhubarb, metals, and crude sugar.

During this period also China had trade relations with her immediate Southern neighbors, Siam, Indo-China, Burma, Malaya, and other South Sea countries, including Java, Borneo, and the Philippines. Trade with Japan was greatly restricted by the Chinese authorities for fear that among her trading agents there might lurk Japanese pirates, who had so often robbed and destroyed Chinese cities and villages, especially in the eastern part of Chekiang Province.

Trade relations between China and the European nations were not established until the beginning of the sixteenth century, a few hundred years after Marco Polo introduced "Cathay" to the Europeans. Briefly, this is how European trade relations developed.

Portugal. In 1516 a Portuguese ship was the first European vessel to arrive at Canton. In the following year, Fernando Perez de Andrade entered the Canton waters with several Portuguese ships and tried to develop trade with China. Later the Portuguese were allowed to settle at Macao on payment of five hundred taels [ounces] of silver as annual rent. During the sixteenth, seventeenth, and eighteenth centuries at least four attempts were made by Portuguese emissaries to go to Peking to establish Sino-Portuguese trade, but with no tangible results. Macao, however, developed into an important trading center and by the early part of the eighteenth century the city had an alien population of more than four thousand.

Spain. The Spanish joined the Portuguese in China trade a few decades later, after occupying the Philippines. Their first visit to China was in 1575. The Spanish trade with China was limited to that conducted by Chinese who traded between Manila and the Fukien ports, such as Amoy, Changchow, and Chuanchow. The Chinese population grew so rapidly in Manila and became so influential and independent of the Spanish administration that the Spanish plotted a series of massacres between 1602 and 1639, in which tens of thousands of Chinese were killed. Thereafter the Chinese population in Manila was limited to 6,000, and trade was adversely affected. Thus the Chinese learned for the first time that European trade was supported by cannon and sword.

The Netherlands. The Dutch, in 1622, seized Formosa off the China coast as a trading base with China, after striving without success for Macao, the Portuguese colony. In 1662, the Dutch were driven from the island, leaving behind them more than a thousand dead, by the independent patriot Cheng Cheng-Kung, known to the Western world as Koxinga, who waged a valiant war against Manchu domination over China. Later. the Manchu government allowed the Dutch to trade at Canton, and it is recorded in Chinese history that the first tea trade was carried on between the Dutch merchants and the Chinese.

England. Although the British trade has dominated China's foreign commerce for the past two centuries, the British came to China one hundred years after the Portuguese got their foothold in Macao. The policy of trading nations in those days, much influenced by the Mercantile school of thought [export promotion], was to restrict the trade of their neighbors in the belief that trade was a stagnant reservoir and that one nation could share the trade only at the expense of another. The Portuguese held Macao for themselves and denied others the trading privilege of the colony. They virtually held a monopoly on Chinese trade.

The first British vessel to reach China was in 1620. By 1637 the British were allowed to trade in Canton, but not until after they had attacked the city with warships. The British tried without much success to develop trade with other Chinese ports, such as Amoy, Foochow, Ningpo, and also with Formosa. By 1684 there was considerable trade in Canton with the British, and 1702 saw the beginning of what was later known as the "Hong" or "Factory" system.

The British China trade was in the hands of the East India Company until the abolition of its monopoly in 1834. Sino-British trade at that time was so flourishing and so profitable that the British traders were no longer satisfied with the restricting "Co-Hong" system, and the resultant struggle led to China's first international conflict, the "Opium War" of 1839–42, when the Chinese government prohibited the importation of the profitable yet dangerous drug—opium—from India, which commodity constituted the bulk of the British export to China. (This will be taken up in the following section.)

France and Italy. French, Italian, and other European traders did not show much interest in the China trade in the early days. Formal commercial relations between China and these countries were not established until a much later date. Most of the traders from those countries came to China under British protection from India.

America. American traders, before the Revolution, had their commercial contact with China through the East India Company. Their first direct connection was established when the "Empress of China," loaded with ginseng, arrived at Canton in 1784. It is estimated that in the following decades Americans shipped millions of dollars worth of silver for the purchase of Chinese tea and silk.

Russia. Russia was the only modern European nation to approach China by land. Trade relations were established after the Nerchinsk Treaty of 1689. This, China's first international treaty, was agreed upon partly to regulate the land trade, but chiefly to recover from Russia the land she had occupied in northern Manchuria. Other diplomatic missions followed in 1693, 1719, and 1727. The land trade was centered around Hiakhata and transacted in barter terms, and the use of coin and specie was prohibited. The frontier land trade with Russia was, from the very beginning, carried on duty-free and was so stipulated in the subsequent trade treaties.

In 1806 Russia sent two ships to open sea trade with Canton, but no further sea trade was allowed to Russia.

Restriction on Trade (Co-Hong and Factory System)

In spite of repeated early demands for the right to trade, on the part of Western merchants, the Chinese government was skeptical about the final aims of the European traders who often resorted to guns and swords when their requests were not met. The Chinese became more suspicious and fearful of their motives when they saw that India was eventually brought under British control after granting Britain trading privileges. The fact that China was self-sufficient in her daily necessities, that the Chinese were accustomed to seclusion within the vast space of their own country, and that the European luxuries and novelties were not indispensable, also contributed largely to the restrictive measures adopted by the Chinese government. This is what is usually referred to as the "closed-door" policy.

In 1702, by edict of the Manchu government, one man each was appointed at Canton and at Amoy to be the sole agent through whom the foreigners should sell and buy. In 1720, the Co-Hong or guild was established at Canton as a body corporate and was given absolute monopoly of all dealings with foreigners. In 1757 Canton was designated as the only port at which foreigners could trade. The power of the Co-Hong was again enhanced in 1760 when its officials were authorized to act as government agents for revenue collection, besides being inter-

mediaries in sales and trade. A due of 200,000 taels of silver was required for admission to membership in the Co-Hong. It is traditionally
stated in Chinese history that the Co-Hong members were thirteen in
number, but as a matter of fact in the heyday of that institution the
membership increased beyond that number.

Foreigners who traded in Canton were confined to a limited area
in the suburbs of the city, where they set up their "factory" (in the old
sense it meant residence or station of the "factor" or agent of the home
company) to serve as countinghouse, warehouse, treasury, and residence. These "factories" were established under the auspices of the
Co-Hong which furnished their contact with the outside world. There
were fifty-nine "factories," thirty-one of which were British. Stringent
regulations to prevent misconduct of foreign traders, even governing
their private lives, were stipulated by the local authorities. For instance,
neither women nor guns, spears, or arms of any kind could be brought
into the factories. Each factory was restricted to the employment of eight
Chinese, and factory traders were forbidden to go on the river or even
to its banks.

When foreign vessels arrived at Canton, the Co-Hong merchants
financed the import duties, ship clearance, unloading, etc. Co-Hong
merchants often paid fees for the ship's entrance as high as £900 for a
boat of 420 tons which, a century later, could be cleared at £25. Besides
the regular high fees, the Co-Hong merchants had to pay gratuities to
numerous field officials to facilitate the regular operation of trade. The
ships were also subjected to daily or monthly fees and various other
charges whenever the local authorities so decided. Notwithstanding all
restrictions on factory merchants and the numerous fees and extortions,
the foreign merchants were well satisfied because of the rapid fortunes
they made out of the trade. The Co-Hong paid its millions, one way or
another, but could recoup its loss many times over. The relations between these Chinese-Western merchants were amicable and fair, which,
on many occasions, led to an exchange of assistance in difficult times.

After the Napoleonic war, however, the British traders began to
realize that the Co-Hong system hampered the growth of Sino-British
trade and in fact was tending to abolish it. The British repeated their
demand for a liberal system of trade, as necessitated by their domestic
industrial expansion and time and again met with a flat refusal from the
Chinese government.

When the East India Company was deprived of its monopolistic position in trade in 1834 and the British government sent a royal mission led by Lord Napier to take over control of China trade, the system was brought under new focus. It was, in British eyes, a system of milking, with the Co-Hong as the milker, extracting from the foreign trade all it was worth, and paying heavily to the officials for the privilege. Friction between the two countries was aggravated by misunderstandings on protocol on the part of Lord Napier's mission.

The struggle for free trade and for importation of opium into China inevitably led to a war between China and England in 1839.

Trade Value and Composition

During the latter years of the Co-Hong system, the annual value of the exports and imports of Canton amounted to twenty to thirty million dollars (silver)

.... The British dominated both the export and import trade. For instance, the value of exports to Britain in 1817 aggregated 9,768,961 dollars (silver), or 62.8 percent of the total export of 15,566,461 dollars. In the same year, imports from Britain constituted as high as 73.3 percent, or 13,694,640 dollars, of the entire import value of 18,693,440 dollars. British trade with China, i.e., Canton, at that time was almost equally shared by the East India Company and private traders. The United States of America each year shipped several million dollars' worth of silver to China for the purchase of Chinese tea.

The rapid growth of the opium trade ... during this period is as noteworthy as the commodity itself is peculiar and infamous. From 1821 to 1830, opium importation formed 40 to 50 percent in value of the entire import trade. Over 90 percent of the opium trade was handled by the British. The British used the opium trade as the chief financial means to offset imports from China.

The Manchu government and the Chinese people were outraged over the traffic, not only because the drug was detrimental to the health of its users, but because millions of dollars' worth of silver were drained out of China annually as a result of the undesirable imports. Several prohibitory edicts were issued during the early part of the nineteenth century with regard to its importation, to the smoking of it, and to its cultivation on Chinese soil.

But in Canton clandestine importation of opium grew by leaps and bounds. Canton's annual importation from 1825 to 1835 of about

19,000 chests of opium rose to 35,000 chests after 1835 (a chest is approximately 133 pounds). More drastic measures were adopted by the Chinese authorities to seize and destroy all the opium stored in Canton and vicinity. British traders in 1839 were forced to give over to the authorities, to be burned, 20,283 chests of opium, worth about six million silver dollars. This led to China's first international conflict, the "Opium War" with Britain, which resulted in 1842 in the defeat of China and the signing of the "Treaty of Nanking."

This treaty marks a new phase in China's international relations. She was compelled to adopt a "liberal," or submissive, policy toward foreign trade. The Co-Hong system was liquidated, and five ports, Shanghai, Canton, Ningpo, Foochow, and Amoy, were opened to the British as trading centers in south China. Hong Kong was ceded to become a British free port in the Far East. Of course, Britain received payment from the Chinese government of six million dollars for the opium destroyed.

Passive Development of Trade before 1913

. . . . China, before the Opium War, secluded herself from commercial relations with other nations, and "closed-door" was the keynote of her foreign policy. The Treaty of Nanking broke down the door. During the ensuing seventy years, up to the outbreak of the First World War, China suffered a series of military reverses in armed conflicts with foreign powers. The major ones were the British-French invasion of 1857–60, the Sino-Japanese War in 1894, and the Boxer War in 1900. More than fifty commercial treaties and their amendments relevant to foreign commerce were signed between China and the major powers, as well as a dozen lesser ones. In these treaties, numerous unequal terms and clauses were imposed on China against the will and interests of her people. As a result of the "most-favored-nation" clause, all of the treaty powers enjoyed all the commercial privileges stipulated in any of the treaties. Thus the "door" of China was not only opened wide, but it was held open without any protection whatsoever against foreign exploitation or competition. Dr. H. B. Morse rightly calls it a period of "submission and subjection."

In spite of continuous efforts on the part of the treaty powers, by armed force and persuasion, to bring China into the international market, the Chinese people showed only passive and slow interest. They had all they wanted of their accustomed daily necessities, such as rice and wheat for food, cotton and silk and fur for clothing, tea and wine for beverage. Moreover, during the early part of that period, the foreign nations had little to offer besides curios like watches and clocks, etc. The nationalist sentiment of the Chinese people, which was opposed to the corrupt and inept Manchu regime and to domination and subjugation by Western powers, as manifest in the Taiping Movement of 1850–64 and the Boxer uprising in 1900, also hampered the development of China's foreign trade during the period under consideration. It was not until World War I, when the strain of war loosened the grip of foreign control over Chinese trade, that the Chinese light industries, like cotton textile and tobacco, regained to a certain extent their home market, and the export of Chinese soyabean and bean products, antimony, tungsten, tung oil, etc., were increased to meet the new world demands. Chinese traders then began to show an interest in foreign trade, and the composition of the trade also changed to a certain extent.

Institutional Arrangements

To begin with, we shall enumerate and discuss briefly the unequal terms forced upon China as embodied in various treaties, which constituted the main institutional arrangements facilitating foreign trade. It should be borne in mind that these institutional set-ups have had far-reaching effects on the Chinese economy and shaped the entire course of her trade.

 Treaty Ports and Extraterritorial Rights. The term "treaty ports" is almost synonymous with "ports open to foreign trade." They are so named because under treaty obligations they were open to foreign trade, although some of them had been opened voluntarily by China. Many of these "treaty ports" are not sea or even river ports, but inland cities.

 Forty-eight treaty ports in all were opened to foreign trade during the period under discussion. By the Treaty of Nanking, five seaports along the south China coast, Canton, Amoy, Foochow, Ningpo, and Shanghai, were first thrown open. Between 1858 and 1880, the major ports in North China and along the Yangtze River were declared open to trade. From 1881 to 1900, pursuant to the provisions of treaties with Britain and France, Southwest China also was brought into contact with the outside commercial world by the opening up of six inland cities, in addition to a dozen new ports in the south and north of China and along the Yangtze River. The vast territory of Manchuria was next forced to trade with other nations, after the establishment of nine treaty ports at the turn of the century. China was then in its length and breadth laid wide open to foreign trade.

In the major treaty ports portions of the city were set aside as a "settlement" or "concession," the administration of which was in the hands of a foreign municipal council for the exclusive benefit and advantage of the represented nation. In Shanghai, Tientsin and Hankow there were several foreign concessions administered by as many countries. . . .

There were more than ten million Chinese residing in these forty-eight treaty ports. The total alien population in China at the time was estimated at 1,486,000, and most of them lived in the treaty ports and special railway zones in Manchuria. Citizens of all the Treaty powers lived in China under the special protection of extraterritoriality and they were subject, if accused of any crime, to trial and punishment only by the consuls or other public functionaries of their respective countries and under their own laws.

These extraterritorial rights were first embodied in the Treaty of Wanghia, signed in 1844 between China and the United States, and [other countries that later signed treaties with China] enjoyed the same privileges. These special privileges have had an important bearing on China trade as well as on the industrial development of the country after the First World War.

Territorial Concession and "Sphere of Influence." "Sphere of influence" or "sphere of interest" of the different Treaty powers in China had its genesis in the territorial concessions made since the Opium War. Britain's possession of Hong Kong and of the lion's share of early trade in Canton made South China her main sphere of interest. France demanded preferential economic treatment in Southwest China after China's tributary state of Indo-China was ceded to her in 1884. The annexation by Russia of the Amur region and the Maritime Provinces by the treaties of 1858 and 1860 developed her special interest in North Manchuria. After the Sino-Japanese war, 1894–95, in which China suffered one of the greatest military defeats in her history, Japan forced China to recognize the independence of Korea, which was then under Chinese suzerainty and was later annexed by Japan, and to cede to

Japan the Liaotung Peninsula, Formosa, and the Pescadores Islands, thus stretching the ever-expanding Japanese interests into South Manchuria and Fukien Province across from the island of Formosa.

It was the Treaty of Shimonoseki with Japan in 1895 which started a new wave of territorial demands or preferential or exclusive rights in different areas by the Treaty powers and which amounted to the actual partition of China. It was mainly due to their periodic industrial overproduction at home that European nations sought desperately at that time to secure their markets in Asia and Africa. England, in addition to obtaining further leased territory in Kowloon, across from Hong Kong, and Weihaiwei in Shantung Peninsula, exacted from the Chinese government an understanding that no part of the rich and vast Yangtze Valley would be ceded to other powers. France in 1898, after having acquired a leased territory in Kwangchowwan, demanded a similar promise in three southwestern provinces in order to safeguard her interests in Tongking. Germany marked out the entire province of Shantung as its sphere of interest. Russia declared that no nation would be allowed to gain a foothold in Manchuria along her frontiers. (Most of Russia's economic and trade concessions and privileges including the bases of Dairen and Port Arthur were, however, transferred to Japan after the Russo-Japanese War.) This series of special rights and immunities granted to different Treaty powers in their respective spheres led in 1899 to a special plea by the United States, a comparative latecomer in the world's commercial arena. The American position was that the Treaty powers should maintain their "open door" policy to secure to the commerce and navigation of all nations equality of treatment within such "spheres."

Within each sphere of interest, the different powers enjoyed preferential or exclusive privileges in railway building, mining, etc. To finance these economic activities, special banking institutions were established.

The distribution of trade in different parts of China among the various Treaty powers was heavily influenced by the "sphere of interest" in each particular area. . . .

Treaty Tariff. Prior to 1842, China had enjoyed the full right of fixing her customs duties, which right is inherent in the sovereignty of an independent state. But in 1843, as a result of the military defeat in the Opium War with England, China was deprived of that right and a flat, rigid rate of 5 percent by value was imposed on all imports. For the sake of convenience in revenue collection, however, most of these duties were made specific.

In 1857, prices began to drop and the customs duty collected appeared to be in excess of the prescribed 5 percent. A downward revision of specific rates was asked by the Treaty powers and was effected in 1858. Again in 1902, after more than forty years had elapsed, another revision was made with a view to raising sufficient revenue to meet the newly imposed obligations of the Boxer indemnities. After years of protracted negotiations, and because of China's participation in World War I, a third revision was effected in 1918, and still another in 1922, before her tariff autonomy was restored in 1929. These revisions could be made only when unanimously agreed upon by sixteen or seventeen powers.

Inasmuch as the greater part of the duty rates were specific, and since commodity prices rose steadily during the entire period after 1858, the average effective rates were often below 3 percent and were never above 4 percent even in the years immediately following the revisions.

The reasons for China's objections to the tariff system were obvious; the unscientific taxation of all commodities alike at 5 percent *ad valorem* did not differentiate between raw materials and manufactured goods, between luxuries and necessities, or between consumers' goods and capital goods. Therefore, it did not permit the application of a protective tariff for fostering infant industries or encouraging basic industries necessary to the economic development of a country. Inflexible and unalterable, it did not permit increase or decrease as the needs of revenue required. Furthermore, being unilateral and non-reciprocal, the tariff imposed restrictions only on China and offered no concession or compensation in international commercial negotiations.

Nor was that all. In addition to enjoying the privilege of a low and flat duty when imported into China, foreign goods since 1858, upon payment of a 2.5 percent transit duty (this being one-half the import duty) could be shipped to any place in China without further imposition of dues or charges of any kind, while Chinese native goods had to pay, up to the year 1931, numerous *likin* charges on land or river routes, each constituting a separate barrier to the free and smooth movement of traffic....

Other Institutions. ... Tariff duties and customs procedures were managed by the Inspectorate General of Customs and its local and field officers. This instrument of the Chinese government was created as early as 1853, when the Taiping Rebels occupied Shanghai and the Customs House was closed. A board of three foreign inspectors was nominated by local Chinese officials to collect the customs revenue. The system appeared to be satisfactory, and an Englishman, Robert Hart, later Sir Robert Hart, was appointed in 1863 as the Inspector-General of Customs, which post he held until his death in 1911. All customs at treaty ports were brought under the control of alien staffs to collect revenue and to handle matters relating to local foreign trade. After 1901, by another treaty provision, all customs receipts, which constituted the bulk of government revenue and were used as a security for Boxer indemnity, were put under the exclusive custody and disposal of the Inspector General of Customs. The Chinese staffs at these customs offices were much larger than the foreign staffs, but their members were kept in subordinate positions and had no voice in the customs administration. . . .

The above were the major institutions established under treaty obligations which shaped to a great extent the course of China's foreign trade, as well as the whole Chinese economy. The unequal treaties were relinquished in 1943 in the midst of World War II.

China's Balance of Payments in the Twentieth Century

Nai-ruenn Chen

The previous reading makes clear why the Chinese refer to the treaties that governed China's relations with the West between 1840 and 1949 as the "unequal" treaties. Undeniably, these treaties imposed tremendous economic costs upon the Chinese. Moreover, the Chinese not only had to pay their own expenses for fighting a losing war, they also had to reimburse the foreigners for their expenses as well. In addition to the pure economic costs, these "unequal treaties" obviously inflicted tremendous political costs upon the Chinese, such as the humiliating loss of sovereignty over areas within their own country. Finally, the forces of modernization that these treaties unleashed upon China undercut and began to tear apart the centuries-old, well-woven fabric of Chinese society and culture. As explained in the sections on history and politics in this volume, in the 1940s the Communists relied upon this history of imperialism to gain considerable support in their campaign for a "united front" against the imperialists—i.e., Japan—and Mao made clear to all Chinese the significance of the Communists' victory in the Civil War when he announced the creation of the People's Republic of China with these simple words: "China has stood up."

It is unlikely that the Chinese will forget the one-hundred-year history of the imperialists in China, or readily forgive the foreigners for what they did. However, some of the widely held anti-foreign memories of that period have become accepted as truth regardless of the facts. For example, there are many complex, interdependent factors that explain China's failure to achieve modernization during the late nineteenth and the first half of the twentieth centuries. Yet, the foreigner and the unequal treaties are often blamed as the major cause for that failure. Rawski, in chapter 47, showed how the economic demonstration effect brought to the treaty ports of China by the foreigner took root in the early decades of the twentieth century, when native Chinese entrepreneurs began establishing their own modern industries. Thus, the unequal treaties did not preclude Chinese industrialization; on the contrary, native industries were being created and growing at an impressive rate in those years.

In this reading, we try to counter another popular argument: as a result of the unequal treaties, the foreigner was plundering China of its wealth and was extracting from the Chinese economy millions of dollars a year. Dr. Nai-ruenn Chen, an economist who until recently worked at the Commerce Department as a specialist on China's foreign trade, analyzes China's balance of payments during the twentieth century. He shows that, contrary to popular belief, China actually had the good fortune of being able to import more commodities than were being exported over a long period of time, while also importing more precious metals than were being exported. This favorable situation was made possible by a unique feature of China's balance of payments: the very large inflow of foreign exchange due to the remittances home from Chinese living overseas.

Following the opening of China to the outside world through the Opium War in the 1840s, especially after the turn of the century, foreign trade gradually emerged as a major factor in the Chinese economy. One striking feature of China's foreign trade in this century was the persistence of unfavorable balances. In no year between 1898 and 1940, did Chinese exports exceed or equal imports. The situation worsened in the 1940s because of war and inflation.... How could an economically underdeveloped country like China finance such a persistent, long-term trade deficit? ...

The answer is tentative because of data limitations. Historical data on China's balance of payments are essential to our investigation, but such data are scarce. There does not exist a systematic, annual estimation of China's international payments accounts. Fortunately, a number of independent estimates were prepared by different authors for individual years....

.... The quality of the existing estimates varies widely; some were carefully prepared while others are no more than rough measures. All estimates were hampered by the insufficiency of information, and hence frequently had to rely on very crude data or bold assumptions. The use of different accounting frameworks and methods of estimation made different estimates often incomparable. In spite of these defects, the existing estimates are basically useful and provide certain general orders of magnitude. These estimates with the support of available qualitative information may enable us to shed some light on how China had managed to offset its chronic trade imbalances. . . .

China's trade levels, measured in U.S. dollars, remained stagnant prior to the early 1880s, and expanded steadily thereafter reaching a peak in the late 1920s. The gain in the trade volume was partly due to the expansion of the treaty port system, and partly to the opening up of Manchuria to foreign trade. World War I also caused exports to rise substantially. Trade declined sharply in the 1930s despite moderate economic progress in these years. The average annual volume dropped from nearly $1.4 billion in the second half of the 1920s to only $380 million a decade later. The decline was attributable to the world depression, the loss of Manchuria to Japan, an upwards revision of Chinese tariffs, and the outbreak of the Sino-Japanese war.

During the last three decades of the nineteenth century China generally maintained a favorable balance of trade, although the export surplus diminished over time. China's balance of trade became unfavorable toward the end of the nineteenth century, and stayed that way every year until 1940. The average annual trade deficit increased rapidly, from $8 million in the second half of the 1890s to a peak of $185 million in the first half of the 1920s. The deficit remained at over $155 million a year in spite of the sharply reduced trade volume because of the loss of Manchuria.

To understand such a persistent pattern of import surpluses, we need to examine the factors underlying the rapid rise of China's imports and the reasons why China's exports could not keep pace with rising imports. . . .

The most fundamental cause for the rapid increase in imports was undoubtedly the imposition of a series of unequal treaties on China following military defeats at the hands of Western industrial powers and Japan. . . . The treaty ports, which had grown to 48 in not only all coastal provinces but also some inland areas, formed an enclave more closely related to foreign countries than to the Chinese economy. Growing foreign direct investment in the enclave, which according to Remer's estimate increased from $503.2 million in 1902 to $1,067 million in

1931, caused producer goods imports to rise. The foreign population in the enclave also expanded rapidly, reaching some 1.5 million in the early 1930s. Most of the foreign residents, with business privileges and rising incomes, had strong demands for high-quality consumer goods, most of which could not be manufactured in China and therefore had to be imported.

The demand for imports was augmented by the emergence in the enclave of relatively rich Chinese who through a demonstration effect tended to imitate the consumption habits of the foreign residents. With the establishment of the treaty port system, there arose a class of *nouveaux riches,* such as the compradore, serving foreign interests or acting as a middleman between the enclave and other sectors of the Chinese economy. Many landlords and other rich Chinese seeking security and convenience were settled in the "concessions" in the treaty ports. An increasingly large number of industrial entrepreneurs were also attracted to the treaty ports where an improved infrastructure provided many external economies and hence profitable opportunities for Chinese-owned factories.

The demand for imports, however, was not limited to foreigners and well-to-do Chinese in the enclave. The Chinese population of the treaty ports expanded rapidly, reaching more than 10 million by the early 1930s. Their demand for food could not be totally met by domestic supplies because of the backward system of land transport with the balance depending on foreign sources. Grain, therefore, had been one of China's leading imports, usually accounting for 5 to 6 percent of the total and reaching over 10 percent in some years.

But backward internal transport was not the only reason for relatively large grain imports. The loss of tariff autonomy until 1929 had provided an impetus for the import of grain and many other commodities.... Further, foreign products were exempted from internal transit taxes, such as *likin* charges to which all Chinese products were invariably subject. Prior to its abolition in 1931, the *likin* often constituted 15 to 20 percent of the value of a given commodity. Thus native products usually could not compete with imports on Chinese markets. Frequently the coastal population found it more economical to buy their food from foreign rather than domestic sources. The same was true in the case of raw cotton. Textile mills in Shanghai, for example, could purchase cheaper cotton from the United States or India than from producing provinces in interior China.

While there were many forces conducive to substantial import growth, the Chinese capabilities to expand exports were limited.... During the six decades from 1871 to 1930 imports grew by more than 7 times, compared to less than 4 times for exports. Incomes derived from exports made up over half of China's total international receipts in the early years of the century but declined to about one-third in the mid-1930s.

China's exports, which were dominated by silk and tea in the nineteenth century, were gradually diversified in the twentieth century, with foodstuffs, raw materials and semi-manufactures becoming predominant. These products constituted about 85 percent of total exports.... Among major categories, only in raw materials had Chinese exports consistently exceeded imports. Even in the foodstuffs and semi-manufactures categories, the trade balance was not always in China's favor. But the most important source of the overall import surplus stemmed from the consistent and large imbalance of trade in manufactured goods. Such an imbalance could only be partially offset by the export surplus in other categories.

The pattern of China's foreign trade, therefore, was typical of an underdeveloped agricultural country where exports, dominated by primary products and semi-manufactures, usually fall short of imports, most of which are manufactured consumer goods and semi-manufactures used for the production of these goods....

But there were other, perhaps more fundamental causes for slow export growth in China. China's export trade was mainly a passive development in response to the growing imports occasioned by the presence of foreign powers. There existed no conscientious national effort to promote exports. The export trade was largely handled by the middlemen in the treaty ports. These middlemen, an often unscrupulous breed of men, in their pursuit for profits tended to take advantage of small producers who were mostly illiterate, inarticulate, unorganized and ignorant of world market conditions. While reaping considerable amounts of profit from the export trade, the middlemen neither invested in export industries in return, nor showed interest in assisting the producer to raise his productivity. Without increased investments and new inputs, the vast agricultural sector in China remained stagnant, thus severely limiting its capability to expand production for exports.

Difficulties in agriculture also manifest the lack of "linkage" between exports and imports. In modern economic growth, imports are often linked to export development by importing producer goods to directly or indirectly facilitate expansion of export industries, which, in turn, help pay for growing imports. In the case of prewar China, as noted above, imports were mostly consumer goods. The relatively small quantities of capital goods imported each year were largely for industrial use in the treaty ports, and had very little to do with agricultural development. Not until the mid-1930s was the Chinese government able to make some attempts to affect the import structure linking it, though still remotely, to export growth.

In sum, the rapid growth of Chinese imports resulting from a series of unequal treaties coupled with the passive nature of export trade and the underdevelopment of the Chinese economy had left China's trade balance constantly in an unfavorable position. From 1901 to 1940 China had accumulated a total deficit of $835 million. This was no small amount in view of the fact that total imports during the same period were only $3,680 million. In other words, only 77 percent of these imports were financed by export earnings. How were the remaining 23 percent of imports paid for? . . .

. . . . The major components of the existing estimates of China's balance of payments . . . [can be organized] into six categories: (1) merchandise trade; (2) gold and silver trade; (3) foreign investments; (4) service transactions; (5) overseas Chinese remittances; and (6) miscellaneous. . . .

To examine the role of capital inflow in financing the trade balance, we have a separate account for foreign investments. The inpayments on foreign investments stemmed from foreign direct investments and foreign loans to the Chinese government while most of the outpayments were distributed between that part of the profit on direct investments remitted to investing countries and amortization and interest payments on foreign loans.

In the service transactions account, on the inpayment side are foreign expenditures in China including those by foreign governments for diplomatic and military purposes and by foreign private sectors such as religious and philanthropic organizations and tourists. Included in the outpayment side are Chinese expenditures abroad, freight and insurance and motion picture royalties.

Overseas Chinese remittances are listed separately because of their unique place in China's international finance. They were in effect a major source of receipts derived from the export of the services of millions of Chinese. The account for the miscellaneous refers to those receipts and payments not listed elsewhere, and include capital flight (in 1934–38) and transfer of government funds (1936–38) as well as errors and omissions.

Usually the movement of gold and silver is taken as a conventional means for offsetting the merchandise trade deficit. Thus one would expect such a deficit to take place in concomitance with an export surplus of gold and silver trade, at least over a prolonged period of time. In the case of prewar China, however, the imbalances in both merchandise trade and specie movement did not necessarily move in the opposite direction. While China consistently maintained a trade deficit throughout the prewar years, an export surplus of gold and silver had not occurred until 1931.

Historically, silver was predominant in China's specie movements.... The movements of silver into and out of China were mainly in response to the changes in its price on the world market. The relatively low gold price of silver abroad in most of the years prior to 1931 resulted in an influx of silver to China, while the rise in the gold price of silver in the United States in the early 1930s led to an efflux of silver from China. The silver influx [before the 1930s] aggravated the already serious problem of continuing merchandise trade imbalances. And in those years when there was a silver efflux, except for 1936, the specie movement could only offset partially the adverse balance of merchandise trade. What, then, were other counter-balancing factors?

Yu-kwei Cheng [author of the previous reading] has contended that "The bulk of China's passive trade balance in her modern history had in fact been counterbalanced by foreign investments in China." He supports his contention by comparing the cumulative value of import surpluses in 1900, 1914, and 1930 with Remer's estimates of foreign investments in China for the corresponding years, and concludes that the two "developed along parallel lines." He further points out that the parallelism also can be found in the case of the cumulative bilateral trade balances with Great Britain, the United States, and Japan and their respective investments in China.

A careful examination of the available data on China's balance of payments will find Cheng's view untenable. As Chi-ming Hou has pointed out, "if one is to find out how the chronic trade deficit was financed, the capital inflow figures (rather than the amounts of foreign investment) are relevant." Hou's analysis shows that especially during the period 1914–36 China's trade deficit continued to expand, but not the inflow of foreign capital. He attributes part of the value of foreign direct investments to reinvestment of profits and the appreciation of the value of properties owned by foreigners in the treaty ports, both of which brought no inpayments to China. He also suggests that neither had much of the increase in foreign loans to the Chinese government resulted in corresponding inflow of foreign capital because it represented interest in arrears, or was raised to repay previous loans, or was advanced by foreign banks in China. Further, some foreign loans were for indemnity payments which, strictly speaking, were not loans made to China but represented unilateral transfer of Chinese resources to foreign countries.

The untenability of the Cheng thesis becomes more apparent if outpayments on foreign investments are considered in connection with inpayments.... The outpayments on foreign investments in the form of the remittance of profits to investing countries and interest charges and amortization of foreign loans overbalanced the inpayments, especially during the period 1928–38. In that period the net balance of outpayments averaged $34 million a year, adding to the already large payments deficit caused by import surpluses.

One significant feature of the development of China's international payments in prewar years was the consistently favorable position which China maintained with respect to the service transactions account where foreign expenditures in China considerably outbalanced Chinese expenditures abroad. The most important item of foreign expenditures in China was those on garrison and naval vessels present in Chinese territories and rivers. Other items included the remittance of foreign funds to China for the acquisition of properties by non-business organizations as well as the expenditures in China by foreign diplomatic missions, merchant marine and tourists. The annual balance of the service transactions account averaged about $45 million a year in the 1910s, $80–90 million in the 1920s and $50–60 million in the 1930s, more than sufficient to offset the negative balance of the foreign investments ... account.

If we combine the foreign investments and services transactions accounts together to measure China's net inpayments from its nontrade transactions with other countries, we find the aggregate balance of these two accounts averaged some $32 million a year. For want of a better term, this combined positive balance may be called "net foreign contribution" to the financing of China's trade deficit.

One other major source of income which was not common to other countries but had long been important to China was overseas Chinese remittances. A large number of Chinese, mostly from Fukien and Kwangtung Provinces, had emigrated to foreign countries, particularly Southeast Asia, to become laborers, businessmen, and entrepreneurs. In the late 1930s the overseas Chinese population reached some 8 millions. They traditionally sent back to China part of their incomes each year to support their families or invest in various undertakings. The individual annual remittances were usually not large, but amounted to millions of dollars in the aggregate.

To show changes over time in the relative importance of net gold and silver exports, net foreign contribution and overseas Chinese remittances in financing the merchandise trade deficit, Table 1 presents data on each of these factors in relation to the trade balance for six year periods from the early 1900s to the late 1930s.

Table 1. Major Sources of Financing the Trade Deficit in China, Selected Periods (in Millions of U.S. Dollars)

	1903–09	1912–13	1920–23	1928–30	1931–36	1937–38
Merchandise Trade Balance	−48.9†	−97.2	−220.4	−123.7	−159.3	−125.9
Sources of Financing						
a. Net gold and silver exports	−1.3	−22.6	−44.5	−54.2	82.1	80.8
b. Net foreign contribution	−2.0	63.7	143.9	27.9	30.8	29.9
c. Overseas remittances	47.6	42.9	90.8	111.8	83.9	129.0
d. Others‡	4.6	13.2	30.2	38.3	−37.5	−113.8

†A negative sign means an expenditure by China, a positive sign means a receipt by China.
‡Included are errors and omissions, capital flight (1934–38) and transfer of government funds (1936–38).

In the 1900s when China began to experience annually an unfavorable balance of trade, the deficit was almost totally offset by overseas remittances. In the early 1910s and early 1920s, when exports expanded more rapidly than imports, there was also an increasingly large negative balance of gold and silver trade, equivalent in size to over 20 percent of the merchandise trade deficit. In these periods net foreign contributions became the most important factor in offsetting the trade deficit, but the amount of overseas remittances was still substantial, constituting over one-third of total inpayments.

In the late 1920s, the annual deficit of merchandise trade was smaller than in the early 1920s, but that of gold and silver trade became larger. Overseas remittances regained the leading position, amounting to $112 million a year, or 90 percent of the trade deficit, while the share of net foreign contributions fell to some 23 percent.

The structure of China's balance of payments changed significantly in the 1930s, mainly because there emerged an export surplus of gold and silver, averaging over $80 million a year and becoming the second largest source of financing the merchandise trade deficit. Overseas Chinese remittances continued to be the leading factor, while net foreign contributions remained basically at the same level as in the late 1920s.

52

Economic Modernization in Contemporary China: Limiting Dependence on Foreign Technology

Robert F. Dernberger

China's long history of relative isolation and belief in its own cultural superiority were challenged in the more recent past, when the material superiority of the West forced the opening of China to the outside world and set the rules that would govern China's dealings with the foreigner. Chinese attitudes toward economic relations with the foreigner, therefore, combine two inconsistent themes. On the one hand, there is the desire to modernize China by means of self-reliant efforts, limiting any role the foreigner might play. On the other hand, there is a recognition of the superiority of Western technology and the desire to borrow that technology and rely on the foreigner's help to catch up with those countries that have already achieved modernization. Throughout the past one hundred years, the policies actually pursued for achieving the modernization of China's economy have followed a cyclical pattern: brief periods of actively borrowing foreign technology and opening the Chinese economy to the foreigner, sooner or later followed by a reaction and a return to isolation and the glorification of self-reliance. This policy cycle became more intense in the period after 1949. Because this issue became a major area of disagreement among China's Communist leaders, the significant and dramatic shifts in political power among the leadership groups in the past thirty-five years have been reflected in extreme and rather shortlived changes in the pattern of China's foreign trade.

These radical shifts in China's pattern of foreign trade in the three decades after 1949, and the extent to which they reflect the ever unstable outcome of the conflict between the forces of isolation and self-sufficiency as against the recognized need to open the economy and rely on the foreigner, are the major themes in the following conference paper by Robert F. Dernberger. The theme of the conference at which this paper was presented in 1975 was the "technological imperative." Those who argue there is a technological imperative believe that modern technology, which was developed in the West in a particular institutional environment, generates forces that undermine the institutions of a different environment into which the technology is transferred. Mao, of course, was very aware of this problem, and Dernberger's article shows how the Maoists tried to avoid the technological imperative by limiting China's foreign trade dependency and the role of the foreigner in China's economic modernization after 1949.

The Problem

Economic development is a primary goal of all societies, both communist and noncommunist. Regardless of the wide variety of cultural values, patterns of social behavior, ideological objectives and constraints, political and administrative institutional organizations, and even specific economic priorities to be found in these societies, the results of empirical research and theoretical reasoning by economists indicate that the accumulation and effective implementation of technological innovations is perhaps the most important and difficult of the necessary conditions for any successful economic development program. By definition, the developed countries are the repositories of advanced technology. The developing countries must rely to a significant extent on borrowing this technology in their efforts to achieve economic development. . . .

Historically this intercultural transfer of technology, a necessary component of modernization for the less-developed countries, has involved serious pernicious effects on the borrowing country's social and cultural system. . . .

The real danger is to be found in the unquestioned and slavish adoption of modern Western technology; the process of defusing its harmful effects lies in its careful adaptation to fit China's needs and environment. Mao's words are as follows:

> China has suffered a great deal from the mechanical absorption of foreign material. . . . We should assimilate whatever is useful to us today not only from the present-day socialist and new-democratic cultures but also from the earlier cultures of other nations. . . . We should not gulp any of this foreign material down uncritically, but must treat it as we do our food—first chewing it, then submitting it to the workings of the stomach and intestines with their juices and secretions, and separating it into nutrients to be absorbed and waste matter to be discarded.

The Chinese have encountered severe problems in their attempt to "digest" foreign technology and history tells us that previous attempts to separate the good from the bad in this manner have often led to the demise of the would-be gourmets. . . .

A Lesson from History: The Failure of Early Modernizers

. . . . By the middle of the nineteenth century, the oldest and most stable cultural and political system in the world's history had begun to crumble. Responsible Chinese leaders, serving an alien rule, went through a considerable period of anguish and soul-searching in the attempt to save China's traditional culture and institutions. These Chinese believed in the superiority of their cultural tradition but were forced to recognize, following a disastrous series of wars and "unequal" treaties, the superiority of Western technology and economic productivity. Thus the solution many of them believed possible was in the adoption of Western "things" to sustain and develop the Chinese "way of life." The popular slogan used to convey the argument was *Chung-hsueh wei-t'i, Hsi-hsueh wei-yung,* which can be translated as "Chinese learning for the fundamental principles, Western learning for practical application."

The efforts of these nineteenth-century reformers were in vain. Not only did it prove most difficult to transplant Western technology, even on a limited scale, into an unmodified traditional Chinese culture and institutional environment without greater official support than they had in these efforts, but these inexperienced indigenous efforts to introduce Western industry were exposed to unrestrained foreign competition when China's domestic economy was finally opened to the forces of "imperialism." . . .

An important contributing reason for the failure of China's early reformers to achieve the objective of *Chung-hsueh wei-t'i, Hsi-hsueh wei-*

yung was the Chinese government's inability to control the foreigners. . . .

Given [the] traditional problem in the transfer of modern Western technology to the non-Western countries, why were Russia, Japan, and even the People's Republic of China relatively successful in coping with this problem, while traditional China was not? A brief review of these countries' experiences indicates that the role played by their governments was critical. Popular sentiment in all four cases would appear to have been strongly antiforeign, but unlike the case of traditional China, the governments in Russia, Japan, and the People's Republic (1) actively pursued the objective of economic development, (2) recognized the need for and advantages of heavily borrowing foreign technology, and (3) effectively controlled and limited the activities of the foreigners within their economies. The fragile balance of control over domestic antiforeign sentiment with simultaneous heavy borrowing of technology from abroad via foreign trade has been one of the striking features of their economic development. In the case of Russia and Japan, this transfer of technology has been eminently successful; these two countries now rank as the second and third largest economies in the world.

It would be premature to claim that the Chinese have been successful, but their prospects for success are very good and their record of past success and expectations of future success owe a great deal to their practice of active borrowing of modern technology from abroad and their ability to control its impact on the domestic economy and society. . . .

The Dominant Theme of Self-Reliance

Policy statements on economic development in China over the past twenty-five years can be compared to a great symphonic work. Self-reliance, the dominant theme, provides the basic framework and the ideological spirit of the piece; heavy reliance on borrowed technology, the minor theme, is an ever-present haunting tune in the background. By definition, the dominant theme is loudly emphasized at certain times, but the minor theme never completely disappears. In fact, at times it threatens to take over as the dominant theme. The merit of the work, however, is the intricate and ingenious weaving together of these two themes.

Thus, during some periods over the past twenty-five years, Chinese policy statements could be interpreted as calling for extreme self-reliance or autarky and, at other times, calling for heavy borrowing of foreign technology from abroad. Furthermore, the advocates of these two conflicting points of view have continued to fight over these differences in determining what particular policy should be adopted. Nonetheless, both a careful reading of their policy statements and an analysis of their actual behavior make it clear that, with the possible exception of the early 1950s, the Chinese communists have continuously followed a policy that represents a compromise: a policy of dual technological development. On the one hand there is the modern sector—the core of China's industrialization, consisting of large-scale, capital-intensive projects, relying heavily on imported technology. On the other hand, there is the rural, small-scale sector, which is very significant in both its contribution to total supply and to China's development potential. The Chinese recognize, however, that this rural industrial sector alone is not a sufficient condition for successful economic development, consisting as it does of smaller-scale, more labor-intensive projects that rely to a greater extent on indigenous technological innovations, which are mostly adaptations of technology available in the modern sector. Although at times they definitely appear to be separated in the thinking of the Chinese economic policy makers, and although Chinese economic development policy may place greater stress on one of these sectors at a particular time, there is considerable interaction between them. It is their emphasis on *both* sectors that represents, I believe, the evolution of a rational and wise approach to the economic development problem in China today. . . .

As for the modern sector, however, three very representative and important examples of the Chinese appreciation of the need for and benefits to be derived from borrowing foreign technology can be cited here: the Chinese First Five-Year Plan, the three short essays by Mao that were required reading during the 1960s, and the authoritative statement on China's economic development policies published at the end of the 1960s.

The First Five-Year Plan (1953–57) represents the most explicit statement of the Chinese leaders' decisions about the means and objectives of China's economic development program following the restoration of the economy in 1952. The language of the plan itself is as follows:

Our industrial capital construction plan which puts the main emphasis on heavy industry is designed to set our technically backward national economy onto the road of modern technology and lay an up-to-date technical foundation for our industry, agriculture and transport. To achieve this aim our plan of industrial capital construction provides for the establishment of new industries equipped with the most up-to-date technique, and for the similar re-equipment of existing industries, step-by-step. This plan is the core of our Five-Year Plan, while the 156 projects which the Soviet Union is helping us to build are in turn the core of our industrial construction plan.

Following their open break with the Soviet Union in 1960 and their agreement that the unquestioned borrowing of the Soviet approach to economic development during the First Five-Year Plan period had been wrong, the Chinese leadership placed much greater emphasis on self-reliance in their public statements of economic policy. Nonetheless, throughout the last decade or so, the three most emphasized required readings from the works of Mao—the brief gospel for one-fourth of mankind—are "Serve the People" (September 1944); "The Foolish Old Man Who Removed the Mountain" (June 1945); and "In Memory of Norman Bethune" (December 1939). These brief essays crystallize the three major "thoughts of Mao": the socialist virtue of dedicating one's life to working for the people; the ability of the people to overcome any obstacle through self-reliance and sacrifice; and the life of Norman Bethune, a Canadian, as an excellent example of not adopting something new just because it is new, but also not ignoring the contributions modern technology (meaning technology brought by a foreigner) can make to China's future. Thus the "thoughts of Mao" stress both self-reliance and borrowed technology.

Finally, an article in the October 1969 issue of *Hung Ch'i (Red Flag)*, entitled "China's Path of Socialist Industrialization," was the most explicit statement of China's economic policy in the period after the Cultural Revolution. This article does indeed stress self-sufficiency as the proper means for achieving economic development. Nonetheless, as always, it admits that lessons can be learned from other countries and are desirable; it is the mere imitation of foreign technology that is wrong, and the Chinese must learn to rely on their own initiative in generating technological progress.

This simultaneous commitment to both rural, small-scale, "native"

industries and urban, large-scale, modern industries is neither schizo-
phrenic behavior nor dishonest propaganda. It is merely sound development policy for the central government of a country with scarce capital
to tell local authorities in underdeveloped rural areas to develop their
areas by utilizing the resources and technology available to them in
small-scale, labor-intensive industrial projects and not look to the central
government for help while the central government is importing advanced technology for large-scale industrial projects in the urban, modern sector.

This ability of China's leaders to conceptually separate these two
sectors and advocate dissimilar technological policies in each is related,
of course, to their ability to control the flow of technology borrowed
from abroad and its utilization in China. In this regard, the institutional
organization of the Chinese economy, as in other socialist economies,
places considerable control in the hands of the central government. For
all practical purposes, since the mid-1950s at least, all industrial enterprises in China are owned by the state and run by managers appointed
by the state. Investment in new industrial projects and the acquisition
of new capital in existing enterprises on any significant scale are also
controlled through the central budgetary process and require the explicit permission of central authorities, that is of the State Capital Construction Commission.

What foreign technology is obtained from abroad, and who uses it
in China, are determined largely, at least in the first instance, by economic agencies directly under the control of the central government.

Although over the past twenty-five years the development policy
of the Chinese has always combined elements of an effort to develop a
domestic industrial sector built through their own efforts while simultaneously building a modern industrial sector incorporating technology
imported from abroad, this dual industrial-sector development was
made possible by the state's centralized control over the importation,
distribution, and utilization of foreign technology. Changes in economic
and in domestic or international political circumstances have resulted
in episodic changes in emphasis from one aspect of this dual policy to
the other.

For example, with the creation of the PRC in 1949, the continued
success of the Chinese Communists depended upon their rapid restoration and development of all industries, but especially the producer
goods industries. Self-sufficiency was out of the question, as was the

piecemeal grafting on of imports to the domestically produced supply of producer goods, given the magnitude of the new industrial capacity required and the time limit for acquiring it if the Chinese hoped to accomplish their goals of national security and industrialization. Thus, even during the period of recovery in 1950–52, the Chinese actively sought and obtained imports of complete and modern plants from their Socialist allies. As pointed out earlier, these imports of complete plants were the core of the First Five-Year Plan for the industrialization of China in 1953–57. At the end of the plan period, due to their failure to achieve significant increases in agricultural production, as well as Mao's desire to speed up the pace of the socialist revolution, the Chinese adopted a new approach in their general attack on the economic development problem.

Known as the Great Leap, this new policy emphasized reliance on the mass mobilization of China's rural labor force in [township-sized] political and economic units—communes—in a guerrilla-type effort not only to increase agricultural output but also to develop small-scale native industries throughout the countryside that would not rely on imports of modern technology, that is, of producer goods. Nonetheless, this new policy also called upon the Chinese to "walk-on-two-legs." Thus large-scale imports of complete plants continued as the Chinese also pursued the expansion of the modern industrial sector, signing agreements in late 1958 and early 1959 that called for additional Soviet deliveries of complete plants in the belief their new development policy had been successful.

By the end of 1959 the failure of the Great Leap became obvious to even the most optimistic of Mao's supporters. The severe agricultural crises of 1959 and 1960 greatly reduced the supply of inputs for industry. These shortages soon generated excess capacity in industry and, in addition, the domestic shortage of foodstuffs created a need for large-scale imports of foodstuffs in order to maintain a minimum standard of living for the Chinese. At the same time, China's foreign exchange earnings were rapidly declining due to the shortage of raw and processed agricultural products for export. Thus both the need for and the ability to obtain imports of machinery and equipment, especially complete plants, declined sharply in 1961, regardless of the existing Chinese policy toward the transfer of technology from abroad or the unwillingness of the Soviet Union to supply complete plants to China after 1960.

There was a considerable time lag between the failure of the Great

Leap and the adoption of a new economic policy to correct the consequences of that failure. A series of secret documents (articles) calling for
specific readjustments in policy were finally issued in 1961 and were
summarized in a speech by Chou En-lai in March 1962. These new
policies called for a retrenchment in the pace of investment, while the
priorities of the previous ten years were to be turned upside down, with
agriculture (the foundation) to receive the highest priority in development. In regard to the transfer of technology, policy statements indicated that self-sufficiency was to be an essential principle.

Despite the emphasis given to self-sufficiency in policy statements,
the new program of readjustment actually supported the continued
borrowing of foreign technology from abroad. China's scientific and
technological establishment was to be strengthened for the purpose of
achieving the desired self-sufficiency, but the efforts of these scientists
were to be rewarded and left relatively free from ideological pressures
in their work. That is, emphasis was once more placed on their being
experts, although lip service was paid to the desirability of being both
"red and expert." This attempt to increase China's scientific and technological capacity, therefore, kept the door open for these scientists to
acquire their expertise by borrowing foreign technology. In addition,
imports of foreign technology by commodity trade were explicitly recognized as an important contribution to China's economic development.

As the level of domestic economic activity and investments in fixed
industrial capital revived in the 1960s, the Maoists' hopes for the socialist
transformation of Chinese society were becoming more and more frustrated. With the approval of guidelines in the "revisionist" economic
program and the active encouragement of those administering that program, bourgeois tendencies stressing skills, increased income differen-
tials, individualism, a vertical chain of authority and responsibility
rather than group responsibility and decision making, enlargement of
the market sector, and all the other complements of "economism" and
"efficiency" became common features of China's economy. In an attempt to revive the goals of their continuous socialist revolution, the
Cultural Revolution in 1966 and 1967 was an open confrontation between the followers of Mao and the Chinese "revisionists."

As a result of this campaign, there was a significant change in
China's policy in regard to the transfer of technology. The policy of
self-sufficiency was emphasized to a much greater extent than previously; that is, it was more widely and frequently expressed as an opera-

tional rule in the short run, rather than as a guiding principle in the long run.

Discussions in the Chinese press during 1970 made it obvious that many of the several radical changes in economic policy that had been proclaimed following the Cultural Revolution either were being seriously reconsidered or had not been effectively carried out. In any event, the economic developments of the early 1970s clearly indicated a return to the policies of the 1950s, at least in the area of transfer of technology. There was a renewal of the decision to strongly push for the simultaneous development of both rural, small-scale industry and modern, large-scale industry. In the 1970s, however, greater emphasis has been placed on the need for improvement in the level of technology utilized in the small-scale industries and for better ties to the modern industrial sector for this purpose. The simultaneous development of these two types of industry is now proceeding in a much more integr′ ted fashion than was true in the 1950s and early 1960s, when the small-scale industries were a more purely local and indigenous effort.

This most recent episode in China's policy regarding the transfer of technology provides strong support for the Chinese reaffirmation of the need for and desirability of large-scale borrowing of modern technology from abroad. As far as the emphasis on self-sufficiency is concerned, the growth of China's foreign trade in the 1970s has rapidly increased China's participation in the world market, to the point where China is currently the largest purchaser of modern technology among the less-developed countries of the world.

This brief review of China's policy in the area of technology transfer clearly indicates that despite the repeated emphasis on self-sufficiency, the large-scale transfer of technology from abroad could easily be considered the dominant theme of that policy, except perhaps in the early 1960s, when economic conditions greatly reduced the need and ability of the Chinese to pursue that policy, and the late 1960s, when zealous Maoists temporarily gained control and began to implement a program of extreme self-sufficiency. This conclusion is made much more convincing by a review of the empirical record of the transfer of technology to China over the past twenty-five years. . . .

Large-Scale Transfers of Modern Technology from Abroad

.... In 1952–73 China imported over $8 billion worth of machinery and equipment, accounting for more than one-fifth of China's total imports. In terms of domestic capital accumulation, these imports were over one-tenth of the total domestic supply of new machinery and equipment over these same two decades. In 1952–60, China's imports of machinery and equipment accounted for over one-third of total imports and over one-fourth of the total domestic supply of new machinery and equipment, compared with less than one-fifth and less than one-tenth, respectively, in the 1961–73 period. Nonetheless, after weathering the ill effects on their industrialization program of the agricultural crisis at the beginning of the 1960s and those of the Cultural Revolution in the mid-1960s, imports of producer goods increased by approximately 40 percent a year between 1969 and 1973, and in 1974 they reached the highest level of any year since 1949.

.... The technological imperatives set loose and reinforced by the transfer of modern technology led to a reaction that found its focus in the Cultural Revolution; however, the need for modern technology in the process of industrialization worked to erode the extreme position of self-sufficiency that was a result of the Cultural Revolution. Once again, the transfer of technology by commodity trade is being carried out on a massive scale, once more raising the serious question of whether or not the technological imperatives of this borrowed technology can be absorbed and controlled by China's leaders. The important point to be made here, however, is that the renewed decision to engage in the transfer of modern technology on a massive scale in the 1970s does not simultaneously imply the abandonment or failure of the Maoist socialist, cultural goals. Although they recognize the many contradictions that exist between the technological imperatives of that technology and those goals, the cohabitation and interdependence of this technological borrowing and social revolution is a key feature of contemporary China ... [and] the attempt to make modern industrial technology and Maoist socialist culture consistent is being carried out with great intensity at the present time [1975].

53

China's Open-Door Policy

Sheree Groves

The previous reading by Robert Dernberger was written for a conference held in 1975, when the struggle between the policies of greater self-reliance versus greater foreign trade dependency had reached a critical point. The energy crises of the early 1970s had resulted in higher energy prices, which in turn led to higher foreign trade prices, especially for China's imports. Thus, in 1974, the Chinese had run up an import surplus in the balance of trade of more than one billion U.S. dollars. When Deng Xiaoping argued that this debt could be paid off by exporting Chinese raw material and energy supplies, the Maoists attacked him for his willingness to turn China into an "economic" colony of the industrial countries. They claimed this import surplus illustrated the negative consequences of an "open economy" policy or strategy of economic dependency. Thus, in early 1976 the Maoists succeeded in removing Deng from his positions of power within the Party and government.

By the end of 1976, however, Mao was dead and the leading Maoists (i.e., the Gang of Four) were arrested, allowing Deng to reemerge and eventually become China's dominant political leader. With his reemergence, Deng continued his attempts to reject the Maoist policy of self-sufficiency in favor of opening the Chinese economy to greater participation in the world economy for the sake of the large-scale acquisition of modern technology from the industrialized West. Thus, from the very beginning of the economic reform program, reforms in the foreign trade sector have been closely identified with and supported by Deng Xiaoping. Economic reforms in the foreign trade sector have consisted mainly of liberaliza-

tion of central controls, i.e.: (1) reducing the monopoly of the centrally controlled, state-owned foreign trade companies over foreign trade transactions, allowing local level foreign trade enterprises and selected state enterprises to deal directly with foreign buyers and sellers; (2) allowing local levels and enterprises to retain some of the foreign exchange they earn from their out-of-plan exports; and (3) setting up foreign exchange markets where those who have earned and retained their own foreign exchange can sell it to those who hold a license to import. These reforms have a way to go before it can be said that the door to China's economy has been opened very wide, but they do signal a rather dramatic departure from the previous two decades when that door was tightly closed.

As a result of this policy, China changed very rapidly from an economy with very limited dependency upon foreign sources of supply to the largest foreign trader of any of the developing countries (see Table 1, below). China's evolution into a major foreign trading country, however, has not been smooth. As controls over foreign trade transactions were relaxed, the pent-up demand for imports by both consumers and producers in China would increase imports far faster than the growth of exports, creating a serious deficit in the balance of trade. (This can be seen in Table 1, below.) The initial reforms in the foreign trade sector created an import surplus of over two billion U.S. dollars in 1979. This was quickly followed by reasserted central controls over import licenses and the allocation of foreign exchange, but only until the growth of exports caught up and balance between exports and imports was restored. Then a new phase of relaxation led to a new crisis in the balance of trade in 1985, followed by another period of centralized control. The relaxation of controls and continuation of reforms in the foreign trade sector in 1987 and 1988 has been followed by the present reassertion of controls to restore balance between exports and imports. Yet, despite this wave-like two-steps-forward-and-one-step-back record of reforms in the foreign trade sector, it is important to note two major facts: (1) Throughout the decade, exports and imports have grown rapidly and China's economy is now very significantly involved in trade relations with other countries of the world. (2) Equally important, despite the pauses or backward steps, at no time (including the present) has the policy of opening been abandoned. The present conservative leadership has taken great pains to assert its intentions of continuing this policy.

In addition to trade transactions, however, the aspect of China's open-door policy over the past decade that has made the growth of China's total trade possible and the open-door policy even more dramatic was the change in policy in regard to foreign borrowing and direct foreign investment. Although China's admission to the IMF, the World Bank, the Asia Development Bank, and other international lending institutions has enabled China to borrow loans that are now said *to total a foreign debt of over $40 billion U.S. dollars, the Chinese have been somewhat disappointed at the relatively slow growth of direct foreign investment (see Table 1). Nonetheless, the following reading prepared by Sheree Groves of the East-West Center in Hawaii for the Center's annual* Asia-Pacific Report, 1989, *indicates rather clearly how the Chinese have pursued the attempt to lure foreign investors. That attempt has not slackened since the emergence of the new, more conservative leadership following the Tiananmen crisis in 1989, but that crisis has caused foreign governments and businesses to be more cautious in extending loans and making direct investments in China. Whether or not this worsening of the "political risk" factor in the foreigner's evaluation of investment prospects in China is a temporary phenomenon or a longer-run change will depend greatly upon future political developments in China, especially their success in creating a stable political environment, ensuring a smooth generational transition in the political leadership, and moving forward with the domestic economic reforms.*

Special Economic Zones (SEZs). To initiate China's drive for foreign trade and investment, in 1979 Chinese leaders set up four export processing zones called Special Economic Zones (SEZs). The SEZs, located in Guangdong province (Shenzhen, Zhuhai, and Shantou) and Fujian province (Xiamen), are aimed at attracting direct foreign investment in wholly owned or joint ventures to provide technology transfer and stimulate exports. Legislation to protect foreign investors and to stimulate foreign trade and investment has been implemented. Such legislation includes a patent law (April 1983), setting up arbitration offices to solve disputes on joint ventures, tax concessions, import duty exemptions, and access to the domestic market. Foreign banks can open branches in the SEZs and can make loans in both *renminbi* (the Chinese currency) and foreign currencies. Foreign banks are also allowed to make loan guarantees and investments within the zones.

Early in 1988, Hainan Island was made a province and declared a fifth SEZ. Hainan is viewed as an area where new experiments in administration and economic reforms can be tried. Foreigners can lease lots of land on the island for up to 50 years and develop them as they see fit. Enterprises will be allowed to export local products that will be exempt from domestic quota restrictions, and foreign banks can set up local branches there. In addition, Hainan with all the advantages of the other SEZs will become almost a free port, or what the Chinese leadership hopes will be the "second Hong Kong."

Open Cities and Coastal Development. In April 1984, China targeted the coastal areas as a means to further encourage economic development and the open-door policy. Nearly a fifth of China's population lives in the coastal regions, and the people here include the best educated and most highly trained workers. Fourteen cities along the eastern seaboard of China were designated as open to foreign capital. The cities (Dalian, Qinhuangdao, Tianjin, Yantai, Qingdao, Ningbo, Nantong, Lianyungang, Shanghai, Wenzhou, Fuzhou, Guangzhou, Zhanjiang, and Beijing), although not having the same status as the SEZs, were permitted to establish "technical and economic districts" that would enjoy the same low taxation rate (15 percent) for projects involving foreign investment as do the SEZs.

By fall 1985, the Chinese government decided that cities would be open to foreign capital based on their ability to absorb the investment. Shanghai, Tianjin, Dalian, and Guangzhou were considered to be already experienced in attracting foreign investment and providing well-developed infrastructure and, therefore, were given priority support by the government.

In addition, three river deltas, one each in Guangdong's Pearl River area, Fujian's river triangle, and around Shanghai's Yangzi River, were designated economic zones in 1985. The purpose of these zones was to facilitate economic and technical cooperation within each area, thereby promoting horizontal and vertical integration of production within the zones. Since then, more and more cities and provinces have applied to open their jurisdiction to handle foreign trade and investment with the outside world.

Other incentives. In October 1986, the State Council furthered its drive to attract foreign investment by promulgating new regulations for joint ventures or wholly owned foreign ventures that are engaged in export or technically advanced enterprises. These incentives include the following:

- Reduced tax rates for those enterprises using advanced technology or that are export producing and a 50 percent tax cut on incomes earned by foreigners living in China.

- Freedom in management decisions, including pay and recruiting and dismissing of staff.

Table 1. China's Foreign Trade and Investment (Current US$ Billions)

A. Foreign Trade

Year	Exports	Rate of Growth (in %)	Imports	Rate of Growth (in %)	Balance	(Exports + Imports)/National Income (in %)
1952-65[a]	1.61	7.4	1.57	4.3	+0.04	10
1966-78[a]	4.72	11.5	4.64	12.9	+0.08	9
1979-88[a]	26.98	17.2	30.94	17.6	-3.97	26
1979	13.66	40.1	15.67	43.9	-2.01	13.6
1980	18.27	33.8	19.55	24.8	-1.28	15.3
1981	22.01	20.5	22.01	12.6	0.00	18.7
1982	22.32	1.4	19.28	-12.4	+3.04	18.1
1983	22.23	-0.4	21.39	10.9	+0.84	18.2
1984	26.14	17.6	27.41	28.1	-1.27	21.3
1985	27.34	4.6	42.25	54.1	-14.90	29.4
1986	30.94	13.1	43.21	1.6	-11.97	32.7
1987	39.44	27.5	43.21	0.7	-3.77	33.1
1988	47.54	20.5	55.25	27.9	-7.71	32.5
1989	52.5	10.4	59.1	7.0	-6.6	(39.5)[b]

B. Utilization of Foreign Capital

Year	Total	Foreign Loans	% of Total	Direct Foreign Investment	% of Total	Other[c]
1979-82[a]	3.12	2.67	85.8	0.29	9.4	0.15
1983-85[a]	3.05	1.68	55.1	1.19	39.0	0.18
1986-88[a]	8.65	5.77	66.7	2.46	28.4	0.42
1989	6.82	2.89	42.4	3.39	49.7	0.54

All data are from Chinese sources.
Notes: [a] Annual average.
[b] Estimated on basis of percentage growth in (exports + imports) and in national income in 1989.
[c] Total—(foreign loans + direct foreign investment).

- Tax-exempt enterprise profits that are remitted and reinvested.

- Exemptions from the usual requirement of import licenses and duties on items used in export production.

- Ability for ventures with foreign investment to obtain hard currency by exporting Chinese goods not made by the venture itself or using *renminbi* to buy foreign exchange from ventures with surpluses [of foreign exchange].

- Priority access to infrastructures and allocations for . . . inputs for which the charge is no more than that for local state enterprises.

Additional incentives for foreign investment were announced in 1987, including in November of that year the approval of five trial centers to test the selling of land-use (lease) rights: Shanghai, Guangzhou, Shenzhen, Tianjin, and Hainan. Later Fuzhou and Xiamen were added to the list, and by the end of 1987 dozens of other cities announced their desire or intentions to sell land-use rights. Under the land-use rights, foreigners can lease plots of land ranging from 50 years (in Shanghai, Guangzhou, and Shenzhen) to 90 years (in Fuzhou) and develop the land as they see fit. Although the land is still legally owned by the state, transfer of mortgage, letting, and subletting are allowed, and the time limit can be extended.

Part 5

Culture

Edited by Kenneth J. DeWoskin

Introduction

Kenneth J. DeWoskin

Ancient Chinese described "culture" as an embroidery. In it patterns from the past are preserved, preserved not as museum pieces but as a framework for living. The patterns of culture give meaning to events, understanding of the world, and order to the people in it. Chinese culture brings a kind of understanding, and cultivates a kind of behavior, that knits the Chinese world together, materially, aesthetically, and socially.

The Chinese word for "culture" (*wen* extended to *wenhua*) appears frequently in the earliest writings with many related meanings. At the center is the idea of "pattern," "organization," "order." It appears compounded with other words to mean "pattern," "written characters," "literature," "ancestors," and "civility." These are the pieces of the embroidery: a population defined by a common ethnic heritage, in possession of a writing system, distinguished by political functions of writing and a corpus of canonical texts, and characterizing itself as a center of order and civility amidst a sea of less "cultured" peoples. From the early Shang oracle-bone inscriptions to the present, Chinese writing communicates a consistent awareness of a central set of cultural values that make China a culture unto itself. It is more than ethnic background, national citizenship, or system of beliefs.

The key characters in Chinese mythology are not gods of the sort familiar in Greek mythology, but *culture heroes,* rulers who advanced Chinese civilization by giving the people the hexagrams of the *Book of*

Changes (Yijing), the writing system, the secrets of raising silkworms, the secrets of growing crops, the mathematics of the calendar and the musical pitches, implements for cooking and building, and the secrets of health and longevity. These key transmissions of knowledge were highly integrative, that is, there was no separation between what we think of as the "humanities" as opposed to the "sciences." Whether they bore on human moral and ethical life or natural philosophy, they made reference to a larger, cosmic framework. The Yellow Sovereign (Huangdi) passed on the secrets of health and longevity in his *Inner Classic (Neijing)*, integrating psychological and spiritual guidance with dietary, calisthenic, and therapeutic instruction. Fu Xi passed on the system of the trigrams, revealing along with that system designs for plows, cooking vessels, the concept of the market place for exchange of goods, and the concept of a written code for governance. Emperor Yao passed on a code for leadership succession, framed by his accomplishments in mapping out the land, revealing seasonal and astronomical correlates, and regulating the economic activities of the people.

Well into China's historical period, in the later bronze and early imperial eras (until the third century A.D.), people of accomplishment were divided into two types, "civil" and "military." The civil types, generally called "Confucians," were the architects of Chinese statecraft and formulators of political ideology. Their world included learning of the past through study of classical history and philosophy, a refined code of behavior, a ceremonial etiquette and system of ritual, a corpus of sanctified music and dance, and a highly systematized set of explanations of the natural world. They wrote extensively about their understanding in all of these areas. Throughout much of pre-twentieth-century China, the collected writings of a learned man would touch upon all of these subjects. At each point of conquest and renewal in the dynastic cycles, military families would come to the throne, but the sheer power of the historical culture invariably required that the rulers demilitarize and become competent in the arts of civilian governance.

Since the days of Confucius, literature and art were recognized for their capacity to educate and shape popular ideology and behavior. Related to this was the claim that the preeminent ruler had the authority to set the agenda for literature and art. China's rulers were almost always patrons of elite literature and art, and, as a result, were arbiters of taste in elite culture. China's rulers also often had an interest in popular literature, theatricals, and other representational entertainments for their potential influence on the people. Even the literature and art of the elite ultimately had an impact on the people by shaping the ideology and behavior of the officials who ministered justice and guidance to them. Good officials of the court were highly educated, and their effectiveness in the field was often described in terms of their ability to "cultivate" or "acculturate" the people under their control. Continuity in these traditions was achieved through an elite education system that trained would-be officials in academies and qualified them through a highly conservative examination system.

Literature and art, in practice as well as theory, have always been closely linked to politics, and they have virtually always been subject to prescription, circumscription, and inquisition. Control of literature and art is not something introduced by the Marxist regime. Mainstream ideas about society have always preferred uniformity of thought to pluralism, compliance and assent to dissent. In early imperial China, the emperor was empowered to resolve all intellectual disputes: the meaning of a text, the authenticity of historical "facts," or proper procedures in ritual events. Throughout history and into contemporary times, ministries of culture and official associations of artists and writers have been committed to the goal of correctness rather than of diversity. One salient characteristic of art and literature in contemporary China is their close link to governance. Shaping forces are the central and provincial governments, through the patronage and regulation of artists and writers.

Also since archaic China, the educated elite had a strong interest in the observation of nature and explanations of natural phenomena. A distinctly Chinese interpretation of nature emerged, by which nature was meaningfully analyzed and man attempted to manage it (see chapter 59). This interpretation emphasized the constancy of change, the unity and polarity of opposites, and the simultaneous interrelatedness of all distinct phenomena. Each of these embodies a paradox and reveals a fundamental dialectic process in Chinese thought. This way of thinking has been a part of China's intellectual tradition since the earliest known records. Even the oracle bones of the Shang dynasty (twelfth–eleventh centuries B.C.) present their divinations in balanced, dialectic pairs, one positive, one negative. The dialectic template of interpretation frames explanations of the phenomenal world in terms of dynamic oppositions that drive the process of change. The first important Daoist classic is a crucial statement of this, the *Daodejing (The Way and Its Power)* of Laozi.

This interpretation of nature and life persisted throughout the history of premodern China. The influences that come to bear on human life are complex and varied. Life is comprehensible in a dialectic framework. In the obvious physical ways—the weather, course of rivers, length of days, and shape of the land—nature controlled the capacity of the Chinese to feed themselves. In less obvious ways—in the movement of the heavenly bodies, climatic anomalies, earthquakes, and a range of other unusual natural phenomena—the Chinese saw heaven expressing approval or disapproval of the course of government. The applied realms of natural science, including medicine, alchemy, and other forms of self-cultivation, as well as musical-instrument making, hydraulic and civil engineering, and a host of other technologies, were seen as interrelated and organized around the set of basic interpretive principles. Significantly, key terms like *yin* and *yang* (the elements of dualism) and *qi* (vital, configured energies) were as fundamental to the discussion of nature as to the discussion of humankind, society, and the arts.

Qi described a vitalizing energy that was both universal and highly particular. Alternately translated "configured energy" and "energetic configurations," *qi* was not divisible along form-matter lines or spirit-substance lines. *Qi* is everywhere in generalized form; yet it has distinct manifestations in which it coincides with the "myriad things." *Qi* is the essence of human life; it is *qi* that makes one painting better than another. *Qi* harmonizes ritual music with the calendar of the heavens; *qi* is the master of human health. *Yin* and *yang* described perfect opposition within a perfect unity, represented by the familiar *yin-yang* sign. Anything at any time at any place will have a *yin-yang* relationship with some other thing, time, or place. True to the dialectic processes of change, that which has reached its peak must decline. That which has reached its nadir must ascend. In virtually every discipline of inquiry in premodern China, these relationships were of primary interpretive value. Female is *yin* to male as *yang*. The moon is *yin* to the sun as *yang*. The north is *yin* to the south as *yang*. Black is *yin* to white as *yang*. The identification and application of polar opposites reached very subtle detail.

The tradition of broad, eclectic intellectual interests and the attraction to dialectic forms of thinking and rhetoric remain strong in contemporary China. Mao Zedong could speak comfortably about statecraft, military strategy, art and literature, science and technology, public health—virtually any area of culture that he felt influenced the course of the revolution. His word and the word of subsequent leaders is definitive, whether on matters of culture, politics, or science. Mao's genius was in a combination of civil and martial talents. What is referred to as Marxism-Leninism–Mao Zedong thought understands the processes of historical change as dialectic. Contradictions move Chinese society forward toward the expressed goal of a modern Socialist society.

The governing apparatus in China today is deeply involved in policy decisions about culture in this broad sense, including public entertainments, public education, the work of artists and writers, the work of scientists, and the development of science and technology. There are now significant forces toward decentralization. But through central agencies like the Ministry of Culture and the State Science and Technology Commission, the leadership in Beijing continues to assert control over the major trends in contemporary culture. New funding for scientific and technological research and development is being provided through new national funding agencies. Yet their independence is always in doubt, and the thrust of the resources they control will accord with overall national development priorities. The most significant science project of the 1980s owes it success, in part, to the visible and unwavering support of Deng Xiaoping (see the discussion below on the Beijing Electron-Positron Collider).

Modernization of Literature and Art

The efforts to modernize Chinese literature began early in this century and crystallized in the May Fourth movement of 1919, a cultural struggle centered on the campus of National Beijing University, under the leadership of a cadre of young, reform-minded intellectuals. Much of the venerated literature of the past was a distinctly elitist literature, written in a classical language that few could master, a language that was detached from everyday speech. The May Fourth reforms were an attempt to escape the confinement of this classical literary tradition. In 1917, while studying for his doctorate in philosophy at Columbia University, Hu Shi published an article entitled "Suggestions for a Reform of Literature" in the influential journal *New Youth*. For several years, the journal *New Youth* was the forum for young intellectuals in their call for literary revolution as well as other reform ideas.

The goal of this reform effort was to breathe new life into literature by replacing the classical language with the vernacular and replacing a literature of the elite with the literary themes and interests of the common people. The reformers criticized the classical tradition as obscure, ornate, and worn-out. In the words of Chen Duxiu, editor of *New Youth*, dean of the School of Letters at National Beijing University, and one of the founders of the CCP, China needed a "plain and lyrical national literature," "a fresh and sincere realistic literature." The change in language and theme would make the new literature accessible to the masses and make it a tool for reforming the thinking and attitudes of the masses. Literary reform was not, in the eyes of the reformers, a luxury, but a social, political, and economic necessity.

Like much of China's modernization efforts throughout this century, the literary movement was born in a kind of ambivalence. China had suffered at the hands of foreign powers since the 1840s, a long history of suffering that itself had been a major force awakening the passion for reform. Yet Western civilization was the main source of inspiration for the reforms, reforms that touched not only upon science and technology but literature and the arts as well. The reform leaders, including Chen Duxiu, Hu Shi, and Lu Xun (pseudonym of Zhou Shuren), fought to negate much of their own intellectual and literary tradition; yet they looked to that tradition, especially the vernacular literature to be found there, as a storehouse of models for the new writing.

The reform efforts were not born suddenly after the fall of the Qing dynasty (1911). Throughout the long demise of the Qing, there was an intense interest in Western and Japanese culture among some Chinese literati. Before the end of the 1920s, ambitious translators like Yan Fu and Lin Shu had introduced hundreds of Western books, ranging from masterpieces like the plays of Shakespeare to more ordinary works like the novels of Rider Haggard. By 1929, 299 important Western works and 50 Japanese works were available in Chinese translation.

Lu Xun's short story "The Madman's Diary" was the first vernacular short story to be written in the new literature. It was not a translation, but drew heavily on Western short stories he had read, especially the works of Gogol. The protagonist of the story suffers from extreme paranoia, fearing his family wants to kill him. He reads in ancient history books and discovers that indeed the Chinese had always professed virtues of kindness and benevolence but practiced the cruelest of acts, cannibalism. The story is not polished; it is actually somewhat clumsy. But its influence was enormous, both as the pioneering experiment in the new literature and a powerful statement on the hypocrisy of China's past.

Mao Dun (pseudonym of Shen Yanbing) emerged as a prominent writer a decade after the May Fourth movement, as the enthusiasm of the early days gradually began to mature into excellence. It was the mid to late 1920s before the new fiction securely took root. Literary societies and journals flourished, representing all major trends in Western writing and criticism. But by the late 1920s and mid-1930s, political events began to dominate the literary scene. The war with Japan, civil strife between the Guomindang and Communists, and other events in the utter turmoil of that decade created a new atmosphere, one in which a concern with realism and accuracy of depiction overshadowed the refined theoretical and generic concerns of the previous decade. Writers built novels from descriptions of Chinese society, family life, and the economic, political, and military tragedies constantly unfolding around them. The titles alone of Mao Dun's trilogy of short novels, published in 1927–28, tell the story: *Disillusion, Vacillation,* and *Pursuit.* The stuff of his work was the conflict between past and present, between revolutionary idealism and the reality, between the pursuit of personal interests and public responsibility.

The search for a "national form," a correct form for the new literature, became an issue as writers grew uncomfortable with their dependence on Western models for fiction. The search took many writers into the vernacular literature of the past, into folk literature, into minority literature, and into drama, storytelling, and other popular literary traditions. Chinese writers, even veteran writers, sought to sinicize their new literature, draw their own inspiration from their own Chinese past, and use their writing as fuel for a broad stimulation of nationalist sentiment. This was another sign of maturation, the earlier fear of the past yielding to recognition of the fact that the writing and arts of old China and the writing and arts of China's masses and minorities were great treasures to be used for enrichment of present works.

Some of the masterpieces of modern Chinese writing were born of this period. It was an interlude between the demise of the Qing dynasty, the old classical writings, and the embryonic May Fourth movement vernacular writings, on one hand, and the dogmatic binding and politicization of writing that took place under Mao's hand at Yan'an in 1942. An important forerunner of this middle period was Lu Xun's collection *Hesitation*, written in 1924–25. "Soap" and "Divorce" are stories dealing less with an abstraction of China's national malady and more with specific descriptions of contemporary life. Passion is replaced by cool and careful craft, polemic with precise description. These same qualities characterize the major pieces of the thirties. Mao Dun's *Midnight* (also translated *The Twilight*), Ba Jin's *Family*, and Lao She's *Rickshaw Boy* (also translated *Camel Xiangzi*) are all works nurtured by close observation of the trials and tribulations of real life in the China of their times.

The Long March and the Yan'an years were a watershed period for the evolution of the CCP. As Mao rebuilt the foundation of his revolution at Yan'an, serious thought was given to shaping literature and art to serve the revolution and serve the people. A special conference on these problems was convened. The diversity of opinions vigorously expressed at the conference was eclipsed by an influential and definitive statement made by Mao, summarizing the issues. The CCP leadership, now quite depleted of the strong intellectuals who had given birth to the movement, asserted its authority over China's cultural agenda without compromise. Mao made perfectly clear that literature and art were to serve the revolution, cultural handmaids to a political master, and that the masses were to be both the subject and the audience of literature and art in post-liberation China. This bonding of literature to politics was not a new event in Chinese culture. Nor was it a very happy event for all the writers who had followed Mao to Yan'an, but by and large China's writers turned their efforts to realizing a new proletariat literature, the style and content of which in a very straightforward way educated the participants in China's revolution in moral, social, political, and economic factors that defined their class and their class struggle.

Over the subsequent decades, the high degree of politicization and authoritarianism took a heavy toll in personal freedom and artistic achievement, and it underscored the emergence of a persistently anti-intellectual bent on the part of those CCP leaders who survived to reach Yan'an. Creative writers and intellectuals generally were vulnerable to political inquisition for what they wrote, and one ideological struggle after another whiplashed the fortunes of China's most important writers and thinkers. Ding Ling, who in 1951 won the Stalin prize for her novel

Sun Shines on the Sanggan River, was summarily tried for rightist tendencies during the antirightist campaign of 1957. The same novel that won the prize was used to discredit her, and she was disenfranchised and exiled to the far north. The most severe movement in literature and art, as in many other endeavors, was the Great Proletarian Cultural Revolution, where wholly inconsistent standards and remedies made it hazardous to be a writer or artist with any history of achievement whatsoever. Most dangerous were signs of Western influence, bourgeois tendencies, or Confucian leanings.

Throughout most of the eighties, writers and artists saw a dramatic relaxation of explicit and implicit controls over literature and art. Although there were new periods of inquisition and reprisal and other menacing events, the writers and artists of China felt that they breathed far freer air than any generation could remember. Four so-called "congresses" of Chinese writers have been held since liberation. In each of these a major theme was sounded that at least influenced the discourse of writers and critics for years after, if it did not actually serve directly to shape the development of creative writing itself. The Congress held in 1984 was attended by 815 delegates representing over 2500 members. The increase in membership alone, essentially triple what it was at the previous Congress in 1979, attests to the vigor of contemporary literature. According to descriptive reports of the Congress, Party leaders acknowledged that there had been too much political interference, too much dogma, and too many unqualified hacks put into influential positions in the officially sanctioned cultural organizations. The key theme of the fourth congress was the call for "creative freedom," and the frequent repetition of this call generated such excitement that writers began to speak of the arrival of a golden age for modern Chinese literature. The Congress saw the ascension to leadership roles of a cadre of writers in their fifties, a changing of the guard that mirrored the replacement of aging leaders on the national political scene. Unfortunately, like the apparent retirement of aging leaders in the center stage of political life, the relaxation of political controls on the arts was neither clear nor enduring.

Until the crackdown after the Tiananmen demonstrations in June of 1989, the general trend was toward liberalization. If this was not by virtue of the intent of the leadership, then it was simply through the force of outside contacts, entrained by economic reform and tolerated by a weakened Party apparatus. Publishing became easier and the control of paper was slackened. Journals proliferated and the underground press surfaced. Major issues in control of the arts were issues familiar to many developed and democratic societies. For example, there was controversy over the display of nudes and the distribution of print and video materials deemed by authorities to be pornographic or violent. Sensitivities and enforcement were uneven. At the end of the eighties, Beijing authorities attempted to ban the display in a park of oil paintings of nudes, even as Tianjin officials put the finishing touches on a huge mural of seminude figures that stretched across the ceiling of the Tianjin central train station. Criticism of the Party and personalities of the leadership carried less risk than any other time in memory. In fact, in the acceleration of events leading up to the military crackdown at Tiananmen, it was evident that there was no official control whatsoever on much of the material printed and circulated.

One important measure of the degree of liberalization reached in China is the evolution of the media. Beginning in the mid-eighties, a new form of reportage emerged, non-fictional narratives about government inefficiency, corruption, and a range of problems that would have been impossible to explore a decade earlier (see chapter 58). Even the official newspapers showed a degree of independence and diversity. In May and early June 1989, for a brief period both the papers and the official television opened up nearly completely, printing stories and showing photos and videos that they had been instructed by the government not to air. A survey of university students at Nankai University immediately prior to the Tiananmen crackdown showed that over 50 percent regularly read the critical literature being produced and over 90 percent knew the most trenchant examples of reportage.

The hard bearing-down that followed the move of the army into Tiananmen has concentrated on the intellectuals who stood in the forefront of the demonstrators. That group includes educators, writers, and researchers. Institutionally, Beijing University and the Chinese Academy of Social Sciences have been under the most intense pressure, both as a direct retaliation for their leadership role in the movement and as demonstrations of the government's power to assert control. The papers and television stations have suffered major changes in leadership and a strengthening of Party presence, and they are engaged in a process of enforced self-examination. As events unfolded in 1990, there appeared to be a hardening of authoritarian policies over culture. Scholars and academics again have obligatory political study sessions. Paper is tightly controlled. Mechanisms to impede the free flow of information are widely enforced.

Most observers agree that the post-1989 scenario is different from the Cultural Revolution and other periods of strong coercive exertions by the authorities, however. Perhaps significant for the future is the fact that most people attached to these key organizations remain defiant and cynical, even if highly visible reform-minded leaders have been forced out from above. At least among urban intellectuals, the appeal to patriotism has not been successful in motivating support for current reactive policies. It is said that a large underground exists in China now, and it is struggling with some success to distribute news and literature. A sizable number of students abroad and overseas Chinese are sympathetic to and supportive of the radical detractors of the present regime. They are organized in a number of different groups, and most are committed to feeding news and information back into China. Most of the students abroad are much less likely to return to China than they were before Tiananmen, awaiting some resolution of the current political uncertainty.

As the arts and letters move into the next decade, there are two battlefronts. The first is the confrontation between government authorities and the present coterie of artists, who increasingly are unwilling to accept the authority of the government over their art. But the second is perhaps the more intractable and complex. Chinese writers and artists continue to seek the optimal balance between their own past and the works they are building for the future. They continue to seek the correct balance between native and Western elements, wanting on the one hand to be part of the international community of artists, but on the other to maintain their distinctive heritage. So even as the translation of Western literature reaches unprecedented levels, Western plays are produced on Beijing stages, Western music is performed nightly by Chinese ensembles and foreign artists, and painting academies introduce courses in oil and acrylic, Chinese writers and artists are strengthening their grasp of their own traditions. New operas are being created in all of the regional forms. Painters and calligraphers are returning to the pinesoot ink and washes of traditional masters. Artists are in some cases even imitating the reclusive lifestyles of past masters.

Chinese literature and art were internationalized during the eighties, and that experience will change them forever. Not only has the culture of the mainland been fully invaded by both elite and popular culture from the West (everything from Madonna to Matisse), but the culture of China, especially the literature and graphic arts, has decentralized, and key writers and artists in significant numbers are working outside China, in the freer and more diverse environments of Asian and Western developed nations. Each year several substantial collections of modern Chinese writing are published in English and other Western languages. Many contemporary Chinese authors have international followings and a new potential to influence world opinion. There are questions as to what this will yield and to what extent it will further the development of literature and art of enduring value. Will the press of political events turn the arts back toward polemics? What are the prospects for the development of artistic quality and the preservation of past strengths?

Writers of fiction are involved in a search for their voices. The vicissitudes of the outside forces bearing on writers since the turn of the century have created a belief that literature and art have been slowed in a substantive sense, that greatness is imminent but not yet here. There is no question that there are more writers working more individually than ever in this century, that there are more experiments with genre and style, more avenues of publication, more critical discussion, and more international exposure and exchange. This is equally true in the arts. A new generation of painters in their forties and fifties is rising to international prominence, local and provincial associations of artists are gaining strength and establishing distinctive aesthetic identities, and the prevalent sense exists that a period of creative freedom is at hand that will unleash tremendous latent energies in the arts.

Modernization of Science and Technology

Concerted efforts to modernize science and technology in China began in a series of reforms roughly coinciding with those influencing literature and art. During the declining decades of the Qing and the early decades of the Republic, Japan and the West, as now, were the impetus for reforms and the sources of knowledge and assistance. Students returning from study in Japan and Europe were the key conduits of new science and technology into China. Western books were translated in large numbers, introducing everything from theoretical physics to the technology of iron smelting. Early in this century, the Chinese were already forming friendships and exchange programs with advanced universities around the world, very much as they are doing in the renewed effort today, trying to accelerate the acquisition of a technology infrastructure and a scientific-research establishment.

Unlike literature and the arts, science and technology require substantial and sustained institutional support and funding to develop strength and gain momentum. And as science develops, the need for increasingly sophisticated support grows, making such high-priced central facilities as observatories, particle accelerators, supercomputers, and satellites indispensable. Prior to 1949, progress in science was made without benefit of stable political or institutional support. Nonetheless, high-quality science was carried out in fields such as chemistry. A literature was developed, research technology was introduced and refined, and scientists and engineers emerged as a professional class. Yet such accomplishments were more a matter of individual achievement than of the development of a research establishment. Despite guidance and funding from foundations outside of China, prior to 1949 political and economic instability retarded the growth of a science infrastructure and the dissemination of scientific research expertise in China.

In the decade immediately after the Communist takeover of China, Western-trained scientists struggled to train students and conduct research, but the political and economic climate was not conducive to success. Scientists were targets of several political campaigns during the fifties and targets as well of the Cultural Revolution, begun in the mid-sixties. After 1949, precisely the same ambivalence toward Japan and the West that had shaped the reform movements of the early decades of the twentieth century emerged in more strident form. The pioneering scientists were attacked for their Westernization, i.e., for the fact that their disciplines and training were essentially imported. But even more troublesome than this xenophobia was an issue that plagued scientific researchers again and again after 1949, an issue that became a signal concern during the Cultural Revolution, namely the complex of problems embodied in the "red" vs. "expert" debates. These debates centered on the issue of elitism in education and professional pursuit. They had an impact on virtually every aspect of scientific research.

The Cultural Revolution sought to shift the emphasis in education and practice from "expert" to "red." Political credentials replaced academic achievement and aptitude as criteria for admission to colleges and research institutions and for selection to key administrative, teaching, and research positions. The populist position of the Cultural Revolution activists stressed that scientific knowledge should be available to the masses, and, by reflection of this position, argued that what was not popularizable and useful to the masses was inimical to the revolution. The placement of politically oriented and scientifically naive "revolutionary scientists" in top administrative positions was an attempt to integrate research and practice, integrate schools and factories, and interrupt a tradition of privilege that had isolated Western-trained scientists from the proletariat, a tradition of "Mandarin scientists." Legions of poorly trained "technicians" and "scientists" emerged during this period, and they continue to dilute human resources and frustrate younger and better trained scientists even today. The atmosphere was one in which pursuit of serious scientific research was not only difficult but hazardous. Outside of a few priority research areas that were protected (those considered of strategic importance for national defense), virtually all scientific research institutes and university research centers were subjected to wholesale decentralizing, disbanding, dismantling, and politicizing.

The National Science Conference, which convened in 1978, addressed the excesses of the Cultural Revolution directly. In fact, exaggerated importance was attached to Jiang Qing and the Gang of Four as the key villains in China's failure to modernize in scientific and technological areas. Theoretical research was again given approval and encouragement. Scientists were declared important workers of the revolution, and the importance of science as an area of international cooperation was underscored. For the last ten years, major efforts have been made to restore efficiency to educational institutions, to install adequately trained personnel in key research and administrative positions, and to encourage leading researchers to participate in international conferences and cooperative scientific undertakings. In recent years, the traditional support sources in the Chinese Academy of Science have been augmented by a new and separate agency, the Chinese Science Foundation, modeled on the National Science Foundation in the United States. Funding for the CSF has been about 130 million RMB per year, but the distribution has been in small grants, many of only 20,000 RMB (about $4,250). Because of dissatisfaction with the size of CSF grants, another program is expected under the Science and Technology Commission that would divide as much as 250 million RMB among a handful of key projects. But the competition for resources is intense, and even research institutes are encouraged to find ways to supplement their grant income with commercial activity.

The Chinese have made several notable achievements in science and technology. They have developed internationally recognized institutions and scientists in high-energy physics, an area of strategic importance that has consistently been well-funded and protected from external interference. Throughout the eighties, right through the Tiananmen events, an intense effort to design and build a modern particle collider was sustained and resulted in the construction of the Beijing Electron-Positron Collider (BEPC), which was officially opened in late 1989 and had an official State Acceptance event in July 1990. The Chinese absorbed and developed sufficient technology in the process of building the BEPC that they are now building and exporting high-precision componentry for similar instruments elsewhere, including the U.S.A., South Korea, Italy, and Brazil. The construction of the BEPC was a top government priority, a sign to the world of China's achievement in pure science research, and a tribute to China's ability to organize and finance a major project in the sciences. At the same time, the BEPC is a dual-purpose instrument, generating synchrotron radiation for a range of medical and industrial uses. In the promotion of the instrument, the Chinese have celebrated it as an example of the close relationship between basic science and technology. The BEPC was opened by Deng Xiaoping himself at a ceremony attended by virtually all of China's top leaders.

China has had enviable achievements in biological controls of agricultural pests, with systematic advantages over Western insecticide and fertilization programs. The Chinese are launching satellites with Long March rockets from facilities in Sichuan and Gansu. Western experts compare the rocket technology to that of fifteen years ago in the NASA program, but it was done with domestic technology and with meager resources. The Chinese claim to have had only one failure in eleven satellite launches since 1974. In April 1990 with the launch of Asiasat-1, China entered the international space market. Nuclear weapons tests are routinely recorded, and Chinese-made armaments fare well in world markets. Throughout the eighties, China experienced a boom in microelectronics and computer manufacture, sustaining phenomenal growth in the number of machines produced and the spread of applications.

But peaks of scientific or technological achievement like the rocket program and BEPC exist among stubborn organizational and regional barriers to their broadest utilization and dissemination. Stronger horizontal integration of China's research institutes, universities, and associations is badly needed for front-line achievements to reach their potential for the nation as a whole.

The most dramatic component in China's science and technology strategy since the 1978 conference is the emphasis on international cooperation and overseas training. Numerous strong ties have been forged between Chinese researchers and scientists in the West and between institutions in China and the West. Significant financial support has been made available by U.S. agencies and foundations to encourage this exchange. Organizations like the Committee on Scholarly Communication with the People's Republic of China (CSCPRC) of the National Academy of Sciences have organized and supported seminars, training programs, international conferences, and orientation meetings on research disciplines, technology transfer, science education, research management, and a host of other central concerns. In the decade following normalization of diplomatic relations in 1979, more Chinese students and scholars will have studied in the U.S. than did so in the century from 1860 to 1949. Nearly 12,000 students and scholars from China worked in the U.S. during academic year 1983–84, representing about 50 percent of all PRC students studying overseas. By the late 1980s, estimates ranged as high as 30,000 students from the PRC in the States. Over two-thirds of these students worked in engineering, physical sciences, health sciences, life sciences, and mathematics, reflecting the heavy commitment of resources to the science and technology areas. In the early eighties, it was estimated that American sources provided roughly 40 percent of the financial support for PRC citizens studying in the States, and this figure has increased sharply. Since the spring of 1989, China has struggled to maintain the high level of science and technology contacts in the face of international censure for its treatment of the demonstrators. In the months immediately following the crackdown, several prominent foreign scientists curtailed their contacts, and several important events were stalled or downsized. Since then, contact through many channels has begun to expand again, but the diversity and productivity of China's alliances with the outside remain far below the level they had achieved prior to June 1989.

The impact of returning students is apparent in many ways. Their contributions to the administration and organization of scientific research are likely to be more significant than their individual research achievements. The present decade, then, is setting the stage for the next generation of researchers, who will not have suffered the training disadvantages of the present cohort. A tide of new journals, societies, and inter-organizational linkages can be directly related to the overseas experiences of returning students. There are still institutional and economic impediments to optimal utilization of returning scientists and engineers, and many students say that they are afraid of becoming intellectually isolated from their professional colleagues when they return. The new funding sources will also influence the shape and quality of funded research. If sustained, the general move from institutional block grants to the funding of individual applicants will remove institutional and bureaucratic barriers and expand the opportunities for younger and better trained scientists to do creative work.

This student and faculty exchange traffic is not without problems. The criteria by which students and faculty win both long-term and short-term study opportunities in the States are sometimes of secondary importance, sometimes quite peripheral to the goals of the programs. In recent years, selection advantages have included proficiency in spoken English, acquaintance with Americans in academic positions, relatives or patrons in Chinese official positions, relatives or patrons in the States willing to provide support, and various fortuitous factors. Secondly, the number of advanced degree recipients reluctant to return to China is growing, a problem engaging the attention of both Chinese planners and the U.S. immigration authorities. Successful students find doors open in the States to both professional and economic rewards that cannot be matched in China. This brain-drain phenomenon has exactly the opposite effect of that intended by the exchange programs—it siphons off the most promising young leaders.

China will continue to surprise the world with achievements in science and technology. There are certain to be an increasing number of accomplishments comparable to the missile and satellite programs and the particle accelerator. It is likely the gaps that separate China and advanced nations in science and technology will narrow. But news-making achievements should not obscure the fact that the problems of modernizing science and technology in China are formidable. An entire generation of researchers, those who would have been trained in the

1960s and would now be reaching the most productive periods of their careers, has suffered from lack of adequate training. In the areas where scientific research is advanced, there is little dissemination of knowledge, an excessively high degree of specialization, and inadequately developed mechanisms for application of results. The notion of innovation by the masses in science and technology is still affirmed by the leadership.

The relative priority of basic research by highly trained researchers in highly specialized laboratories, as opposed to application-oriented research by technicians and workers in "open-door" factories, remains a troublesome issue. Social and generational differences as well as gross training discrepancies among researchers complicate the efficient utilization of human resources. Policies vacillate between highly centralized planning, with national priorities in focus, and decentralized planning, with local and often parochial interests guiding the way. Real resources are still extraordinarily limited in light of the enormity of the challenge. Leaders recently have cited the need to increase scientifically based decision-making, improve the flow of expert information, and establish ways to break through long-existing bureaucratic deadlocks in the overall effort to make science and technology policy.

This cycle of inefficiency is difficult to escape. The lack of infrastructure itself leads to a high percentage of waste of the inadequate but precious resources that the Chinese are able to commit to both education and equipment. All over China, one sees expensive laboratory equipment and computer facilities unused, improperly used, or inadequately maintained. Overspecialization or inadequate preparation often limits the benefits gained by participants in international conferences. Regional imbalances, bureaucratic and political obstacles, lack of information, and lack of requisite funding all conspire to distort the distribution of resources and diminish the return on the investment being made. Growth at the contemplated rate is very difficult to sustain and even more difficult to balance.

Still, there is change in the science and technology area that echoes that in literature and art. There is full exposure to outside scientific work. Students and visiting scholars often return from abroad with great prestige and are working major structural changes in their professional worlds. Changes underway in funding will nurture the creative efforts of younger scientists. In the final analysis, the goals of recent Five-Year Plans and the accomplishments projected at the National Science Conference have already proven to be unrealistically ambitious, designed more to fuel ardent hopes than to chart orderly achievement. Yet there is today widespread belief that science will continue to progress in China, essentially free from overt ideological pressures, and that solutions to organizational problems are being found.

Conclusion

In culture resides the basic tension of China's struggle to modernize. The strengths of China's past are vast, and many of them must be preserved to be the strengths of China's future. These are what the Chinese think of as their ongoing virtues, the ways of life, beliefs, and objects that make them Chinese. There is in China today a very high degree of confidence in these strengths, a confidence that China can martial whatever it is that makes them Chinese (past and present) and overcome. But at the same time, there is anxiety about that very tradition and the limitations it might impose. In both arts and sciences, there is an explicit commitment to blending knowledge from China's past but moving into a decidedly distinct future. The Chinese experience of this century has shown to be unattainable the expressed desire of late Qing reformers, a spiritual life that was largely Chinese and a material life that was largely Western. In both arts and sciences, decisions are made within a wide and complex framework of political, social, and ideological factors, among which national and regional pride, public welfare, and political philosophy are not insignificant.

Today, Chinese intellectuals in their writings often compare China and the West, and they often compare their own past to their own present. In these comparisons, they recognize some features of the past as obstacles to the future and some aspects of international culture as inappropriate to their situation. To the extent China can plan her development, building the future will require both sorting through the Chinese past and confronting a foreign-made present. This requires painstaking effort to examine, to select, to discard, and to reform. From some perspectives, it seems a slow process, from others, a rather quick one. But judging from dramatic changes in the coastal cities, it is an accelerating process, and one that will bring the Chinese very close to their identity as a people.

Literature
and the Arts

54

"K'ung I-chi"

Lu Hsün

Lu Xun (Lu Hsün, pseudonym of Zhou Shuren, 1881–1936), is regarded as the greatest writer of fiction in the decades following the literary revolution. He studied Western medicine in Japan, after China's defeat by Japan in the Sino-Japanese War. Deciding that China needed a spiritual and intellectual cure more than a physical one, Lu Xun returned to China in 1909, abandoned medical practice, and dedicated himself to healing the country as a whole. During the May Fourth Movement, he was lecturing at Beijing University and immediately joined forces with other proponents of the Literary Revolution, calling for writing in the vernacular rather than literary language and urging writers to explore themes of immediate relevance to Chinese intellectual and social concerns. Lu Xun was an important critic and literary historian as well as a creative writer, lecturing at the university on the history of Chinese fiction. Among his voluminous writings is A Short History of Chinese Fiction, *a study that established popular fiction written in premodern China as an important component of China's traditional literature. "Kong Yiji" (K'ung I-chi) is one of many short stories Lu Xun wrote satirizing the traditional intellectual in order to underscore the infirmity of traditional Chinese ways and the pressing need for a realistic program of reforms. Kong, who shares a surname and is the implied descendant of the architect of China's traditional culture, Confucius, wears a long gown and displays all of the pretensions of the traditional scholar. But he is "unable to make a living . . . , practically a beggar." Kong is a liar and a thief. His only accomplishment is his calligraphy, but he is too unreliable to earn a living at the menial task of copying. The influence of works like "Kong Yiji" on both the language and thematic scope of modern Chinese literature has been enormous and enduring.*

The wine shops of Luchen are arranged rather differently from those in other places. They all consist of a huge L-shaped bar facing on the street inside of which hot water is kept ready for warming up the wine. At noon and at evening the laborers coming from work would invariably stop to spend four cash for a bowl of wine—that was twenty years ago, and the price has now risen to ten cash—and, standing up against the bar, would imbibe its comforting warmth. If one were willing to spend an extra cash, one might have a dish of salted bamboo shoots or of spiced beans to accompany the wine. If one could afford ten or more cash, one might have a meat dish. But these customers were all of the short-coated class, and were very rarely so extravagant. It was only the long-gowned gentlemen who would step through to the inner adjoining room, order wine and meats, and sit down for a leisurely drink.

From the age of twelve on, I served as an apprentice in the Prosperity Wine Shop. The barkeeper remarked that my manners were too crude for waiting on the long gowns, so I was given work on the outside. It was easy enough to get along with the short-coat customers, and yet among them, even, there were a good many fussy and garrulous ones. These were never satisfied unless they were permitted to see with their own eyes the dipping of the yellow wine from the jar to make sure by examination that there was no water in the bottom of the pot and to personally supervise the placing of it in the hot bath. Under such rigorous inspection it was, of course, extremely difficult to water the wine, so, after a few days, the barkeeper decided that I was equally inept at this job. Fortunately I had been recommended by an influential person. Since he could not dismiss me, he transferred me to the single uninteresting operation of warming up the wine.

Thereafter I stood the whole day long inside the bar attending to my one responsibility and, although I was kept employed, nevertheless I found the work monotonous and tiresome. The barkeeper was a stern-faced man, and the customers were not very genial, so that I could not be lively. It was only when K'ung I-chi came to the shop that I was able to laugh a little, and for that reason I still remember him.

K'ung I-chi was the only long-gowned customer we had who stood at the bar to drink. He was a very large man with a scraggly, unkempt gray beard and a sallow face whose wrinkles were generally full of scars. He was dressed in a long gown, to be sure, albeit a most dirty and ragged one which seemed not to have been mended for more than ten years— nor washed, either. His speech was heavily interlarded with classical particles which people only half understood. Because his surname was K'ung, he had been given the nickname I-chi, from the meaningless line in the elementary copybooks: *"Shang ta jen k'ung i chi."*[1]

As soon as K'ung I-chi arrived in the shop, all the drinkers would look at him and laugh and someone would call out, "K'ung I-chi! You've added a few new scars on your face."

He never answered but would call across the bar, "Warm up two bowls of wine and give me a dish of spiced beans." Meanwhile he laid out nine large cash.

Then they would deliberately set up a shout. "Well, well! You've been stealing again, that's for sure!"

K'ung I-chi would open his eyes wide and say, "How can you thus groundlessly defame the spotless—"

"Spotless, eh? Why, day before yesterday with my own eyes I saw you strung up and beaten for stealing someone's books!"

K'ung I-chi would grow red in the face while the veins stood out on his forehead. "The larceny of books," he protested, "cannot be classed with stealing.... The larceny of literature! ... That is a scholar's business. Can it be considered theft?" He would continue in a string of unintelligible phrases, something about "Sit philosophus indigens," a succession of "wherefores" and "whereases," until the whole crowd would burst into laughter and the shop was filled with merriment.

Gossip had it that K'ung I-chi had studied books all right, but that he hadn't ever been to a proper school and was unable to make a living. He had grown poorer and poorer with time until he was practically a beggar. Luckily he wrote a good hand and could earn a bowl of rice by copying out manuscripts for people. But he had one unfortunate trait:

---

1. Literally this could mean "Above the great man—" followed by three meaningless syllables, *k'ung-i-chi.* *K'ung* was the surname of Confucius and since many Chinese names are trisyllabic, the people of the place gave these three syllables to the old man as his surname and given name. Actually all calligraphic copybooks began with these characters simply because they included all the basic strokes needed for learning how to write Chinese characters. Since many had begun to study but never gotten far, the words were widely known, even by the unlettered.

he loved drinking and was averse to work. He would have been at his copying only a day or two when books, paper, pen, and inkslab, as well as copyist, would all vanish completely. After a few such incidents, no one could be found to give him further copying work to do, and K'ung I-chi had no recourse but to indulge in a little occasional thievery. When at our shop, however, his behavior was exemplary. That is to say, he never failed to settle his account and, although he was sometimes temporarily without ready cash and had to be posted on the blackboard, still it was never more than a month before he was all clear and the name of K'ung I-chi was erased from the board.

After K'ung I-chi had drunk half a bowl of his wine and his face had gradually lost its fiery expression, one of the bystanders asked him, "K'ung I-chi, can you really read characters?"

K'ung I-chi gazed at his questioner with a look of lofty disdain.

"How did it happen," they asked him again, "that you couldn't manage even half a degree for yourself?"

K'ung I-chi appeared immediately to droop uncomfortably, and his face turned ashen gray. He made some remark, but this time it was so entirely literary that no one understood a word. Again the whole crowd burst into laughter and the shop was filled with an air of merriment.

At times like these I could join in the laughing without being rebuked by the barkeeper. The barkeeper himself, in fact, on seeing K'ung I-chi would invariably ask him some question to give the others a laugh. K'ung I-chi realized that he could not converse with any of them but must confine himself to the children. Once he said to me, "Have you studied? Then I shall examine you. How do you write the character spice in the word 'spiced beans'?"

I thought to myself that it was no business of a beggarly fellow like that to examine me, so I turned my face away and paid no further attention to him. K'ung I-chi waited a long time, then spoke pleadingly.

"Can you not write it? Then I will teach you. Now remember! You should commit such characters to memory because when you are a barkeeper later on you will need to write them in the accounts."

I reflected that I was a long way from being barkeeper and that in any case our barkeeper never charged up spiced beans on the bills, so with a mixture of impatience and amusement I replied lazily, "Who wants instruction from you? Isn't it the character *'hui'* meaning return, with the grass radical over it?"

K'ung I-chi appeared highly pleased and, tapping on the bar with two long fingernails, nodded his head. "Right! Right! Now there are four ways of writing the character 'hui.' Do you know those?"

I grew more impatient, and, pursing my lips, walked away from him. K'ung I-chi had just dipped a finger in his wine and was preparing to write on the surface of the bar, but noting that I was not in the least interested he heaved a sigh and looked very crestfallen.

On some occasions the children of the neighborhood would be attracted by the sound of laughter and would gather about K'ung I-chi. He would present them with spiced beans, one bean for each child. When they finished eating, their eyes remained fixed on the dish. Once K'ung I-chi grew alarmed and spread out his five fingers over the plate, at the same time bending down to say, "There are not many more. There are not many left for me."

Then he straightened up and inspected the beans, shaking his head sadly, "Not many! Not many! Lo, are there indeed many? Nay, forsooth, there be not many!" Whereupon the crowd of children ran laughing away.

Such a man was this K'ung I-chi, one to make others merry. And yet without him the world went on just the same.

One day—it must have been two or three days before Mid-Autumn—the barkeeper was slowly casting up his accounts and had taken down the board, when he suddenly exclaimed, "K'ung I-chi has not been here for some time! He still owes nineteen cash!"

I realized it to be a fact that we had not seen him for a long period.

"How can he come?" remarked one of the customers. "He's had his legs broken."

"Oh!" said the barkeeper.

"He would keep on with his stealing. This time it was his own foolhardiness. He got into the home of Mr. Ting, the provincial scholar. You can't steal things in that house, you know."

"Then what happened?"

"Then?—first he had to write a confession. Then they beat him. They beat him more than half the night. And then they broke his legs."

"What happened after the legs were broken?"

"What happened? Who knows? Probably he's dead."

The barkeeper had no further questions but resumed his slow calculation on the accounts.

After Mid-Autumn the wind grew daily colder until the beginning of winter seemed at hand. Though I stuck close to the fire all day long,

I still had to put on a quilted coat. One afternoon, when there were no customers, I was sitting with closed eyes when I suddenly heard a voice, "Warm up a bowl of wine!"

The voice was very low, but none the less familiar. There was no one in sight. I stood up and peered outside. K'ung I-chi was sitting on the floor by the door. His face was haggard and dark; he looked awful. He was wearing a thin lined coat wrapped around his legs. A piece of coarse sacking and some grass ropes supported these from around his shoulders.

"Warm up a bowl of wine," he repeated at sight of me.

Thereupon the barkeeper put out his head. "Is it K'ung I-chi?" he inquired. "You still owe us nineteen cash!"

K'ung I-chi lifted his face and replied humbly, "That? I'll settle everything next time. This time it's cash and I want good wine."

The barkeeper laughed in his usual way and said, "K'ung I-chi, you've been stealing again!"

This time he offered no vigorous denial, saying merely, "Don't jest."

"Jest? If you weren't stealing, how did you get your legs broken?"

"I fell and broke them." K'ung I-chi replied in a low voice. "I had a fall. . . . I. . . ." His eyes seemed pleading with the barkeeper not to mention the matter again.

By this time a few others had gathered to share the amusement with the barkeeper. I warmed the wine, carried it out, and set it on the doorstep. From his ragged pocket he dug out four large cash and placed them in my hand. I saw that his own hands were covered with dirt. He had, in fact, come pulling himself along with his hands.

A few minutes later he had finished the wine and again, amidst the laughter of the bystanders, he went slowly off, crawling with his hands.

K'ung I-chi was not seen after that for a long time. At the end of the year the barkeeper took down the board and said, "K'ung I-chi still owes us nineteen cash!" The next year at the fifth of the fifth moon, he said again, "K'ung I-chi still owes us nineteen cash!" But at Mid-Autumn he said nothing, nor did we see K'ung I-chi at the end of that year.

I myself have never seen him since. It is most probable that this time K'ung I-chi is really dead.

Translated by George A. Kennedy

55

Talks at the Yan'an Conference on Literature and Art

Mao Zedong

The CCP retreat to Yan'an saw not only the revitalization of the military, political, and economic strength of the Communist movement. The Yan'an Conference on Literature and Art, held in the spring of 1942, was a defining moment for the new culture of Mao's China, making the artist's responsibility to promulgate ideology of the revolution an explicit doctrine. Though the writers and artists who participated voiced diverse views on the issues and considerable criticism of the party leadership, Mao's conclusion, quoted here, was unambiguous and dogmatic, clearly an effort to discipline the writers and artists of the revolution. Mao defined the audience for the new literature and art and declared that its content was to derive from popular life. He instructed artists to go among the people for their inspiration and materials, a design to escape from what he saw as the elitism of China's traditional literature and art. Finally, the arts, according to Mao, must obey the political demands of class and party. Mao declared culture to be not the most significant area of revolutionary work, but an indispensable one nevertheless. As views evolved over the post-Yan'an decades, the interpretation and emphasis of discussion of Mao's statement evolved as well. Even the text of his speech was revised in 1953. But Mao's talk at Yan'an has been quoted and discussed innumerable times in post-liberation China as the definitive comment on what China's writers and artists should do and how they should do it.

Comrades! Our conference has met three times this month, and in our search for truth several dozen party and non-party comrades have spoken, producing heated debates, bringing problems into the open and making them concrete; I believe that this will prove beneficial to the whole movement in literature and art. . . .

Well, then, what is the central issue facing us? In my opinion, our problem is fundamentally one of serving the masses and how to do this. If we do not solve this problem, or if we do not solve it properly, then our workers in literature and art will not be attuned to their circumstances and responsibilities and will come up against a string of problems both internal and external. My conclusion will consist of some further explanation with this problem as the central issue and will also touch on a few other problems related to it.

1

The first question is: who are the people our literature and art are for? . . .

There is indeed such a thing as literature and art that serves exploiters and oppressors. The literature and art that serve the landlord class are feudal literature and art, that is, the literature and art of the ruling class in China during the feudal era. This kind of literature and art still has considerable influence to this day. The literature and art that serve the bourgeoisie are bourgeois literature and art; although people like Liang Shiqiu, who was criticized by Lu Xun, talk about some kind of literature and art that transcends class, in practice they uphold bourgeois literature and art and oppose proletarian literature and art. The literature and art that serve imperialism, represented by people like Zhou Zuoren and Zhang Ziping, is called slave culture or slave literature and art. There is also another kind of literature and art, which serves the Special Branch and may be called "Special" literature and art: it may be "revolutionary" on the surface, but in reality it belongs with the three categories above. For us, literature and art are not for those groups mentioned above but for the people. As we have said before, the new culture of China at its present stage is an anti-imperialist, antifeudal culture of the popular masses under the leadership of the proletariat. Whatever genuinely belongs to the masses must be under the leadership of the popular masses. New literature and art, which are part of new culture, are naturally in the same category. We do not by any means refuse to use the old forms of the feudal class and the bourgeoisie, but in our hands these old forms are reconstructed and filled with new content, so that they also become revolutionary and serve the people.

Well, then, who are the popular masses? The broadest section of the people, who constitute more than ninety percent of the total population, are workers, peasants, soldiers, and the petty bourgeoisie. Therefore, our literature and art are in the first place for the workers, the class that leads the revolution. Secondly, they are for the peasants, the broadest and firmest allies in the revolution. Thirdly, they are for workers and peasants who have taken up arms, namely the Eighth Route Army, the New Fourth Army, and other popular armed forces; these are the chief strength in war. Fourthly, they are for the petty bourgeoisie, who are also allies in the revolution and can cooperate with us on a long-term basis. These four kinds of people constitute the largest sector of the Chinese nation and the broadest popular masses. We should also make alliances with the anti-Japanese elements in the landlord class and bourgeoisie, but they do not support democracy among the broad popular masses. They have a literature and art of their own, while our literature and art are not for them and are in any case rejected by them. . . .

2

. . . . Reaching a wider audience and raising standards are both worthy activities, but from what source do they arise? Works of literature and art, as conceptualized forms on whatever level of operation, are the result of the human mind reflecting and processing popular life; revolutionary literature and art are thus the result of the revolutionary's mind reflecting and processing popular life. Rich deposits of literature and art actually exist in popular life itself: they are things in their natural forms, crude but also extremely lively, rich, and fundamental; they make all processed forms of literature pale in comparison, they are the sole and inexhaustible source of processed forms of literature and art. They are the sole source, because only this kind of source can exist; no other exists apart from it. Someone may ask whether works of literature and art in book form, classical or foreign works, aren't also a source. Well, you can say they are a source, but a secondary and not a primary one; it would be a distorted way of looking at things to regard them as primary. In fact, books and other works already in existence are not the source but the flow, they are things that the ancients and foreigners processed and fabricated from the literature and art they perceived in popular life in their own time and place. We must absorb these things in a discriminating way, using them as models from which we may learn what to accept or what to reject when we process works of literature and art as conceptualized forms from the literature and art in popular life in our own time and place. It makes a difference to have this model, the difference between being civilized or vulgar, crude or refined, advanced or elementary, fast or slow; therefore, we certainly may not reject the ancients and foreigners as models, which means, I'm afraid, that we must even use feudal and bourgeois things. But they are only models and not substitutes; they can't be substitutes. Indiscriminate plagiarization, imitation, or substitution in literature and art of dead people or foreigners is an extremely sterile and harmful literary and artistic dogmatism, of the same basic nature as dogmatism in military, political, philosophical, or economic matters. Revolutionary Chinese writers and artists, the kind from whom we expect great things, must go among the masses; they must go among the masses of workers, peasants, and soldiers and into the heat of battle for a long time to come, without reservation, devoting body and soul to the task ahead; they must go to the sole, the broadest, and the richest source, to observe, experience, study, and analyze all the different kinds of people, all the classes and all the masses, all the vivid patterns of life and struggle, and all literature and art in their natural form, before they are ready for the stage of processing or creating, where you integrate raw materials with production, the stage of study with the stage of creation. Otherwise, there won't be anything for you to work on, since without raw materials or semiprocessed goods you have nothing to process and will inevitably end up as the kind of useless writer or artist that Lu Xun in his will earnestly instructed his son never to become. . . .

3

Since our literature and art are for the popular masses, we can now discuss two further questions, the first concerning the relationships within the party, i.e., the relation between party work in literature and art and party work as a whole, the other concerning relationships that go outside the party, i.e., the relation between the party and nonparty work in literature and art—the question of the united front in literature and art.

Let us start with the first question. In the world today, all culture or literature and art belongs to a definite class and party, and has a definite political line. Art for art's sake, art that stands above class and party, and fellow-travelling or politically independent art do not exist in reality. In a society composed of classes and parties, art obeys both class and party and it must naturally obey the political demands of its class and party, and the revolutionary task of a given revolutionary age; any deviation is a deviation from the masses' basic need. Proletarian literature and art are a part of the whole proletarian revolutionary cause; as Lenin said, they are "a screw in the whole machine," and therefore, the party's work in literature and art occupies a definite, assigned position within the party's revolutionary work as a whole. Opposition to this assignment must lead to dualism or pluralism, and in essence resembles Trotsky's "Politics—Marxist; art—bourgeois." We do not support excessive emphasis on the importance of literature and art, nor do we support their underestimation. Literature and art are subordinate to politics, and yet in turn exert enormous influence on it. Revolutionary literature and art are a part of the whole work of revolution; they are a screw, which of course doesn't compare with other parts in importance, urgency, or priority, but which is nevertheless indispensable in the whole machinery, an indispensable part of revolutionary work as a whole. If literature and art did not exist in even the broadest and most general sense, the revolution could not advance or win victory; it would be incorrect not to acknowledge this. Furthermore, when we speak of literature and art obeying politics, politics refers to class and mass politics and not to the small number of people known as politicians. Politics, both revolutionary and counterrevolutionary alike, concerns the struggle between classes and not the behavior of a small number of people. Ideological warfare and literary and artistic warfare, especially if these wars are revolutionary, are necessarily subservient to political warfare, because class and mass needs can only be expressed in a concentrated form through politics. Revolutionary politicians, professional politicians who understand the science or art of revolutionary politics, are simply the leaders of millions of mass politicians; their task is to collect the opinions of mass politicians, distill them, and return them to the masses in an acceptable and practical form; they are not like the kind of aristocratic or armchair "politician" who acts as if he had a monopoly on brilliance—this is the difference in principle between politicians of the proletariat and the propertied classes, a difference that also exists between their respective politics. It would be incorrect not to acknowledge this or to see proletarian politics and politicians in a narrow or conventional way. . . .

Since we must join in the new era of the masses, we must thoroughly resolve the question of the relationship between the individual and the masses. Lu Xun's couplet, "Stern-browed I cooly face the fingers of a thousand men, Head bowed I'm glad to be an ox for little children" should become our motto. The "thousand men" are the enemy, we will never submit to any enemy no matter how ferocious. The "children" are the proletariat and the popular masses. All Communist Party members, all revolutionaries, and all revolutionary workers in literature and art should follow Lu Xun's example and be an ox for the proletariat and the popular masses, wearing themselves out in their service with no release until death. The intelligentsia must join in with the masses and serve them; this process can and definitely will involve a great many trials and hardships, but as long as we are resolute, these demands are within our grasp.

Translated by Bonnie S. McDougall

56

"The Wounded"

Lu Xinhua

Lu Xinhua, born in 1954, is considered to be among the finest of China's new generation of writers. At age 14, he worked on an army farm and subsequently was an agricultural worker in Jiangsu. His story "The Wounded" was originally rejected for publication by People's Literature, *but Lu "published" it himself, by posting it on Fudan University bulletin boards. It was soon printed and became the flagship piece of a genre of post–Cultural Revolution writing known as "Literature of the Wounded," stories that combine harsh criticism of the Gang of Four and the radical excesses of the Cultural Revolution with a poignant if not melodramatic self-examination by individuals who were caught up in it. This story explores the complex strains on Wang Xiaohua, a young girl of sixteen, whose widowed mother had been branded a renegade. In 1969, Xiaohua denounces and abandons her mother in a struggle to gain peer acceptance and membership in the Communist Youth league. But at the demise of the Gang of Four she is forced to confront the meaning of her decision. She acknowledges her natural affection for her mother and the commitment to family that inheres in a Chinese filial ideology far more enduring than the fleeting radicalism of the Cultural Revolution. The set of concerns explored in "The Wounded" is found in many novels, stories, dramas, films, and paintings of the late 1970s and early 1980s. It testifies to the deep moral and emotional significance of the Cultural Revolution years, from which virtually none of China's now middle-aged artists escaped.*

On this last night of the year, nothing could be seen from the train window. Colored lights faded in and out of view, red, white, some near, some far. Here it was, already the spring of 1978!

Xiaohua's gaze returned from the window.[1] She let her head drop to look at her watch. The hands stood precisely at midnight. She gathered some loose hair at her forehead, and tucked her long black braid behind her ears. Rubbing her bloodshot eyes, she turned to her bag hanging on the window and took out a small square mirror. She moved her head about, facing it to the faint light from the carriage lamps, and looked at her face in the mirror.

Xiaohua had a plump, squarish, pale white face. Her straight nose and thin lips fit well in their respective places. Her chin pushed forward just a little bit, and below wispy black eyebrows she had a pair of deeply and darkly quiet eyes, which all of a sudden would glisten with a watery gleam of light. She had never before examined with such care this young and beautiful face. But as she looked and looked, she suddenly realized that her eyes had begun to fill with tears. Taking hold of herself, Xiaohua held the mirror to her chest and quickly looked about her, only to see that everyone was sound asleep as the train churned along. Certainly no one had noticed what she had just done. With a breath of relief, she tucked the little mirror right back in its original place in her bag.

She was tired, but all night she had been unable to fall asleep. She put her head down on the tea table between the seats for what could not even have been three minutes, when she lifted it up again.

A young engaged couple, off to visit relations, sat across from her. All along the way they had carried on excited discussions about their studies, work, and the great events of the last year. Now they were so tired that they fell asleep leaning on each other. On the other side, a woman in her thirties from the city slept with her head on the table. Lying next to her was a four or five year old little girl. Suddenly, the little girl kicked her feet up and cried out from her dreams, "Mama!" The mother woke in an instant and leaned over to kiss her daughter's face: "Little one, what is it?" The little girl did not peep again, but waved her little hands a bit, shifted about, and dropped off to sleep.

Everything became peaceful and quiet once more. Before long there was only the rhythm of the train as it rocked along, a sound like a mother very softly humming a lullaby. And the train was the mother's hand rocking the cradle. Every passenger on the train had journeyed deep into the land of sweet dreams, unconscious, drifting, and peaceful.

---

1. The protagonist's name, Xiaohua, might be translated "Dawning China."

Xiaohua was still not interested in sleep. She was suddenly oppressed by a feeling of loneliness and isolation, as she looked at the engaged couple and the mother and daughter. It was like a knife through her heart when the little girl had cried "Mama!" Those two syllables—"Mama"—sounded very strange to her now, but at the same time stirred up a fully passionate hope for her life. She could imagine her mama's hair, already grayed, and her mama's face, now all covered with wrinkles. Xiaohua wanted very much to throw herself into her mama's arms and beg forgiveness: "But . . ." Again her soft tears rolled out from deep within her eyes, but this time she would not give into them. She took a deep breath, and with her elbows on the table and her slightly jutting chin in her hands, she fixed her gaze outside the window again.

"Nine years." With real pain she thought back to the time she had forced herself to control her indignation against her "Traitor Mama." With an extremely ambivalent mind, she reported for work in the countryside before completing her schooling. She could not imagine how her mama, a revolutionary of many years, could turn out to be a character like Dai Yü in *A Song of Youth*, crawling out of an enemy dog hole. She had read the book, and that Dai Yü was a totally deplorable creature.

Xiaohua hoped that this might be a false charge. When her father was alive, he had told her how her mama braved the lethal danger of enemy guns, rescuing wounded soldiers on the battlefield. How could she have turned completely about during her time in enemy prison?

From the time her mama was judged a traitor, Xiaohua began to lose her very closest colleagues and friends, and her family moved into a dark little room. At the same time, she lost her Red Guard status because of her mama, and she became the victim of cold treatment and discrimination that she had never experienced before. This made her hate her mama all the more, hate her for the weak and shameful acts in her past. Even so, she still thought of her mama's deep love for her. From as early as she could remember, her mama and father treasured their only daughter as they would treasure a bright and precious pearl. Now this too was only an ugly scar struck on an otherwise fair complexion, something that only made her feel more ashamed. She was obliged to listen to both the voices within and without her, criticize her own petit-bourgeois thoughts and feelings, and draw a clear boundary between herself and her mama. She had to leave her right away; the faster she left and the farther she went, the better.

When she left Shanghai on the train that year, she was only a six-teen-year-old girl with a childish face and two pigtails. Among all of the other students who went into the countryside, the combination of her immature face, with its adolescent fervor, and her thin and willowy body made her look particularly young and frail.

She sat alone in the corner of that train, her eyes unflinching as she stared out the window. No other students came to speak to her, and she didn't make conversation with them. Only when the train entered a tunnel did she look up for a second at the two pieces of luggage on the luggage rack, a canvas traveler's bag and a bedroll, things she had gotten together bit by bit without her mama's notice. Her mama was still completely in the dark, right up to the time she and her fellow students boarded the train. By now, she imagined, her mama had probably returned home and discovered the note Xiaohua had left on the table:

> I am making a complete break with you and with this whole family. There's no point in trying to find me.
>
> Xiaohua
> June 6, 1969

She thought to herself that perhaps her mama would cry and perhaps be deeply wounded. She also could not keep herself from thinking about the affectionate care her mama had lavished on her from the time she was little. But then, who made her mama become a traitor! She finally decided that she should not pity her, even though it was her own mama.

By that time, the train had gradually become quiet. Only then did she look at the students surrounding her. Some leaned against the seats and slept; others studied. Sitting across from her was a young man, about her age, who stared intently with a look of surprise in his eyes. Embarrassed, she looked down, but he spoke to her in a friendly way, "What class are you?" Xiaohua raised her head to reply, "Class of 1969." "1969?" he queried with obvious curiosity, "Then you . . ." "I graduated ahead of schedule," she interrupted, finishing his sentence. Her bright eyes came alive for a moment, as if expressing thanks for the concern shown by his questions. She also took the opportunity to muster her courage and look at this young man's face. He was of medium build and had a pale face, shaped like a ginkgo nut, with innocent but lively eyes under a pair of rather fine eyebrows. "What's your name?" Xiaohua asked. "Su Xiaolin. What's yours?" "Wang Xiaohua," she answered, but even as she said her name, she couldn't help but blush a bit out of embarrassment.

Overhearing this conversation some of the students who had been studying broke in. "Wang Xiaohua, how did you ever graduate early?" She was dumbstruck for an instant, then thought maybe she would say whatever necessary to lie her way through. But she had never been able to lie well, and, her face reddening with embarrassment, she told them the whole truth. She finished speaking and looked down, knowing deep within her that she was going to be treated very coldly. In fact, her fellow students were warm and understanding, and they comforted her. Xiaolin said even more enthusiastically, "Xiaohua! You did exactly the right thing. Don't worry. When we get to the countryside, we will all help you out." She looked up at them and nodded gratefully.

In the embrace of warm communal living, Xiaohua gradually forgot the family life that had made her suffer so. Along with other students from Shanghai, she put down roots in a farming village in Liaoning Province on the coast of the Bohai Sea. She progressed quickly, and in only her second year she filled out an application form to join the Communist Youth League. But in a million years she would not have anticipated the rejection of her application, another result of her mama being a traitor.

When she learned of this, she went with tears in her eyes to see the branch league secretary. "I have no mama. I have already broken off all connection with my family. You know this. . . ." Su Xiaolin and other fellow students stood by her side to testify, "Just last year, her mama learned that Xiaohua had come here, and she sent her a big package of clothes and food. She didn't even open it, but sent it right back in the original package. Not only that, time and again the letters her mama sent have gone unopened. Whenever they come, they are sent right back."

"Still . . ." the branch league secretary replied, a pained expression on his face and both hands spread open, "our league committee has received an external investigation letter from Shanghai, and the province level has stressed all along. . . ." His face bore a distressed grin.

There was nothing Xiaohua could do.

In spring of the fourth year, she finally managed to get herself into the league, but by that time her zeal for it had already cooled somewhat.

New Year was here again, always the most painful time for Xiaohua. All of the other young people returned home to visit families. Xiaohua was left completely to herself in the dormitory. Outside, fire-crackers exploded to welcome the New York, and the air was thick with the pungent smell of gunpowder smoke. You could hear the children jumping with delight, singing and calling, while gongs and drums banged and clanged.

Although it was a holiday, Xiaohua was only able to get a bit of the holiday spirit from warmly disposed "aunts" and "uncles" who took her in. But when she returned to the empty, desolate dormitory, she imme-diately felt a boundless pain pressing upon her.

The only thing that gave her any comfort was the fact that the poor, lower class peasants of the area showed such sincere concern for her. They took her in; they encouraged her. When she was rebuffed by the Youth League, they got together again and again and collectively wrote letters to the committee demanding that she be approved. Also, Xiaolin often came to see her. Over the years of living and working together, the two of them had developed an ever-deepening shared love in the revolution. Xiaolin was delighted by her combination of candor and naivete, on one hand, and her very practical, realistic devotion to ardu-ous effort on the other. She considered Xiaolin to be the most depend-able "relation" she had, and she would often pour out to him all of the frustration and pain she held within her. There was one night on the beach, during the mid-autumn festival, when the two of them spoke heart-to-heart as they walked. Since then, she felt even more strongly about him.

After they had walked along the water's edge for a long while, they sat next to each other on the sandy beach. There in front of them, under the moonlight, the water gently lapped up on the beach with a rhythmic washing sound, and the breeze carried with it wave upon wave of sea smells. After a silence, Xiaolin asked unexpectedly, "Xiaohua, do you think about your family?" Stunned, she looked up and said "No! How could you ask that?" Xiaolin looked down and said softly, "I think you ought to write to your mama to find out how she is. Lin Biao destroyed a lot of old cadres. Couldn't your mama have been one of those?"

"No! Not possible!" Both hands picked at the corner of her jacket, and she shook her head in obvious pain. "I had thought about that too before. But it is not possible. I heard that my mama's case was decided by Zhang Chunqiao. No. It is not possible." And she just continued to shake her head.

Xiaolin blew out a breath of air and mumbled to himself with exasperation, "Chairman Mao had said, 'There are factors derived from a person's origins, but you cannot talk solely about a person's origins. The emphasis should be on one's political actions.' Now look what we're doing! If the old man's a hero, then the kid'll be tough too. If the old man's a traitor, then the kid's a bum for sure."

The weather was getting chilly. Xiaolin noticed that Xiaohua was wearing only a thin jacket. "Are you cold?" "No. Are you?" She looked up and stared at him with deep emotion. "I'm OK." His head dropped down again, and he silently watched the moonlight glistening on the wave tops. Then he said very seriously, "Xiaohua, do you think that revolutionaries can be people without a shred of emotion?" She didn't answer the question, lost in thought about her entire situation, feeling the deep wounds in her heart.

Xiaolin turned to see tears welling up in her eyes. He tried to comfort her. "Xiaohua. Don't be depressed about this." But he couldn't hold back himself, and he wiped tears from the corners of his eyes. Finally, he blurted out what he had been holding in his heart under great pressure for a very long time, "Xiaohua, you don't have any family. If you trust me, let's . . . let's be friends!"

"You mean it? You don't . . . ?" Her heart would not stop pounding as she asked dubiously, her eyes open wide with a mix of delight and surprise.

"I mean it." Xiaolin assured her with a nod of his head. Reaching out a warm and friendly hand, he said, "Xiaohua, believe me." Without thinking, she fell into his embrace.

Now Xiaohua's face bore a renewed smile. No matter where she was, inside or out, there was the sound of her singing. Her face shown with a ruddy vitality, enriching all the more her spring-like, youthful beauty.

In autumn of the second year, Xiaohua was moved to the people's school in the village to be a teacher, because her health was not good and teachers were needed. Xiaolin was transferred to the commune office.

One afternoon, after Xiaohua had attended a teachers meeting in the commune office, she went to Xiaolin's dormitory room. The door to the room was open even though no one was there. She picked up some of the clothes he had thrown on the bed in order to wash some things for him, and she turned her head and saw his diary lying at the head of the bed. she casually picked it up and flipped through the pages, noticing that yesterday's entry said:

> Today, I really had a headache! This morning, Secretary Li said to me that the prefectural committee was planning to transfer me to the propaganda department to work, and they were right in the midst of investigating me. He said that the prefectural committee was emphasizing my relationship with Xiaohua, saying that this was a problem with worldview and with class line. In the event the relationship continued, they would simply have to give my transfer to the propaganda department some more thought. I truly cannot understand. . . .

Xiaohua read to this point and stood as still as a wooden post, stunned. Then in a rush she closed the book, and immediately ran out of the little room. Almost in a stupor, she went back to her school. She waited until she lay down in her own bed in her own dormitory room to begin an uncontrollable bout of wounded crying.

The next morning, when she got out of bed to dress and make-up, she felt the pain deep inside her temples, and her eyes had swollen up.

After breakfast, she requested a break, and went down to the commune to find the commune secretary. She spoke to him with an odd calm, "Secretary Li, my relationship with Xiaolin is completely broken off, as of today. Please do not let anything to do with me influence his future."

After this, she was like a different person, even more morose and laconic than she had been years ago. Numbness showed on her face. Even though Xiaolin refused to accept the transfer because of her and maintained his true love for her all along, she intentionally avoided him and refused to see him.

It was as if she now really understood her place and position in life. Although contact with her family was completely broken off, never would she be able to throw off the rope wrapped around her by being in the family of a "Traitor Mama." She had become clear about something else—if she fell in love with someone, this same rope would entangle him as well. Because of this, and because of her genuine love for Xiaolin, she felt she ought not involve him. Xiaohua even had chest pains resulting from lobular hyperplasia, which the doctors told her again and again might get better once she married. But now she would rather sacrifice all of that. She had already decided, she would close the window to love in her heart and would never again open it for anyone.

From this point, she gave to her children in the school what fragments remained of a young woman's feelings. She would eat a little less and otherwise be frugal; she took a sizable part of her own resources to buy school supplies for the children. In the evenings, she would often go to their homes to help them prepare for class. The strength of feeling she built in this way with the children helped her forget, for the time being, everything that came before.

Another two years went by. Her melonseed-shaped face had matured beyond adolescence and become a woman's, and her body too, in all respects, had filled out. She was already a full-fledged young woman. Especially after the smashing of the "Gang of Four," Xiaohua gradually began to feel a bit more relaxed, even to the point of showing a little smile. After taking part in a self-organized mass demonstration, she felt that emotionally she had never before been so moved and so stimulated. But then, sometimes she would lapse into darker thoughts, and her face would become indescribably melancholy.

One day, when she was correcting exercise books, one of the teachers unexpectedly handed her a letter that had been mailed from Jiangsu. Who wrote it? Curious, she tore it open to see. It turned out to be from her mama, but the address was different. Prior to this time, she might have immediately torn it up, but this time she could not help herself from reading it.

Xiaohua:

It has been eight years since you broke off with your mama. I cannot blame you. In this letter I want to tell you, under the brilliant leadership of Chairman Hua, the injustice done me has been cleared away. The criminal label of "traitor" was identified as part of the plot of the "Gang of Four" and their cohorts to grab power. They took the label "traitor" and forcibly stuck it on me! The true story is now completely revealed.

My child, thanks to Chairman Hua, I have also returned to my former work as a school leader. The unfortunate part is that my health was destroyed by them over the last few years; it is really no good. Not only do I have a very serious heart condition, I also suffer from rheumatoid arthritis. Still, I have resolved to do my utmost in working for the party.

My child, it has already been more than eight years since we have seen each other. I very much would like to come see you, but my health will not permit it. So, I hope you will come see me for a while, just so I can lay my eyes on you again. My child, please come as soon as possible.

With love
Mama
December 20, 1977

As she read the letter, she was stunned. "Is this true? Is this true?" Her heart began to pound.

That evening, when it was nearly ten o'clock, she still clutched her mama's letter in her hand. She was lying on her bed, reading it and thinking. Xiaohua drifted off. She was already back home, pushing open the door. She saw her mother hunched over a table writing something. When she saw her daughter had returned, she called out in surprise, "Xiaohua," and rushed over to her. With a mix of every sort of feeling, she clutched her mother in her arms. After a very long time, Xiaohua lifted her head and wiped the tears from her eyes, "Mama, what are you writing?" "Nothing . . . nothing at all." Her mama suddenly looked a little panicked and hurriedly cleared the papers from the desk. So Xiaohua suspiciously stepped right over, grabbed the paper and read a few large words very clearly written on top: "Supplementary Confession of my Problem as a Traitor." Xiaohua glared at her and angrily cursed, "How shameful!" With that she spun around to run out. "Where are you going?" "It's no concern of yours." But her mama had already rushed forward to block the door, her hair now completely disarrayed. "Ahh!" With that startled cry, Xiaohua was jolted awake and sat up abruptly in bed. She could not help from holding both hands to her wildly beating heart. "Shall I go back or not?" She was completely unable to decide.

Two days prior to New Year, she received an official letter from her mama's unit. Then she hastily packed up some things, left school, and got herself on that day's train.

Now, as she sat on this train bound for Shanghai, how could she possibly be calm? She was excited; she was overjoyed. But she also was suffering and depressed.

In the morning, a little after six o'clock, the train charged into the sunshine of the New Year, and proudly entered the Shanghai station with a long blast of its whistle. After getting off the train, Xiaohua first helped the mother carrying the small child find her way out of the station and get on a bus. Then, throwing her yellow shoulder bag over her back and lifting her suitcase, she got on the #18 trolley to return home.

From the trolley she looked out at the streets and buildings she had often walked by and often watched as a child. Her heart beat unusually fast, as her whole body was filled with that special and indescribable joy that one feels when walking once again on home ground. Today was New Year's Day. What was mama doing at home right now? Mama was not one to sleep late, so she was certainly already up. When she unexpectedly appeared in the doorway, perhaps mama would be facing the other way, eating her breakfast. If so, she would very quietly call, "Mama!" Her mama would certainly spin around with complete surprise. "Yaa! Xiaohua!" And tears of joy would certainly well up over her face.

With these exciting thoughts, she climbed off the trolley and walked into lane 954. She counted the door markers, #16, #18, #20. She stopped there and waited for a second. Then she walked right up to the dark door, still fresh in her memory. Controlling her excitement and deep feelings, she stretched out her hand and with her fingers tapped lightly a few times on the door. There was no answer. "Mama has not gotten out of bed yet?" She let her knuckles rap the door a little more soundly, but still there was no response. She began to panic. She banged on the door with her fists, but inside the house it was still as quiet as death.

"Who are you looking for, Miss?" Suddenly there was a little girl at her side, with a piece of cake in hand, eating the cake and staring at Xiaohua. "Uh, little sister . . . the people who lived here. . . ." Licking her thin lips, the little girl replied, "Moved away, just three days ago." "Moved where?" Xiaohua asked nervously. "Umm. . . ." The little girl's eyes looked up and rolled around; then she spun about and ran back into her house. Very shortly, a thirty-year-old woman came out.

"Um, are you looking for Principal Wang? She's moved to lane 816 house #1." Having said this, she asked with suspicion, "Who are you?" Xiaohua paused for a second, then replied with a smile, "I have a little business with her. Thank you." She took off immediately.

When she located lane 816 #1, it was a newly built worker's residence. In the doorway of #1 was a flower pot with a cultivated winter palm tree. When she saw these flowers, she knew she was home, for her mama's favorite was the winter plum.

The yellow painted door was still closed. She knew that her mama's health was not good. Perhaps she was still resting. So once again she walked up to the door and curled her fingers to knock. But before she did so, she was called to by a middle-aged man from house #2 who was right in the middle of brushing his teeth. Turning and looking at her with twinkling, warm eyes, he asked, "Are you looking for Principal Wang? There's no one there. Yesterday she became ill and was moved to the hospital." Xiaohua gasped with shock, and quickly asked, "What department? What room?" "I'm not sure," replied the man, shaking his head ever so slightly. She quickly asked, "Comrade, could I leave these travel bags with you for a while?" and ran off toward the hospital.

It was New Year; the halls of the hospital were abandoned. She ran right up to the information desk, but nobody was there. She turned around to see several white-coated doctors turning a corner in the hall, walking and chatting about something. She went right up to them and asked, "Doctor, where is Principal Wang?" One of the doctors, a thin man wearing glasses, simply stared at her for a moment. Then, as if he had remembered something, he revealed a note he had in his hand and said, "Ah, very good. You must be from Principal Wang's school, right? That's good. May I trouble you to send a telegram to Principal Wang's daughter—here is the address—tell her that her mother passed away just this morning. Have her. . . ."

"What? What?" Xiaohua gasped with her mouth open, her gaze transfixed. Suddenly, she began to stumble forward; she ran a few steps, then suddenly stopped again. She turned around and glared, then asked with a stammer, "Which . . . which room?" "Number two." The same doctor answered her. Startled, he gestured with his hands, "Internal medicine, number two. Go straight ahead, then turn left."

She ran to number two as if she had gone mad. She slammed open the door with a bang, and all of the people inside immediately turned around. She couldn't care less who these people were. She just pushed her way through the crowd and right up to the side of the bed. Her hands shook as she drew aside the white sheet covering her mama's head.

"Ahh. . . . This is mama. Mama, I missed her for nine years. I will miss her forever."

Her pale, thin face was framed with white hair. Among the deep wrinkles of her brow were the traces of her wounds, faintly revealed. And her eyes, utterly still, were half-opened in a peaceful gaze, as if waiting to see something.

"Mama! Mama! Mama! . . ." She cried out in the most heartrending way, calling that name she had not called in so very long. "Mama! Look! Look! I've come back . . . Mama! . . ."

She furiously shook her mama's arms, but there was no response at all.

After a long while, after she had cried her eyes dry, she stood up and looked mutely at the others in the room. They were all crying with her. Suddenly from this crowd of people she recognized a very familiar form, someone of medium build. His face was ginkgo nut shaped, bearing an elegance that was somber but not completely without a childish quality, and eyes clearly red from crying. "Su Xiaolin!" His name nearly escaped her lips, but first she heard that voice well-known to her saying, "Xiaohua, it's all right. . . ."

The evening of the next day, mama's remains were cremated at the Longhua crematorium. On the walk back to the house, Xiaohua, her eyes swollen and tender from crying, went with Xiaolin to the bund where she had often walked when young.

It was already late at night, and the wind came in piercing gusts off of the Huangpu River. For the first time, walking very close to him, Xiaohua let the deep breath of his spring-like youth warm her cold, grave, nearly suffocated heart. Xiaohua felt grateful. When Xiaolin was visiting his family, he had learned that her mama had been absolved of her crimes, so he made a special point of going to see her. Not only that, but on New Year's Eve he braved the bitter cold to go to the hospital to look after her. It was a small comfort to Xiaohua to think that before her mama died, she was able to see Xiaolin, and that Xiaolin was able to see mama in her stead.

They walked along in silence under the street lamps. Xiaolin produced a diary. He thumbed to the last page on which anything was written and handed it over to Xiaohua. "Xiaohua, this is what your mother wrote the evening of the day before yesterday." She took it immediately, and, under the dim glow of the street lamp, read her mama's familiar script:

I've been hopeful right up to this very day, but Xiaohua has still not come back. Seeing Xiaolin makes me think all the more of her. Although my child has physically not suffered the lashings of the leather whip that I bore under the "Gang of Four," I know that the wounds suffered in my child's heart are perhaps deeper than those that have scarred my body. This is why I am more eager for my child to come back. I know that I cannot hold on much longer, but still I will struggle to hold on for a few days, because I must certainly wait for my child to return. . . .

Her eyes blurred. She immediately released Xiaolin's arm and ran to the edge of the river. Leaning over the cement wall of the embankment, she stared dumbly at the water. The lamps glistened like a million stars on the river, and she watched them twinkle in and out of view.

After a long time, Xiaohua raised her head. The pain on her face suddenly become a kind of anger. In complete silence she took Xiaolin's hand and held it tightly. Then, with her eyes wide open and blazing with fire, she spoke, from deep within her heart, slowly, word by word, "Mama, my dear Mama, you rest in peace. Your daughter will never forget who inflicted these wounds that have scarred both your heart and mine. And I will certainly never forget the kindness of Chairman Hua. I will stay close to the Central Committee headed by him and contribute my life's strength to the work of the party."

Night. It was still. The water of the Huangpu River rolled along to the east. Suddenly from a distance came the angry howl of a steam whistle from a giant ship. Xiaohua felt the blood in her whole body surging. So, she held Xiaolin's arm tightly, walked down the stone steps, and with bold steps headed toward the bright lights of Nanjing Road.

Translated by Kenneth J. DeWoskin

57

"Ancient Temple,"
"In the Ruins"

Bei Dao

Bei Dao, the pen name of Zhao Zhenkai, was born in Beijing in 1949, the year of the CCP takeover. By the late 1970s, he was already gaining recognition as a talented and courageous young writer, working in both lyric poetry and fiction, looking to literature to escape the political turmoil of the Cultural Revolution and the ideological constraints with which the party wished to bridle writers. Bei Dao's poetry is representative of a genre called "Misty Poetry" by critics, who hailed it as a new poetry of a new generation. Misty poets sought to revive the evocative qualities, the ambiguity, and the rich visual imagery of China's great poetic tradition, while enjoying freedom in form and choice of subject. His short stories likewise attempt to reach a deeper reality than the ideological tracts he read as a youth. The poem and story that follow both take place in ruins, an attractive symbol to writers who struggle with the prospects of a spiritual rebirth, a new China, to rise from the ruins of the old. "The Ancient Temple" is a pure lyric, evoking the sense of China's ancient and weighty traditions through a meeting of the living eye and broken stone tablets. "In the Ruins" brings together many themes familiar to post-Cultural Revolution writers: the ruins that remain of China's past; the fracture of parent and child bonds; the vicissitudes of individual fortunes that are both cruel and meaningless; and the relationship between the intellectual and the peasant. But it treats these themes in a new and subtle way, capturing the ambiguity of real life and leaving uncertain the significance of each moment and the very outcome of the events that triggered the tale. Neither tragic nor comic, neither hopeful nor hopeless, the story is flavored with the bitterness of the Cultural Revolution experience and the simple sweetness of young life.

Ancient Temple

Vanishing bell tolls
forming webs, around cracked lacquer columns,
spread layers of year-counting rings.
Remembering nothing, stones
In hollow mists of the mountain valley, cast back sounds;
The stones, remembering nothing.
Once, when a small way circled this place,
the dragon and strange bird flew off,
carrying off chimes silent under the eaves.
Wild weeds, each year once more
grow long, so unconcerned
they do not care what master bends them,
a cloth shoed monk or just the wind.
The stone tablet broken, inscription worn and lost,
as if only a glaring blaze
could make it readable again. Perhaps
upon the light of a living eye,
the dark turtle will return from the mire to life, and
bearing dark and weighty secrets, come crawling through the gate.

Translated by Kenneth J. DeWoskin

In the Ruins

Two hours had passed.

It was autumn, but the fields were a picture of bleak desolation. A few sparrows perched on the overhead lines, crying endlessly from an old abandoned shed; the sound seemed unduly loud and clear under the cloudless sky.

He looked at his watch again. He really did not understand what he was expecting himself. It was as if he still hadn't freed himself from the mechanical concept of time that professors had; the empty echo, the dust on the bookshelves, and the mist-wrapped lamplight were still waiting for him. Yes, past time had slipped by in his hands like an old monk's rosary beads, rubbed bright and shiny. And now, what meaning had time for him?

"Wang Qi, old-line British spy and reactionary authority, report to the organ of mass dictatorship tomorrow morning at eight o'clock, pending criticism and denunciation. This order must be promptly obeyed!"

In fact, when he saw the order, he was extremely calm, as calm as a bystander, horribly calm. At the time, digging out a bit of broken brick with the tip of his shoe, his arms folded together, he had stood firmly before the red paper, reading it carefully several times over. The handwriting was not bad, but one could tell it had been written by a young man. Over his name was a yellow cross. He inwardly congratulated himself that the characters of his name had not been written upside down—as far as he was concerned, that was the most extreme form of insulting behavior.

He groped for a cigarette, and again his hand touched the photograph of his daughter as a child which he had hurriedly taken from the photo album just as he was leaving home. His daughter had left home almost two months ago; after formally denouncing her relationship with her father, she had moved to live at school in the city. At mealtimes, he laid bowl and chopsticks as usual in the empty place; he would not allow anyone to sweep his daughter's room, but would shut himself inside and stare blankly ... he did not know why, but since his daughter left, he could not recall the likeness of her laughing face. It troubled him so much that he would spend the whole night lost in unhappy thought, often getting up during the night to open the photo album. But as soon as he closed it, the impression would disappear immediately. And trivial events from her childhood spun in his brain throughout the night. Some of the details were so distinct, he even wondered whether they were not the result of his own fabrication. Look, the smile that filled her slight dimples was offset by the puzzled frown between her eyebrows, as if she already had a premonition of misfortune in her young soul.

"Papa, I won't have my picture taken with a doll."

"Why not?"

"I'm grown-up now."

"Then have one with Papa."

"No, your mustache prickles me, I want one by myself."

He put the photograph back in his pocket, lit a cigarette, and sat down on a dry bank at the side of the road. The irrigation water and time had flowed past here together, carrying mayflies, grass and leaves, perhaps even a few carefree little fish. Everything would pass. Sometimes, people's choices could be terribly simple; there could be no regrets because of haste or avoidance because of fear.

He closed his eyes: a strong light focused on the balding crown of his head, the coldly gleaming lead wire engraved itself into his neck, the black dumbell at the end of the wire rocked back and forth. Behind were rows of faces shining with excitement and a crimson curtain as bright as if it were dripping with blood. . . . At the time he saw everything too clearly, never moving his eyes away although his whole body was trembling: he thought he saw his own end in the body of this old friend. Yes, he understood too well his old fellow-student from Cambridge. The death that night of this hefty six-footer, who had once been a sensation as a university softball star, was not because of physical torture, but because of shame, grief, and indignation. It was then he learned to understand everything completely, it was only through learning to understand that one truly experienced things personally. The light roasted the top of his own head, the lead wire was engraved in his own throat, the large beads of sweat streaked with blood dripped down his own face. . . . He had already died once, ten times, a hundred times! He believed that if he could choose to live again, his old friend would die with dignity, without compromise.

For two weeks the spotlight kept pursuing him. He hid, he ran, until he was completely exhausted. What was the use? The light fell on his head in the end. He looked up, gazing at the sun, gazing in that dazzling direction until his eyes, smarting with pain, shed tears.

He wrapped his windbreaker tightly around him and walked on again. This time, he felt a sudden pity for that boy who'd written the order. He couldn't have been more than twenty. Ah, so young, his life had just begun. He would regret it. Perhaps, waking in the dark from a nightmare, the shifting lights and shadows on the ceiling would arouse associations with the past; perhaps it would come from an individual's unhappiness, his eyes blurred by tears beside a friend's coffin; perhaps after he kisses his girlfriend for the first time, the passionate, meaningless low murmuring would suddenly break off, and the emptiness that follows needs certain genuine sentiments to fill it . . . what would the boy

say then? Lord, even if such a time would come, he could console himself and the girl by his side: "At that time, I was still young."

"When Papa gets old, you should get married too."

"Stop it, I won't, I'll stay with you for the rest of my life."

"What if Papa dies?"

"You're just saying silly things!"

"Dear girl, Papa's only teasing."

His eyes were moist with tears. Already, at this very moment, he
couldn't distinguish the limits of imagination and reality clearly, nor did
he care about the reliability of memory. He only hoped that her tender
expression and voice would reappear, allowing him to savor a certain
kind of delight amidst the numbness.

On a secluded little path in the university grounds just now he had
bumped into Wu Mengran, the head of the history department, sweeping up fallen leaves. This time he didn't make a detour but walked
straight on. Wu Mengran hung his head, strenuously wielding the big
broom. Two deep, intersecting furrows had been shaven through the
white hair he had once been so proud of, and now it was uncombed and
full of dust, like a handful of withered grass covered with hoarfrost.
Seeing him coming, Wu Mengran hesitated a moment, pulling his eyes
away from the toes of his shoes.

"You?" Wu Mengran looked up and down nervously. "You'd better
keep away!"

"You and I will be the same tomorrow."

"That's impossible, you've been earmarked as a key object for protection."

"Protection? You're a Harvard Ph.D."

Wu Mengran forced a smile. As in the past he brought up his hand
majestically to smooth his white hair, but as soon as he touched the
furrows on the top of his head he involuntarily withdrew his hand.

"Our problem will be clarified eventually," Wu Mengran said.

"Perhaps."

"Where are you going?"

"Going?" he responded like an echo and walked off. After walking
some distance, he turned his head and saw Wu Mengran still standing
there, holding the broom like an old soldier dragging a gun.

He climbed a slope, not thinking about where he was going. The
side of the slope facing the sun was warm and sunny, tall straight little

poplars clustered around him. Climbing to the top of the slope, he felt a little tired. He felt in his pocket for his handkerchief, but drew out a piece of rope. What, had he come to hang himself? Death: he repeated the unfamiliar and well-known word in several different ways until it lost all meaning, leaving only an empty sound. A blue mist wavered before his eyes, the whole sky wavered for a moment and he clutched at a small sapling beside him.

... The first time he met Jie was at the school reunion dance. The dim wall-lights spun around, casting long shadows; the brass instruments in the orchestra-pit gleamed, the conductor's slender shadow alternating on the wall, the waving baton extending to the ceiling. He felt Jie's breath brush his face, and under her half-closed eyelids gleamed an elusive light.

A sound of wings beating the treetops. In the twinkling of an eye twenty years passed, and his daughter had grown up, as pretty as her mother in those years. He couldn't help his fist touching the photograph in his coat pocket.

"Papa, do you like Mama?"

"Yes."

"Mama likes crying."

"We all have our weak moments."

"I don't like crying."

"You haven't reached the time for crying yet."

"Even then I won't cry."

No, child, you will cry. Tears will soak a person's conscience, tears will ease the weight of suffering and let one's life become a little more relaxed.

A light breeze drifted past, and he breathed in a deep mouthful. Blending all the flavors of autumn, it dispelled some of the painful bitterness in his breast. He raised his head and stared in surprise: opposite, on the hillock opposite, was a group of stone ruins—the Yuanmingyuan. He didn't understand how he had got here. It had been a completely unconscious act. No, he remembered someone saying that consciousness existed in the midst of unconsciousness. Probably it was true that a kind of summons from the unseen world had drawn him there in spite of himself.

He walked toward the ruins.

The sun, which had lost its warmth, had already sunk behind the jagged edge of the distant hills. In no time, it would disappear to finish the other half of its journey. Amidst the rubble, an ancient Roman-style archway stood tall and upright, its huge shadow lost in the rustling weeds.

Standing before him was China's history, the history of the last decades, or even of the last centuries or millenia. The endless arrogance and revolt, dissipation and vice; the rivers of blood and mountains of bones; the sumptuous yet desolate cities, palaces, and tombs; the thousands upon thousands of horses and soldiers mirrored against the huge canopy of the heavens; the ax on the execution block, dripping with blood; the sundial with its shadow revolving around the glossy stone slab; the thread-bound hand-copied books piled in dusty secret rooms; the long, mournful sound of the night watchman beating his wooden rattle ... all these together formed these desolate ruins. However, history would not stop at this scene of ruin, no, it would not, it would proceed from here, and go on into the wide world.

He touched the cooling stone pillar. Finished, he thought, this once-illustrious palace, which had been the celebration of an age, had collapsed, and once it had collapsed, it was no more than so many pieces of stone. And he himself was just a little stone among them. There was nothing to be lamented; in the midst of a people's deep suffering, individuals were negligible.

He gazed sentimentally at the distant hills. Goodbye, sun, but I hope that tomorrow you shine on a different world. A pity I won't see it, it doesn't matter, I'll die, but my books will live, they haven't paled into insignificance through years of criticism; on the contrary, they have proved even more that they are worth surviving. As long as one's thoughts are spoken and written down, they'll form another life, they won't perish with the flesh.

He thought again of the autumns of those years, the autumn of his prime, the autumn of richly blossoming chrysanthemums on his desk, the autumn of the bowknot dancing in his daughter's pretty hair.

"Papa, some people say you're bad, is it true?"

"Yes."

"Why?"

"Because I speak the truth."

"You can't tell lies?"

"No."

"Suppose you don't speak?"

"Only when I'm dead, silly child."

He walked down the hillside. In a clearing, a red-gold smoke tree soughed in the wind. A little pool of rainwater reflected his changed shadow and the azure sky. He lit a cigarette. His hand, a hand covered with blue veins, calmly shielded the flame, then this movement suddenly seemed to stop, come to a standstill. Time congealed, and everything around him lay still on the glassy smooth water. The wind dropped, the leaves made no sound, and even the birds' wings came to rest in the air. At length, the match fell into the pool, giving off a little stream of white smoke. Time began to flow again, and everything returned to its original state. He now felt a kind of calmness he had never experienced before.

He drew the rope from his pocket, skillfully tied a sailor's knot (he had learned this the year he went to London, when he had been a temporary deckhand on the packet-boat *Victoria*) and threw one end of the rope toward the fork of the tree. His action was as deft as if he had been doing this all his life.

Everything was set. He breathed a sigh of relief, walked to one side, and lit his extinguished cigarette again. Suddenly he gave a start, almost dropping his cigarette. Not far away, in the clump of trees opposite, stood a little peasant girl, staring at him curiously. Beside her was a wicker basket filled with grass.

"Hello," he said tentatively.

The little girl didn't move, but stood there unflinchingly.

"What are you doing here?"

"Cutting grass."

He walked a little closer. "What's your name?"

"Erya."

"How old are you?"

"Eight."

"Do you go to school?"

"No, Ma says that it's all a mess now, maybe next year."

"Your home's near hear?"

"Over there," she pointed a grubby finger in the direction east of the woods. "Across the vegetable patch."

"You're cutting grass for the goats?"

"For the rabbits. They're so crafty, they prefer this grass here." She rubbed her nose with her little fist, raised her head and gazed at the noose. "Uncle, what are you catching?"

He smiled grimly.

"Are you catching birds?"

"Yes, I'm catching an old bird."

"Old—bird—" she repeated in a singsong. "There are owls near here, their call makes my flesh creep."

"Hurry back home, your Papa's waiting for you."

"My Pa's dead," she said expressionlessly. "Last month, on the sixth, he was tied up and beaten to death by Erleng, Shuanzhu, and the others from the north end of the village."

"Why?"

"My Pa stole some of the brigade's watermelons."

He went over, clasped the child in his arms, and impulsively pressed his face against the little girl's startled face, big teardrops starting from his eyes. This was the first time in many years that he's shed tears. The little girl gave a cry of alarm, kicked and struggled to free herself, and plunged deep into the woods.

Night fell. In the darkness, the outline of the ruins could still be distinguished clearly. He sat on a piece of stone for a long time, then stood up and silently went away.

The noose swayed in the wind.

Translated by Bonnie S. McDougall and Susette Ternent Cooke

58

People or Monsters?

Liu Binyan

Until his departure from China several years ago, Liu Binyan was an aggressive investigative reporter for China's leading newspaper, The People's Daily. *Born in 1925 in Jilin Province, six years before the Japanese invasion following the Mukden Incident, Liu was largely self-taught and became active in the Communist Party at age 18. A well-known and controversial literary figure at least since the "Hundred Flowers" movement in 1956, Liu was in and out of favor many times, always speaking out boldly against Party bureaucratism and corruption as well as framing issues in theory and criticism for fellow writers. By the late 1970s, he was playing a significant role in the administration of the Chinese Writer's Association. The following piece comes from a narrative exposé based on actual investigation of Wang Shouxin, a brazenly corrupt Party official in Bin County, Heilongjiang Province. Published in September 1979, it was an immediate sensation among readers and provoked severe criticism of Liu, especially from cadres in Heilongjiang. "People or Monsters" does not focus exclusively on the misfeasance of a single official, but searches for the social and political conditions that made such corruption and bureaucratism familiar to Chinese all over the country. The piece exemplifies the courage of a writer and reporter seeking a new level of truth in a time when public taste and public policy were shifting rapidly and increasingly out of synch with each other. Before the end of the 1980s, Liu Binyan had been expelled from the Communist Party, relieved of his duties at* The People's Daily, *and essentially forced into exile.*

The selection here is excerpted from a much longer piece. Prior to the section below, Liu describes the miserable economic conditions of Bin County and the appearance of a new Party secretary, Tian Fengshan, an honest and widely-loved official who lasted in his position but two years before being forced out by rampaging Red Guards.

Wonderful Exchange

On the day that Wang Shouxin first took over as manager and Party secretary of the coal company (which was later called the fuel company), some workers were digging trenches for oil pipes. Some members of the county work team were playing chess in the office. When she saw this Wang Shouxin flared up. "Well I'll be damned," she yelled. "You play chess while others work. What kind of work team is this?"

Zhou Lu, now the assistant manager, was shocked; Wang Shouxin had never yelled at anyone like that before. What he didn't realize was that someone at that very moment was observing *him,* and that this person was also shocked by certain changes. The observer was the old Party secretary at the coal company, Bai Kun, and there was something he couldn't figure out: this guy Zhou Lu had never been very good at his job—once when he was driving a car he had lost a wheel and didn't even notice it. That I can forgive, mused Bai Kun, but—though I always thought highly of his character and even felt I could train him to take over for me—suddenly he appears to have changed entirely. He fawns over Wang Shouxin like crazy, patting the woman's ass whenever she speaks. It must have been the same, all this flattering and fawning, when he worked for me. But because it made me feel comfortable, I always felt it was a virtue. How could I have failed to see through him all these years?

There were many things that had not been seen through. Just look at Wang Shouxin—she too had seemed to change completely. Formerly she had been lazy and useless, but now she was the first one on the job and the last to leave. Even her clothing changed drastically—she wore a cotton jacket and rubber shoes. All day long she would be running in and out of the office, busy as a bee, laboring along with the workers who were unloading coal or cleaning up.

Over the years Wang Shouxin had come to know this tiny coal company thoroughly, and to become thoroughly bored with it. Yet once she became boss, all that changed; everything now seemed to take on a strange radiance. Jet black coal piles, glistening lumps of coal—how

delightful! No longer was she bored with those who were busy unloading the coal, weighing it or collecting payment for it. Everything now
belonged to her, and everybody obeyed Wang Shouxin's orders.

Of course Wang Shouxin supposed that she was "serving the people." But "the people" were various: they differed in quality and rank.
The first reform she carried out was to sell coal according to a person's
position. She arranged to have the top-grade coal picked out and packed
in waterproof straw bags for delivery by truck directly to the doors of
the County Party secretary and the members of the Standing Committee. This was coal that caught fire quickly and burned well—just right
for cooking dumplings at New Year's. And payment? "What's the rush?
We'll discuss it later. . . ."

As for the people's armed forces, no question about it—nothing was
nearer and dearer to Wang Shouxin's heart than the brown padded
coats of the military. Soldiers were on the top rung of her class ladder.
Right below them came the Organization Department. These people
were sent the best grade of coal, delivered in special trucks, and were
treated to meals to boot. Next in line were those concerned with personnel, finance, and labor.

Wang Shouxin was a warmly sentimental woman with clearly defined likes and dislikes. Her tens of thousands of tons of coal and her
nine trucks were the brush and ink that she used every day to compose
her lyric poems.

The distilleries and provisions factories produced the sweet, entic-
ing smells of famous liquors, pastries, and candies. Wang Shouxin was
not a glutton; no, what she sought from these sweet smells was only the
smiling faces of provincial-, prefectural-, and county-level "connections." For this reason, such factories could rely on a never-ending supply of fine-quality coal at low prices. Wang Shouxin couldn't care less
about the bearings factory or the porcelain factories. These produced
nothing but cold, hard little knickknacks. Who would ever want gifts like
that? So these factories got low-grade coal, with prices jacked up at that.
What if a factory was losing money? Going bankrupt? What if the coal
could not burn hot enough to heat large vats? None of *that* had anything
to do with the great Wang Shouxin!

One year in January the county hospital ran out of coal. A man was
sent to seek out Manager Wang. After looking over his letter of introduction, Wang Shouxin raised her eyebrows and questioned the man.
"How come your top man didn't come?"

"He's busy, he didn't have time . . ."

"A man named Gao Dianyou from your hospital has informed against my son. No coal for you!"

The man begged and pleaded, but Wang Shouxin wouldn't give an inch. "Your Gao Dianyou accused my son of adultery," she continued. "The County Party Committee has been investigating for two months already, and my son is still the vice-director of the Xinli Commune, isn't he? Don't think you can slip one past Old Lady Wang! This exposé of my son is the work of Fang Yongjiu of Xinli Commune and was prepared by Director Rong of the Commune's Health Department. Gao Dianyou is just their mouthpiece!"

When word got back to Gao Dianyou, he immediately wrote a letter to the County Party Committee: " . . . There is obviously something fishy going on here. How could Wang Shouxin know so much about my exposé of Liu Zhimin? I request the County Committee to give this matter their closest attention and to take measures to assure my physical safety."

This was not the first time, nor would it be the last, that an accusation against Wang Shouxin fell into the hands of Wang Shouxin. It was also not the first or last time that Wang Shouxin brazenly used the coal she controlled as a weapon for revenge.

Trucks were also important instruments in Wang Shouxin's system of rewards and revenge. Every fall people in Bin County had to go up in the mountains for firewood and down to the villages for vegetables in order to get through the winter. And in a county seat with a population of 30,000, trucks were hard to come up. Yet this was an ordeal every family had to undergo every year.

Inspector Yang Qing of the County Inspectorate had that year asked a driver to go to the mountains for firewood. His family prepared a complete banquet for the returning driver—no mean feat on a salary of about thirty dollars a month. When it was almost dark, they could hear the truck returning, and the whole family rushed out for a look. The truck had come back empty! The driver's face revealed his displeasure. "Roads were blocked," he said, and drove his truck back home. How would this family get through the winter? They were on the verge of tears. Husband and wife looked helplessly at the banquet spread, which was getting colder and colder.

Then in their hour of despair, who was it that lent them a helping hand?—Old Lady Wang. How could the whole family not be grateful?

Wang Shouxin was deeply concerned about the difficulties of people in Bin County. The county cadres' wages hadn't risen for over ten years, and every family felt the pinch. Many had borrowed anywhere from several hundred to nearly a thousand dollars of public funds. In 1975 the County Committee, on instructions from above, insisted on a deadline for the return of the public funds. Enter Wang Shouxin, the "goddess of wealth." She always carried with her a passbook for an unregistered bank account. and she could produce ready cash just by reaching into the drawer of her office desk.

People she could use didn't even have to open their mouths; Wang Shouxin would approach *them:* "Having problems? Short of cash?" The rebel leader Wen Feng and his pals, as well as the leaders of many important offices, all "borrowed" public funds that Wang Shouxin had appropriated without the niceties of bookkeeping, and then used that money to repay their own debts to the public. A new relationship arose from this transfer of the proletarian state's money: first, Wang Shouxin, rather than the state, assumed the creditor's role; second, Wang Shouxin's money did not necessarily have to be returned. In fact, she preferred that it not be returned, because then people would owe her their loyalty and future favors. But even if the money was returned, the debts of favor would remain. The favorite method of repaying these obligations was for the debtor to use his own power for Wang Shouxin's convenience. This caused the debtor no material loss, and for Wang Shouxin it was more than she could buy for a thousand pieces of gold. So why not do it this way, since it had such benefits for both sides?

At bottom, all this was an exchange of goods that was effected by trading off power. One form of this barter involved the direct handling of goods. For example, Wang Shouxin raised a large number of pigs, pork being another item in her power-brokering. But where could she get fodder for the pigs? Just seek out the vice-director of the Grain Bureau, of course! More than five tons of corn, bran, soybeans, and husks were sent right over. Later on, Wang Shouxin needed flour, rice, and soybean oil for partying and gift-giving. No problem! Just call the vice-director again! And thus it happened that, in the short span of one year, another five tons of rice, flour, and soybean oil passed into her hands. In return, the vice-director could "borrow" money or bricks from Wang Shouxin, or "buy" complete cartloads of coal on credit. Payment was never required, and in fact no payment was ever made.

In this county, the organs of the "dictatorship of the proletariat" served Wang Shouxin's "socialist" enterprises extremely well. Wang Shouxin would dispatch carts loaded with meat, fish, grain, oil, or vegetables to Harbin, in violation of county regulations. When this happened, the chief of the Section for Industry and Commerce, who was also second-in-command of the "rebels," would give special approval under his own signature. From 1973 on, her vehicles could come and go unhindered. In return, this fellow received a "loan" of four hundred dollars plus a variety of presents. On one occasion Wang Shouxin had to "safeguard" some cash that properly belonged to the central government. She needed it for her private dealings and building, so she couldn't put it in a bank account; that was when the deputy chief of the Finance Section, another of her "rebel" friends, opened account number 83001. To it she diverted hundreds of thousands of dollars, which were always at her disposal in a perfectly legal and protected place. To repay this man, Wang Shouxin arranged to have his son-in-law transferred from the temporary labor force to a permanent job. Then she admitted his son to the "Camp for Educated Youths" she had set up and, after falsifying his credentials, arranged his admission to a university.

For years this trading of influence went on between Wang Shouxin and dozens of officials—perhaps a hundred—on the County Party Committee, County Revolutionary Committee, and at the district and even the provincial levels. Many of these people used their status as the capital for their trade. Once Wang Shouxin, in order to set up a "nonstaple foodstuffs base," needed to take over more than thirty-three acres of good land that belonged to the Pine River Brigade of the Raven River Commune. This infuriated the commune members and local cadres. The head of the County Agricultural Office, who lacked the power to approve this deal, arranged a meal where he brought Wang Shouxin together with the leaders of the commune, the brigade, and the production teams that were involved. This gave the impression that the County Revolutionary Committee supported the discussions and acquiesced in the illegal dealings. Thus a huge tract of arable land changed hands.

This kind of "socialist" exchange does indeed demonstrate great "superiority" over capitalist exchange; neither party has to have any capital of his own, there is no need to put up private possessions as collateral, and no one needs to run any risk of loss or bankruptcy. Everybody gets what he wants.

One thing was completely clear, however. Not a single one of these exchanges could have been made without a departure from Party policy, or without either causing direct loss of socialist public property or breaking Party regulations and national laws. In some cases all of these violations occurred. Eventually, this had to harm the socialist system and discredit the Party's leadership. Through the incessant bartering, Party and government cadres slowly degenerated into parasitical insects that fed off the people's productivity and the socialist system. The relationship between the Party and the masses deteriorated greatly.

How Can a Single Hand Clap?

Language is a strange thing. When Commissar Yang pointed to Wang Shouxin as having a "completely red family," he had meant to praise her. Yet, in the mouths of the common people, the same phrase— "completely red family"—was said as a curse. When they went down the list of Wang Shouxin's family and asked how each had entered the Party or risen to official positions, they rejected all of these relatives one by one.

Her eldest son, Liu Zhimin, was a lazy oak who could think only of women. He almost always looked half-drunk. What could possibly have qualified him to become a member of the Chinese Communist Party? And how did he become vice-director of Xinli Commune? When he tried to rape a girl, why was it that he was treated with such leniency, and even assigned thereafter to the County Committee "to make policy?" Wang Shouxin's second son entered the Party from a cadre school that had only a temporary branch, one without the power to recruit Party members. And what about her youngest, that totally unqualified young dandy who got appointed assistant manager of the photography studio? Even stranger was Wang Shouxin's younger sister, who, shortly after being expelled from the Communist Youth League, managed to enter the Party! . . .

Since the people loved the Party, they were of course going to be upset when they saw these shady characters sneak into it! From 1972 onwards, any time a political campaign came along, people would flock to the Party Committee to put up big-character posters with their questions about Wang Shouxin and her "completely red family."

Yet the Party organization of Bin County could not be reformed until there was a change in the Party leadership. The opportunity for this came in 1970. Early in the year, because of his success in "supporting the Left," Commissar Yang was appointed head of the security task force for all of Heilongjiang Province. He was succeeded as Bin County Party secretary by an old cadre named Zhang Xiangling. Zhang was a solidly built, middle-aged man, with a pair of big, thick-soled feet. In 1945 he had *walked* all the way from Yan'an to Baiquan County in Heilongjiang. Now he was preparing to make use of his big feet again to take the measure of Bin County. Despite a severe stomach ailment, he could cover as many as thirty-five miles in one day.

But he quickly discovered one place where he could hardly take a single step, and that was inside the courtyard of the Party Committee. For Commissar Yang, even after receiving his transfer orders, hung on in Bin County for several months; he had reorganized administrative power so that each important position at the section level and above was filled by a "rebel" member. Most of the regular cadres of Bin County were still down in the countryside or were under house arrest.

Whenever Zhang Xiangling tried to free one of these cadres, the "Cultural Revolution Group" would inform him that they planned to hold a criticism and struggle session concerning that cadre the next day, and they requested Zhang's attendance. The power of the "Cultural Revolution Group" was much like that of the Beijing group of the same name [headed by Mao Zedong and his wife Jiang Qing]; its deputy leader also happened to be a woman—Wang Shouxin's daughter-in-law.

This woman was in her twenties, not very tall but slender and pretty. Her smile disclosed a pair of comely canines that made her even more attractive. As a typist at the County People's Committee she was fine. But once Commissar Yang appointed this poorly educated, minimally capable woman to be deputy head of the Cultural Revolution Group, she suddenly became another person altogether.

Nothing causes self-delusion quite so readily as power. The very day this woman achieved power, she began—mistakenly—to convince herself that she had the education, the moral stature, and the ability that such a position called for. The vanity, narrowness, and jealousy that had lain dormant in the typist's heart were all suddenly awakened. Her lovely eyes now flared with suspicion and hatred, as they followed and searched out her potential enemies. The tears she had shed at the departure of Commissar Yang now changed to enmity for Zhang Xiangling. Whenever a meeting took her to Harbin, she always went to see Commissar Yang, and in this way Bin County remained subject to Yang's will through a kind of remote control.

For a while Zhang Xiangling had only this one power: he could absent himself from criticism and struggle sessions. His situation bore a startling resemblance to the position of Chinese magistrates under the puppet regime of Manchukuo [occupied northeast China, 1932–45], where real power lay in the hands of the Japanese. Yet unlike those days, when there was only one Japanese deputy magistrate, now there were "Japanese" all over the place. The "rebels" who held the deputy positions in each of the sections had greater power than that of the formal section heads.

In order that readers have no misunderstanding, I must do a little explaining about the "rebels" of Bin County. The Bin County high school students who had been "Red Guards" had long ago been quelled by the "Unified Program to Defend Mao Zedong Thought." The Red Guards' crime had been that they were "anti-Army." Those who took over the power also called themselves "Red Guards" at first, and wore red armbands. But actually they were stubble-bearded cadres, many of them well over forty and old enough to be grandparents. They belonged to the generation of the Red Guards' parents. The important distinction, however, was not that of age. It was primarily that they all had families to feed and were much more interested in economics than the young-sters had been. Second, many of them had "rebelled" because of the frustration of having failed, after many years in officialdom, to enter the Party or to be promoted. These people could think of nothing but their desires for material improvement, political power, and influence.

What worried Zhang Xiangling most was that not only the leader-ship but the whole Party organization was growing more corrupt daily. One married couple who entered the Party in 1969, right after Wang Shouxin had, were overheard fighting with each other in this fashion: "What're you so uppity about? A few bottles of good liquor were your ticket of admission to the Party!"

"Goddamn it, you're worse than I. You think you could have joined without that pretty face of yours?"

Only by doing his utmost, and at the risk of his own Party member-ship, was Zhang Xiangling finally able to remove from office a few of the most detested "rebel" leaders. In 1970 there was a resolution to reinvestigate the pack of rascals who had entered the Party in 1969. Yet, when he left Bin County in 1972, Zhang had to admit that he had failed to change the balance of political power in Bin County. Not long thereafter, those he had removed from power came back; his resolution to purge bad elements from the Party was never put into effect.

Zhang Xiangling left behind several newly constructed factories in Bin County. He could hardly have imagined that these factories would lose money year after year and would make little contribution to the central government treasury, but would help line the pockets of grafters, thieves, and powerholders.

Science and
Technology

59

Chinese Science: Explorations of an Ancient Tradition

Nathan Sivin

Until the last centuries of Imperial China, the Chinese had a continuous and coherent tradition of science and technology that was unparalleled in the world. This tradition has been systematically introduced to the West by one of the great scholarly undertakings of the twentieth century, Joseph Needham's Science and Civilisation in China, *an ongoing, multivolume research project. Theories and applications are known from the earliest extensive written records in China, pertaining to mathematics, harmonics and astronomy, medicine, alchemy, astrology, and geomancy. In the early Chinese view, two distinct theoretical principles underlay the events of nature. The first, mutation theory, examines the qualitative changes in both physical existence and superphysical states or conditions and relates them to structural schemata that are highly numerological, such as the hexagrams and trigrams of the* Book of Changes. *The second, resonance theory, examines the categorical associations and correspondences that govern the interactions in the physical and spiritual world, also relating them to numerological structures with considerable geometric significance. One important value in the study of traditional science and technology is the understanding it brings of the current evolution of scientific work in China. Though increasingly dominated by the theoretical and experimental norms of the international scientific community, science and technology in China will remain a distinct blend, in substance as well as social context. In this excerpt, Nathan Sivin introduces a basic categorization of early Chinese science and discusses its salient features.*

667

.... Although every culture must experience much the same physical world, each breaks it up into manageable segments in very distinct ways. To make a long story short, at the most general level of science (natural philosophy, it used to be called) certain basic concepts became established because of their very general usefulness in making nature comprehensible. In Europe after Aristotle's time among the most important of these notions were the Four Elements of Empedocles and the qualitative idea of a proper place that was part of the definition of each thing. In ancient China the most common tools of abstract thought were the yin-yang and Five Phases concepts, implying as they did a dynamic harmony compounded out of the cyclical alternation of complementary energies [The Five Phases is a network of relationships, keyed to fire, water, metal, wood, and earth, that links everything in the phenomenal world—*Ed.*]. Today scientists use a much wider range of well-defined concepts, embracing space, time, mass, energy, and information.

Thus the fields of science in a given culture are determined by the application of these general concepts, suitably refined, reinterpreted if necessary, and supplemented by more special concepts, to various fields of experience, demarked as the culture chooses for intrinsic and extrinsic reasons to demark them.[1]

It is natural to expect that, given roughly the same body and much the same range of malfunctions likely to befall it, every culture will draw the boundaries of medicine more or less similarly. Actually this is far from true. One can find no consensus even among modern physicians in the wealthy countries as to how seriously emotional factors must be weighed when treating somatic disease, and vice versa. The student of intellectual issues can distinguish various schools of thought, and the anthropologist can locate conventional views among those who prefer not to think too deeply about these questions, although even the cliches have changed drastically over the past century. But the decisive mutual interaction of emotional and somatic states has been one of the most constant doctrines of Chinese medicine. In fact we find intricately developed theories in areas that lie almost completely outside the intellectual horizons of the modern doctor. There was, for instance, a strict correla-

---

1. One remembers the puzzlement of a great European historian of China when he discovered that the Five Phases system in medicine did not quite correspond to that in astronomy. The difference is quite comprehensible in terms of the specialization of concepts.

tion of variations in the body's energetic functions with the cosmic cycles of the day and the yearly seasons. Beginning in the T'ang it was further elaborated in the *yun ch'i* theory to take into consideration in diagnosis the effects of unseasonable variations in climate and weather.

Then what fields of science did the Chinese themselves organize in the course of conceptualizing the phenomenal world? I would propose more or less the following list of major disciplines:

1. Medicine *(i)*, which included theoretical studies of health and disease *(i ching*, and so on), therapeutics *(i fang*, and so on), macrobiotics *(yang sheng)* or the theory and practice of longevity techniques, sexual hygiene *(fang chung*, on the whole an aspect of macrobiotics), pharmacognosy *(pen-ts'ao)*, and veterinary medicine *(shou i)*.. Pharmacognosy, the study of materia medica, incorporated a large part of early knowledge of natural history as well as approaches to biological classification; Needham and his collaborator Lu Gwei-djen generally refer to it as "pharmaceutical natural history." Acupuncture, which has recently been seized upon by the mass media in their endless quest for novel misinformation, was (and still is) on the whole only a minor branch of therapeutics....

2. Alchemy *(fu-lien*, and so on), the science of immortality, which overlapped greatly in practice with medical macrobiotics. Immortality was thought of, in fact, as the highest kind of health. The two major divisions were "external alchemy" *(wei tan)* and "internal alchemy" *(nei tan)*. In the former, immortality drugs were prepared by techniques largely based on the natural processes by which minerals and metals were believed to mature within the earth, but in the laboratory they were carried out on a telescoped scale of time. A year of cyclical treatment by the alchemist might correspond to a cosmic cycle of 4320 years. In internal alchemy, by a different sort of analogy the interior of the adept's body became the laboratory and the "cyclical maturation of the elixir" was carried out by meditation, concentration, breath control, or sexual disciplines....

3. Astrology *(t'ien-wen)*, in which anomalous celestial and meteorological phenomena were observed and interpreted in order to detect defects in the political order. This science was based on a close correspondence between the cosmic and political realms. In the "field allocation" *(fen yeh)* theory of the second century B.C., this was an actual mapping of sections of the sky upon political divisions of the civilized world. In astrology the Emperor was the mediator between the orders of na-

ture and humanity. Like a vibrating dipole, the ideal monarch drew his charisma from the eternal order of the cosmos, radiating it in turn to inspire virtue—defined implicitly as values oriented toward hierarchical order—in society. Because of his centrality, the harmony of above and below depended critically upon the Emperor's ability to maintain his ritual and moral fitness. Omens in the sky were thus an early warning that his responsibility as Son of Heaven needed to be taken more seriously.

4. Geomancy *(feng-shui)*, the science of "wind and water," which determines the auspicious placement of houses and tombs with respect to features of the landscape. While alchemy uses the yin-yang, Five Phases, and other concepts mainly to study the temporal relations involved in maturing the Great Work, geomancy adapts them predominantly to topological configurations. Geomancy has been shrugged off as mere superstition, but perhaps more to the point is the rationale it provides for expressing the status or wealth of a family in terms of control of its physical environment in life and death. Nevertheless geomancy, which has no Occidental counterpart, is much more than an arbitrary excuse for demonstrating social clout. Geographers have found it intrinsically interesting as the world's only time-proven theoretical approach to the aesthetics of land use. In other words, it succeeds consistently in producing sites that, in addition to their supramundane virtues, are beautiful. No serious historical study or conceptual analysis of geomancy has yet been published in any modern language, including Chinese.

5. Physical studies *(wu li)*. The shape of this composite field has more in common with that of Greek or Islamic natural philosophy than with that of post-Newtonian physics. In general this is the area in which fundamental concepts were adapted and applied to explain particular physical phenomena, as well as chemical, biological, and psychological phenomena that were not distinguished or were thought to be closely related. We can distinguish three overlapping exploratory approaches, which at various times and in various circumstances served much the same function in Chinese thought as elementary physics today—as well as other functions with which modern physics does not concern itself. Their free use of numerology should not obscure their essentially qualitative character.

The two major early approaches to the theoretical principles behind the events of nature might be called "mutation studies" and "resonance studies." The first uses the conceptual apparatus of the commentaries to the *Book of Changes,* and is in general as concerned with the social and political spheres as with nature. The second, which unlike the others has been studied from the viewpoint of the history of science, has its own literature, going back to the second century B.C. The resonance *(hsiang lei)* treatises elaborate the notion that physical interactions are prompted by or controlled by categorical associations and correspondences, set out in terms of yin-yang and the Five Phases. The third approach is "correspondence studies" *(ko chih, ko wu)*, which attained prominence much later as part of the program of Chu Hsi (1130–1200) and other Neo-Confucian philosophers. This tendency brought to bear on interesting natural phenomena not only the more sophisticated concepts of the Neo-Confucians but their concern for the didactic applications of their insights, for they were committed to the integration of nature, society, and the individual psyche. The term *wu li* (literally, "the pattern-principles of the phenomena") was ultimately redefined to become the standard equivalent in modern Chinese for "physics."

In addition to these qualitative sciences there were others concerned with number and its applications:

6. Mathematics *(suan)*, which was on the whole numerical and algebraic in its approach rather than geometric, and oriented toward practical application rather than toward exploration of the properties of number and measure for their own sake. The search for the deeper meaning and implication of number seems to have remained within the province of what we would call numerology.

7. Mathematical harmonics *(lü* or *lü lü,* Needham's "acoustics") was perhaps the field in which mathematics and numerology were applied in closest combination. It arose from discoveries about the simple numerical relations between sound intervals, which had also suggested to the Pythagoreans that the basis of regularity in nature was numerical. In China the relations explored were mainly those of the dimensions of resonant pipes. The importance of music in ceremonial made harmonics part of the intellectual trappings of imperial charisma. This tied it to other kinds of ritually oriented charisma, guaranteed it sponsorship, protected its study, and petrified it institutionally. The very special nature of its connections with other kinds of activity tied to dynastic legitimacy, particularly mathematical astronomy and metrology, needs to be studied further. Attempts were made, for instance, to use the standard pipes as basic measures of length, capacity, and (indirectly) weight.

8. Mathematical astronomy *(li* or *li fa)* was, especially in early times, thought of as closely related to harmonics. In some of the dynastic histories the state of the two fields is surveyed in a single *Treatise on Harmonics and Calendrical Astronomy [Lü li chih]*. Astrology and astronomy, on the other hand, were treated separately except in the first of the histories (*Shih chi,* ca. 90 B.C.). Astronomy and harmonics both dealt with phenomena governed by simple but constant numerical relations. It was usual in early astronomy to rationalize and account metaphysically for the observed periodic constants by "deriving" them through numerology from the categories of the *Book of Changes.* It is perhaps most useful to think of mathematical astronomy as aimed at making celestial phenomena predictable and thus removing them from the realm of astrology, which interpreted the ominous significance of unpredictable phenomena. The ties of both disciplines to ritual thought and institutions, which depend in their essence upon precedent, often tended to blur the boundary by retaining astrological significance for phenomena that astronomers had learned to predict. The sky's eternal changes, especially the fine variations underlying the gross regularities of the solar and lunar motions, prompted the most sophisticated technical developments of which Chinese mathematics was to prove capable. . . .

This crude topography of the Chinese sciences can at least serve to remind us of a truth that we easily forget when we focus our attention narrowly on the anticipations of modern chemistry, physics, biology, and so on. When Needham speaks of internal alchemy, the art of perfecting the Elixir within the adept's body, as a "proto-biochemistry," he has already scrupulously depicted its methods as a variety of breath manipulations, sexual disciplines, and psychic meditations; but it will be interesting to observe how many writers in the next decade or so describe the initiates as if they would be more at home in a university laboratory than in a mountain abbey. There is no surer road to triviality than to forget that, although many Chinese concepts and attitudes can be found in science today—and, very likely, others in science tomorrow—the disciplines in which they were originally embedded were drastically different from our own in aim, approach, and organization.

60

Science in Contemporary China

Leo A. Orleans

Though Mao's thinking was in many respects conducive to the development of science and technology, a dramatic and explicit recommitment to their accelerated development quickly followed his death in 1976. Science and technology were paired as one of the "Four Modernizations" that would lead China into the next century. Discussion of current modernization efforts should begin with the Cultural Revolution and its impact on the higher education system. In recovering from the severe interruptions of the Cultural Revolution, the Chinese have launched a rigorous, multifaceted program, including investment in key universities and research institutes and a massive program of international exchanges, overseas training, and importation of expertise. The importance of international partnerships in China's drive to modernize science and technology is clear in Leo A. Orleans' book, Science in Contemporary China, *published as a result of years of cooperative analysis and assessment of China's current strengths and needs in science and technology. The core of the book is a collection of reports on various scientific disciplines, each done by an expert in the field from outside China. The essays demonstrate not only the technical issues confronting each field of development, but the economic and social ones as well, as various sciences and technical areas compete for scarce financial and human resources. In the following selection, Orleans presents an overview of China's achievements and prospects in modernizing its science and technology.*

. . . . The PRC is by no means a typical developing country. China's long and distinguished history, its ancient civilization, its complex social and political systems that go back to premodern times, its people's long-standing respect for knowledge and scholarship, have all contributed to a real sense of national pride and identity—attributes that often have to be created artificially in other developing countries. Joseph Needham's *Science and Civilisation in China* documents the high level of cultural and technological development in traditional China. In our own century, thousands of Chinese intellectuals have selected careers in science as a means of advancing both themselves and their country. With the establishment of the People's Republic in 1949, China not only had a certain tradition in the sciences but already had a substantial number of Western-trained, urban-based scientists and engineers.

Many of Mao Zedong's notions have been compatible with contemporary development theories. He emphasized the need to expose China's whole population to basic science and technology; to adapt programs to local conditions, resources, and needs; to place more stress on middle-level manpower; and, most of all, to "walk on two legs"—to use a variety of approaches to solve basic problems. Mao wanted to see greater emphasis placed on "science for the masses," so as to alter some of the peasants' traditional resistance to change and make them more amenable to accepting "scientific methods." To smooth out the differences between the city and the countryside and between mental and physical labor, Mao initiated some disruptive movements, notably the Great Leap Forward of 1958–59 and the much more damaging Great Proletarian Cultural Revolution of 1966–69. We cannot know where China's science and technology might be today had the scientific establishment and higher education not suffered so severely from these interruptions.

But all that is prologue. Mao's death in September 1976 was quickly followed by the appointment of Hua Guofeng as the new Chairman, the purge of the Gang of Four, the second ascendancy of Deng Xiaoping in July 1977, and the all-out effort to make up for the years when economic growth was subordinated to politics and ideology. At the National Science Conference in March 1978, China defined its developmental goals in the "four modernizations" policy, in which science and technology, one of the "modernizations," was seen as playing a key role in propelling the other three: agriculture, industry, and national defense.

By 1979 many developments that would have seemed almost inconceivable a few years earlier were being reported by Chinese news sources and foreign visitors. The Chinese were even publishing economic statistics (unavailable for some two decades) and reporting demonstrations for human rights and improved living standards. New scientific institutes and publications were flourishing, and Chinese scientists were touring the West and frankly discussing China's scientific and human problems. Scholarly, governmental, and commercial contacts with China were formalized, and there was a concomitant demand for more and better information about China's science and technology. . . .

Developments in U.S.–China relations have progressed at an unprecedented rate since normalization in January 1979 and are continuing to do so. Cooperation in science and technology has become increasingly complex, involving important governmental agreements stemming from cabinet-level missions to the PRC, extensive participation by the U.S. business community, and independent agreements between academic and research institutions. The CSCPRC, now only one of many organizations pursuing scientific and technological exchanges, is finally sending individual scholars to travel, study, and do research in China, conducting bilateral scientific symposia, and sponsoring reciprocal lectures by American and Chinese scientists. The United States has reached a new plateau in its relations with China, and Americans have reached a new stage in their study of Chinese science. The "viewing of science from horseback," to paraphrase Mao, is over and an era of on-the-spot, collaborative work with Chinese scientists has begun. . . .

It is clear that the adverse effects of the Cultural Revolution and the subsequent rule of the Gang of Four (1966–76) on the educational system will continue to hamper China's progress in science and technology throughout the 1980s. Since 1949, China's older generation of Western-trained scholars and to a lesser extent those trained in the Soviet Union, have occupied key positions in the Chinese Academy of Sciences (CAS) and its research institutes, and have been responsible for most of the scientific and technological progress. The best of these scientists are as good as can be found anywhere in the world, but they are aging and their numbers are rapidly dwindling. Who will take their place? The current effort to raise the quality of higher education and to upgrade the competence of the middle-level professional cohort (aged 30–45), and the program of sending promising students to the United States and other industrial nations for advanced training, are the first steps in a process that will take many years.

There is less agreement . . . about the familiar conflict between basic and applied research—an argument well known to most developing nations. Mao believed that scientists should focus all their efforts on meeting China's practical needs. This resulted in periods of considerable friction between administrators and scientists but nevertheless research was, for the most part, dictated by national priorities. Some ... deplore this virtual absence of basic research in their discipline in China; others believe that during China's "catch-up" phase basic research should be undertaken only when the scientific lag in a particular field is less than five years. Whichever side is right, Beijing seems to be gradually relaxing restrictions on basic research. No doubt the government's emphasis will continue to be related to immediate economic plans and social goals, but Chinese scientists are now confident that basic and long-range research will not be neglected.

Because China's first priority after 1949 was the improvement of people's living conditions, science had to play an important role in improving public health and increasing food production. The achievements in health have received international notice, and progress in agriculture has been much better than many observers anticipated. In both fields the research and innovations by China's scientists have elicited considerable interest on the part of their Western colleagues.

As social conditions improved, China was able to concentrate an increasing proportion of its scientific and technological resources on its three other priorities, which have essentially remained unchanged over the years. One is the rapid development of the Chinese economy, and many of the most capable Chinese scientists have spent years endeavoring to make China's industry, mining, transport, and other economic sectors more efficient and productive. A second is the emphasis on national defense, a priority that protected scientists working in military-related nuclear and space research even during the height of the Cultural Revolution. The third is international recognition and prestige, a goal that permits some scientists to pursue work that may not be practical but can attract worldwide attention. One example is the excellent work of Chinese surgeons in the reimplantation of severed limbs—seemingly a low-priority activity in a nation with only one Western-trained physician for every 10,000 people. Another, criticized by some Western physicists, is the effort going into high energy physics. Yet another is the orbiting of a small satellite whose sole apparent purpose beyond demonstrating China's capabilities in this area was to advertise

China's ideology to the world below by playing the song "The East Is Red."

Practical considerations, however, have led to great imbalances within specific disciplines. In chemistry, for example, there has been a high-quality effort in such areas as pharmaceutical research, polymers, materials, and gas chromatography—all important in China's economic production plans—but little or no work in quantum and theoretical chemistry, molecular spectroscopy, organometallic chemistry, and other areas of chemistry that have no immediate economic benefits.

There seems to be unanimous agreement about the obsolescence of equipment in Chinese laboratories. But although some ... believe that future progress ... will depend on how much instrumentation China can import from abroad, others are impressed by how much the Chinese are able to accomplish despite this handicap—for example, by how completely Chinese scientists were able to identify and analyze most mineral and rock samples without modern petrographic microscopes, modern x-ray equipment, and electron microprobes. All agree, however, that China's inadequate and mostly antiquated computer technology is a major handicap—a view widely held by the Chinese themselves. Computers represent a priority area in China's eight-year plan, and the country is increasing both domestic production and imports of larger and more sophisticated equipment. . . .

As a postscript, it must be stressed that during the 1980s the vital question for China (and for the world) is not whether it will be able to achieve its stated purpose of catching up with the advanced countries by the year 2000. That goal is unrealistic and almost incidental. The rhetoric is essentially for domestic consumption and is characteristic of slogans designed to stimulate enthusiasm among the people by introducing a concrete reason for hard work and sacrifice. In connection with national modernization, China has many more immediate and serious problems than catching up and overtaking the rest of the world. Two of them stand out above all others.

China's first concern is nothing less than a matter of survival, for all its publicized plans presume that it will be able to maintain a reasonable balance between food and population. Despite rationing, China has admitted that between 1957 and 1977 there was a decline in the per capita production of grain; and despite earlier birth control campaigns, only in the mid-1970s did officials publicly acknowledge a direct relationship between population growth and China's ability to achieve the stated economic goals. Thanks to the priority being given to the allocation of resources to agriculture, and to the apparent initial success of intense propaganda and even coercion in reducing China's birthrate to a level unheard of in other developing countries, there are grounds for cautious optimism. But the balance will continue to be precarious; and a bad crop year or any relaxation of pressures in family planning could create serious setbacks.

China's second concern for the 1980s and 1990s is the impact that modernization is bound to have on Chinese institutions, lifestyles, and values. Is it possible to introduce sophisticated science and technology into the economy without radically altering the material expectations of China's workers and peasants? Can the PRC be opened up to sustained Western contact without far-reaching effects on its political system? Do China's leaders agree on a particular balance between modernization and revolution? Can China achieve its goal of "four modernizations" without also introducing the "fifth modernization"—a liberalization of the system? The answers that the Chinese leaders eventually find for these questions are likely to be crucial not only to China's developmental course, but to its stability.

China must overcome innumerable domestic and international difficulties. Yet this is no reason for pessimism; one should never underestimate the talents and resources of the Chinese people.

61

National Plan for the Development of Science and Technology (1975–1985)

Fang Yi

In March 1978, China held the National Science Conference with a dual purpose: to marshal China's resources internally to support a renewed commitment to science and technology, and to signal the outside world of China's seriousness in the area. In his address to the Conference, Fang Yi, who served as the Minister of the State Sciences and Technology Commission from February 1978 to September 1984, presented a rough development plan for 1978–85, covering both goals and strategies for the period. High-speed development of key areas, the fastest possible increase in the number of professional researchers, the expeditious construction of modern research centers, and the creation of a nationwide system to facilitate research were goals to be achieved through several means. Among these Fang Yi emphasized consolidation of existing institutions, new and open policies of recruiting and training potential scientists, rewards for accomplishment of science and technology, tolerance of diverse and contending ideas, rapid application of new knowledge and rapid dissemination of information, and an open-door policy toward overseas training and academic exchanges. Few outside observers believed that the goals articulated by Fang Yi and repeated throughout the conference were realistic. In fact, they served more to underscore the deficiencies of China's present situation and recent policies than to provide attainable goals. Nevertheless, during the years since 1978, China's accomplishments in key areas of development and the levels of activity reached in international exchange have far surpassed what most observers thought possible.

Chairman Mao and Premier Chou mapped out a gigantic plan for us to make China a modern, powerful socialist country. By the end of this century, all departments and localities in China that can use machines must be fully mechanized, electrification must be realized in both urban and rural areas, the production processes in major industrial departments automated, advanced techniques extensively applied, labor productivity raised by big margins, and a radical change brought about in industrial and agricultural production so that our national economy can take its place in the front ranks of the world. We must equip our armed forces with the advanced achievements in science and technology and greatly enhance our national defense capabilities. We shall build a vast army of working-class scientists and technicians who are both red and expert, and we must have our own experts in science and technology who are first rate by world standards. It is also necessary to acquire the most sophisticated equipment for scientific experimentation so that we can approach advanced world levels in most branches of science and technology, catch up with them in some branches, and take the lead in certain others. With the accomplishment of these tasks, we can say that we have realized by and large our objective of modernizing agriculture, industry, national defense, and science and technology. China will radiate even more brilliantly throughout the world.

The eight years from now through 1985 are crucial for this long-term plan. We must foster lofty ideals and set high goals, work out a strategic plan, fully mobilize all positive factors, and organize all our forces well.

Our plan should serve the needs of realizing the four modernizations, which hinge on modernizing science and technology. The plan on science and technology must dovetail with the plan on production and construction, and the two must be organically combined. Research in applied sciences and in basic theories and the immediate and long-term tasks must be properly arranged to avoid over-emphasizing one to the neglect of the other.

Our plan should be aimed at high-speed development. Compared with advanced world levels in science and technology, our country is now lagging fifteen to twenty years behind in many branches and more still in some others. Modern science and technology are developing rapidly. Only by developing at a higher speed can we catch up with or surpass the capitalist countries. We fulfilled five years ahead of schedule the major targets specified in the twelve-year plan for the development of science and technology mapped out in 1956. In the mid-1960s we approached advanced world levels at the time in some scientific and technical spheres, which helped the popularization of some new techniques and the building of some new rising industries. Now that we have much better conditions and a more solid foundation than in those days, a much higher speed is entirely possible.

Our plan should be one with the present-day advanced levels as its starting point. We must be good at learning from the advanced. We should conscientiously assimilate the experience and lessons of our predecessors so as to avoid the detours they went through. In carrying out the first plan for the development of science and technology, we took semiconductor technology, which was an advanced branch of science at the time, as our starting point for studying and developing electronic computers. As a result, we soon passed the stage of the electron tube and gained time. In the years to come, we must work hard to raise all our scientific research work to advanced levels as quickly as possible. Scientific experiments by the masses should also be steadily improved on the basis of popularization.

Since last June, departments under the State Council and various localities and units have, through repeated discussions and revisions, mapped out a draft outline National Plan for the Development of Science and Technology, 1978–85.

The draft outline plan sets forth the following goals to be attained in the next eight years:

1. Approach or reach the advanced world levels of the 1970s in a number of important branches of science and technology.
2. Increase the number of professional scientific researchers to 800,000.
3. Build a number of up-to-date centers for scientific experiment.
4. Complete a nationwide system of scientific and technological research.

The eight-year outline plan (draft) makes all-around dispositions for the tasks of research in twenty-seven spheres, including natural resources, agriculture, industry, national defense, transport and communication, oceanography, environmental protection, medicine, finance and trade, culture, and education, in addition to the two major departments of basic and technical sciences. Of these, 108 items have been chosen as key projects in the nationwide endeavor for scientific and technological research. When this plan is fulfilled, our country will approach or reach the advanced world levels of the 1970s in a number of important branches of science and technology, thus narrowing the gap to about ten years and laying a solid foundation for catching up with or surpassing advanced world levels in all branches in the following fifteen years.

The eight-year outline plan (draft) gives prominence to the eight comprehensive scientific and technical spheres, important new techniques, and pace-setting disciplines that have a bearing on the overall situation. It calls for concentrating all forces and achieving remarkable successes so as to promote the high-speed development of science and technology as a whole and of the entire national economy.

Agriculture. In accordance with the principle of "taking grain as the key link and ensuring an all-around development," we will in the next three to five years actively carry out comprehensive surveys of our resources in agriculture, forestry, animal husbandry, sideline production, and fisheries, study the rational exploitation and utilization of the resources and the protection of the ecological system, and study the rational arrangement of these undertakings.

We should implement in its entirety the Eight-Point Charter for Agriculture (soil, fertilizer, water conservancy, seeds, close planting, plant protection, field management, and improved farm tools) and raise our level of scientific farming. We should study and evolve a farming system and cultivating techniques that will carry forward our tradition of intensive farming and at the same time suit mechanization; and study and manufacture farm machines and tools of high quality and efficiency. We will study science and technology for improving soil, controlling water, and making our farmland give stable and high yields. In order to improve as quickly as possible the low-yielding farmland that accounts for about one-third or more of the country's total, we must make major progress in improving alkaline, lateritic, clay, and other kinds of poor soil, in preventing soil erosion, and in combating sandstorms and drought. We will study projects for diverting water from the south to the north and the relevant scientific and technical problems; study and develop new compound fertilizers and biological nitrogen fixation, methods of applying fertilizer scientifically, and techniques for

drainage and irrigation; breed new seed strains, work out new techniques in seed breeding, and improve the fine crop varieties in an all-
around way so that they will give still higher yields, produce seeds of
better quality, and can better resist natural adversities. We should
quickly develop new insecticides that are highly effective and are harm-
less to the environment, and devise comprehensive techniques for preventing and treating different kinds of plant diseases and pests.

We need to step up scientific and technological research in forestry,
animal husbandry, sideline production, and fisheries. We should provide new tree varieties and techniques that will make the woods grow
fast and yield more and better timber; develop multipurpose utilization
of forest resources, and study techniques and measures for preventing
and extinguishing forest fires; step up research on building pasture-
lands, improving breeds of animals and poultry, mechanizing the process of animal husbandry, increasing the output of aquatic products,
breeding aquatic products, and marine fishing and processing.

We will set up up-to-date centers for scientific experiments in agriculture, forestry, animal husbandry, and fisheries.

We must lay great emphasis on research in the basic theories of
agricultural science, and step up our studies of the applications of agricultural biology, agricultural engineering, and other new techniques to
agriculture.

Energy. We must make big efforts to accelerate the development of
energy science and technology so as to carry out full and rational exploitation and utilization of our energy resources.

We have our own inventions in the science and technology of the
oil industry, and in some fields we have caught up with or surpassed
advanced levels in other countries. We must continue our efforts to
catch up with and surpass advanced world levels in an all-around way.
We should study the laws and characteristics of the genesis and distribution of oil and gas in the principal sedimentary regions, develop theories
of petroleum geology, and extend oil and gas exploration to wider areas;
study new processes, techniques, and equipment for exploration and
exploitation and raise the standards of well drilling and the rate of oil
and gas recovery; and actively develop crude oil processing techniques,
use the resources rationally and contribute to the building of some ten
more oilfields, each as big as Taching.

China has extremely rich resources of coal, which will remain our
chief source of energy for a fairly long time to come. In the next eight

years, we should mechanize the key coal mines, achieve complex mechanization in some of them, and proceed to automation. The small- and medium-sized coal mines should also raise their level of mechanization. Scientific and technical work in the coal industry should center around this task, with active research in basic theory, mining technology, technical equipment, and safety measures. At the same time research should be carried out in the gasification, liquefaction, and multipurpose utilization of coal, and new ways explored for the exploitation, transportation, and utilization of different kinds of coals.

To improve the power industry is another pressing task. We should take as our chief research subjects the key technical problems in building large hydroelectric power stations and thermal power stations at pit mouths, large power grids, and super-high-voltage power transmission lines. We must concentrate our efforts on comprehensive research in the techniques involved in building huge dams and giant power-generating units and in geology, hydrology, meteorology, reservoir-induced earthquakes, and engineering protection, which are closely linked with large-scale key hydroelectric power projects.

New sources of energy should be explored. We should accelerate our research in atomic power generation and speed up the building of atomic power plants. We should also step up research in solar energy, geothermal energy, wind power, tide energy, and controlled thermonuclear fusion, pay close attention to low-calorie fuels, such as bone coal, gangue, and oil shale, and marsh gas resources in the rural areas, and making full use of them where possible.

Attention should be paid to the rational utilization and saving of energy, such as making full use of surplus heat, studying and manufacturing fine and efficient equipment for this purpose, and lowering energy consumption by every means and particularly coke consumption in iron smelting, coal consumption in power generation, energy consumption in the chemical and metallurgical industries.

Materials. Steel must be taken as the key link in industry. It is imperative to make a breakthrough in the technology of intensified mining and solve the scientific and technological problems of beneficiating hematite. We should speed up research work on the paragenetic deposits at Panchihhua, Paotow, and Chinchuan, where many closely associated metals have been formed; solve the major technical problems in multipurpose utilization; intensify research on the exploitation of copper and aluminum resources; make China one of the biggest producers of titanium and vanadium in the world; and approach or reach advanced world levels in the techniques of refining copper, aluminum, nickel, cobalt, and rare-earth metals. We should master new modern metallurgical technology quickly, increase varieties, and improve quality; study and grasp the laws governing the formation of high-grade iron ore deposits and the methods of locating them; establish a system of ferrous and nonferrous materials and extend it in the light of the characteristics of our resources.

We should make full use of our rich natural resources and industrial dregs and increase at high speed the production of cement and new types of building materials which are light and of high strength and serve a variety of purposes; step up research in the technology of mining and dressing non-metal ores and in the processing techniques; lay stress on research in the techniques of organic synthesis with petroleum, natural gas, and coal as the chief raw materials; step up our studies of catalysts and develop the technology of direct synthesis; renovate the techniques of making plastics, synthetic rubber, and synthetic fiber; and raise the level of equipment and automation in the petrochemical industry. We must solve the key scientific and technical problems in producing special materials necessary for our national defense industry and new technology, and evolve new materials characteristic of China's resources.

We should devote great efforts to basic research on the science of materials, develop new experimental techniques and testing methods, and gradually be able to design new materials with specified properties.

Electronic computers. China must make a big new advance in computer science and technology. We should lose no time in solving the scientific and technical problems in the industrial production of large-scale integrated circuits, and make a breakthrough in the technology of ultra-large-scale integrated circuits. We should study and turn out giant computers, put a whole range of computers into serial production, step up study on peripheral equipment and software of computers and on applied mathematics, and energetically extend the application of computers. We aim to acquire by 1985 a comparatively advanced force in research in computer science and build a fair-sized modern computer industry. Microcomputers will be popularized, and giant ultra-high-speed computers put into operation. We will also establish a number of computer networks and data bases. A number of key enterprises will use computers to control the major processes of production and management.

Lasers. We will study and develop laser physics, laser spectroscopy, and nonlinear optics in the next three years. We should solve a series of scientific and technical problems in optical communications, raise the level of the routine laser quickly, and intensify our studies of detectors. We expect to make discoveries and creations in the next eight years in exploring new types of laser devices, developing new laser wave-lengths, and studying new mechanisms of laser generation, making contributions in the application of the laser to studying the structure of matter. We plan to build experimental lines of optical communications and achieve big progress in studying such important laser applications as separation of isotopes and laser-induced nuclear fusion. Laser technology should be popularized in all departments of the national economy and national defense.

Space. We should attach importance to the study of space science, remote sensing techniques, and the application of satellites; build modern centers for space research and systems for the application of satellites; step up the development of the vehicle series, and study, manufacture, and launch a variety of scientific and applied satellites; actively carry out research in the launching of skylabs and space probes; and conduct extensive research in the basic theory of space science and the application of space technology.

High-energy physics. We expect to build a modern high-energy physics experimental base in ten years, completing a proton accelerator with a capacity of 30,000 million to 50,000 million electron volts in the first five years and a giant one with a still larger capacity in the second five years.

We should from now on set about the task in real earnest and make full preparations for experiments in high-energy physics, with particular stress on studying and manufacturing detectors and training laboratory workers. We should step up research in the theory of high-energy physics and cosmic rays; consciously promote the interpenetration of high-energy physics and the neighboring disciplines; actively carry out research in the application of accelerator technology to industry, agriculture, medicine, and other spheres; and pay attention to the exploration of subjects which promise important prospects of application.

Genetic engineering. We must in the next three years step up the tempo of building and improving the related laboratories and conduct basic studies in genetic engineering. In the next eight years, we should combine them with the studies in molecular biology, molecular genetics, and cell biology and achieve fairly big progress. We should study the use of the new technology of genetic engineering in the pharmaceutical industry and explore new feasible ways to treat and prevent certain difficult and baffling diseases and evolve new high-yield crop varieties capable of fixing nitrogen.

We must grasp firmly and effectively the above eight important spheres. But this in no way means that we can neglect work in other spheres. All branches of science and technology have their specific positions and roles in our socialist construction, and none can be dispensed with or replaced. We should grasp the key spheres well on the one hand and make overall planning and give all-around consideration on the other. Make all-around arrangements while laying emphasis on the key points—this is our policy.

Here I would like to mention in particular the question of multipurpose utilization. Chairman Hua has given this instruction: "We must attach importance to multipurpose utilization which makes full use of natural resources and alleviates pollution of the environment. The three industrial wastes (liquids, gases, and dregs) will bring harm if they are discarded but will become treasures if they are turned to good account." People working in all professions and trades should go in for multipurpose utilization, and the departments concerned should be organized to concentrate their forces on tackling major scientific and technical problems.

The march toward the modernization of science and technology means in essence a comprehensive and fundamental technical transformation of all fields of material production in our country. This is a great technical revolution that history has entrusted to us. Accomplishment of this revolution depends on leadership by the Party and on the people of the whole country. Our Party organizations at all levels, first of all the leading Party groups of the ministries and commissions under the State Council and the Party committees of the provinces, municipalities, and autonomous regions, must earnestly implement the instructions of Chairman Hua, simultaneously grasp the three great revolutionary movements of class struggle, and struggle for production, and scientific experiment, and do the following work well in a down-to-earth manner.[1]

---

1. These are the subheadings of separate sections of Fang Yi's speech.—*Ed.*

1. Consolidate the Scientific Research Institutions and Build Up a Scientific and Technological Research System. . . .
2. Open Broad Avenues to Able People and Recruit Them Without Overstressing Qualifications. . . .
3. Institute Regulations for Training, Appraising, Promoting, and Rewarding Scientific Technical Personnel. . . .
4. Uphold the Policy of Letting a Hundred Schools of Thought Contend. . . .
5. Learn Advanced Science and Technology from Other Countries and Increase International Academic Exchanges. . . .
6. Ensure Adequate Work Hours for Scientific Research. . . .
7. Strive to Modernize Laboratory Facilities and Information and Library Work. . . .
8. Close Cooperation with an Appropriate Division of Labor. . . .
9. Speed Up Popularization and Application of Scientific and Technical Achievements and New Techniques. . . .
10. Make Big Efforts to Popularize Science. . . .

62

DOS ex Machina:
The Microelectronic Ghost in China's Modernization Machine

Richard Baum

The Chinese have been most enthusiastic about inviting visits from expert foreign observers and consultants in key areas of science and technology, and they have generally been forthcoming in providing access to the sites and data necessary for assessing the state of various fields. There has been much interest in the current state of electronics in China, especially in computer technology. China's development plans place heavy emphasis on electronics and computers, and failure to maintain currency in computers and electronics will cause an ever-growing lag in many other sciences and technology industries. Given the significance of developments internationally in the last ten years, assessing China's accomplishments in computer areas provides a good measure of whether China is winning or losing the race to modernize. Strategic applications, including military electronics, command up to half of China's annual electronic production and significantly shape the direction of technological development, yet they may not be as important ultimately as development of a strong foundation in chip-fabrication, microcomputer design and manufacture, the dissemination of engineering skills, and the adjustment of the Chinese language and communication practices to the capabilities of new technology. In the following article, Richard Baum reviews the last decade of accomplishment in the microcomputer industry and considers the prospects for this technology to influence the fundamental organizational and structural features of Chinese technology, communications, and politics.

A Chinese microelectronic revolution of some note has taken place in the 1980s. Since the turn of the decade, domestic Chinese production of integrated circuits (ICs) and microcomputers has on average doubled annually; in the same period, computer imports have risen almost a hundredfold. By early 1986, China had manufactured almost as many personal computers as the Soviet Union; computer boutiques in Peking and Shanghai were selling the latest in 16-bit foreign and domestic micros; a computer dating service had opened in the Chinese capital with the blessings of the local Communist Party branch; and Chinese college students were relaxing between classes, playing "Flight Simulator" and "Space Invaders" on fully equipped IBM PC-XTs in modern computer labs. For all this surface glitter, however, China's computer revolution remains in virtual infancy, its progress severely constrained by a number of technical and developmental problems. Consequently, though the computer's potential impact on Chinese society is enormous, its actual consequences to date have been quite limited.

The first Chinese-made computers were bulky vacuum-tube models, copied from Soviet prototypes supplied in the 1950s. By the mid-1960s, Chinese engineers had designed and developed a second generation of transistorized machines; and, in the early 1970s, the first Chinese IC-based third-generation computer was successfully trial-produced. Despite rapid advances in basic technology, by the close of the 1970s Chinese computer R&D remained an estimated fifteen years behind that of the West, with the gap being most apparent in the areas of IC production, external storage, input/output peripherals, and applications software.

In 1979, there were an estimated 1,500 computers installed throughout China. The vast majority of these machines—including the country's main production-line models—were based on foreign designs and prototypes, reverse-engineered in Chinese laboratories. Most computers in the Chinese inventory were large, expensive mainframe or minicomputers dedicated to numerical data processing and scientific computation; a smaller number were utilized for industrial process control, primarily in the defense sector.

China's Microcomputer Boom

The onset of the Chinese computer boom in the early 1980s coincided with the spread of a worldwide revolution in microchip technology. As small, low-cost 8-bit desk-top computers and microprocessors became readily available on the world market, the PRC's computer inventory jumped five-fold in just two years—from 2,300 units in 1981 to more than 10,000 in 1983. At the same time, Chinese manufacturers began to incorporate imported semiconductors and subassemblies into their finished products. As a result, China's domestic computer output registered an 8-fold increase between 1981 and 1983, from less than 700 units annually to almost 6,000. From mid-1984 to the spring of 1985, the microelectronics boom gained fresh momentum as Deng Xiaoping's newly expanded "open-door" policy *(kaifang)* resulted in a fresh wave of hard-currency imports and high-tech joint ventures. By the time the wave subsided in the last half of 1985, there were an estimated 100,000 computers in the country, the vast majority of which were desk-top PCs—approximately one-third of which had been domestically manufactured or assembled.

So rapid was the buildup of China's microcomputer inventories that, by the beginning of 1986, some 40,000 PCs were stacked in warehouses throughout the country "owing to lack of trained personnel to operate them." Beijing alone reportedly had 20,000 computers on hand early in 1986—almost ten times more than the entire 1981 Chinese national inventory....

By 1985, the 16-bit architecture of the IBM PC had emerged as the micro industry standard in China, displacing the older 8-bit Apple II. In that same year, the bulk of the PRC's microcomputer production consisted of final assembly of partially knocked-down, imported components and subassemblies. Average output of finished machines at each of the country's 111 computer-assembly plants in 1984 was less than 1 computer per day, as compared with almost 1,000 a day at Apple's automated Macintosh plant in Silicone Valley.

Along with the outbreak of microcomputer fever there has occurred in China a less well-publicized—but no less significant—advance in the field of large-scale integrated (LSI) technology, used in the manufacture of so-called "supercomputers." LSI research began in China in 1975, culminating in the successful trial manufacture of the PRC's first two fourth-generation supercomputers in 1983—the "Galaxy" and the "757." Although China's LSI program is still in the experimental stage, and Chinese computer technology continues to lag several years behind the West and Japan in such important areas as manufacturing techniques, software, and peripheral devices, the gap has clearly been narrowing.

The rapidity with which PC fever spread to China in the early 1980s, and the considerable enthusiasm with which Chinese state planners, managers, and technical intellectuals welcomed the dawning of the new microcomputer age, stood in marked contrast to the more ambivalent, conservative response evinced by Soviet authorities. Despite sharing similar Marxist doctrines and Leninist institutions, China and Russia have diverged markedly in their basic approaches to the acquisition, allocation, and end-use of computer technology. . . .

Ghosts in the Machine

Despite the steady upward trend of recent years, it is highly unlikely that the phenomenal growth rates of the past half-decade can be sustained—or even approximated—over the next several years. For one thing, the Chinese government in the spring of 1985 began severely to curtail hard-currency expenditures on imported consumer durables. As a result, Western computer sales to China slacked off considerably in the second half of the year. Another constraint on growth is the lack of competent technical personnel. One authoritative Chinese source, noting that a great many of the PRC's current stock of 100,000 computers remain idle for lack of qualified programmers, operators, and maintenance/repair personnel, wrote that "to solve the personnel shortage problem, even with a very optimistic estimate it would take China at least five years to train 100,000 qualified people to work on those computers." Currently, China is graduating qualified computer technicians and programmers at the rate of around 10,000 per year.

The extremely low personal income of the vast majority of Chinese people (average income of China's 100 million urban blue-collar and office workers in 1985 was around US $350/year), coupled with the extremely high price of PCs sold in China, militates strongly against any major surge in the Chinese home-computer market. The average selling price of a fully equipped, dedicated IBM PC Model 5550 in China in early 1985 was around US $15,000 (equivalent to more than 30 years' income for the average Chinese college teacher or mid-level manager), while a locally manufactured 16-bit IBM PC-XT clone, the "Great Wall" model 520A, sold for about $7,000. A Chinese copy of the Apple II + (the "Venus") was available for around $2,500, while Taiwanese-made

Apple knock-offs were reportedly priced below $1,000. A locally cloned Z-80 CP/M machine constituted the bottom of the microcomputer line, and could be purchased in Peking for as little as $400, still more than a full year's income for the average worker.

To a certain extent, the prohibitive cost of purchasing a foreign-made computer in China reflects the regime's deliberate attempt to pursue a policy of high-tech import substitution. In order to promote Chinese co-manufacture (or assembly) of finished computer products—and thereby to stimulate the process of transferring needed manufacturing technologies from abroad—the PRC in 1985 imposed a tariff of 100 percent on all fully assembled computer products brought into China (up from 50 percent in 1984), while at the same time retaining substantially lower import duties of 25 and 7.5 percent, respectively, on partially pre-assembled and completely knocked-down units.

Despite repeated efforts to raise Chinese industry standards for domestically produced PCs, foreign computers continue to be in much greater demand than their local look-alikes—notwithstanding the substantially lower prices of the latter. The workmanship, reliability, repair, and maintenance record of Chinese-made machines remain generally poor—far below current Taiwanese, South Korean, or Hong Kong standards. For this reason, few Chinese end-users, offered a choice, opt for domestic products. Indeed, the overwhelming majority of mini- and microcomputers seen by visitors in Chinese government offices, enterprises, universities, and research labs in recent years have been of foreign manufacture; much the same also holds true for mainframes.

A rare glimpse into the frustrating world of Chinese computer end-users was provided in a poll conducted by the fledgling China Computer Users' Association in October 1984. Members of the Association were asked to rate 38 computer products—28 domestic and 10 foreign-made—according to 6 criteria: product quality, technical competence of company personnel, written documentation, spare parts availability, repair and maintenance service, and warranty reliability. Not one of the 38 products evaluated in the survey was rated "good" by consumers in as many as 4 categories; only 8 were judged good in 3 categories. By far the most widespread source of consumer dissatisfaction the survey revealed was the area of written documentation, in which only one native product—a Suzhou-made clone of the Nova 1200—rated a high mark. Second worst overall ratings were in the category of spare parts, where only 8 of the 38 rated products were deemed satisfactory. Best overall performance was in the category of manufacturer's warranty reliability, wherein 23 of the 38 products received high marks.

The results of this survey reveal a Chinese computer market plagued by lack of adequate technical support, written documentation, spare parts, and after-sales service. Compounding these difficulties are a number of endemic problems such as poor software support (reflecting a severe shortage of off-the-shelf programs capable of processing Chinese characters); insufficient numbers of trained computer operators, programmers, and technicians; inadequate and irregular electric-power supplies (making expensive constant-voltage transformers and battery back-ups virtually indispensable for reliable computer operations); poor telephone transmission quality (rendering high-speed data transfers via modem all but impossible); and high concentrations of particulate air pollution in most Chinese cities (making an air-conditioned environment a virtual necessity for trouble-free computing). All these factors combine further to reduce the salutary impact of the micro revolution on the prospective Chinese end-user.

In addition to these various developmental obstacles, still other difficulties confront the Chinese in their effort to leap forward into the age of mass microelectronics. Amusing—and often poignant—anecdotes abound concerning the use, misuse, non-use, and abuse of computers in China. A recent review article summed up the highly checkered Chinese "state of the art":

> China's computer industry is far behind. The largest domestically produced RAM chip in wide use holds just 1 kilobit.... Central processing chips are early 8-bit designs.... Virtually all microcomputers now made in China ... use imported parts for most of the critical components.... Prices are high.... The profusion of incompatible models afflicts China just like everywhere else.... Hardly anyone in China is familiar with applications software.... Nearly all users write their own programs in BASIC or FOR-TRAN; even statistical programs running on the mainframes servicing ministries in Peking are written locally in BASIC. Duplication and triplication of effort are the norm. Users rarely communicate with one another, much less share their work, even if they are in the same city....
>
> In offices and factories, an extreme shortage of competent managers often makes the few available micros ineffectual.... State-run businesses are little concerned with efficiency or profit and loss, so decision-making is much less analytical than in capitalist countries....
>
> Some users, lacking manuals and access to knowledgeable help, don't

even know how to start up their computers. . . . All too often, expensive imported equipment is purchased without allowance for maintenance and repair; mainframes designed for twenty users can be reduced to a handful of working terminals as disk drivers fail, and frequently no hard currency can be found to buy replacement parts. Even worse is the presence of off-beat equipment that has been foisted off on innocent buyers.

All this is compounded by a highly bureaucratized, rigidly compartmentalized, organizationally redundant Chinese R&D system that makes interagency communication difficult at best and renders the nationwide coordination of computer planning, research, and production virtually impossible.

Given such constraints, it would be unwise to render predictions of a trouble-free future for Chinese computerization. Yet the microelectronic revolution is almost certainly irreversible; the computer—no matter how mixed the blessing—is here to stay; indeed, it has already left a visible, if embryonic, imprint on Chinese society. . . .

China's Emerging Microculture

One obvious reason for the lack of effective, interactive LANs [local area networking systems] in China is the extreme paucity—and awkwardness—of applications software capable of processing Chinese characters. Several proprietary Western software programs (for example, WordStar, SuperCalc, and dBASE II) are readily available in (mostly unlicensed and often bug-ridden) Chinese versions in Hong Kong and the PRC. Some of these programs make use of abbreviated *pin-yin* romanization to represent individual Chinese syllables (of which there are only a few hundred, exclusive of tonal variation); once the proper syllabic abbreviation is entered at the keyboard, a character-based menu containing a number of tonally grouped homophones "pops up" on the screen, requiring at least 2 further inputs from the operator to select the desired character. Other programs make use of 4-digit numerical codes, entered via the computer's keyboard, to represent individual Chinese characters (as opposed to syllables), which are then graphically displayed on the screen. This scheme, while obviously involving fewer discrete keyboard operations than the 3-step phonetic/syllabic technique, is not without drawbacks, since it requires the operator either to memorize several thousand 4-digit codes or to look up the code for each individual

Chinese character before entering it at the keyboard. Other schemes for processing Chinese characters have been developed both in China and abroad. Most of these systems require either a great deal of operator experience and expertise or a relatively large number of separate keyboard inputs.

Because Chinese character processing is still in its relative infancy, the task of writing new software—or adapting existing software to Chinese requirements—continues to be slow and tedious. For this reason, English has remained the language of choice for Chinese computer programmers and end-users involved in word-processing, database management, and electronic communications. Only in such highly specialized fields as computer-assisted design (CAD), industrial process control, and quantitative data processing has the language barrier proved to be relatively insignificant.

For all the above reasons the average Chinese computer user has yet to find the world of microcomputing particularly accessible or hospitable. Once Pac-Man and Space Invaders have been mastered (some computer programs are omni-lingual), the fact remains that precious few "user-friendly" software applications are currently available to the non-specialist in China. . . .

Conclusion: Communism and the Computer

We turn, finally, to what many observers regard as the most important—and most enigmatic—political variable affecting China's computerization drive: the CCPs monopolistic control over the media of mass communication. Precisely because computers make it technically feasible to circumvent official, approved channels of communication in the dissemination of ideas and information, they are sometimes seen as posing an innate threat to the power of Communist elites and institutions. Christopher Evans thus argues that the spread of cheap, universal computer power will erode traditional restraints on the flow of information in Leninist systems by "encouraging . . . the spread of information across the base of the social pyramid." Such a development, he argues, "favors the kind of open society which most of us in the West enjoy today, and has just the opposite effect on autocracies." And he predicts that, by the end of the 1980s, "even the most ardent Marxist will probably have to bow to the overwhelming [democratizing] testimony of the microprocessor."

Not all analysts, however, are so certain of the corrosive effects of the information revolution on Communist Party control. Erik Hoffmann argues that the process of computerization will almost surely *not* produce major changes in the Soviet polity, since "modern information technology is likely to be integrated or absorbed into existing bureaucratic value systems and behavioral patterns." By carefully controlling both access to and end-uses of computers, he argues, Soviet elites can ensure that control over electronic data processing will remain in the hands of "generalist" politicians and loyal party technocrats, thereby serving to "reinforce and intensify centralized control over strategic decisions." With computers remaining a narrowly confined producer good rather than a freely available consumer good, there is relatively little danger, Hoffmann avers, of a significant, computer-driven erosion of Soviet political power.

To date, the Soviet experience has proven inconclusive. Few knowledgeable observers of Soviet affairs have claimed to detect any substantial diminution in the degree of bureaucratic control or Communist Party domination in recent years. Yet, the much-publicized *glasnost* (openness) campaign of Mikhail Gorbachev has raised profound questions about the causal relationship between an ever-rising flow of secular communications in Soviet society (facilitated, *inter alia,* by the spread of telephones, television, computers, and other technological carriers of the "information revolution") and the generation of internal pressures for political democratization.

If the Soviet case seems ambiguous, the Chinese case is, in some ways, even more perplexing. On the one hand, China is clearly at a more primitive stage of technological development than the USSR, its economy less information-dependent than the latter. With only about 6 telephones per 1,000 population, China lags well behind both the Soviet Union (92 telephones per 1,000) and Taiwan (210 per 1,000). In this connection, a leading Western expert on the "information revolution" has argued that the critical point beyond which an autocratic regime finds it difficult to maintain its power monopoly is when 20 percent of its population have telephones. Measured against this rather impressionistic yardstick, China is at least one or two decades away from the threshold of political criticality.

Television, on the other hand, has become an immensely popular and readily available medium of mass communications in the PRC. With almost 50 percent of China's urban households reportedly owning TV sets, it has been estimated that the 1985 Superbowl may have had a larger potential viewing audience in China (where it was nationally broadcast several months after the event via microwave relay) than in the United States. Other things being equal, it would appear that television has far greater potential as an electronic disseminator of new ideas, information, and values than computers, which are, after all, both exceedingly rare in China today (0.1 per 1,000 population, compared with 50 TV sets per 1,000) and almost exclusively *danwei*-owned and operated. Moreover, an ordinary xerox machine (of which there were an estimated 10,000 in China in 1985) is capable of making more copies of a given document—whether authorized text or underground *samizdat*— in a single hour than a high-speed dot-matrix printer attached to a ·computer can print out in an entire day. And, finally, while it is certainly true that the technology embodied in the microcomputer is revolutionary indeed, the nature and magnitude of its effects upon the state/Party apparatus and political culture of Communist systems has yet to be demonstrated with any clarity.

For all these reasons, it seems advisable to resist the temptation to overstate the probable political impact of the computer in China. In the long term, the ongoing global revolution in information technology (of which computerization is an important part) may well be subversive of Communist monocracy, and perhaps even fatally so; but the near-term effects of the computer per se upon the organization and operation of the Leninist polity remain both highly problematical and extremely difficult to document.

Part 6

The Future

Edited by Steven M. Goldstein

Introduction

Steven M. Goldstein

Predicting China's future is a hazardous business. For example, few would have thought that the Communist stragglers who reached the north of China after the legendary Long March of the 1930s would be ruling China in 1949. The only thing predictable about China is that, more likely than not, developments there will take an unpredictable course. There is another pitfall in Chinese futurology: the historic tendency among Americans to predict China's future in accord with their own prejudices and hopes, and then to turn against China when these hopes—usually unrealistic—are not realized. On and off during the last one hundred years, we have seen China becoming "more like us." Each time such expectations are raised, China has dashed them by once more changing direction, causing disillusionment and, frequently, hostility on the American side.

Most recently, there have been signs that this syndrome is once more in operation. During the height of the post-Mao reform, the national media depicted China as finally going down the path of capitalism. President Reagan spoke of the "so-called Communists" in Beijing. Deng Xiaoping was lionized as the "pragmatist" who would bring China back into step with major global currents. Then came the April–June 1989 events in Tiananmen. Overnight American images of China changed.

Instead of being the epitome of what reform in socialist countries should be like, China was seen as regressing in the hands of orthodox

"hardliners." Deng the reformer was vilified. As change swept the socialist countries of the Soviet Union and Eastern Europe, China seemed
hopelessly out of step. American hopes for China had once more been
dashed. Would the cycle of mutual hostility be started once again?

In the readings that follow we present a sampling of the debate
that developed regarding the proper response to the events at
Tiananmen, which some American specialists on China feared might
rekindle the hostility of the past. This controversy points up the importance of the American public coming to grips with two central challenges: understanding the factors shaping the course of the changes
occurring in China and defining the limits of the influence which outsiders have to affect that change.

China's Reform Movement: To Tiananmen

From 1978 to 1989 the political, economic, and social fabric of China
was dramatically transformed. A reform process such as this, which
seeks to restructure long-standing attitudes and institutions, poses an
enormous challenge to political leadership and institutions. Reforms as
ambitious as these make three demands on the reformers: they must
have a consistent policy, a strong political apparatus to apply it, and the
leadership unity and determination to persevere during times of political and social disturbances. Events at Tiananmen demonstrated that
China's reform effort was deficient in all three respects.

In formulating reform policy, the leadership seemed aware of the
destabilizing effects of a too-rapid dismantling of the planned economic
system. Seeking to cushion the shocks of inflation, unemployment, and
bureaucratic resistance, the decision was made to carry out a partial or
gradual reform. In the realm of prices, a "dual price" structure was
created, whereby some goods traded at both market and state-controlled
(usually lower) prices. In respect to supply, some goods continued to be
allocated by state bureaucracies and others traded on the market. Finally, seeking to cushion the impact of the market, the government
committed itself to continuing subsidies of individuals and enterprises.

Such partial policies backfired. The existence of a dual economy
was an invitation to official corruption, as continuing bureaucratic control over resources led to speculation, bribery, and the granting of special favors to family or friends. The inevitable inflation that accompanies
even the limited introduction of market prices was made worse not only

by the existence of such speculation, but also by the increases in money supply required by rising subsidies and declining revenues. By the summer and fall of 1988, overambitious local investment had contributed to an overheated economy. Inflation in China was running as high as 40 percent, with evidence of panic buying in the major cities. Widespread corruption and nepotism were an acknowledged fact.

Of course, many of these problems were not simply the result of poor policy. They could be ascribed to weaknesses in the Chinese polity. For example, the corruption suggested deeper pathologies in the Chinese political system; government deficits that necessitated inflationary policies could be ascribed to a weak banking and tax structure; the uncontrollable local investment suggested poor central control of local economies, and so forth. Thus, in the years from 1978 to 1989, it became apparent that Deng's efforts to create efficient government instruments for economic change had failed.

In that decade a final problem with the Chinese reform effort became apparent. The course of the reforms began to take its toll on leadership unity and resolve. The reform movement was begun in the late 1970s by a group of senior leaders, some of whom had, since the early 1960s, been formulating a program for the reform of China's socialist system. Their fate during the Cultural Revolution only increased their determination to effect reform. Joined by a number of talented younger cadres, they provided the necessary prestige and bureaucratic connections to promote the cause of reform. However, by 1985 it became apparent that there were divisions within this leadership. Some were concerned about the destabilizing impact of further reform and argued for a slowing down of the process of change. Others stressed the importance of continuing the reform and seemed prepared to tolerate greater social instability as a necessary price for change. Deng played an uncertain role. Sometimes he intervened on the side of the reformers, but at other times, such as when he accepted the removal of a possible successor, Hu Yaobang, he seemed prepared to slow or halt reform when his prized political and social stability seemed to be in danger. In short, as the accumulated political and social pressures of a decade of reform pressed upon the leaders, they became more disunited and less certain of China's course.

A crucial juncture was reached more than six months before the public demonstrations in Tiananmen. Many in the leadership believed that reform was moving too quickly and pushing China to the brink of

crisis. Growing inflation, an overheated economy, and signs of consumer uneasiness led to a decision in the summer of 1988 to call a halt
to some basic elements of the reform. The more conservative Premier
Li Peng replaced the reformist Party chief Zhao Ziyang in the day-to-day
management of China. In the months that followed, price reform was
put on hold, central economic controls were re-established, and credit
was tightened. It was in the midst of this more conservative drift in
policy—during April of 1989—that the reformist Hu Yaobang died, and
the demonstrations in Tiananmen began, which would continue until
their ugly suppression on the night of June 3–4.

The issues behind the demonstrations were complex. On the one
hand, the demonstrators were protesting against many of the problems
that had been created by the reform effort—inflation, corruption, and
nepotism (see chapter 24). But they were also concerned that the brief
interlude of consolidation under Li Peng might presage a halt to the
reform movement and regression to a less liberal economy and polity.
The occasion of Hu Yaobang's funeral seemed an appropriate time
rekindle the demand for forward movement in reform. In a sense, then,
the protesters were reacting both to too little as well as to too much
reform.

For nearly two months the Chinese leadership equivocated. This
lack of action can be attributed to concern over the impact of any coercive actions on the international community (Soviet leader Gorbachev
visited in May and brought the world's media to Beijing); to the chilling
impact repression might have on China's intellectuals; and, most of all,
to divisions within the leadership. However, there was never any real
readiness on the part of most of China's leaders to make concessions.
Deng Xiaoping and other leaders' overarching concern with the importance of stability to China's reform effort precluded any concessions.
Moreover, the humiliating fact that the nation's leaders often lacked
access to a major public area during the Sino-Soviet summit and the
undoubted sense of Cultural Revolution *déja vu* that Deng and his colleagues must have felt as masses of people swarmed through the middle
of the city, could only have strengthened the resolve to restore order.

In the year after Tiananmen, China changed in some very fundamental ways. Although economic reform discussions continued, except
on the subject of privatization, there was really very little forward movement in that area. Pointing to the necessity of stabilizing the economic
environment, the leadership reimposed many central-planning controls,

tightened credit, increased control over foreign trade, forced the curtailment of projects not considered essential to the economy, and moved very cautiously on price reform. However, these were measures intended to stabilize an economy suffering from the effects of the previous reforms. They did not, by any means, represent a wholesale repeal of the reforms of the previous years. Indeed, much of the previous economic reform program remained—particularly in the rural areas and in regard to foreign trade and investment. It was in the political realm that major changes—indeed retrogression—occurred after the spring of 1989. Talk of political reform virtually stopped. The campaign against "bourgeois liberalization" made it clear that the boundaries of the permissible had once more narrowed. More ominously, the enhanced role of the Party and the growing power of the military and police suggested a considerable tightening of the authoritarian controls of the Chinese regime.

China's Reform Movement: Beyond Tiananmen

To its own people and to the world as a whole, the Chinese leadership after Tiananmen sought to present an image of a nation in which nothing had changed. A plot by "domestic and foreign hostile forces ... to overthrow leadership by the Chinese Communist Party, subvert the socialist system, and turn China into a bourgeois republic and a dependency of developed capitalist countries" had been foiled. China could now return to the business of reform and economic construction. However, it was not that simple. Tiananmen marked a new period in the development of post-Mao China. It will cast a long shadow over China's development in the years ahead.

This is attributable to four factors operating at the leadership level. First, as a result of Tiananmen, a fundamental shift occurred in the political configuration at the top. With the purge of Zhao Ziyang, the balance of political influence tilted towards those in the leadership who were either flatly opposed to further reform or who viewed reform with reservations. Second, the fact of Zhao's purge and the irregular manner in which it occurred suggest a significant escalation in the stakes of political conflict over reform as well as uncertainty about the institutions in which such conflict might occur. Third, as commentators such as Lowell Ditmer have noted, as result of the events at Tiananmen there has been a strengthening of bureaucracies opposed to reform at the expense of those that might promote it. The more conservative military, central-planning, and police bureaucracies have become more influential, even as some of the scientific academies and think-tanks that spawned much of the reform program have been closed down or have seen their activities curtailed. Fourth, Tiananmen and the events that followed in Eastern Europe have stigmatized reform in the eyes of China's current leaders. In their minds, reform must be implemented with extreme caution while maintaining authoritarian political control, lest the turmoil of Tiananmen recur or, even worse, they suffer the fate of the ousted leaders of Eastern Europe. For them, the central lesson of Tiananmen is that reform is something to be implemented cautiously and slowly—if at all.

Of course, the events surrounding Tiananmen also had an impact on the population. For many urban dwellers, the inflation and corruption that precipitated the demonstrations might have engendered a similar lack of enthusiasm for renewed reform. Moreover, it seems clear that in Beijing, at least, the impact of the reforms has been to engender considerable cynicism regarding the regime and a decided lack of responsiveness to its renewed ideological appeals. This attitude seems particularly prevalent among the many intellectuals who have borne the brunt of post-Tiananmen political campaigns.

These will be the major factors shaping the future of China in the near term. While portions of the population seem sullen and unresponsive to ideological appeals, it is unlikely that any new mass outbursts will occur. At the elite level, the political balance among China's top leaders and institutions suggests that the basic thrust of policy in the near term will be that of muddling through. Conservative by nature and shaken by the disturbances of Tiananmen, where they confronted the consequences of reform, China's leaders lack the political will to initiate any major reform efforts for fear that they might destabilize the current calm. However, it is also unlikely that they will undo major aspects of the economic reform. Under the rubric of "consolidation" they can be expected to maintain many of the earlier policies—and even initiate some new reforms—as long as it seems consonant with their emphasis on political stability and vigilance against ideological erosion. China may well come to look like Brezhnev's Russia: a country in which an aging leadership shaken by earlier reform efforts (those of Khrushchev) presided over a sputtering, partially reformed system.

Of course, as was the case in the Soviet Union, there are natural limits to such a future. A year after Tiananmen, the Chinese economy was starting to exhibit some of the problems that motivated the reform effort in the first place, as well as others that are the result of the post-1988 retrenchment policies. It is unclear whether incrementalism and muddling through will be a sufficient response to them. But most importantly, China will soon be addressing the issue of the succession to China's paramount leader, the eighty-six-year-old Deng Xiaoping. Deng has dominated Chinese politics since 1978, and his passing will pose the greatest challenge to the political system since Mao's death.

It was an awareness of the gravity of this challenge that motivated Deng to seek to settle the succession issue before his passing. However, as we have seen above, in large part because of his own impatience with his chosen successors, this has not been accomplished. Although in the wake of Tiananmen, he tapped yet a third candidate for successor, Jiang Zemin, former Party Secretary in Shanghai, most observers believe that a bitter political struggle will follow Deng's death. While it is impossible to predict the course that this struggle will take, the past decade of reform in China and the events elsewhere in the socialist world suggest three likely scenarios for the near future.

The first draws on the political legacy of Tiananmen. During that turbulent period, bitter elite divisions seemed to override the political institutions and procedures that Deng had sought to put into place during the previous decade. In a succession struggle, with the political stakes raised by Deng's death, elite divisions would be even sharper and the conflict more bitter. And, as has been the case in the past, differences at the very top might stimulate renewed activism from below—not only from the masses but from the localities of China. In this most dire scenario, elite divisions and social conflict could, as it did during the Cultural Revolution, result in a form of civil war and near breakdown of the polity.

A second near-term scenario also assumes a succession process shaped by Tiananmen, but the outcome is less apocalyptic. Fear of the consequences of bitter conflict at the top might actually bring the post-Deng leadership together and generate a consensus to continue the cautious, more conservative approach to reform characteristic of the post-Tiananmen period. While there would be no bold reform visions or initiatives, there might be some tinkering with economic mechanisms, even as political control is strengthened. In this scenario, there would be a somewhat marketized economy working within the context of a strengthened economic plan and greater limits on private enterprise. There might be greater controls over the foreign business presence in China and stronger government intervention in the agricultural sphere. Finally, there would have to be a continued lowering of popular expectations, both in regard to maintaining past rates of economic improvement and, for the intellectuals, in respect to political reform, which would almost certainly be avoided. Whether the leadership would have the will and the unity to implement such a program and whether it could be economically and politically viable are, of course, major questions regarding this scenario. However, this scenario of semi-reform draws strength not only from the aversion of both the elite and the masses to the uncertainties of a more sweeping reform, but also from its strong resonances with important themes in Chinese political culture: economic nationalism, desire for stability, and authoritarian control from above.

The third and final scenario is premised on the fact that succession struggles in Communist states are frequently times of political ferment when radical new ideas come forward. It assumes that conservative economic and political measures are not successful and that the economy once again shows the pathologies of Soviet-style planning. Stability becomes stagnation and popular dissatisfaction grows, due to the failure of an authoritarian government to deliver an improved economy. This scenario recognizes that there are constituencies in China that might benefit from reform and that, despite the lack of reform action after Tiananmen, many of the reformers have continued to work and publish their views. A bold, vigorous leader with a reform vision could exploit the economic difficulties of a semi-reformed economy and draw on the backlog of past reform proposals to effect dramatic change in China, much as Mikhail Gorbachev did after the stagnation of the Brezhnev years. The precise nature of this change would be impossible to define. It would simply mean that China, like the Soviet Union and Eastern Europe, would resume its navigation of the uncharted waters of reforming a centrally planned economy—with all the hazards identified earlier.

The United States and China

The discussion thus far has been based on the assumption that China's future will be shaped exclusively by domestic factors. This is, of course, misleading. To be sure, China is not like Eastern Europe, where the major impetus for change in 1989 came from external events—primarily developments in the Soviet Union. However, neither has China been immune from international developments. As the events at Tiananmen demonstrated, the previous decade of liberalized contact with the outside world—both socialist and capitalist—profoundly shaped the thinking and aspirations of many Chinese. By travel and study abroad as well as through the electronic media, once isolated Chinese were able to measure themselves and their system against world standards.

As Martin Whyte argues in chapter 63, this process reopened for many Chinese the historical dilemma of defining their own place—and that of their nation—in that world. For China's leaders, it rekindled a long-standing dilemma: to what extent could China import *technology* from abroad without also leaving the country open to foreign *ideas* that might change its very essence? The article by Liu Maoyin (chapter 65) demonstrates that concern in very blunt language: to the post-Tiananmen leadership, the West sought to use China's involvement in the world economy to achieve a "peaceful evolution" away from socialism and towards capitalism. They were determined to increase ideological vigilance and monitor international contacts to guard against such an eventuality.

For the United States, China's growing involvement in the world community posed equally difficult dilemmas. Post-Mao foreign policy was, for the most part, a welcome change for American business people and politicians alike. The economic open door seemed to be the beginning, at last, of access to the fabled China market. And although Washington and Beijing never saw completely eye-to-eye on global and regional politics, an involved, constructive Chinese foreign policy was certainly preferable to the hostility and frequent isolation of the Mao period. In 1978–89, Sino-American relations seemed to be building on a solid and multi-faceted foundation. For American policy-makers, the brutal suppression of the Tiananmen demonstrators was a rude shock and presented them with a difficult question: what is the proper balance to be struck between expressing justifiable outrage at the treatment of the Tiananmen demonstrators and preserving the accomplishments of the past decade of Sino-American relations?

The section that follows presents a sampling of opinion on this question, particularly as related to the issue of economic sanctions against China. The questions raised are complex ones. They highlight the difficulties of pressuring leaders who seem indifferent to international opinion and ready to use foreign disapproval to mobilize the potent force of Chinese nationalism; of reconciling the necessity of registering some American disapproval with the danger that basic links between the two countries might be endangered; and, finally, as with the issue of China's "most favored nation" status, of measuring the efficacy of direct efforts to shape the direction of change in China versus more passive postures (such as simply keeping open economic and cultural links that might strengthen certain political constituencies or orientations within China).

There are no easy answers to these questions. China is continuing a process of transformation that began more than two hundred years ago and which, while conditioned by the nature of the outside world, has been decisively shaped by domestic factors. If the past is any guide, outsiders will find themselves consistently frustrated in their attempts to shape China's evolution. More often than not, those outside the nation must resign themselves to the role of observers, who, while having a vital interest in the evolution of China, have precious few resources to influence it.

China's Prospects

63

Evolutionary Changes in Chinese Culture

Martin K. Whyte

One of the most enduring—and unresolved—issues on the Chinese political agenda has been that of defining the nature of the prevailing cultural orthodoxy. In this essay, written before the events surrounding Tiananmen, Martin K. Whyte of the University of Michigan discusses this issue in the context of broader evolutionary changes in Chinese culture. His cautionary statements regarding the volatile nature of this question seem justified in the wake of the events of April–June 1989.

Does China need a uniform set of values and cultural practices to remain unified as a nation and develop and prosper? If so, what combination of traditional Chinese customs and values, Marxist-Leninist (or Maoist) practices, and Western influences should be used to mold Chinese culture in the reform era? Is it even possible to forge a new cultural orthodoxy out of such disparate elements? Should any such cultural orthodoxy be allowed to emerge naturally out of the competition among different ideas and cultural systems, or should the central authorities strictly control what cultural elements are allowed and attempt to define and impose their vision of a cultural orthodoxy on the population? Many countries in Asia and elsewhere have grappled with the problem of how to combine native and foreign cultural elements into a cohesive whole. But in China during the reform both the fact that not two but three distinct cultural alternatives are under contention—traditional Chinese, Marxist-Leninist/socialist, and Western—and that there have been such erratic swings in governmental preference for and suppression of these alternatives in the past makes the problem of defining and developing a cultural orthodoxy particularly difficult. . . .

Mao's Revolution and Chinese Culture

At first glance, it might appear that the victory of the Chinese Communist Party (CCP) in 1949 marked a fundamental victory of alien Western culture over traditional Chinese culture. After all, the CCP itself was a product of the May Fourth Period, when Mao Zedong and other founders of the CCP vigorously denounced the evils of traditional Confucian ways, eagerly read recently translated Marxist texts, and tried to follow events in the newly established Soviet Union. When the CCP came to power in 1949, Marxism-Leninism (or Marxism-Leninism-Mao Zedong Thought) was proclaimed the new orthodoxy, and Confucianism and a whole range of traditional customs and values were denounced and suppressed.

The hostility of the CCP toward traditional Chinese culture only reached its zenith during the last ten years of Mao's life. During the early years of the Cultural Revolution (1966–69), Red Guards, inspired by Mao, ransacked private homes and vandalized temples and monuments in an effort to eliminate the "four olds"—old ideas, culture, customs, and habits. . . .

The Overlap between Maoist Rule and Chinese Tradition

It would be oversimplifying things to view the period of Mao's rule as an overall assault on traditional Chinese culture and the reform era as primarily a revival of this long-suppressed traditional culture. The reality is much more complex. Even though the CCP espoused a Western ideology, Marxism-Leninism, the establishment of the People's Republic in 1949 in no way constituted a victory for wholesale Westernization and a repudiation of traditional Chinese values. In certain very basic respects, Maoist rule emphasized fundamental Chinese traditions and defended these against rival Western ideas. It may not be too far-fetched to argue that Maoism in power represented a last effort, now abandoned (at least for the moment), to defend traditional Chinese culture against Western cultural influence.

To be sure, the CCP was not simply a traditional dynasty disguised in Marxist-Leninist slogans. A variety of far-reaching institutional changes were made in Chinese society; many traditional customs and cultural practices (such as arranged marriages, burials, spirit mediums, and kowtowing to elders) were discouraged or banned; and new ideas, concepts, and cultural forms were forcefully introduced, in some cases in the face of popular resistance or incomprehension. . . .

But in certain respects Maoist rule was not really so iconoclastic and, in fact, was deeply rooted in Chinese tradition. Ancient Chinese assumptions about social order were built upon and reinforced, even though they began to be interpreted in Marxist-Leninist, rather than in Confucian, terms. Society was conceived of a vast bureaucratic hierarchy in which every individual was to have a place and be subordinated to the social group (now termed a *collective*) in which he or she was enmeshed. National unity was to be fostered by developing a coherent set of values (to which the specifically modern term *ideology* would apply) that would mandate how to behave, rather than by promulgating a national code of laws and administrative procedures. Primary duties of political leaders at every level, as in imperial China, were to maintain the coherence of the official ideology, to indoctrinate the population, and to enforce compliance. Any conception of autonomous subgroups, independent cultural innovation, or a free-wheeling competition of ideas was directly contrary to the Maoist ethos, as it was to the traditional imperial doctrines.

So the content of the culture in Maoist China was in many ways new, but the idea that China required a uniform culture to survive as a nation and that the authorities should enforce an orthodoxy to maintain cultural, and thus political, cohesion was very old. Indeed, the vigor with which Mao and those around him imposed their new orthodoxy reflected the fact that their Marxist-Leninist convictions in this instance reinforced traditional Chinese assumptions. Socialism entails central planning and regulation not only of economic production but also of all social life, including culture and values. In contrast to traditional Chinese thought, the prevailing image of society in Marxism-Leninism is a society as a single, well-regulated factory, rather than as a hierarchical chain of human relationships, but the implications are much the same. There is one correct way for society to be organized, and cultural unity and officially imposed ideology play central roles in maintaining societal cohesion. Allowing alternative values and cultural practices would hinder the pursuit of socialism and communism and foster political disunity.

Enforcing a New Cultural Orthodoxy

In spite of the considerable overlap between traditional Chinese and Marxist-Leninist assumptions about cultural unity, there is also a basic difference in practice. The CCP, using modern technology, a huge central bureaucracy, and organizational practices learned from the Soviet Union, had the wherewithal to put these ideas into practice much more thoroughly than its imperial predecessors ever could have dreamed. The result was much tighter central control over schooling, the mass media, literature, the performing arts, social life, and even styles of dress and leisure activities. Even prior to the Cultural Revolution, the CCP had successfully used its increased powers to change traditional Chinese culture. From suppressing secret societies to campaigning against mah-jongg, from reforming Chinese opera plots to purging and standardizing school textbooks—all facets of Chinese cultural life witnessed the activist efforts of China's communist revolutionaries. Still, the goal was to forge a Chinese society united around a common set of values and ideas—a very traditional goal.

The Maoists used the power of the state vigorously to exclude Western cultural influences and, after 1960, even Soviet influence. . . .

The CCP did not exclude all foreign influences entirely (although during the Cultural Revolution it nearly did). Foreign influences penetrated China only in a manner that the government chose and on the government's terms. Western orchestras on tour and Western exchange students were allowed, whereas listening to foreign radio broadcasts and independent travel abroad were not. Special hotels, stores, and travel arrangements were developed in the 1950s under the pretext of shielding foreign visitors form the hardships of Chinese life, but their more basic purpose was to protect most of Chinese society from possible "contamination" by foreign guests. The desire of China's nineteenth-century modernizing elite to carefully screen foreign influences and selectively admit only those elements deemed practical had eluded them but came much closer to being realized by their post-1949 successors. . . .

The Reforms and Chinese Culture

The death of Mao Zedong in 1976 and the implementation of the reform program by his successors have produced a rethinking of all aspects of the Maoist social order. This, in turn, has resulted in a reaction against the rigid and impoverished cultural straitjacket that characterized China during Mao's last decade in power. In most respects, the reformers have allowed and encouraged a very broad cultural liberalization.

Writers have been permitted to explore the dark side of society and to depict themes, such as romantic love and distaste for politics, that Mao's partisans had tried to ban during the Cultural Revolution. Artists have been allowed to revive traditional styles and to experiment with a variety of Western forms, including abstract and surrealistic art. Freedom of religious belief and practice has been reinstated, and Buddhist temples, Islamic mosques, and Christian churches have been revived and refurbished with official approval and are to be staffed by both rehabilitated religious leaders and new graduates of reopened monasteries and seminaries. School curricula have been revamped with a renewed emphasis on pure academics and the establishment of formerly proscribed or neglected fields, such as law, sociology, political science, and business management.

The mass media have witnessed an explosion; a few tightly controlled and highly politicized publications have been replaced by a bewildering variety of new, specialized journals, catering to those interested in calligraphy, classical Western music, the martial arts, weightlifting, and other decidedly nonpolitical realms. . . .

Official tolerance of differing ideological ideas has also increased. Ideas that would have been risky to express a few years ago, such as having officials be bound by laws, recognizing and allowing interest groups to compete in the political arena, or making divorce easier, can now be expressed. Controls over the communications technologies that facilitate the transmission of ideas and cultural products independently of the state have been relaxed. Computers and printers, cassette recorders, mimeograph machines, photocopying machines, and videotape recorders are not found everywhere, but an increasing number of them are in the hands of private individuals and local organizations who use them in a variety of ways, not all of which please the authorities.

Of course, there are clear limits to the reform-era liberalization.

Perhaps the most important, the ideas and cultural products of the late Mao era are for the most part now proscribed, and there is political risk in advocating them.... Still, the growing diversity and liveliness of cultural life in the post-Mao era is indisputable.

Impact on Chinese Traditional Practices

The traditional cultural legacy has been a major beneficiary of the post-Mao liberalization. There are signs everywhere in China today of a revival of a variety of traditional Chinese practices. A vast amount of new research and publishing on ancient and imperial China is under way. The past no longer has to be portrayed as a simple conflict between heroic but oppressed peasants and evil and cruel landowners and officials. Traditional operas, music and dance, and performance troupes and associations dedicated to the preservation of these arts, have been revived. Traditional-style painting, calligraphy, and other fine arts have enjoyed a renaissance as well, and there is a new pride emerging in China's artistic heritage. Many tombs, monuments, and temples have been renovated and reopened, and they are less likely now to be accompanied by signs describing the exploitation and misery the common people suffered during their construction.

Confucius has also been "rehabilitated." His ancestral temple and adjacent facilities have been refurbished, new journals and associations devoted to the study of his writings have been established, and international symposia have been convened on the lessons of Confucian ideas for the modern world. An underlying theme in this "neo-neo-Confucianism" is that the great philosopher's values must have played a role in explaining the economic successes of the other East Asian Confucian societies (Japan, Taiwan, South Korea, Hong Kong, and Singapore); therefore, the People's Republic could benefit as well from renewed respect for his legacy. In addition to the possible material benefits, it is argued that greater stress on Confucian values like moderation, benevolence, harmony, and filial piety will help to overcome the social conflicts and frayed nerves that are legacies of the Mao era.

Of course, the authorities do not look positively upon all the traditional Chinese practices that are reviving, such as lavish weddings and funerals, siting graves in arable fields, investment by peasants in constructing new ancestral lineage halls instead of schools; secret societies and Daoist sects; fortune tellers, spirit mediums, and traffickers in women; and female infanticide. Some forms of corruption that appear to be widespread in the reform era, involving demands for bribes and manipulation of personal connections, are also perceived as reflecting harmful traditional "feudalist" influences.

Western Cultural Influences

The relaxation of official controls and the open-door policy have fostered a major new infusion of Western cultural influences. The reform policies have increased the number of diplomats, foreign businessmen, teachers, and tourists in China and have resulted in tens of thousands of Chinese traveling to the West, either on short business trips or for extended periods of study. Contacts have intensified with Chinese living abroad who have already made their accommodations with Western cultural practices, and particularly with Chinese from Hong Kong and Macao and those visiting from Taiwan. The number of Taiwanese returning to visit has been increasing since 1987. . . .

Most foreign broadcasts are no longer banned or jammed, and in fact listening to them is an approved way to help develop valuable foreign language skills. Foreign movies and television series are now regularly shown in China, although the selection criteria are obscure. . . .

Along with these forms of Western cultural influence, there are also officially sanctioned efforts to gain a new appreciation for Western institutions and values. Simplistic analyses of the America run by Wall Street conspirators have given way to efforts to understand how the American electoral system works, how Congress does its business, the role of think tanks and foundations, the influence of religious organizations, and other long-neglected topics. American Studies has been booming in Chinese academe, and the study of other foreign countries has also enjoyed a renaissance. . . .

However, not all of the Western influences in China today have new and external sources. In the reform era, those Chinese who were trained in the West or who were influenced by Western culture and ideas prior to 1949 have resurfaced, just as have champions of China's traditional culture. Surprisingly, these people not only show little sign of having been affected by decades of "thought reform" but also, in some cases, enthusiastically take up where they were so rudely interrupted by the revolution. Proposals and manifestoes drafted forty or more years ago are dusted off and aired for public discussion, friendship contacts overseas are reestablished, and writings disowned in the Mao era as tainted by bourgeois values are prepared hastily for republication. Similarly, communities that appeared earlier to have renounced their Christian faith have now resumed a vibrant level of religious activity, with few apparent losses of membership despite the long years of official persecution. And musicians trained in Western classical styles before 1949 have hurried to relearn their discarded repertoires and display their fondness for Mozart, Beethoven, and Bach once again. Thus the reform era has revealed that an important domestic constituency for Western culture survived the Mao era and is eager to lend its support to the new openness toward Western influence.

As with the revival of traditional Chinese culture, the authorities are by no means pleased with all of the new forms of Western cultural influence. Considerable debate has surrounded the appearance in China of such things as bodybuilding and beauty contests. Critics cite a long list of harmful influences that have erupted in China at least partly as a result of the open-door policy.... The open door, it is argued by critics, has fostered doubt about the virtues of socialism, China's institutions, and the leadership of the CCP, and may be creating perceptions that the institutions and values of foreign societies are superior. The same theme was sounded in the early 1950s—Chinese must be dissuaded from the notion that "the American moon shines brighter than the Chinese moon."

Even though there have been persistent efforts to monitor and control foreign contacts and to prevent harmful ideas and practices from entering, the increase in foreign influence has been so rapid, and its forms so massive and diverse, that it has proved impossible for the authorities to effectively monitor and control everything. To some extent this inability is inherent in the reform process itself, for the granting of local autonomy that is vital to the economic reforms inevitably leads to activities and influences that are outside of the range of central controls.

Cultural Dilemmas

Given the increased cultural liveliness and diversity in recent years, the questions persists as to how much the basic rules of the system have changed. Does the increased "blooming and contending," involving traditional Chinese and Western alongside socialist cultural practices and

symbols, indicate that the authorities' efforts to impose cultural uniformity have ceased? This is far from being the case, although the issue
could be debated. There are, to be sure, some intellectuals and some
reformers who come close to adopting a Western "marketplace of ideas"
argument—that the open door and other current policies are good because they introduce many new ideas and cultural practices, that the
competition among ideas and practices will be a healthy way to weed
out bad or outmoded elements, and that as a result a modified and
stronger, more dynamic Chinese culture will emerge.

Two points should be noted about this sort of argument. First, it
seems to represent the view of a minority, with most participants in the
cultural debate being uncomfortable with the sort of unbridled cultural
competition being advocated. Second, even in this minority view, competition and variety in the cultural realm are perceived as necessary but
temporary. The necessity arises from China's need to recover from the
isolation and cultural impoverishment that Mao led the nation into in
his final years. Once the elements of a modified and revitalized Chinese
culture have been identified, the competition would be curtailed, with
a new and improved cultural orthodoxy dominant. In other words, even
in this minority and apparently proto-Western view, permanent cultural
competition of the sort that appears to reign in the West is rejected as
too chaotic for China.

Many if not most participants in the debate on the future of Chinese
culture are not even willing to go as far as this minority position. Even
the temporary, free competition of ideas and values is seen as threatening to the social order. To those who hold this view, Chinese culture
needs to be modified and changed, but this should be done in a careful
and controlled manner. Individuals, groups, organizations, and localities should not have too much autonomy to experiment with new ideas
and practices. Rather, the authorities should identify those new elements that are suitable to modern life under Chinese conditions and
foster experimentation and innovation in those areas; other elements
that are not deemed so suitable should continue to be proscribed. This
is a familiar formula. It is very much a continuation of the "Chinese
learning as the foundation, Western learning for its practical applications" notion advocated by China's nineteenth-century modernizing
elite.

Critics of recent cultural trends differ on whether the resurgence
of traditional practices or the influx of Western influences is more prob-

lematic and potentially harmful. Some argue that China's most serious problems arose from the way centralized state socialism reinforced the worst, feudal tendencies of the traditional legacy, producing "little emperors" ruling over factories, offices, and schools throughout China. For such critics the revival of traditional cultural forms and the new respect given to Confucian ideas is particularly worrisome, since these can only make the effort to eliminate the "feudal remnants" from contemporary China more difficult.

Others argue, however, that Western influences pose more of a threat than the revived traditional practices. In addition to the greater familiarity of the traditional heritage, there is also the comfortable (but probably mistaken) view that harmful traditional practices are the products of backwardness and ignorance; therefore, with time, modernization, and rising educational levels, these will gradually disappear. No such assumption can be made about foreign influences. In addition to their being more alien to begin with, they are found in societies that are more modern and well educated than China. The dilemma for the screeners of such foreign influences, then, is how to identify which elements of Western culture are required by any modern society and thus have to be allowed to develop in China and which elements are unnecessary for China's modernization effort. Where do neckties, rock music, premarital sex, or for that matter electoral democracy and competitive individualism fit?

As the central authorities have struggled with these problems, they have been unable to come to a consensus. Clearly, the more radical among the reformers feel that China benefits from most of the new Western cultural infusions and that the resulting changes in Chinese practices to date have been too slow. In other words, the new influences have still only had a partial and superficial effect, mostly among the young and urban intellectuals, but have not yet had much impact on the deep recesses of Chinese organizations, families, and individual psyches. More conservative leaders perceive the infusions of Western influence to date as excessive and undesirable. They see the open door causing both a rising tide of social problems and a loss of national pride and faith in the system. These conservatives argue that the loss of centralized control over cultural innovation and transmission is even more dangerous than the specific kinds of harmful phenomena fostered, for it spells the doom of any serious attempt to forge cultural orthodoxy and will thus lead to political fragmentation and social chaos.

Twice in the 1980s these conservatives have managed to launch campaigns designed to gain greater control over Chinese cultural life and punish those involved in spreading "unhealthy" Western influences—in the Anti-Spiritual Pollution campaign of 1983–84 and the Anti-Bourgeois Liberalization campaign of 1987. That each of these conservative initiatives faltered after a few months, after claiming a few prominent victims and intimidating many others, does not mean the debate is now over. It merely indicates that for the moment the conservatives have not managed to gain sufficient support within the elite for a more thorough cultural crackdown.

Meanwhile, the ordinary population is confused and uncertain. The Chinese man and woman on the street (and rural lane), while generally appreciative of improved consumption standards and less oppressive political controls, often find the lack of clear consensus on values and cultural forms unsettling. For people who have grown up in a highly didactic and moralistic society, being faced with options and with no clear standards for selection is unfamiliar. Should they cultivate an interest in Western classical music, rock, traditional operas, Chinese folk tunes, or perhaps favorite martial tunes from the socialist tradition (or all of the above)? Should they wear the latest Western fashions or retain the proletarian drab of the Mao era? Should they push their children down the "white road" toward academic learning and expertise, the "yellow road" toward business success and financial wealth, or the "red road" toward political activism and party membership? How should they celebrate a family wedding or a funeral? How would they react if a son came home and announced he wanted to leave a state job to go into private business, live together with his girlfriend without benefit of marriage, or go into training to become a Buddhist monk?

This uneasiness of the general population has several sources. It is not simply that people are unfamiliar with being faced by such choices. Nor is it solely a matter of being nervous in the face of the uncharacteristic restraint of the CCP and worried that in the future, if this restraint is abandoned and cultural uniformity is again forcefully imposed, they may be criticized for having made the wrong choices. As much as anything else, this popular uneasiness can be attributed to the fact that both in imperial times and in the Maoist era, Chinese were accustomed to living in a society in which habits and cultural forms were infused with political and moral meanings that flowed from the cultural orthodoxy— a trait still very much alive. Even though China is an avowedly atheistic state, in a certain sense, until the reform era, China was a minimally secularized society. The sort of secularized, pragmatic societies in which Westerners have grown up, in which most spheres of daily life and culture are seen as detached from higher moral battles, has never been part of the Chinese experience. For this reason many Chinese have the gnawing feeling that they are sailing into uncharted seas without a clear moral rudder. Today's situation may then be interpreted not so much in terms of new freedoms and choices, but as a moral vacuum in which, for example, individuals are encouraged to get rich without experiencing the restraints of socialist, traditional Confucian, or Western moral values.

The efforts of the reformers to alleviate these concerns by formulating a revised ideological and moral framework to guide China in the new era have so far not been very convincing or satisfying to the population. The Chinese people are told that various ideas and practices are good or bad, but they are not given a clear set of principles to live by that would allow them to tell the difference. The concept of China being in the "primary stage of socialism," popularized by the reformers in 1987, does not seem to provide the needed moral guidance. This concept mainly justifies allowing traditional Chinese and Western capitalist, as well as socialist, practices to coexist for some time to come, as long as they contribute to modernization.

Many Chinese are skeptical of the idea that their society can be guided by a moral framework that simply says that whatever works economically is good and whatever does not is bad. Some Chinese thinkers are attempting to fill the moral void by adapting portions of Confucianism, the writings of the early Marx, and Western doctrines of individual rights and dignity to form a new amalgam they call Chinese humanism. However, these efforts are still at an early stage, and what guidance these new humanist ideas might provide for meeting a variety of problems in life is still not very clear. So, as yet, no coherent set of moral standards has emerged to replace those discredited by the excesses of the Cultural Revolution. The reformers worry that their conservative opponents may be able to play on public unease about the moral vacuum and cultural confusion to engineer a return to a more closed-door society with an imposed and anti-Western cultural orthodoxy.

China has struggled for more than a century to cope with the problems involved in adapting Chinese culture to the modern world. Because the Chinese define "being Chinese" in cultural terms and both the elite and the masses believe that forging a unifying cultural orthodoxy is vital, cultural debates have constantly spilled over into the political realm. Similarly, political leaders in imperial, Republican, Maoist, and reform-era China have all had devising and implementing the proper cultural policy high on their political agenda. But in spite of this century of efforts, the debate, particularly in terms of how Chinese culture will accommodate Western influence, is still unresolved, and arguments in this realm remain volatile. It is still very unclear whether a well-defined cultural orthodoxy will emerge from the new round of debates on these issues in Deng Xiaoping's China and what form that orthodoxy might take.

64

The Impact of Tiananmen on the Political Climate of Economic Reform

Nina P. Halpern

In the months after Tiananmen, many Western commentators were quick to declare the end of the Chinese reform movement. In the essay that follows, Nina Halpern of Stanford University suggests that such pronouncements might be premature. Through a careful study of post-Tiananmen policy, she demonstrates that while political reform has ceased and the climate for economic reform has certainly worsened, it appears that economic reform has been put on hold rather than removed from the political agenda altogether. A changed political environment could very well bring the reform issue back to the fore.

Following the brutal crackdown June 3–4, 1989 on the political demonstrations of the prior six weeks (these demonstrations, which centered on Tiananmen Square in Beijing, and the subsequent crackdown will hereafter be referred to as "the Tiananmen incident") and the initiation of the campaign against "bourgeois liberalization," many Western scholars pronounced the death of Chinese economic reform. Although such declarations had been made several times in the past and proved faulty (such as during the economic retrenchment of 1981–82 and the campaign against spiritual pollution in 1983–84), this time the case seemed far more plausible. The military-political crackdown of summer 1989 was far more severe than any of the earlier post-Mao responses to political dissent; the decision to initiate it brought back onto the political stage a group of relatively conservative Party elders (such as Chen Yun) who had earlier seemed to lack political clout; it resulted in the purge of CCP head Zhao Ziyang, widely regarded as the most enthusiastic and influential proponent within the leadership of far-reaching economic reform; and one could easily imagine (as many Western observers have) that the shaken Chinese political leaders would attribute the political demonstrations that almost caused their downfall to the economic reforms previously implemented and their legacy of problems such as inflation and corruption.

Although there were many signs that even prior to Tiananmen, the economic reforms were already in trouble for economic reasons—particularly skyrocketing inflation—many believe that Tiananmen was the final blow because it added to these more pragmatic economic concerns significant *political* obstacles to reform: particularly, an ideological bias against market-oriented reform. This anti-reform bias was said to be produced both by empowering more conservative leaders (e.g., Chen Yun) and by altering the thinking of formerly reformist ones (e.g., Deng Xiaoping). In the summer of 1989 there seemed good reason to expect the reversal of many of the reform measures introduced earlier, and a long-term retreat to a more centralized, planning-based approach to economic development.

Nevertheless, one year after Tiananmen, evidence is growing that once again Western observers have overestimated the extent of the policy reversal in China. Rather than a retreat from reform and return to a more conservative path, the economic policies of the past year appear to be a short-term attempt to cope with the economic crisis of the prior period. The major barrier to successful economic reform in the future does not appear to be the emergence of a new leadership consensus in favor of more central planning, but rather the same one that existed prior to Tiananmen: the absence of any real consensus within the leadership about which economic policies will resolve China's current economic problems while promoting future economic development. To be sure, Tiananmen has influenced the political climate of economic reform in several negative ways. . . . But in the future, these negative influences will be seen primarily in the difficulties of implementing economic reform measures and the continued failure of these measures to produce desired results, rather than in removal of economic reform from the political agenda.

How did the Tiananmen events and subsequent reaction to them influence the political setting of economic reform? Following the military crackdown on the demonstrators and removal of Zhao Ziyang as Party leader, the leadership was confronted with three major domestic political tasks. The first was essentially factional: to eliminate the political influence of Zhao Ziyang and those allied with him. The second was ideological: to forge a new consensus within the Party and government that would allow the leadership to work in a unified manner in addressing the country's problems. The third was to restore political control over the urban population and ensure future social stability. Intentionally or not, the CCP's responses to these three tasks have significantly affected the political environment of economic reform. . . .

. . . . The analysis will suggest that the leadership has been more successful in achieving its factional goals and in reasserting social control than in forging any new policy consensus. Although I will argue that the post-Tiananmen leadership generally lacks the ideological bias against economic reform often attributed to it, its political actions of the last year nevertheless suggest that the future of economic reform does not look very bright.

The Attack on Zhao Ziyang and the Elaboration of a New Policy Consensus

Zhao Ziyang's decision to defect from the hardline approach of the rest of the leadership, thereby encouraging the political demonstrations and slowing leadership efforts to address them, was a key element in the growth of the popular movement and the ultimate military confrontation. Thus, the post-Tiananmen leadership sought to solidify its own rule by eliminating the influence of Zhao Ziyang and his supporters, within both the elite and the population as a whole. In addition to arrests of some of his supporters, dissolution of some organizations and a reshuffling of the leadership of others, a barrage of articles began reassessing his ideas and legacy. Because the economic reform program was recognized as Zhao's most important legacy, the media campaign primarily involved a critique of certain reform ideas associated with Zhao and an illumination of their supposed negative consequences. . . . Even prior to Tiananmen, Zhao's influence over economic policy had waned considerably. As Premier Li Peng sought to assert himself as the primary economic decisionmaker, he also attempted to replace some of Zhao's policy formulations with his own. . . .

In the aftermath of Tiananmen, new ideological formulations regarding economic policy did appear in the media. Moreover, these were presented in such a way that few could doubt that they were explicitly intended to critique past policies associated with Zhao. However, after some months of media discussion, it became clear that these new formulations did not provide any clear direction for actual policy. Nor did they succeed in putting an end to the basic intellectual divisions over reform policy, which had characterized the pre-Tiananmen period.

A number of articles blamed Zhao for promoting "bourgeois liberalization." Because the primary purpose of these articles was to discredit Zhao and his followers, not to criticize the idea of economic reform, great efforts were made to argue that economic reform must be distinguished from "bourgeois liberalization," and that only the latter was being criticized. A *Renmin ribao (People's Daily)* editorial pointed out:

> The reform and opening up we speak of are reform and opening up on the basis of adhering to the four cardinal principles. However, in the past few years certain people have looked at reform and opening up from the viewpoint of bourgeois liberalization and opposed adhering to the four cardinal principles. The "reforms" they speak of actually mean changing to the capitalist road; the "opening up" they speak of actually means turning China into an appendage of imperialism.

This kind of statement is basically contentless, as far as setting a new direction for economic reform is concerned. Its purpose is essentially political: to separate the notion of economic reform from the leaders (especially Zhao Ziyang) with whom it was formerly identified, to reclaim the mantle of "real reformers" for the current leadership, and to discredit Zhao Ziyang and his allies politically. . . .

As the campaign against Zhao Ziyang and "bourgeois liberalism" progressed, several more specific issues emerged. These included different forms of ownership of the means of production, the role of planning and administration measures in the state's means of controlling enterprise behavior, and the appropriateness of income disparities between different segments of society and within particular groupings. In these discussions one can discern something of the vision of economic reform that Li Peng and others sought to promote. However, by commenting in different ways on these issues and specific economic reforms, economists managed to some extent to push their own particular agenda for reform. The campaign, intended to promote ideological and political unity, became instead a vehicle for continued intellectual debate, although in a much more constrained manner than before Tiananmen. This can best be illustrated through the discussions surrounding the issue of "privatization," [where a] large-scale campaign against the notion of "privatization" laid out no clear agenda for the future direction of economic reform. Although removing total privatization of state enterprises from the list of legitimate reform ideas, the campaign left ambiguous the status of stock markets, shareholding schemes, and bankruptcy, and the scope and treatment of private enterprises. Such ambiguity did not set a clear leadership agenda for action, end intellectual debates, or assure those engaged in these reform experiments any protection from unhappy cadres. . . .

The household responsibility system was one of the reforms always mentioned by top leaders as unchangeable, but as with the private economy, despite assurances of stability in policy, it soon became clear that a new formulation for thinking about the responsibility system was far more ambiguous, leaving room for some to push farmers in the direction of recollectivization. Again, the responsibility system could be (but not necessarily should be) blamed for real economic problems, such as neglect of infrastructure and inefficient, excessively small-scale operations. However, these problems were not addressed simply in economic terms, but rather by suggesting a new formula regarding the implications and significance of the responsibility system. As a January 1990 *Guangming ribao* article put it: "The rural production responsibility system with household operation as the basis does not contradict development of the collective economy but constitutes the realistic basis for its development." Despite the affirmations of long life for the responsibility system, the new approach suggested that ultimately, the purpose was to return the peasantry to collective farms—albeit this time on a voluntary basis. . . .

In both urban and rural policy, although the new ideological formulations did not reverse existing policy, and despite repeated official statements about the importance of continuing the responsibility system and private enterprise, it proved impossible to maintain popular faith that the policies would be continued. By reintroducing the criteria of "socialist and capitalist" rather than economic effects, and by introducing new, ambiguous and double-sided ideological formulations, the leadership left room for some to attack and oppose these reforms. Consequently, the campaign was more effective in attacking Zhao Ziyang than in achieving a clear basis for future reform or generating a consensus (even an imposed one) among leaders and intellectuals. Nor did it manage to assure the population that even the most widely agreed-upon reforms would remain stable.

Political Reform

In the second half of 1986, it was widely agreed within the elite that continued progress in economic reform required further political reform. In the course of the discussion that took place at that time, two distinct views of political reform emerged. One focused on political issues, calling political reform necessary for its own sake, and often emphasizing the importance of democratization. This strand of the discussion helped produce student demonstrations for democracy in the winter of 1986–87, which led to the fall of Party General Secretary Hu Yaobang. The more dominant strand of the discussion, clearly more in line with the views of Deng Xiaoping (and probably Zhao Ziyang), instead emphasized the need for political reform to contribute to furthering economic reform. These authors deemphasized democratization, viewing it as something for the future, and instead stressed reforms that would increase the efficiency of the government and economy. The three key reforms agreed on at this time were: separation of Party and government (as well as Party and economy); streamlining the administrative structure; and reform of the cadre system. . . .

Although one can debate how successful these reforms would have been, and what impact they might have had on economic reform if carried out, there seems little doubt that Tiananmen has reversed or at least greatly slowed this political reform process. After dismantling about one-fourth of the Party core groups by Spring 1989, an August post-Tiananmen decision was made to restore them. The media at this time repeatedly emphasized the need to strengthen Party leadership. The status of the reform to abolish overlapping departments is uncertain; the Beijing Municipal Party Committee, at least, retained its education and agriculture departments, and it seems likely that this reform has not moved ahead. The civil service reforms began trial implementation in six ministries and commissions in December 1989, but it probably will be some time before they achieve wider implementation.

Most obvious . . . is the new unwillingness to undertake reforms that might weaken the role of the Party within the enterprises. Instead, articles emphasize the need for stronger political and ideological leadership. Despite frequent arguments that strengthening Party leadership and political education in no way weakens economic reform or contradicts such reforms as the "factory director responsibility system," in this area one can see a clear reversal of the leadership's earlier position. . . . The felt need to restore political control within the factories . . . undermined the earlier reforms designed to lessen Party control over day-to-day running of the factories in two ways: first by insisting on a greater emphasis on political work within the factory, and second by giving critics of the management reforms a vehicle to attack them.

In sum, the leadership's political reaction to the Tiananmen Incident affected the economic reforms both directly, by causing them to alter the ideological formulations for economic policy (albeit largely for factional purposes), and indirectly, by causing them to reverse some of the political reforms adopted earlier in order to facilitate economic reform. . . .

Conclusion

As suggested earlier, following Tiananmen, the CCP had a three-part political agenda: eliminating the influence of Zhao Ziyang and his "faction"; forging a new leadership ideological consensus to guide future policy; and reestablishing political control over the population and ensuring social stability. Of these three tasks, the first and third have been fairly well accomplished, at least for the near term, but each of these efforts has had negative spillover effects on the economic reforms. The first, in addition to personnel and organizational changes, involved a media campaign designed to discredit Zhao's ideas and policies. Intentionally or not, this campaign has permitted some to voice positions that are quite anti-reformist, encouraging Western (and Chinese) impressions of a significant policy reversal. The third has been reflected both in media statements and in institutional changes designed to reinforce Party control over society, negating some earlier political reforms adopted to facilitate economic reform. Both of these political changes of the past year have made successful implementation of economic reform far more problematic.

However, the leadership has not had notable success in accomplishing the second major task: forging a new ideological consensus that could provide a basis for a coherent set of economic policies, market-oriented or otherwise. The media campaign presents no clear message on what types of policies will be acceptable or desirable in the future. Although ruling out total privatization of state enterprises (a policy unlikely to be put into effect anyway), the media discussions reveal no clear direction from above on how or whether to proceed with those economic reforms already underway, such as development of a sizable private sector, planning reforms, and even household-based farming. The apparent lack of direction from the top has permitted lower-level actors—economists and cadres—to push their own diverse arguments for and against various economic reforms, but has not succeeded either in assuring the population and foreign businessmen that the existing reforms will be maintained, or in providing a coherent plan for addressing current economic difficulties.

The failure to set forth a new ideological vision that could successfully guide future economic policy might result from a deadlock at the top between anti-reformers and those more committed to reform. If so, the spring 1990 deemphasis of retrenchment policies and reintroduction of some reform measures (for example, in May 1990 it was announced that price reform would be speeded up) would be due to shifting power within the new political coalition that formed after Tiananmen: i.e., the gradual lessening in influence of those conservatives opposed to reform and rise in power of the more reformist group. However, there is no obvious political reason for this shift in power relationships: if anything, the 1989–90 political changes in the Soviet Union and Eastern Europe, especially Romania, should have strengthened the hand of the more conservative elements in the leadership. Indeed, there has been no obvious shift in the direction of political reform to match the reintroduction of economic reform measures. On the contrary, there have been many signs of a political tightening up, particularly around the time of the first anniversary of the Tiananmen incident and in anticipation of the Asian Games to be held in Beijing in fall 1990.

The alternative explanation favored by this author is that outside observers had overestimated the ideological shift which took place following Tiananmen. To be sure, some within the leadership (such as Chen Yun) *are* opposed to many of the economic reforms on ideological grounds, and these individuals have been more visible in the past year. However, the dominant grouping within the leadership which made the decision to restore order through military means (including Deng Xiaoping and Li Peng) has given little evidence of sharing that ideological opposition to economic reform. Deng's views on the ideologically permissible degree of economic reform have been remarkably obscure over the past ten years. Li Peng's opposition to Zhao's reforms has always had a heavy overtone of political opportunism, rather than ideological motivation. Accordingly, the most likely reason why no clear position has emerged on desirable reform policies is a *lack* of vision (or ideology) regarding economic policy, not the triumph within the leadership of a new, anti-reformist one. Likewise, the recent revival of some individual reform policies seems more likely to be a pragmatic response to changed economic conditions (lessening of inflation, but growing concern with unemployment) than a shift in underlying policy.

To be sure, the argument that observers have overestimated the degree of change in leadership ideology and economic policy, and that the current leadership looks more for policies that will work than ones that are ideologically correct, does not mean that the future of economic reform in China is a rosy one. For several reasons, the prospects for successful economic reform in China do not look very bright. First, although the current leadership is not obviously biased *against* reform, neither does it have the ideological (and political) commitment *to* far-reaching reform that Zhao Ziyang possessed. Moreover, it is heavily preoccupied with other tasks, particularly ensuring political stability. Thus, we are unlikely in the future to see the kind of political push behind reform policies that Zhao provided, and these policies, once introduced, will be far more readily subject to reversal when they encounter difficulties. Second, the absence of any coherent program for future policy means that reforms will continue to be adopted in a piecemeal way that will almost ensure that they do encounter such difficulties or fail to bring desired results. Finally, the leadership's concern about the causes and possible recurrence of the Tiananmen uprising has led it to reverse some of the corollary political reforms designed to facilitate economic reform. This, too, will help ensure that the economic reform policies adopted in the future will fail to produce the desired results;

indeed, they will face many of the same problems that motivated these political reforms in the first place.

Thus, the future of economic reform in China looks much like its past. One can anticipate cycles of introducing new reform measures which because of their partial nature and leadership unwillingness to introduce necessary related political and social changes fail to produce the desired results, while giving rise to new problems, followed by periods of retreat and policy reformulation attempting to cope with these problems. At least until exogenous political events produce some major new political alignment which can build a consensus upon a particular direction for economic policy, China appears trapped upon what Gertrude Schroeder has labeled "the treadmill of reform."

65

American Policy
after Tiananmen and
the Chinese Response

Michel Oksenberg / James D. Seymour / Winston Lord
Liu Maoyin

In the aftermath of the ugly denouement at Tiananmen, a vigorous debate developed in the United States regarding the proper posture toward China in the wake of this tragedy. The excerpts that follow are a sample of that debate as well as of the Chinese response to it. We begin with Congressional testimony by Michel Oksenberg of the University of Michigan, in which he tries to define the appropriate response in light of American interests in China. Next, James Seymour of Columbia University's East Asian Institute discusses the general issue of sanctions, while Winston Lord, former United States Ambassador to China, addresses the specific question of whether or not to continue to grant most favored nation status (MFN) to China. We close with the Chinese regime's post-Tiananmen view of Western motives in promoting economic exchange and criticizing human rights violations. Such actions, Liu Maoyin argues, are a continuation of the Cold War strategy of overthrowing socialism through the "smokeless war" strategy of peaceful evolution.

American Policy toward China after the Beijing Tragedy

Michel Oksenberg

A political crisis now exists in China. Beijing is under martial law. Believing they had lost control of their capital city, in early June, the leaders of China callously ordered heavily armed forces to penetrate and occupy the center of Beijing, and in the inevitable resulting turmoil, untold thousands of unarmed civilians and soldiers were killed and wounded. In subsequent days, the leaders have unleashed the instruments of totalitarian rule in the major cities.

There is much about the current situation that is unknown: exactly who at the top is in charge of what, how the army feels about all of this, what the attitudes of provincial officials are, and most importantly what the populace is thinking. But amongst the many uncertainties, three conclusions are unmistakable: first, there has been a massive failure of governance in China; second, the leaders of China are once again attempting to force their people into an ideological straitjacket; and third, the leaders of China have done immeasurable damage to their stature in world affairs.

All this poses a challenge to American foreign policy. The challenge affects both our principles and our national interests. The challenge to fundamental American values is clear. The leaders have terminated a ten year record of gradual and halting improvements in their respect for human rights and in establishment of a legal system. Recognizing the human rights abuses in China, we welcomed the progress and based our approach on encouraging and nurturing positive trends. Now we must ask: How should we react to a deteriorating situation?

With respect to our interests, we have asserted for seventeen years that we are served by a secure, modernizing, effectively and humanely governed China that contributes to the peace and stability of the Asia-Pacific region. That is still the case. But how do we react to a China whose leaders seem intent on doing damage to themselves and their country? In the past ten years, the leaders of China were welcomed into the council of nations. Now the President of the People's Republic Yang Shangkun and the Premier Li Peng probably would not be well received in a single leading nation of the world; it will be quite a while before a major foreign leader will wish to visit the Chinese capital.

Until this spring, the leaders of China were seen around the world as responsible, balanced, credible individuals. Some exceptions existed, such as over their handling of Tibet or their reaction to earlier student demonstrations. But they were basically respected for their judgment; their words counted. In a few days, through their precipitous and violent deeds, they lost much of their international standing. International norms of behavior demand that we exhibit disdain toward leaders who order an army to fire upon their own people when other courses of action are available to them. . . .

[In the formulation of American policy] our interests with respect to China are discernible and extensive. . . . Let me enumerate them:

—We expect China to help maintain stability in East Asia and to contribute to the global balance-of-power. This means we count on China to retain a realistic sense of Soviet foreign policy, to help sustain peace on the Korean peninsula, to demonstrate patience and seek a peaceful evolution of the Taiwan issue, to abide by its agreement with Britain over the future of Hong Kong, to assist in a solution of the Cambodian problem that will bring peace and independence to that tragic land, to abide by its commitment not to engage in nuclear proliferation, to refrain from destabilizing but lucrative arms sales in the Middle East, and to support arms control measures where China's interests are involved. This is a long list indeed. China's generally constructive position on these issues has been quite helpful in the past decade. A return to previous postures would complicate our foreign policy considerably. But we cannot take Chinese cooperation for granted; it requires nurturing, consultation, and mutual understanding.

—We also need Chinese cooperation in addressing problems that transcend national boundaries: dealing with the greenhouse and ozone effects, controlling communicable diseases, preventing the growth and marketing of narcotics, halting illegal population migration across national boundaries, limiting population increases, raising enough food, and so on. The cooperation of the government of one-fourth of humanity—no matter how odious—is essential for these issues to be addressed. Scientific cooperation with China on these issues should go forward, though in ways that do not serve the propaganda interests of the leaders.

—We also have an interest in a humanely governed China and in a China committed to policies of economic and political reform. This is not dictated solely by sentimental, moralistic or humanitarian concerns. Rather, China can neither play a responsible role in world affairs nor address the problems of global interdependence unless it has a unified, effective government. And its government cannot be effective unless it enjoys the support and trust of its people. This means the government must accord its people the dignity they seek, be responsive to popular opinion and give its people the role in their governance that they demand. That is primarily why I advocate promoting human rights in China: not to remake China in our image or to interfere in Chinese internal affairs, but in recognition that how the leaders of China treat their own people affects the stability of China and its ability to play a constructive role in world affairs.

　　—Finally, we have a commercial interest in China. We seek a share of China's growing market, as China secures access to our markets. I do not believe in neo-mercantilism, but I do believe China should recognize the generosity with which we have welcomed Chinese entry into our markets since 1978. And I believe that American business firms should not work at a handicap in securing market shares at this early stage in China's development vis-à-vis our competitors.

　　In short, we have major strategic interests with China. It is a great power that sets it apart from, for example, Bulgaria, Czechoslovakia, or Romania. It is a nuclear power. And it is a nation with which we are unprepared to sustain an adversarial or animosity ridden relationship. Our strategy toward China since 1971 has been to draw it out of its isolation and to integrate it in the international community. Underlying this strategy was the recognition that the burden of keeping China poor, weak, and isolated in world affairs—our strategy of the previous twenty years—had proven too costly. Our calculus was that by building strong links to China strategically, intellectually, commercially, and even militarily in this early stage in its rise, we would reduce the chances of China's becoming a disruptive, expansionist power as it grew stronger militarily. Our expectation was that a forthcoming posture toward China would prompt its leaders gradually to accept and abide by international standards of behavior.

　　That is why a vigorous response to the events of May and June is necessary. Not since 1975–76 has the government of China been as scornful of internationally accepted codes of conduct, and it is important to remind the leaders of China that when they depart from the norms of the international community, a severe price is paid. . . .

　　I believe for the most part that the response has been appropriately tough to date. I particularly approve the suspension of weapons sales, the delay in issuance of concessional interest rate loans to China by the United States and our allies, the delay in processing new World Bank loans, the postponement of the GATT [General Agreement on Tariffs and Trade] negotiations, and the postponement of any further relaxation of export controls. . . .

I [also] believe no more should be done at this time, though if human rights abuses persist, emigration is restricted, or China's international behavior becomes irresponsible, it may be necessary to apply further sanctions—such as withdrawal of MFN [most favored nation] status or tightening export control restrictions. I am not averse to applying additional sanctions out of principle. I simply think prudence dictates seeing whether what we have already done will be sufficient. . . .

What considerations should therefore govern our approach to China at this point? Here is the list that I would keep in mind:

—Let our expressions of moral indignation recognize that most of the Chinese officials who receive our statements probably share our grief and dismay toward the tragedy. Too many of our pronouncements are self-righteous and do not acknowledge that our sentiments are felt by many Chinese as well. Human life and dignity are as precious to Chinese as they are to Americans.

—Let us not inadvertently drive the leaders of China into isolation or evoke their strong inclinations toward xenophobia and nativism. Excessive rhetoric on our part or application of the harshest economic sanctions available to us *could* return us to an adversarial relationship with China.

—Let us not so weaken our ties with China that, if a similar abandonment of reform policies were to occur in the Soviet Union, the natural and only course for Moscow and Beijing would be to forge a close relationship. It is important that we continue to engage in dialogue with the Chinese and consult with them on matters of mutual concern.

—Let us not become entwined once again in a Chinese civil war. A number of Chinese intellectuals and students, for totally understandable reasons, seek to overthrow their government and wish to enlist us in their cause. Even as we sympathize with their plight and give them refuge in our midst, as we must, let us recognize that their interests and ours do not coincide.

—Let us therefore retain a balanced posture, mindful of both interest and principle. Let us not be governed by the emotion of the moment but keep in mind—as President Bush has sought to do—our longer term strategy, pursued by five Presidents, of seeking to integrate China into the international community.

—But let the leaders of China confront the consequences of their actions. Deny them the opportunity to blame China's intensifying economic difficulties on Western actions. Let the burden rest on the leaders for their inability to confront inflation, deficits, unemployment, and problems in agricultural and energy production.

—Keep the United States in step with Western Europe and Japan. Do not depart from our allies, and do not become a special target of Chinese animosity. The Japanese position is particularly crucial. Historically, we know the price to be paid when our China policy departs dramatically from that of Japan.

—Do not undertake measures that do more harm to the people of China than to its government. Let us remember the target and whose minds we are seeking to change. And let us not do more damage to ourselves than to the Chinese government. I put withdrawal of MFN status or Commodity Credit Corporation financing in this category.

—Maintain scholarly communications with China. Sending our scholars to China, if serious research is possible, will help us better understand that country, and continuing to welcome their scholars here will position us well when normalcy returns.

—Finally, let us preserve our flexibility. We will wish to respond with alacrity should the situation improve. Writing President Bush's sanctions into law may not give him the flexibility he will need in the conduct of our China policy.

All of these injunctions point in one direction. The Administration appropriately has imposed numerous punishing economic sanctions. The time has come to wait and watch, to test and probe for signs of improvement, to be prepared to apply additional sanctions, and to preserve flexibility. There is much about the current situation that dictates prudence, caution, and balance. . . .

Sanctions or Subdued Relations: The International Response to the 1989 Massacre

James D. Seymour

What is the international community to do when a government's domestic behavior is utterly offensive and in violation of established international norms? To respond by committing an act of war is clearly out of the question. Are there any suitable lesser punishments? The question is particularly vexing when, as in the case of China and the United States, the nations of the antagonistic governments have strong emotional attachments to each other.

Relations between the United States and the People's Republic of China (PRC) divide easily and sharply into two periods, and are defined largely by American conservatives' attitudes toward China. (Liberals have been consistently ambivalent toward the PRC, and have had little impact on American policies toward the country.) The two eras are demarcated by Henry Kissinger's secret visit to China in 1971. Before that year, there was little in the way of a political relationship between the two countries, and virtually no economic relationship. The United States did make occasional propagandistic reference to the undemocratic nature of the Chinese system, but both subjective and short-term strategic considerations always have been much more weighty considerations. Thus, Secretary of State James Baker was making something of an understatement when he said that although he deeply regretted the executions of protesters, human rights "is not the only principle which determines our foreign policy." Lacking here is a sense that long-run American interests depend on the friendship of the Chinese *people*. The example of South Korea suggests that if America is seen as backing a repressive regime, the anti-Americanism that is engendered could last much longer than the repressive regime itself. China once exemplified this anti-Americanism.

The 1950s and 1960s were what can be called a period of total sanctions against China. American conservatives felt betrayed by a China that did not appreciate the many years of support for Chiang Kai-shek's Republic, and they had equally irrational fears of the Sino-Soviet and then Sino-Vietnamese alliance. Whatever the intended effect of the sanctions, they were not only ineffective, they were counterproductive and helped drive the country into the arms of the Soviet Union.

In terms of human rights, the late 1960s and early 1970s comprised the worst period in Chinese history. Although political violence did seem on the decline in 1971, for the people who had been brutalized and imprisoned, there was still no hint of restoration of rights. The fact that the shift in U.S. policy toward China came in 1971 when extreme human rights abuses continued, demonstrates how little Washington cared about the question of democracy.

The promise that a more open China would be a more humane and free one seemed to be borne out—until 1989. Then came the slaughters, first in Lhasa, and then in Beijing, Chengdu, Xian, Lanzhou, and elsewhere. The reaction of the Bush administration was measured: the United States "cannot ignore the consequences for our relationship with China." The president, who fancies himself a China expert, tried to display enough anger to appease the Congress, which was being prodded by human rights organizations and Chinese exiles to impose heavy sanctions. However, he was reserved enough not to produce unnecessary headlines.

Bush canceled the sales of weapons to China, and suspended direct contact between senior U.S. and Chinese officials. However, the decision to allow the sale of dual-use items such as satellites and airliners (which are often used to shuttle troops to martial-law areas) reduced the significance of these steps.

The American response was no more tepid than that of some other countries. Japan was slow to criticize the massacre and only briefly cut off economic assistance to China. Other countries (albeit those with less clout), such as Australia, Canada, France, Great Britain, and Sweden, were willing to make greater sacrifices. For example, France, which had been one of the first Western countries to establish diplomatic relations with the PRC, now became a particularly hospitable haven for dissident exiles. Only time will tell whether the attitude of Paris or Washington is more farsighted.

Certainly, in the short run, Bush's caution has gained nothing. The Chinese authorities, who claim not to care at all about sanctions, seem upset with the United States for three general reasons. First, Americans are held at least partially responsible for the anti-government movement. Second, the United States and other countries have been assailed for extending the visas of students from China. Finally, Beijing does not like the way the media portrayed the turmoil. The Voice of America (VOA) reporting has come under particularly heavy criticism. As a result concrete measures were taken, such as jamming VOA, postponing the start of the Peace Corps program in China and canceling plans for Fulbright scholars to teach there. The cancellation of the Fulbright scholars' stay is a rare example of China failing to encourage the continuation of cultural exchanges which, in general, are going forward.

Should more in the way of economic sanctions have been imposed? First it must be said that no great claim can be made for sanctions against foreign governments. About half the time they do not work at all, and the other half the results are difficult to measure. Still, sanctions enable one to do *something* when no good alternatives are available. This at least satisfies the home demand for a political response. And in the case of China, where modernizers place great stress on economic relations with the United States, economic sanctions would touch a particularly sensitive nerve.

Sanctions will probably be less damaging to China's economy than will the purely risk versus reward decisions of Westerners not to increase activities there. International and Japanese banks have cut lending in the belief that, because of the unrest and stalled economic reforms, the PRC is a poor credit risk. Likewise, China's grain imports and textile exports seem in jeopardy. Tourists and investors are shying away from China. The resulting decline in the country's hard currency reserves makes it difficult to buy foreign products.

Still, the sanctions may be suitable in the face of serious human rights violations. The type and timing of sanctions against China can be judged according to the following criteria:

(1) *The importance of trade in specific areas to Chinese leaders.* Yang Shangkun, author of the massacre, sorely needs military equipment and technology. At this moment, gun sales to the United States are doing well. Sanctions against the gun trade would be effective, especially since they primarily would hurt China's offending military-industrial complex. As for commerce in general, Mao Zedong proved that China can survive without international trade. However, such commerce now accounts for almost 20 percent of China's gross national product.

(2) *The hardship inflicted on the public.* In the case of China, a grain embargo would be inappropriate since the general population would be adversely affected. But a halt in the sale of airplanes to China would target the military without harming the Chinese people as a whole.

(3) *The political implications of non-economic relations.* In the cases of athletic and cultural exchanges, the value of the exchanges in keeping China open must be weighed against the luster they add to the regime.

(4) *The strength of the statement about unacceptable government behavior.* There is little point in imposing sanctions if they are accompanied by an apologetic chorus from prominent members of the ruling party.

(5) *Multilateral support.* There must be participation by nearly all of China's trading partners for economic sanctions to be effective. So far sanctions against arms sales and military or high-level contacts have

received international support. Broad-spectrum commercial sanctions, however, would not receive international approval, thereby hurting China less than the country imposing such sanctions.

(6) *Support in the sanctioning country to sustain the sanctions until the human rights situation improves.* Sanctions accomplish nothing if they are backed away from before there is any improvement. Furthermore, ineffective sanctions hand the offending government a propaganda victory.

In measuring the value of sanctions one must take a long-range view. Their imposition stands primarily as a warning that the international community will extract a price from future irresponsible rulers who engage in serious human rights violations. The price is as much symbolic as monetary. As we have noted, the real economic impact comes not from sanctions but from the chilling effect that the overall situation has on business. Thus, in the final analysis, the value of sanctions lies in the moral stance taken and the signal sent. . . .

Few wars ever settle matters of principle, but World War II was an exception. Primarily as a result of international revulsion over the Holocaust, the principle was established that governments do not have absolute sovereignty, and there are international limits to the abuses which they are permitted to commit against their own citizens. Nothing is more important than upholding that principle, which was established after such a terrible sacrifice. After the 1989 China massacre, many governments rose to the occasion, though the United States and Japan were not among them. But it must be borne in mind that the problem is not primarily one of relations among states. Rather, the fundamental issue is between tyranny and humanity.

In a more immediate sense, the problem is between the Chinese authorities and the Chinese people. The Chinese Communist Party has lost much of its legitimacy; knowledgeable people overwhelmingly support the goals and means of the Tiananmen workers and students. According to one poll of Beijing residents, only 1 percent found the protesting students' demands unreasonable. In this situation, Washington must choose sides wisely, if at all. Although some argue that geostrategic interests require our maintaining good relations with China's rulers, this view springs from the needs of a bipolarity which no longer exists. Indeed, given China's close relations with the Khmer Rouge, they hardly make an attractive ally, whereas the Soviet Union is becoming increasingly easy for us to get along with. . . .

It surely would be helpful if American liberals reclaimed a voice in the matter. Sino-American relations are too important to be subject to erratic swings at the hands of American conservatives. The latter have made their belated contribution; the Sino-American economic relationship has grown phenomenally. However, the political relationship has been awkward. The conservatives in Washington and the conservatives in Beijing have had an odd symbiotic relationship, but public opinion, especially the opinion of intellectuals in both countries, increasingly has been operating on a different wavelength from that of the leaderships. For the first time, the American public views the Soviet Union more favorably than China. If Washington would place itself more clearly on the side of political reforms, that would render the present Beijing leadership "odd man out," which is the way it should be.

Sanctions and moral posturing may not be as effective as we and the Chinese people might like. Still, it would be foolish for Western countries, through unrestricted trade and business-as-usual diplomacy, to slow down the process of dynastic decline. This would only delay the return to China of the politics of decency.

Bush's Second Chance on China

Winston Lord

June 3 marks the first anniversary of the massacre of innocents in the streets of Beijing. It is also the deadline for President Bush to decide whether to recommend continued most-favored-nation trade treatment for China.

This irony poses a dilemma—and offers a major opportunity—for the Administrators. In one stroke, President Bush can close the breach between Capitol Hill and the White House on China policy, forge a common American front and promote Chinese human rights and U.S. national interests.

He should invite Congress to join him in crafting a joint statement for the first weekend in June. The essential components:

• An eloquent tribute to the Chinese who demonstrated and died for the aspirations America has supported elsewhere in the world.

• Extension of most-favored-nation trade status *for one year,* with the openly expressed purpose of supporting progressive forces in China, protecting concrete American interests and maintaining the framework for future American-Chinese relations. (This status entitles China to the standard treatment that the U.S. grants almost all other trading partners.)

• Explicit reaffirmation of such existing measures as the suspension of military ties, the freeze on liberalization of technology exports and the postponement of World Bank loans.

• Determination to move ahead on related issues, such as positive consideration of Taiwan's application to the General Agreement on Tariffs and Trade and enlarging future immigration opportunities for Hong Kong citizens.

• A substantial increase in Voice of America funding to overcome jamming of programs beamed to China.

• A meeting between President Bush and selected Chinese studying in America to exchange views on China and American policy.

There are solid grounds for revoking most-favored-nation status.

Both the preamble to the relevant statute and its legislative history include concerns for human rights.

The situation in China has greatly deteriorated this past year: executions, purges, imprisonment, surveillance, political indoctrination, the rollback of many economic reforms—all cloaked in the Big Lie.

The xenophobic regime has launched attacks on Western values and crude invective against the U.S. It muzzles foreign correspondents and jams the Voice of America.

Revoking most-favored-nation treatment, which would increase pressures on Beijing, would be the strongest signal of censure to date.

There is also the specific legislative criterion of free emigration. While many are still allowed to leave China, new restrictions have curtailed others, including students and scholars. Obviously, both dissidents in our embassy and tens of thousands in jail cannot move. Countless Chinese have no chance of getting exit papers or dare not even try.

In any case, the most potent argument for revocation is that extension of most-favored-nation status could be misconstrued by China's hardliners. In internal policy debates, they could argue that they can repress and reap commercial benefits, too.

Unfortunately, this view has been reinforced by Bush Administration actions: its unrequited conciliatory gestures; the double standard between China and support for democracy in Eastern Europe, Latin America and South Africa.

Beijing might conclude that there is no limit to our toleration of its abuses. So might Mikhail Gorbachev, as he contemplates his policies toward the Baltic states and his summit meeting with Mr. Bush on the eve of June 3.

For these reasons, simply extending most-favored-nation treatment would be a grave mistake. If the other steps outlined above are not undertaken, this trade status should be ended.

On balance, the arguments favor extension of most-favored-nation treatment—if embedded in a larger package. Termination would trigger serious consequences.

First, it would hurt the wrong people in China, reducing their leverage in the struggle for its future.

The most severe impact would be on the sectors we wish to support—entrepreneurs, business people, Chinese in the coastal areas and open cities. They are the ones most dependent on foreign trade and investment and most committed to reform and contact with the outside world.

The regime, meanwhile, would use America as a handy scapegoat for China's floundering economy.

Second, termination would undermine Hong Kong. Seventy percent of China's $12 billion in exports to the U.S. passes through there. Millions working in Hong Kong and southern China would be affected. As Hong Kong residents look with trepidation toward 1997, when Britain turns Hong Kong over to China, this is not time to deal them additional economic and psychological blows.

Third, it would harm many Americans. Consumers would pay more for certain products; importers would need to look elsewhere; exporters would face retaliation by China. Business people in China and Hong Kong would lose markets and investments, perhaps permanently. Competitors in Japan, Europe, South Korea, Taiwan and elsewhere—where governments would not follow our lead—would profit, at America's expense.

Fourth, it would undercut our long-term objectives. While granting China new privileges would be wrong, we should be wary of dismantling frameworks like most-favored-nation treatment and the related overall trade agreement that were carefully constructed during the 1980s.

Once commercial and personal links with progressive forces are severed, repairing them would be difficult. We will need them in place when a more moderate regime allows us to resume full cooperation. That time is not far away.

President Bush has an opportunity to heal wounds on the single foreign policy issue where he has provoked heated debate and about which he may care most deeply. He can align himself solidly with the Chinese people for the first time and restore the bipartisan approach that marked our China policy for two decades through five Administrations. Congress, torn on the trade issue, would respond positively to a Bush initiative that made clear where this nation stood. Together, the President and Congress can send a powerful message to the transitional leaders in Beijing and to the Chinese people who herald a more hopeful future for their country.

Guard against the Smokeless War

Liu Maoyin

Although people have been highly vigilant against the smokey, devastating wars launched by the bourgeoisie and reactionaries of the West, they often are unaware of the smokeless war—"peaceful evolution"—the latter carried out through ideological infiltration and economic inducement and coercion. We must be aware of this war. Commenting on the "peaceful evolution" strategy, a noted U.S. political figure said: "Increasing trade and contacts with the Soviet bloc may promote peaceful evolution within that bloc. The more contacts we have with the East, the more they will be influenced by the examples presented by the West. This will certainly strengthen the internal forces which support evolution. While there were virtually no changes in Eastern Europe during the long and frigid years of cold war confrontation, significant changes have taken place after the cold war." This shows that, as the cold war comes to an end, "peaceful evolution" becomes the major strategy of the bourgeoisie of the West to subvert and undermine the socialist states. We must be highly alert against this strategy.

"Peaceful Evolution," a Very Sinister and Ruthless Strategy

Compared with other strategies, the "peaceful evolution" strategy is even more sinister and ruthless and more penetrating and deceptive, and thus it is even more dangerous to socialist countries. The five principal tactics with which the bourgeoisie of the West carries out its "peaceful evolution" strategy are as follows:

First, they use international broadcasts to intensify their ideological infiltration and political influence and to fan up "resistance sentiments" in socialist countries. They believe that "installing new transmitters and equipment to beam programs to the East is more important than deploying guided missiles." A U.S. Congress document points out: "Radio broadcasts are the one and only means capable of subverting the socialist system." Take the "Voice of America," for example. During the upheaval and rebellion in China in the late spring and early summer of 1989, it beamed its programs to China three times and more than ten hours each day, using endless rumors to shake the people's communist convictions, demoralize people, and subvert China's socialist system. Second, they have intensified their ideological infiltration of intellectuals through academic and cultural exchange programs. The U.S. Government has publicly indicated that U.S.-Chinese cultural exchange "is meant to fill the void of Western thinking and concept of values caused by thirty years of isolation and open anti-Americanism among the Chinese people" so that a large number of Chinese scholars and students will become "disseminators and interpreters of the Western system and concept of values." Their tactics include: (1) sponsoring all types of academic symposiums and relevant international conferences and giving out various kinds of honors and monetary awards to those scholars who worship Western democracy and freedom so that they can influence more people with their fame and status; (2) giving direct financial aid to institutes of social sciences in socialist countries so that they will undertake research projects useful for the propagation of Western democracy, freedom, and human rights; (3) taking advantage of scholar exchange programs they publicize the contributions and progressiveness of founders of the democratic system of the West and depreciate communist leaders by "criticizing their autocratic and brutal rule." Such tactics are extremely sinister and ruthless. Some "disseminators and interpreters of the Western system and concept of values," like Fang Lizhi, Yan Jiaqi, Liu Xiaobo, and the like have indeed appeared in China in recent years. Shouting slogans of so-called "democracy, freedom, and human rights," they attack and slander the CCP as being "dictatorial" and "autocratic," smear China's socialist system as being a "cradle of monarchy" and a "hotbed of corruption," and advocate "the establishment of a pluralistic political system and a government by the elite." They also go all out to propagate the concept of values of the bourgeoisie of the West and promote such ideas as "individualism," "personal struggle," and "money is almighty." All this is the stock in trade of the bourgeoisie of the West.

Third, through subsidizing and recommending, Western governments and their press and publishing departments have sent a large number of newspapers as well as books and magazines containing political, philosophical, and social ideas to socialist countries in an effort to shake their people's socialist beliefs. This can be proved by the fact that many people who are unable to distinguish right from wrong have been poisoned by the decadent ideas and living styles of the bourgeoisie as result of the influx of books and magazines into China. Fourth, they support "independent political organizations" in socialist countries so that "free and democratic forces can come into being and develop gradually." They directly support people's representatives in communist parties who worship the type of democracy and lifestyle of the West and support reputable liberals so that they can become so-called "seeds of freedom," which they use to influence people in society and young people and encourage them to set up independent political and social groups advocating liberalization. To infiltrate socialist countries, they also encourage nongovernmental groups in the West, such as labor unions, trade unions, and churches, in establishing ties with counterpart organizations in socialist countries. These tactics could be clearly observed during the upheaval and rebellion that occurred in China in the late spring and early summer of last year. Fang Lizhi, Yan Jiaqi, Liu Xiaobo, Wang Dan, and the like were their so-called "seeds of freedom," and such illegal organizations as the "Autonomous Federation of University and College Students" and the "Autonomous Federation of Workers' Unions" were "independent political organizations" they supported. Fifth, they encourage so-called "democratization" and try to gradually change the socialist countries' nature by taking advantage of their reform and open policies. They have carried out economic inducement and coercion in the name of providing financial assistance and carrying out technical exchange, trying to "achieve political results by using the economic strength of the West." A U.S. leader once said that the United States is assisting socialist countries in response to their quest of freedom, and the assistance is based on these countries' "economic and political pluralization." Capitalist countries in the West recently openly declared that their assistance to socialist countries was based on these five prerequisites: "These countries must have a legal system, they must respect human rights, they must have a pluralistic political system, they must have free elections, and they must practice market economy." To put it simply, they want a capitalist system in the socialist countries. This strategy has been fully exposed by the fact that the bourgeoisie of the West clamored to impose economic sanctions against China after the Chinese Government suppressed the rebellion. In short, all the tactics relevant to "peaceful evolution" are very sinister and ruthless, and "peaceful evolution" is a smokeless war conducted within the ideological sphere.

The Struggle Between "Peaceful Evolution" and "Counter-Peaceful Evolution" Will Be a Protracted One

The struggle between "peaceful evolution" and "counter-peaceful evolution" is essentially a struggle between the socialist system and ideology on the one hand and the capitalist system and ideology on the other.

First of all, the change of the bourgeoisie in the West from carrying out "armed intervention" against socialist countries to promoting "peaceful evolution" is only a change of strategy. As their basic intention to subvert and undermine the socialist countries remains unchanged, our basic principle of opposing their subversion and sabotage also remains unchanged. Thus, this struggle will certainly go on for a long time. Ever since the founding of the Soviet Union, the first socialist country in the world, it was considered a thorn in the flesh of the bourgeoisie and the reactionary forces the world over. They immediately organized 14 countries to launch a military offensive against the Soviet Union, but failed. When more socialist countries appeared in the world after the Second World War, the capitalist world became even more panic-stricken and they resolved to wipe out all socialist countries by using their strong military force [in China, Korea, and Vietnam]. . . . They learned the painful lesson that they cannot wipe out socialism with force alone, but that, while using force, they must also resort to a "peaceful evolution" strategy. This being the case, we must clearly realize that the bourgeoisie of the West has never changed its intention to subvert and undermine socialism and China, and that we must be prepared to wage a protracted struggle.

Second, over the last seventy years and more, capitalism has not been able to swallow up socialism but neither is capitalism on the verge of death. Thus capitalism and socialism remain in a state of "coexisting in struggle" and this situation will continue for a long time to come. As an institution and a world system, it will take a long time before capitalism dies. This historical process will take decades, and even centuries. . . . Although the subversion carried out by the bourgeoisie has been successful at times in certain regions and countries in the world, socialism as a world system cannot be annihilated no matter how ferocious the capitalist subversion and counterattacks may be and no matter what kinds of measures they take. More importantly, the socialist system itself is constantly improving and developing. In China, for example, owing to its reform and open policies, it has achieved enormous success in the political and economic areas over the past decade and its socialist system is full of vigor. This being the case, the state of "coexistence in struggle" between capitalism and socialism will continue for a long time to come.

Third, class struggle in the socialist countries will continue to exist for a long time in certain areas. For example, after China accomplished its socialist transformation, remnant elements and other hostile elements of the exploiting classes continued to exist, such as those forces in Hong Kong and Taiwan hostile to socialism as well as the degenerates in our party and among our people, including the proponents of bourgeois liberalization and other decadent elements. The class struggle in the ideological sphere, in particular, will also continue for a long time to come. These hostile forces, and the capitalist forces the world over, will certainly echo each other and do everything possible to subvert socialism. Because of this, class struggle will continue to exist for a long time to come in certain spheres and may even sharpen under certain conditions.

For these reasons, the struggle between the socialist system and capitalist system will continue for a long time to come and "peaceful evolution" will become a special feature of this struggle. Therefore, our struggle against "peaceful evolution" will also be long one.

Upholding the Four Cardinal Principles, the Magic Weapon to Smash the "Peaceful Evolution" Conspiracy

The most important characteristic of the "peaceful evolution" scheme of the bourgeoisie in the West is that it exerts its effect through the internal degeneration of socialist countries. Therefore, if we are to guard against and smash their "peaceful evolution" conspiracy, we must consolidate and develop the socialist system and prevent this bastion from being penetrated from within. The only magic weapon that will help us do that is upholding the four cardinal principles. The fundamental objective of the bourgeoisie in the West in promoting the "peaceful evolution" conspiracy is to make the socialist countries renounce the Marxist guiding ideology, give up communist leadership, and abandon proletarian dictatorship and the socialist system and to incorporate the socialist countries into the Western capitalist framework. We must not treat this matter lightly or lower our guard; instead, we should give tit for tat. In the realm of ideology, we must firmly resist and eliminate the various reactionary bourgeois ideas, world outlook, and values that have sneaked in, educate our cadres and people in Marxism and Mao Zedong Thought, immunize them against the "peaceful evolution" conspiracy of the bourgeoisie in the West, and foster among them a strong conviction that socialism and communism are invincible. In politics, we must firmly criticize the "multiparty system" as well as the assorted bourgeois ideas about an abstract "democracy" and "freedom" that transcend classes and uphold communist leadership and the socialist system. In economics, we must firmly oppose private ownership and free economy and instead uphold planned socialist commodity economy in which public ownership remains dominant. At the same time, in order to ensure that the socialist bastion remains secure, we must uphold people's democratic dictatorship. If hostile elements attempt to subvert or sabotage the socialist system on our soil, we must firmly and mercilessly crack down on them.

With the four cardinal principles, we have a firm stand and a clear orientation for all our work. On the question of our attitude toward reform and opening to the outside world, we have declared clearly to the world: China's reform and opening up is for the purpose of self-improvement of the socialist system. China's introduction of advanced science and technology, funds, and advanced management know-how from the West is for the purpose of developing socialist productive forces and injecting vitality into socialism. We will not renounce Marxism, abandon socialism, or abolish the Communist Party, and instead practice capitalism in return for the Western bourgeoisie's alms.

Suggestions
for Further Reading

Part 1: History and Geography

Bodde, Derk. *China's First Unifier: A Study of the Ch'in Dynasty.* Hong Kong: Hong Kong University Press, 1967. The standard account of the origins of empire and the career of Ch'in Shih Huang Ti and his policies.

Cannon, Terry, ed. *The Geography of Contemporary China.* London: Routledge, 1990. A useful multi-author survey, stressing recent changes.

Fairbank, John K. *The United States and China.* Fourth edition. Cambridge: Harvard University Press, 1983. The best single brief thematic introduction to China's history, geography, civilization, and contemporary evolution. Includes an extensive annotated bibliography.

Fairbank, John, K., and Edwin O. Reischauer. *East Asia: Tradition and Transformation.* Boston: Houghton Mifflin, 1989. The broad sweep of Chinese history by two leading scholars; a detailed account of events and trends from origins through the Cultural Revolution.

Fitzgerald, C. P. *China: A Short Cultural History.* Third edition. New York: Praeger, 1961. One of the best of many summary accounts, with special attention to what its title promises.

Gasster, Michael. *China's Struggle to Modernize.* Second edition. New York: Knopf, 1981. A brief, clear survey of the period since 1842.

Geelan, P. J. M., and D. C. Twitchett, eds. *The Times Atlas of China.* London: Van Nostrand Reinhold, 1974. The best detailed maps of China by province and by topical coverage: climate, agriculture, transport, etc., with a high standard of cartography.

Goodrich, L. C. *A Short History of the Chinese People.* Third edition. New York: Harper, 1959. Another excellent survey effort, brief, authoritative, and well written, stressing social and cultural history.

Hsu, Immanuel. *The Rise of Modern China.* Fourth edition. New York: Oxford University Press, 1990. The major standard survey of the period since 1842, detailed and authoritative.

Lattimore, Owen. *Inner Asian Frontiers of China.* Second edition. New York: American Geographical Society, 1951. The geographical and historical context of China's interaction with Xinjiang, Mongolia, and Manchuria, from their beginnings to modern times.

Loewe, Michael. *Imperial China: The Historical Background to the Modern Age.* New York: Praeger, 1966. Another first-rate survey treatment.

Meisner, Maurice. *Mao's China and After.* New York: Free Press, 1986. The best general history, surveying all aspects of the years from 1949 to Mao's death in 1976.

Meskill, John, ed. *An Introduction to Chinese Civilization.* Boston: D. C. Heath, 1973. A good general survey, focused on history but with essays by specialists on major topics, including geography.

Murphey, Rhoads. *The Fading of the Maoist Vision: City and Countryside in China's Development.* London and New York: Methuen, 1980. Tensions and conflicts as a peasant revolution has had to confront the problems of modern development.

Smith, Christopher J. *China: People and Places in the Land of One Billion.* Boulder: Westview, 1990. A basic human geography.

Spence, Jonathan. *The Search for Modern China*. New York: Norton, 1990. A clear, well-written, long account of the roots of the present, from the rise of the Manchus in the seventeenth century to the Beijing massacre of 1989.

Part 2: Politics

Barnett, A. Doak. *Cadres, Bureaucracy, and Political Power in Communist China*. New York: Columbia University Press, 1967. A fine description of the party/state system as it operated on the eve of the Cultural Revolution. It provides important insights that are still useful for understanding this system.

Chan, Anita, Richard Madsen, and Jonathan Unger. *Chen Village: The Recent History of a Peasant Community in Mao's China*. Berkeley: University of California Press, 1984. The impact of rural policy on one village during the past twenty years.

Chang Chung-li. *The Chinese Gentry*. Seattle: University of Washington Press, 1955. A classic study of the nature and role of the gentry.

Ch'u T'ung-tsu. *Local Government in China under the Ch'ing*. Cambridge: Harvard University Press, 1962. A meticulous study of the structure and personnel of local government.

Deng Xiaoping, *Selected Works of Deng Xiaoping, 1975–1982*. Beijing: Foreign Languages Press, 1984. The views of the principal architect of post-Mao China.

Fairbank, John K., et al. *Cambridge History of Modern China*, volumes 10–15. New York: Cambridge University Press, various dates. Covering the period from 1800 to the 1970s, these volumes contain important articles by prominent scholars on the development of the Chinese polity.

Feuerwerker, Albert. *State and Society in Eighteenth Century China: The Ch'ing Empire in Its Glory*. Ann Arbor: Center for Chinese Studies, 1976. A splendid description of the traditional Chinese system during one of its highpoints.

Frolic, B. Michael. *Mao's People: Sixteen Portraits of Life in Revolutionary China*. Cambridge: Harvard University Press, 1980. The personal stories told by these Chinese provide innumerable insights into social, political, and economic developments.

Hamrin, Carol. *China and the Challenge of the Future: Changing Political Patterns*. Boulder: Westview, 1989. A study of the development of reform politics in China and some speculations on the future.

Harding, Harry. *China's Second Revolution: Reform after Mao*. Washington: Brookings Institution, 1987. Although written before the events surrounding Tiananmen, this stands as the best study of the post-Mao reform movement.

————. *Organizing China: The Problem of Bureaucracy, 1949–1976*. Stanford: Stanford University Press, 1981. A book that offers more than its title suggests. It provides a comprehensive picture of the evolution of China's political structure.

Lee Hong Yung. *The Politics of the Chinese Cultural Revolution: A Case Study*. Berkeley: University of California Press, 1978. A useful study of the interaction of social tensions and political developments during the Cultural Revolution.

Lieberthal, Kenneth, and Michel Oksenberg. *Policy Making in China: Structures and Process*. Princeton: Princeton University Press, 1988. A series of case studies of policy making in regard to the energy area provides the basis for an important study of politics in post-Mao China.

Mote, Frederick W. *Intellectual Foundations of China*. New York: Knopf, 1971. A useful overview of the major schools of thought in ancient China.

Nathan, Andrew. *Chinese Democracy*. New York: Knopf, 1985. Post-Mao political developments are placed in the perspective of the historical development of Chinese conceptions of democracy.

Oksenberg, Michel, Lawrence R. Sullivan, and Marc Lambert, eds. *Beijing Spring, 1989: Confrontation and Conflict*. Armonk, N.Y.: M.E. Sharpe, 1990. Documents and commentary on the background to—and nature of—the events of April–June, 1989.

Perry, Elizabeth. *Rebels and Revolutionaries in North China, 1845–1945*. Stanford: Stanford University Press, 1980. An excellent study of a century of popular movements in the north of China.

Schram, Stuart. *The Political Thought of Mao Tse-tung*. New York: Praeger, 1969. Although dated, this is still the best treatment of the subject.

Schwartz, Benjamin. *The World of Thought in Ancient China*. Cambridge: Harvard University Press, 1985. A magisterial study by one of the most insightful intellectual historians of China.

Shue, Vivian. *The Reach of the State: Sketches of the Chinese Body Politic*. Stanford: Stanford University Press, 1988. A provocative study of the nature of state power in the countryside from imperial times to contemporary China.

Siu, Helen F., and Zelda Stern, eds. *Mao's Harvest*. New York: Oxford University Press, 1983. A collection of writings of social criticism that appeared in China during the post-Mao period.

Spence, Jonathan. *The Death of Woman Wang*. New York: Penguin, 1978. A reconstruction of life in one county during the early years of the Qing dynasty.

———. *Emperor of China: Self-Portrait of K'ang Hsi*. New York: Vintage, 1979. Using imperial court records, Spence reconstructs the thinking of one of China's great emperors. This is truly the "view from the top" on a number of topics.

Tiewes, Frederick C. *Leadership, Legitimacy, and Conflict in China*. Armonk, N.Y.: M.E. Sharpe, 1984. Elite politics from Mao to Deng. This is a view from the top in post-1949 China.

Townsend, James. *Political Participation in Communist China*. Berkeley: University of California Press, 1969. A classic study of the place of citizen participation in the Chinese political system.

Part 3: Society

Baker, Hugh. *Chinese Family and Kinship*. New York: Columbia University Press, 1979. The best available general summary of our knowledge about Chinese family life and kinship organization. It deals primarily with family patterns in urban and rural China in the late imperial and republican periods.

Bianco, Lucien. *Origins of the Chinese Revolution, 1915–1949*. Stanford: Stanford University Press, 1971. A French social historian provides an overview of the variety of tensions and social conflicts in the republican period which helped to bring about the rise to power of the Chinese communists.

Chance, Norman. *China's Urban Villagers*. New York: Holt, Reinhart, & Winston, 1984. An anthropologist who conducted a brief field study of a prosperous commune in the suburbs of Beijing just prior to the decollectivization of agriculture describes the patterns of life and work there, and the mixture of benefits and problems that state penetration of the countryside has brought.

Croll, Elisabeth, Delia Davin, and Penny Kane, eds. *China's One Child Family Policy*. New York: St. Martin's, 1985. In a set of papers from a conference held in England, the enforcement of the one-child policy introduced after 1979 and its social consequences are examined by a variety of experts.

Davis-Friedmann, Deborah. *Long Lives*. Cambridge: Harvard University Press, 1983. An examination of the revolution's effect on the lives of the elderly in rural and urban China, based upon interviews in Hong Kong and fieldwork in China in the late 1970s.

Fried, Morton. *The Fabric of Chinese Society*. New York: Praeger, 1953. An anthropologist looks at the way in which personal ties and social networks provided the glue that held urban China together in the pre-communist period; based upon fieldwork in a town in Anhui province in 1947–48.

Hinton, William. *Fanshen: A Documentary of Revolution in a Chinese Village.* New York: Monthly Review Press, 1966. A classic account of land reform in Long Bow village in North China in the years 1946–48, by an American who conducted extensive interviews there as the campaign was being completed. Hinton vividly describes the process of mobilized class struggle used to carry the campaign forward.

————. *Shenfan.* New York: Vintage, 1984. Hinton returns to the site of his original study and reports on developments in the village over the thirty years after land reform.

Honig, Emily, and Gail Hershatter. *Personal Voices: Chinese Women in the 1980s.* Stanford: Stanford University Press, 1988. A very systematic treatment of the situation of urban women in the PRC and how the reforms have affected their lives. The authors are two American social historians who lived and conducted research in China. This book is based upon interviews as well as a thorough combing of Chinese newspaper and journal articles dealing with women.

Hsiao Kung-chuan. *Rural China: Imperial Control in the Nineteenth Century.* Seattle: University of Washington Press, 1960. A massive study which examines the Qing dynasty effort to produce order and community in rural villages, and the forces that made this effort less than fully successful.

Huang Shu-min. *The Spiral Road.* Boulder: Westview, 1989. This is a detailed study, by an anthropologist originally from Taiwan, of a suburban village outside of Xiamen (Amoy) during the mid-1980s. The history of the village and the impact of the reforms on peasant life are described through the eyes of the village's party secretary.

Liang, Heng, and Judith Shapiro. *Son of the Revolution.* New York: Vintage, 1983. The life story of a young man who grew up in post-1949 China and experienced the turmoil and social conflicts caused by Mao's policies. His marriage to an American teacher in China, his co-author, made it possible for him to leave and tell his story.

MacInnis, Donald. *Religion in China Today*. Maryknoll, NY: Orbis, 1989. This is a compilation of official documents on religious policy in China in the post-Mao period and articles and interview selections describing actual religious practices. The author is a long-time student of policies toward religion in the PRC, and both native and foreign-origin religions are covered.

Naquin, Susan, and Evelyn Rawski. *Chinese Society in the Eighteenth Century*. New Haven: Yale University Press, 1987. Two American social historians provide a general overview of Chinese society during the last dynasty, and before the impact of foreign imperialism. Their study details changes underway during the height of Manchu rule, showing that the China that existed before the arrival of foreign gunboats was not mired in tradition.

Parish, William, and Martin K. Whyte. *Village and Family in Contemporary China*. Chicago: University of Chicago Press, 1978. A comprehensive study of social change and continuity in rural Guangdong province, based primarily on interviews conducted in Hong Kong in the mid-1970s.

Pruitt, Ida. *A Daughter of Han*. New Haven: Yale University Press, 1945. A life history of the sufferings and family conflicts of a Chinese working woman in the republican period, based upon oral interviews by a Westerner who resided in China for many years.

Rosen, Stanley. *Red Guard Factionalism and the Cultural Revolution in Guangzhou (Canton)*. Boulder: Westview, 1982. Much of the hostility and violence of the Cultural Revolution can be traced to the feelings of class hatred stimulated by government policy. In this study a political scientist examines in extraordinary detail how students in high schools in one city, Canton, were induced to enter into this byzantine struggle.

Rowe, William. *Hangkow, Commerce and Society in a Chinese City, 1796–1889*. Stanford: Stanford University Press, 1984; and *Hangkow, Conflict and Community in a Chinese City, 1796–1895*. Stanford: Stanford University Press, 1989. This magisterial work describes the social fabric and dynamism of one of China's major cities in the waning years of the Qing dynasty. Through sensitive comparisons with the development of European cities such as London and Paris, the author challenges simple notions that Chinese cities were backward and retarded China's development compared to the West.

Strand, David. *Rickshaw Beijing: City, People and Politics in the 1920s.* Berkeley: University of California Press, 1989. This account by a political scientist examines how guilds, unions, chambers of commerce, and other organizations evolved and transformed the nature of urban life in Beijing in the early republican era. Through rich anecdotal material as well as a wealth of pictures, the author provides a real feel for social life in the city in that period.

Walder, Andrew. *Communist Neo-Traditionalism: Work and Authority in Chinese Industry.* Berkeley: University of California Press, 1986. A sociological analysis of factory organization and work-unit life in the late Mao period illustrates the near total dependence upon bureaucratic superiors that the post-1949 changes produced.

Whyte, Martin K., and William L. Parish. *Urban Life in Contemporary China.* Chicago: University of Chicago Press, 1984. A comprehensive study of urban society and economy under Mao.

Wolf, Margery. *Revolution Postponed.* Stanford: Stanford University Press, 1985. An anthropologist looks at the role of women in China in the early 1980s and finds that in many ways sexual inequality is still a pervasive part of Chinese life.

Zhang Xinxin and Sang Ye. *Chinese Lives: An Oral History of Contemporary China.* New York: Pantheon, 1987. The authors, two Chinese journalists, emulated Studs Terkel and compiled this collection of more than sixty accounts of diverse individual lives in reform-era China. The excellent translations of their accounts provide vivid windows onto contemporary Chinese social life.

Part 4: The Economy

de Crespigny, R. R. C. *China: The Land and Its People.* New York: St. Martin's, 1971. Highly readable economic geography with a good "Guide to Further Reading."

Elvin, Mark. *The Pattern of the Chinese Past*. Stanford: Stanford University Press, 1973. Interpretative analysis of the long sweep of China's economic evolution, with emphasis on the explanation for the alternating stages of technological advance and stagnation.

Fei Hsiao-tung and Chang Chih-i. *Earthbound China*. Chicago: University of Chicago Press, 1945. Classic statement of China's economic problems in the twentieth century written by Western-trained Chinese observers. Based on field study in villages.

Feuerwerker, Albert. *The Chinese Economy, ca. 1870–1911*. Ann Arbor: Center for Chinese Studies, 1969; and *Economic Trends in the Republic of China, 1912–1949*, Ann Arbor: Center for Chinese Studies, 1977. Brief but useful texts which cover economic developments in the final decades of the Ch'ing dynasty and in the years between the Revolution of 1911 and the rise to power of the Communists in 1949.

Gurley, John G. *China's Economy and the Maoist Strategy*. New York: Monthly Review Press, 1976. Collection of writings presenting author's favorable interpretations of Mao's economic policies and economic developments in China after 1949.

Ho Ping-ti. *Studies on the Population of China, 1368–1953*. Cambridge: Harvard University Press, 1967. Somewhat scholarly, but detailed and interesting on China's demographic history in the past six centuries, with emphasis on major migrations within China.

Howe, Christopher. *China's Economy: A Basic Guide*. New York: Basic Books, 1978. A good and readable summary of economic developments since 1949, based upon results of scholarly studies but written for the layperson. Also includes a good selection of references for further reading.

Liu Suinian and Wu Qungan, eds. *China's Socialist Economy: An Outline History (1949–1984)*. Beijing: Beijing Review Press, 1986. A rather detailed chronological account of economic developments and policy changes in China since 1949. Appendices contain English versions of several important documents over the same period.

Myers, Ramon H. *The Chinese Economy Past and Present.* Belmont, Ca.: Wadsworth, 1980. Author's summary presentation of research by others on China's economic history, intended for the nonspecialist.

Perkins, Dwight H., ed. *China's Modern Economy in Historical Perspective.* Stanford: Stanford University Press, 1973. Collection of articles on various aspects of China's pre-1949 economy in relation to contemporary developments.

Rawski, Thomas G. *Economic Growth in Prewar China* (Berkeley: University of California Press, 1989. A statistical evaluation of growth and development in the main economic sectors during the period between the First and Second World Wars. Presents the arguments for a more favorable interpretation for the record of economic growth in this period.

Riskin, Carl. *China's Political Economy: The Quest for Development since 1949.* New York: Oxford University Press, 1987. Textbook which analyzes developments since 1949 according to the different policy regimes implemented since that time. Somewhat sympathetic, yet critical, interpretation of the various Maoist economic campaigns and economic principles.

Tawney, R. H. *Land and Labor in China.* Boston: Beacon, 1966. Classic statement of China's economic problems in the twentieth century, written in the 1930s by a Western observer who was not a specialist on China's economy.

The World Bank. *China: Socialist Economic Development.* A World Bank Country Study. Washington: The World Bank, 1983. The initial detailed statistical and institutional description of China's economy done by the staff of the World Bank after China joined that institution. Originally consisted of a main, summary report and eight sector studies.

Zweig, David. *Agrarian Radicalism in China, 1968–1981.* Cambridge: Harvard University Press, 1989. Very good analysis of the process of policy and institutional change in the rural areas as a result of the Cultural Revolution and the reasons for the failure of the radicals' program.

Part 5: Culture

Literature and Art

Bei Dao. *Waves*. Bonnie S. McDougall and Susette T. Cooke, trans. New York: New Directions, 1990. A collection of stories by the one of the most innovative and important Chinese poets and writers of his generation. Seven stories demonstrate Bei Dao's rich literary and ironic treatment of themes and plots familiar to readers and the author's escape from the propagandistic dictates of his predecessors.

Chinese Literature: Fiction, Poetry, Art. A journal published by the Beijing Foreign Languages Press in several languages, including Chinese and English, that covers contemporary developments in literary and graphic arts. While sometimes lacking critical rigor in the selection of materials, it provides a wide assortment of recent short stories, poems, and critical essays, as well as plates and comments on rising artists.

Feuerwerker, Yi-tsi Mei. *Ding Ling's Fiction.* Cambridge: Harvard University Press, 1982. A detailed study of China's most important woman writer that deals not only with Ding Ling's life and the chronological development of her fiction but also issues of political and social context in which writers worked. Ding Ling's works are analyzed with considerable critical sophistication, providing one of the best introductions to twentieth-century Chinese literature available.

Goldblatt, Howard, ed. *Chinese Literature for the 1980's: The Fourth Congress of Writers & Artists.* New York: M. E. Sharpe, 1982. Collected translations of the major addresses given at the Fourth Congress in late 1979, with a brief introduction by the editor. Provides the most extensive official statement of prescribed lines and anticipated trends in literature and the arts for the decade of the 80s.

Isaacs, Harold, ed. *Straw Sandals: Chinese Short Stories 1918–1933.* Cambridge: MIT Press, 1974. A collection of key short stories from the formative early decades of modern Chinese literature. The translations are readable and accurate. Includes a foreword by Lu Xun.

Lim, Lucy, ed., *Contemporary Chinese Painting: An Exhibition from the People's Republic of China*. San Francisco: Chinese Culture Foundation, 1983. An exhibition catalogue featuring the works of thirty-six contemporary painters working in traditional media. Essays by Lim, James Cahill, and Michael Sullivan, as well as selected translations of essays by the artists, provide a concise and beautifully illustrated introduction to the most important painters on the contemporary scene in China.

Liu Binyan, *"People or Monsters?" and Other Stories and Reportage from China after Mao*. Perry Link, ed. Bloomington: Indiana University Press, 1983. Stories and reportage by this looming figure in contemporary Chinese life. Includes a broad selection of Liu's work written over several years, demonstrating the evolution of press freedoms and writing styles.

McDougall, Bonnie S., ed., *Popular Chinese Literature and Performing Arts in the People's Republic of China, 1949–1979*. Berkeley, University of California Press, 1984. A collection of essays arranged historically and dealing with drama, fiction, films, poetry, and folk arts in post-liberation China. Includes a three-decade retrospect by the editor that reviews trends among writers, their works, and their audiences from social, political, and artistic perspectives.

Science and Technology

Needham, Joseph. *Science and Civilisation in China*. Cambridge: Cambridge University Press, 1954– . One of the great scholarly undertakings of this century, this multivolume work, still in progress, explores the nature and development of Chinese science and technology from the earliest times to the end of imperial China. The volumes are organized according to fields of inquiry, with special attention to comparative developments outside China.

Orleans, Leo A. *Chinese Students in America: Policies, Issues, and Numbers*. Washington, D.C.: National Academy Press, 1988. A study of one of the most significant issues shaping China and shaping Sino-American relations and activities in science and technology. Orleans explores many facets of Chinese students abroad, including their backgrounds, their fields of study, their career prospects, and their funding.

Orleans, Leo A., ed. *Science in Contemporary China*. Stanford: Stanford University Press, 1980. A large volume, consisting of an introduction by Orleans reviewing salient points about the development of science in modern China, field reports by a large number of specialists who did intensive on-site surveys, and translations of key statements on current science policy.

Simon, Denis F., and Merle Goldman, *Science and Technology in Post-Mao China*. Cambridge: Harvard University Council on East Asian Studies, 1989. This conference volume includes fourteen essays that update many important issues in S&T, including reorganization of science and technology, the progress of applications, and the refinement of systems for technology transfer. An additional concluding essay looks at the future for China's S&T efforts.

Sivin, Nathan. *Traditional Medicine in Contemporary China*. Ann Arbor: Center for Chinese Studies, Science, Medicine, and Technology in East Asia Series, no. 2, 1986. A translation of a standard textbook for traditional Chinese medicine that is currently used in Chinese medical universities. In an extensive scholarly introduction, Sivin explores medical education in contemporary China and the approaches to integrating traditional Chinese practice and Western medicine.

Suttmeier, Richard P. *Science, Technology, and China's Drive for Modernization*. Stanford: Hoover Institution, 1980. A concise volume that surveys the current status of many fields of science and technology, the policy trends, and the growing role of international exchanges.

Part 6: The Future

Asiaweek. An important weekly magazine devoted to developments in Asia.

Asian Survey. A monthly journal published at the University of California, Berkeley, with frequent articles on contemporary China.

Beijing Review. A weekly magazine published in China that covers both domestic and international developments.

The China Quarterly. A major journal concerned with China published by the Contemporary China Institute at the University of London.

Far Eastern Economic Review. Published in Hong Kong, this magazine has frequent feature stories on China's domestic and foreign policy.

Kane, Anthony, ed. *China Briefing, 1990.* Boulder: Westview, 1990. This is the latest volume in a series sponsored by the China Council of the Asia Society, which commissions articles on developments in China (politics, economy, foreign policy, etc.) during the previous year.

Problems of Communism. This journal, published by the United States Information Agency, regularly carries scholarly and semi-scholarly articles dealing with China.

Studies in Comparative Communism. An academic journal with frequent contributions on China.

Sources

Part I: History and Geography

Chapter 1: "The Old Order" from *The United States and China*, 4th edition, by John K. Fairbank. Cambridge: Harvard University Press, 1979. © 1948, 1958, 1971, 1972, 1979 by the President and Fellows of Harvard College. Excerpted by permission of the author and publishers.

Chapter 2: "Sung Society: Change within Tradition" by E. A. Kracke, Jr., *Far Eastern Quarterly* 14: 4 (August 1955). © 1955 by the Association for Asian Studies, Inc. Reprinted by permission.

Chapter 3: "Traditional China at Its Peak: Achievements and Problems" is excerpted from *The Great Chinese Revolution, 1800–1985* by John K. Fairbank. New York: Harper & Row, 1986. © 1986 by John King Fairbank. Reprinted by permission of HarperCollins Publishers.

Chapter 4: "China's Response to the West" from *China's Response to the West: A Documentary Survey, 1839–1923*, edited by Ssu-yu Teng and John K. Fairbank. Cambridge: Harvard University Press, 1954. © 1954 by the President and Fellows of Harvard College; © 1982 by Ssu-yu Teng and John K. Fairbank. Reprinted by permission of the publishers.

Chapter 5: "Modern China in Transition, 1900–1950" by Mary C. Wright, *Annals of the American Academy of Political and Social Science*, January 1959. © 1959 by the American Academy of Political and Social Science. Reprinted by permission.

Part II: Politics

Chapter 13: "The Chinese Revolution" is excerpted from "The Present Situation and Our Tasks" and "The Vision of the Great Leap" by Mao Zedong, in *The People's Republic of China: A Documentary History of Revolutionary Change*, Mark Seldon, ed. New York: Monthly Review Press, 1979. © 1979 by Mark Seldon. Reprinted by permission of Monthly Review Foundation.

Chapter 14: "The Constitution of the Communist Party of China, 1982: General Program" from *Contemporary Chinese Politics: An Introduction*, 3rd edition, by James C. F. Wang. Englewood Cliffs, NJ: Prentice-Hall, 1989. © 1989 by Prentice-Hall. Reprinted by permission.

"Take a Clear-Cut Stand against Bourgeois Liberalization" in *Fundamental Issues in Present-Day China* by Deng Xiaoping. Beijing: Foreign Languages Press, 1989.

"Advance along the Road of Socialism with Chinese Characteristics" by Zhao Ziyang. Report to the Thirteenth Congress of the Communist Party of China, October 25, 1987. *Beijing Review*, November 9–15, 1987.

"Report on the Work of the Government" by Li Peng. *Beijing Review*, March 20, 1990.

Chapter 15: "China after Mao" by Steven M. Goldstein, Kathrin Sears, and Richard C. Bush, in *The People's Republic of China: A Basic Handbook*, 4th edition. New York: Council of International and Public Affairs, 1984. © 1984 by The Asia Society. Reprinted by permission.

Chapter 16: "Institutionalizing the Post-Mao Reforms" from *China's Second Revolution: Reform after Mao* by Harry Harding. Washington, D.C.: Brookings Institution, 1987. © 1987 by the Brookings Institution. Reprinted by permission.

Chapter 17: "The Origins of China's Pro-Democracy Movement and the Government's Response: A Tale of Two Reforms" by Yasheng Huang, *Fletcher Forum of World Affairs* 14: 1 (Winter 1990). Reprinted by permission.

Chapter 18: "Two Models of Law" is excerpted from "The Evolution and Development of the Chinese Legal System" by Victor H. Li, in *China: Management of a Revolutionary Society*, John M. H. Lindbeck, ed. Seattle: University of Washington Press, 1971. © 1971 by the University of Washington Press. Reprinted by permission.

Chapter 19: "Law in Imperial China" from *Law in Imperial China* by Derk Bodde and Clarence Morris. Cambridge: Harvard University Press, 1967. © 1967 by the President and Fellows of Harvard College. Reprinted by permission of the publishers.

Chapter 20: "Mr. Wang vs. Mr. Ch'en: A High Ch'ing Parable" from "High Ch'ing: 1683–1839," by Frederic Wakeman, Jr., in *Modern East Asia: Essays in Interpretation*, James B. Crowley, ed. New York: Harcourt Brace Jovanovich, 1970. © 1970 by Harcourt Brace Jovanovich, Inc. Reprinted by permission of the publisher.

Chapter 21: "The One Who Loved Dog Meat" from *Mao's People* by B. Michael Frolic. Cambridge: Harvard University Press, 1980. © 1980 by the President and Fellows of Harvard University. Reprinted by permission of the publishers.

Chapter 22: "Liberalizing Political Life" from *China's Second Revolution: Reform after Mao* by Harry Harding. Washington, D.C.: Brookings Institution, 1987. © 1987 by the Brookings Institution. Reprinted by permission.

Chapter 23: "Political Participation in Communist China" from *Political Participation in Communist China, New Edition* by James R. Townsend. Berkeley: University of California Press, 1969. © 1969 by the Regents of the University of California. Reprinted by permission.

Chapter 24: "Fang Lizhi: An Interview with Tiziano Terzani" in *Seeds of Fire: Chinese Voices of Conscience*, Geremie Barmé and John Minford, eds. New York: Farrar, Straus, and Giroux, 1988. © 1988 by Geremie Barmé and John Minford. Reprinted by permission of Hill and Wang, a division of Farrar, Straus, and Giroux, Inc.

"Soldiers, Look How Profiteering by Government Officials Is Eating You Up" and "Ten Questions" from *Cries for Democracy: Writings and Speeches from the 1989 Chinese Democracy Movement*, Han Minzhu, ed. Princeton: Princeton University Press, 1990. © 1990 by Princeton University Press. Reprinted by permission.

Chapter 25: "Deng Xiaoping's Remarks to Martial Law Officers on June 9" from *Cries for Democracy: Writings and Speeches from the 1989 Chinese Democracy Movement*, Han Minzhu, ed. Princeton: Princeton University Press, 1990. © 1990 by Princeton University Press. Reprinted by permission.

"Killings, Arrests, and Executions since 3 June 1989" from "Preliminary Findings on Killing of Unarmed Civilians, Arbitrary Arrests, and Summary Executions since 3 June 1989," Introduction, August 1989, and Preface to April 1990 update, *China: The Massacre of June 1989 and Its Aftermath* by Amnesty International Publications. © 1990 by Amnesty International Publications. Reprinted by permission.

Part III: Society

Chapter 26: "Family Instructions" edited from *Chinese Civilization and Society*, Patricia Buckley Ebrey, ed. New York: The Free Press, 1981. © 1981 by The Free Press, a division of Macmillan, Inc. Reprinted by permission.

Chapter 27: "The Family" excerpted from *The Family* by Ba Jin, translated by Sidney Shapiro. Beijing: Foreign Languages Press, 1954

Chapter 28: "Urban Workers' Housework" by Wang Yalin and Li Jinrong, *Social Sciences in China* 3: 2 (June 1982). Beijing, Chinese Academy of Social Sciences.

Chapter 29: "Zhao Xiuyin: Lady of the Sties" by Mary Sheridan, in *Lives: Chinese Working Women*, Mary Sheridan and Janet Salaff, eds. Bloomington: Indiana University Press, 1984. © 1984 by Indiana University Press. Reprinted by permission of the author and publisher.

Chapter 30: "Courtship, Love, and Marriage: The Life and Times of Yu Luojin" is a shortened version of "Private Issues, Public Discourse: The Life and Times of Yu Luojin" by Emily Honig, *Public Affairs* 57: 2 (Summer 1984). © 1984 by the University of British Columbia. Reprinted by permission.

Chapter 31: "Urban Social Control" by Sybille van der Sprenkel, in *The City in Late Imperial China*, G. William Skinner, ed. Stanford: Stanford University Press, 1977. © 1977 by the Board of Trustees of the Leland Stanford Junior University. Reprinted by permission of the publishers.

Chapter 32: "The Commune as a Social System" by Martin K. Whyte, from *China: A Country Study*, Frederica M. Bunge and Rinn-sup Shinn, eds. Washington, D.C.: U.S. Government Printing Office, 1981.

Chapter 33: "A Chinese Hospital" from *The Chinese Hospital* by Gail E. Henderson and Myron S. Cohen. New Haven: Yale University Press, 1984. © 1984 by Yale University Press. Reprinted by permission.

Chapter 34: "My Neighborhood" from *Mao's People* by B. Michael Frolic. Cambridge: Harvard University Press, 1980. © 1980 by the President and Fellows of Harvard University. Reprinted by permission of the publishers.

Chapter 35: "An Exploration of Relying on Connections" by Zheng Yefu, *Shehuixue yu Shehui Diaocha* [Sociology and Social Investigation], no. 2/3, 1984.

Chapter 36: "Subethnic Rivalry in the Ch'ing Period" by Harry J. Lamley, in *The Anthropology of Taiwanese Society*, Emily Martin Ahern and Hill Gates, eds. Stanford: Stanford University Press, 1981. © 1981 by the Board of Trustees of the Leland Stanford Junior University. Reprinted by permission of the publishers.

Chapter 37: "The Position of Peasants in Modern China's Social Order" by Sulamith Heins Potter, *Modern China* 9: 4 (October 1983). © 1983 by Sage Publications, Inc. Reprinted by permission of Sage Publications, Inc.

Chapter 38: "The Class System of Rural China: A Case Study" by Jonathan Unger, in *Class and Social Stratification in Post-Revolution China*, James L. Watson, ed. Cambridge: Cambridge University Press, 1984. © 1984 by Cambridge University Press. Reprinted by permission of Cambridge University Press.

Chapter 39: "Birth Control: A Grim Game of Numbers" is an edited version of chapter 9 from *Broken Earth: The Rural Chinese* by Steven W. Moser. New York: The Free Press, 1981. © 1981 by The Free Press, a division of Macmillan, Inc. Reprinted by permission of the author and publisher.

Chapter 40: "Saturday Night in Baoding" is excerpted from *Saturday Night in Baoding* by Richard Terrill. Fayetteville: University of Arkansas Press, 1990. © 1990 by the University of Arkansas. Reprinted by permission.

Part IV: The Economy

Chapter 41: "The Chinese Peasant Economy" from *The Chinese Peasant Economy: Agricultural Development in Hopei and Shantung, 1890–1949* by Ramon H. Myers. Cambridge: Harvard University Press, 1970. © 1970 by Ramon H. Myers. Reprinted by permission.

Chapter 42: "Marketing and Social Structure in Rural China" by G. William Skinner, *Journal of Asian Studies* 24: 1 (November 1964). © 1964 by the Association for Asian Studies, Inc. Reprinted by permission.

Chapter 43: "The Commune System before Reform" by Frederick W. Crook, in *The Chinese Economy in the Eighties*. Papers presented to the U.S. Congress Joint Economic Committee. Washington, D.C.: U.S. Government Printing Office, 1986. Reprinted by permission.

Chapter 44: "Socialist Agriculture is Dead; Long Live Socialist Agriculture! Organizational Transformation in Rural China" by Kathleen Hartford, in *The Political Economy of Reform in Post-Mao China*, Elizabeth J. Perry and Christine Wong, eds. Cambridge: Council on East Asian Studies, Harvard University, 1985. © 1985 by the President and Fellows of Harvard College. Reprinted by permission.

Chapter 45: "China's New Rural Reform Experiments" by Francis C. Tuan, *CPE Agriculture Report* 2: 3. Reprinted by permission.

Chapter 46: "The Foreign Establishment in China in the Early Twentieth Century" from *The Foreign Establishment in China in the Early Twentieth Century* by Albert Feuerwerker. Ann Arbor: Center for Chinese Studies, The University of Michigan, 1976. © 1976 by the Center for Chinese Studies, University of Michigan. Reprinted by permission.

Chapter 47: "China's Transition to Industrialism" is excerpted from *China's Transition to Industrialism* by Thomas G. Rawski. Ann Arbor: University of Michigan Press, 1980. © 1980 by The University of Michigan. Reprinted by permission.

Chapter 48: "China: The Economic System" in *China: Socialist Economic Development,* vol. 1: "The Economy, Statistical System, and Basic Data." A World Bank Country Study. Washington, D.C.: The World Bank, 1983. © 1983 by the International Bank for Reconstruction and Development / The World Bank. Reprinted by permission.

Chapter 49: "China's Economic Reforms" by Robert F. Dernberger, in *Asia-Pacific Report 1989, Focus: China in the Reform Era*, Charles E. Morrison and Robert F. Dernberger, eds. Honolulu: East-West Center, 1989. Reprinted by permission.

Chapter 50: "Foreign Trade and Industrial Development of China" excerpted from *Foreign Trade and Industrial Development in China: An Historical and Integrated Analysis through 1948* by Yu-Kwei Cheng. Washington, D.C.: University Press of Washington, 1956. © 1956 by Yu-Kwei Cheng. Reprinted by permission of Cherokee Publishing, Inc.

Chapter 51: "China's Balance of Payments in the Twentieth Century," excerpted from "China's Balance of Payments: The Experience of Financing a Long-Term Trade Deficit in the Twentieth Century," by Nai-ruenn Chen, in *Conference on Modern Chinese Economic History.* Taipei: The Institute of Economics, Academia Sinica, 1977. Reprinted by permission.

Chapter 52: "Economic Development and Modernization in Contemporary China: The Attempt to Limit Dependence on the Transfer of Modern Industrial Technology from Abroad and to Control Its Corruption of the Maoist Socialist Revolution" by Robert F. Dernberger, in *Technology and Communist Culture: The Socio-Cultural Impact of Technology under Socialism*, Frederic J. Fleron, Jr., ed. New York: Praeger, 1977. © 1977 by Praeger Publishers. Reprinted by permission of Greenwood Publishing Group.

Chapter 53: "China's Open-Door Policy" by Sheree Groves, in *Asia-Pacific Report 1989, Focus: China in the Reform Era*, Charles E. Morrison and Robert F. Dernberger, eds. Honolulu: East-West Center, 1989. Reprinted by permission.

Part V: Culture

Chapter 54: Lu Hsün, "K'ung I-chi," in *Straw Sandals*, Harold R. Isaacs, ed. Cambridge: MIT Press, 1974, © 1974 by MIT Press. Reprinted by permission.

Chapter 55: "Talks at the Yan'an Conference on Literature and Art" by Mao Zedong, in *Mao Zedong's "Talks at the Yan'an Conference on Literature and Art": A Translation of the 1943 Text with Commentary*, Bonnie S. McDougall, trans. Ann Arbor: Center for Chinese Studies, The University of Michigan, 1980. © 1980 by the Center for Chinese Studies, University of Michigan. Reprinted by permission.

Chapter 56: "The Wounded" by Lu Xinhua, translated by Kenneth J. DeWoskin for this volume. © 1986 by Center for Chinese Studies, The University of Michigan.

Chapter 57: "Ancient Temple" by Bei Dao, translated by Kenneth J. DeWoskin for this volume. © 1986 by Center for Chinese Studies, The University of Michigan.

"In the Ruins" by Bei Dao, in *Waves: Stories by Bei Dao*, Bonnie S. McDougall, ed; Bonnie S. McDougall and Susette Ternent Cooke, trans. New York: New Directions, 1990. © 1985, 1986 by The Chinese University of Hong Kong. Reprinted by permission of New Directions Publishing Corporation.

Chapter 58: "People or Monsters?" by Liu Binyan from *"People or Monsters?" and Other Stories and Reportage from China after Mao*, Perry Link, ed. Bloomington: Indiana University Press, 1983. © 1983 by Indiana University Press. Reprinted by permission.

Chapter 59: "Chinese Science: Explorations of an Ancient Tradition" by Nathan Sivin, from the Preface of *Chinese Science: Explorations of an Ancient Tradition*, Shigeru Nakayama and Nathan Sivin, eds. Cambridge: MIT Press, 1973, © 1973 by MIT Press. Reprinted by permission.

Chapter 60: "Science in Contemporary China" is excerpted from "Introduction" by Leo A. Orleans, in *Science in Contemporary China*, Leo A. Orleans, ed., with the assistance of Caroline Davidson. Stanford: Stanford University Press, 1980. © 1980 by the Board of Trustees of the Leland Stanford Junior University. Reprinted by permission of the publishers.

Chapter 61: "National Plan for the Development of Science and Technology, 1975–1985" by Fang Yi. Address to the National Science Conference, March 1978.

Chapter 62: "DOS ex Machina: The Microelectronic Ghost in China's Modernization Machine" by Richard Baum, in *Science and Technology in Post-Mao China*, Denis Fred Simon and Merle Goldman, eds. Cambridge: Council on East Asian Studies, Harvard University, 1989. © 1989 by the President and Fellows of Harvard College. Reprinted by permission.

Part VI: The Future

Chapter 63: "Evolutionary Changes in Chinese Culture" by Martin K. Whyte, in *Asia-Pacific Report 1989, Focus: China in the Reform Era*, Charles

E. Morrison and Robert F. Dernberger, eds. Honolulu: East-West Center, 1989. Reprinted by permission.

Chapter 64: "The Impact of Tiananmen on the Political Climate of Economic Reform" by Nina Halpern, forthcoming in *Issues and Studies: A Journal of China Studies and International Affairs*. Reprinted by permission.

Chapter 65: "American Policy toward China after the Beijing Tragedy" by Michel Oksenberg. Testimony before the U.S. House of Representatives Subcommittees on Human Rights and International Organizations; Asian and Pacific Affairs; and International Economic Policy and Trade, July 19, 1989.

"Sanctions or Subdued Relations: The International Response to the 1989 Massacre" by James D. Seymour, *Fletcher Forum of World Affairs*, 14: 1 (Winter 1990). Reprinted by permission. An expanded version appears as "The International Response to the Crackdown in China," *China Information* (Leiden), April 1990.

"Bush's Second Chance on China" by Winston Lord, in *The New York Times*, May 9, 1990. © 1990 by The New York Times Company. Reprinted by permission.

"Guard against the Smokeless War" by Liu Maoyin, *Zhejiang Ribao*, February 13, 1990. Reprinted from *Foreign Broadcast Information Service Daily Report*, March 23, 1990.

Chronological Table
of Readings

This table provides a breakdown of the readings by historical period. Chapters 6, 7, 8, and 10, which are geographical, rather than historical, are omitted. The three chapters in Part 6 (The Future) are listed by subject area in the Deng Era.

	Part 1 History	Part 2 Politics	Part 3 Society	Part 4 Economy	Part 5 Culture
Imperial Period	1, 2, 3, 4, 9	11, 12, 18, 19, 20	26, 31, 36	42	59
Republican Period	5		27	41, 46, 47, 50, 51	54
Mao Era		13, 21, 23	28, 29, 30, 32, 33, 34, 37, 38	43, 52	55, 56, 60
Deng Era		14, 15, 16, 17, 22, 24, 25, 64, 65	35, 39, 40, 63	44, 45, 48, 49, 53	57, 58, 61, 62

The Editors

Robert F. Dernberger has been a professor of economics at the University of Michigan for the last twenty-five years, serving as Director of the Center for Chinese Studies from 1983 to 1985. He received his formal training in Chinese studies and economics at the University of Michigan and Harvard, earning a doctorate at Harvard in 1965. He has also taught at the University of Chicago, where he chaired the Committee of Far Eastern Studies and edited the journal *Economic Development and Cultural Change*. In 1984 he served as president of the Association for Comparative Economic Studies. Having made over fifteen visits to China, Professor Dernberger has written more than forty articles and books on the problems of economic development and on comparative economic systems, with special reference to the Chinese economy. His most important publications include an edited conference volume, *China's Development Experience in Contemporary Perspective*, several contributions to the volumes of collected papers on China's economy periodically released by the Joint Economic Committee of the U.S. Congress, and monographs on *China's Future* (with Allen Whiting) and *Financing Asian Development* (with Richard Eckaus).

Kenneth J. DeWoskin is Professor of Chinese, Chair of the Department of Asian Languages and Cultures, and Professor of International Business at the University of Michigan. He did his graduate work at Columbia University, at Kyoto University, and at the Inter-University Program in Taipei, earning his doctorate from Columbia in 1973. His research interests focus on early Chinese literature and cultural history, and he has published on a diverse range of subjects, including Chinese historiography, aesthetics, and science and technology. In recent years, Professor DeWoskin has been active in both public and private sector exchange activities in China, and he is engaged in research on issues relating China and the outside in both historical and contemporary time frames. His major publications include *A Song for One or Two: Music and the Concept of Art in Early China* and *Doctors, Diviners, and Magicians of Early China: Biographies of Fang-Shih*. In progress are an edited volume on entertainments in early China and a volume on music archaeology, as well as a study of the Beijing Electron-Positron Collider.

Steven M. Goldstein is Professor and Chair of the Department of Government at Smith College, where he joined the faculty in 1968. He has also taught at the Fletcher School of Law and Diplomacy and at Columbia University, where he earned his Ph.D. in 1972. In addition, he was Director of the China Council of the Asia Society from 1983 to 1984. He has written a number of works dealing with a broad range of topics related to contemporary Chinese politics, including peasant revolution and elite politics. However, his major field of interest is Chinese foreign policy. He has written on Sino-American and Sino-Soviet relations. His most recent books are *Single Sparks: China's Rural Revolutions* (co-edited with Kathleen Hartford) and *The Minidragons* (editor).

Rhoads Murphey is Professor of History at the University of Michigan, where he has also served as Professor of Asian Studies and Geography and as Director of the Center for Chinese Studies. He earned his B.A., M.A., and Ph.D. at Harvard University. He lived in China from 1942 to 1946, working with the Friends Ambulance Unit, and he has returned several times since 1972, most recently in 1990. He has served as president of the Association for Asian Studies, whose journal he edited for several years. His interests include all of Chinese history from its beginnings to the present, as well as urbanism and ecology. His main research, however, centers on Chinese interactions with the West since the eighteenth century. His books include *Shanghai: Key to Modern China; A New China Policy; Approaches to Modern Chinese History* (coeditor); *The Treaty Ports and China's Modernization; The Outsiders: Westerners in India and China* (which won the 1977 Best-Book-of-the-Year Award); *The Fading of the Maoist Vision;* and, most recently, *A History of Asia*.

Martin K. Whyte is Professor of Sociology at the University of Michigan, where he has been a member of the faculty since 1970. He studied physics at Cornell University and then Russian studies and sociology at Harvard University, where he earned his doctorate in 1971. He is particularly interested in the comparative institutional development of the Soviet Union and China and in the evolution of grassroots social life in the People's Republic of China since 1949. He is also involved in research and teaching in the field of family sociology, and he recently directed a survey investigation of mate choice and marriage relations patterns in Detroit. He has served as Director of the Universities Service Centre in Kowloon, Hong Kong. A frequent traveler to China, he has written dozens of articles on contemporary China. His books include *Small Groups and Political Rituals in China; The Status of Women in Preindustrial Societies; Dating, Mating, and Marriage;* and, with William Parish, *Village and Family in Contemporary China* and *Urban Life in Contemporary China.*

Index

Note: The index is intended only as a supplement to the table of contents, which should be consulted to locate entire readings devoted to a particular topic.